The Farmer's Age: Agriculture
1815–1860

THE ECONOMIC HISTORY OF THE UNITED STATES
Edited by Henry David, Harold U. Faulkner, Louis M. Hacker, Curtis P. Nettels, and Fred A. Shannon

Curtis P. Nettels: THE EMERGENCE OF A NATIONAL ECONOMY, 1775-1815

Paul W. Gates: THE FARMER'S AGE: *Agriculture, 1815-1860*

George Rogers Taylor: THE TRANSPORTATION REVOLUTION, 1815-1860

Fred A. Shannon: THE FARMER'S LAST FRONTIER:
Agriculture, 1860-1897

Edward C. Kirkland: INDUSTRY COMES OF AGE:
Business, Labor, and Public Policy, 1860-1897

Harold U. Faulkner: THE DECLINE OF LAISSEZ FAIRE, 1897-1917

George Soule: PROSPERITY DECADE:
From War to Depression, 1917-1929

Broadus Mitchell: DEPRESSION DECADE: *From New Era Through New Deal*

THE
FARMER'S AGE:
AGRICULTURE

1815-1860

By PAUL W. GATES

VOLUME III
The Economic History of
the United States

M. E. SHARPE, INC.

Armonk, New York   London, England

Cover photo courtesy of Westchester County Historical Society.

This book was originally published as volume III of The Economic History of the United States series by Holt, Rinehart and Winston in 1960. It is here reprinted by arrangement with Holt, Rinehart and Winston, Inc.

Library of Congress Cataloging-in-Publication Data

Gates, Paul Wallace, 1901-
   The farmer's age

   Reprint. Originally published: New York : Holt, Rinehart, and Winston, 1960. (The economic history of the United States ; v. 3)
   1. Agriculture—Economic aspects—United States—History—19th century. 2. United States—Economic conditions—To 1865. I. Title. II. Series: Economic history of the United States ; v. 3.
HD1761.G255   1989   330.973'05   89-10671
ISBN 0-87332-100-6

Printed in the United States of America

ED   10   9   8   7   6   5   4   3   2   1

Foreword

WHEN this series of nine volumes on the economic history of the United States was first conceived, the nation's economy had reached a critical stage in its development. Although the shock of the depression of 1929 had been partially absorbed, the sense of bewilderment which it produced had not yet vanished, and the suffering and the bitterness of its first years were being transformed into less substantial, though still anguished, memories. Reform measures, either in operation or proposed, were being actively debated, but with less sense of urgency than earlier.

To the Editors of this series a fresh consideration of America's economic history was justified by more than the experiences of the recent past or the obscurity of the future. Rich contributions to the literature of American history had been made through cooperative series dealing with the political, social, and cultural aspects of American life. Numerous single-volume surveys of the country's economic development have been written. But, as late as the end of the fourth decade of the twentieth century, the world's foremost economic power had not yet produced an integrated, full-length, and authoritative treatment of its own economic history.

Scholarly concern with American economic history has been constantly growing during the past half century, and chairs of economic history have been established in leading universities. A more profound understanding of the role of economic forces in the nation's history has not only been developed by historians and economists, but has also won some measure of popular acceptance. The earlier thin trickle of monographs has broadened in recent years into a flood of publications. At present, such specialized studies, the many collections of documentary materials, and the mountains of government reports on different facets of American economic life, are staggering in their richness and scope.

This series has been planned to utilize these available sources in the preparation of a full-scale, balanced, cooperative, and readable survey of the growth of American economy and of its transformation from one of primitive character to world pre-eminence in industry, trade, and finance. Clearly, in nine volumes all aspects of the nation's economic life cannot be treated fully. But such a series can point the way to new fields of study and treat authoritatively, if not definitively, the main lines of economic development. Further, the series is intended to fill a present need of those professionally concerned with American economic history, to supplement the economic materials now available in general school and college histories of the United States, and finally to provide the lay reader with the fruits of American scholarship. If these objectives are attained, then the efforts which have gone into the creation of this economic history of the United States will have been amply repaid.

Contributors to the series have been chosen who have already established their competence in the particular periods they are to survey here; and they are, of course, solely responsible for the points of view or points of departure they employ. It is not intended that the series represent a school of thought or any one philosophical or theoretical position.

The Farmer's Age is the appropriate title for Volume III of the series, devoted to agriculture between 1815 and 1860. The title is appropriate, as Professor Gates makes clear, in two ways. On the one hand, the period between the War of 1812 and the Civil War was a time when the typical American farmer might well have felt that—on balance—"everything appeared to be going his way." On the other hand, there were clear signs in 1860 that "the great age of the American farmer was drawing to a close."

Public land policies, while enriching urban speculators, also served most farm owners. These tended to regard "their land as the means of quickly making a fortune" and were ready to move on whenever they saw a chance to reap bigger profits from virgin land farther west. The westward movement intensified the clamor for new transportation to carry the burgeoning output to market, and farmers bore a heavy share of the costs attending the transportation revolution with minimum protest. New methods and new species—some the product of Yankee ingenuity and some of Europe's more scientific agriculture—were as much a part of the frontier as new land. Agricultural technology was advanced by the states and, to some degree, by the Federal government; by seed, fertilizer, and implement companies and journal publishers, all seeking profits like the farmers themselves; and by the farmers' own societies.

Like the nation as a whole, however, the farmers were divided against themselves: large landowners against small; landlords against tenants; creditors against debtors; growers of one crop against those of another; and, most serious of all, partisans of one section against their fellow citizens elsewhere. Professor Gates sets forth these divisions with particular brilliance and cogency—not only the sectional differences that speeded the coming of the Civil War but also the disunity that foreshadowed an end to *The Farmer's Age* just when "everything appeared to be going his way." In 1860, when the population of the United States was still more than four-fifths rural, it could not find a common solution to its chronic problems of cyclical instability, high transportation costs, and inadequate sources of credit.

THE EDITORS

Preface

FEW historians have had their way better prepared for a major project than one who undertakes a general history of agriculture for the antebellum period. Bidwell and Falconer for the North and L. C. Gray for the South wrought admirably, producing histories that will last though later writers may not necessarily accept their emphasis, allocation of space, or even interpretation in all matters. An abundance of monographs and articles have appeared since their publication which make necessary different treatment, the inclusion of new subjects, and a reassessment of older ones.

My obligations in the preparation of this study are many. James B. Hedges and Frederick Merk were most responsible for attracting me to agricultural history. Everett E. Edwards, Herbert Kellar, Wendell Stephenson, L. C. Gray, Charles S. Sydnor, and Joseph Schafer offered encouragement and provided intellectual stimulation. It was a great privilege to attend Dr. Gray's seminar in Land Economics at the Brookings Institution. Over the course of a full year of close association Leonard Arrington shared with me his intimate knowledge of economic progress in territorial Utah. My graduate students, especially David M. Ellis, Neil A. McNall, Harry J. Brown, Allan G. Bogue, Margaret Beattie Bogue, Richard M. Bliss, and Gould Colman have taught me much about farmers and farming. The editors of this series have been appropriately helpful. My grandfather, who successfully tilled his New Hampshire farm, made 400 gallons of maple syrup, and hundreds of pounds of sugar annually, sold butter, cheese, apples and garden products in a nearby city, gave me unforgettable experiences which have ever been an inspiration and a delightful memory. My wife, notwithstanding the responsibility of four children and her own intellectual interests, has given of her time and attention as no one but a wife should be asked to do.

I am indebted for many favors to the staffs of the United States Department of Agriculture, the National Archives, the Indiana State Library, the Wisconsin State Historical Society Library, the Louisiana State University Library the Alabama State Library, the Kansas State Historical Society Library, the Bancroft Library, and the Huntington Library, as well as the various Cornell University Libraries. During a year at the Huntington Library where most of this study was written I borrowed through inter-library loan a host of books with the kind assistance of Miss Marion Chevalier.

Fellowships of the Social Science Research Council, the Guggenheim Foundation, and the Huntington Library gave me time to pursue my research in peaceful environments away from the bustle of college life. Donald Young, Henry Allen Moe, and John E. Pomfret can never be forgotten by the many they have aided. Cornell University has materially helped in the pursuit of this work.

PAUL W. GATES

Ithaca, New York
March, 1960

Contents

CONTENTS

Illustrations

BETWEEN PAGES 140–141

BETWEEN PAGES 300–301

Tables

The Farmer's Age: Agriculture
1815–1860

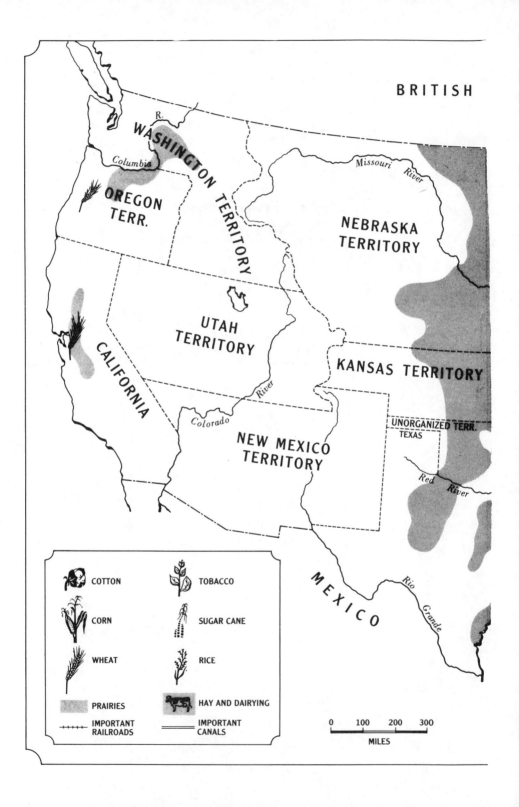

BRITISH

WASHINGTON TERRITORY

R.

Columbia

OREGON TERR.

NEBRASKA TERRITORY

Missouri River

CALIFORNIA

UTAH TERRITORY

KANSAS TERRITORY

River

Colorado

NEW MEXICO TERRITORY

UNORGANIZED TERR.
TEXAS

Red River

MEXICO

Rio Grande

COTTON

TOBACCO

CORN

SUGAR CANE

WHEAT

RICE

PRAIRIES

HAY AND DAIRYING

IMPORTANT RAILROADS

IMPORTANT CANALS

0   100   200   300

MILES

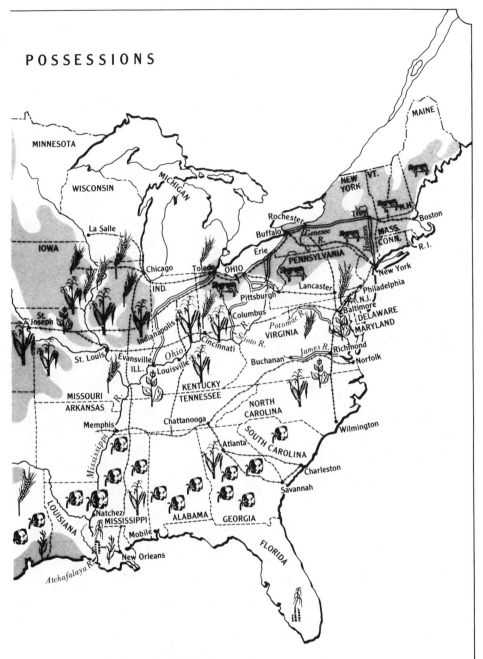

POSSESSIONS

MINNESOTA

WISCONSIN

MICHIGAN

MAINE

NEW YORK

VT.

N.H.

IOWA

La Salle

Rochester

Troy

Boston

Buffalo

Genesee R.

Hudson

MASS.

CONN.

Erie

R.I.

Chicago

Toledo

OHIO

PENNSYLVANIA

New York

IND.

Lancaster

Philadelphia

Pittsburgh

N.J.

St. Joseph

Columbus

Baltimore

DELAWARE

Indianapolis

Cincinnati

Scioto R.

Potomac R.

VIRGINIA

MARYLAND

St. Louis

Evansville

Ohio R.

ILL.

Louisville

KENTUCKY

Buchanan

James R.

Richmond

Norfolk

MISSOURI

TENNESSEE

ARKANSAS

Chattanooga

NORTH CAROLINA

Memphis

SOUTH CAROLINA

Wilmington

Atlanta

Charleston

Mississippi R.

Savannah

LOUISIANA

Natchez

MISSISSIPPI

ALABAMA

GEORGIA

Mobile

New Orleans

FLORIDA

Atchafalaya R.

AGRICULTURE

IN THE UNITED STATES, 1860

CHAPTER I

The South in 1815

AN unrivaled sweep of land-hungry men was unleashed into the trans-Appalachian West by the close of the War of 1812. By that time, British intrigues among the Indians had been eliminated, the western frontier had been pacified, and interference by the Spanish had been reduced. Hundreds of thousands of people left their homes and struck out into the wilderness in search of cheap, fertile land in new communities untroubled by a concentration of land ownership, inequalities, and lack of economic opportunities. This burst of population into the West swept five new states, not including Maine, into the Union in six years. It brought millions of acres of new land into competition with the farms of older states. The United States was no longer considered an Atlantic coastal confederation but a continental nation. All the coastal states except New York and Georgia, which had frontiers of their own and an abundance of land to settle, were seriously affected by this pull of the West. They lost part of their rural population, and consequently there was a diminishing demand for land and farms. They suffered from a shortage of farm laborers and from the competition of tobacco, cotton, wheat, and wool produced on the cheap virgin land of the West.

In 1815 America's population of 5,500,000 to 6,000,000 people lived in the seaboard states, in Vermont, in parts of Kentucky, Tennessee, and Ohio, in the St. Louis area, and along the lower Mississippi. Of these areas only eastern Pennsylvania and New York, most of New Jersey, and southern New England were intensively developed in terms of agriculture.[1] Few Americans were far from direct contact with the soil. The Census of 1810 showed only eight cities with a population in excess of 10,000 and only 6 per cent of the population living in communities of

[1] *Statistical Atlas; Twelfth Census of the United States,* prepared under the direction of Henry Gannett (Washington, D. C.: United States Census Office, 1903), Plates 4 and 5.

1

5,000 or more. Smaller communities down to the crossroads hamlet were inhabited chiefly by people engaged in satisfying the farmers' wants or processing his goods. Among them were millers, sawyers, cobblers, harness makers, drovers, merchants, blacksmiths, glaziers, brickmakers, carpenters, tinsmiths, and unskilled workers. Many of these people lived on generous-sized lots or on small farms adjoining the towns; they usually kept gardens, a pig, a cow, and perhaps a horse. They were in reality part-time farmers. The occupation of the great mass of the people was agriculture or was related to agriculture. Agriculture provided the basis of much of America's foreign and domestic trade, and the opportunities it offered constituted the principal attraction to immigrants. Out of the problems of agriculture were to come bitter sectional strife, dissolution of the Union, and the Civil War.

In 1815 there was no one pattern of agriculture prevailing throughout the country or throughout any of its physiographic provinces. Pioneering —the making of a farm in a new community—had certain basic similarities whether conducted on the frontier of Maine, the back country of Kentucky, or the canebrakes of Mississippi: trees were cleared or girdled, a small patch of corn was hoed in, the piece was fenced, and a crude log hut was erected. After the initial years, during which a considerable acreage was cleared and fenced, trails were constructed over which hogs and cattle could be driven and wagon loads of grain or tobacco could be hauled. As the pioneering stage ended throughout the various sections, differentiation in agricultural patterns produced well-defined stereotypes. There was the Yankee hillside farmer with his mixed economy; the Pennsylvania "Dutch" farmer with his large, well-fed cattle, level and productive wheat fields, and big barns; the tobacco planter with his slave labor; the cotton farmer of the Georgia Piedmont; and the Buckeye corn and hog farmer.

All these types of farmers had certain basic attitudes in common: a yearning to own land in abundance, a love of freedom and a contempt for restrictive measures that denied them the rights they claimed, a pragmatic outlook on life, a distrust of urban politicians, and a tendency to become more conservative as their property increased in value. With the exception of the Pennsylvania German farmer, all these types discarded the Old World respect for the soil as something to be cherished, and looked upon land as a means to a quick fortune. If wheat, tobacco, rice, or cotton were marketable and returns from their cultivation were satisfactory, the one-crop system was introduced, no matter what the effect upon the soil. When the land was no longer profitable to operate, the farmers, with a certain fatalism, sold it to others or let it grow up to brush and moved on to exploit new areas.

WASTEFUL FARM PRACTICES

European travelers who surveyed American rural life condemned the wasteful and destructive practices they observed. They came from countries where land was intensively and conservatively used, where the pressure of population upon land was great and increasing, where land values were high and labor costs low, where forests were dangerously depleted and what remained had to be carefully husbanded. The idea that the forest was an enemy that must be destroyed was shocking to Europeans. Isaac Weld commented upon this aversion to trees which led settlers to cut and destroy without regard to future needs.[2] Travelers criticized the practice of lightly scratching the soil and sowing grain or tobacco year after year without applying restoratives, not realizing that the very abundance of cheap tillable land and the high cost of labor made such methods almost unavoidable. To them deep and horizontal plowing, utilization of animal manures, elimination of weeds, maintenance of hedgerows, and prudent use of the forest were basic to proper agriculture. In 1815 American farm practices were indeed primitive and destructive although generally rewarding to the first generation who used the land.

In the coastal states, soil-exhausting farm practices had by 1815 already created serious agricultural problems for which many farmers saw only one solution: fresh land. Farmers from the older settled areas had long been moving westward into the Piedmont, the Great Valley and then into the trans-Allegheny country from the South, and across New York State from New England. Internal migration had become a well-established feature of American life. Turner's conception of a fluid mobile population perennially moving and re-establishing itself on successive frontiers remains intact, no matter what other parts of his frontier interpretation may be open to question. A detailed examination of the state of agriculture in the various sections of the United States in 1815 will show that their problems and the tendency of their populations to migrate into new areas had a variety of causes, of which worn-out land was but one. Soil and topography, previous land policies, land and capital requirements of staple crops, fluctuations in European demand for American products and in European tariffs, technological changes, and established social patterns were all factors that influenced in varying degrees the prospects of agriculture in the various sections and the readiness of the population to take up new land in the West.

Oldest of the settled regions of the United States was the coastal plain

[2] Isaac Weld, *Travels through the States of North America and the Provinces of Upper and Lower Canada During the Years 1793, 1796 and 1797* (London: J. Stockdale, 1799), pp. 23–24, 29.

of Virginia. Endowed with a soil only truly productive in the alluvial river bottoms, this region had long since passed its prime as a result of exhaustive planting of tobacco and wheat. Sterilizing the soil of seedbeds for tobacco by burning brush on it, and clean cultivation of the fields to which the tobacco was transplanted had killed the soil-binding plants and permitted the heavy rains to erode the topsoil from the bare fields, while continued cropping had depleted the minerals in the soil. Gradually tobacco planting had moved into the Piedmont, and wheat had replaced it in the coastal plain. The Napoleonic Wars—which had not favored tobacco producers—had induced some to make this change. There was, however, little profit in the cultivation of wheat, which yielded only four to seven bushels an acre on badly abused land and required from one half to one bushel of seed. And corn on the worn-out lands was said to yield but eight to fourteen bushels to the acre.[3] Continued cropping to wheat, once tobacco was abandoned, resulted in the accumulation of wheat parasites. In 1817 one third of the wheat in Virginia was reported to have been destroyed by the Hessian fly.[4] Eventually both tobacco and wheat had to be given up for corn and mixed farming. Corn, with its cross cultivation, carried soil damage further. Exhausted fields were then abandoned to scrub pine. Livestock might have aided Virginia farmers in maintaining the fertility of their soil, but they concentrated upon the production of staples and made little or no effort to utilize the manure of the animals they did have.[5] Clearing fresh land seemed more important than liming, manuring, and rotating crops. Some forward-looking planters had begun to use more grass crops and to apply gypsum, but their example was not extensively followed. The historian of soil exhaustion in Virginia observes that contemporary sources deplored the "continuance of exhausting cultivation, of wasted lands, abandoned fields, neglected stock and shifting crops" for the years 1785 to 1820.[6]

The Maryland tidewater region went through much the same experience. Land no longer useful for tobacco or cereal production was permitted to grow up into weed timber. Nature was attempting to make up for the sins of man by covering the scars left by his activities.

[3] François Alexandre Frédéric de La Rouchefoucauld-Liancourt, *Travels through the United States of North America* . . . (2d ed., 2 vols.; London: R. Phillips, 1800), II, 52, 106.

[4] D. B. Warden, *Statistical, Political and Historical Account of the United States of America* . . . (2 vols.; Edinburgh: Archibald Constable & Co., 1819), II, 208-218.

[5] Johann David Schoepf, *Travels in the Confederation*, Alfred J. Morrison, trans. and ed. (2 vols.; Philadelphia: William J. Campbell, 1911), II, 32, and *passim*.

[6] Avery Craven, *Soil Exhaustion as a Factor in the Agricultural History of Virginia and Maryland, 1606-1860* (University of Illinois *Studies in the Social Sciences*, Vol. XIII; Urbana: 1925), p. 82.

PLIGHT OF THE TOBACCO-GROWING AREAS

Agriculture was in a chronic state of depression in 1815 in the tobacco-growing areas of Virginia and Maryland. Overproduction, marketing problems, low prices, declining yields, and heavy debts had brought a once-proud area to near insolvency. This is not to say that no farmers or planters prospered; those who were more efficient, more able, more modern did well, or at least maintained their equity. But others, including some of the outstanding statesmen of the Old Dominion, were faced with increasing obligations and had to sell some of their slaves and land and ultimately lost most of their possessions. Well known is the plight of Jefferson, Madison, and Monroe, whose long-neglected and ill-used plantations failed to yield them an adequate income in their retirement.

THE WESTWARD TREK

As the yield of their lands declined, the tobacco and wheat planters of Virginia and Maryland had to be prepared to purchase or develop new land to which they might move their hands when the old was no longer sufficiently productive to operate. Many of the better small holdings were purchased by the large planters or, if tenancies, were consolidated by them. Small farmers whose holdings were thus swallowed up, or the children of small farmers who saw no reason to remain in regions seemingly destined for planters and slaves, sought new homes in the West, taking with them little more than a gun, a hoe, an ax, a cow, oxen, and a wagon filled with miscellaneous household articles. Joining them in the westward trek were other small farmers who found their lowered social position unattractive, and large numbers of young people pouring out of the immensely fecund families of the upland and hill sections where the land resources were insufficient to absorb their energies. At the same time, planters dissatisfied with the declining yield from their heavy investment in land and slaves, or younger sons who could not expect to inherit the family plantations, were moving west to establish in new communities substantial plantations stocked with slaves, sheep, horses, cattle, and all essential agricultural implements.

Also joining the westward trek were numerous planters who did not intend to give up their residences in older communities. They acquired lands in newly opened areas with the expectation of creating, at some future date, a second tobacco or cotton plantation which would be managed by an overseer and to which they would move the surplus slaves that could no longer be gainfully employed on the home plantation. If, in the meantime, squatters settled upon their land there was nothing to be lost by permitting them to remain for a few years. They would surely clear a few acres, erect a rude hut, and thereby increase the value of the land. Often two years' free use of the land was followed by rental agreements which brought the landlord some income in the form of tobacco or wheat. Tenancy was not uncommon in the Piedmont and Great Valley of Virginia in the eighteenth century. Great landlords like Washington, Fairfax, and Carter had scores of tenants. However, when the landlords needed the land on which to establish their slave economy, which was no longer profitable on the worn soils of the older plantations, the tenants had to go.[7] Both the planter and the man of small means thus joined in the development of the new West.

In the broad coastal plain of North Carolina, agriculture was still in a rude state in 1815. After tobacco had taken toll of the land it was moved to newly cleared tracts, and for a time corn continued to provide worth-while returns. An Edgecombe County scribe in 1811 said that farmers and planters tried to clear and put in grain as much land as possible and to "exhaust it as fast as a series of grain crops can do it." The task of clearing the land to replace that which was to be abandoned absorbed all efforts. There was no time for manuring the land, for sowing clover in rotation, or for proper attention to livestock. The only good stock was horses.[8]

On the Carolina frontier, corn was raised in abundance but had little commercial value because of the remoteness of the frontier communities and the lack of transportation. A good portion of it was distilled into whiskey. One frontier county—Iredell—could boast fifty-nine stills in 1800.[9] Cattle grazing had once been a chief source of livelihood. Cattle and hogs ran wild in the woods, the owners allowing them to take their chances against the attacks of wild animals, Indians, and cattle rustlers. A little grain was given them in the winter when forage was gone, but only enough to assure survival, not enough to put them in good shape for market. Under such conditions stock degenerated into scrub animals of low value.

North Carolina was sandwiched in between two states with navigable rivers and good harbors which drew off its products. It had no sizable urban centers of its own to provide markets and processing plants for foodstuffs, tobacco, and cotton. Hogs and tobacco were driven or hauled to Virginia markets, and cotton and rice were floated to South

[7] Willard F. Bliss, "The Rise of Tenancy in Virginia," *Virginia Magazine of History and Biography*, LVIII (October, 1950), 427–441.

[8] A. R. Newsome, "Twelve North Carolina Counties in 1810–1811—Sketch by Jeremiah Battle of Edgecombe County," *North Carolina Historical Review*, VI (January, 1929), 82–85.

[9] Hugh Hill Wooten, "The Land Values of Iredell County in 1800," *North Carolina Historical Review*, XXIX (October, 1952), 536; Newsome, "Twelve North Carolina Counties . . . ," *loc. cit.*, p. 85.

Carolina centers. Transportation costs delayed the development of commercial agriculture, and careless farm practices ruined land lightly tilled in corn and tobacco. In 1819, before North Carolina had enjoyed any extensive prosperity, a leading agricultural reformer said that its "state of agriculture is at the lowest ebb" as a result of its "land killing system." [10]

These were the circumstances that stimulated the first great rush of North Carolinians to Alabama's fast-growing and exciting cotton country. A resident of the North Carolina Piedmont spoke in 1817 of the "anxiety and confusion that pervades all ranks of people in this section of country to remove" to Alabama. Numbers had already sold their property and left for Alabama and many more were anxious to follow. Land was diminishing in value and the state was losing "many of its most enterprising and respectable inhabitants." [11] It was estimated at that time that the amount of abandoned land in the state was equal to, if not greater than, the amount of land in cultivation.[12]

In South Carolina, rice and indigo planting had flourished in the eighteenth century, but only rice survived into the nineteenth. Its cultivation was narrowly limited to coastal areas washed by the tide above the salt-water level. Cotton, both long and short staple, had also been grown in small quantities until the invention of the cotton gin, when the short-staple variety became extensively planted. In the coastal areas of South Carolina the average plantation of 1795 contained 725 acres. Colonial land policies, under which generous donations had been made to influential people and headrights had been granted in proportion to the number of white servants and slaves they brought to America, had made possible the accumulation of substantial holdings of land. Even in the upcountry, where small farmers were more common, the average farm or plantation contained 225 acres.[13]

COTTON PLANTING

When the cotton gin was perfected, cotton swiftly became the miracle crop that surpassed all others in importance in the South. The

[10] C. O. Cathey, "Sidney Weller, Ante-Bellum Promoter of Agricultural Reform," *North Carolina Historical Review*, XXXI (January, 1954), 5n.

[11] James Graham, Lincoln Vesuvius Furnace, near Statesville, August 10, 1817, to Thomas Ruffin, in J. G. de Roulhac Hamilton, ed., *Papers of Thomas Ruffin* (4 vols., *Publications* of the North Carolina Historical Commission; Raleigh: 1918), I, 194–195.

[12] Wooten, "The Land Values of Iredell County . . . ," *loc. cit.*, p. 531; Cathey, "Sidney Weller . . . ," *loc. cit.*, p. 5.

[13] William A. Schaper, "Sectionalism and Representation in South Carolina," *Annual Report* of the American Historical Association, 1900 (Washington, D. C.: Government Printing Office, 1901), I, 391.

gin made practicable the use of the seedy short-staple cotton which could
be raised in upland areas more easily and cheaply than long-staple
cotton could be raised in the lowlands of South Carolina and Georgia.
Cheaper cotton and technological improvements in the manufacture of
the fiber permitted the substitution of cheap cotton fabrics for woolens
and linens. Between 1790 and 1815 the new demand for cotton led to
a sixtyfold increase in its production, from 3,135 to 208,986 bales. Supply
did not catch up with demand for many years, and the price remained
well above ten cents a pound except for an unusual year, 1811, and
perhaps 1812.[14] Cotton planting swept everything before it as planters and
farmers with one accord turned to it to reap the profits which high
prices and swiftly accelerating demand assured them. Favorable prices
and high gross returns—in 1815 $18,526,589—provided planters with
capital for expansion that was phenomenal.[15] Slaves were imported in
large numbers into the South Carolina and Georgia Piedmont and
tobacco plantations, mixed farms and squatters' holdings were replaced
by extensive cotton plantations. Here was the center of the cotton
kingdom in 1815.[16]

As a result of the scramble for good cotton land, the patterns of
settlement and the problems they produced became rather different in
the cotton-growing South from those in other areas. Outside the lowland
cotton region the squatter had always been as characteristic of the South
as hogs and hominy. Public or ungranted lands had been the refuge of
the redemptioner; to them had gravitated the Scotch-Irish, the German
immigrant, and other folk who were being crowded out of the older
settled areas. The southern states had tolerated, even encouraged, the
settlement of squatters on the frontier. When a squatter was so unfortunate as to settle on the property of some absentee owner he might
be evicted unless he would accept the landlord's terms. A squatter
generally found it difficult to raise the money to buy either from the
government or from a private owner. With luck he might sell some skins
or furs, he might even sell some of his crops to a nearby fort, Indian
trader, or government agent, or perhaps to a man with capital who was
getting his plantation under way. If he was near a river, he could float
his crop to market by flatboat. He might even make a little money from
labor performed on public works such as river improvements, canals, or
roads. In time he might create a self-sufficient farm and obtain title to

[14] O. E. Baker, ed., *Atlas of American Agriculture* (Washington, D. C.: Govern-
ment Printing Office, 1918), Part V, sec. a, Table IV, p. 18; Lewis Cecil Gray,
History of Agriculture in the Southern United States to 1860 (2 vols.; Washington,
D. C.: Carnegie Institution, 1933), II, 1035.

[15] Baker, *Atlas of American Agriculture*, Part V, sec. a, pp. 16, 18.

[16] Ulrich Bonnell Phillips, *American Negro Slavery* (New York: Appleton-
Century-Crofts, Inc., 1927), pp. 150–163.

it, provided in the meantime that competition for the land did not send
its price up rapidly. Unfortunately for the squatters, the latter phenom-
enon was occurring in the newer South. Planters with capital and
speculators either forestalled squatters by purchasing in advance of need,
or forced market values up to such levels that the squatter could neither
buy nor afford to retain ownership if he did acquire title.

The exodus of small freehold farmers from the coastal plain and the
Piedmont of Carolina and Georgia was also hastened by the expansion of
the cotton economy. Slaveowners tended to crowd them out. Potential
cotton land brought from five to more than ten dollars an acre, clearing
cost eight to fifteen dollars, fencing three to six dollars. Small farmers
with meager resources could not meet these expenses, build the
necessary house and shed, provide the essential farm implements and
stock, and subsist until returns from the first crop were received. With
no labor but his own, the small farmer could make only slow progress.
To support his family he had to raise corn, not cotton. Only when his
farm operations were well under way could he afford to turn to cotton.[17]
This is not to say that small farmers did not survive planter competition
in most good cotton areas, but the pressure upon them was always
present and many gave up and sold out. The piney woods area of southern
Georgia and later the upland hill sections of northern Georgia
provided a refuge for some of these small farmers who found little opportunity in the Piedmont. In some instances, however, poor whites and
freedmen became established in a small way in the cotton areas as farm
tenants, day laborers, or squatters who were tolerated until their lands
were wanted by the planters. As tenants they cultivated old fields
which the plantation owner had abandoned, paying a small rent. As
squatters they were sometimes permitted to use planter-owned land
which did not interfere with the large-scale slave operations; for this
privilege they might be required to perform small tasks.[18]

The rapid expansion of cotton planting in Georgia was facilitated
by the prodigal distribution of its public lands and by the removal of
the Creek and Cherokee Indians, who had long persisted in retaining
land admirably suited to the growth of the fiber crop.[19] Georgia was one
of the most profligate states in the disposal of its public lands. Although
the intent of the Georgia law was to restrict grants to 1,000 acres,

[17] M. B. Hammond, The Cotton Industry (Publications of the American Economic Association, New Series, No. 1; New York: The Macmillan Company, 1897),
pp. 101–102; Roger W. Shugg, Origins of Class Struggle in Louisiana (Baton Rouge:
Louisiana State University Press, 1939), pp. 81 ff.

[18] Guion Griffis Johnson, Ante-Bellum North Carolina (Chapel Hill: University
of North Carolina Press, 1937), pp. 68–72.

[19] The production of cotton, prices, and amount produced in the various states
are found in Baker, Atlas of American Agriculture, Part V, sec. a, pp. 16, 18.

individuals had secured numerous rights that permitted them to gain possession of tracts ranging from 10,000 to 1,000,000 acres. Later, when new cessions were acquired from Indians, land was granted or sold in 200-acre allotments for small sums through the operation of lotteries. Efforts were made to prevent allotments from falling into the hands of large owners but without much success.[20]

The Georgia Creeks and Cherokees clung most tenaciously to their ancestral homes, but the demand of cotton farmers for land was inexorable, the more so as the areas first brought into use soon wore out under the continued cropping to which they were subjected. It was the efforts to oust the Indians and the resistance of the Creeks and Cherokees to the pressure of the planters, small farmers, and speculators who sought their land that Ulrich B. Phillips considered to be the central theme of early Georgia history.[21]

A general weakness of American agriculture that showed itself markedly in Georgia was the tendency of farmers and planters, after accumulating considerable land and cropping the best of it for several years, to sell and move on to other locations. Continued farm- or plantation-making thus absorbed their attention. They skimmed the cream off the land, and, unwilling to maintain it by better farm practices, they left it for others with more patience and with knowledge of scientific farming to restore it to profitable use. The first group went on to other regions after taking two profits: one from mining the land and the other from rising land values, the result of improvement and the subsequent inrush of settlers. Such a practice was not materially different from that followed on a small scale by the squatter who sought out a desirable location on the public land, made a minimum of improvements while waiting for the demand for land that would make his claim valuable, and then sold. The squatter was not, however, exhausting land though he might be somewhat destructive of its timber.

NEW LANDS IN THE TRANS-APPALACHIAN STATES

After the War of 1812 the Georgian looking for new lands to exploit naturally turned to neighboring Mississippi Territory, where land was being opened to sale and settlement. Settlers from the Carolinas and

[20] Enoch Marvin Banks, The Economics of Land Tenure in Georgia (Columbia University Studies in History, Economics and Public Law, Vol. XXIII, No. 1; New York: 1906, passim; Niles' Register, XXXII (June 23, 1827), 277; Milton Sydney Heath, Constructive Liberalism: The Role of the State in Economic Development in Georgia to 1860 (Cambridge, Mass.: Harvard University Press, 1954), passim.

[21] Ulrich Bonnell Phillips, "Georgia and States Rights," Annual Report of the American Historical Association, 1901 (2 vols.; Washington, D. C.: Government Printing Office, 1902), I, 15 ff.

Virginia also rushed into the region that soon became Alabama. In fact, all the original southern states contributed heavily of their population to the newly developing commonwealths west of the Appalachians. Kentucky and Tennessee had been the first areas to attract residents of the older South. They had surpassed Georgia in population by 1810 and were to surpass South Carolina by 1830 and North Carolina by 1840. The phenomenal growth of these trans-Appalachian states is not easy to explain in view of the confusion in land titles and the great speculative landholdings which existed.

An aristocratic and concentrated pattern of landownership had been established in the tidewater states by lavish grants and abuse of the headright system; in Kentucky and Tennessee large grants, unrestricted sales and generous military bounties permitted an equally concentrated pattern of landownership to develop. L. C. Gray has shown that 60 per cent of the Virginia grants in Kentucky were for 1,000 to 5,000 acres, and 4 per cent were for 5,000 to 10,000 acres. There were 250 grants of 10,000 to 20,000 acres, 89 grants for 20,000 to 40,000 acres, 44 grants for 40,000 to 100,000 acres, and 4 grants in excess of 100,000 acres. In addition, speculators secured more than one grant; some had as many as fifty or more ranging from a few hundred acres to many thousands. The early land grants made by Kentucky itself were on an equally lavish scale. Seven persons acquired a total of 1,732,000 acres or an average holding of 247,427 acres.[22]

Grants made in such a reckless manner, carelessly assigned and inaccurately surveyed and recorded, frequently only after long delay, resulted in widespread confusion over titles. This insecurity of titles led the Kentucky legislature to provide in 1811 that all claims to land were to be produced and put on record within five years from adoption of the measure; none were to be admitted thereafter. Overlapping claims were to be referred to commissioners appointed by the legislature; in the meanwhile, all transfers were to be recorded. Unfortunately, the damage was done, and Kentucky, despite its excellent soil and favorable location, was by-passed by many westward movers for areas where land titles were more certain. Kentucky in 1815 still had wide areas almost untouched by settlers. Further title complications were provided by squatters who disliked absentee ownership and saw no reason why they should not set up counterclaims to the land they were improving.

[22] Gray, *History of Agriculture in the Southern United States*, II, 624. I have corrected the number of grants in excess of 100,000 acres. See Willard Rouse Jillson, *The Kentucky Land Grants* (*Filson Club Publications*, No. 33; Louisville: The Standard Printing Company, 1925), pp. 15–139 and the same author's *Old Kentucky Entries and Deeds* (*Filson Club Publications*, No. 34; Louisville: The Standard Printing Company, 1926), *passim*.

Lawyers' and court fees were high for years as a result of long-sustained litigation over titles. Sympathetic to squatters' rights, the legislature provided that the occupier of the land who lost a title dispute and was ejected should be reimbursed for the improvements he had made.[23]

The great speculator landlords showed discrimination by locating their holdings in the heart of the fertile Bluegrass region: in Fayette, Madison, Bourbon, Clark, and Scott counties. By the labor of squatters, tenants, small purchasers, and slaves, land was cleared, fenced, and put in cultivation. Wheat was easily and abundantly produced on these limestone- and phosphorus-bearing soils and it became the first cash crop. Livestock prospered in the area, and the raising of horses, mules, cattle, and swine was undertaken in a large way, thereby providing a type of mixed farming that was not hard on the land and at the same time produced an easily marketable surplus. The increasing tax burden, the demand for land, and rising land values induced division and sale of some of the speculative holdings. As late as 1816, however, as one indignant visitor noted, many thousand acres of undeveloped land in Kentucky were being held for $30 an acre by a "rich gentleman in Virginia, or . . . some other opulent, non-resident land jobber. . . ." [24] From the outset the unit of farm management in the Bluegrass country was large. The vitriolic Thomas Ashe, not distressed at the concentration of ownership and liking the aristocracy which had established itself in the vicinity of Lexington, commented on the neatness of the farms which "affect the English manner." [25]

Elsewhere in Kentucky, on poorer land, farmers with small means were taking up tracts of 50 to 200 acres under state legislation which permitted purchase at prices varying from five to forty cents an acre. By far the larger proportion of the 143,228 separate grants in Kentucky that Jillson lists were of this order. The near-subsistence farming practiced

[23] John Melish, *Travels through the United States of America* (2 vols.; Philadelphia: John Melish, 1815), II, 2–9, 226. Kentucky adopted laws recognizing squatters' rights in 1797, 1812, 1819, and 1820. William Littell and Jacob Swigert, *Digest of the Statute Laws of Kentucky* (2 vols.; Frankfort: Kendall & Russell, 1822), II, 724–728, 957, 961, 963–964.

[24] Samuel R. Brown, in his *The Western Gazetteer or Emigrant's Directory Containing a Geographical Description of the Western States and Territories* (Auburn, N. Y.: H. C. Southwick, 1817), p. 112, maintained that the "evil" of land speculation in Ohio, Pennsylvania, New York, and the western counties of Virginia as well as in Kentucky was a "disgrace of our legislation, which grant every facility to the rich, without consulting the interests of the poor." He noted that farms around Lexington were selling in 1816 for as much as $100 an acre.

[25] Thomas Ashe, *Travels in America, Performed in 1806, for the Purpose of Exploring the Rivers Alleghany, Monongahela, Ohio, and Mississippi, and Ascertaining the Produce and Condition of Their Banks and Vicinity* (London: R. Phillips, 1809), pp. 184 ff.

by these pioneers soon gave way to the cultivation of tobacco, which became their principal cash crop. Most of the early settlers in Kentucky and Tennessee were from North Carolina and Virginia, where they had concentrated upon tobacco and it was natural that they should raise the "weed" in the new commonwealths. Second to tobacco, whiskey—bourbon —was the most important item the Kentuckians sold.[26] Their 2,000 distilleries, one for every 200 people, produced more than five gallons of liquor for every person in the state in 1810. Only Pennsylvania, which produced eight gallons for every person, exceeded this record. North Carolina had more stills than any other state, but its production was little more than half that of Kentucky. The distilleries provided a growing demand for large quantities of barley, rye, oats, corn, and wheat, which farmers were glad to satisfy.

PRINCIPAL WHISKEY-PRODUCING STATES IN 1810

State	Number of Stills	Gallons
Pennsylvania	3,594	6,552,284
Virginia	3,662	2,367,589
Kentucky	2,000	2,220,775
New York	591	2,107,243
Massachusetts	—	1,628,326
North Carolina	5,426	1,386,691

Source: Compiled from the Census of 1810 (Philadelphia: Tench Cox, 1813). North Carolina had 1 still for every 111 people. Massachusetts led in the production of rum, which was distilled from West India molasses.

LAND POLICIES IN TENNESSEE

Chance played an important role in determining the nature of land which early settlers, planters, and speculators acquired. The immigrants to the Tennessee country were forced by circumstances to take up land in the thin-soiled, rugged, or steeply sloped and infertile eastern part. There farmers raised grain to feed cattle, the principal product they could market. Drovers annually purchased their surplus animals and drove them over the mountains for sale in North Carolina and Virginia. When better land in the Nashville Basin became available, many of these first emigrants undoubtedly moved on to try life there. Others remained, destined to suffer from the opening up of superior land elsewhere, an eroding soil that was producing ever poorer yields, isolation, distance from markets, low land values, a poor tax base, inadequate educational and other social facilities, and poor nutrition. Those on the worst land,

[26] Henry Bradshaw Fearon, Sketches of America . . . (3d ed.; London: Longmans, Hurst, Rees, Orme, & Brown, 1819), pp. 237–238.

suffering from malnutrition and hookworm and finding their efforts produced little, became lazy, shiftless, "no account," perhaps "poor white trash," the "southern mountaineer." Those on somewhat better land struggled hard to improve their position, had better returns from their labor, were able to vary their diet somewhat more, improve their homes, even expand their ownership of land. By the second or third generation the descendants of both groups were pressing on the supply of cultivable land, and many of the younger men were attracted elsewhere by better land. Division of the larger holdings was resorted to in some instances, but in eastern Kentucky and Tennessee the parceling of tracts never went to the extremes found in Ireland or on the Continent. Americans rarely became so wedded to an area that they would stay there when it became overcrowded.

The record of land distribution and use in Tennessee is not unlike that in Kentucky. By favoritism, fraud, and misuse of authority, and by taking advantage of loosely drawn laws in an area where the jurisdiction of North Carolina and Tennessee overlapped, speculators and land companies had acquired most of the best land, including the Nashville Basin and the choice tract in western and southwestern Tennessee, which was to be intensively developed in cotton. Holdings of 100,000 to 300,000 acres were established, though no person could retain ownership of such large tracts for long after taxes were levied. Most large holders found that their expectations of sales were rarely fulfilled and that meanwhile interest and taxes had run away with their resources. Only prompt sales or renting could save them. Those who sold early might only make a small profit, but they could come out with a whole skin. Others who held too long were forced to sell their land at distress prices that did not cover all costs in the transactions. About 1813, speculator-owned land in Tennessee was selling for 12½ cents an acre.[27] Unfortunately, actual settlers seeking small tracts were rarely able to pick up land at these prices. Large owners who wanted to retain and develop their holdings, but who lacked the necessary capital and slaves to do so, resorted to tenancy to achieve their aims. They made agreements with tenants, generally recent arrivals or squatters, to build log houses and to clear, fence, and cultivate land for a period of years rent-free, at the end of which time the tenants were

[27] Thomas Perkins Abernethy, in his *From Frontier to Plantation in Tennessee* (Chapel Hill: University of North Carolina Press, 1932), finds greed for land a central theme in Tennessee political history, but he gives little detail concerning the distribution of land by the governments of Tennessee and North Carolina. Cf. Samuel Cole Williams, *Beginnings of West Tennessee: In the Land of the Chickasaws, 1541–1841* (Johnson City: The Watauga Press, 1931), p. 99; "Recollections of Memucan Hunt Howard," *American Historical Magazine*, VII (January, 1902), 55–68; Carl S. Driver, *John Sevier, Pioneer of the Old Southwest* (Chapel Hill: University of North Carolina Press, 1932).

either to pay a share or cash rent or give up their improvements. In the Tombigbee Valley of Alabama, farms of 200 acres with 25 or 30 acres in crops rented in 1812 for 200 bushels of corn or $100.[28]

Persons who located in the Nashville Basin had much in their favor. Endowed with a soil that was rich in both humus and minerals, well drained yet comparatively level, and not too difficult to bring into cultivation, this area was destined by nature to become a land of grain, livestock, and tobacco farms and plantations. The limestone soils of the Nashville Basin, like those of the Kentucky Bluegrass area, produced favorable yields of wheat, corn, and rye, much of which was used locally for human and livestock consumption.

There was less concentration upon a single crop in these trans-Appalachian states than in the lower South or in parts of the Old Dominion, but systematic rotation of crops and fertilization of the soil were not generally practiced. Increased production of cotton in the lower South created a demand for baling cloth and rope. There was therefore a good market for hemp, another cash crop which, like tobacco and cotton, could be raised to advantage on the plantation system. Gray states that by 1810 flax had become the "grand staple" of Kentucky. In Tennessee, flax was raised more extensively than hemp, but in Kentucky both crops were established as major features of the agricultural pattern. Despite the early concentration of landownership, small farms were numerous, their owners rubbing elbows with their neighbors, the great planters. Slaves were brought in early, and with their labor rich yields of tobacco, grain, livestock, hemp, and flax were brought forth.[29]

In addition to the staple crops of tobacco, rice, and hemp in Kentucky and tobacco and cotton in southwestern Tennessee, these states were important food producers for the lower South. When cotton and sugar prices were favorable in this latter area, the planters leaned heavily upon the corn, hogs, cattle, wheat, and hay of Kentucky and Tennessee as well as of the states north of the Ohio. But when cotton and sugar prices were less favorable, the staple producers of the lower South sought to make themselves self-sufficient. That they never succeeded was well for the food-producing states of the upper Mississippi Valley.

THE LOWER SOUTH AND SUGAR

The lower South, a recent addition to the United States where boundaries were not yet clearly defined, was a section of great social and eco-

---

[28] Lewis Sewall, St. Stephens, August 3, 1812, to Edward Tiffin, in Clarence Edward Carter, ed., *The Territorial Papers of the United States* (Washington, D. C.: Government Printing Office, 1938), VI, 316.

[29] Gray, *op. cit.*, II, 821–823.

nomic contrasts in 1815. In Mobile and New Orleans was to be found an easygoing Latin society and in Natchez, a small British aristocracy. Although the Latin civilization was deeply influenced by the influx of acquisitive and land-hungry Americans, it was able to assimilate them to its mode of life. These cosmopolitan communities were surrounded by illiterate Cajuns (descendants of Acadian exiles) and crude American frontiersmen. In the area from New Orleans to Natchez, highly developed plantations created by slave labor poured out their wealth in sugar or cotton for their planter-owners, but the little peasant farms which stretched back from the bayous in narrow strips barely sufficed to maintain their Cajun occupants. A variety of land systems and land policies— Spanish, French, English, and American—made for prolonged litigation which lasted in notable instances for half a century.

These contrasting states of civilization were well delineated in 1817 by William Darby, a Natchez planter from 1799 to 1804 and government surveyor in Louisiana:

A journey from New Orleans to the mouth of the Sabine, exhibits man in every stage of his progress, from the palace to the hut, and inversely. . . . The rapid transition from the superb mansions of the wealthy citizens of New Orleans and its vicinity, to the rudely constructed log cabin, on the Sabine and Calcasieu, will suggest matter for the deepest reflection. . . . On a space of three hundred miles can be found human beings from the most civilized to the most savage. In the city of New Orleans, four or five of the most elegant of the living languages of the earth are now spoken in all their purity; and there is now enjoyed all that luxury and learning can bestow. Upon the banks of the Mississippi many of the sugar and cotton planters live in edifices, where . . . are exhibited all that art, aided by wealth, can produce. In Attacapas and Opelousas the glare of expensive luxury vanishes, and is followed by substantial independence. . . . The farm houses are generally rough, but solid buildings, in which the inhabitant enjoys good, wholesome, and abundant food, and excellent beds.

In the western parts of Opelousas are found those pastoral hunters who recall to our imagination the primitive times of history.[30]

At an early date French families had located on the alluvial soils on both sides of the Mississippi above and below New Orleans. Experiments with tobacco, indigo, and sugar cane showed that the first, except for richly flavored perique, did not do well on fertile soils in a hot climate, but that indigo and sugar cane flourished. Market changes, the ravages of parasites, and severe competition with other areas better adapted to their production brought these crops into disrepute and they were largely abandoned after the American Revolution. Then a fortunate development wrought a swift change in the agriculture of the lower Mississippi: the

[30] William Darby, The Emigrant's Guide to the Western and Southwestern States and Territories (New York: Kirla & Mercein, 1818), p. 61.

perfection by Étienne Boré, on his plantation six miles from New Orleans, of the process of granulating sugar from the juice of the cane.

Planters from Baton Rouge to below New Orleans took up the raising of sugar cane and the production of sugar and molasses with highly profitable results. Governor W. C. C. Claiborne reported in 1806: "The facility with which the sugar Planters amass wealth is almost incredible. . . . It is not uncommon with 20 working hands to make from 10 to 14 thousand Dollars, and there are several Planters whose field negroes do not exceed forty who make more than 20,000 Dollars each year." One planter, Jean Noel d'Estrehan, was reported to have an annual income of $30,000 from his sugar and $6,000 from his real estate in New Orleans.[31] Sugar planters in the Mississippi Delta soon began to erect the "elegant and commodious" houses which have attracted the attention of travelers from that day to this.[32]

When the famous naturalist, Thomas Nuttall, visited Louisiana in 1819, he commented on the plantation of Julien Poydras on Bayou Sara, on which between 400 and 500 slaves were employed in the production of sugar. At this early time he estimated Poydras's estate to be worth several million dollars. In his will Poydras provided for the gradual emancipation of his slaves, said to number 1,200 in 1824.

Among the Americans who came early to Louisiana and acquired large tracts of land were John McDonogh, Daniel Clark, and Wade Hampton. Clark, who had a number of well-developed plantations, sold the largest and most valuable of them to Hampton in 1811 for $300,000. Abundant sugar and cotton crops, technical proficiency in making sugar, ease of marketing, and deals in land and city property made all three millionaires.[33]

[31] Dunbar Rowland, ed., *Official Letter Books of W. C. C. Claiborne, 1801–1816* (6 vols.; Jackson, Miss.: State Department of Archives and History, 1917), III, 361 ff., especially p. 363; Henry Ker, *Travels through the Western Interior of the United States from the Year 1803 up to the Year 1816* (Elizabethtown, N. J.: Henry Ker, 1816), p. 44; Charles Gayarre, *History of Louisiana: The Spanish Domination* (New York: W. J. Widdleton, 1854), pp. 347–349.

[32] Thomas Nuttall, *A Journal of Travels into the Arkansa Territory during the Year 1819* (Philadelphia: T. H. Palmer, 1821), p. 237; Helen Tunnicliff Catterall, *Judicial Cases concerning American Slavery and the Negro* (5 vols.; Washington, D. C., *Publication* No. 374, Carnegie Institution, 1932), III, 393–394, says the Poydras estate had a value of more than a million dollars at the owner's death in 1824; Alcee Fortier, *Louisiana Studies: Literature, Customs and Dialects, History and Education* (New Orleans: F. F. Hansell & Bro., 1894), pp. 7–16.

[33] Christopher Fitzsimons, Charleston, May 15, 1811, to Wade Hampton, Charles E. Cauthen, ed., *Family Letters of the Three Wade Hamptons, 1782–1901* (Columbia: University of South Carolina Press, 1953), pp. 14–15. Thomas Nuttall reported in 1819 that Hampton had over 400 slaves and produced in a single year 500 hogsheads of sugar and 1,000 bales of cotton worth $150,000. It is not clear whether he included Hampton's South Carolina plantations in these estimates.—Nuttall, *op. cit.*, p. 239.

Large profits permitted sugar planters to purchase numerous slaves, build levees to shut out flood waters, and clear increasing amounts of land. So valuable was the alluvial land along the Mississippi that by 1820 a levee six to nine or more feet broad at the base and four to six feet high had been built stretching for 130 miles on the eastern side and 170 miles on the western side of the river.[34] The wealth that sugar had brought to the D'Estrehan, Marigny, Bouligny, Poydras, and Trepagnier and other family groups enabled them to erect their magnificent plantation homes, to travel, to educate their children abroad, to patronize the arts, and to establish a high state of culture in a frontier wilderness.

One hundred and fifty miles north of New Orleans by land, and 322 miles by the Mississippi was Natchez, the center of the cotton culture of the Mississippi Valley. To Natchez, after a decade spent on a plantation near Baton Rouge, came William Dunbar, with numerous slaves. Dunbar raised indigo, corn, tobacco, rice, and cotton, but by the 1790's he was concentrating on cotton. By 1810 he was raising more than 500 bales, in addition to quantities of corn for domestic consumption. Dunbar combined the qualities of a harsh slave-driver, a persistent land-grabber, and a shrewd and resourceful businessman with a conservative political temperament, a keen interest in science, and a wide learning.[35]

To Natchez also had come wealthy families from New Jersey, Pennsylvania, and New England, bringing with them many slaves and capital with which to establish a flourishing aristocratic society.[36] Winthrop Sargent, for example, the puritanical and autocratic Federalist governor of Mississippi territory who had arrived in 1798, by marriage, settlement rights, and purchase had soon built up an estate of 8,000 acres of well-located and highly productive land near Natchez, on which he raised cotton. Despite his background, he had no more difficulty in reconciling himself to the employment of slave labor than did other immigrants who came from the North. Sargent claimed that his slaves brought him an annual return of $270 each, which would make his income high indeed.[37]

---

[34] Warden, *Statistical, Political and Historical Account of the United States*, II, 507; Adam Hodgson, *Letters from North America* (2 vols.; London: Hurst, Robinson & Co., 1824), p. 162.

[35] Dunbar's journal and letters in the Mississippi State Department of Archives and History have been published in Mrs. Dunbar Rowland, *Life, Letters and Papers of William Dunbar* (Jackson: Mississippi Historical Society, 1930), *passim*.

[36] J. F. H. Claiborne, *Mississippi as a Province, Territory and State* (Jackson: Power & Barksdale, 1880), p. 107; Major Samuel S. Forman, *Narrative of a Journey Down the Ohio and Mississippi in 1789-1790*, Lyman C. Draper, ed. (Cincinnati: R. Clarke & Co., 1888), pp. 19-63; Robert T. Thompson, *Colonel James Neilson* (New Brunswick, N. J.: Rutgers University Press, 1940), pp. 48 ff.

[37] For Sargent's purchase, see Adams County Deed Records, F:165 and G:367; for the income from slave labor see letter of François X. Martin, March 22, 1811, to

Natchez, like New Orleans, was a wealthy and cosmopolitan community developed in the midst of a frontier wilderness by capitalists who came as pioneers.

Because these early Mississippi and Louisiana planters did so well with their staple crops, they made little effort to raise grain and livestock for their own consumption, preferring to buy from the operators of flat-boats who brought supplies from Kentucky and Ohio. The ideal of self-sufficiency that was to motivate their successors in a later day was not a factor in their economic policies. The flourishing cotton business made southwestern Mississippi, like the lower Delta region, a fast-growing area. A census of 1816 showed that the four southwestern counties, of which Natchez was the center, contained 14,599 slaves, or 69 per cent of the Negro population of the state.[38]

Two other areas in which the plantation system was developing in the Southwest were the Huntsville region of the Tennessee Valley, then Madison County, Alabama, and the lower Tombigbee and Alabama Valleys. Madison County had 4,000 slaves in 1816.[39] Around Mobile and northward for a considerable distance on the Tombigbee and Alabama were centered the Spanish and British grants. In this area, where a considerable concentration of ownership had developed, cotton and sugar cane were planted.

The Acadians who came to the bayous of Louisiana after 1763 crowded tightly into a solid pattern of small farms having narrow frontages on the streams and extending back forty arpents (or slightly less than a mile). Lacking capital and, some said, enterprise, they improved little land but subsisted on slight cultivation, a few cattle that fed on the prairies, hunting, fishing, and trapping. Although they had originally acquired desirable land, they were early pushed out by late-comers and were left in possession of swamp and overflowed land which was not commercially feasible to drain; they were also left with prairie land useful for little more than grazing livestock.[40]

On the richly grassed prairies of Calcasieu and St. Landry Parishes were grazed large herds of cattle descended from the early Spanish importations. Vacheries, or great cattle farms of five, ten, and fifteen thou-

Col. John Hamilton, in Ulrich B. Phillips, *Plantation and Frontier, 1649–1863*, in John R. Commons, *et al.*, *A Documentary History of American Industrial Society* (11 vols.; Cleveland: Arthur H. Clark Company, 1910–1911), II, 197.

[38] Carter, ed., *The Territorial Papers of the United States*, VI, 730.

[39] *Ibid.*, V, 684–692; VI, 730.

[40] The *Planter's Banner and Louisiana Agriculturist*, Franklin, La., September 23, 1847, has a strongly worded criticism of the Acadians for their poverty and lack of enterprise and intelligence. See also William Henry Sparks, *The Memories of Fifty Years . . . Spent in the Southwest* (3d ed.; Philadelphia: Claxton, Remsen & Haffelfinger, 1872), Chap. 26, "Acadian French Settlers."

sand acres, had been blocked out on these prairies by the Fontenot, Wick-off, and Andrus families. By 1811 these farms had between 15,000 and 20,000 cattle and several hundred horses and mules.[41] Another area where cattle raising was a major industry was the piney woods region of southern Mississippi.

FARMING IN THE NEWER SOUTH

In the newer parts of the South, whether in the Bluegrass region of Kentucky, the limestone soils of central Tennessee, the upcountry of Georgia, or the cane and alluvial lands of Alabama, Mississippi, and Louisiana, the early experiments in farming had by 1815 shown great possibilities for future development. In the older portions of the South, the cultivated areas were badly depleted but there was much good land still unutilized. For those planters and farmers who loved their land and tried to develop a rational plan of agriculture to offset declining yields, there was hope in crop rotation, the use of lime and marl, abandonment of tobacco and the cultivation of new crops including clover, and the sale of slaves to the new South. To other practical farmers who could see no limit to the expansion of the United States and no alternative to cultivating staple crops, the new lands beckoned.

The cropping system which the South had developed on its tobacco, cotton, rice, and sugar plantations called unceasingly for more new land and an increasing supply of labor. Continued emphasis upon staple-crop agriculture and the production of ever-increasing quantities of these goods which, except for sugar, the domestic market could not absorb, forced attention upon foreign markets. Cotton, tobacco, and wheat (and wheat flour) constituted America's chief export items.

VALUE OF EXPORTS, 1815

Cotton	$17,529,000
Tobacco & tobacco products	12,809,000
Wheat & flour	7,209,000
Rice	2,785,000
Total	$40,332,000
Value of all exports	45,974,403

Source: Timothy Pitkin, Statistical View of the Commerce of the United States (2d ed.; New York: James Eastburn & Co., 1817), Chap. 4.

[41] Claims for 52,000 acres were confirmed to these three families. Compiled from American State Papers, Public Lands (8 vols.; Washington, D.C.: Gales and Seaton, 1832–1861), Vols. II, III, and IV; William Darby, Geographical Description of the State of Louisiana (Philadelphia: John Melish, 1816), p. 89.

Nothing could be of more importance to the South than the assurance that this flow of produce to foreign markets would not be interrupted. The Napoleonic Wars and American foreign policy had brought some interruption, but they had also brought higher prices. During the wars the Louisiana Territory and a part of West Florida had been acquired. If Calhoun for a time and Clay throughout his life were to support such sophistries as were embodied in the arguments for protection, others who were more aware of current trends and more farseeing were marshaling their forces in opposition. Large-scale farming as practiced in the South, except for the sugar, flax, and hemp plantations, made for no alternative to free trade.

CHAPTER II

Northern Agriculture in 1815

AGRICULTURE in the northeastern states, particularly in the New England states, was early displaced in importance in the minds of their statesmen by commerce and industry. Consequently, its problems were given little attention in Congress and in the press. Neither the devastation of the potato blight nor the calamitous effects of pleuropneumonia on the dairy herds, both of which wrought havoc in Massachusetts, stirred the lofty Webster or the high-minded Sumner to action. In contrast, leading Southerners like Clay, Calhoun, and Slidell never let an opportunity pass to argue the needs of the growers of hemp, flax, cotton, or sugar cane. One may search in vain for references to potatoes, onions, apples, and cheese in Congressional discussions but allusions to southern staples cannot be missed. The country was surfeited with literature relating to plantation economy but few heard or thought about the problem of the northern farmer.

One explanation for the neglect of the northern farmer is that slavery drew public attention to the plantation economy of the South. Neither abolitionists nor advocates of slavery could talk about it without discussing also the staple economy of the South which depended on it. When Southerners replied to attacks upon their peculiar institution they sought to turn the tables on their opponents by describing in lurid detail the "wage slavery" in the cotton mills of Massachusetts. European travelers also paid great attention to southern agriculture. These visitors brought with them aristocratic notions, a distrust of democracy, and a desire to associate only with the better class of people. The southern planter's big house, income, and leisure permitted him to extend generous hospitality and entertainment to guests as the working northern farmer could not. Even critics of slavery were likely to be captivated by southern hospitality. Only in a few spots outside the northern cities was comparable hospitality available. Travelers took full advantage of the Wadsworth home in Geneseo, Otsego Hall and Hyde Hall on Otsego Lake, John Greig's mansion in Canandaigua, and Stephen Van Rensselaer's palatial home in Troy, New York. Except in these localities they saw little of northern farm life save through the meager windows of stage coaches.[1] Had they been properly aware, they would have realized that northern farming was more important to the economic growth of the United States than the plantation economy of the South on which they lavished their attention.

THE LAND OF NEW ENGLAND

New England's touring Yankee peddlers, strident abolitionists, social reformers, and forceful leaders who sought to impose their theological and political philosophy on other sections of the country aroused deep resentment in the West and South. Western land and settlement promoters and southern politicians counterattacked by presenting a distorted picture of the Northeast. New England's thin, unproductive soil covered with rocks and boulders, its steep and rugged slopes that made the use of oxen and horses almost impossible, its long, harsh winters that isolated farmers for months, its early frosts and short growing season, its nagging women, fretting children, tight-fisted and hard-hearted farmers, and shrewd storekeepers ever ready to cheat the unwary were all part of the caricature of New England shaped by its critics.[2]

Much of New England had thin and infertile soil over a granite base. In addition to the mountainous country of western Massachusetts, northern New Hampshire, and the Green Mountain spine of central Vermont, there were other extensive areas not suited for anything but forest growth. Furthermore, except for the lower portions of southern New England, the growing season was short. These handicaps did not, however, prevent New England from developing into an agricultural region which supported a larger population than any state save New York until 1850. New England, without Maine, maintained in an area much smaller than Virginia an agricultural population 50 per cent greater than that of the Old Dominion, and New England's deficiencies did not prevent her from feed-

[1] One hostile critic of European travelers, himself an intelligent commentator on the American scene, said this of foreign observers: "They fly through the country in stages and steam-boats; make half their tour in the night-time; see nothing but the highways and a few great cities, the inhabitants of which are half foreigners; talk with a dozen foolish would be aristocrats, who give them dinners, and instil into them their own superficial notions, and then return to set themselves up as judges. . . ."—James Kirke Paulding, Letters from the South (2 vols.; New York: Harper & Brothers, 1835), II, 107.

[2] See the doggerel in the Little Rock Arkansas Gazette, April 30, 1826, about

"Such barren lands, such rocks and sands,
    And then, good Lord! so hilly."

ing in addition the rapidly growing population of her commercial and industrial cities, although with the aid of some grain and meat brought in from New York and Ohio.

New England's disadvantages of geography were offset to some extent by the advantage arising from the fact that land speculation had occurred to only a limited extent in that section. In the rest of the country speculative land companies or landlords commonly intruded themselves between the government, as the first owner of the land, and the pioneer owners. These speculator interests increased the cost of farm making, induced men to buy land on credit, exacted heavy interest payments that absorbed the fruits of the farmers' labor for many years, and skimmed off the profits of rising land values resulting from the settlers' own improvements. Their activities retarded the transition from subsistence to commercial agriculture by withholding undeveloped areas from settlers and delaying the coming of internal improvements.

It would not be correct to say that speculation was nonexistent in New England. Town proprietors in some communities accumulated large holdings, speculation in the New Hampshire grants was extensive, and in Maine large sales were made by Massachusetts.[3] William Bingham's purchase of two million acres was the largest, but other big holdings were established, mostly of timber land unsuited for settlement.

Squatters, tenants, landlords, and debt-ridden farmers as well as land speculators were known though not common. Timothy Dwight lists a town in Maine in 1807 which had 1,044 settlers, all of whom were squatters. One half the farms in Stonington, Connecticut, he found to be operated by tenants paying rents in produce worth from $100 to $700 a year. Another traveler commented on the "very extensive farm, and an entire village named Weathersfield," Vermont, owned by the wealthy William Jarvis.[4]

Notwithstanding these instances of extensive land accumulation in New England, on the whole, land was distributed on a more equitable basis there than elsewhere. There was therefore less tillable land undeveloped, fewer debt-ridden farmers and mortgages. Tenancy, squatting, absentee and alien ownership, and anti-rent wars were not the issues they were elsewhere. Settlers could devote their energies and their capital to the task of improving the land. Dwight sang a paean of praise for the

[3] Lewis D. Stilwell, Migration from Vermont, 1776–1860, Proceedings of the Vermont Historical Society, V (1937), 84; Florence May Woodard, The Town Proprietors in Vermont: The New England Town Proprietorship in Decline (New York: Columbia University Press, 1936), passim.

[4] Timothy Dwight, Travels in New-England and New-York (4 vols.; New Haven, Conn.: T. Dwight, 1820), II, 221; III, 24; and Benjamin Silliman, Remarks Made on a Short Tour between Hartford and Quebec in the Autumn of 1819 (New Haven, Conn.: Converse, 1820), p. 390.

New England system that assured "that every man in this country, almost
without an exception, lives on his own ground. The lands are universally
holden in fee-simple; and descend, by law, to all the children in equal
shares. Every Farmer . . . is the little monarch of a dominion sufficiently
large to furnish all the supplies of competence. . . ." [5]

Critics of New England wrote off its agricultural potentialities too
readily. They did not take into sufficient account the considerable areas
where high farming could profitably be practiced. The Connecticut Valley, which broadens into a level plain south of Northfield and has a growing season longer by a month than the upland sections bordering it, was
such an area. Here prosperous farms with fertile fields were early established. By 1815 these valley farms were becoming known for their truck
gardening and for their tobacco, dairy cattle, and even wheat. Onions for
the West Indian market constituted a profitable crop.[6] The Champlain
Valley of Vermont was another richly productive area having, as Elkanah
Watson said in 1805, "a range of excellent farms occupied by substantial
houses, and every appearance announcing the abodes of high-minded,
intelligent, republican farmers. A few elegant seats exhibited the presence
of affluence and taste." [7] Extensive and high-yielding timothy and clover
pastures helped to make this region a wealthy sheep and horse-breeding
area. An English traveler noted on his way from Boston to Canada by
way of Keene, Middlebury, and Burlington, the well-cultivated farms,
quantities of livestock, neat houses, and the steadiness and industriousness
of the farmers.[8] Elsewhere in the Housatonic, the Merrimack, the Black-
stone, and numerous smaller valleys, agriculture flourished. Aroostook
County in northern Maine, which had the largest extent of first-rate arable
land in New England, was, in 1815, a wilderness, not to be settled for years
to come.

Outside the valleys was rolling countryside where the thin, less fertile
soil was liberally sprinkled with stones. Yet these areas could produce
fine grass, potatoes, fruit, rye, and, at lower altitudes, corn. On these
plateau or rolling lands a more diverse program of land use had been
developed. Because they were farther than the valley lands from centers
of population, only articles of high value in relation to bulk, like butter,

[5] Dwight, op. cit., I, 17, 214–215.

[6] John Donald Black, The Rural Economy of New England (Cambridge, Mass.:
Harvard University Press, 1950), p. 181; Dwight, op. cit., I, 225. Cf. Edward Augustus
Kendall, Travels through the Northern Parts of the United States in . . . 1807 and
1808 (3 vols.; New York: I. Riley, 1809), I, 84.

[7] Winslow C. Watson, ed., Men and Times of the Revolution, or, Memoirs of
Elkanah Watson (New York: Dana and Company, 1856), p. 353.

[8] John Lambert, Travels through Canada, and the United States of North America,
in the Years 1806, 1807, & 1808 (3 vols., 3d ed.; London: Baldwin, Cradock & Joy,
1816), II, 301 ff.

cheese, or meat on the hoof, could be transported to market. The execrable roads in existence in 1815 did not encourage long hauls of any kind, and the new turnpikes were not much better.[9] Occupants of these plateau and rolling lands, after the first generation had cleared the more level areas, fenced the meadows, pastures, and crop land, and erected homes; they had few complaints and were not inclined to migrate elsewhere, although their younger sons might do so.

A third class of land was the steep and broken hillsides through whose thin, gravelly soils extensive outcroppings of granite base protruded. Huge glacial boulders were to be found on these hillsides, which were covered with heavy stands of mixed hard and soft woods. These timbered tracts were made useful possessions. Potash derived from the burning of the logs cut for clearing constituted a product of value that could be bartered for essential items the farmer could not produce.[10] Fuel wood early became an important item in the economy of farmers near Long Island Sound, who could ship it to the New York City market. Elsewhere it was hauled to nearby country villages and cities, to be sold for use in fireplaces and kitchen stoves. After coal had replaced wood as the major fuel in cities, cordwood still sold extensively throughout the northern states. In 1839, the first year for which statistics are available, 3,217,000 cords were thus sold. In Boston and New York the wood brought from five to eight dollars a cord.[11] Maple sugar was another important item on northern farms. Timothy Pitkin reported that from the maple trees of the North, principally New England and New York, was produced one seventh of the sugar consumed in the United States in 1810, which was almost as much as the cane sugar made in Louisiana.[12]

On these hill farms small islands of gravelly loam left by the glaciers existed here and there. These could be cleared and cropped, but most of the land in these hill farms was too broken and too rugged to be worth cultivating. Heavy pelting rain washed the top soil off or leached away the scant supply of essential minerals from the cleared ground. Declining yields showed farmers how unwise their fathers had been in investing labor in the backbreaking work of clearing such land. Tillage proving unprofitable, the occupants turned to raising sheep and beef cattle to utilize the still well grassed pastures.

[9] Percy Wells Bidwell, Rural Economy in New England at the Beginning of the Nineteenth Century, Transactions of the Connecticut Academy of Arts and Sciences, XX (1916), 311–318.

[10] Lambert, op. cit., II, 526–527.

[11] Sixth Census; or Enumeration of Inhabitants of United States (Washington, D. C.: Blair and Rives, 1841), p. 360; Boston Cultivator, February 2, 1839. The New York Herald of March 2, 1836, said fuel wood was "exhorbitantly high" with very little available. Prices were quoted at $5 to $7 a load.

[12] Timothy Pitkin, A Statistical View of the Commerce of the United States of America (2d ed.; New York: James Eastburn & Co., 1817), p. 283.

Livestock, particularly sheep, enabled farmers to remain on these hill farms for a second generation after their tillage capacity was gone. Livestock improvement was fostered by the Massachusetts Society for Promoting Agriculture, which offered a prize of $50 for the introduction of a superior ram or ewe from abroad.[13] In the first two decades of the nineteenth century some of the best Spanish Merino sheep were brought to New England. These, together with its Morgan horses, enabled that region to become a leader in the breeding and sale of high-quality stock. Sheep farming required larger pastures, better fences, good-blooded stock, and protection from killer dogs. All this took considerable capital and led to the consolidation of small farms.

Even before the transition to sheep farming was made, life on these hill areas had begun to yield a crop of discouraged and dissatisfied people. Hill farmers listened entranced to the blandishments of the representatives of the Holland Land Company or the Ohio Land Company, who optimistically described the lush soils and economic opportunities of the Genesee Valley of New York or the Muskingum Valley of Ohio. From these hill farms of southern New England, called by Thomas Cooper "the northern hive," went a growing stream of emigrants, younger sons at first, and finally entire families, to seek homes in western New York, Ohio, Michigan, northern New England, and elsewhere.[14] In his travels in New England on behalf of the Holland Land Company, John Lincklaen found a Vermont farmer who, although he had spent a considerable part of his life in creating a farm from the wilderness and who had not yet completed his new house, had bought a Genesee Valley tract in New York for a tenth or twentieth of the price he could get for his farm. At the age of fifty he was planning to move and to start anew with a much larger tract. Such was the ambition of restless Yankees who were not content with small holdings of inferior land when farther west they could acquire more and better acreage.[15]

New England cities, with their flourishing industries and commerce,

[13] *Papers on Agriculture Consisting of Communications Made to the Massachusetts Agricultural Society* (Boston: Young and Minns, 1801), p. 6.

[14] Thomas Cooper, *Some Information Respecting America* (London: J. H. Johnson, 1794), p. 8. For other promotional pamphlets, see Robert Munro, *A Description of the Genesee Country in the State of New York* (New York: The Author, 1804); and Charles Williamson, *Description of the Settlement of the Genesee Country, in the State of New-York* (New York: T. & J. Swords, 1799). Also see Richard J. Purcell, *Connecticut in Transition, 1775–1819* (Washington, D. C.: American Historical Association, 1918), pp. 139–158; and Jarvis Means Morse, *A Neglected Period of Connecticut's History, 1818–1850* (New Haven, Conn.: Yale University Press, 1933, Chap. 1.

[15] Helen Lincklaen Fairchild, ed., *Travels in the Years 1791 and 1792 in Pennsylvania, New York and Vermont: Journals of John Lincklaen, Agent of the Holland Land Company* (New York: G. P. Putnam's Sons, 1897), p. 83.

produced a demand for grain, flour, dairy products, vegetable crops, beef, pork, and mutton in addition to hay and grain for dray and driving horses. In 1815 this urban demand was limited, however, for it was still common for city and town residents to keep dairy cattle and hogs and to have vegetable gardens or perhaps small farms on the outskirts of the communities. Analysis of the goods brought to Boston from the Merrimack Valley by way of the Middlesex Canal in 1805 shows that "cyder" constituted the chief farm product sent to the city. But grain, apples, barrels of beef, flax seed, lumber, barrels, hoops, and ashes were also shipped to market.[16]

New England farmers found other markets for their surplus goods. New York City drew quantities of supplies from farms in Connecticut and Rhode Island as well as from western Massachusetts. Also, the rice and cotton plantations of South Carolina and Georgia and the planters of the West Indies took quantities of butter, cheese, lard, beef, pork, and livestock.[17]

Travelers and critics agreed that New England's farm methods and practices were inferior to those of old England. Dwight censured his own section for slovenly preparation of the soil, failure to practice rotation of crops, insufficient use of manures, and neglect of weeds. Most of these failures could be attributed, he felt, to the shortage of farm labor. Intensive cultivation or high farming would scarcely have paid, except on farms close to the larger cities and it is doubtful whether farmers could, with all their tasks, have undertaken more.[18]

That New England farmers were not altogether unprogressive was the view of Rodolphus Dickinson, of Greenfield, Massachusetts, who wrote a *Geographical and Statistical View of Massachusetts Proper* in 1813 to counteract unfair charges against his section. He pointed out that except in areas of high land values close to cities and on navigable rivers, Yankee farmers preferred to cultivate the land extensively. He contended that greater attention was being given to manures than formerly, that clover was being successfully introduced, and that plaster of Paris was widely used in improving the land. Despite the "humiliating picture of our agricultural economy, that is often drawn by interested strangers," he held that the farmers derived "as much profit from their farms in proportion to the capital employed, as those in the most prosperous, fertile, and best cultivated parts of Europe." [19]

[16] Christopher Roberts, *The Middlesex Canal, 1793–1860* (*Harvard Economic Studies,* No. 61; Cambridge, Mass.: Harvard University Press, 1938), p. 161.

[17] Bidwell, *Rural Economy,* pp. 294–302.

[18] Dwight, *Travels in New England,* I, 108–109; Bidwell, *op. cit.,* pp. 319 ff.

[19] Rodolphus Dickinson, *A Geographical and Statistical View of Massachusetts Proper* (Greenfield, Mass.: Denio and Phelps, 1813), p. 9. Corroborating evidence concerning the use of gypsum on New England farms is found in Kendall, *Travels through the Northern Parts,* I, 231.

Farm land values in New England, even for the poorer sort of country, were high, as compared with those elsewhere. Population density, the resulting pressure upon the supply of land, and the growth of towns all tended to maintain farm values at high levels. Edward Augustus Kendall, after a tour of Connecticut in 1807 and 1808, placed the average value for farm land in that state at between $40 and $50 an acre. A few years earlier Pitkin had given an average value of $15 for Connecticut and $7 for all of New England. The Connecticut figure far exceeded the average value of farm land in any other state except Rhode Island, and the average of New England was likewise greater than that of other states, except New Jersey.[20] These high values were doubtless for the better lands. They did not lead to tenancy, as high values did in other areas at a later time, but they did make the way to farm ownership difficult for succeeding generations and encouraged emigration to other states.

LAND SPECULATION IN NEW YORK

If land speculation was limited in extent in New England, it was rampant in New York. In the colonial period the governing clique had acquired by favoritism and collusion large tracts of land in eastern and southern New York. These holdings had been improved by squatters or by tenants, who were offered a period of free use after which regular rents were due.[21] Some of these large estates, owned by Tories, had been confiscated during the Revolution and partially broken into small holdings, but others had been sold in large tracts; the net effect was not to democratize landownership to any great extent.[22]

In the Military Tract of central New York, land bounties ranging from 500 to 5,500 acres had been granted to soldiers and officers who had

[20] Kendall, op. cit., I, 311; Pitkin, Statistical View of Commerce, p. 417; Fairchild, op. cit., pp. 82, 87.

[21] Charles Worthen Spencer, "The Land System of Colonial New York," Proceedings of the New York State Historical Association, XVI (1917), 150–164; Ruth L. Higgins, Expansion in New York with Special Reference to the Eighteenth Century (Ohio State University Studies, No. 14; Columbus: 1931); Irving Mark, Agrarian Conflicts in Colonial New York, 1711–1775 (Columbia University Studies in History, Economics and Public Law, No. 469; New York: Columbia University Press, 1940); David Maldwyn Ellis, Landlords and Farmers in the Hudson-Mohawk Region, 1790–1850 (Ithaca, N. Y.: Cornell University Press, 1946); Edith M. Fox, Land Speculation in the Mohawk Country (Cornell Studies in American History, Literature and Folklore, No. 3; Ithaca, N. Y.: Cornell University Press, 1949).

[22] Harry A. Yospe, The Disposition of Loyalist Estates in the Southern District of the State of New York (Columbia University Studies in History, Economics and Public Law, No. 469; New York: Columbia University Press, 1939), passim. The Livingston, Schuyler, Van Rensselaer, Clarke, and Duane holdings remained intact, occupied by hundreds of tenants.

fought in the Revolution. Not until eight years after the close of the war was the Indian title to the region cleared, and by then most veterans had been driven by economic necessity to dispose of their rights. John Maud visited the tract in 1800 and reported that common gossip had it that the rights had been "bought up by the speculators, who very rarely gave more than eight dollars" for a 500- or 600-acre warrant.[23] The largest single holding in the tract was 101,400 acres. The fifteen largest holders of land owned or controlled 370,000 acres.[24] Speculator ownership resulted in slow development of the area, squatterism, tax delinquency, title disputes, and tension between original owners and subsequent purchasers. It was to be many years before the large holdings were to pass completely into the hands of small farmers.

In New York the colonial policy of permitting individuals or groups of proprietors to acquire large tracts of land for resale to small farmers had been followed by both New York and Massachusetts. New York sold 3,625,000 acres of land to Alexander Macomb, and Massachusetts sold 6,000,000 acres of its New York land to Phelps and Gorham. These and other large purchases were resold in smaller quantities to a number of energetic promoters, among whom William Cooper, James Wadsworth, the Holland Land Company, and the Pulteney Associates are the best known.[25]

New York's land speculators undertook to colonize their tracts with people drawn from the decaying hill country of southern New England. Agents were sent there to bring these tracts to the attention of discouraged hill farmers who might easily be induced to sell out and migrate to the new frontier.[26] The rush of settlers to the Genesee country was to a con-

[23] John Maude, *Visit to the Falls of Niagara in 1800* (London: Longmans, Rees, Orme, Brown, & Green, 1836), pp. 38–39. Maude reported that the soldiers' rights, which sold at eight dollars in 1788, brought thirty dollars in 1792, and in 1800 were worth from three to five dollars an acre.

[24] Wayne H. Merrick, "The Military Tract of New York State," manuscript, Syracuse University Library. Merrick's tabulation is made from the *Balloting Book and Other Documents Relating to Military Bounty Land in the State of New York.*

[25] A map of New York State showing the location of "land grants patents and purchases" is found in Joseph Bien, *Atlas of the State of New York* (New York: Joseph Bien & Co., 1895). Also see Neil Adams McNall, *An Agricultural History of the Genesee Valley, 1790–1860* (Philadelphia: University of Pennsylvania Press, 1952), pp. 13 ff.; William Cooper, *A Guide in the Wilderness; or the History of the First Settlement in the Western Counties of New York* (Dublin: Gilbert E. Hodges, 1810), p. 13; James Fenimore Cooper, "Reminiscences of Mid-Victorian Cooperstown and Sketch of William Cooper," *Publications* of the Otsego County (New York) Historical Society, No. 1 (1936), p. 46.

[26] For the promotional activities of New York land companies and individual landowners, see Paul Demund Evans, *The Holland Land Company, Publications* of the Buffalo Historical Society, Vol. XXVIII (1924); Helen I. Cowan, *Charles William-*

siderable degree the result of the promotional work of these speculative groups.[27] Between 1790 and 1820 more than 800,000 people, one seventh of the population increase for the entire country, were added to the population of the upstate counties. New York by 1815 had become the major farm state, truly the Empire State.

When the canal fever struck New York, the great landholders and their agents actively sought state aid for favored projects. In addition, the Holland Land Company made a generous donation to aid the building of the Erie Canal, as did some individual speculators. Settlement promoters of the type of Cooper and Wadsworth were empire builders in a small way as well as speculators.

Aristocratic landed proprietors and representatives of absentee speculators moved in person to the New York frontier to participate in developing the wilderness. William Cooper, father of James Fenimore Cooper, settled at Cooperstown; William Church came to Angelica; James and William Wadsworth to Geneseo; Charles H. Carroll and William Fitzhugh to Groveland; [28] and Arnold Potter and the Rose family to the region west of Seneca Lake.[29] The migration of these families to the New York frontier was very different in character from the usual movement of pioneers to the West, and they were almost as important as the more numerous small farmers in its development. La Rochefoucauld-Liancourt says of Arnold Potter, who owned 25,000 acres near Penn Yan, that he lived in an "elegant and gentleman-like manner," maintaining several servants and renting his land to tenants.[30] Guy H. McMaster, an early local historian, wrote of the "not a few Virginia planters, with their great households, [who] abandoned their barren estates beyond the Potomac" and migrated to the region west of Seneca Lake where "there was an abundance of gentility . . . both sham and genuine." [31] A more recent historian, Dixon Ryan Fox, waxed sentimental in his description of aristocrats like David A. Ogden, Henry Van Rensselaer, the Parishes, and the Whites, who built

son, *Genesee Promoter—Friend of Anglo-American Rapprochement, Publications* of the Rochester Historical Society, Vol. XIX (1941); and McNall, *op. cit.*

[27] Orasmus Turner, *Pioneer History of the Holland Purchase of Western New York* (Buffalo: Jewett, Thomas & Co., 1849), pp. 454–464.

[28] Orsamus Turner, *History of the Pioneer Settlement of Phelps & Gorham's Purchase, and Morris' Reserve* (Rochester, N. Y.: W. Alling, 1852), pp. 365, 396.

[29] R. Sheldon Rose, "The Rose Family in Geneva," *New York History,* XXIII (January, 1942), 24–32.

[30] François Alexandre Frédéric de La Rouchefoucauld-Liancourt, *Travels through the United States of North America, the Country of the Iroquois and Upper Canada in the Years 1795, 1796 and 1797* (2d ed., 2 vols.; London: R. Phillips, 1800), I, 226–227.

[31] Guy H. McMaster, *History of the Settlement of Steuben County, N. Y.* (Bath, N. Y.: R. S. Underhill & Co., 1853), pp. 148–150.

NEW-YORK
CANAL LANDS
ON SALE.

THE unsold part of that extensive tract bounded on the *East end of Lake Ontario*, extending North from the mouth of *Salmon River*, to the Towns of *Henderson* and *Adams*, watered by the *Big Sandy* and *Little Sandy* Creeks, and their innumerable tributary streams; every part of the tract being within one day's easy drive of the *Erie Canal*. at the Village of Rome, and at Salt Point or Salina, and will be accessible to it by water, (from the outlets on the Lake) as soon as it shall be united to the Lake at *Oswego*, which it is supposed it will be in two years.

That part of the tract more particularly recommended to the notice of Settlers of industrious and steady habits, includes the Town of *Ellisburgh*, and number one of *Lorraine*, forming the south-west part of the *County of Jefferson;* and the Township *No.* 10, *of Richland*, north of Salmon River, and *Nos.* 6, 7, *and* 11, *of Orwell*, making the north part of the *County of Oswego*.

It contains about two hundred thousand acres, more than one half of which is now under actual improvement, and a great portion of it paid for and deeded; and having been from 10 to 15 years regularly advancing in settlement, has a numerous population, and possesses most of the advantages of old countries, as to schools, public worship, mills, distilleries, mechanics, manufactories, &c

Betterments, or partially cleared farms, may be had reasonably. The price of wild lands has always been held very moderate, and will be continued so until the whole are settled. A reasonable chance as to pay will be afforded, and the same fair and liberal treatment toward settlers, as has been heretofore practised, will be continued, of which information can be best obtained on the spot.

The present price (the choice *as to quality* allowed to the purchaser) is from two dollars fifty cents, to three, four, and five Dollars per acre, according to situation. The lowest rates are for Lands most distant from the Lake, and the Villages, which as they recede to the east, beyond the alluvial lands, gradually become more swelly and elevated; every part, however, is susceptible of cultivation, there not being a mountain or considerable hill on the tract.

The soil is strong and durable, adapted to grain, grass, and fruit trees. The more it is cultivated and known, the better it is esteemed. No country can possess a more *healthy climate*, or a greater abundance of living springs, and streams of *the purest water*, than this part of the tract; the prevailing Timber is a sufficient indication of the soil, being Sugar Maple, Beach, Ash, Elm, &c. the most profitable kinds for Ashes, which, if carefully saved, will defray the cost of clearing and fencing.

No part of the state of New-York is better adapted for *Cattle ;* the *air is so dry*, and the *temperature so uniform*, that they do not require to be housed during any part of the winter; and vegetation becomes abundant for their support by the 15th to 25th of April: it is rarely, if ever, necessary to fodder after that date. The prosperous state of the settlement may be inferred from the fact, that more than two thousand head of horned Cattle, and Horses, have been received by the proprietor within the last three years, from settlers on this tract, in payment for Land, and sold in the southern district of this state, and will be continued, as heretofore, to be received in pay, together with Ashes, Grain, Pork, Butter, &c.

The direct route to these Lands, for those who come from the East, is through *Utica* and *Rome*. Settlers, on arrival, will find local agents and others. who will assist them to make selection of their Land, after which they will apply for writings to the *General Land Office*, at *Ellisburgh*, under the superintendance of *William Constable Pierpont*, son of the proprietor, who will also be present at several stated periods, in the course of the year, at which office any information will be afforded, and business transacted, relating to other tracts of Land, owned by the subscriber, also on sale, on moderate terms, and in prosperous course of settlement, in the adjoining *Counties of Lewis, St. Lawrence, and Franklin.*

Apply to Agents in the respective towns—at the Land Office at Ellisburgh—or to the Subscriber, residing on Brooklyn Heights, opposite the City of New-York.

HEZ. B. PIERPONT.

October, 1823.

(Courtesy, Regional History, Cornell University)

themselves "mansions looking upon extended parks and prim formal gardens" in northern New York.[32] These aristocratic and wealthy pioneers brought with them the capital to clear and place in cultivation hundreds of acres of land. They also brought conservative political ideas, culture, refinement, and knowledge of the outside world, with which they kept in contact by visits, correspondence, and reading.

There was much land for sale in New York, and many companies and landlords were looking for purchasers in 1815. Competition among sellers and the inducements offered to settlers by the Ohio country made it inadvisable to hold land at high prices or to expect cash for small transfers. A broadside issued by thirty-three owners of land in St. Lawrence County, who met in New York "to adopt plans to promote views of persons disposed to emigrate" to northern New York, gives some idea of the competition for purchasers. The owners offered lands at $1 to $8 per acre, asked small down payments, gave as much as nine years' credit, and offered to accept potash, cattle, and merchantable wheat in payment.[33]

The Holland Land Company and the Pulteney Associates, being alien owners whose right to hold property in New York was under attack, deemed it advisable to push sales rapidly and to make their charges reasonable.[34] They offered some land as low as $1.25 an acre, although for most of their holdings they charged from $2.00 to $4.00, the price depending roughly upon demand, location, proximity to towns and roads, and the quality of the soil as determined by contour, forest cover, and general appearance.[35]

To ease the path of the pioneer and to make the price more acceptable, several years' credit was offered, only small down payments were required, roads and mills were constructed, and subsequently land buyers were given aid in marketing their livestock and crops. When payments became delinquent, leniency was generally shown, as it was not advisable for foreign or even domestic landlords to arouse against themselves the ire of numerous debtors.

[32] Dixon Ryan Fox, *The Decline of Aristocracy in the Politics of New York* (Columbia University *Studies in History, Economics and Public Law*, No. 86; New York: Columbia University Press, 1919), pp. 130 ff.

[33] Broadside, "Lands in the County of St. Lawrence, State of New York," (Regional History, Cornell University), ca. 1815.

[34] At a meeting in Genesee County, November 25, 1819, "the extravagant prices demanded" by the Holland Land Company were condemned, the amount of money being drained from the country by the payments of the principal and interest was deplored, and it was recommended that steps be taken to require foreign owners to provide their fair share of taxes for roads and schools. At this meeting the usual frontier position that increasing land values were to be attributed to improvements made by the farmers was expressed. See Broadside in Regional History, Cornell University.

[35] Evans, *op. cit.*, pp. 222 ff.

To refugees from New England's high-valued land, $1, $2, and $3 an acre did not seem extortionate, but payments were not easy to meet. The sheer task of clearing a forty-acre piece involved the heaviest of labor with tools not of the best. Fencing was essential to keep livestock from destroying the crops, but this task might be delayed in areas where there were few or no cattle. The cost of clearing and fencing land was variously stated by authorities of the time to be from $6 to $25 an acre; a fair estimate would be between the two extremes.[36] One pamphlet advertising land stated conservatively that the essential equipment of a pioneer consisted of a log house costing $50 if the construction work was hired; a yoke of oxen, $70; a cow, $15; farming tools which would include a hoe, a plow, an ax, and a saw, $20; and an oxcart, $30—making a total of $185.[37] Domestic furnishings could be fashioned largely on the farm but to make them took additional time. Faced with these unavoidable expenses, the pioneer's first attention was to take care of them and to provide subsistence for his family, not to make payments on his land. For years after his initial improvements the pioneer struggled toward his goal, an unencumbered title to his land. In New York State some of them never realized that goal because of the level of land prices.

The first returns which the pioneer obtained from his land came from the sale of the wood ashes accumulated in the process of clearing and burning the hardwood on his land. There was a ready market for either wood ashes, or potash and pearlash made from them, and crossroads storekeepers and itinerant peddlers vied with each other for such amounts as were available. Choice wood ashes brought as much as fourteen cents a bushel, while potash and pearlash were quoted in the Ithaca market in 1821 at $90.00 a ton and in the New York market at $121.25 a ton.[38] In the hope of stimulating improvements and getting their rent, landlords even furnished their tenants with kettles in which to make the potash. The two dozen kettles issued by James Wadsworth to his tenants doubtless contributed to the 3,653 barrels of potash that Rochester shipped east in 1818. Thereafter New York could boast of a potash production worth from $300,000 to $1,000,000 a year.[39]

[36] William Cooper, *A Guide in the Wilderness,* p. 32; Thomas Cooper, *Some Information Respecting America,* pp. 119, 143; Ellis, *op. cit.,* pp. 74–75; McNall, *op. cit.,* pp. 173 ff.

[37] Cowan, *Charles Williamson,* p. 157.

[38] *American Journal,* Ithaca, August 15, 1821; *Ithaca Journal & General Advertiser,* August 15, 1827; Jared Van Wagenen, Jr., *The Golden Age of Homespun* (Ithaca, N. Y.: Cornell University Press, 1953), pp. 165–168.

[39] Ulysses Prentiss Hedrick, *A History of Agriculture in the State of New York* (Albany: New York State Agricultural Society, 1933), pp. 139–141; McNall, *op. cit.,* pp. 5, 28, 89, 96. John Lincklaen, agent of the Holland Land Company, reported that three men at Whitestown made twenty tons of pearlash a year. The logs of seven to ten acres would make a ton of pearlash.—Fairchild, *op. cit.,* p. 71.

Skins and furs were another source of income to the frontiersman. A Finger Lakes newspaper listed prices paid for furs in 1821. They ranged from one to two shillings for mink skins to $2.50 to $2.75 for beaver skins.[40]

Wheat, for which most New York land was well suited, was the first crop the pioneer produced in quantity. It was valuable in proportion to its bulk, it could be transported long distances, and it was always in demand. It could be sown early in the development of the farm, did not need the attention that cotton or corn required, and after reaping could be threshed when time permitted. The greatest cost in producing wheat was in clearing the land and bringing it into cultivation. Land clearing could be accomplished by the labor of the settler, and his crop could be harvested with simple home-made tools, the sickle and the flail, though with immense labor.

Farmers near the Hudson or Mohawk could easily transport their grain to market or could sell to local millers or itinerant buyers. Genesee wheat flowed through Rochester and by way of Lake Ontario and the St. Lawrence to Montreal. Down the Chenango, Chemung, and Susquehanna rivers went boats, rafts, and arks loaded with wheat from the southern tier for Harrisburg and Baltimore, where it was milled into flour.[41] Arks seventy feet long and sixteen feet wide with a draft of two feet, operated by four hands, could carry 1,200 bushels of wheat by way of the Cohocton and Susquehanna rivers to Havre de Grace, a distance of 350 miles, in five to seven days. From there the grain was transported by canal to Baltimore.[42] A miller has told how during the first decade of the nineteenth century he purchased the surplus grain of farmers in Steuben County, ground it into flour, and in the spring shipped the flour in four to eight arks down the Canisteo and Cohocton rivers to the Susquehanna and on to Baltimore. When the Embargo disrupted the export trade in flour, he opened a distillery in which he converted the grain of the region into whiskey, gin, brandy, and cordials. He also bought cattle which he fattened and drove to Philadelphia. Enterprising middlemen found ways of conducting business, no matter how dull the markets appeared.[43]

Continued cultivation of wheat attracted the parasites and pests which prey upon it. The Hessian fly, the midge, the rust—all took toll. Careless farming, failure to keep livestock or to use animal manure if it was available, light tillage, inadequate weed control, and erosion of the topsoil so reduced yields that ultimately wheat ceased to be the basic crop in the New York farmers' economy.

[40] *American Journal,* Ithaca, August 15, 1821.

[41] William Cooper, *A Guide in the Wilderness,* p. 13.

[42] Maude, *Visit to the Falls of Niagara,* p. 57.

[43] Reminiscences of George M'Clure in McMaster, *Settlement of Steuben County,* pp. 138 ff.

Another item which had a ready market was whiskey distilled from rye, wheat, or corn. It was essential for public occasions such as house raisings, political gatherings, and weddings, and was liberally quaffed at inns and taverns by travelers and residents. Rye whiskey brought 25 cents a gallon in Ithaca in 1821, but when imbibed at inns it was more expensive. The demand for whiskey was so extensive on the frontier that it may be doubted that any substantial part was shipped to New York City. Distilleries were not difficult to set up and most communities could boast one or more. Landed proprietors like the Wadsworths and Charles Williamson found it desirable to set up stills in which they could use a part of the grain paid as rent. The Census of 1845 revealed 221 distilleries in New York State with a heavy concentration in Orange, Ulster, Ontario, and Otsego counties. In that year $3,162,580 worth of grain was used in the manufacture of whiskey, which represented a very considerable part of the entire grain output of the state.[44]

LANDLORDISM AND TENANCY

Landlordism and tenancy were flourishing features in New York at the opening of the nineteenth century. In 1807 in four counties (not including New York County) more than half of the people qualified to vote were tenants. In 1814 this was true in eight counties and in 1821 in fifteen counties. A solid block of ten counties in the Holland Land Company's purchase had more tenants than freeholders. The ratio of tenants to freeholders was three to one in Alleghany County and two to one in Genesee County. In northern New York and in the Hudson Valley, where Yankee farmers had become tenants of the Rennselaers, Livingstons or Schuylers, the number of freeholds was small. For the entire state except for New York County the Census of 1821 showed 105,577 freeholders and 80,274 tenants.[45]

Many persons listed as tenants were undoubtedly attempting to buy land. Since it was a common practice to give title when land was sold and to take a mortgage as security for future payments, this incumbrance, with accumulated interest, became increasingly heavy in cases of delinquency. When hard times fell and money was scarce, as in 1807 or in 1819, it was almost impossible for debtors to meet their obligations. Pressure by creditors might take the form of seizure of crops and livestock or foreclosure. The debtors, faced with the loss of their homes and the labor

[44] *American Journal*, Ithaca, August 15, 1821; *Ithaca Journal & General Advertiser*, November 14, 1827; *Census of the State of New York for 1845* (Albany: Carroll & Cook, 1846), *passim;* McNall, *op. cit.*, p. 91; Cowan, *Charles Williamson*, p. 154.

[45] *Census of the State of New York for 1855*, prepared by Franklin B. Hough (Albany: Charles Van Benthuysen, 1857), pp. ix–x.

NO OPPRESSION !
Justice to the old
Settlers!

ANANIAS WELLS and SETH EDDY, opposed to the Aristocratic measures of the Agents of the Pulteney and Hornby Estates.

From the Lyons Countryman, of Oct. 12.

The following correspondence relates to a subject of much interest to the people of this county, and affecting materially the principles of a just public policy. We are gratified with the general view presented, in the reply of the respectable anti-masonic candidates for assembly in Wayne. These gentlemen have both purchased lands of the estates in question, and have thought much and closely upon the operation of the course of proceeding adopted by the agents of those estates. We shall be glad of further light, in this concern, and will not fail to lay before our readers all the intelligence we may receive respecting it.

LYONS, 1st Oct. 1830.
To Ananias Wells and Seth Eddy.

GENTLEMEN—Several members of the County Convention held here yesterday, by which you were nominated as candidates for the next Assembly, have requested us to lay before the public an authentic expression of your sentiments, on the subject of the enquiry, or controversy, now pending between the contractors for the land of the Pulteney and Hornby estates, and the Agents of those estates. Having learnt those sentiments themselves, by private conversation, they wish to have them made public. And trusting from the frankness of

ject, are, and at the same time, to authorise us to make those views public, if the principles of justice, or a becoming desire to correct misrepresentation shall seem, to us, to demand it.

We are with much respect, Gent. your ob't. servants,
MYRON HOLLEY,
WM. VOORHIES,
J. A. HADLEY,
County Corresponding Committee.

[*Messrs. Wells and Eddy's Answer.*]
October 6, 1830.
To the Committee of Correspondence of Wayne County.

GENTLEMEN,—We have received your note of the 1st inst. and have no objections, frankly, to make the expression you ask for, nor to your publishing that expression, if you think it will promote the interest of our fellow citizens.

We are both of us interested, in the inquiry or controversy, to which you allude, and are not more indifferent spectators of it. And we think the purchasers of the Pulteney and Hornby lands, as a body, have reason to

2d. Because compound interest has been uniformly demanded.

3d. Because all payments are required to be made in money, and no part of them in any country produce.

4th. Because the monies paid have not, in any equitable measure, been laid out to improve the country, by the labor of which they have been accumulated.

This last cause has been shown, by experience, as we think, to be of vastly more consequence than could have been foreseen; and is the great, though not the only reason, why the other causes have operated oppressively. The difference, in effect, upon any agricultural country, arising from having nearly all the money earned by its labors, paid over to those who carry it out of the country to foreign owners, and from having the same money laid out in improving the country from whose industry it proceeds, is immense. In the one case, that of carrying off the money, the country is necessarily impoverished : in the other case, that of laying out the money in improving the country, it is enriched. The first

second case operates like returning, every year, to the soil of a field, as much nourishment, for a future crop, as the crop of the year after it is gathered in, has deprived it of; which every farmer knows, will preserve the land, in good heart, forever.

To have enabled the country, covered by these estates, to prosper, after buying its lands upon the terms deprofits of its labor, over and above what was required to subsist the laborers, should have been laid out in constructing and repairing roads, erecting and maintaining bridges, building mills, supporting schools and other public establishments, *in the country itself.* But this has not been done, and the prosperity of the country has, therefore, been greatly retarded. We are of opinion that the Legislature of the state may do something to relieve the settlers ; and shall always, whether elected to the Legislature or not, earnestly promote every measure which we shall think honest, and calculated to afford the settlers that relief to which they are justly entitled.

We are, respectfully, yours,
ANANIAS WELLS,
SETH EDDY.

Settlers' complaints against the Pulteney and Hornby Estates (Courtesy, Regional History, Cornell University)

of years, pleaded with their creditors to write off back interest, grant extensions, accept produce in lieu of cash for payments, and postpone eviction. Tension between landlords and tenants or debtors frequently flared up in political attacks, efforts to tax large estates heavily, especially those owned by aliens, newspaper bickering, and, at times, mob violence. Few states before or since 1815 have been so troubled by anti-rent wars as was New York.[46]

[46] There is much material concerning tenancy, rental agreements, and landlord-tenant relations in New York in Ellis, *Landlords and Farmers in the Hudson-Mohawk Region,* pp. 16–55. Also see Henry Christman, *Tin Horns and Calico: A Decisive Episode in the Emergence of Democracy* (New York: Henry Holt and Company, 1945), *passim.*

VENDUE!

The subscriber will sell, at **Public Vendue**, on SATURDAY, the 3d day of April, at 10 o'clock A. M., at the residence of William P. Young, in the town of [Guilderland, half mile north of the **Reformed Dutch Church**, the following property, viz:

1 Bay Mare,
1 Sorrel Mare,
1 Yearling Colt,
2 New Milch Cows and Calves,
1 Heifer,
1 Pair Steers,
1 Bull, (extra)
4 Sheep, 4 Shoats, 45 Fowls,
10 Bushels Buckwheat,
100 Bushels Oats,
100 Bushels Rye,
23 Grain Bags,
15 Bushels Corn in the Ear,
6 Bushels Wheat,
3 Horse Blankets,

1 Lumber Wagon,
1 Lumber Sleigh,
1 Set Double Harness,
2 Ploughs,
1 Harrow,
1 Log Chain,
1 Horse Rake,
4 Forks,
1 Dung Fork,
1 Shovel,
2 Ox Yokes,
1 Lot of Hay,
1 Lot of Straw Bundles,
1 Lot loose Straw and Fodder,
1 Lot Seed Potatoes,

Together with a lot of Scythes, Snaths, Hoes, Ploughs, Shears, Barrels, and other articles too numerous to mention.

Terms of Sale:

A credit of nine months will be given on all sums over $5, six months without interest if paid when due, if not interest from date with approved endorsed Notes. All sums of $5, and under, Cash. No property to be removed until the terms of sale are complied with.

WILLIAM P. YOUNG.

Guilderland, March 18th, 1858.

Albany Morning Express Print, 52 State Street, cor. Green.

Inventory of stock, grain, and equipment on a New York farm, 1858 (Courtesy, New York State Historical Association)

Tenancy worked badly in the hill areas of eastern New York. The requirement that rent be paid either in wheat or in cash brought about continued cultivation of wheat, the one important cash crop. Having no equity in the land aside from their improvements and under the necessity of meeting their rent, the tenants cropped the land to destruction. Declining yields made it difficult for them to make their payments and caused unrest that ultimately broke out into open warfare.

In other parts of New York tenancy flourished. The proprietors of the Fonda Patent, Baron Steuben, the Pierrepont-White estate, the Wadsworths, Charles Carroll, and the Fitzhughs all rented their large estates in whole or in part. The 40,000-acre Clarke estate in the vicinity of Otsego Lake went through interesting transformations. The leases for three lives originally granted the tenants were gradually changed into short-term leases with high rents, and tenants were required to farm the land and maintain improvements as the owner dictated. The estate with its hundreds of tenants was retained until the late eighteen eighties, and a small portion was held by the Clarkes into the twentieth century.[47]

In the Genesee country permanent landlordism flourished. Here men of capital determined to erect for themselves and their families estates to be held in perpetuity. Land was sold only to raise essential capital for further improvements on other land or because it was not desirable to hold certain remote or separate tracts. Because of the craze for Genesee land the landlords had no difficulty in securing tenants or in making agreements with squatters already on their land. After a short period of free use of the land, the landlords exacted 24 bushels of wheat per 100 acres. Later, the rent became 8 bushels an acre, and eventually a share rent was substituted for what had been essentially a cash rent.

In their frontier mansions in Geneseo, Bath, Canandaigua, and Angelica the great landlords were able to live in opulent style in the pattern of the English landed gentry. With domestic servants and hired hands to perform the work in the big house and at the stables, and with tenants to cultivate the fields, the master of the estate had only to supervise and handle the business details of marketing his crops and livestock; his leisure could be spent in fox hunting. Tenants had to have their grain ground at the landlord's mill and sell their products to him in the absence of other outlets. On each of these transactions the landlord exacted a profit. If tenants became delinquent or needed funds for some purpose and borrowed from him, he required heavy interest compounded regularly. Frequently he owned or controlled the local store, dispensed legal advice, became justice of the peace or county judge, member of the legislature, and local political boss.[48]

[47] Fox, *Land Speculation in the Mohawk Country, passim.*
[48] Edward Noyes Westcott, *David Harum: A Story of American Life* (New York:

Although the growth of freehold tenure in New York State lagged, many factors were working in its favor. If full ownership could not be attained, the disillusioned farmer was likely to give up the struggle, abandon his equity or sell it if possible, and strike out to the West for another attempt. The fear of losing tenants, purchasers of lands, or even farm laborers was a factor that induced landowners to deal leniently with them, sell at lower prices, and pay higher wages. Landlords and land agents could not fail to realize the harm that would come to them if wholesale migration of distressed and disillusioned tenants were to take place. Willingness to abandon unpromising farms is early apparent, even in the frontier period of development. For example, a group of residents of Ovid Township in the Military Tract of New York petitioned Congress in 1806, at which time they could have been living on their land for only a few years, asking the privilege of buying a township of land in Ohio to which they might move.[49]

Other factors were working against the continued growth of tenancy. Rising tax burdens, opportunities for investment in other enterprises, and the slow returns from land all encouraged the liquidation of large holdings. Estates came to be divided by inheritance; others were lost by foreclosure, the result of too sanguine borrowing upon them. The net effect was to make easier the road to ownership for many small farmers.

Despite the flood of immigrants into its upstate counties, New York in 1820 still had much undeveloped land. High land prices, the exactions of landlords, and the fact that the best land had been taken up by the first-comers and that the remainder was inferior to cheap public land farther west tended to discourage the purchase or rent of these poorer lands. Not until the frontier had moved beyond New York were people content to take them up and improve them.

FARM-MAKING IN PENNSYLVANIA

Pennsylvania was more fortunate than New York in that its colonial administrators had followed an enlightened land and immigration policy that encouraged wide ownership of land in small tracts, and at the same time allowed men of means and influence to establish manors to which they brought numerous tenants.[50] Toward the end of the eighteenth century the legislature had breached this liberal policy by allowing unlimited

---

D. Appleton & Company, 1898), a novel about an upstate landed magnate who acquired numerous farms through loans and foreclosure.

[49] *American State Papers, Public Lands* (8 vols.; Washington, D. C.: Gales and Seaton, 1832–1861), I, 288.

[50] Elizabeth K. Henderson, "The Northwestern Lands of Pennsylvania, 1790–1812," *Pennsylvania Magazine of History and Biography*, LX (April, 1936), 131–160.

purchase of land. By 1815 this policy had resulted in a concentration of ownership in parts of northern and western Pennsylvania quite in contrast to the more democratic distribution of land in much of the remainder of the state. For example, eighteen individuals and partnerships thus acquired more than 4,200,000 acres, much of which fell into the hands of three companies: the North American Land Company, the Holland Land Company, and the Pennsylvania Population Company.[51]

Of these three, the Holland Land Company was the most active in promoting settlement, chiefly because it feared its title was not sound and it wanted to dispose of its holdings before the validity of the title was denied. The company built and maintained stores stocked with necessary supplies for settlers, advanced money to immigrants to enable them to get started, constructed mills on and roads through its lands, and advertised the advantages of western Pennsylvania.[52]

Immigrants swarmed into these unimproved, speculator-held lands in northern and western Pennsylvania, convinced that the title was invalid because the owners had not conformed to the settlement requirements of the Act of 1792 and they refused to purchase or to pay rent on their claims. Not having security for their claims and fearing ejectment, these squatters did not make permanent improvements. They cared not for the preservation of either the forest or the soil and made a shambles of their claims, which they planned to abandon when better land with good titles should become available across the Ohio.[53] A traveler through the region in 1815 declared that "many small farms, which had been cleared some years ago . . . are completely deserted: and the solitary buildings, or the burnt spots where they stood, fill the passenger with melancholy reflections. Even the improvements of former years, now occupied are retrogressive. The chief part of the remaining inhabitants remind us of exiles. . . ."[54] After working through the original sources of this sorry conflict over titles, Paul Evans summed up its results:

The log cabins were more shabby, the clearings smaller and more slovenly, the fields more carelessly tilled than in almost any other frontier community of the day. Many of the settlers were half starved for lack of proper food; the ma-

[51] Compiled from William Henry Egle, ed., *Warrantees of Land in the Several Counties of the State of Pennsylvania, 1830–1898, Pennsylvania Archives,* Third Series, XXVI (1897), 701–905; Sherman Day, *Historical Collections of the State of Pennsylvania* (Philadelphia: G. W. Gorton, 1843), pp. 261–262; Evans, *The Holland Land Company,* Chaps. 4 and 5. The Dutch capitalists had a large share in the Pennsylvania Population Company.

[52] Nina Moore Tiffany and Francis Tiffany, *Harm Jan Huidekoper* (Cambridge, Mass.: The Riverside Press), p. 107.

[53] Henderson, "The Northwestern Lands of Pennsylvania," *loc. cit.,* pp. 156–160.

[54] David Thomas, *Travels through the Western Country in the Summer of 1816* (Auburn, N. Y.: David Rumsey, 1819), pp. 41–44, 268–270.

jority were clad in the most miserable clothes. Abject poverty held the whole country in its grip. As the farmers had neither oxen nor horses they were unable to cultivate their lands; they could only scratch over the surface with a hoe. The crops of grain were hardly sufficient to supply the settlers' families with bread for half the year.[55]

By 1799 the democratic forces had ousted the Federalists from control of the legislature and courts of Pennsylvania. Under the pressure of western equalitarians, every possible legal obstacle was placed in the way of speculators and land companies trying to make good their titles. Not until property-conscious John Marshall had an opportunity to deal with the question of the rights of the speculators was there any security for their investment. Even with Marshall's utmost aid, they had to compromise with the squatter-settlers because the state courts were not inclined to follow the Federalist line on property rights. Ultimately both sides gave way, the squatters agreeing to make modest payments which neither wrecked their hopes of financial independence nor brought to the speculators the profits they had anticipated. The struggle between the landlords and the squatters was long and costly to both sides, and litigation and angry feeling lasted well into the twenties and thirties.[56]

A somewhat similar situation existed in northeastern Pennsylvania, where the usual squatter-tenant animosity toward the landlord was complicated by the overlapping claims of Connecticut and Pennsylvania. The resulting "Pennamite Wars" and the long and involved litigation did not end until well into the nineteenth century, by which time many landowners had paid for their land two or three times over in an effort to get clear title.[57] Meanwhile they had found it difficult to sell the disputed land.

As late as 1824 William Bingham, the well-known Philadelphia aristocrat and land speculator, was advertising for sale at $2.50 to $3.00 an acre 250,000 acres of land in Bradford and Tioga counties with ten years to pay, the first three of which carried no interest charges. Undoubtedly a good portion of this land, along with 500,000 acres in Potter, McKean, Lycoming, Armstrong, and Jefferson counties which was available at $2.00, was timbered, mountainous, thin soiled, and infertile.[58]

Notwithstanding the retarding effect of the difficulties between landlords and tenants and between rival landlords upon the agricultural devel-

[55] Evans, The Holland Land Company, pp. 161–162.

[56] Tiffany and Tiffany, op. cit., pp. 126 ff.

[57] Louise Welles Murray, History of Old Tioga Point and Early Athens, Pennsylvania (Athens: 1908), contains documentary materials relating to the land squabbles. At his death in 1832 Carroll still held 27,691 acres in Pennsylvania.—Kate Mason Rowland, Life of Charles Carroll of Carrollton (2 vols.; New York: G. P. Putnam's Sons, 1898), II, 399.

[58] New England Farmer, III (August 7, 1823), 16.

opment of the state, Pennsylvania had achieved remarkable progress by 1815. Wheat was the principal cash crop, its cultivation being well adapted to the soil and climate of most of the arable land. Yields of wheat were quite generally low, ten to twelve bushels to the acre being common. Thomas Cooper noted that this was about half the yield of good English farms. He was aware, however, as many other critics of American agriculture were not, that though this seemed a low yield per acre it was high in relation to the amount of labor expended.[59]

Farm practices of the Pennsylvania "Dutch" in southeastern Pennsylvania, notably in Lancaster and York Counties, were superior to those commonly found elsewhere. Here early German immigrants had obtained the best limestone soils which, heavily endowed with mineral and vegetable elements, compared favorably with the best soils in the country.[60] Frugal, hard-working, methodical, skilled in the best farm practices of the day and having a profound respect for the land, these German-speaking Americans were the best farmers in the New World. The very richness of their land made it possible for them to satisfy their creditors without mining the soil. As their clearings progressed they were stoutly fenced and the stumps were removed, not left to obstruct the plow while they rotted. The practice of allowing land to lie fallow was adopted and soil building was begun well before the opening of the nineteenth century. Red clover with its humus and nitrogen-building qualities was introduced. Deterioration of the soil from constant raising of grain crops was prevented by careful rotation, light pasturing of the clover, which was kept over two years, and the spreading of lime, gypsum, and manure on the fields. A system of rotation commonly practiced called for corn, oats, wheat, and clover. Seed was selected, weeds were destroyed, and meadows were irrigated.[61] Good breeds of cattle were maintained, housed in great stone barns that were generally superior to the homes of the owners, and manure was carefully husbanded.[62] The stone barns were functionally designed to provide the most convenient use of space, the greatest comfort for the livestock, and ease of work for the farmer. All hay, straw,

[59] Thomas Cooper, *Some Information*, pp. 113–115.

[60] Henry Francis James, *The Agricultural Industry of Southeastern Pennsylvania* (Philadelphia: 1928).

[61] Thomas Cooper, *op. cit.*, p. 157. Rayner Wickersham Kelsey, ed., *Cazenove Journal, 1794: A Record of the Journey of Theophile Cazenove through New Jersey and Pennsylvania* (Haverford: Pennsylvania History Press, 1922), pp. 29, 35, 77; Albert Bernhardt Faust, *The German Element in the United States* (2 vols.; Boston: Houghton Mifflin Company, 1909), I, 131 ff.; Richard H. Shryock, "British Versus German Traditions in Colonial Agriculture," *Mississippi Valley Historical Review*, XXVI (June, 1939), 29–54.

[62] Stevenson Whitcomb Fletcher, *Pennsylvania Agriculture and Country Life, 1640–1840* (Harrisburg: Pennsylvania Historical and Museum Commission, 1950), pp. 132 ff.; *Farmers' Cabinet*, I (September 1, 1836), 52–53.

stock, and carriages were housed in the barn instead of being left outside or kept in outbuildings, and fresh and abundant straw litter was continually supplied.[63]

In 1817 Henry Fearon noted the "excellent breed and condition of livestock and superior cultivation" of the German-speaking farmers, their "substantial barns, fine private dwellings," well-improved land, rotation, and fine orchards. The Germans were "excellent practical farmers, very industrious, very mercenary, and very ignorant," and many were rich.[64] This was high praise from a critical Englishman. Fearon found farm land in this area to be worth $200 an acre. This figure of course reflected the boom in land prices following the War of 1812. Superior farming techniques, frugality, and hard labor enabled the thrifty Pennsylvania Germans to monopolize the limestone soils and to displace earlier Scotch-Irish settlers, not only in Pennsylvania but also in parts of Maryland.[65]

In his investigation of American agriculture made in 1801, William Strickland was particularly concerned about land values, profits, rents, and rental agreements about which he made some shrewd observations. "Very little land is let," he said of Pennsylvania and New Jersey, "few of the people born in the country being ever willing to become tenants. . . . Custom or ignorance can alone cause this objection; since they who purchase land, purchase it with money that would otherwise afford them seven or eight per cent, at the least; whereas if they rented land, it would be at a rate that would not pay more to the owners of it, than an interest of three or four per cent. . . ." So great was the difficulty of procuring what he called "regular tenants" that landlords were letting their surplus tracts on a share basis which he said "nothing but extreme poverty, or extreme ignorance, can vindicate." The advantages of share renting in regions where commercial agriculture has made little progress were not understood by Strickland; nor could he foresee that this method of leasing farm land was to become the prevailing one in the United States when the country had passed into a more highly developed economic state.[66]

Lancaster County wheat and flour early found their way to Baltimore

[63] *Farmers' Cabinet,* II (October 2, 1837), 74–75.

[64] Henry Bradshaw Fearon, *Sketches of America: A Narrative of a Journey of Five Thousand Miles through the Eastern and Western States of America* (London: Longmans, Hurst, Rees, Orme & Brown, 1819), pp. 181–183. Cf. *Niles' Register,* VIII (May 6, 1815), 172–173; and Charles L. Fleischmann in *De Bow's Review,* XXVII (November, 1859), 503.

[65] Walter M. Kallmorgen, "The Pennsylvania German Farmer," in Ralph Wood, ed., *The Pennsylvania Germans* (Princeton, N. J.: Princeton University Press, 1942), pp. 29–55.

[66] William Strickland, *Observations on the Agriculture of the United States of America* (London: W. Bulmer and Co., 1801), pp. 16–18.

by way of the Susquehanna and to Philadelphia by the overland route. So heavy became the shipments that they were a factor in bringing about the construction of the Philadelphia and Lancaster Turnpike, the first great modern road built in America. Lancaster was Pennsylvania's richest and most productive farming county, but York, Chester, Bucks, Berks, Northampton, and Adams, where the German element was strong if not predominant, also were well developed in 1815; together they constituted the granary of America, the center of the wheat belt.

The corn, oats, and clover or timothy that were raised by the Pennsylvania Germans in rotation with wheat were fed to stock and cattle. Cattle from poorer regions were driven to Lancaster and neighboring counties to be fattened for market, and cattle feeding became an important feature of the economy of the area. Representatives of the Holland Land Company annually drove a herd of cattle, received in payment on land from its buyers, from western Pennsylvania to the feeding grounds in the southeastern part of the state. When moving through settled areas they paid from two to four cents a head for overnight pasture. Driving through the mountains was hárd on the animals because of the scarcity of forage.[67] A long grueling journey of 400 miles reduced the weight of the cattle and left them in poor market condition. German farmers could buy them cheaply, fatten them for the Philadelphia butchers on the grain and pasture they had in abundance, and make a good profit. To meet urban demands for milk and cheese, dairy cattle were maintained, and together with the feeder cattle provided the manure essential for adequately feeding the soil.

Farming in eastern Pennsylvania had attained in 1815 a high and profitable state of development. The combination of superior soils, climate, excellent farmers, growing markets, and natural and man-made transportation facilities made possible good yields, intensive utilization, rising standards of living, and modest wealth for many. Most important, perhaps, is the fact that this prosperity was enjoyed not by great planters, alien land speculators, or other absentee owners, but by owner-operators. Here democratic ownership was early achieved.

Although western Pennsylvania was still wracked by tensions and ill feeling between landlords and tenants or debtors, and its resources were still being drained away by absentee owners, by 1815 these problems were gradually diminishing. The demand for grain, pork, and beef in New Orleans and in the East, as well as the cheapness of transporting goods by flatboat down the Ohio and Mississippi, was having an effect on the region. Pittsburgh was coming into its own as a center of trade, manufacturing, and population.

In 1800 the total assessed value of all land in New York exceeded the

[67] Tiffany and Tiffany, *Harm Jan Huidekoper*, pp. 164–165.

total in Pennsylvania, but the average per acre of assessed value was $6.09 for Pennsylvania and $4.56 for New York. The Pennsylvania average was only exceeded by the three states of southern New England and by New Jersey. The best average for a southern state was $3.97 per acre for Maryland.[68] In 1814 the average assessed value of land in Pennsylvania as adjusted by the legislature was $12. The highest averages for the farm counties were $52 for Lebanon, a small county just north of Lancaster; $48 for Lancaster; $40 for Lehigh; $37 for Chester; $36 for Bucks; $35 for Berks; and $33 for Montgomery. The counties with the lowest average values contained large tracts of land owned by the Holland Land Company, among them being Warren and Potter, with average values of $1.75, and Jefferson and McKean, with average values of $1.50.[69]

FARMING IN NEW JERSEY

Most of the problems discussed in connection with the distribution of the land in New York and Pennsylvania existed in equal degree in New Jersey. Large grants of land had been made to persons planning to establish estates or to resell to others, and a landed aristocracy had developed whose holdings were farmed by indentured servants, slaves, and tenants. Small purchasers struggled to keep up their payments on tracts they had bought on credit. Squatters resisted landlords' efforts to eject them or to make them sign contracts to buy or rent their claims. Gradually the large estates were broken up and transferred to small operators. By 1811 share tenancy had become fairly common, the renter being required to pay the taxes, one third of all grain, flax, and potatoes, and one half of the hay and fruit he produced. Agreements which provided that no hay or manure was to be sold off the farm indicate that landlords were becoming sufficiently concerned about their investments to attempt to assure better farm management.[70]

New Jersey farmers, being close to markets, raised wheat, the principal cash crop in the North and its worst scourge. Economic necessity undoubtedly was responsible for this overemphasis upon grain, but until the farmers had paid for their land, constructed comfortable homes for themselves, and built fences to enclose livestock, they had no other choice. When the farm had been paid for and the necessary improvements made—generally by the end of the first generation—the owner began to diversify and to improve his farm techniques. He had capital to invest in

[68] Pitkin, *Statistical View*, p. 417.
[69] *Niles' Register*, VIII (May 6, 1815), 172–173.
[70] Hubert G. Schmidt, *Rural Hunterdon: An Agricultural History* (New Brunswick, N. J.: Rutgers University Press, 1945), pp. 55 ff.; Andrew D. Mellick, *The Story of an Old Farm* (Somerville, N. J.: The Unionist-Gazette, 1889), p. 307.

better livestock and income to purchase guano, lime, marl, or other soil-improving minerals.[71] He doubtless recognized and regretted that his earlier cultural practices had not maintained soil quality. Much damage had been done, some of which could be rectified by soil-building practices, but it is difficult to see how, given the nature of the early land-distribution policies in existence in New Jersey, New York, and some parts of Pennsylvania, it could have been avoided.

New Jersey, fortunately situated between the two greatest markets in the United States and with much of its area accessible to coastal or river navigation, developed its agricultural possibilities early. By 1815 there was not much room for further improvement except through more intensive and more careful use of the land. The assessed value of its 2,788,282 acres of farm land in 1800 was substantially greater than the assessed value of 23,306,746 acres of farm land in South Carolina and Georgia and was nearly equal to that of North Carolina.[72] If assessed value of farm land is an index of rural conditions, one may conclude that New Jersey agriculture was well advanced at the opening of the nineteenth century.

GROWTH OF OHIO

Beyond the Ohio new communities were developing in 1815 whose growth was made possible by the increasing flow of immigration from older states. Land-hungry people swarmed into those areas where Indian titles had been surrendered—all of Ohio except its northwestern corner, southern Indiana, and southern Illinois. In southern Ohio around Marietta and in northeastern Ohio where the Connecticut Land Company held sway, the new communities with their Congregational churches, town meetings, schools, academies or colleges, and small farms based on a mixed agricultural economy were outposts of New England culture. Wealthy Virginians had come to south central Ohio with their pockets stuffed with land warrants of war veterans. There in the Virginia Military Tract they had created large estates on which livestock provided the principal source of income. Elsewhere, in the region of the Miami River and farther west in southern Indiana and Illinois, settlers had drifted in from the South, bringing with them an attitude toward life that struck the thrifty, hard-working, serious New England farmer as shiftless and irreligious.

Four fifths of Ohio was covered with heavy stands of hardwoods, principally oak, beech, ash, cherry, walnut, and hickory, which provided

[71] Schmidt, op. cit., pp. 112 ff.
[72] Pitkin, op. cit., p. 417.

superb timber for household furniture, buildings, and fuel, but made the task of clearing the land a herculean one. As in the region farther east, hardwood ashes and their derivatives, potash and pearlash, brought the pioneer good returns, but this source of income soon ended.

Pioneers first encountered small prairies in Ohio, where perhaps one fifth of the land was barren of trees. The prairies of northwestern Ohio and of Indiana and Illinois were avoided in 1815 because they were poorly drained, and there was a high rate of illness among the inhabitants. Problems of cultivating such land, moreover, had yet to be solved. Southern Indiana and southern Illinois, unglaciated and poor in soil quality, except for the alluvial lands along the streams, yielded only meager returns to the pioneers who developed them.

Lacking roads of any kind, the early settlers sought land close to the streams flowing into the Ohio and its tributaries, which provided them with transportation facilities, and all too commonly they built their homes and villages on bottom lands. As clearings farther inland were enlarged, the land held back less and less of the heavy rains, and these locations became subject to destructive floods that carried off livestock and buildings and sometimes took the lives of inhabitants. Later generations, after long struggles to protect these homes and communities by levees, were forced to move back to higher lands.

Pioneer farmers moving into new communities lacking crossroads stores or accessible gristmills were forced to produce foodstuff for themselves and their livestock and to resort to primitive methods of preparation. Few could transport any very heavy equipment and none was available to them at their destination. Consequently, they had to rely on their own ingenuity to improvise simple tools and household utensils. In the first year of farm making, the settler had the crucial problem of how to divide his time between home construction, making tools and furniture, clearing, planting, fencing, guarding the few livestock from predatory animals, and perhaps putting time into road building.

Fortunately, nature had generously supplied the region with game that for a time could provide much of the sustenance of the pioneers. Squirrels, racoons, bears, deer, fish, turkeys, and passenger pigeons were found in such abundance that, unlike later experiences, the poor subsisted on a diet of protein rather than carbohydrates. Salt for the preservation of meat was hard to obtain. Consequently, salt licks or saline springs were highly valued and were reserved for public use.

Corn and hogs, for which much of the settled portion of the old Northwest was admirably adapted, early became the basis of farm life, particularly in the more central and southern portions. Pioneers brought with them a little corn, a hog or two, and almost inevitably seed of the pumpkin and other vegetables, and in their narrow clearings they were soon producing quantities for domestic consumption. Farther north, wheat yielded sufficiently well so that when ways were found to get it to market its extensive planting was assured. The tall grasses of the Scioto prairies provided feed for herds of cattle destined for the Philadelphia and Baltimore markets. Elsewhere hogs constituted the principal livestock.

In 1817 Henry Fearon's caustic pen etched a picture of the Ohio farmer's attitude toward his work:

> The management of farms is full a century behind that of England, there being here a want of improved machinery for the promotion of economy in time and labour; and no regular attention to the condition of live stock, while the mode of culture in general appears slovenly and unsystematic. Cows are milked sometimes twice, sometimes once a day; at others four times a week. Barns are erections which you would not know by that name, and which must materially deteriorate the annual receipts. . . .[73]

A major problem of interior farmers was marketing. Thomas Ashe tells of an English farmer coming into the Miami country, where he did well in establishing a successful plantation but who said that "the best he could do in the western country, or that any farmer could do, *was just not to starve.*"

> The price of produce was so low and that of labour so high, that very little profit attended the most laborious exertions of industry. Indian corn, in particular carried a value so mean, that he never offered to sell it, and for his wheat, he made it into flour, he could get but about three dollars per barrel, and that had, for the most part, to be taken in goods for which he had not always a consumption or use.[74]

Nevertheless, by 1815, arks, flatboats, keelboats, and steamboats were carrying the produce, still small in amount but rapidly growing, down the Ohio and Mississippi to the lower river communities.

Frontier Ohio, but twelve years a state in 1815, already had produced a landed aristocracy bearing such distinguished names as Longworth, Massie, Worthington, and Symmes. In addition to their extensive and well-developed holdings, absentee owners held almost one half of the land in private ownership.[75] Furthermore, a large portion of the people of Ohio were in debt for their land either to the federal government or

[73] Fearon, *op. cit.*, p. 223.
[74] Thomas Ashe, *Travels in America* . . . (London: R. Phillips, 1809), p. 220.
[75] William T. Utter, *The Frontier State*, Vol. II in Carl Wittke, ed., *The History of the State of Ohio* (6 vols.; Columbus: Ohio State Archaeological and Historical Society, 1942), *passim.* Federal lands were exempt from taxation for a period of five years after sale. The proportions of resident- and nonresident-owned land given here are therefore not entirely accurate.

to the various land companies and owners. Yet the road to ownership was open to all and many were rapidly meeting their obligations.[76]

FARMING IN INDIANA, ILLINOIS, AND MISSOURI

Farther west in the territories of Indiana, Illinois, and Missouri, except for the St. Louis area, farming was fairly primitive and settlement was sparse, scarcely emerging from the pioneer stage. While clearing and fencing their land and erecting their homes, farm makers had time only to raise foodstuffs sufficient to satisfy immediate wants. They possessed few or no livestock and depended on game, fish, and wild fowl for a considerable part of their food. The small surpluses brought but slight returns because of transportation difficulties and because neighbors had no cash and had to depend on their own skill in the hunt or in tilling the soil. Barter was common, prices were low.[77]

Few could have predicted in 1815 that these three territories, which had a population density of slightly more than one to three square miles in the census of 1810, were to enjoy a rush of settlers that in a few years enabled them to be admitted into the Union as thriving and rapidly developing states.

[76] I have relied on Utter, *The Frontier State* and R. Carlyle Buley, *The Old Northwest* (Indianapolis: Indiana Historical Society, 1950), Vol. I, for this summary treatment of agriculture in the old Northwest in 1815.

[77] D. B. Warden, *Statistical, Political and Historical Account of the United States of America* . . . (2 vols.; Edinburgh: Archibald Constable & Co., 1819), II, 308; Solon Justus Buck, *Illinois in 1818, Illinois Centennial Publications,* Introductory Volume (Springfield: The Illinois Centennial Commission, 1917), pp. 113 ff.

CHAPTER III

Public-Land Policies

UNCLE SAM'S acres were numerous and far flung by 1815. The business of surveying, sectioning, advertising, selling, and collecting the proceeds constituted the largest single area of economic activity in the country and a major obligation of the federal government. It is difficult for people of later generations to realize the extent to which the government was engaged in the land business in the nineteenth century. After the individual states claiming the trans-Allegheny region had surrendered their rights, the public domain of the United States amounted to more than 200,000,000 acres. This was increased to a billion acres by the Louisiana Purchase and the acquisition of Florida, Texas, Oregon, and California. No problem so continuously absorbed the attention of Congress for the next century as that of the management, sale, and donation of this great empire.

By the close of the War of 1812 the administration, sale, and donation policies of the public domain were fairly well defined. Before opening public lands to settlement, the occupancy rights of Indian tribes claiming them were recognized and treaty negotiations similar to those with foreign nations were conducted for the surrender of these rights. Payment for Indian claims ranged from a fraction of a cent to a dollar an acre and was made in the form of rations, annuities and trust funds for the tribes, and presents to important chiefs. Grants or rights to land given by predecessor governments were confirmed after their validity had been established, and settlers within newly acquired areas who were without title to land at the time of transfer were given free homesteads of 400 or 640 acres. Well in advance of demand, land was surveyed into townships and ranges, sections and quarter sections. At appropriate times land was advertised for sale at public auction and sold to the highest bidder offering the minimum price or more. Land remaining unsold was thereafter "offered" land which was subject to purchase at the minimum price:

two dollars an acre between 1800 and 1820, one dollar and a quarter thereafter.[1]

OHIO ENABLING ACT

A precedent of major importance established in the Ohio enabling act of 1802 conceded to the states created out of the public domain a share, though a small share at the outset, in the disposal of the public lands. In return for its agreement to levy no taxes on lands for five years after they had been sold by the federal government, Ohio was given section sixteen in each township for common schools; salt springs and surrounding lands; and one twentieth of the net proceeds from the sale of lands within its borders were also granted for the building of roads. Increasing generosity was thereafter shown as state followed state into the Union until as much as one seventh of the land was given to new states on their admission. They failed, however, in gaining their chief aim: complete control over the lands within their boundaries. Additional conditions were imposed for the grants to the states: they were not to discriminate against absentee owners in assessing taxes, they were to disclaim all right and title to the unappropriated land within their borders, and they were not to tax the lands of the federal government.[2]

On the assumption that it was better to purchase the Indian occupancy rights and to remove the Indians before white settlers began to penetrate their reserves, treaty negotiations were begun with Ohio Indians in 1795. During the next twenty years all of Ohio except a number of small reserves, southern Indiana and Illinois, southeastern Michigan, most of Missouri, central Alabama and southern Mississippi, most of Louisiana, and northern Arkansas were freed of Indian claims by some twenty-five treaties. By 1820 it was estimated that 191,978,000 acres had been divested of Indian occupancy rights.[3] The demands of settlers and speculators for land was thus anticipated for a time, but there was to be no letup in the pressure upon the Indians for their land east of the Great Plains. Though they were pushed from frontier to frontier in these treaty negotiations, the Indians acquired such skill in dealing with officials of the Indian Office that in later negotiations they succeeded in wresting from reluctant officials prices that were at least generous in comparison with what their fathers had received a generation earlier and with

[1] Payson J. Treat, *The National Land System, 1785–1820* (New York: E. B. Treat & Company, 1910); Benjamin Horace Hibbard, *History of the Public Land Policies* (New York: The Macmillan Company, 1924).

[2] Acts of April 30, 1802, and March 3, 1811. 2 *U.S. Stat. at Large* 175, 665.

[3] *American State Papers, Public Lands* (8 vols.; Washington, D. C.: Gales and Seaton, 1832–1861), II, 462.

what frontiersmen thought unimproved wild land was worth. The Miami and Pottowatomie Indians, for example, who with related tribes ceded most of Ohio in 1795 for the equivalent of about a cent an acre, sold their claims in Indiana in the late thirties for one dollar and a quarter an acre. The rations, supplies, and annuities the Indians received for their lands made them increasingly dependent upon government bounty and therefore more tractable, more willing to give way under pressure. Thus the way was paved for the rapid expansion of white settlement westward.[4]

PRIVATE LAND CLAIMS

The first task of the United States government in the management of the public domain acquired from England, France, and Spain was the adjudication of a mass of confused, ill-defined, overlapping, and inadequately documented claims to land, the legacy of previous governments. At Detroit, Kaskaskia, Vincennes, St. Louis, and on both banks of the Mississippi, the Red, the Atchafalaya, the Ouachita in Louisiana, the Alabama and Tombigbee in Alabama, and the St. Johns in Florida, grants ranging from city lots to a million and more acres had been made, some with conditions, others without. Congress promised confirmation of all claims for which there existed any actual proof, but the records of many transactions were in such bad shape as to make it difficult, sometimes impossible, to produce evidence of title.

Anxiety to conciliate the French, Spanish, and English residents suddenly transferred to American control without their approval, and the political influence of the larger claimants, many of them speculators who had bought out original owners, led to increasing liberality in confirming titles. Once- and twice-rejected claims were given reconsideration and confirmed. Many of the fabricated titles based on forged documents were rejected and those in excess of 100,000 acres were given close legal investigation. Yet almost 1,500,000 acres were confirmed to the Forbes family in Florida and 346,000 acres to the Arredondo family. Furthermore, where delay in settling ownership had permitted settlers to acquire rights on land, the heirs of the original owners were granted scrip to be used for other land: the Dauterive heirs received 212,000 acres in Louisiana; the McDonogh heirs, 104,000 acres in Louisiana; and the Clamorgan heirs, 196,000 acres in Missouri. Cajun claims in Louisiana

[4] For maps showing Indian land cessions, see Charles C. Royce, *Indian Land Cessions in the United States* (*Eighteenth Annual Report* of the Bureau of American Ethnology, 1896–1897, Part II; Washington, D. C.: Government Printing Office, 1899). For the reasons why the Miami and Pottawatomie Indians received such high prices for their claims, see Nellie Armstrong Robertson and Dorothy Riker, eds., *The John Tipton Papers* (3 vols., *Indiana Historical Collections*, Vols. XXIV–XXVI; Indianapolis: Indiana Historical Bureau, 1942), Vol. I, Introduction.

were mostly for less than 200 acres; other settlement rights generally ranged from 400 to 640 acres. The delay in confirming titles and the resulting confusion made it easy for individual Anglo-American speculators and planters to take advantage of the Creoles with their slight knowledge of American land law and land values. Unscrupulous persons thus acquired as many as five, ten, twenty, even thirty-five claims. In this way ownership of much of the best cotton and sugar land in Louisiana and Mississippi became concentrated in few hands.[5]

SURVEYING THE PUBLIC DOMAIN

In the meantime, Congress had, in 1812, assigned to the newly created General Land Office, a bureau in the Treasury Department, responsibility for surveying the public domain, making sales and collections, and granting patents. At the outset its staff consisted of a commissioner, eleven clerks, and two surveyor generals who were placed in charge of surveying districts where the actual running of the lines was done by assistants.[6] Territories and states were divided into land districts in which local land offices operated as branches of the General Land Office. There were twenty-one land offices in 1818, thirty-six in 1822, and seventy-eight in 1860. Each land office had a register who had charge of the tract books, the surveyors' plats with their valuable descriptions, and the entry books wherein were recorded all purchases of land; and a receiver, who recorded all payments on land and maintained a set of books which, in effect, were duplicates of those maintained by the register, thereby giving the clerks in Washington and the frequent inspectors sent to the local offices ample opportunity to check one by the other. Receivers were responsible for the money they received until it had sufficiently accumulated to warrant traveling to the nearest bank of deposit, which might be hundreds of miles away. Compensation of the local land officers was $500 annually plus 1 per cent commission on all receipts for the register and 1.5 per cent for the receiver. In active districts the receiver's compensation exceeded $5,000 in some years.[7]

Surveying the townships and ranges, the sections and quarter sections, marking the corners, taking notes on land formation, forest cover, drainage, minerals, and other facts that might be useful to settlers was a

[5] Harry L. Coles, Jr., "The Confirmation of Foreign Land Titles in Louisiana," *Louisiana Historical Quarterly*, XXXVIII (October, 1955), 1–22, and his "Applicability of the Public Land System to Louisiana," *Mississippi Valley Historical Review*, XLIII (June, 1956), 183–204; Paul W. Gates, "Private Land Claims in the South," *Journal of Southern History*, XXII (May, 1956), 183–204.

[6] *House Document* No. 23, 14 Cong., 1 Sess., 1815–1816, pp. 2–3; *American State Papers, Public Lands*, III, 312.

[7] *American State Papers, Public Lands*, III, 312.

task requiring many skilled surveyors, chain bearers, axmen, flagmen, and woodsmen. Contracts for surveying were awarded faithful party supporters who, in notable cases, performed their tasks in irresponsible fashion, carelessly running the lines, insufficiently marking the corners, and making serious errors of calculation. Many a frontiersman with the merest rudiments of surveying secured contracts or subcontracts which his limited knowledge and experience did not permit him to carry through in proper fashion. Later generations were thus caused many angry boundary disputes and much litigation. So inaccurately had the lines been run and the corners marked the first time that in not a few instances the land had to be resurveyed.

The surveyors were the first white men who systematically studied the land on the outer edge of the frontier and acquired a discriminating knowledge of the tracts most suitable for settlement, small-farming operations, cotton plantations, or lumbering and mining. Because of this prior knowledge the surveyors not infrequently became (1) "landlookers" who sold their knowledge for a fee, (2) agents prepared to enter lands for capitalists on a partnership basis or for ten or twenty dollars a quarter section, or (3) petty or substantial capitalist speculators who acquired the choicest lands they spied out in their surveying work.[8]

Western political pressure kept the surveyors operating generally far in advance of the squatters, settlers, and speculators, though in some instances, notably in eastern Iowa in 1836 and in eastern Kansas in 1855, they followed rather than preceded the potential land buyers. In 1820, 72,805,000 acres had been surveyed in nine states and territories, of which 18,601,000 acres had been sold.[9] Throughout the century the disparity between the number of acres surveyed and the number sold was to continue to increase.

REVENUE LAND POLICY

The revenue emphasis in shaping land policy was responsible for the high price of two dollars an acre that prevailed from 1800 to 1820. Furthermore, the smallest purchasable unit was 320 acres until 1804, when 160-acre sales were allowed, and 1817, when the smallest unit became 80 acres.[10] Since few land seekers could pay two dollars an acre

[8] Useful on the surveyor and the local land officer is Verne E. Chatelain, "The Public Land Officer on the Northwestern Frontier," *Minnesota History*, XII (December, 1931), 379–389, and Roscoe Lokken, *Iowa Public Land Disposal* (Iowa City: State Historical Society of Iowa, 1942), pp. 13–64; Thomas Donaldson, "The Public Domain," *House Miscellaneous Document* No. 45, 47 Cong., 2 Sess., 1884, pp. 178–195.

[9] *American State Papers, Public Lands*, III, 460.

[10] Treat, *National Land System*, pp. 121, 138.

cash when they began making improvements, credit was allowed: one twentieth was due on the day of sale, one fourth in forty days, and the balance in two, three, and four years. Five full years' use of the land was permitted before delinquents would lose their equity.[11]

Advocates of a revenue land policy could argue that the two-dollar price was not unduly high in view of the excited purchasing at that price which occurred, particularly in 1816–1818. On the other hand, the settler who arrived in the West with little capital had to use his resources to buy tools, stock, seed, and food until his crops came in, and could neither afford to make the payment of one fourth nor reasonably expect to raise the balance during the next few years when he was struggling to make a farm of wild land. In the cotton-growing South, where marketing problems were not as serious as they were for the grain-producing regions in the upper Mississippi Valley, the risk in buying and improving on such terms was not perhaps as great, but any major change in the price of cotton might offset this advantage. Credit was instituted to aid the hardy pioneer, and doubtless it did enable many to get started and, with the leniency shown delinquents, allowed them ultimately to get title. On the other hand, it encouraged men of small means to overbuy and contributed largely to the great orgy of speculation in which whole areas of the public domain went into private ownership and unproductive use.

Early framers of federal land policies saw nothing wrong in men of capital engrossing large areas and holding them for a rise in value. Indeed, it was expected that the primary purchases of land would be made by capitalists, and not for improvement or development but for speculation. Small purchases were not permitted, and during the period of Confederation special terms were given to large and influential buyers. The credit terms to the government permitted speculators to hold great acreages with only a slight payment. During these intervals, when the scramble for land was active, as it was after 1815, they might resell to other speculators or to actual settlers at higher prices, again on credit. Credit, then, in periods of rapid turnover was a boon to the speculator, who could hold from three to twenty times as much land as he had the means to purchase outright. But what was their gain was the actual settler's loss. The speculators' ventures were undertaken not without risk, for no one could foretell how long the flush times would last and how soon a reduction in the demand for land might set in. True, some who overbought at the auctions and did not find the anticipated market were either able to forfeit before they made any payment or sustained only the loss of the initial 5 per cent payment they had made.

[11] *American State Papers, Public Lands,* III, 277.

Prior to 1815 the area of public lands open to sale had been largely confined to Ohio, and most sales had been to actual settlers. Sales totaled 4,824,375 acres in Ohio, 638,748 acres in Indiana, 253,528 in Alabama, and 329,440 in Mississippi.[12]

SPECULATION IN PUBLIC LAND

Speculation in public land was stimulated in the flush years 1815–1819 by the extraordinarily high prices which cotton, sugar, tobacco, and wheat brought. Twenty-five- and thirty-cent cotton, nine-cent sugar, fourteen-cent tobacco, and two-dollar wheat were sufficient to turn the attention of many from normal pursuits to the scramble for land capable of producing these crops. Never again were such prices to prevail in the ante-bellum period, except perhaps in 1857, and only twice later was there to be such wild excitement on the part of petty and large capitalists anxious to invest in land.[13]

A third major factor contributing to the speculation in land was the easing of credit restrictions and the expansion of banking facilities. Within two years from its establishment in 1816 the Second Bank of the United States had placed its paper in circulation to the amount of $8,300,000 and had loaned $41,000,000 on real property and bank stock.[14] The circulation of all banks increased from $45,000,000 in 1812 to $100,000,000 in 1817.[15] The sorry story of stock jobbing, lending for speculation in land and stock on collateral appraised at inflated figures, and inordinate note issues for which the officers and directors of the Second Bank of the United States were responsible, was reproduced throughout the country by officials of state-chartered and state-owned banks. Primitive banking theories then largely prevalent permitted the establishment of note-issuing and lending agencies whose directors and stockholders actually paid in little specie, borrowed on their stock to speculate in lands and in turn borrowed on their newly acquired lands to purchase additional lands and pyramid their holdings. The Secretary of the Treasury, William E. Crawford, observed in 1820 that banks had been incorporated "not because there was capital seeking investment . . .

[12] *Ibid.*, p. 420.
[13] The quotations are from Lewis Cecil Gray, *History of Agriculture in the Southern United States to 1860* (2 vols.; Washington, D. C.: Carnegie Institution, 1933), II, 1027 ff.
[14] David Rich Dewey, "The Second United States Bank," *Publications* of the National Monetary Commission, Vol. IV, "Banking in the United States before the Civil War," *Senate Document*, No. 571, 61 Cong., 2 Sess., 1910–1911, pp. 236, 246.
[15] Fred Albert Shannon, *America's Economic Growth* (New York: The Macmillan Company, 1951), p. 196.

but because men without active capital wanted the means of obtaining loans, which their standing would not command. . . ."[16] By such means men with limited resources could take advantage of the credit terms allowed for the purchase of land and build up impressive holdings though their equity rested on a weak foundation.

The combination of government credit, high agricultural prices, expansion of bank credit, and note issues during the postwar years produced the first major period of land speculation that extended from 1815 to 1819. Whereas public land sales had averaged 359,031 acres from 1800 to 1814, in the midst of this rush to acquire real property they bounded to new heights, reaching 5,475,648 acres in 1819.[17]

In Ohio and Indiana it was chiefly men of small means who bought land at this time, though many of them were lured by the spirit of the time into more extensive ventures than their resources warranted. It was their hope that before the five years allowed for payment expired, good crops and fair prices might make it possible to meet their payments, or that they might be able to sell a surplus quarter at a profit which would take care of their obligations. Some extensive purchases, however, were made in Ohio. For example, the 13,753 acres bought by Nicholas Longworth and associates were developed with tenants and became the basis of the Longworth fortune; 20,000 acres were acquired by Oliver W. Spencer, and 22,000 acres by Samuel McCord.[18]

These purchases of Congress lands, as the public lands were called in Ohio, were not large in comparison with the extensive holdings acquired in Ohio by speculators using land warrants in the Virginia

NUMBER AND SIZE OF FARMS IN THE VIRGINIA
MILITARY TRACT IN 1860

County	Farms over 1,000 acres	Farms 500–1,000 acres	Average size of farms (acres)
Champaign	0	13	146
Fayette	10	40	202
Madison	24	48	191
Pickaway	6	20	138
Pike	6	6	166
Ross	6	42	185
State of Ohio	112	485	114

Source: Computed from *Eighth Census of the United States, 1860, Agriculture* (Washington, D. C.: Government Printing Office, 1864), *passim*.

[16] C. F. Emerick, *The Credit System and the Public Domain, Publications* of the Vanderbilt Historical Society, No. 3 (Nashville: 1899), p. 8.

[17] Statistics of land sales are from *American State Papers, Public Lands*, III, 420.

[18] *Ohio Cultivator*, IX (January 1, 1853), 15.

Military Tract somewhat earlier. The counties containing these large holdings, which in some instances were in excess of 100,000 acres, showed the effects of this concentration of ownership as late as 1860. Among these results were large farms and a thin rural population. The 21 counties in the tract, roughly one fourth of the 88 counties in the state, contained 66 per cent of all the farms of 1,000 acres or more in the state, 52 per cent of the farms of 500 to 1,000 acres. The average size of farms in six of the counties in the tract ranged from 138 to 202 acres as compared with 114 for the state.

It was fortunate that speculators were not attracted to the newly opened parts of Ohio and Indiana in the first third of the century, when the lands were brought into market. As a result, actual settlers—small farmers—had much better opportunity to get established in these areas than they did in Mississippi and Alabama, where the story was very different.

Following the War of 1812 the most intensive scramble for land occurred in Alabama and Mississippi. With English manufacturers again actively bidding for cotton, the price of the staple doubled between June of 1814 and June of 1816. Planters and farmers, working strenuously to meet this demand, more than doubled the nation's yield of cotton between 1814 and 1819. Unparalleled prosperity thus descended upon the planter who joined with others to acquire as much as possible of the public lands.

High cotton prices and tales of tremendous profits being made in growing the staple in Mississippi and Alabama attracted a motley crew of speculators, gamblers, dispossessed farmers who had lost their land to more successful neighbors, and planters from the older states. Petty dealers in claims who had purchased and hoped to resell the rude improvements of squatters before the lands were offered at the government auction were likewise in attendance. To the land-office towns also flocked the note shavers, the moneylenders prepared to lend funds at usurious interest, politicians big and small who invariably dabbled in speculation in the public lands, and local planters who wished to enlarge their holdings and open up new plantations. The state bank notes being issued at this time by Kentucky and Tennessee banks provided them with easily obtained credit.

This combination of abundance of money and credit and "the infatuating prospect of a continuance of great and extravagant prices for cotton" produced the most excited competitive bidding at government land sales in all American history. One who participated in this rush for land maintained that tracts acquired for a few dollars an acre would in four years bring $50 or $60, possibly more, per acre. Speculators who appeared in abundance at the Huntsville sale first organized an association to prevent competitive bidding and for a time succeeded to the point that the officials ordered sales stopped. When they reopened, the rush for land was so great that the association could no longer control its members. In the excitement that followed, prices were bid up to fantastic levels, as a numerously signed petition later said, by "a rapacious horde of speculators (who seemed disposed to monopolize the whole country, for

PRICE AND PRODUCTION OF COTTON IN MISSISSIPPI AND ALABAMA

	Weighted average price of cotton	Production of cotton in bales of 500 lbs.	Sales of public land in Mississippi and Alabama	
			Acres	Average price
1807	16.4	167,189	74,831	$2.00
1808	13.6	156,740	17,492	2.00
1809	13.6	171,369	87,635	2.22
1810	14.7	177,638	77,035	2.05
1811	8.9	167,189	81,913	2.01
1812	—	156,740	144,872	2.07
1813	15.5	156,740	30,260	2.00
1814	16.9	146,290	41,272	2.00
1815	27.3	208,986	27,254	2.00
1816	25.4	259,143	490,873	2.25
1817	29.8	271,682	744,419	2.59
1818	21.5	261,233	695,848	5.34
1819	14.3	349,007	2,278,045	4.21

Sources: Data on price and production of cotton are taken from Lewis Cecil Gray, *History of Agriculture in the Southern United States to 1860* (Washington, D. C.: Carnegie Institution, 1933), II, 1026–1027. The quantity of land sold and the amount for which it was sold in the period from 1807 to 1819 is found in *American State Papers, Public Lands.* (Washington, D. C.: Gales and Seaton, 1832–1861), III, 420.

the purpose of retailing it out again, upon their own terms, to those who were desirous to become permanent settlers therein) . . . outbidding people who attended the sale to purchase lands for settlement." Speculators drove prices to such levels that actual settlers were prevented from getting their tracts or could buy only a small part of them.[19]

John Brahan, receiver of the Huntsville office, was one of the most

[19] Picturesque accounts of the factors behind the excited bidding at the Alabama auctions, especially the Huntsville sale, may be found in the memorial of the Alabama legislature of November 22, 1820, urging that relief be granted to purchasers who were unable to meet their payments to the government, and the petition of numerous citizens of Lawrence and Franklin Counties, in *Senate Document* Nos. 18 and 40, 16 Cong., 1 Sess., 1820–1821, Vol. I. Also see Gordon T. Chappell, "Some Patterns of Land Speculation in the Old Southwest," *Journal of Southern History*, XV (November, 1949), 463 ff.

grasping of these "rapacious speculators," though he later excused himself by saying that he was only trying to keep the land from falling into the hands of the big speculators. In 1818 he bought 44,169 acres for $317,622, or an average of $7.19 an acre. His first successful bid was on a fractional section (of 611 acres) within a few miles of Huntsville which was purchased at $27 per acre. On that same day, February 2, he was high bidder on fifteen parcels containing 3,487 acres for which the average price was $17.97. He continued to buy throughout the year, his total number of transactions being 264, of which 178 were for more than the minimum price. The highest price he paid was $30.72 for a quarter section in Limestone County. Brahan was taking advantage of his position in the land office to control no small part of the land being offered, and other dealers had either to outbid him publicly or to pay him privately for his services. He also bought improved land from settlers unable to make the first payment on their claims and in the excitement of the time was able to resell, always on credit, at greatly increased prices. When his customers could not meet their obligations to him, the rascally Brahan defaulted on his obligations to the government to the amount of $81,963. To secure the payment of this sum a lenient government required him to turn over $42,021 worth of mortgages and notes he held against others. Doubtless this paper netted only a small fraction of its face value, and the 1,260 acres of land and some lots and improvements in Huntsville which were also surrendered were to go begging for the next five years.[20]

Brahan's action in levying tribute on settlers and other purchasers was rivaled by General John Coffee's sale of the advance information he gained from conducting the government surveys of the Tennessee Valley land to speculators either for a share in the investment or for a cash consideration. Control over the information in the surveyors' notes and plats made Coffee and Brahan the key figures in the district, and to them came numerous requests from people desiring to capitalize upon their positions. Coffee did so well that he was able to purchase for himself and groups he represented a total of 22,887 acres.[21] Andrew Jackson, a close friend of Coffee, had watched carefully the progress of the surveys, had selected land he wished to own, and arranged his military duties in such a way as not to interfere with his speculative propensities. He attended the sale and bought a section at the minimum price, "No person bidding against me," he gleefully reported to a crony, which,

[20] Documents relating to Brahan's default, including the description of land purchased by him, are in American State Papers, Public Lands, III, 552–560.

[21] Gordon T. Chappell has an account of Coffee's land speculations in "The Life and Activities of General John Coffee," Tennessee Historical Quarterly, I (June, 1942), 125–146.

with the "unanimous shouts of a numerous and mixed Multitude," he took as an expression of gratitude for his official acts.[22] For two other quarter sections, however, he had to pay $10.05 and $3.00 an acre, respectively. The territorial governor of Mississippi and first governor of the state of Alabama, William Bibb, and his brother, Thomas, who was president of the Alabama Senate and subsequently governor, together purchased in the Huntsville and Cahaba districts 33,000 acres. The action of Brahan, Coffee, Jackson, and the two Bibbs, in either employing the information and power available to them by virtue of the offices they held or in selling or permitting friends and political associates to do so, was not uncommon at the time; only men of the finest sensibilities drew sharp lines between their public and private business.[23]

Prominent at the Huntsville sale was the banker, moneylender, or "loan shark" who attended to lend his credit or paper money to desperate squatters fearful of losing their improved claims. Malcolm Gilchrist was of this type. For a generation Gilchrist and others like him, who represented banks, land companies, and capitalists anxious to lend funds at the high rates of interest obtained on the frontier, attended all the major land sales, purchased heavily, reconveyed to the squatters the land they had purchased for them burdened now with a mortgage. They left behind them hundreds of indebted settlers who could but sigh for the more generous terms of credit that the government itself granted the large speculators and those able to make a down payment and purchase from it direct. Gilchrist was high bidder on 23,000 acres at this exciting sale.

The high point in the Huntsville sale came when two single quarter sections were knocked down at $69.00 and $69.99 an acre. Unless there was a possibility of establishing a town on land thus bought, there was no justification for such fantastic prices or anything approaching them, and it is doubtful whether much agricultural land in the area again attained this price level in the nineteenth century. The participants, hardened speculators and moneylenders, eager to put their funds into land, had completely lost their sense of proportion for the moment.

The combination of speculators that prevailed at the Alabama land offices did not succeed in keeping land prices down but did prevent most of the land from getting into the hands of settlers. The squatters were helpless in the face of the organized competition. After the sales the speculators permitted the squatters to buy their claims but at a sub-

[22] Jackson, Hermitage, November 24, 1818, to Isaac Shelby in John Spencer Bassett, ed., *Correspondence of Andrew Jackson* (7 vols.; Washington, D. C.: Carnegie Institution, 1926–1935), II, 401–402.
[23] Statistics of land entries are compiled from the abstracts of land entries of the various land offices, now in the National Archives.

stantial advance in price, although credit was granted them.[24] In this way the cost of land to small farmers was increased and their chances of gaining full ownership diminished.

Some of the features of these Alabama public land sales were often to be noted at other land auctions held prior to 1860. A combination of public officials anxious to sell their influence or inside information, well-financed speculators, and land company agents dominated the public auctions, intimidated men ignorant of their rights, and made difficult the way of the person of little means who hoped to get title to his improvements. Pioneer settlers learned, however, to counteract these activities by organizing claim associations which effectively massed their power and enabled them to acquire their claims. After the public auction was over, "private entries" could be made on lands unsold, but these were likely to be the less desirable or remote lands that were not wanted.

ABANDONMENT OF THE CREDIT SYSTEM

In 1819 economic conditions swiftly changed for the worse. Cotton fell to less than one half its former high price, credit dried up, loans became uncollectible, debtors defaulted, banks closed their doors, paper money became valueless, specie was unobtainable, and crops could be moved only with difficulty because of the financial stringency. Land that had sold for $10 to $69 an acre now would bring only $2. Distressed buyers of government land petitioned for a moratorium on collections, for extensions of payments, for reduction in price, and for the right to surrender a part of their land and to have the payments already made applied to the remainder.

Payments on credit purchases of land had begun to fall into arrears from the start. Distressed settlers, faced with the loss of their land at the end of five years if they had not completed payments, pressed for relief. As early as 1806 relief was extended to 309 delinquent settlers. Prior to 1820 eleven further relief acts were adopted to aid buyers who had overpurchased and were threatened with the loss of their holdings because of delinquent payments. The downturn in the economic cycle in 1819 and the widespread inability to make payments on government land contracts brought into existence a politically powerful group that sought the adoption of legislation to give liberal extensions of credit. There followed ten relief measures that permitted relinquishments of part of one's purchases and the application of the payments already made to the remainder, allowed a 37.5 per cent discount and the remission of interest for prompt payment, and gave further time for payments.[25] The unwieldy

[24] American State Papers, Public Lands, IV, 528; V, 376–386.
[25] Emerick, op. cit., p. 14. Treat, National Land System, pp. 101 ff.

debt on land contracts of $21,000,000 was in this way reduced by the relinquishment of 4,502,573 acres and payments on the balance. Most of the lands which had brought the higher prices were thus forfeited, 50 per cent being in Alabama and 40 per cent in Mississippi. Never again was the government to experiment with credit sales.[26]

Disillusioned by the difficulties that stemmed from the credit policy, Congress in the Land Act of 1820 required full payment for land at the time of purchase and reduced the minimum price from the high level of $2.00 to $1.25 an acre. Criticism of the credit system for encouraging speculation by men of small as well as large means and for creating a group-conscious class of debtors who exerted increasing pressure for extensions led to its abandonment rather than to its reform. The change was fundamental but its wisdom was doubtful. The usual frontiersman who was trying to create a farm for himself in the wilderness had little or no capital with which to operate. Farm making called for considerable capital as well as for much labor regardless of whether undertaken in wooded hills, overflowed alluvial lands, or prairies.[27] A frontiersman who had to buy land at $2.00 or even $1.25 an acre at the beginning of his operations was deprived of much needed working capital. If he could have free use of the land for a number of years while he was improving it he might acquire sufficient capital with which to buy it. This, in effect, was the pre-emption principle. Unfortunately, the Act of 1820, under the guise of striking at speculation—and most members of Congress found it desirable to condemn the "rapacious speculators"— accomplished nothing of the sort but did immeasurable damage to the farm maker.

Ninian Edwards, himself a considerable speculator in land and a senator from Illinois, charged that by ending credit and reducing the price, Congress was aiding speculators, that he personally would benefit, that "large landholders in the West" had written in behalf of the change letters which were "exhibited as disinterested testimony . . . for the purpose of convincing our minds . . . of the absolute necessity for its speedy adoption." [28] He would prefer "confining the sale of the public lands altogether to actual settlers" but knew full well that speculators were too powerful within and without the halls of Congress to permit such a radical change.[29] Efforts to grant pre-emption rights and to gradu-

[26] *American State Papers, Public Lands*, V, 347; VI, 456.

[27] Clarence Danhof, "Farm Making Costs and the 'Safety Valve': 1850–1860," *Journal of Political Economy*, XLIX (June, 1941), 317–359.

[28] *Debates and Proceedings in the Congress of the United States*, 16 Cong., 1 Sess., 1819–1820, I, 443 ff., especially 482.

[29] *Ibid.*, p. 452.

ate the price of land in proportion to the length of time it had been on the market also failed at this time. The legislation to extend relief to land buyers by permitting them to surrender part of their purchases and to have all payments applied to their remaining holdings enabled substantial holders to retain ownership of much land. Small men, hurt by the abandonment of credit, had to seek relief in other ways.

BOUNTY LAND ACTS

Meantime, Congress used the public lands to induce enlistments in the army and to reward veterans of the War of 1812. Each enlisted man between the ages of eighteen and forty-five received a bounty of 160 acres. To prevent creditors or speculators from obtaining the soldiers' bounty, the warrants were made unassignable, were to be located by lot in military tracts in Michigan, Illinois, or Arkansas, and were to be subject to sale only when the patent had issued to the warrantee. If held by the patentee or his heirs, the lands were tax-free for three years after the patent had been issued but were taxable when sold.[30]

The inalienability clause was presumably included in the bounty land acts to induce the veteran to settle upon his land, but very few ever did. Like the Revolutionary War veterans who were given land bounties in the New York Military Tract and in the Virginia and the United States Military Tracts in Ohio, a very large proportion of the soldiers of the War of 1812 disposed of their rights by power of attorney for small considerations, and the lands were grabbed up by speculators and land companies.[31] Because the bounty land tracts were located far beyond the region then attracting settlement, immigration was slow and the demand for land light. After the Panic of 1819 most of the speculators and land companies who had loaded up with large amounts of these remote tracts found themselves unable to pay the taxes on their land or to meet the interest on their borrowings. Tax liens were issued against the land, and within a short time titles became so involved as to add heavily to the costs of carrying the land and to the prices subsequent settlers had to pay. For a generation, residents of the military tracts were badgered by litigation over patent titles, tax titles, squatters' or occupying tenants' rights, and other liens.[32]

[30] Acts of December 24, 1811; May 6 and June 11, 1812; April 29, 1816; 2 *U. S. Stat.* 344, 669, 672, 728; 3 *U. S. Stat.* 332.

[31] For a list of persons to whom patents on the bounty lands of Illinois were delivered, see *House Executive Document* No. 262, 26 Cong., 1 Sess., 1840, Vol. VII.

[32] Theodore L. Carlson, *The Illinois Military Tract: A Study of Land Occupation, Utilization and Tenure* (Urbana: University of Illinois Press, 1951), pp. 40–64.

GROWTH OF TENANCY

Both absentee and resident ownership of large blocks of land for speculation led to tenancy. Owners, pressed to meet costs but unwilling to sell until they could realize their expected profits, arranged with squatters on their tracts to pay taxes, and perhaps a little rent. The more the tenant improved the land by constructing a house, breaking the prairie, or clearing the forest cover and fencing, the more he was committed to it and the more likely he was to agree to the landlord's terms rather than to suffer eviction. What started out as a temporary arrangement by the squatter developed into permanent tenancy. The Military Tract of Illinois, in particular, showed this tendency early, but it was not the only area of the public domain where speculation was prevalent and tenancy was under way.[33]

Notwithstanding the continued emphasis upon revenue in land disposal, the extensive acquisitions of land by speculators and promoters, and the early development of tenancy, the land system was slowly being bent in the direction of the settlers' needs. Tracts as small as forty acres could be purchased by 1832. New land offices were opened on the frontier to make it easier for the widely scattered pioneers to file their entries. In some areas lands were withheld from the market for a time to permit settlers to take them up, improve them, and buy them when offered at public auction.[34] Increasingly, laws against intrusion upon the public lands were not being enforced.[35]

The states of the new West objected to the federal government's retaining ownership of public lands within their borders. Had not the older states kept full control over their lands and was it not unfair and discriminatory to deny new states the same power? Federal control meant, the West argued, slow development, the continuation of high prices, the punishment of intruders, the establishment of speculators' holdings, and the creation of a class of settlers burdened with heavy debts. States with public lands that did not have full control of them worked for liberal grants for education, for internal improvements and railroads, for reduction in the price of lands, and for a pre-emption right to entitle actual settlers

[33] Paul W. Gates, "Land Policy and Tenancy in the Prairie Counties of Indiana," *Indiana Magazine of History*, XXXV (March, 1939), 1–26; Gates, "Land Policy and Tenancy in the Prairie States," *Journal of Economic History*, I (May, 1941), 60–82; Gates, *Frontier Landlords and Pioneer Tenants* (Ithaca, N. Y.: Cornell University Press, 1943), p. 3.

[34] This point is made by Dallas Lee Jones, "The Survey and Sale of the Public Lands in Michigan, 1815–1862." Master's thesis, 1952, Cornell University Library, pp. 44 ff.

[35] *American State Papers, Public Lands*, III, 78; Act of May 10, 1800. 2 *U. S. Stat.* 78.

to buy at the minimum price without having to bid at auction. Finally, they demanded free homesteads. All these objectives they ultimately obtained except cession of the public lands to the states, but this they gained partially through the donation to them of considerable portions of the public lands within their borders for specific purposes.

With outright cession unobtainable and free homesteads and reduction or graduation in price remote, the western folk concentrated upon securing the right of pre-emption, that is, the privilege of settling upon public land and developing it for one or more years before they were required to purchase it. By moving upon the public lands well in advance of the auction, the settler could erect a small cabin; clear, fence, and cultivate a little land; and, if given sufficient time, might, with luck, save enough money to purchase his claim. If he failed he could sell his improved claim to someone who had the necessary funds with which to purchase it at the approaching auction, and begin on another tract, but this time with some capital. The West's increasing political power enabled it to obtain a series of measures, mostly local in their application, which granted the right of pre-emption to squatters in specified areas. Altogether, thirty-three special pre-emption laws were enacted between 1799 and 1830.[36]

Though limited in their application, these special pre-emption acts prepared the ground for general acts, the first of which was passed in 1830. In that year it was provided that settlers living in 1829 on public lands they had improved should have a pre-emption right. On four later occasions—1832, 1834, 1838, and 1840—Congress forgave illegal trespass on the public lands by granting pre-emption rights to settlers, but it refused to concede prospective pre-emption which would sanction squatting anywhere on the surveyed public lands. Conservative eastern and southern people feared prospective pre-emption in the same way they feared at a later time that free homesteads would produce a concerted rush to the public lands, adversely affect land values in older areas, and produce a rapidly growing West that could not be assimilated, absorbed, or dominated politically.

In the absence of pre-emption laws, squatters on public lands protected their claims by organizing claim associations that virtually policed the auction sales and prevented speculators and loan sharks from bidding against them. The claim associations had numerous functions other than preventing competitive bidding on squatters' claims. They provided a title registry system before the extension of local government that made it possible to convey claims with safety, made certain that settlers whose claims did not coincide with land-office surveys would convey and reconvey parts of their quarters to neighbors, and provided a court which

[36] *House Executive Document* No. 303, 25 Cong., 2 Sess., 1838, IX, 4-6.

could settle claim disputes with dispatch and deal summarily with claim jumpers. Claim or squatter associations appeared on the frontier at least by the middle twenties, were common in the thirties, and continued to exist long after prospective pre-emption was enacted.[37]

Prospective pre-emption was won only in 1841, when it was linked up with distribution, which the West abhorred as much as the East disliked pre-emption. Distribution—the division of the net proceeds from public land sales to the states in proportion to their population—was designed to rid the federal treasury of land revenues and to forestall demands for reduction of the price of land and of customs duties.

The Pre-emption Law of 1841 has sometimes been misunderstood. It was not evidence that Congress placed settlement above revenue, and it did not retard the engrossment of lands by speculators.[38] As is explained in a later chapter, the greatest era of land jobbing came in the eighteen fifties, and the pre-emption law did nothing to prevent it.

The broad policies of public land distribution were laid down by 1830. There were no restrictions on the size of purchases; in fact, local land offices gave preference to large buyers on occasion: their purchases could be taken care of more easily than those of numerous small buyers, and the fees were larger. Pre-emption rights were given squatters from time to time; when these were not conceded, the squatters protected their "rights" by using claim associations. Free grants were made only to persons residing on land in alien territory that was acquired by the United States. Credit was not given after 1820, but squatters often

[37] Sanford C. Cox, *Recollections of the Early Settlement of the Wabash Valley* (Lafayette, Ind.: Courier Steam Book and Job Printing House, 1860), pp. 17–19; *Michigan Sentinel*, Monroe, September 16, 1825; Elijah Hayward, Commissioner of the General Land Office, May 15, 1833, to Louis McLane, Secretary of the Treasury, National Archives; Herbert A. Kellar, ed., *Solon Robinson: Pioneer and Agriculturist* (2 vols., *Indiana Historical Collections*, Vols. XXI and XXII; Indianapolis: Indiana Historical Bureau, 1936), I, 68–69; *Register of Debates*, 24 Cong., 2 Sess., 1836–1837, Vol. XIII, Pt. I, pp. 547–549; Benjamin F. Shambaugh printed the records of an Iowa claim association in *Constitution and Records of the Claim Association of Johnson County, Iowa* (Iowa City: Historical Society of Iowa, 1894). Also see Allan G. Bogue, "The Iowa Claim Clubs: Symbol and Substance," *Mississippi Valley Historical Review* XLV (September, 1958), 231 ff.

[38] Cf. Roy Marvin Robbins, *Our Landed Heritage: The Public Domain* (Princeton, N. J.: Princeton University Press, 1942), p. 91, and his "Pre-emption: A Frontier Triumph," *Mississippi Valley Historical Review*, XVIII (December, 1931), pp. 331 ff. Unfortunately, the General Land Office failed to distinguish in its statistics of land sales between those lands acquired under pre-emption and those purchased under the cash sale law of 1820. For the period between 1830 and 1838 we may conclude that pre-emption sales were of slight importance compared with cash sales; the ratio seems to have been about one to twenty. See "Land Sold under Pre-emption Laws . . ." *House Executive Document* No. 303, 25 Cong., 2 Sess., 1838, IX, 7.

had a year or more of free use of the land before they had to purchase it. Efforts to control or make compact settlement in the West were abandoned, the Indians were being pushed rapidly westward, and intrusion laws were being nullified. The very liberality of the system drew people from the older parts of the country and from Europe to the new West, which was growing at a rapid pace.

CHAPTER IV

The Business in Land: Public-Land Policies, 1835-1861

SPECULATION in public lands of the United States reached three peaks: in 1818–1819, 1836, and 1855–1856, as is shown in the accompanying chart. Preceding and making possible these periods of frenzied scrambling for land were the favorable balance of trade from the sale of quantities of American food and fiber abroad; loose experiments in state banking which produced huge increases in the circulating medium and bank credit; a swelling tide of immigration and of westward migration; and, for the second and third peaks, extraordinary expenditures of public and private funds on internal improvements. Until the era of big business, large capitalization, and million-share companies, the favorite medium of speculation was land, whether corner lots in existing or prospective towns and cities or wild lands on the frontier.

After each peak of excitement in land purchases there followed a great letdown accompanied by a sharp decrease in the demand for land and a depreciation in land values. Overoptimistic investors who had expected to sell at a profit before interest and taxes made their investments a burden to them often found they could not meet their obligations. In the liquidation of their poorly managed and inadequately financed accounts, many investors lost their holdings to persons claiming through tax titles, occupying tenants' rights, or foreclosure of mortgages. Over the course of years their lands were acquired by stronger capitalists or by actual settlers.

The pressure of capitalists anxious to acquire favorable locations in new regions and the need of the government at times for additional revenue induced it to push the surveys far in advance of the needs of actual settlers. Great tracts of land were offered for sale during the inflation

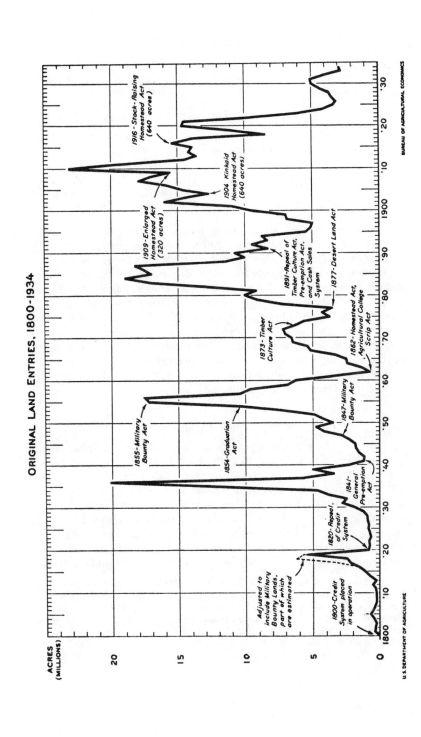

ORIGINAL LAND ENTRIES, 1800-1934

ACRES (MILLIONS)

1800 - Credit System placed in operation

Adjusted to include Military Bounty Lands, part of which are estimated

1820 - Repeal of Credit System

1841 - General Pre-emption Act

1847 - Military Bounty Act

1855 - Military Bounty Act

1854 - Graduation Act

1873 - Timber Culture Act

1862 - Homestead Act, Agricultural College Scrip Act

1891 - Repeal of Timber Culture Act, Pre-emption Act, and Cash Sales System

1877 - Desert Land Act

1909 - Enlarged Homestead Act (320 acres)

1904 Kinkaid Homestead Act (640 acres)

1916 - Stock-Raising Homestead Act (640 acres)

U.S. DEPARTMENT OF AGRICULTURE

BUREAU OF AGRICULTURAL ECONOMICS

years of the thirties on which few or no improvements had been made by squatters. By 1835 almost four times as much land had been offered at auction as had been sold.

LANDS—CEDED, SURVEYED, OFFERED, AND SOLD TO SEPTEMBER 1, 1835

Ceded lands	268,348,942
Surveyed and offered land	166,897,462
Surveyed and unsold land	122,397,462
Land sold	44,499,620

Source: American State Papers, Public Lands (Washington, D. C.: Gales and Seaton, 1832–1861), VIII, 424.

Numerous agencies sprang up to enable eastern investors to make entries of public lands. As few as 160 acres could be purchased through these agencies, which offered to make the entry, secure the patent, pay the taxes, protect the property from depredations, collect the rents if any, and sell when ordered—all for a commission on each transaction.[1] It was no more difficult to buy a tract of land in Illinois, Iowa, Michigan, or Minnesota for speculation than it was to buy shares in United States Steel in the nineteen twenties, and perhaps was accompanied by no greater risk. True, the agent who made the entry, particularly if it was a small one, would give little time to selection, not through any malice but because the fee was small, and the owner might find the land worthless or nearly so when later he investigated.

MONEYLENDING TO SQUATTERS

At the public auctions of government land in Illinois, Indiana, Michigan, or Missouri in 1835 and 1836, the usual squatters appeared seeking to protect the small improvements they had made on their claims. Capitalists or representatives of combinations of capitalists from the older states were also present to bid for the new tracts just coming into the market. Contrary to much that has been written about some of these exciting sales, there was little conflict within or between these two groups. Claim associations resolved difficulties between squatters, and tacit agreements among capitalists obviated any competition that might have threat-

[1] Eastern newspapers, such as the National Intelligencer and the New York Tribune, are replete with advertisements of land agents prepared to invest in western lands for eastern capitalists. See especially advertisements of George Megquier of Warrenton, Va.; David Clark, of Bloomington, Iowa; L. D. Stockton, of Burlington, Iowa; Cook & Sargent, of Davenport, Iowa; Henry McKenty, of St. Paul, Minn.; and Leonard & Everett, of Council Bluffs, Iowa; in the National Intelligencer, October 12, 1836; July 20, 1841; January 11, 1842; December 10, 1847; and January 9, 1856.

ened. Capitalists, not anxious to invoke the wrath of squatters, were quite prepared to lend them the funds with which they could purchase their tracts, but at a high price.[2] If the squatter met his payments to the lender, a high return was obtained on the investment; if not, an improved and perhaps a choice piece of land was obtained. The squatters, knowing that their claim association could not protect their right to their improvements beyond the auction, were ready to pay any interest the capitalist—"loan sharks" or "pelt gatherers," as they were called—might charge to enable them to purchase their claims. One desperate Iowa squatter, writing about the difficulty of raising funds with which to meet the purchase price of his government claim in 1841, said he could spare five yoke of oxen, two or three cows, a good horse, 3,000 pounds of pork, and 400 to 500 bushels of corn, but in the absence of a market he did not see how he was to save his property.[3]

Lending funds to squatters to enable them to purchase their claims, though it was not without risk, was a surer investment than purchasing land for speculation, and proved to be one of the most lucrative business opportunities on the frontier. To evade state and territorial usury laws limiting interest to 10 and 12 per cent, it was the practice for the lending agent to enter the land in his own name for the squatter, and to give a bond obliging him to convey title to the squatter at the end of one or two years when the original price, plus a heavy premium together with the maximum interest the law allowed, had been paid. In this way the actual interest ranged up to 30 and 40 per cent in the thirties and as high as 120 per cent in the fifties. Ten per cent, which was about the minimum charged in new communities, was only on the very best of security.[4]

In the prosperous years of 1835 and 1836 and again in 1854–1856, when agricultural prices were high and land values were swiftly rising, settlers on the frontier rashly entered into such high-interest-bearing obligations. If they had anything to sell it might bring good returns and they could hope that with the continuation of favorable weather and

[2] Mary Young has shown how effectively residents, settlers, and speculators collaborated at land sales in Mississippi in the eighteen thirties in Chapter 8, "Public Land Sales and the Cession in Trust," in her unpublished doctoral dissertation, "Redskins, Ruffleshirts and Rednecks: Indian Allotments in Alabama and Mississippi, 1830–1860," 1955, Cornell University Library.

[3] Ophia D. Smith, "Life and Times of Giles Richards, 1820–1860" (*Ohio Historical Collections*, Vol. VI; Columbus: Ohio State Archaeological and Historical Society, 1936), pp. 68–69; *Iowa Territorial Gazette and Burlington Advertiser*, September 21, 1839.

[4] The 10 per cent interest per month was not common but was by no means unknown. The *Arkansas Gazette & Democrat*, November 3, 1854, says that 100 and 200 per cent were being paid for money to enable squatters to enter graduation lands. The "time entry" business, as it was called, is described in Paul W. Gates, "Southern Investments in Northern Lands," *Journal of Southern History*, V (May, 1939), 161 ff.

prices they might meet their notes when due. Many succeeded but others did not: the extortionate interest charges ate up all they made.

Representative of the larger lenders were Miles and Elias White of Baltimore and James Stone Easley and William W. Willingham of Halifax, Virginia. These capitalists, who had accumulated considerable wealth in commerce, began lending in the late forties to squatters on the prevailing frontier terms. The Whites' total entries were 165,000 acres; those of Easley and Willingham and others for whom they acted were 350,000 acres. Some of this land may have been acquired for speculation, but the larger part was entered for squatters who had no other way of buying their land. Between three and four thousand people were accommodated in this way by these two groups of financiers. A considerable portion of the land reverted to the creditors and was sold by them over the remainder of the century. Perilous indeed was the position of a squatter who had to arrange financing with a loan shark. The Whites, Easley, and Willingham kept their business largely in their own hands and made frequent trips to the West to supervise the operations of their agents, who were required to get their approval for every loan, every compromise, and every sale.[5]

Another group of capitalists lending eastern funds was Cook & Sargent of Davenport, Iowa, and their various western associates. With Boston funds they established a bank, issued currency, and made entries for squatters and for absentee investors to the amount of 170,000 acres. Their business prospered for more than a decade, enabling them to establish branches at every land-office town in Iowa, to push aggressively the Mississippi and Missouri Railroad (the present Rock Island), and to become one of the most powerful banking and real-estate firms in Iowa. Over-commitments and too sanguine expectations brought them to bankruptcy in 1859.[6] They had numerous rivals in Iowa, including former surveyors, registers and receivers of the land offices, and politicians, but competition in lending funds to squatters seems not to have brought interest rates down at any time before the Civil War.

PANIC OF 1857

The Panic of 1857 and the resulting decline in farm commodity prices was felt immediately in the West. With their income drying up, farmers

---

[5] Gates, "Southern Investments . . . ," *loc. cit.*, pp. 160 ff.; Gates, *Wisconsin Pine Lands of Cornell University* (Ithaca, N. Y.: Cornell University Press, 1943), pp. 82 ff.

[6] There is some material of a jaundiced character on Cook and Sargent in Milo M. Quaife, ed., *The Early Days of Rock Island and Davenport: The Narratives of J. W. Spencer and J. M. D. Burrows* (The Lakeside Classics, No. 40; Chicago: The Lakeside Press, 1942).

were unable to meet payments on obligations which fell into default. A despairing Illinois farmer wrote:

> The financial panic of the East has cast its dark shadow over Illinois. There is little money in circulation. . . . Everything down to the lowest figure. We are overflowing with grain of all kinds and it is worth little or nothing. Wheat down to 50 cts., oats 17 cts., and still going down; cows that could not be bought for $30, three months ago, are now down to $18.[7]

Default on mortgage obligations and tax delinquency was widespread. An Iowa moneylender gave public notice to 109 debtors early in 1860 of his intention to foreclose the mortgages he held on their land.[8] In Minnesota a highly successful banker, note shaver, and moneylender foreclosed thirty-nine of fifty-eight mortgages drawn between 1857 and 1861; nineteen were paid in full.[9] The Whites, Easley, Willingham, and numerous other eastern capitalists likewise had to protect their equities in thousands of scattered farms by foreclosing. Persons losing their farms through failure to pay were permitted to remain on them as cash tenants until they could buy again or until other buyers appeared. In this way the frontier became saddled with debt, and tenancy appeared early and continued to increase as capital costs of farming grew.

The policies of the Buchanan administration deepened the farmers' distress. In his efforts to raise additional revenue from the public lands during the depression years following 1857, Buchanan ordered into the market great tracts of land in Iowa, Wisconsin, Kansas, Nebraska, and Minnesota on which many thousands of settlers had established their claims. Thus he cast aside an administrative policy toward which the government had been working: a policy that assured the settlers that land would not be brought into the market in hard times and that assured them free use of their claims for two or more years before being called upon to buy them. Settlers had been going to loan sharks since public sales began but generally in good times, when there seemed a prospect that they could repay their obligations when due. In former periods of depression they had sought postponement of sales and not uncommonly their pleas were answered. Now, in 1857–1860, with a catastrophic drought in Kansas and a nearly complete crop failure, with the price of wheat so low that it scarcely paid the cost of transportation to market, and with no prospect of improvement in the near future, the farmers begged for postponement of the sales without effect.

[7] *New England Farmer*, X (January, 1858), 23; Paul W. Gates, *The Illinois Central Railroad and Its Colonization Work* (Cambridge, Mass.: Harvard University Press, 1934), p. 256.

[8] *New York Tribune*, February 7, 1860.

[9] Margaret Snyder, *The Chosen Valley: The Story of a Pioneer Town* (New York: W. W. Norton & Company, 1948), p. 158.

Meantime, land reformers in the East like George Henry Evans, a prominent workingman's advocate, and Horace Greeley, powerful editor of the crusading *New York Tribune,* joined forces with such western agrarians as George W. Julian, Andrew Johnson, and other political liberals in a campaign to secure the enactment of a free homestead measure which would halt the sale of public lands and provide free grants to actual settlers. Their efforts led to the passage by both houses of Congress of an emasculated measure that was not satisfactory to any land reformers but made easier the road to ownership by reducing the price of land. Buchanan's veto of this bill destroyed the last hope of the settlers on the frontier for relief from Washington. Consequently, they had to turn to the loan sharks and make such terms as they could for loans to safeguard their rights in lands they had improved. Buchanan's sales policy and his veto of the greatly weakened homestead bill forced a large mortgage debt upon the farmers which they never forgot. Nothing contributed so largely to turn them from the Democratic party as these steps, the results of which they felt for years.[10]

In pressing additional lands on the market, at least in good times before 1855, the government was in a sense only carrying out the wishes of most Westerners, who wanted the Indians removed from their midst, the Indian lands ceded, surveyed, sold and developed as speedily as possible, and placed on the tax list to provide revenue for schools and roads. Westerners maintained, however, that it was improvements which gave value to land and that the $1.25 an acre exacted by the government for land, no matter what its quality, was beyond its true value. In exacting this price the government placed an additional hurdle in the path of the pioneer. Early in the process of farm making, all settlers had to meet the $200 payment for their quarter section in addition to all other capital costs. In the long run, the frontier rate of interest on the loan that many a settler contracted to enable him to purchase his land proved the greatest of his costs. Horace Greeley may not have been far wrong in maintaining that the two hundred million dollars paid into the Treasury for public lands "cost the settlers and improvers of those lands Five or Six Hundred Millions, in the shape of usury, extra price, Sheriff's fees, costs of foreclosing mortgages, etc. . . ."[11] Yet it was not until the best of the humid lands

[10] Some postponements were made where it seemed essential for the administration to aid local Democratic wheelhorses, but in Kansas, where the party had already been overwhelmed by the voters, the sales were held.—Paul W. Gates, *Fifty Million Acres: Conflicts over Kansas Land Policy* (Ithaca, N. Y.: Cornell University Press, 1954), pp. 72 ff. For the land-reform movement, see Helene Sara Zahler, *Eastern Workingmen and National Land Policy, 1829–1862* (New York: Columbia University Press, 1941), *passim.*

[11] *New York Tribune,* January 26, 1860; Paul W. Gates, "From Individualism to Collectivism in American Land Policy," in Chester McA. Destler, *Liberalism as a*

had passed into private hands that agrarian spokesmen came forth with proposals for the establishment of government banking schemes to provide low-cost credit to farmers.

Prior to 1860 free lands constituted the ultimate demand of the West, but this goal could not be achieved until southern opposition was stilled by secession.[12] Opposition in the South and to some degree in the Northeast, like earlier opposition to pre-emption, was based on fears that free lands would accelerate migration to the West, drain off population from older areas, and thus lower land values there. This in turn would create additional competition for farm products, swamp Congress with radically minded western representatives, and upset the old balance between the North and the South. *The Planters' Banner* of Franklin, Louisiana, summarized the grounds for opposing free homesteads, as follows: the policy would result in a large national debt, would draw paupers and criminals to America, would colonize the West with a "low and degraded" people, all speaking different languages and un-American in tastes, habits, and feelings.[13]

STEPS TOWARD FREE LAND

Though free homesteads were not to be had, a number of steps were taken in the late forties and fifties that substantially lowered the price of government lands and contributed further to speculation in them. The first of these steps was a series of acts adopted between 1847 and 1855 to grant land bounties of 40 to 160 acres to persons enlisting in the Mexican War and to veterans of earlier wars. Military bounty warrants for 61,000,000 acres were thus donated to veterans, a large number of which were promptly sold for prices that ranged from 70 cents to $1.10 an acre. The warrants were quoted regularly in the New York papers and in *Thompson's Bank Note Reporter*, and virtually passed as land-office money though their abundance and restrictions on their use depressed their value. At all the western land offices were agents of brokers prepared to sell land warrants, which thus became the principal means of acquiring land at less than the established minimum price. From the enactment of the first warrant act in 1847 until the adoption of the Graduation Act in 1854 twice as much land was acquired with warrants as with cash.[14]

Force in History: Lectures on Aspects of the Liberal Tradition (Henry Wells Lawrence Memorial Lectures, Vol. III; New London: Connecticut College, 1953), pp. 17 ff.

[12] George Malcolm Stephenson, *The Political History of the Public Lands from 1840 to 1862* (Boston: Richard G. Badger, 1917), *passim*.

[13] *Planters' Banner*, August 3, 1854. Cf. the *Baton Rouge Gazette*, May 29, 1852, for a favorable editorial on the homestead bill.

[14] Arthur H. Cole's valuable "Cyclical and Sectional Variations in the Sale of Public Lands, 1816–1860," *Review of Economic Statistics*, IX (January, 1927), 41 ff.,

Next in the process of lowering the cost of government land was the Swamp Land Act of 1850, which authorized the donation to the states of the swamp and overflowed portion of the public lands, in the expectation that the states would provide for their drainage. Instead, the states permitted the 64,000,000 acres to filter through their hands to private owners, frequently at prices substantially less than the government minimum and without any assurance that the lands would be drained.[15] A considerable part of the "swamp" lands were wet only in the spring and needed little more than drains, but others in the Kankakee Valley, for example, could be cultivated only after great co-operative and government-aided drainage districts had been created.

Finally, in 1854, Congress graduated the price of land in proportion to the length of time it had been on the market. Land offered and unsold for ten years was priced at $1.00 an acre, and by progressive downward steps the price was reduced to 12½ cents for land on the market for thirty or more years. For newly offered land or land subject to purchase for less than ten years the minimum price of $1.25 remained in effect. Although lands subject to graduation had been picked over and left unentered by settlers over these long periods, many tracts were fair to good and, like the swamp lands, only needed large amounts of capital to develop them.[16]

The table showing the Acreage of Public Land Entries, 1845–1860, is inserted for the light it throws on the working of an increasingly complex land system. The entries of land of 1840 to 1847 as shown in the table and chart were largely made by settlers under the pre-emption law or by the purchase of land after the auction, and in the absence of large speculative activity may be considered as the normal amount of land being taken up and improved by settlers. Following 1847 an increasing proportion of land being sold was acquired by speculators. It reached a high point in 1854 and 1855 and continued large until 1862. Entries with military warrants, which cost less than cash entries because of the low market value of the warrants, displaced cash entries in 1848. Graduation sales from their appearance in 1855 exceeded the regular cash entries in all

---

needs reconsideration because it neglects the large amount of land acquired with military bounty warrants from 1848 to 1860. True, the government received nothing but fees on the entry of land with warrants, but what is important is the rate of transfer of land from public to private ownership, not the amount the government received.

[15] Margaret B. Bogue, "The Swamp Land Act and Wet Land Utilization in Illinois, 1850–1890," *Agricultural History*, XXV (October, 1951), 169 ff.

[16] In addition to the progressive lowering of the price of government land through the use of land warrants, the Graduation Act, and swamp-land sales, the ratio of the inflexible government minimum price for newly offered land to the high price level of farm products in the years preceding the Panic of 1857, as well as in the middle thirties, was highly favorable to farm makers.

years except 1856. The large cash entries at $1.25 for 1854–1856 are partly to be explained by the fact that lands previously withdrawn from entry to allow railroads to select out of them their land grants were now being reoffered. It should be noted that the many million acres of swamp lands and other lands granted to the states for various purposes—which were being disposed of at an unparalleled rate in the fifties—do not appear either in the table or the chart.

ACREAGE OF PUBLIC LAND ENTRIES, 1845–1860

Year	Cash entries		Warrant entries	Scrip entries
	At $1.25 or above	Graduation sales		
1845	1,843,527			
1846	2,263,731			
1847	2,521,306		239,880	55,903
1848	1,887,553		2,288,960	57,249
1849	1,329,903		3,405,520	53,935
1850	1,405,839		2,167,680	
1851	1,846,847		2,454,000	
1852	1,553,071		3,201,314	115,682
1853	1,083,495		6,142,360	9,427
1854	7,035,735		3,402,620	14,182
1855	7,009,152	8,702,373	1,345,580	
1856	5,230,586	3,997,293	8,382,480	
1857	1,622,730	2,520,014	6,283,920	
1858	817,529	2,957,379	5,802,150	
1859	511,478	3,450,103	2,914,700	
1860	601,160	2,860,044	2,782,780	

Source: Compiled from *Annual Reports* of the Commissioner of the General Land Office, 1845–1860.

Western settlers and their representatives in Congress were not content with these measures for lowering the cost of land and, as has been seen, attempted to push through Congress a free grant measure. Diminishing opposition in the Northeast seemed to make certain the success of this move, but southern emasculation of the measure and Buchanan's veto delayed the final triumph of the reformers till 1862.

Meantime, the General Land Office had pushed the survey of public lands as rapidly as appropriations permitted. Kansas and Nebraska territories were opened to settlement in 1854 before an acre of land had been surveyed, yet so speedily were surveys run thereafter that they reached 272 miles west of the Missouri-Kansas border within six years. True, there was Indian land farther east which, until surrendered, could be neither surveyed nor settled. Great areas in California, Washington, Oregon, practically all of Iowa, Wisconsin, Missouri, Arkansas, most of Louisiana and

Florida, and a large part of Minnesota had been surveyed into townships and ranges, sections and quarter sections. Settlers continued to precede the surveyor, but their unlawful intrusions on unsurveyed land were winked at so long as they were not made on Indian reserves. In 1853 and 1854 pre-emption rights were conceded to settlers on unsurveyed land in California, Washington, Oregon, Kansas, Nebraska, and Minnesota, and in 1862 were extended to settlers on all unsurveyed lands to which Indian title had been surrendered.[17]

LAND SPECULATION IN THE FIFTIES

A combination of events in the fifties and the lowering of land prices produced a rush for the public domain that surpassed anything in previous history. Frantic railroad building, particularly in the upper Mississippi Valley, the great influx of Germans, Scandinavians, and Easterners into the West, and a new era of banking experiments which greatly increased available credit all contributed to the demand for land. Optimistic settlers bought as much as their resources permitted without regard to the possibility of utilizing the land they thus acquired or of meeting taxes and interest on borrowed funds. Eastern funds poured into the West, seeking the elusive quick profits which so frequently seemed to escape speculators in the land.

Everywhere the hand of the speculator was felt, especially in the upper Mississippi Valley. Wisconsin and Missouri lands were purchased in large amounts, but it was Iowa and Illinois prairie lands which the speculators preferred. The productivity of the prairies was just beginning to be recognized, railroads were being pushed throughout Indiana, Illinois, and eastern Iowa, the demand for labor was greater than the supply despite the big influx of immigrants, capital or credit was abundantly provided by new banks, and values of both improved and unimproved land were zooming upward. About 28,000,000 acres passed directly into the hands of settlers and speculators in these two states in the fifties; in addition, considerable quantities of swamp, railroad, and internal-improvements grant lands were sold. If one deducts from the total acreage of Illinois and Iowa the acreage in farms as of 1860 and the acreage held for railroads, swamp, and river improvement, unsold government land in Iowa, and 2,000,000 acres for town and city property, there is a remainder of 24,000,000 acres, a large part of which was owned by speculators.

The entry books of the government land offices show both the speculative purchases of small investors and those of individuals, partnerships,

[17] In the *Annual Report* of the Commissioner of the General Land Office for 1860 are maps showing the progress of surveys in all the above-mentioned states.— 10 *U. S. Stat.* 246, 268, 305, 310, 576, and 12 *U. S. Stat.*, 413.

and companies who made large purchases in the period before 1860. In Iowa, for example, 101 persons and groups acquired 2,786,000 acres. A considerable amount of this acreage was entered by agents of eastern capitalists for settlers, but a large part was purchased for speculation. Similarly, in Illinois 112 individuals and groups bought or otherwise directly entered at the land offices 2,045,000 acres. In Michigan 70 parties entered 955,000 acres.[18] Many more investors who bought land in amounts ranging from a full section to 5,000 acres are not included in these figures.

In the southern public-land states large-scale buying was very noticeable in the thirties, particularly in Alabama and Mississippi. In one of the eight land districts of Mississippi for which there is detailed information, 62 purchasers acquired ownership of 1,399,000 acres. Fifty-seven buyers of Creek and Chickasaw allotments in amounts of 10,000 acres or more acquired 3,019,486 acres. An additional 2,604,451 acres were acquired by purchasers in amounts ranging from 2,000 to 10,000 acres. Finally, a large part of the 4,863,915 acres sold at the Columbus and Chocchuma land offices in Mississippi went into the hands of middlemen and speculators.[19]

The anatomy of land speculation needs further study and can only be briefly discussed here. Practically all classes of the population in frontier communities speculated in the public lands. Squatters who brought no capital with them and had no credit made small improvements on quarter sections and sold their claims when the rush of settlers appeared. Then, contrary to the spirit of the pre-emption law, they moved on to another frontier, once more to anticipate settlers who planned to remain on the land. On the outer edge of settlement, squatters commonly engaged in such speculative practices. One whose capital was not sufficient to develop a single quarter section nevertheless bought on credit two or three quarters, thereby "pushing the school house away from his children and the mill and store away from his neighborhood in the hope of making a big profit. . . . ," as Horace Greeley critically observed.[20] Next came the men of small means who, whether located in frontier communities or in older established areas, invested a few hundred dollars either directly or through one of the numerous land agents. Then there was the eastern capitalist who had five or ten thousand dollars for which he sought a lucrative investment, but had no plan to develop the land he acquired with it. Moneylenders, like James S. Easley, who put out many thousands of

[18] These totals are the tabulation of cash, scrip, and warrant entries taken from the abstract books of the various land offices in the National Archives.

[19] Data concerning the Creek and Chickasaw allotments and the Pontotoc sale are from Mary Young, "Redskins, Ruffleshirts and Rednecks: Indian Allotments in Alabama and Mississippi, 1830–1860." The original purchasers at the Columbus and Chocchuma sales are given in *American State Papers, Public Lands* (8 vols.; Washington, D. C.: Gales and Seaton, 1832–1861), VII, 377 ff.

[20] *New York Tribune*, February 3, 1860.

dollars in loans, also speculated by buying outright large acreages of wild land. Finally, there were the great land companies whose operations covered many states and included both purchase and sale of unimproved wild lands and city lots, in addition to considerable publicity, promotion, and sometimes development work.

One such company was the American Land Company, organized in 1835 by a group of New York and Boston men with a capital of $1,000,000. This company called in payments on its stock and allocated $400,000 for investment in Mississippi cotton lands, $250,000 for Arkansas lands, and the balance for city lots and rural property in six other western and southern states. Well over 200,000 acres were acquired and retailed during the next generation, not, however, with the anticipated results.[21] The New York and Mississippi Land Company, with a capital of $500,000, also invested heavily in Mississippi cotton lands in the middle thirties. The sales record of its 206,000 acres was no more favorable than that of the American Land Company.[22] Other intersectional land companies of this period had suggestive names: New York, Mississippi, and Arkansas Land Company; Boston and New York Chickasaw Land Company; Boston and Mississippi Cotton Land Company; New York and Boston Illinois Land Company; Boston and Indiana Land Company; and Boston and Western Land Company.[23] One of these companies claimed to own 900,000 acres; the total holdings of all of them would run to a number of million acres.[24]

The character of the intricate land deals in which eastern capitalists became involved is shown by the investments of Erastus Corning. Beside his investment in the New York and Mississippi and the American Land Companies, Corning had an interest in the New York Land Company, which controlled a large part of the Half Breed Tract in southeastern Iowa; he also acquired a one-sixth interest in the Fox and Wisconsin Improvement Company, which had a land grant of 338,000 acres; and his share in the 563,000-acre grant of the St. Marys Falls Ship Canal Company which built the Soo Canal was more than 100,000 acres in Michigan. In addition, he owned directly several thousand acres in Indiana and Michigan and was a heavy investor in the Burlington Railroad, which

[21] *First Annual Report of the Trustees of the American Land Company* (June, 1836), pp. 9 ff. An influential trustee of the American Land Company was Erastus Corning. Irene Neu, in her "Business Biography of Erastus Corning," an unpublished doctoral dissertation in the Cornell University Library, 1950, has a section on the American Land Company.

[22] Mary Young, "Redskins, Ruffleshirts and Rednecks," has a chapter on the New York and Mississippi Land Company.

[23] James W. Silver, "Land Speculation Profits on the Chickasaw Cession," *Journal of Southern History*, X (February, 1944), 85 ff.

[24] *For Sale. The Following Parcels of Land Situate in the Military Tract of Illinois and Belonging to the New York and Boston Illinois Land Co.* [no date, no place].

had a land grant in Iowa and Nebraska.[25] Corning's biographer was not able to determine the profits and losses in the numerous land deals in which he invested but concludes that he continued to regard western lands as a good investment throughout his life.[26]

Immigrants arriving in frontier communities soon learned that speculators had anticipated them by selecting many of the best-situated tracts. Almost everywhere they were met with advertisements offering "choice, well-located land" at well above the government price and were warned that government land was available only in inaccessible and distant areas. Examples are Cook and Sargent of Davenport; W. J. Barney and John W. Taylor of Dubuque, who offered, respectively, 128,000 acres in fifty-one counties in Iowa, 70,000 acres in northern Iowa and "nearly 100,000 acres . . . generally well and judiciously selected" land for sale.[27] In Illinois, Richard P. Morgan offered 1,000,000 acres along the Chicago and Alton Railroad, Andrew J. Galloway offered 200,000 acres, and numerous other dealers and speculators advertised land in amounts from 5,000 to 70,000 acres.[28] In Indiana, the Cincinnati, Peru, and Chicago Railroad offered the 100,000 acres it had received in exchange for its stock.[29] A Milwaukee firm announced it held 600,000 acres for sale in Wisconsin.[30] Landlookers in Alabama could not but notice David Hubbard's advertisements of 100,000 acres of fresh cotton lands for sale.[31] More disillusioning to the immigrants must have been the advertisements of the land-grant railroads offering land within fifteen miles of their line from $5 to $25 an acre, the price depending upon the distance from the line.[32]

The total volume of small-scale speculation in claims before the

[25] Neu, op. cit., pp. 195 ff.

[26] Ibid., p. 252.

[27] Catalogue of Lands in Iowa, Wisconsin, Minnesota, etc., for Sale by Cook & Sargent, Davenport, Iowa (Davenport: 1858); Northern Iowa: Containing Hints and Information of Value to Emigrants, by a Pioneer (Dubuque: 1858); John W. Taylor's Descriptive Pamphlet. No. 1. The West. Description of Iowa. Information for Those Seeking New Homes or Profitable Investments (Dubuque: 1860).

[28] Some other Illinois agents and speculators with the acreage they offered: John Shaw Hayward, 55,000 acres; John S. Greene, 50,000; W. N. Coler, 40,000; James Mix, 35,000; the Illinois Land Company, 30,000; D'Wolf, MaClay & Quimby, 45,000; Solomon Sturges, 70,000; G. W. Yerby, 55,000; George Fuller & Co., 100,000; Gridley & Helm, 25,000; J. E. Garrels, 20,000.—Advertisements of these individuals and firms in the Chicago Daily Democratic Press and the Bloomington, Ill., Pantagraph, 1855–1857.

[29] Wabash Weekly Intelligencer, August 30, 1854.

[30] Valuable Information Important to Emigrants and Strangers Intending to Settle or Make Investments in the State of Wisconsin (Milwaukee: 1852).

[31] Tuscaloosa, Ala., Flag of the Union, August 4, 1841.

[32] The Illinois Central Rail-Road Company Offer for Sale over 2,400,000 Acres . . . (New York: John W. Ammerman, 1855), p. 9; The Hannibal and St. Joseph Railroad Company Have Received by Grant from Congress over 600,000 acres . . . (Hannibal, Mo.: 1859), p. 7.

public sale and in small purchases at the sales was large, but it is impossible to give any accurate figures without the most detailed examination of the land-office books. Before and after the sales in eastern Kansas in 1859–1860 "vast bodies of land" were said to be held by speculator-squatters acting either for themselves or for men of means. As late as 1878 much of this land was still withheld from development by speculators waiting for the long-anticipated profits.[33] The tendency of Americans of all classes to speculate in land was observed by an Englishman resident in the United States:

> Speculation in real estate has for many years been the ruling idea and occupation of the Western mind. Clerks, labourers, farmers, storekeepers, merely followed their callings for a living, while they were speculating for their fortunes. . . .
>
> The people of the West became dealers in land, rather than its cultivators. . . . Everyone of any spirit, ambition, and intelligence (cash was not essential), frequented the National Land Exchange. . . . Millions of acres were bought and sold without buyer or seller knowing where they were, or whether they were anywhere; the buyer only knowing that he hoped to sell his title to them at a handsome profit.[34]

The American land system which placed no restriction upon the quantity of public land an individual could acquire with cash or land warrants, and required no settlement condition to be fulfilled before patent, facilitated the creation of speculative holdings. As the surveyors pushed westward, great areas of surveyed land remained untilled, unimproved, and often untaxable. Speculators' deserts they were called.[35] Such undeveloped tracts, held as they were for high prices, forced incoming immigrants to go farther afield in their search for cheap land, dispersed population over a wide area, brought about intrusions into the Indian reserves, and led the government to concentrate Indian tribes on ever smaller reserves. In thinly populated communities cursed by extensive absentee ownership, churches, roads, schools, and local government came slowly, and the cost of maintaining them bore heavily upon the resident owners. Poorly developed rural communities meant thin farm development, promised little freight for prospective railroads, and made subsidies necessary if they were to be built in such areas. To bring rail-

[33] White Cloud *Kansas Chief*, August 20, 1857; *Indiana Farmer*, XI (April 29, 1876), 4; L. D. Burch, *Kansas as It Is* (Chicago: C. S. Burch & Co., 1878), p. 113.

[34] D. W. Mitchell, *Ten Years in the United States* (London: Smith, Elder & Co., 1862), pp. 325–327; also see Levi Beardsley, *Reminiscences* (New York: C. Vinten, 1852), pp. 253 ff.

[35] *New York Tribune*, February 3, 1860; Judge Albert Miller, "Thomas L. L. Brent," *Collections* of the Michigan Pioneer and Historical Society (Lansing: 1886), IX, 192–196.

roads to their regions, speculators and real-estate promoters induced the federal government to vote lavish railroad land grants and persuaded counties, towns, and cities to bestow bond subsidies on the railroads.[36]

ABSENTEE OWNERS

Western newspaper proprietors, who represented the small business interests of their communities as well as the predominant political party whose patronage made their papers possible, welcomed absentee capital, whether it was intended for speculation, for development, or for loans to squatters.[37] Not all rural folk thought similarly, however; some looked upon the speculators as "public enemies" whose operations ought to be frustrated in every possible way.[38] These feelings were increased when interest on mortgages owned by these absentees could not be met and foreclosure followed, or when absentee holders did not meet their taxes, tried to upset assessments, and made no effort to develop their tracts or to contribute to the growth of the community.

In the midst of these waves of "antimonopoly" feelings politicians vied with each other in condemning absentee owners and in demanding action to force them either to disgorge their property or to improve it. Agrarian-minded precursors of Henry George tried to exempt improvements from taxation and to place the tax burden entirely on land as a means of shifting taxes from farm makers to speculative and absentee owners. Such a policy, said the Iowa *Bloomington Herald,* "will make the taxes so onerous upon non-resident lands that the holders will be glad to sell at fair and reasonable prices to those who will improve" them.[39] The territory of Iowa actually experimented with such a law. Most western states and territories were not willing to go as far as Iowa, which quickly withdrew from its advanced position, but did adopt legislation to tax mortgage instruments; permit delinquent debtors to plead usury against their creditors; prevent or delay foreclosure proceedings; and

[36] Paul W. Gates, "The Role of the Land Speculator in Western Development," *Pennsylvania Magazine of History and Biography,* LXVI (July, 1942), 314 ff.

[37] The *Michigan Sentinel,* Monroe, September 23 and December 9, 1825, welcomed a number of robust capitalists from New York who had come to purchase lands.

[38] For the pillorying of absentee speculators and landlookers employed by them, see Mrs. C. M. Kirkland, *Western Clearings* (New York: Wiley and Putnam, 1845), pp. 2–14.

[39] *Bloomington Herald,* October 23, 1846, and January 8, 1847, cited in John E. Brindley, *History of Taxation in Iowa* (Iowa Economic History Series, 2 vols.; Iowa City: State Historical Society of Iowa, 1911), I, 370. Much the same sentiments were expressed in the Little Rock *Arkansas Gazette & Democrat,* November 11, 1853, and July 21, 28, 1854. Years later a Nebraska resident said that "the speculators are getting tired of building school houses, so that they are offering their lands for sale very low and on reasonable terms."—Monticello, Ill., *Piatt Republican,* February 5, 1874.

give greater validity to the tax titles which were issued year after year on much of the absentee-owned land.[40]

Agrarian radicalism reached a high point in the bad years of 1857 to 1860. Land speculation, in which it seemed almost everyone had indulged, was now widely condemned, and earlier efforts to limit the amount of land individuals could buy from the government or could hold were revived.[41] Normally conservative organs of corn-belt business and farm interests castigated the "demon of land speculation . . . that seizes the choice spots . . . in advance of the emigrants' arrival, separates the settlers' cabins by wide tracts of unreclaimed wilderness, and encircles every embryo town and populous city with leagues of waste land as absolutely wild as when the deer and the Indian were its only inhabitants." Another prairie organ wrote:

We hate this land monopoly;—it is an evil and a curse. It compels the hard handed, toiling cultivator, to produce wealth, whether he will or no, to fill the pockets of the non-resident, non-improving, non-laboring speculator, who owned the land around him.[42]

Speculators were called an "unmitigated evil," "a withering, blighting influence," responsible for the depression because they drained money from the West and had created the inflated land values which kept the farmer from owning land. An indignant Kansas editor expressed the hope that "the land of non-residents who never intend to live here, will be taxed so steeply and the owners harassed so vigorously that they will be glad to dispose of them." [43] A more cautious proposal was that a limit should be placed on the amount of land individuals could own and the owners of land in excess of 160 acres should be compelled to sell their surplus. At the same time it was proposed to restrict the right to inherit land.[44]

[40] Brindley, op. cit., I, 8, 25, 33, 43. The compiler of History of De Witt County, Illinois (Philadelphia: W. R. Brink, 1882), p. 59, commenting on the 11,000 acres owned by nonresidents at the time the county was organized in 1839, observed that these lands were usually assessed "a little higher" than those of actual settlers, as was commonly done in "new" counties.

[41] Both Wisconsin and Minnesota sought to place limits on the amount of land individuals could acquire. Springfield Illinois State Register, March 11, 1851; St. Paul Minnesota Democrat, April 15, 1851; Brownville Nebraska Advertiser, July 23, 1857; De Soto Pilot, Nebraska, May 18, 1858; New York Tribune, June 9, 1859; Monticello Spectator, Illinois, August 1, 1860; Annual Report of the Secretary of the Interior, Senate Executive Document No. 1, 33 Cong., 1 Sess., 1853–1854, I, 53; House Miscellaneous Document No. 89, 35 Cong., 1 Sess., 1857–1858.

[42] Bloomington, Ill., Pantagraph, March 8, 1859; Neosho Valley Register, Kansas, February 21, 1860.

[43] Neosho Valley Register, February 21, 1860; Margaret Beattie Bogue, "Patterns from the Sod: Land Use and Tenure in the Grand Prairie, 1850–1900." Unpublished doctoral dissertation, 1955, Cornell University Library, pp. 49 ff.

[44] Ohio Cultivator, VI (March 15 and April 15, 1850), 84–85, 117.

Unimproved absentee-owned land was commonly plundered by settlers who cut their firewood and fence rails from it, even stripped it of its valuable timber, and pastured their livestock on it. An Iowa emigration association actually gave publicity to this possibility of utilizing speculators' lands in its advertising literature:

There are plenty of lands [in northern Iowa] . . . belonging to speculators on which settlers can pasture their cattle and cut their hay for several years to come. A farmer can buy a small piece, break it up and enclose it . . . and the speculator will furnish the meadow and pasture and pay the taxes on it.— A very great convenience to a new beginning in a new country.[45]

In similar fashion a large sheep owner of Illinois told of cutting prairie hay on unsold government land and on that of speculators who did not occupy it.[46] At a later time even resident owners of large estates were attacked by the more advanced antimonopolists, who disliked the landlord's opposition to "every public enterprise that has ever been projected, even to the public school. . . ."[47] In view of the West's tendency to plunder the land of absentee owners it is not surprising that the American Land Company which had a large investment in Arkansas land should have appropriated a thousand dollars "in aid of the religious, moral and intellectual interests of the territory of Arkansas," which was not noted for its law-abiding character.[48]

Westerners early learned that in areas where absentee speculators were almost the only actual owners of the soil it was easy to spend public funds for roads, schools, county buildings, poorhouses, and salaries for officeholders. Only a very few people were needed to create local governments; after a county was organized, the offices and construction contracts could be passed around among the residents, who could sell bonds and issue scrip or tax-anticipation warrants to finance such activities. One critic of these practices charged that a number of western Iowa counties having a mere baker's dozen of residents had built roads "equal to the Simplon and not inferior to the Appian Way," and schoolhouses that were veritable châteaux. All such activities were characterized as a "swindling farce."[49] Local residents came to regard the speculative holders as largely responsible for their plight during periods of depression and saw nothing wrong in voting large appropriations for roads, obtaining con-

[45] Dubuque Emigrant Association, *Northern Iowa: Information for Emigrants* (Dubuque: 1858), p. 12.

[46] Albany *Cultivator* in *Farmer's Monthly Visitor*, VIII (January 31, 1846), 12–13.

[47] Bloomington, Ill., *Leader*, October 18, 1872.

[48] *First Annual Report of the Trustees of the American Land Company*, p. 32.

[49] *Lafayette Daily Journal*, January 11 and 24, 1862. The practices thus described in Iowa were later developed and refined in Wisconsin and Kansas frontier counties and were by no means unusual.—Gates, *The Wisconsin Pine Lands of Cornell University*, pp. 137 ff.

tracts for road work at high prices, and building expensive schoolhouses so long as most of the burden could be passed on to absentees.[50]

Absentee investors were not without defensive weapons. They paid their taxes with depreciated county orders, permitted their taxes to become delinquent and their lands to be advertised for sale, and would then attack the assessments as discriminatory and have them set aside. Sometimes they would attempt to compromise with local authorities by offering to pay a small part of the assessment, which officials would accept, so great was the need of money. In efforts to set aside assessments, they argued that local officers, who were not the best of legal minds, had not followed exactly the procedure for making assessments and that official notice of the taxes had not been received. Faulty procedures in making assessments sometimes led the courts to suspend the collection of taxes. This both demoralized local government and created additional expense in the matter of titles. To meet this situation states legalized faulty assessments and provided that ignorance of assessments could not be offered as a reason for setting aside penalties.[51]

Absentee owners, particularly small investors who could not supervise their land matters closely, were often careless about remitting funds for taxes and permitted their holdings to become tax delinquent and to have tax titles issued against them. They complained that western tax laws did not allow sufficient time to elapse between assessment, the levying of the tax, and the final date when it had to be paid to enable them to remit funds. Many columns of official advertisements appeared in western newspapers each year announcing the sale of hundreds, even thousands, of tracts for taxes.

Western legislators were sensitive to the rights of squatters. Long before 1841, when the federal government conceded prospective preemption on surveyed land, states and territories recognized the rights that squatters had acquired by living upon and improving public land and held conveyances of these rights or claims to be as valid in law as conveyances of the fee. Local governments were thereby recognizing rights to land that was legally subject to control and disposal only by the federal government. The West went further by giving squatters protection for improvements they made on absentee-owned land. For a few cents an acre, squatters living on such tax-delinquent land could acquire tax titles which gave them a "color of title," with the full right to all improvements they put on the land. If the absentee owners of patent titles brought ejectment proceedings, the defendant was entitled to the full

[50] D. B. Brett, Stevens Point, Wisc., March 13, 1860, to Charles Mason, Mason MSS, Iowa State Historical Department, Des Moines, Iowa.

[51] Laws of Iowa, Fifth General Assembly, 1855, p. 246, and Laws of Iowa, Seventh General Assembly, 1858, p. 320.

value of his improvements, minus any depreciation of the land through timber cutting that resulted from his occupation. In a few years' time, if taxes were paid and improvements continuously made, the rights of the occupant could become of greater value than the patent title. Thus the absentee owner's rights could be eroded away, and the patent title come to have little more than a nuisance value.

RAILROAD LAND GRANT POLICIES

Westerners, eager for railroads, were ready to help finance them by all possible means. Early experiments in state financing and building railroads having failed, however, in the thirties, this method was not again to be tried, except by Missouri, but county and municipal subscriptions to the securities of railroads were widely granted and few middle western railroads were built without some aid of this character. In Indiana, Illinois, and Wisconsin, mortgages on farms and other real property were exchanged for the stock of railroad enterprises, with disastrous results for the participating farmers.[52] Most successful of western methods for aiding the construction of railroads was the land grant. Though land grants to eastern companies—for all major railroads were built with the aid of and controlled by eastern capitalists—meant absentee ownership and land speculation on a scale bigger than anything the West had yet seen, the West felt the benefits to be expected from the building of the railroads would be greater than the troubles anticipated from this absentee ownership. Nevertheless, Westerners watched with concern the early land policies of the railroads and tried to compel early sales.

The Illinois Central Railroad, the northern part of the Chicago and Mobile line which Congress strove to get under way with a generous grant in 1850, was the greatest capitalistic enterprise in the West at the time it was under construction. The 2,595,000 acres of land granted this road had been subject to entry for years, but had been passed over because it was prairie land with little timber and remote from navigable rivers. The building of the railroad, it was expected, would create a demand for this land and permit it to be sold at prices well above the government minimum.

Fearing that the railroad might withhold the land for speculation for years to come, the Illinois legislature specified that all lands unsold ten years after completion of the road should be offered at auction annually until completely sold. It also provided that pre-emptors who had

[52] For the extension of railroads through the prairies of Illinois in the fifties, see the annual maps and tables in Frederic L. Paxson, "The Railroads of the 'Old Northwest' before the Civil War," *Transactions* of the Wisconsin Academy of Sciences, Arts and Letters, Vol. XVII, Pt. I (October, 1912), pp. 248 ff.

made improvements on land later selected by the Illinois Central should have the right to buy their claims at $2.50 an acre. A week after the charter of the railroad was approved, the Illinois Central was prohibited from laying out towns on or near its line. The first and third of these limitations were to be successfully evaded.[53]

The task of selecting the lands, appraising them, and setting up a sales system was not easy, and people of the state became restive at the slowness of the Illinois Central in placing its land on sale. Early in 1852 a meeting of those opposed to land monopoly along the line of the railroad demanded that the company sell its lands only to actual settlers.[54] Had this demand been heeded, some of the worst results of the railroad's sales policies would have been avoided. In 1854 a strong movement in the state legislature to compel the company to sell one fifteenth of its lands yearly was defeated by only one vote after heavy lobbying.

Recognizing that the people wanted the railroad lands sold and improved and realizing at the same time that its own future as a transportation company depended on the development of its territory, the Illinois Central followed a vigorous policy of attracting immigrants and selling its lands that established the pattern to be followed by later land-grant railroads. Seven years' credit was allowed to settlers, and only a small down payment was required. In fact, settlers had two years' use of the land at an advance payment of only 4 per cent, which was almost as generous as the pre-emption policy of the government. The lands were priced at from $6 to $24 an acre, the bulk of them being held for $6 to $10 an acre. These prices appear to be decidedly high in view of the fact that the same lands had gone begging just a few years before, but in the meantime railroad connections with Chicago and the East had been provided and a veritable price revolution had occurred. When the lands were placed on sale in 1854 and 1855 there was a rush to buy them, almost a third being sold on credit. When the Panic of 1857 struck and prices of wheat, corn, and hogs fell disastrously, farmer-buyers could not meet their payments. The officials of the Illinois Central were lenient with the settlers, granting them extensions, taking their produce for payments, and allowing them to forfeit contracts and apply their installments on portions of the original purchase.[55]

A succession of poor crops and continued low prices brought many farmers, as well as the railroad officials, to despair. Farmers came to feel that the prices they had contracted to pay in the halcyon days before the panic were too high. At a meeting at St. Anne, in October, 1859, the attending farmers called to the attention of the Illinois Central "the criti-

[53] *Charter of the Illinois Central Railroad Company* (Chicago: 1878), pp. 7 ff.

[54] *Bloomington Intelligencer,* Illinois, quoted in *Prairie Farmer,* XII (May, 1852), 244.

[55] Gates, *Illinois Central Railroad,* pp. 270 ff.

cal position of the settlers on her lands" and asked for relief. Four consecutive crop failures and the continued low prices of produce made it impossible for them to meet their payments, and the accumulation of interest on delayed payments was actually making their situation worse. They urged a reduction in the price of unsold land and a rebate on those for which contracts had already been issued.[56] Nothing came of their demands, and when inflation came in the sixties, prices were boosted further.

When Congress had just passed or was considering the enactment of a railroad land grant it was the practice of the General Land Office to withdraw from sale the public lands within the probable limits of the grant until the line was determined and the lands were selected. The withdrawals were to prevent speculators and settlers from anticipating the railroad by entering the lands. Since the area of withdrawal was thirty or more miles wide and since Congress passed numerous measures providing land grants between 1852 and 1856, a large part of the public lands was thus closed temporarily to settlers seeking pre-emption rights. Only two railroads, the Illinois Central and the Hannibal and St. Joseph, completed their lines with reasonable despatch, the alternate reserved sections were restored to market and were promptly grabbed up by speculators and placed on the tax roll.

Elsewhere, because of the inability of promoters to raise funds for construction and the failure of many companies in the Panic of 1857, the lines were not built for years; hence the withdrawn lands were not earned and could not be sold for they were not open to entry under the public-land laws nor had the railroads earned title to them. Instead, then, of contributing to the growth and prosperity of the regions they were intended to aid, the first effect of the grants, with the exceptions noted, was to repel immigrants and to retard growth. The *Milwaukee Sentinel,* in expressing strong opposition to the land-grant policy, spoke of it as a "most mischievous policy" that is "disastrous to individuals and detrimental to the interests of the State." [57] At the time this represented a minority opinion, for the West wanted railroads so badly that it was willing to accept conditions it later regarded as intolerable.

The unfortunate effects of withdrawals were to be more apparent after 1860, when many tens of million acres were out of the market. Settlers' grievances against the railroads for their failure to earn their lands, take title to them, and have them placed on the tax roll, and for their refusal to sell at reasonable prices, combined with grievances over freight rates and discriminatory shipping practices produced the anti-railroad movement of the seventies, with its demand for the forfeiture of the un-

[56] Middleport, Ill., *Iroquois Republican,* October 20, 1859.
[57] *Milwaukee Sentinel,* June 11, 1856.

earned grants, taxation and forced sale of the earned lands, and the end of the land-grant policy.[58]

FARM MORTGAGES

Westerners were keenly concerned about the availability of capital for farm makers and for rising business interests. It had long been a moot question on the frontier whether usury laws were effective. A Democratic paper of Des Moines called the Iowa statute making the maximum rate of interest 10 per cent and authorizing persons who had paid more to recover in the courts a "dead letter [that] is openly and notoriously violated every day" with rates of interest running as high as 50 per cent.[59] Lenders also evaded usury laws, as has been seen, by entering land for squatters, taking title in their own name, and reselling to the squatters for a premium of $25 or more on a quarter section plus the maximum interest the law allowed. When squatters were anxious for loans to buy their land, legislatures were less inclined to adopt restrictive measures; when hard times appeared, they tried to help the debt-ridden farmers by tightening up the usury laws.[60] Thus Wisconsin in good times fixed the rate of interest at 12 per cent and "repealed all laws forfeiting the principal, if interest beyond this sum be agreed on." [61] When depression struck, the state reversed its action by adopting a rigorous law. Debtors were authorized to sue for treble the amount they had to pay beyond the 12 per cent maximum. Little relief actually was accorded debtors, however, for the act did not apply to mortgages negotiated prior to its adoption if they conformed to previous legislation.[62]

Both Wisconsin and Iowa adopted stay laws to extend the period of time following default on a mortgage payment before foreclosure proceedings could be carried out. Wisconsin gave debtors a year's time, and Iowa nine months, after the filing of a complaint of nonpayment, before foreclosure could be completed. The period in which a mortgagor could

[58] *Dubuque Herald,* January 23, 1862, cited in Brindley, *History of Taxation in Iowa,* II, 391–392; Gates, *Illinois Central Railroad,* p. 306; David M. Ellis, "The Forfeiture of Railroad Land Grants, 1867–1894," *Mississippi Valley Historical Review,* XXXIII (June, 1946), 27 ff.; Fred A. Shannon, *The Farmer's Last Frontier,* pp. 64 ff. Volume V in this series.

[59] Des Moines *Iowa Star,* November 21, 1850; *Davenport Gazette,* February 9, 1859.

[60] The Kansas legislature in 1859 authorized any rate of interest, whereas the Minnesota legislature made the legal maximum 12 per cent. *Laws of Kansas Territory,* Fifth Session, 1859, p. 487; *Laws of Minnesota Territory,* 1860, p. 226.

[61] Tom O. Edward, "The Progress, Conditions and Prospects of Wisconsin," *Collections* of the State Historical Society (Madison: 1856), II, 500.

[62] Act of April 5, 1859, *Laws of Wisconsin,* 1858, p. 165. The following year the maximum interest was reduced to 10 per cent.

recover his lost property was also extended.[63] The *Menasha Conservator* commented on the beneficial effect the law had in saving "many an honest settler from being swept from his possessions by the mercenary and unprincipled." [64]

More radical action was taken by successive Wisconsin legislatures to protect some 6,000 farmers who had exchanged farm mortgages for stock in various railroad enterprises they were anxious to have constructed. Misled by a combination of fraud, distortion, and slick exaggeration, whereby they were promised a higher rate of interest on their stock than they would pay on their mortgages, the usually cautious farmers had been grossly imposed upon by the agents of the railroads. Extravagance and mismanagement brought the lines into bankruptcy, and the stock from which so much was expected became practically worthless. Meantime, the mortgages had been sold to third parties, who expected their interest payments made regularly. Believing that they had been unfairly treated, the farmers rushed into politics for relief.

The political instrument through which the distressed farmers worked was the Home League, a typical agrarian organization like the anti-rent movement which flourished in New York. Similar anti-landlord associations came into existence on the Half Breed Tract and the Des Moines River lands of Iowa and on the Cherokee Neutral Tract and the Osage Reserve of Kansas. Threats of violence and political retribution led the Wisconsin legislature to authorize mortgagors defending suits of foreclosure to plead fraud and misrepresentation and, if sustained, to have judgment. Held unconstitutional by the courts, the measure was repealed but re-enacted in broader form in 1861. For years the railroad farm-mortgage question continued to roil Wisconsin politics and erected a base on which the Granger movement of a decade later was to be built.[65]

What can be said of the results of federal land policy before 1862? Did it achieve the Jeffersonian goal of making America a nation of farm owners, or did the revenue features create a "Land Nobility . . . overbearing and oppressive," who leased to dependent tenants their surplus acres not tilled by "hirelings"? [66] Did it provide a relatively simple and uncomplicated method of transferring ownership from government to

[63] *Laws of Wisconsin*, 1858, pp. 134–135; *Laws of Iowa*, Eighth General Assembly, 1860, p. 145.

[64] *Menasha Conservator*, January 29, 1859. The measure was opposed by the *LaCrosse National Democrat*, June 8 and 18, 1858, and the *Richland County Observer*, June 15 and 22, 1858.

[65] *Laws of Wisconsin*, 1858, pp. 46–47; *Laws of Wisconsin*, 1859, p. 249; *Laws of Wisconsin*, 1860, pp. 204–208; *Madison Argus* in *New York Tribune*, January 26, 1859. Frederick Merk, *Economic History of Wisconsin during the Civil War Decade* (*Studies* of the State Historical Society of Wisconsin; Madison: 1916), pp. 238 ff.

[66] *Ohio People's Press* in *Cincinnati Daily Gazette*, July 6, 1836.

purchaser, as it appeared to do on paper, or was the road to ownership filled with ruts of legal entanglements? Did speculation and large grants to canals, roads, and railroads tend to prevent or delay and make impossible family farm ownership for many?

Where there was no contest over the patent, the transfer was simple and generally uncomplicated. The exceptions, however, were so numerous that officials of the General Land Office and its local agents in the districts had to devote much of their time to adjudicating disputes. Preemptors claimed the same quarter section, and settlers claimed land as open to entry which agents of a land-grant railroad claimed as part of its grant; state, counties, and settlers argued over whether a tract was a swamp, a railroad, an internal improvement, or an education grant; original owners of land warrants filed caveats claiming that their warrants had been obtained fraudulently by the assignees. Furthermore, because the land system was never systematically reorganized while new features, frequently irreconcilable with old, were added to it, there appeared numerous conflicting ideas that led to confusion, overlapping claims, and a vast deal of litigation.

MALFUNCTIONING OF THE LAND SYSTEM

Because Congress granted veterans of the War of 1812 rights to land in the Military Tract of Illinois almost a generation before the warrantees or their assignees were prepared to develop them, the area became a vast speculators' desert for a time; then, when settlers did begin to penetrate the tract, it turned into a lawyers' paradise. Tax delinquency became chronic, titles were involved, and court calendars were filled with cases between owners of tax titles, judgment titles, liens, occupying claimants' titles, and patent titles. In this state of confusion only the lawyers flourished. A former New York resident who was living in the Military Tract in 1856 wrote, "What lots of lawyers there are in the West! Every little place of one hundred inhabitants supports some six or eight." [67] Citizens of Missouri and Arkansas had no more reason than those of Illinois to be grateful for the establishment of military tracts within their boundaries.

Careless drafting of land-grant measures and failure to consider adequately how they might affect existing rights produced a series of settler conflicts and anti-rent wars. Most notable of these occurred in the grants

[67] Olive Cole Smith and Addison James Throop, *Ancestral Charts of George Addison Throop, Deborah Goldsmith: Many Historically Interesting Letters from the Old Traveling Bag Saved throughout the Years by James Addison Throop* (East St. Louis, Mo.: 1934), p. 238. The standard work on title questions in the Illinois Military Tract is Theodore L. Carlson, *The Illinois Military Tract: A Study of Land Occupation, Utilization and Tenure* (Urbana: University of Illinois Press, 1951).

given for the canal between the Fox and Wisconsin rivers and for the improvement of the Des Moines River. Controversies over intent of the granting acts, failure to carry out the will of Congress or the states, and other issues delayed patenting the lands, settlers' claims were made on them, and the usual controversy between angry pioneers seeking to maintain long-held and improved land and absentee-owned corporations followed. On the 119,000-acre Half Breed Tract in southeastern Iowa a bitter controversy developed between settlers claiming pre-emption rights and the New York Land Company, which acquired ownership of most of the tract.[68] The land grant to the Burlington and Missouri Railroad of Iowa brought the railroad into acrimonious dispute with settlers who claimed the lands they had settled upon were "swamp" lands acquired from the county. When the Burlington brought ejectment proceedings many years later, open warfare was threatened.[69]

The error that proved most explosive in its results was the opening of Kansas territory to settlers before there was an acre of land along the eastern border subject to settlement and when numerous intruded Indian tribes still had reserves they refused to cede. When settlers poured across the Missouri border looking for land they found a confused and complex variety of policies differently interpreted by the Office of Indian Affairs and the General Land Office, by the carpetbag officials sent in from Washington, and by the local people trying to establish their own government. Conflicts over claims, attempts to buy entire reserves, and disputes over the location of land offices, the territorial capital, the terminals of prospective land-grant railroads, and the Indian allotment problems all played their part in the jayhawking and bushwhacking era that followed.[70]

Land engrossment by railroads, groups of capitalists, and individual speculators reached a high point on the eve of the Civil War and, combined with the increased capital costs of farm development, placed a major hurdle in the way of those who wanted to make farms for themselves. Immigrants coming to the West found it increasingly difficult to buy land and commence farming on their own. Instead, many took jobs as construction laborers or as farm laborers on the farms of those who had started earlier or who had come with resources sufficient to buy and improve land. The Census of 1860 reveals that between 20 and 30% of the total number of people engaged in agriculture in the states and territories of the upper Mississippi Valley were farm laborers. In California the proportion of farm laborers was even higher. These percentages

[68] Irene Neu has considerable material on Erastus Corning's part in the management of the Half Breed Tract, the Fox and Wisconsin, and the Des Moines River grants in her "Business Biography of Erastus Corning," p. 195.

[69] *Glenwood Opinion*, January 20, 1866, February 21, 28, 1888.

[70] Gates, *Fifty Million Acres, passim.*

would be somewhat reduced if the farm owners' children from the age of sixteen upward were omitted from this calculation, but the result would still be large. Both permanent and migratory farm labor had come to the rural areas of the West well before the public lands had been disposed of and when much of the area was still untouched by the white man.[71]

Farm tenancy, another result of the intrusion of speculators, land companies, and railroads between the government and the actual settler in the disposal of the public lands, was also becoming extensive by 1860. The census gives no statistics on tenancy before 1880, but evidence of its extent is to be found in emigrant guidebooks, in the advertising literature of the West, in leases recorded at the county seats, in increasing allusions to tenant problems in the newspapers and rural journals,[72] and in the frequent advertisements announcing land or farms for rent. For an example, an advertisement appeared in an Iowa paper less than three years after the first public land sales were held in that territory offering "Three farms for rent to good tenants." "Thirteen improved farms for sale and rent, also four farms for rent," all within twelve miles of the Mississippi River, advertised a land agent in Davenport, Iowa, in 1852. In Rock County, Wisconsin, Orrin Guernsey offered two "well fenced" farms to let.[73]

Landlords were renting their holdings to tenants on a crop-share or cash-rent basis or were allowing tenants to have free use of land for one to three years in return for stipulated improvements they were to make. The *Bloomington Pantagraph* drew to the attention of local speculators who were *not* improving their land the activities of Matthew Scott, who was spending many thousands of dollars in fencing, breaking, and

[71] *Sioux City Register*, January 12, 1861; *Eighth Census of the United States, 1860, Population* (Washington: Government Printing Office, 1864), pp. 662–663.

[72] In their advertising circular of 1838, Curtis and Ellsworth of Lafayette, Ind., stated: "Any quantity of land enclosed, with the accommodation of a small cabin, can be rented, and one-third of the crops allowed by the tenant."—Henry W. Ellsworth, *Valley of the Upper-Wabash, Indiana, with Hints on Its Agricultural Advantages* (New York: Pratt, Robinson and Co., 1838), p. 174. *Valley Farmer*, IV (May, 1852), 172; *Country Gentleman*, X (July 23, 1857), 64; and XI (February 25, 1858), 131. Calvin Fletcher, an Indianapolis banker and landlord, maintained that out of 155,000 voters in Indiana, one third were tenants, day laborers, loafers, or young men who had acquired no property.—Letter of Fletcher, Indianapolis, March 23, 1846, to McFarlin, Fletcher MSS, Indiana Historical Bureau, Indianapolis.

[73] Bloomington *Iowa Standard*, April 29, 1841; *Davenport Gazette*, January 29, 1852; Janesville, Wisc., *Gazette*, March 27, 1851. A Missouri landlord, with 2,500 acres, rented 160-acre tracts to German immigrants, who were to break up the land, put it into cultivable shape, and have the free use of it for three years, and for each of the next two years were to pay 75 cents an acre for the land under cultivation.—Henry G. Brokemeyer, *A Mechanic's Diary* (Washington, D. C.: E. C. Brokemeyer, 1910), p. 97.

planting corn or wheat on his great estate and erecting housing for tenants.[74] Farther south in Christian County, E. E. Malhiot, a Louisiana
sugar planter, was developing a large estate of 22,000 acres to which he
brought some 100 French Canadian families as tenants.[75]

On both sides of the Indiana-Illinois line in the Kankakee Valley
large estates operated by tenants were developing. Some land was held
for sale, but at $6 to $20 an acre, a price far beyond the means of the
average man looking for land to make into a farm. If prospective buyers
wished to go no farther in their search they could rent a small piece here,
but they could do nothing without a team of horses, a plow, some lumber,
fencing material, and food to carry them until their first harvest. From
the heart of this area where H. L. Ellsworth had his large holding came
a plaintive letter to the *Ohio Cultivator* in 1857, complaining about the
speculator, the high price of land, and saying "Pity the poor renter who
does not do well here." Tenants were in debt for their horses and were
making little progress in improvements or acquiring ownership.[76]

By the fifties, renting had become sufficiently common in Illinois and
Iowa so that it is possible to generalize about terms. Rental charges for
improved land in Illinois ranged from $1.50 to $3.00 an acre for country
farms and from $3.00 to $5.00 an acre for suburban farms and gardens.[77]
In Iowa improved land rented for $1.25 to $2.00 an acre.[78] Even more
important as showing the demand for land by men of small means were
advertisements appearing in the local papers under the caption, "Farm
Wanted." [79] For better or for worse, tenancy was becoming a major feature of western agriculture.

Concern over the number of large estates and the growth of tenancy
found expression in Indiana when landlords tried to secure from the state
legislature a measure that would give them a lien upon the crops of their
tenants as assurance that rents would be paid. Angry criticism of the proposal was expressed by representatives of counties in southern Indiana
having small farms, who declared in 1857 that if enacted it would "build

---

[74] Bloomington, Ill., *Pantagraph*, May 2, 1855; *Neosho Valley Register*, February
21, 1860; Bogue, "Patterns from the Sod," pp. 154 ff.

[75] *Country Gentleman*, IX (March 19, 1857), 195; X (July 2, 1857), 17–18; XI
(January 28, 1858), 68.

[76] *Ohio Cultivator*, XIII (June 1, 1857), 164.

[77] *Prairie Farmer*, VII (April, 1847), 120; LaSalle *Independent*, March 4, 1854;
Fred Gerhard, *Illinois as It Is in 1855* (Chicago: Keen and Lee, 1857), p. 404.

[78] N. Howe Parker, *Iowa as It Is in 1855* (Chicago: Keen and Lee, 1855), p. 67;
G. C. Beman, Croton, Lee County, Iowa, January 12, 1853, to D. Kilbourne, Kilbourne MSS, Iowa State Historical Department, Des Moines.

[79] *Cincinnati Daily Gazette*, February 3, 1837; Monticello, Ill., *Prairie Chieftain*,
November 4, 1852; Bloomington, Ill., *Pantagraph*, February 8, 1854, and November
5, 1856.

up in our country a kind of landed aristocracy . . . [and was] in favor of capital, the rich, and against labor, the poor." [80] Defeated in 1857, the measure was revived in 1859 and after being denounced as a bill "to enable landlords to oppress indigent tenants" was again defeated. Though brought up in session after session it was not until 1881 that a lien act was finally adopted in Indiana.[81] Meantime, in Illinois, Iowa, Wisconsin, and Kansas as well as in Indiana the extensive accumulations of land by wealthy capitalists, their refusal to sell, and their rental policies produced resentment and efforts to prevent further engrossment.[82]

Notwithstanding all this malfunctioning of the public-land system, followers of Jefferson's agrarian ideas might have been relatively satisfied with the way the system had worked throughout the ante-bellum period. Examination of the original census schedules for 1860 shows that to a very large degree farmers in the northern public-land states owned the land they tilled, though it does not appear what proportion of the farms was mortgaged and for what amounts. Furthermore, farmers owned considerable livestock, they were acquiring farm machinery to lighten the drudgery of hand labor, the improvements on their land were returning increasing yields, and, in so far as records permit generalization, their standards of living may be said to have been good.

[80] So said Michael Kerr.—*Indianapolis Daily State Sentinel,* January 23, 1857.
[81] *Brevier Legislative Reports,* Fortieth Session of the Indiana Legislature, 1859, p. 79.
[82] Paul W. Gates, *Frontier Landlords and Pioneer Tenants* (Ithaca, N.Y.: Cornell University Press), *passim.*

CHAPTER V

The Border South: Tobacco, Flax, Hemp

IN the states of the upper South the staples of commercial agriculture were corn, wheat, tobacco, flax, and hemp. The production and value of these staples stood in this order throughout the ante-bellum period.

Corn, not cotton or tobacco, was the chief staple of the South, as is shown by the acreage planted to it, the amount produced, and the value of the product. This was true of the states of the South as a whole as well as of the upper South. In 1849 the South had approximately 18,-000,000 acres in corn, 5,000,000 in cotton, 400,000 acres each in sugar and tobacco, and 70,000 in rice.[1] A much smaller acreage was in flax and hemp. In 1855, a year for which there are statistics of crops, the value of the southern corn crop exceeded that of cotton, tobacco, sugar, and rice together. The corn crop was valued at $209,000,000; cotton, at $136,000,000; tobacco, at $17,500,000; sugar, at $35,350,000; and rice, at $10,000,000.[2] Furthermore, the value of the South's wheat crop in 1855 was equal to the combined value of the tobacco, rice, and sugar crops.

Corn was largely used on the farm or plantation of origin or shipped as shelled grain or as pork to the Deep South, which could not meet its own needs. Wheat likewise was consumed locally but not to the same

---

[1] Calculated from *Eighth Census of the United States, 1860, Agriculture* (Washington, D. C.: Government Printing Office, 1864), p. 189, and *Hunt's Merchants' Magazine*, XXXV (August, 1856), 250, quoting the *New York Herald*.

[2] The figures of production and value of crops given by D. J. Browne of the Agricultural Division of the Patent Office are for the entire country; hence I have applied the proportion of the crop the South yielded in 1849 to determine the values of Southern crops in 1855.—*Hunt's Merchants' Magazine*, XXXIV (February, 1856), 253. Cf. Donald L. Kemmerer, "The Pre–Civil War South's Leading Crop, Corn," *Agricultural History*, XXIII (October, 1949), 236–239.

extent as corn. Virginia was the principal southern state producing a surplus of wheat. In 1849 its wheat was worth double its tobacco. Because the corn and most of the wheat of the South were consumed locally and did not become a part of the complicated economic, political, and even diplomatic relations between the South, the Northeast, and England, and also because corn and wheat were never popularly identified with slavery, as were tobacco, rice, sugar, and cotton, these crops have not received much attention in histories of the South. Corn was not called "king"; nor was any region called the corn kingdom; no journal was named the *Southern Corn Planter;* and, more recently, there has appeared no "Corn Bowl." And yet corn is as basic to southern history as were Thomas Jefferson and John C. Calhoun. Since, however, corn growing is the same north of the Mason-Dixon line as it is south of it, the treatment of that grain and as well as of wheat is left to a later chapter which deals with grain farming throughout the United States.

TOBACCO: A PROBLEM STAPLE

Tobacco had long been the problem staple in southern economy because of the difficulties in producing and marketing it and the effects of its cultivation on soil. Tobacco is an intensive crop that draws heavily upon the soil but at the same time it produces a high yield and brings a high price in relation to its bulk and to the acreage involved. For example, the gross value of the average per acre yield of tobacco in 1850 was $54.40, whereas the value of the average yield per acre of wheat was $10 or $12.[3] Planters who had abundant land were more concerned with the output per slave than with the output per acre. Nevertheless, the high value per acre of the tobacco crop was a major factor in fastening the cultivation of that crop upon regions adapted to it.

The high rate of return caused planters to disregard the fact that tobacco so depleted the soil's resources that it could be planted on a tract for no more than three or, at the most, four years. By the end of that time the humus had been subtracted, the phosphate and potash had been partly leached away by weathering and partly lost in plant growth, and the topsoil, made dry and powdery by the surface cultivation, was easily dissolved and washed away by heavy, pelting rains. Through careful

---

[3] From Lewis Cecil Gray, *History of Agriculture in the Southern United States to 1860* (Washington, D. C.: Carnegie Institution, 1933), II, 1038–1039. I have borrowed price data which are not quite applicable, as they are Richmond or New Orleans prices, but they are indicative of the differences in the per acre value of the tobacco crop as compared with the wheat crop. Cf. Joseph Clarke Robert, *The Tobacco Kingdom: Plantation, Market and Factory in Virginia and North Carolina, 1800–1860* (Durham, N. C.: Duke University Press, 1938), p. 249.

plowing and cultivation and the use of cover crops, such as clover, in rotation, the loss of the topsoil could be partly controlled. Tobacco was, however, the important money crop. In the presence of a seemingly inexhaustible supply of good land, planters saw no reason to concern themselves with the destructive effects of tobacco cultivation. Soil was regarded as an expendable commodity, not as a permanent investment that should be maintained, cherished, and built up. Thomas Jefferson expressed this view in 1793 when he declared that he did not use manure "because we can buy an acre of new land cheaper than we can manure an old acre. . . ." [4] It would have been impractical to transplant the better agricultural methods used in England and Germany, where land values were high and labor costs low, to the tobacco country, where these conditions were reversed.

It did not take twentieth-century historians or agricultural economists to discover the destructive character of the tobacco economy in the South. European travelers and progressive planters continually deplored the wasteful and destructive methods of tillage. Washington, Jefferson ultimately, and other southern leaders expressed grave concern about contemporary farm practices in the tobacco country and tried on their own lands to rotate crops, plow horizontally on hillsides, save straw, use manures and plaster, sow clover, make careful selections of seed, and cultivate frequently during the growing season. Washington wrote as early as 1791: "To say with us, that great quantities of tobacco are raised in any tract of country, implies without more, that the land is wasted, and no surplus of any thing made in it but tobacco." [5] In 1819 Jefferson spoke of the "constant culture without any aid of manure" which had brought his land to a low state and said that unless soil-building practices were instituted, planters would have to abandon their land and "run away to Alibama [sic], as so many of our countrymen are doing, who find it easier to resolve on quitting their country, than to change the practices in husbandry to which they have been brought up." [6]

From the first appearance of the *American Farmer* in 1819 and the *Farmers' Register* in 1833, abuse of the soil by destructive tillage and constant cropping to tobacco or wheat was a major theme in their pages. Olmsted, a not altogether friendly critic of the South, who differed from other travelers in concentrating more upon what he regarded as the evils of the plantation system than upon the blighting effects of slavery, wrote caustically about Virginia agriculture:

[4] Edwin Morris Betts, *Thomas Jefferson's Farm Book* (Princeton, N. J.: Princeton University Press, 1953), p. 194.

[5] Quoted in *Farmers' Register,* V (October, 1837), 331.

[6] Jefferson to Joel Yancy, January 17, 1819, and to Richard Peters, March 6, 1816, in Betts, *op. cit.,* pp. 42–43.

From the beginning the planting aristocracy has merely been living on its capital; the whole labor of the country . . . continued to be engaged in nothing else but transmuting the soil . . . into tobacco—which was sent to England to purchase luxuries for its masters—and into bread for the bare support of its inhabitants, without making any return.[7]

Tobacco planters were not slovenly farmers but hard-headed businessmen who knew that their methods of tillage, while destructive, were economically sound from their point of view. To have rotated crops with grain and with clover plowed in would have prevented the economical use of the labor of their slaves. To have maintained and protected the soil by the use of manures and fertilizers would have called for more livestock, for which there was no demand, and would have reduced the amount of tobacco they could raise, and hence their cash income. Since the tobacco planter had accustomed himself to the living standard made possible by the bounty of virgin soil, it was diffiult for him to accept a lower return. Olmsted cited the case of a Virginia planter who, thoroughly aware that his method of raising tobacco depleted and wore out the land, maintained that he was "well paid for it and did not know why he should not wear out his land."[8] Much land in the tidewater and piedmont regions of Virginia and Maryland had been subjected to this exhausting treatment and reduced to a dismal state.

As tobacco workers could care for only two or three acres at the most, the patches in crop in any one year on most plantations were small. But in the course of a lifetime a farmer or planter might wear out thirty to fifty acres for himself and for each additional worker. Such a process of land utilization involved a good deal of land clearing, the abandonment of worn-out land or perhaps the use of wheat or other grain or grass on it for a time. It also required that a farmer or planter should have sufficient land to meet his needs throughout his lifetime.

Because tobacco requires a long growing season in which to mature, and intensive and careful labor, from the preparation of the seedbed to the curing, packing, and marketing, it was well adapted to the employment of slaves in small numbers. The crop year began early in the spring with the preparation of small, carefully selected seedbeds or "plant patches" of upland soil on which trash or piles of wood were burned to sterilize the soil and destroy all weeds. This was necessary because the tobacco seed contains no reserve food and when sprouted cannot stand competition from weeds. The soil was then finely pulverized, horse manure worked in, the seeds delicately planted, lightly covered, and the ground firmed by boards or the dancing feet of the labor force.

[7] Frederick Law Olmsted, *A Journey in the Seaboard Slave States, with Remarks on Their Economy* (New York: Dix & Edwards, 1856), pp. 272–274.
[8] *Ibid.*, p. 90.

Fertilizer might be lightly scattered over the seedbed and brush piled on to prevent frost in the early season. In May or June, depending upon the condition of the soil, the growing tobacco was transplanted to previously prepared hills. Many plants were lost at this time through ravages of cutworms, beetles, and drought, and they were replaced with new transplantings. Then followed continued cultivation with hoes, plows, harrows, and cultivators to eliminate weeds and keep the soil loose. Pinching off the suckers, pruning the lower leaves to force growth into those higher on the stem, and topping the main stem to prevent the plants from going to seed were essential to assure quality leaf. The most unpleasant task was the weekly worming of the plants. Parasites and disease were endemic, but in the absence of effective insecticides the only remedy was to pick off the worms and destroy their eggs. No staple crop was so demanding.

When ready for harvesting, the tobacco was cut, dried, sorted, and packed for shipment into hogsheads holding from 1,200 to 1,500 pounds. From seedbed to market, tobacco provided steady employment the year round. Indeed, the new crop had to be put in before some of the hardest work on the old crop had been completed. This overlapping of crop years made it difficult for the planter to adjust the extent of his planting to the market.[9] It assured, however, constant employment of slaves without much letdown, seasonal or otherwise. Tobacco, like all the southern staples, kept the hands busy the year round and stands in sharp contrast to northern staples, particularly wheat, which required intensive labor for only short periods at seeding, harvesting, threshing, and marketing time.

Tobacco was the poor man's stand-by as well as the rich planter's income-producer. Requiring no expensive equipment or special type of soil, it could be raised as efficiently on the small holding as on the large. Good-quality tobacco called for the most diligent supervision, according to Joseph Robert:

Carelessness in handling was perhaps more costly here than in the case of any other staple; few products showed such a wide price range between mediocre and better grades. To send to market a profitable "parcel" required a sober crop master who kept a critical eye on the usual laborer.[10]

[9] *American Cotton Planter and Soil of the South,* New Series, II (June, 1858), 176; "Tobacco: Directions for the Cultivation and Management," condensed from *Farmers' Register,* in Commissioner of Patents, *Annual Report: Agriculture, 1854* (Washington, D. C.: Beverley Tucker, 1855), pp. 209–212. Modern treatments are Joseph Clarke Robert, *The Story of Tobacco in America* (New York: Alfred A. Knopf, Inc., 1949), and Nannie May Tilley, *The Bright-Tobacco Industry, 1860–1929* (Chapel Hill: University of North Carolina Press, 1949).

[10] Robert, *Tobacco Kingdom,* p. 18.

Unlike the cotton or sugar plantations, where numerous slaves could be efficiently utilized under an overseer or a driver, the tobacco plantation required a small, closely supervised labor force.

Tobacco prices moved in sympathy with the general index level of business, except in years of partial crop failure or bumper crops. Three periods of favorable prices were the years from 1815 to 1819, 1833 to 1841, and 1849 to 1860. Unfortunately, as soon as the price assured profit to producers, planters who had turned away from the crop during poor years resumed its production while others enlarged their operations. Overproduction was therefore a continuous threat. During the twenties and again in the forties, efforts were made to institute crop controls, which had been experimented with in the colonial period, but tobacco was produced in so many states that no promising plan could be framed.

Planters were no more successful in controlling the marketing of their tobacco than they were in limiting production. Small producers had to sell their staple locally to the general merchant in nearby communities, who received it in exchange for debts already accumulated. The bulk of the tobacco of North Carolina and Virginia was shipped in hogsheads to the public or private warehouses, where it was inspected by state officials, graded, and either passed or rejected. If rejected because of dampness, improper curing, poor handling, or trash contamination, the tobacco could not be exported and would therefore be sold to local manufacturers.

From being a crop that was largely exported in the colonial period, tobacco came in the nineteenth century to be increasingly manufactured in the American market for domestic consumption. Plug tobacco for chewing took much of the crop. Centers for the manufacture of plug, snuff, and cigars were developing at Richmond, Petersburg, Lynchburg, and Danville. Here were employed in numerous small plants most of the 11,382 workers whom the Census Bureau found engaged in the manufacture of tobacco in Virginia in 1860.[11]

Overproduction, depression prices, high costs, and declining yields hit Virginia and Maryland planters hard during the recurring periods of economic distress. Jefferson's correspondence shows the troubles of an Albemarle County tobacco planter. Before his retirement from public life, Jefferson went through all the usual difficulties of an absentee proprietor with his overseers, including unsuccessful management of slaves, poor packing of tobacco, slowness in getting it off to market, and failure to get all the crop cut before the frost struck it. Jefferson early abandoned tobacco at Shadwell and Monticello because the poor yields and low prices did not justify continuing it when he could do better with wheat. On his Bedford County plantation, tobacco was the major crop, but the income from it and from his wheat and flour did not free him

[11] Robert, *Tobacco Kingdom*, p. 164.

in his later years from continued worry about debts he could not meet.[12] The economic trials of Madison and Monroe on their Albermarle County lands were equally severe.

In the older tobacco areas, parasitic infestations generally occurred when land was planted to tobacco year after year, making more labor necessary to ensure a fair crop. At the same time the cost of slave labor was rising as a result of the closing of the slave trade in 1808 and the opening of the Gulf states, where there was a heavy demand for slaves. In the Old Dominion, capital in slaves was no longer as profitable on tobacco plantations as it had been earlier, and this development caused some persons to question the economic feasibility of slavery. Some planters floundered in economic despair, not understanding the cause of their plight and not attempting to improve their farm practices.[13] It was therefore easy for them to yield to the slave traders, who offered them prices that did not justify keeping their slaves on their abused and worn-out land. Despite compunctions they might have had against breaking up families of bondsmen, the threat of bankruptcy and of losing their land forced many to sell the younger and abler of their Negroes to the traders, who carried them to Alabama, Mississippi, or Louisiana.

Other planters and farmers, believing their chances of survival to be unfavorable, and fearing complete defeat if they remained, determined to emigrate before their equity was eaten up by taxes and interest. They sold their plantations and took their slaves with them to the new Eden west of the mountains. In Kentucky and Tennessee, in the counties on the north side of the Missouri in the state of Missouri, and in the extreme southern counties of Ohio, Indiana, and Illinois bordering on the Ohio River, new tobacco communities developed which demanded their share of the market. Here tobacco was raised on fresh soils, in some instances without slave labor. At a later time the new Southwest drew heavily from the older states of the South. Vast areas of land suitable for staple crop production could be obtained there at low prices, or even free, as in Texas, and emigrants by the tens of thousands moved westward. It was in 1835 that the family of Thomas Dabney, with its two hundred slaves, and friends and relatives moved from tidewater Virginia to Hinds County, Mississippi, to set themselves up in cotton planting;[14] William Clark and Lewis Thompson of North Carolina invested large sums in the Louisiana sugar bowl;[15] John F. Scott of Richmond, Virginia, bought 22,000 acres in

[12] Betts, *Thomas Jefferson's Farm Book*, passim.

[13] Robert, *Tobacco Kingdom*, p. 29; Olmsted, *Journey in the Seaboard Slave States*, p. 58.

[14] Susan Dabney Smedes, *Memorials of a Southern Planter* (Baltimore: Cushings, Bailey, 1887), pp. 42, 93.

[15] Clark's two plantations on the Red River, containing 5,180 acres, passed into the hands of his son-in-law, Lewis Thompson. There were 365 slaves on these

Mississippi; [16] and many other planters of the tobacco country invested heavily in sugar and cotton land in Arkansas, Alabama, Mississippi, and Louisiana. Numerous advertisements offering plantations for sale in Virginia and North Carolina began with "Having determined to send my negroes to Alabama," "Wishing to employ my negroes in making cotton," "Having determined to move to the Southwest," or "Desirous to emigrate south." [17]

The loss to the older states of population, both white and black, and of capital was heavy.[18] While the United States as a whole had a population increase of 32 per cent in the thirties, Virginia, North and South Carolina, and Maryland had increases of only 4 per cent, 2 per cent, 2 per cent, and 7 per cent, respectively. Virginia had 20,670 less slaves in 1840 than in 1830. These proud states, whose leaders had ruled the country at an earlier date, now found themselves diminishing in political importance as well as in economic well-being. Declining population, income, and political power induced these older and somewhat decadent states to question the value of the Union and of nationalism, and to retreat into the Constitution as they thought it existed in 1789.[19]

Careless use of the soil, which had appeared essential in the seventeenth and eighteenth centuries because of scarcity of labor, competition, overproduction, and low prices, was increasingly criticized in the older areas as the nineteenth century wore on. Vested interests in farms and plantations as homes had been created; in fact, a whole social pattern was erected upon them which was dependent upon their proper use. Low-priced land suitable for the South's staple was still available, but it was remote, it required a heavy investment of capital to bring it into cultivation, and it was in an area where disease and high mortality were common and where the amenities of life were not available. It was a heavy and, indeed, dangerous undertaking to transport one's family,

plantations in 1850.—Joseph Carlyle Sitterson, "Lewis Thompson, a Carolinian and his Louisiana Plantation, 1848–1888: A Study in Absentee Ownership" (*The James Sprunt Studies in History and Political Science*, Vol. XXXI; Chapel Hill: University of North Carolina Press, 1949), pp. 16–27.

[16] Scott's purchase is taken from the abstract of land entries for the Mt. Salus Office, National Archives.

[17] These are random samples of a theme that runs throughout advertisements for the sale of farms and plantations in Virginia.—*Richmond Enquirer*, January 3, 1829; June 17, September 30, October 7, 1836; June 11 and September 10, 1841.

[18] Frederic Bancroft, *Slave-Trading in the Old South* (Baltimore: J. H. Furst Co., 1931); Rosser Howard Taylor, "Slaveholding in North Carolina: An Economic View" (*The James Sprunt Historical Publications*, Nos. 1–2; Chapel Hill: University of North Carolina Press, 1926), pp. 53 ff.; J. Winston Coleman, *Slavery Times in Kentucky* (Chapel Hill: University of North Carolina Press, 1940).

[19] Jesse Carpenter, *The South as a Conscious Minority* (New York: New York University Press, 1930).

slaves, and other valuables to Arkansas or Louisiana. Stories that came back to the older states about the rise in land prices, the amount that land speculators were holding, and the paucity of first-rate land remaining in public ownership all contributed to make a move to the new territories and states less inviting.

CHANGES IN FARM PRACTICES

Agricultural reformers and farm journals argued strenuously that it was cheaper to rebuild a run-down farm than to commence farming anew on virgin land in the new states and territories.[20] Farm papers in the older states from which emigration was flowing stressed the possibilities and the economy of farm rebuilding and drew attention to the high mortality and the incidence of disease in the newly developing areas, and to the lack of social facilities. Thus a writer in the *Farmers' Register* in 1837 scorned "the squatter population, the horse thieves and counterfeiters of the west" with whom decent people had to associate, and commented on the dangers from Indians, the scalping knife and tomahawk, pestilential marshes, and yellow fever in new communities.[21] With the western outlet not quite so attractive as formerly, planters turned their attention to the agricultural improvements they had so long rejected.

Heretofore, only "gentlemen farmers" had been inclined to break loose from the one-crop system and to experiment with new methods, but now in the "agricultural revival," to borrow Craven's term, practical men took up the movement. This revival has been attributed to the influence of notable agricultural reformers like Edmund Ruffin; to the farmers' journals that stridently argued for rotating crops, the use of clover, lime, guano, marl, plaster, for contour and deeper plowing; and to the agricultural fairs and wider education.[22] None will deny that these had their share in bringing about such improvement as came, but equally important was the recognition by hard-headed farmers and planters that the dangers and hardships of starting farming anew in remote sections might be greater than the task of rationalizing existing farm practices. Previously, it had not been necessary to use improved methods as long

[20] Richard Bardolph, "A North Carolina Farm Journal of the Middle 'Fifties,'" *North Carolina Historical Review*, XXV (January, 1948), 87–88; James C. Bonner, "The Plantation Overseer and Southern Nationalism as Revealed in the Career of Garland D. Harmon," *Agricultural History*, XIX (January, 1945), 8.

[21] *Farmers' Register*, V (May–June, 1837), 9, 117, 127.

[22] Avery Craven, *Soil Exhaustion as a Factor in the Agricultural History of Virginia and Maryland, 1606–1860* (University of Illinois *Studies in the Social Sciences*, Vol. XIII, No. 1; Urbana: 1925); and Craven, *Edmund Ruffin, Southerner: A Study in Secession* (New York: Appleton-Century-Crofts, Inc., 1932).

as fresh land was easily available. Now it was slowly becoming apparent that it was neither necessary nor advisable to follow outmoded ways of farming.

Where tobacco continued to be grown as the major crop, improved methods of producing and curing the leaf were introduced. A light yellow tobacco that caught the fancy of smokers was perfected in the fifties. It grew best on the light sandy soils of the Roanoke Valley of Virginia and North Carolina, where tobacco planting was becoming increasingly centered. Demand for this variety and the prosperity of the fifties pushed prices out of the depression range of the years 1842–1848 until, by 1857, they had tripled. Flue curing was introduced to assure better control in the curing and hence a better quality of tobacco. Rotation with grain and clover to put nitrogen and humus back into the soil and to assure partial control of harmful soil organisms and destructive parasites came to be commonly practiced.[23]

Both within these tobacco counties and elsewhere in Virginia and Maryland diversified farming developed. Wheat became a second cash crop; on many farms, the first. Increasing attention was paid to the quality of livestock and to dairying. Experiments were made with alfalfa, then called lucerne, a leguminous plant which enriched the soil with the nitrogen it drew from the atmosphere.[24] Imported guano and local manures came into use, and marl, lime, and gypsum were applied to the soil to counteract its acidity. In Fairfax County alone, between 500 and a 1,000 tons of guano were used annually. John A. Washington, master of Mt. Vernon in 1852, declared that the application of guano to his worn and sandy lands and on farms elsewhere in the vicinity increased wheat yields to ten or fifteen bushels an acre.[25] Other improvements included better plows, the use of reapers, and other machinery, deep plowing to loosen the subsoil, and contour plowing to hold back the runoff.[26]

Changes introduced on two Maryland farms indicate that diversified farming was beginning to replace the production of tobacco and wheat. With respect to his 1,735-acre plantation in Carroll County, which had been badly abused before he took it over in 1825, George Patterson reported 160,000 bushels of lime had been put on the land, the low places had been drained, stones had been removed, and fine horses, Devon cattle,

[23] Robert, *Story of Tobacco*, pp. 58–63.

[24] *American Farmer*, X (April 25, 1828), 43; *Farmers' Register*, I (October, 1833), 286; III (August, 1835), 251; VI (August, 1838), 315; and VIII (June, 1840), 321–323, 383, 384; *Southern Cultivator*, IV (June, 1846), 108; *New England Farmer*, VIII (October, 1856), 461; *Rural Register*, I (November 1, 1859), 131.

[25] Letter of Washington, August 30, 1852, in *Prairie Farmer*, XII (October, 1852), 464–465.

[26] Craven, *Edmund Ruffin*, pp. 49 ff.

Berkshire hogs, and Southdown sheep introduced.[27] In the other instance, Charles Calvert, president of the Maryland State Agricultural Society, told of the changes he had brought about on his 2,000-acre farm near Washington. After tobacco cultivation had badly exhausted the land, it was brought back to a high state of productivity by rotation of crops, with heavy emphasis upon grass for the dairy cows whose milk constituted the principal item of sale. Tobacco was no longer an important crop on the farm.[28]

These changes in farming practices optimistically described by Avery Craven have led him to say that soil exhaustion was no longer a problem in Virginia in 1860, that the land had come "largely" into the hands of the small farmer, and that a new prosperity had been "established upon a restored fertility." [29] Both Virginia and Maryland made progress in the forties and fifties, particularly in the latter decade, in improving their agricultural position. Each increased its tobacco production by 54 per cent between 1839 and 1859; Virginia increased its wheat production by 29 per cent, Maryland by 85 per cent; Virginia increased its corn yield by 10 per cent, Maryland by 63 per cent. There was also some increase in the number of cattle, although the number of hogs and sheep declined. During the fifties the area in improved land in farms in Maryland was enlarged 7 per cent and in Virginia 10 per cent. Better farm practices made headway, and the states were supporting a larger number of independent farmers. In the fifties the number of farmers in Virginia increased by 15,592; in Maryland, by 3,634.

WHEAT AND TOBACCO PRODUCTION IN MARYLAND, VIRGINIA,
NORTH CAROLINA

	Maryland	Virginia	North Carolina
Wheat (bu.)			
1839	3,345,783	10,109,716	1,960,855
1849	4,494,680	11,212,616	2,130,102
1859	6,103,480	13,130,977	4,743,706
Tobacco (lbs.)			
1839	24,816,012	75,347,106	16,772,359
1849	21,407,497	56,803,227	11,984,786
1859	38,410,965	123,968,312	32,853,250

Source: Taken from Censuses of 1840, 1850, and 1860.

[27] Cultivator, New Series, II (July, 1845), 204–215.
[28] Southern Cultivator, X (January, 1852), 405.
[29] Craven, Soil Exhaustion, p. 161. A Lancaster County farmer of Pennsylvania, returning from a tour to Richmond, wrote of Virginia farms which were "most miserably cultivated," exhausted by tobacco planting, lacking in storage for fodder, and having little hay and that stacked in the field.—Pennsylvania Farm Journal, I (July, 1851), 119.

That rural decline was not halted in some areas of Virginia is shown by the fact that, despite the high prices tobacco brought in the fifties, twenty-four of her counties suffered losses in population in this decade. Less than half of these losses can be accounted for by the creation of new counties. The counties which did not lose population were those in which farms and plantations were large and where some division of farms was taking place. Nevertheless, there still remained in Virginia more farms in excess of 500 acres than were to be found in any other state except Georgia.[30] Nor does the average size of farms in the Old Dominion—324 acres—indicate that the small farmer controlled most of the land. True, the average had diminished somewhat from the previous decade, but so had the size of farms in all the older states save New Hampshire. It is important to note that the greatest concentration of ownership and the largest number of extensive plantations existed in those counties having the most valuable land and the highest yield of principal cash crops, tobacco and wheat.

PRINCIPAL TOBACCO PRODUCING AREAS

In the counties of the Roanoke Valley in North Carolina and Virginia, where the soil was peculiarly suited to the bright yellow tobacco, ownership of the land was concentrated in the hands of the great planters to a degree that was only exceeded in the rice and sugar country in the Gulf states. Samuel Hairston, one of the wealthiest men in the country, who was said to own between 1,600 and 1,700 slaves and to have the management of 1,000 more belonging to his mother-in-law, owned plantations in this area. In 1855, his plantations were valued at $600,000 and his total wealth was estimated at from $3,000,000 to $5,000,000.[31] Disregarding multiple ownerships, to which the Census Bureau gave no heed, there were in thirteen counties in this area 156 plantations exceeding 1,000 acres in size and 737 containing between 500 and 1,000 acres. Small holdings, it should be added, were far more numerous and were being somewhat increased.[32]

[30] Comparison of population data in the Seventh and Eighth Censuses. In 1841 George A. Smith, of Orange County, Va., advertised 700 acres of land for sale as he wished "to divide his farm and retain only a sufficient quantity . . . for his own force to cultivate." A portion of the bottom land, he maintained, "can be cultivated uninterruptedly in tobacco without exhausting it."—*Richmond Enquirer*, June 8, 1841. The following year Burwell Stark of Hanover County, "having more land . . . than he can profitably manage," offered 775 acres for sale.—*Richmond Enquirer*, October 14, 1842. A study of wills and transfers of property would be useful in determining the amount of change in landownership and in testing the validity of Professor Craven's assumption.

[31] *Richmond Whig* in *De Bow's Review*, XVIII (January, 1855), 53; and in *Alabama Beacon*, Greensboro, June 2, 1854.

[32] Compiled from *Eighth Census of the United States, 1860, Population, passim.*

The nature of tobacco production in the seven principal tobacco counties of Virginia in 1859 may be seen from statistics worked out by Robert. In the seven counties in the Roanoke Valley, 90 per cent of the farmers raised tobacco. The average yield was 5,802 pounds which, to borrow Robert's figure of 660 pounds to the acre, was the product of between eight and nine acres and the labor of three or four slaves. In the sample county of Charlotte, 36 per cent of the planters produced 8 per cent of the tobacco, whereas at the other end of the scale 17 per cent produced 57 per cent of the crop. There were some large plantations of a thousand acres and more, and some planters owned numerous plantations, but smaller operators flourished at the same time, whether they owned slaves or not. The strong comeback of tobacco in the fifties led Robert Russell to say, "The great upholder of slavery in the Northern States [Virginia, Maryland, and North Carolina] is the cultivation of tobacco, and not the breeding of slaves." [33] There is much to be said for this position, for slaves were increasingly concentrated in the progressive tobacco counties of the "Old Bright Tobacco Belt" in Virginia and North Carolina.

In Maryland also the new prosperity of the fifties seemed to be confined to the counties in which there was the greatest concentration of farm-land ownership and the most numerous large farms and plantations. Prince Georges County, which produced more tobacco than any other county in the entire country and ranked sixth among Maryland counties in wheat production, had two farms over 1,000 acres, sixty-one over 500 acres, and 60 per cent of its farms over 100 acres, whereas in the entire state only 48 per cent of the farms had over 100 acres. All other counties having high yields in tobacco and wheat had similarly high averages of farm size. Montgomery County was turning from tobacco cultivation and substituting dairy farming and vegetable crops. Charles Calvert had made this transition by 1852 on his much-fertilized 2,000-acre plantation near Washington, where he had over one hundred cows, mostly purebred Shorthorns, Jerseys, and Ayrshires, the milk of which brought twenty-five cents a gallon. His supply of salable slaves doubtless made possible the transition from tobacco to dairying.[34]

Not far distant from these well-to-do Maryland counties with their great estates was the richest agricultural county in the United States—Lancaster County, Pennsylvania, which had only two farms over 500 acres and 76 per cent of its farms smaller than 100 acres. In comparison with the northern states it is not accurate to say that Virginia and Maryland "had come largely to the small farm and the small farmer." [35]

[33] Robert Russell, *North America: Its Agriculture and Climate* (Edinburgh: Adam & Charles Black, 1857), p. 140.
[34] *Southern Cultivator*, X (January, 1852), 4–5.
[35] Craven, *Soil Exhaustion*, p. 161.

Virginia had made a notable agricultural comeback by 1860, but it still showed the tragic results of past errors. Although it had much more land in farms than any other state, it ranked fifth in the total value of its farms and in their number, and twentieth in the average value per acre of its farm land, being exceeded by six other slave states. Virginia was eighth in the value of its livestock, seventh in the value of its agricultural machinery. Only in the production of tobacco and in the income from the sale of slaves into the Deep South did Virginia surpass other states, and who among Virginians would have boasted of this last item? [36]

One reason for its low average value per acre of farm land was that Virginia had more unimproved land in farms than any state except Texas. Purchasing and holding land in excess of operating needs to profit from an anticipated increase in value at its resale, to permit larger operations when economic conditions improved, to replace worn-out and depleted soils, to make provision for children, or to assure greater social prestige was a common practice with tobacco, cotton, rice, and sugar planters and one that was continually deplored by practically all critics of American agriculture. The ownership of this unproductive land, which was used only for pasture or to supply fuel, tied up capital, scattered population widely, depressed assessments because of lack of improvements, made more difficult the financing of internal improvements, and prevented utilization of the land by small farmers. By 1860, Virginia had 36 per cent of its farm land improved and North Carolina had 27 per cent. In contrast, New York and Pennsylvania had 68 per cent and 61 per cent improved. As later developments were to show, Virginia and North Carolina were capable of supporting a far larger farm population than they had in 1860.

The estimated per capita income of farmers and planters in the new southern states was well in advance of that of Virginia.[37] Either Virginia's planters and farmers were unenterprising or, what is more likely, landownership was concentrated in the hands of planters who were not motivated to enlarge their operations. Their best land was already in use or had been exhausted, and to improve poorer land and bring it into cultivation to wheat and tobacco in competition with better soils elsewhere might not have paid. "The grand incentive of *necessity*" had not driven the wealthy planters to strive to attain the best agricultural practices as it did farmers in other sections of the country, where the

[36] Bancroft, *Slave-Trading in the Old South*, p. 386, estimated that 9,371 slaves were sold annually from Virginia in the period from 1830 to 1860. His estimate of slaves sold from Kentucky into the Deep South in the fifties is 3,400 annually.

[37] There are no figures for the per capita income, but some approximation can be secured from analysis of the census data for 1860. By using the price data in Gray, *History of Agriculture in the Southern United States*, it appears that the gross income of agriculture in Mississippi, Alabama, Louisiana, Kentucky, and Tennessee was ahead of that of Virginia, and that the per capita income was far greater.

wealth and the security of the owners were not so well established, a writer in the *Southern Planter* observed.[38]

The average-sized Virginia farm of 324 acres was worth in 1860 slightly less than the average-sized New York farm of 106 acres. The low prices attracted some New York farmers, who thought it possible to bring the land they acquired back to a high state of cultivation by the application of modern practices. One of these Yankee farmers later expressed his disappointment at the results he had on his 700-acre farm in Powhatan County. He concluded that the investment of labor and capital in New York brought a better return than in Virginia, and attributed his lack of success among other things to the high cost of providing education for his children in a community where public schools did not exist, and to the higher prices he had to pay for necessities and for transportation of his crops to market. Spotty and thin utilization of the land caused these great costs.[39]

The large farm units, the small proportion of land in cultivation, the low land values, and the small production of basic crops in relation to acreage all combined to delay the construction of roads, canals, and railroads in Virginia and North Carolina. While New York and Pennsylvania were building an intricate pattern of roads, canals, and railroads that were bringing most of their farms within easy hauling distance of such facilities, many Virginians still had to depend on the uncertainties of river transportation. By 1850 New York had four times, and Pennsylvania three times, as many miles of canals and railroads as Virginia could boast. By building a canal along the James River, Virginia sought to gain some of the tremendous advantage the Erie Canal was bringing to New York, but had difficulty in raising funds, the expected traffic did not appear, and the results were not outstanding. Similarly, Maryland began the construction of the Chesapeake and Ohio Canal to parallel the Potomac River with results little more favorable. These canals did reduce the cost of bringing tobacco and wheat from the interior to the eastern portions, but their construction was not followed by the great burst of commercial and agricultural development that followed the building of the Erie Canal. In 1860, Virginia had one mile of railroad for 37 square miles of land; New York and Pennsylvania each had one mile for 17 square miles of land.[40]

North Carolina fell into depression in the eighteen thirties without

[38] *Southern Planter* XVIII (April, 1858), 231–236.

[39] *Cultivator*, VII (April, 1850), 154.

[40] Balthasar Henry Meyer, *History of Transportation in the United States before 1860* (Washington, D. C.: Carnegie Institution, 1917), pp. 264–271; Wayland Fuller Dunaway, *History of the James River and Kanawha Company* (Columbia University *Studies in History, Economics and Public Law*, Vol. CIV, No. 2; New York: Columbia University Press, 1922), *passim;* George Rogers Taylor, *The Transportation Revolution, 1815–1860,* p. 79. Volume IV in this series.

having enjoyed the heights of prosperity that Virginia had earlier attained. The low price tobacco had brought in the twenties and early thirties had done little to wean planters away from it, and continued cropping had ruined many places. Emigration from the state was so heavy that 283,077 natives of North Carolina were living elsewhere in 1850. Planters were advertising their land for sale in exchange for slaves which they would take with them to the Southwest. It was said that nine tenths of the farm land in the state was available for sale in 1833.[41] The poorest of all the Atlantic states in the per acre value of its farm land in 1860, North Carolina never excelled in the production of any of the staple crops. In 1860 it ranked ninth in cotton, fifth in tobacco, and third in rice. Although it had never become a great producer, much of its land was regarded as exhausted as early as the thirties and forties. In 1833 a critical observer commented on North Carolina's "wasted fields, her deserted farms, her ruined towns, and her departing sons," though undoubtedly with some exaggeration.[42] North Carolina's great day in the production and processing of tobacco was still to come.

Well before the Civil War, Virginia's eminence in tobacco production was being challenged by Kentucky. Earlier transportation and marketing difficulties had been solved by shipping the tobacco on flatboats down the Mississippi and its tributaries to New Orleans, which was fast becoming a primary market. Fresher land, smaller-sized farms and plantations, fewer slaves, more direct supervision and participation by white owners in the process of tobacco production, and lower fixed charges combined to make Kentucky the second tobacco state. Tennessee was a fair third in 1860. It was in the poorer land of western Kentucky and Tennessee, outside the Bluegrass region, the Nashville Basin, and the cotton area of southwestern Tennessee that the larger part of the tobacco of these states was grown.

In the entire country the leading tobacco counties were, as is shown in the table, four in Maryland on the lower Potomac, a group in Kentucky and Tennessee north and south of their mutual border, and a group in the Roanoke Valley of Virginia and North Carolina. Though its total crop was much smaller, Hartford County, Connecticut, had the best yield per acre and secured the best price. J. D. B. DeBow, no warm friend of New England, pictured the valley lands in this county as being "equal to any in the world for the production of the Tobacco plant." Two thousand pounds to the acre was not an unusual yield, he was told, or

---

[41] Taylor, "Slaveholding in North Carolina," *loc. cit.*, pp. 53, 57.

[42] *Fayetteville Observer*, Fayetteville, N. C., December 17, 1833, in Taylor, "Slaveholding in North Carolina," *loc. cit.*, p. 68; J. G. de Roulhac Hamilton, ed., *Papers of Thomas Ruffin* (4 vols., *Publications* of the North Carolina Historical Commission; Raleigh: 1918–1920), II, 59, 77.

approximately three times the average in Virginia. Hartford County tobacco lands rented for $25 to $50 an acre; the net returns, DeBow figured, after all costs on such a crop, would be $92.50 an acre.[43]

TOBACCO PRODUCTION IN LEADING COUNTIES, 1859

County	Area in sq. miles	Improved land (acres)	Pounds tobacco
Prince Georges, Md.	485	182,468	13,446,550
Christian, Ky.	726	158,092	11,409,016
Halifax, Va.	808	277,913	8,544,532
Henderson, Ky.	440	92,814	7,938,836
Pittsylvania, Va.	1,022	247,156	7,053,962
Calvert, Md.	219	81,301	6,204,524
Warren, N. C.	445	122,074	6,148,321
Anne Arundel, Md.	417	144,211	6,039,910
Granville, N. C.	543	197,498	6,025,574
Weakley, Tenn.	576	79,915	6,015,104

Source: *Eighth Census of the United States, 1860, Agriculture* (Washington, D. C.: Government Printing Office, 1864), passim.

None of the staple crops of Kentucky encouraged the development of the great plantations that characterized parts of Virginia and the richer cotton-producing sections of the Deep South. That is not to say that Kentucky was primarily a land of small farms. Large holdings were created in the early years of the state's history, many of which were divided and subdivided, but this early concentration played its part in shaping the development of the land use and ownership pattern of the nineteenth century. In the eleven top tobacco-producing counties in western Kentucky were 23 farms of 1,000 acres or more and 119 which contained between 500 and 1,000 acres. In the Bluegrass counties, where hemp plantations and livestock production flourished, the greatest concentrations of farm ownership and large holdings were to be found. Fayette and Bourbon, the leading counties, had 63 and 79 farms respectively between 500 and 1,000 acres and 12 holdings in excess of 1,000 acres. Staple-crop production as practiced in the southern way on the large farms and plantations required numerous hands whose labor could be assured only by ownership and the whip.[44]

HEMP AND FLAX

While tobacco was raised in the counties less abundantly endowed by nature, hemp, and to a somewhat less extent flax, were produced in

[43] *De Bow's Review*, II (October, 1846), 253–254.
[44] Coleman, *Slavery Times in Kentucky*, p. 45.

the rich limestone counties of central Kentucky. Hemp was in demand for bagging and rope for the cotton crop and for yarn. It required less labor in the field than did tobacco and cotton, for when the seeds were sown thickly, as was the custom, the plants ran up straight without branches but with such thick crowns as to prevent weeds from flourishing.[45] Time-consuming cultivation was therefore not needed. From harvest, however, until the dried hemp was ready for market, it required much labor and attention. Cutting at just the right time in its growth was followed by shocking, drying, and retting (the dew-rotting process which made possible the separation of the lint from the woody part of the stalk). Breaking, drying, pressing, and baling required constant labor from December until April, when the finished product was ready for market and planting time had arrived once more. In 1843, Adam Beatty, vice-president of the Kentucky Agricultural Society, reported instances of good crops of hemp on the same land fourteen years in succession without any decline in yield. Beatty was familiar with the depleting effect on soil of corn, wheat, and tobacco culture, but he could not see that hemp had the same effect, and offered some quite unscientific reasons to substantiate his ideas. Since his hemp grossed him from $35 to $70 an acre it is understandable why he did not question the doctrine of inexhaustibility to which too many other frontier farmers were firmly committed.[46]

The Census Bureau enumerated 3,520 hemp plantations in Kentucky which produced most of the crop of 17,787 tons in 1839. Prices, which fluctuated from $90 to $180 a ton, did not always assure profits, but hemp production continued to be a major factor in the economy of the Bluegrass region throughout the ante-bellum period.[47] By levying substantial duties on the importation of foreign hemp that were adjusted up and down nine successive times between 1824 and 1861, Congress encouraged its production, though not altogether consistently. Farmers in Missouri, finding hemp a profitable crop, were beginning to raise it in increasing quantity toward the end of this period, especially in Pike County and the river counties in the western part of the state.[48]

[45] Commissioner of Agriculture, *Annual Report, 1864* (Washington, D. C.: Government Printing Office, 1865), p. 28.

[46] Adam Beatty, *Southern Agriculture, Being Essays on the Cultivation of Corn, Hemp, Tobacco, Wheat, Etc. and the Best Method of Renovating the Soil* (New York: C. M. Saxton & Company, 1843), p. 113.

[47] James F. Hopkins, *History of the Hemp Industry in Kentucky* (Lexington: University of Kentucky Press, 1951), pp. 109 ff. The author has discarded the census figures of hemp production for 1859 because of obvious errors.

[48] "Report from the Secretary of the Navy, in Compliance with a Resolution of the Senate, Relative to the Cultivation and Manufacture of Hemp," *Senate Executive Document* No. 6, 27 Cong., 3 Sess., Vol. II, January 29, 1842; Brent Moore, *A Study of*

The manufacturers of hemp into rope, bagging, yarns, and cordage centered in Lexington and Louisville. Lexington boasted ten bagging and bale rope mills employing 500 men in 1828. A large part of the hemp was made into cotton bagging and shipped down the Ohio and Mississippi to New Orleans, where it was used to cover cotton after it came from the gin and press.[49]

Flax had been cultivated by American farmers to a limited extent since colonial days, but by 1815 it was proving not well adapted to American agriculture. Unlike hemp, flax is a tender crop. It not only required special fertilization, but could not be grown in successive years; instead, it had to be spaced by a number of years in other crops. It was easily overwhelmed by weeds, heavy winds blew it down, and the cost of harvesting and retting the fiber was heavy. The amount of labor and the close supervision required of the water-retting process did not appear justified when cotton cloth could be bought cheaply. The cultivation of flax was largely confined to those areas where farmers attempted to meet all their own needs. Elsewhere, it was the demand for linseed oil made from the seed of the flax plant that kept the crop from disappearing. Kentucky, Virginia, and New York were first in the production of flax fiber; Ohio excelled in the production of flaxseed. During the Civil War, when the cotton famine was keenly felt, Congress ordered "investigations to test the practicability of cultivating and preparing flax or hemp as a substitute for cotton." The resulting report by the Commissioner of Agriculture was more a scientific treatise than a practical document that might encourage extensive cultivation of the two crops. Only with the artificially high prices that prevailed during the Civil War was it possible to make much from raising flax.[50]

---

the Past, Present and Possibilities of the Hemp Industry in Kentucky (Lexington: Press of J. E. Hughes, 1905), Appendix I.

[49] Moore, Hemp Industry, p. 43.

[50] Gray, History of Agriculture in the Southern United States, II, 821; S. S. Boyce, Hemp (New York: Orange Judd Company, 1900), p. 54.

CHAPTER VI

Rice and Sugar

COMMERCIAL agriculture before the Civil War reached its fullest development in the rice, cotton, and sugar planting areas of the Deep South. Here, in contrast to the tobacco, wheat, and hemp regions of the upper South, the operating units were larger, the number of slaves and the amount of capital invested in equipment greater, and the gross returns higher.

RICE

Rice plantations were chiefly found on the lower reaches of the Savannah, the Altamaha, the Edisto, the Santee, and the Combahee rivers in Georgia and South Carolina on land above the salt-water level but capable of being overflowed by fresh water pushed back by the tide. In a limited area extending up these rivers, from five to twenty miles from the ocean, were some 500 or 600 planters who produced the bulk of the American rice crop. The actual area in rice was not more than 60,000 or 70,000 acres, though the rice plantations included a much greater acreage which was used for other purposes or was uncleared.[1]

Rice was an exotic crop requiring much crude labor, skillful management, and a large investment of capital. After the land was cleared it had to be surrounded by substantial embankments five or more feet in height and fifteen feet in breadth at the base; elaborate drainage ditches had to be dug and cumbersome sluice gates installed. Maintaining the

[1] Albert Virgil House, *Planter Management and Capitalism in Ante-Bellum Georgia: The Journal of Hugh Fraser Grant, Rice Grower* (New York: Columbia University Press, 1954), pp. 18 ff.; Lewis Cecil Gray, *History of Agriculture in the Southern United States to 1860* (Washington, D. C.: Carnegie Institution, 1933), II, 721 ff.

embankments, clearing the drains and canals, and repairing the valves and sluices required frequent supervision and much labor. Though transportation was generally by river and canal, some difficult and expensive road making was necessary.[2]

The quantity of agricultural implements used in growing rice was almost negligible, so primitive were the methods of preparing the soil, sowing the seed, cultivating, and harvesting the grain. Plows were rarely employed, preparation of the soil for planting being done with the hoe. Seeding, intensive weeding, and cultivating required a great deal of labor; hence the ratio of slaves to acreage was high. Successive floodings accomplished part of the work of weed control, but hand weeding was also employed in the flooded fields to eliminate the volunteer rice which sprang up from the previous year's rice seeds. When it was allowed to mature, the volunteer rice produced red kernels that, mixed with other rice, reduced the market value of the crop. Flooding needed the attention of an expert because a miscalculation could do serious damage to the crop. When it was ready for harvest, the hands cut the grain with the sickle, tied it in bundles, and hauled it to the barn or rice mill by oxen.

Paradoxically, the ancient and the modern were found side by side on the rice plantations: the hoe to cultivate and the sickle to harvest; and expensive thrashing, grinding, and polishing machines operated by tidal power or by steam. To operate these machines and keep them in repair, blacksmiths able to forge a new part or repair a broken one and possessing the rudiments of engineering skills were needed. Slaves who could handle such tasks were cherished and gently treated. Only the very large producers could grind their own rice. Small planters arranged to have it ground at a neighboring mill or sold their crop without milling it. The machines and the large number of slaves required on rice plantations and the high value of the land when improved brought the total investment in a successful plantation to from $50,000 to $500,000.[3] Rice was not a poor man's crop.

The greatest concentration of slaves in America was in the rice-producing counties of the South Carolina and Georgia coast. Here in 1860 were twenty of the seventy-four estates that had 300 to 500 slaves, eight of the thirteen that had 500 to 1,000 slaves, and the only estate of more

[2] Frederick Law Olmsted, *A Journey in the Seaboard Slave States with Remarks on Their Economy* (New York: Dix & Edwards, 1856), pp. 466 ff.; Robert Russell, *North America: Its Agriculture and Climate* (Edinburgh: Adam & Charles Black, 1857), p. 177.

[3] House, *Planter Management*, pp. 42 and 51, uses the figures $50,000 to $100,000 in one place and $100,000 to $500,000 in another. Basil Hall, *Travels in North America in the Years 1827 and 1828* (2 vols.; Philadelphia: Carey, Lea & Carey, 1829), II, 213 ff., found the area in rice generally ranged from 50 to 200 acres. He reported threshing done in 1826 with the flail.

than 1,000 slaves in the South.[4] Nowhere except on the sugar plantations of Louisiana were there such large and fertile estates amply stocked with slaves and such conspicuous display of luxury as in this rice country.

The most successful of the planters, like the Heyward, Manigault, Allston, and Potter families, acquired a number of plantations, some for the production of rice and some, on higher ground, for other grain, cotton, and livestock. They endeavored to produce much if not all the foodstuffs necessary for their numerous slaves. Nathaniel Heyward, who died in 1851, left an estate containing 5,000 acres of riceland, a much larger amount of timberland, and well over 1,000 slaves. With livestock and other property it was valued at $2,018,000.

Robert Allston had seven plantations containing 4,000 acres, one fourth of which was suitable for rice cultivation; in addition, he owned 9,500 acres of pasture and timberland.[5] Thomas Allston put together into one plantation 4,257 acres on the Savannah River in Georgia, which he brought to a high state of productivity. A large rice mill was added, an extensive canal was built to shorten transportation routes, and other improvements were introduced. In 1845, six hundred acres in rice were made to yield, through intensive application of labor and efficient management, a return of $324 for each of 215 slaves. Profits were reinvested in further improvements, including the draining of additional land and the construction of canals and embankments to control the flow of water. Upon the death of the last son in 1862, the appraiser found 1,372 acres of riceland worth $100 an acre, 442 slaves, and other property that brought the value of the estate to $527,081.[6] These were unusually large holdings, but they show the tendency to create extensive properties in the rice counties of South Carolina and Georgia that is more fully revealed in the census figures. The average size of farms and plantations in Georgetown County, South Carolina, which produced 30 per cent of the rice crop of the United States in 1859, was 1,841 acres; the average amount of land in cultivation per farm was 234 acres.[7]

Questionable but perhaps unavoidable farming practices were characteristic of rice planting. The heavy investment in improvements and the rising value of slaves, resulting from demands in the cotton belt and the sugar country, necessitated cropping schemes that were exhausting to

[4] *Eighth Census of the United States, 1860, Agriculture* (Washington, D. C.: Government Printing Office, 1864), pp. 237, 247.

[5] Duncan Clinch Heyward, *Seed from Madagascar* (Chapel Hill: University of North Carolina Press, 1937), pp. 81 ff.; James Harold Easterby, *The South Carolina Rice Plantation as Revealed in the Papers of Robert F. W. Allston* (Chicago: The University of Chicago Press, 1945), p. 22.

[6] Savannah Unit, Georgia Writers' Project, Works Projects Administration, "Colerain Plantation," Pts. II–IV, especially Pt. IV in *Georgia Historical Quarterly*, XXV (March and September, 1941), 29–66, 120–140, 225–243.

[7] *Eighth Census, Agriculture*, pp. 128, 214.

both land and labor. It was not easy to rotate crops on land suitable for rice cultivation, though long-staple cotton was used at times, and it was not uncommon to permit fields to lie fallow for a season. Declining yields, hurricanes, flood and tidal damages to the dikes and ditches, low prices in some years, and diminished profits beset the planters. The expansion of clean-culture crops—cotton and corn—in the uplands and piedmont of the Carolinas caused soil erosion which did appreciable harm to the ricelands of the lower valleys when sterile soil silted over them. This silting, combined with the declining fertility of the older ricelands of South Carolina, resulted in lower yields and led planters to seek fresh lands in Georgia, where yields were higher. To increase the productivity of their lands and to reduce costs, some planters resorted to the plow in place of the hoe in preparing seedbeds for sowing the seed, paid greater attention to the elimination of weeds and volunteer rice, introduced new varieties of rice, permitted fields to lie fallow regularly, applied chaff, straw, rice flour, marsh mud, guano, and other fertilizers to their soils and rotated their crops. On the other hand, as late as 1850 William A. Carson, on his Cooper River tract, planted all his rice, potatoes, corn, and oats on a thousand acres solely with the use of hoes.[8]

The rice counties seem not to have produced a surplus of slaves quite as early as did the older tobacco- and cotton-producing areas, possibly because of the unhealthy character of the rice plantation and the higher death rate prevailing.[9] Exhaustion of the soil and the high prices paid for slaves in the new areas farther west encouraged some men to sell their slaves or to remove with them to those areas. Some planters built up substantial holdings of land in Alabama, Mississippi, and Louisiana, to which they moved some of their slaves but held their properties as absentee owners. Phillips cites a letter from the *Charleston Mercury* of February 13, 1861, that comments on this great movement of slaves from the rice country:

> Within ten years past as many as ten thousand slaves have been drawn away from Charleston by the attractive prices of the West. . . . The slaves from lighter lands within the states, have been drawn away for years by the higher prices in the West. They are now being drawn from rice culture. Thousands are sold from rice fields every year.[10]

[8] Herbert Anthony Kellar, *Solon Robinson: Pioneer and Agriculturist* (*Indiana Historical Collections*, Vols. XXI and XXII; Indianapolis: Indiana Historical Bureau, 1936), II, 350; Communication of R. F. W. Allston of Matanza Plantation on the Pee Dee River in Commissioner of Patents, *Annual Report, 1850* (Washington, D. C.: 1851), pp. 323–325.

[9] House, *Planter Management*, p. 52; *Flag of the Union*, January 3, 1838.

[10] Ulrich B. Phillips, *Plantation and Frontier*, in John R. Commons, *et al.*, *Documentary History of American Industrial Society* (10 vols.; Cleveland: Arthur H. Clark Company, 1910), II, 176–177.

The combined slave and white population moving out of South Carolina was so great that in 1860 41 per cent of the people born in that state were living elsewhere. Only Vermont had a higher percentage of its native-born living outside the state. Of course, many of the westward-moving South Carolinians were from the cotton country, dispossessed by factors different from those affecting the rice country.

Rice reached its high price and brought its most favorable returns in 1815-1819, but planters received good prices in 1836-1840 and 1845-1857. Competition from oriental rice tended to keep the level of prices moderate. Over half the rice was shipped to the West Indies and to Europe where, because of its superior quality, it found a ready market. Planters sold to factors in Charleston or Savannah or to mills or commission houses.

Rice as the staple crop of a restricted area of South Carolina and Georgia was not holding its own in the fifties, owing to a number of factors. In South Carolina diminishing fertility of long-used land was seen in declining yields. Owners of slaves whose price was rising rapidly were uneasy about using them in unhealthy occupations such as cultivating the wet and soggy riceland. More favorable cotton prices were inducing planters to put their land into the fiber crop if the land were adaptable to it, or to sell or transfer their slaves to cotton-producing land. Between 1849 and 1859 the South Carolina rice crop shrank from 74 per cent to 63 per cent of the total United States crop. Georgia, on the other hand, with its newer rice area, enjoyed an expansion in this period that brought its percentage of the total crop from 12 to 28. The total for the country declined from 215,313,497 pounds in 1849 to 187,167,032 pounds in 1859.[11] No other staple crop offered as little promise for the future as rice.

SUGAR

Sugar production was centered on land bordering on the lower Mississippi, the Lafourche, the Atchafalaya, and Bayou Teche in twenty-four parishes in southern Louisiana. This limited area enjoyed a long growing season and a well-distributed precipitation of sixty inches, both essential for raising sugar cane.[12] Alluvial land close to the streams was best suited for the crop. To protect it against high water, levees had to be erected and maintained. The task of clearing the rank subtropical forest of cypress, tupelo, gum, clinging vines, and lush undergrowth with the ax and grub hoe was a heavy one that could be accomplished only

[11] *Eighth Census, Agriculture*, pp. 185, 189.
[12] J. Carlyle Sitterson, *Sugar Country: The Cane Sugar Industry in the South, 1753-1950* (Lexington: University of Kentucky Press, 1953), *passim*.

with an enormous expenditure of labor, even on small tracts. Drainage ditches had to be dug, roads laid, and numerous bridges constructed. For example, on a plantation of 1,360 acres it was estimated there were 100 miles of ditches, 25 miles of roads, and 200 bridges. Steam-operated scoop wheels were used to remove the surplus water behind the levees.[13] Steam- or horse-powered mills for grinding the cane, and apparatus for evaporating the moisture, crystallizing the sugar, and purifying the molasses might cost as much as $40,000 to $100,000.[14] Small planters whose equipment was somewhat obsolete had higher costs of manufacture and turned out an inferior product.[15]

Valcour Aime, one of the most successful of the sugar planters, who was responsible for important innovations in the industry, made some interesting observations in an article on sugar culture in 1847. The amount of capital necessary to buy the land, make the necessary equipment, and set in motion a 300-hogshead (1,000 pounds each) sugar plantation would range from $75,000 to $100,000. On such large plantations the usual yield was 5 to 8 hogsheads to each hand. Some small planters were said to have produced as much as 10 hogsheads to the hand, but Aime was convinced that they did not include their own labor or that of other members of their family. Small farmers with crude equipment had made 10 or 15 hogsheads of sugar, but they were doubtless exceptions.[16]

In the process of reducing the cane juice, some 600 gallons of molasses were made for each 1,000 pounds of sugar. While the best grade of molasses might sell for fifteen or twenty cents a gallon, the returns from it do not seem to have entered largely into the profits and losses of the planters. Much of the molasses was consumed locally. Portions were doled out to slaves as rewards for good behavior and for the extremely hard labor and long hours they had to put in during the grinding season. The cheapness of molasses made it a common item in the diet of the poorer class of white farmers.

Sugar, like rice, required a high degree of technical skill at certain points in its productivity, particularly in the refining process. The cane needed the longest possible growing period, but delay in cutting it in late fall was to run the risk of losing it because of frost. Equipment for grinding and refining had to be ready the moment the cutting was begun,

[13] Kellar, Solon Robinson, II, 165; Commissioner of Patents, Annual Report, 1848 (Washington, D. C.: Wendell and Van Benthuysen, 1849), p. 287.

[14] Olmsted, A Journey in the Seaboard Slave States, pp. 229–270; Kellar, Solon Robinson, II, 179.

[15] Judah P. Benjamin discusses the problems of sugar planting and the technical details of the various refining processes in De Bow's Review, II (November, 1846), 322–345.

[16] De Bow's Review, IV (November, 1847), 385–386.

and spare machine parts had to be available in the event of a breakdown. Long before sugar making began, woodcutters had to prepare and haul to the boiler hundreds of cords of fuel wood, and coopers had to make the sugar hogsheads and molasses barrels for the finished product. When the cane was ripe, the entire force of a plantation worked at high speed —days, nights, and Sundays—to get it cut before the black frost struck and to put it through the grinding machine and the sugar-making process. Delay meant loss in quantity and quality. Most important was the sugar boiler, usually a hired expert, though sometimes a skilled Negro, who had immediate charge of the refining process. Slight changes in the heat applied to the boilers and wrong timing in applying the lime in the clarification process might considerably reduce the quality of the sugar. The manager or overseer, or possibly an owner who had too much at stake to leave all responsibility at this crucial time to another, had not only to handle all these details at their proper time but also to be good at getting the most out of the men.

At less rushed periods the hands were turned to clearing out the drainage ditches; maintaining the roads in good shape for the heavy hauling of the cane; fortifying the levees, which were sometimes weakened or breached by the spring floods on the streams; and making careful selection of strong and disease-free seed cane. The owner or overseer had to be sure there was an adequate supply of hands to carry through the arduous work of harvesting and refining. He had to plan the over-all agricultural operations, including the decisions respecting the acreage to be placed in cane, cotton, and corn; he had to make up for any deficiencies in corn and pork on the plantation by purchases from up-river boats. He had to determine whether to sell the sugar and molasses on the plantation or to ship it to New Orleans, New York, or elsewhere to be assigned to a factor for sale, and to arrange for shipment, insurance, and other costs. He might be managing a number of plantations to which he had to give personal direction to integrate their operations as much as possible. He might even be renting some of his land to small farmers who functioned on a crop-share basis with the land, mules, plows, and seed provided by the landlord. He might be somewhat of an innovator in introducing new grinding and refinery machinery, or in experimenting with the use of guano, with rotation of crops, with seed selection. Finally, he might turn to politics to secure relief from what he thought were unfair exactions of the factor or to press for tariff protection.

Throughout the ante-bellum period there were both large and small planters engaged in sugar production in an area which came later to be called the "sugar bowl." The larger planters enjoyed the major advantages. They had their own mills and did not have to waste time or endanger the amount and quality of sugar by waiting to get their cane ground and the juice reduced at custom or community houses; moreover, they had a dependable labor supply which in the event of impending flood damage or frost could move swiftly to safeguard their crops. The conservatism of the planters led them to be slow in adopting new methods and acquiring new machines for making sugar; yet, under the stimulus of good prices, they generally expanded their operations and introduced new machines that the small operator could not afford. Small planters continued to use the old wooden rollers operated by horse power to press out the juice from the cane instead of iron rollers operated by steam, and the open kettle instead of the more efficient vacuum pan, the cost of which was well beyond their resources. As late as 1856 more than a quarter of the sugarhouses were operated by horse power. Greater sources of credit enabled the larger planters to withhold their sugar from the market when the price was not right.[17] They could also experiment more readily with guano. Col. John S. Preston, for example, one of the largest producers of sugar, applied fifty tons of guano at a cost of $2,500 in successive years to his holdings in Ascension Parish and was convinced it resulted in greatly increased crops.[18]

If 1853 was an abnormally good year, 1856 was an unusually bad one. A heavy frost killed many plants and a terrific hurricane swept down both sugar cane and sugarhouses in a number of parishes and brought the yield to the smallest since 1838. Twenty-three per cent of the sugarhouses produced less than $3,100 worth of sugar; a few made only two or three hogsheads worth $110 each. The total yield was less than one sixth that of 1853. The twin catastrophes struck unevenly in the sugar parishes and produced the highest recorded price for sugar in the ante-bellum period.

Swift expansion in the sugar industry more than quadrupled production in the decade between 1843 and 1853. The number of planters having sugarhouses reached a peak in 1849—1,536—and thereafter slowly declined. Efficiency of large-scale production and growing capital costs were squeezing out the small man so that, by 1859, 228 plantations either had shifted to other staples, had been consolidated into large units, or, because of flooding, frost, or other calamity, had not made a crop.[19]

The biggest crop year by far was 1853, when, not surprisingly, the price of sugar reached the lowest point between 1834 and 1860. With sugar at a little more than four cents a pound, only the most efficient and

[17] *Planters' Banner*, September 20, 1845, in Commissioner of Patents, *Annual Report, 1845* (Washington, D. C.: Ritchie & Heiss, 1846), p. 298.

[18] *American Cotton Planter*, III (April, 1855), 116.

[19] V. Alton Moody, "Slavery in Louisiana Sugar Plantations," *Louisiana Historical Quarterly*, VII (April, 1924), 201, offers the following tabulation of sugar producers for 1853: Less than 50 hogsheads, 142; between 50 and 200 hogsheads, 547; between 200 and 500 hogsheads, 498; between 500 and 1,000 hogsheads, 217; over 1,000, 43.

largest operators could survive. Following this big crop with its low price came the sharpest drop in the number of operating plantations. The crop of 1858, much short of that of 1853, yielded the highest money return, the 1,298 plantations averaging $19,319. At least forty-one individuals and partnerships turned out over 1,000,000 pounds of sugar apiece, each worth $70,000 at the lowest.[20]

Outstanding among the larger producers were the numerous members of the Pugh family, whose production in 1858 was close to 6,000,000 pounds, and the Bringier family, which produced 3,380,000 pounds. J. L. Manning, son-in-law of Wade Hampton, had an output of 1,900,000 pounds, and John Burnside, who bought the larger portion of Houmas just a year before for $1,500,000 had a yield of 4,170,000 pounds.[21] Dr. Stephen Duncan, America's greatest cotton planter, produced 1,630,000 pounds of sugar on two plantations. On the other hand, Laurent Millauden and other planters in the lower delta lost their crops as a result of a bad break in the levee, a hazard that, with early frosts, made sugar planting anything but a secure business.[22]

ECONOMICS OF SUGAR PLANTATIONS

Despite the hazards of breaks in the levees, early frosts, hurricanes, and destructive fires, the sugar plantations flourished in much of the ante-bellum period. J. Carlyle Sitterson estimates that gross returns of Louisiana planters on their capitalization before deduction of expenses were 17 per cent in 1828, 13.7 per cent in 1844, 9.2 per cent in 1859, and 11.9 per cent in 1861. From these percentages well-informed planters deducted 6 per cent for operating costs. These figures do not take into account the income from the sale of and the value of the molasses used domestically. More important, they disregard the rapid appreciation in the value of slaves and land. Some plantations increased in value by more than 100 per cent in the fifties. The growth of capitalization in the sugar plantations, which resulted from rising value of land, improvements, and slaves, and the reinvestment of earlier earnings are evidence of the remarkable prosperity the large planters enjoyed though the actual net profit appears not to be large.[23]

[20] P. A. Champomier, *Statement of the Sugar Crop Made in Louisiana, 1856–57* (New Orleans: Cook, Young & Co., 1857), *passim;* William Howard Russell, *My Diary North and South* (2 vols.; London: Bradbury & Evans, 1863), I, 389, 395.

[21] Gray, *History of Agriculture in the Southern United States,* II, 1033–1034.

[22] Statistics of sugar yield are from Champomier, *Annual Statements of the Sugar Crop Made in Louisiana, 1845–1859.*

[23] To arrive at an estimate of the net profit of the planters, attention would have to be given to the income from molasses (the above figures include only income from the sale of sugar), and to the appreciation in capital value of the land and slaves. The table is compiled from Sitterson, *Sugar Country,* pp. 181 ff.

The wholesale price of sugar at New Orleans ranged from 11⅛ cents a pound in 1820 to 4 cents in 1840. Among the factors affecting the price were the extent of the Cuban sugar crop, fluctuations in tariff rates, the weather, and the size of the Louisiana production. One half of the Louisiana crop was shipped to New Orleans, where it had to be sold within thirty-six hours of being unloaded on the levee to make space for other sugar and cotton. This worked hardship for those who were so unfortunate as to have their sugar offered at a time when freights to the North were high and exchange and the condition of the money market were unfavorable.

GROWTH AND PROFITS OF THE LOUISIANA SUGAR INDUSTRY

	Capitalization	Sugar produced (pounds)	Value of sugar	Gross profit (%)	Net profit (%)
1828	$ 34,000,000	110,000,000	$ 5,775,000	17	11
1844	60,000,000	205,000,000	8,200,000	13.7	6.7
1859	180,000,000	255,000,000	16,575,000	9.2	3.2
1861	200,000,000	530,000,000	23,850,000	11.9	5.9

Source: J. Carlyle Sitterson, *Sugar Country* . . . (Lexington: University of Kentucky Press, 1953).

Sugar profits were reinvested in enlarging the plantations or in acquiring others, consolidating operations where possible, and introducing the latest and most modern grinding and evaporating equipment. Some planters, on the other hand, wasted away their profits through extravagant living, archaic and inefficient operations, and high interest costs on their indebtedness.

Small sugar planters or farmers were being eliminated by the introduction and perfection of improved and expensive refining machinery, the rising cost of slaves, and the greater advantages of large-scale operations. Acadians and Creoles having small narrow tracts fronting on the streams and extending back 40 arpents (a linear arpent approximates 63¼ yards) had long been subdividing their little units as generation followed generation, making them less and less able to compete with the large plantations. A planters' organ commented disparagingly on these "Cajuns" on Bayou Black who "led an indolent life, fishing, hunting, pasturing cattle and raising a little corn—until the intelligent, money-loving, go-a-head Americans came, and drove them before them. . . ." So it was with the "Cajuns" of Attakapas and Opelousas.

Instead of settling on the rich woodland of the country, they occupied the prairies, which the more enterprising Creoles and Americans are now taking up and fencing in. Even the Swamps, on which they depended for wood, have been taken up by capitalists and the Acadians who have not the intelligence to pursue a proper system of farming, wander on the prairie, hard pressed for pasturage and even firewood. . . . Their present condition is extraordinary, in a country in which agriculture, trade, manufacture and professions are daily extending their means of employ, and premiums of success. We can only attribute their present declining conditions to their want of intelligence! [24]

It is easy to understand though not necessarily to sympathize with the harshness of the tone which a paper representing the planter position should take toward these people who stood in the way of "progress," expansion of the plantation system, and accumulation of wealth in the hands of the few.

Large planters were anxious to close out the small holdings, not only because they coveted the land but also because they disliked the poor white owners, whom they wished to expel from the neighborhood. Worthless land was even acquired at high prices to assure the removal of poor farmers from the planters' neighborhood. [25]

There was almost continuous work for slaves on sugar plantations the year round. Fresh land was continually being cleared, and the wood was used for construction or for fuel in the sugarhouses or was sold to steamboats. Levees had to be raised; ditching and draining were never completed. Planting, numerous hoeings, cutting, loading and unloading the cane, putting it through the mill, feeding the boilers, moving the huge hogsheads of sugar and molasses and drawing them to the boat landing, setting aside the seed cane, hauling the bagasse to the fields—all this took much labor. Before the end of work of one crop year another had begun with the preparation of the soil for new plantings. Life on the sugar plantation was harsh, the labor more difficult and more constant than that on tobacco and cotton plantations. [26]

The slave diet of corn and pork was not what modern nutritionists would regard as satisfactory. Long hours of hard, debilitating labor from before sunup to sundown, combined with a poor diet, made the Negro an easy prey to malaria and to the periodic outbreaks of deadly cholera and the dreaded yellow fever. For example, Bishop Leonidas Polk on Bayou Lafourche lost 70 of 440 from cholera in 1848 and William J. Minor noted the loss of 37 "men & women & children" by cholera on his southern Louisiana plantation in 1851. [27] One is not surprised to find that Louisiana

[24] *Planters' Banner and Louisiana Agriculturist,* Franklin, La., September 23, 1847.

[25] Roger W. Shugg, *Origins of Class Struggle in Louisiana* (Baton Rouge: Louisiana State University Press, 1939), pp. 95 ff.; Jewell Lynn de Grummond, "A Social History of St. Marys Parish, 1845–1860," *Louisiana Historical Quarterly,* XXXII (January, 1949), 23 ff.

[26] Sitterson, *Sugar Country, passim;* and Moody, "Slavery in Louisiana Sugar Plantations," *loc. cit.,* pp. 191 ff.

[27] Kellar, *Solon Robinson,* II, 201; J. Carlyle Sitterson, "The William J. Minor Plantations: A Study in Ante-Bellum Absentee Ownership," *Journal of Southern History,* IX (February, 1943), 67. John C. Jenkins on his River Plantation, near Natchez,

had the highest death rate in the Union in 1849 and was exceeded only by Massachusetts in 1859.[28]

Extensive absentee ownership, continued cropping to cane, pressure on the overseer to produce the largest possible volume to enable his high-living employer to disport himself in Natchez, New Orleans, or elsewhere were characteristic of much of the sugar country. Not every sugar planter was guilty of abusing the soil. Some experimented with the use of manures, lime, and gauno, deep plowing, and different kinds of improved plows. New varieties of cane were introduced, new methods of cultivation were tried, and peas were used as a cover crop.[29]

Wealthy planters with much at stake in the existing order naturally supported the party that favored the least change, or, to put it differently, that best represented the interests of the larger property owners.[30] The Democratic party, which was more liberal on such issues as banking, land policy, immigration, naturalization, and control of monopolies, attracted them little. The Whig party, on the other hand, was "sound" on these issues and, more important, favored protecting the American market for American producers, including the sugar producers. Protection affected the American price but lightly if at all, even in the years of highest protection, 1842–1846, but the sugar planters were positive that without it they would suffer losses.[31] It was easy, therefore, for them to attribute the low prices after 1846 to the Walker Tariff, which reduced the import duty on sugar substantially. Cotton was also so low in price at the same time that some planters shifted to sugar production. Indeed, the *New Orleans Delta* reported in late 1848 a considerable shift from cotton on worn-out lands in West Feliciana Parish to cane, which was doing very well. One of the principal sugar, hence protectionist, organs, the Franklin *Planters' Banner and Louisiana Agriculturist*, gave the situation away when it condemned the planters for their poor agricultural practices which already had greatly diminished the yield of sugar on the older fields.[32]

---

lost twenty slaves out of ninety from cholera in 1849. Jenkins expressed much grief the following year at the death of a slave from "dirt eating." He observed that many other planters had suffered so much from deaths and illness that they had not been able to plant their crops.—Plantation diary of Jenkins, Louisiana State University Library, notation of August 29, 1850.

[28] *Eighth Census, Population*, p. 41.

[29] Walter Pritchard, "Routine of a Louisiana Sugar Plantation under the Slavery Regime," *Mississippi Valley Historical Review*, XIV (September, 1927), 168–178; Sitterson, *Sugar Country, passim.*

[30] Shugg, *Origins of Class Struggle*, pp. 121–156; Arthur Charles Cole, *The Whig Party in the South* (Washington, D. C.: American Historical Association, 1913), *passim.*

[31] Gray, *History of Agriculture in the Southern United States*, II, 144–148.

[32] *New Orleans Delta* quoted in *Southern Cultivator*, VII (January, 1849), 5; *Planters' Banner and Louisiana Agriculturist*, August 25 and September 23, 1847.

Improving economic conditions and the growing demand for sugar restored prices to a favorable level, in 1857, to the highest point since 1820. Further tariff reduction in that year did no serious harm to the industry. That sugar brought prosperity to the planters, despite their frequent complaints about prices and low tariff protection, is evident from their way of life, the continuous expansion in the industry until 1854, and the demand for slaves that boosted prices to new highs successively in the forties and fifties. With such favorable conditions prevailing under Democratic administrations and with the Democratic leaders showing an increasingly benevolent regard for property rights and less inclination to be influenced by the more agrarian sentiments of the predominantly small-farm parishes, the lines separating leadership in the two parties weakened. Planter-aristocrats could feel safe under either party.[33]

ATTEMPTS AT ECONOMIC SELF-SUFFICIENCY

Along with their economic nationalism the sugar planters had as their goal as near self-sufficiency on their plantations as it was possible to achieve. The *Planters' Banner and Louisiana Agriculturist,* published at Franklin in the heart of the sugar country, repeatedly scolded the planters for overemphasis upon one major cash crop and urged them to diversify and to produce their own foodstuffs.[34] Instead of buying corn and pork from Kentucky or Indiana farmers, who could produce and market them in Louisiana for less than the planters could raise them in Louisiana, the latter were urged to devote to its cultivation land ill adapted to corn and to raise sufficient hogs to provide the essential pork for their slaves. And this the planters sought to do. Corn produced at the rate of sixteen bushels to the acre, the average for Louisiana, Mississippi, Alabama, South Carolina, North Carolina, and Georgia, in comparison with the average of thirty bushels for Ohio, Kentucky, and Indiana was expensive, particularly when cotton brought nine or ten cents and sugar six or seven cents. Furthermore, there was considerable risk for the planters in having many hogs on their places: their slaves had a peculiar fondness for stealing and roasting the young pigs.[35] True, the argument for self-sufficiency was linked with diversification and better farm practices, but these were not given the same emphasis. The *Planters' Banner* carried the argument even further, maintaining not only that planters should provide their own food-stuffs but that they should manufacture yarn, thread, cloth, ironware, and

[33] Shugg, *Origins of Class Struggle,* pp. 155–156.
[34] *Planters' Banner and Louisiana Agriculturist,* November 4, 1847; May 11, 1848; and June 20, 1850.
[35] *New Orleans Price Current,* May 19, 1855; Russell, *North America: Its Agriculture and Climate,* p. 265.

other materials they were then buying from the North.[36] Southern hostility to northern abolitionists entered into this desire for self-sufficiency. In the face of their aggression the South was urged to use its major weapon, the economic boycott.

The experience of Bishop Leonidas Polk in attempting to make his plantation self-sufficient is instructive. On his great plantation on the Bayou Lafourche, where he produced 1,200,000 pounds of sugar in 1853, the bishop, an experimenter by nature, tested out various plows, introduced new laborsaving methods into his grinding mill, manured his land, and plowed into the soil the rotted bagasse left from the grinding. Although his yield of corn was only 26 bushels to the acre, he insisted on raising a full supply for his 370 slaves, 75 mules and horses, numerous oxen, hogs, and beef cattle; he never realized his goal of producing the half pound of pork he daily allotted each of his slaves. Plows, hoes, carts and wagons, and the shoes and clothing of the slaves were made upon the plantation. It is not clear whether the good bishop, whose views seem to have coincided with those of his fellow planters on everything except slavery, ever questioned whether his area in corn might yield more profit in sugar cane, or whether the time his slaves spent in making plows might more profitably be devoted to draining land.[37]

BUYING AND SELLING OF SUGAR PLANTATIONS

There was a good deal of speculative buying and selling of improved plantations in the lower Mississippi country in much the same way that unimproved land was dealt in. When a good crop was made and prices were favorable, the net returns might be sufficient to warrant expanding one's operations by buying another plantation. Olmsted related the story of a man who bought a sugar plantation on the Red River, substantially enlarged it by purchasing adjoining holdings of several poor people, increased the force of slaves, modernized the sugar works, and produced three good crops in succession, the last of which amounted to 650,000 pounds. With one more good crop he would be free of debt on the transaction. He paid 10 per cent interest on his debt but made 25 per cent annually in those three years (1851–1853) on his full investment.[38]

Through speculation in Spanish land claims and the development and sale of alluvial lands on the lower Mississippi two of the largest estates in the South were accumulated. Much of the great wealth of Daniel Clark

[36] *Planters' Banner and Louisiana Agriculturist*, November 4, 1847, May 11, 1848, and June 20, 1850.

[37] Kellar, *Solon Robinson*, II, 201–204; Champomier, *Statement of the Sugar Crop Made in Louisiana in 1853–54*, p. 27.

[38] Olmsted, *A Journey in the Seaboard Slave States*, pp. 660–662.

and John McDonogh came from shrewd real-estate deals and appreciation in the value of their holdings. Joseph Erwin, a wealthy Tennessee planter, moved to Louisiana in 1807, where he began buying and selling small improved farms and plantations. Over the next twenty years he made scores of deals involving some 27,000 acres for a total of $1,000,000. Heavy financial losses produced by the flooding of his sugar land brought him to despair and suicide. Despite his losses and large donations to his children during his lifetime, Erwin left an estate, somewhat encumbered, but valued at $300,000.[39] That doughty fighter for southern rights, John A. Quitman, bought and sold plantations in Louisiana and Mississippi over many years. In 1840 his debts resulting from reckless purchasing of land and endorsements for others threatened to overwhelm him, despite the fact that his income was $45,000. Two years later he advertised for sale two plantations of 2,000 acres each. At his death in 1858 Quitman had 12,634 acres in six plantations in as many Mississippi counties.[40]

Absentee ownership was more common for sugar and rice plantations than for cotton and tobacco plantations, partly because the risks to health were greater on the former. Many of the larger sugar planters lived in New Orleans but might have homes on their land, which they would visit in cool weather. Wade Hampton and his son-in-law, owners of Houmas, retained their residence in South Carolina, William J. Minor and his son John, Dr. Stephen Duncan, and James and Francis Surget, all substantial owners of cotton plantations in Mississippi and residents of Natchez, owned from two to five or more sugar plantations in Louisiana. Herbert Weaver has prepared a list of forty-two Mississippians, many of them residents of Natchez, who owned plantations containing 1,000 acres or more in six parishes in Louisiana in 1860. Their total holdings in Louisiana were 119,308 acres. Sugar was the principal crop raised on these plantations in the more southern parishes, and cotton in the northern parishes. More detailed analysis of ownership of sugar plantations would doubtless show numerous additional nonresident planters.[41]

[39] Alice Pemple White, "The Plantation Experience of Joseph and Lavinia Erwin, 1807-1836," *Louisiana Historical Quarterly,* XXVII (April, 1944), 343–478, especially 354 ff.

[40] John A. Quitman, January 27, 1840, to J. F. H. Claiborne, in J. F. H. Claiborne, *Life and Correspondence of John A. Quitman* (New York: Harper & Brothers, 1860), I, 186; *Natchez Free Trader,* February 4, 1842; papers relating to the Quitman estate, File Box 167, Adams County Probate Records, Natchez. Mention might also be made of Bennet H. Barrow, wealthy cotton planter of the Bayou Sara area, who bought and sold plantations.—Edwin Adams Davis, *Plantation Life in the Florida Parishes of Louisiana, 1836–1846, as Reflected in the Diary of Bennet H. Barrow* (Harry J. Carman and Rexford G. Tugwell, eds., Columbia University *Studies in the History of American Agriculture,* No. 9; New York: Columbia University Press, 1943).

[41] Herbert Weaver, *Mississippi Farmers, 1850–1860* (Nashville: Vanderbilt University Press, 1945), p. 109; Sitterson, "The William J. Minor Plantations," *loc. cit.,* p. 67.

Absentee ownership, with its pressure for profits, tended to exagger-
ate the evils of southern staple economy: the concentration upon one
crop, mining of the soil, failure to build up a sturdy yeoman-farmer base,
and dependence upon slave labor. The narrowly concentrated profits permitted a very few planters the luxury of fine homes in Natchez, New
Orleans, and Charleston, staffed with numerous domestic slaves, and the
social prestige which all the realism of a later generation has not removed
from the memory of man.

CHAPTER VII

Cotton

IF sugar and rice were the aristocrats of southern crops, tobacco and cotton were the commoners. Except for the border states and Virginia, cotton was produced extensively in all the slave states. In the area of its greatest production, the lower South, there were few counties which did not yield some of the staple. It could be raised on almost any well-drained land having a sufficiently long growing season. Noah B. Cloud even succeeded in raising cotton profitably on the pine barrens of Macon County, Alabama, by continued soil building, contour plowing, and rotation of crops. Nor did cotton require a large investment of capital to make land suitable for its cultivation and to handle the crop. Hence it was raised by squatters, tenants, mortgaged farmers, full owners, by yeoman farmers, medium planters, and owners of great estates.

COTTON PLANTING

Long-staple or sea-island cotton differed materially from upland green, short-staple cotton as to the areas in which it could be planted, the amount and costs of labor devoted to its production, and price. Grown first on the sea islands off the South Carolina and Georgia coast, long-staple cotton was a fine cotton, difficult to produce and prepare for market. Careful selection of the best strains of seed led to gradual improvement of the lint but reduced the yield to an average of 150 pounds to the acre of cotton ready for market. Since delicate cotton lint was easily ruined by heavy driving rains, the fields had to be picked frequently to avoid damage even though the results might be meager. A picker of sea-island cotton was expected to gather 25 to 100 pounds a day in contrast to 200 pounds or more of upland cotton. These factors, which, added to the greater cost of extracting the seed from the lint, made sea-island cotton expensive to produce, were offset by the premium price it brought. The choicest quality of sea-island cotton sometimes sold as high as $1.25 a pound; usually, however, it brought between 20 and 40 cents, or three or four times the price of upland cotton. The area suitable for sea-island cotton was very small, and the quantity raised did not amount to 1 per cent of the short-staple crop.[1]

In few regions of the United States were farm practices as primitive as on the plantations in the sea islands. As on the rice plantations, the plow was rarely used, and when it was employed it was a most inadequate, futile device that did little more than gently stir the soil. Instead of being hauled by a mule it was drawn by a cumbersome and slow pair of oxen. Edmund Ruffin, while in South Carolina, was quoted as saying, "The small use of the plow—indeed its total disuse in many cases and the substitution of the hoe and hand labor, is to a stranger the most remarkable and novel feature of the agriculture of the lower districts." [2] In 1853, however, Robert F. Allston, of South Carolina, was pleased to note that although the old foot or treadle gin, which could turn out only twenty-five pounds of cotton a day, was still commonly used, the improved roller gin operated by horse power or steam was being introduced. He also reported the use of plows and scrapers on some Georgia and Florida plantations.[3]

Newly cleared land was put into cotton for a number of years in succession, and when its productivity declined sharply, fresh land was utilized. Rotation, fallowing, and the use of soil builders were not common. Fanny Kemble, whose husband had a plantation devoted to sea-island cotton, when told in 1839 by older slaves that the yield had greatly diminished over the course of years, speculated as to the future prospects of the owner and his slaves on depleted land. She also found the work of the slaves on the sea-island plantation less harsh, less grueling, less killing than that on the rice plantation on which she had lived for a time.[4] Realizing the destructive effects of their practices, some planters began to apply marsh mud, guano, and other fertilizers to their soils and made some efforts to rotate their crops. Unfortunately, the crop they needed the most was corn for their stock and their slaves, and the land did not

[1] James L. Watkins, *King Cotton: A Historical and Statistical Review, 1790–1908* (New York: James L. Watkins & Sons, 1908), pp. 80, 102; Lewis Cecil Gray, *History of Agriculture in the Southern United States to 1860* (2 vols.; Washington, D. C.: Carnegie Institution, 1933), II, 1025, 1032; J. A. Turner, *The Cotton Planter's Manual* (New York: C. M. Saxton and Company, 1857), pp. 128–129, cites a planter whose crops averaged 137 pounds to the acre and grossed $83 per hand.

[2] Watkins, *op. cit.*, p. 79.

[3] *American Cotton Planter*, II (July, 1854), 196–197.

[4] Francis Anne Kemble, *Journal of a Residence on a Georgia Plantation in 1838–1839* (New York: Harper & Brothers, 1863), pp. 163 ff.

prove well adapted to it. Planters had, therefore, to buy corn, pork, and beef to meet their needs, as did the rice planters.[5]

The area open to upland cotton was limited only by isothermal lines and quantity of rainfall, or, as later developments were to show, the availability of water for irrigation. Cotton was planted on land so hilly that it was necessary to terrace it. Unlike tobacco, rice, sugar cane, and sea-island cotton, which all required expert, and at times the most delicate, attention to assure high quality and abundant crops, the short-staple variety made no such demands. Planting, chopping, frequent cultivating, picking, ginning, baling, and hauling took constant labor but little skill. The crop was thus well adapted to production on any scale.

As with other slave-produced crops, cotton planting employed fairly primitive methods. It required a large volume of labor and little mechanical aid to supplement it. The simple bull-tongue or scooter plows slowly replaced the hoe but were not efficient. Since cotton seed as yet had little value it was sown lavishly and covered with the hoe. This made it necessary to chop or remove the surplus plants at a later time. Scraping, chopping, thinning, and laying-by were all designed to thin the plants to permit them to gain the fullest possible growth, to keep the soil stirred up, and to eliminate the moisture- and nutriment-absorbing weeds. Once the cotton was up, these operations, whether done by hand as in the early part of the century or partly by cultivators, scrapers, and plows as at a later time, required much labor.[6]

COTTON PICKING

Picking cotton was most time consuming and took more labor than any other task. On the plantations, all field hands, including women and young children, were pressed into service, and on small farms whites and blacks of all ages turned to picking. The season was long, ranging over as much as five months, during which the fields were picked three or more times,[7] but rainy weather, muddy fields, and wet cotton reduced the amount of time in which picking could be done. After picking, the cotton was dried in the gin house or in the sun, then put through the gin to re-

[5] Guion Griffis Johnson, *A Social History of the Sea Islands* (Chapel Hill: University of North Carolina Press, 1930), pp. 49 ff.

[6] Communication of R. Abbey, Boston Plantation, Yazoo City, Miss., in *De Bow's Review*, II (September, 1846), 132–142; Turner, *Cotton Planter's Manual, passim*; Gray, *History of Agriculture in the Southern United States*, II, 700 ff.; Ulrich B. Phillips, *American Negro Slavery* (New York: Appleton-Century-Crofts, Inc., 1918), pp. 205–227.

[7] In 1844 John C. Jenkins began picking cotton on his Mississippi plantations on July 19 and ended on November 22. Two years later picking continued until January 1. See his diary for these dates in the archives of the Louisiana State University.

move the seeds, and compressed into bales in a screw press. Long tedious hours were required to get the cotton ginned and baled, and continued experiments were made to improve operating efficiency. Small farmers, not being able to afford such equipment, had to haul their cotton long distances to custom gins and lose time waiting to get their cotton processed.

The amount of land to be put into cotton was restricted by the capacity to pick. There was considerable variation in the ratio of land in cotton to hands, the variables being other obligations required of slaves, such as care of land in corn and maintenance of livestock, the degree to which the slaves were driven, and their age and physical capacity. A fair estimate of the ratio of land to laborers might be from six to nine acres in cotton and half as much in corn per person.[8]

Ulrich B. Phillips' belief that "one-horse farmers and hundred-slave planters competed on fairly even terms, acre for acre," in cotton farming is not wholly acceptable.[9] The small planter or farmer working in the field avoided costs of supervision and might, by example, drive his hands harder and save the labor of, and investment in, one slave. On the other hand, he frequently had to till poorer land and pay higher interest on his debt. A broken plowshare might set him back a number of days, whereas the large planter who had his own blacksmith to make repairs was not delayed by accidents to equipment.[10] The small man had to take his turn at the custom gin and press, could not withhold his cotton for higher prices (though neither could many large planters), was less inclined to experiment with manures and new equipment, and was more seriously affected by the loss of a slave.[11]

[8] Charles S. Sydnor, *Slavery in Mississippi* (New York: Appleton-Century-Crofts, Inc., 1933), p. 14. Hugh Davis on his Perry County, Ala., plantation regarded twelve acres to each hand as the proper ratio.—Weymouth T. Jordan, *Hugh Davis and His Alabama Plantation* (University: University of Alabama Press, 1948), pp. 30, 133. John H. Dent, a Yankee planter in Barbour County, Ala., who drove his Negroes hard, held that fifteen acres could be properly handled by each slave, but after further experience realized that this was too high. See his plantation journal for 1840–1841, in the Library, University of Alabama.

[9] Ulrich B. Phillips, *Life and Labor in the Old South* (Boston: Little, Brown & Company, 1929), p. 128. Cf. Roger W. Shugg, *Origins of Class Struggle in Louisiana* (Baton Rouge: Louisiana State University Press, 1939), pp. 97 ff.

[10] Bennet H. Barrow, a substantial cotton planter in East Feliciana Parish, had between 15 and 25 plows, in one year bought 15, employed his own blacksmith, whether black or white, to keep plows, gins, threshers, carts, and wagons in working order.—Edwin Adams Davis, ed., *Plantation Life in the Florida Parishes of Louisiana, 1837–1846, as Reflected in the Diary of Bennet H. Barrow* (Harry J. Carman and Rexford G. Tugwell, eds., Columbia University *Studies in the History of American Agriculture*, No. 9; New York: Columbia University Press, 1943), pp. 33–35.

[11] A. H. Stone, "The Cotton Factorage System of the Southern States," *American Historical Review*, XX (April, 1915), 563.

FARM MANAGEMENT PRACTICES

What can be said of the differences between the farm management practices of the large and the small planters and farmers? Were the planters of the ante-bellum period able to pursue a better program of land use than did the small operators? With both groups there were strong incentives for pushing cotton planting to the limit, especially in the early period when debts, heavy interest charges, the need for funds to purchase equipment, stock, and slaves and to construct and furnish a permanent home all called for money. On most cotton land there was no other staple crop that could be used in rotation for which there was a sufficient demand and an adequate price. In part of Louisiana, sugar cane could be substituted and, during the fifties, thousands of acres were shifted from cotton to cane, but this opportunity existed only within a restricted area. Corn was in demand in the South and millions of bushels were being imported annually from the North, but alluvial land or black prairie of Alabama or Mississippi did not yield good crops of corn. The failure of a cotton crop meant disaster to a small farmer unless he had some grain and livestock on which to depend. Consequently, it was unwise for him to put all his eggs in one basket. A planter would be hurt by cotton failure but, unless he was greatly overextended, could worry along without too much difficulty for another year.

Although he needed diversification less, it was the planter, rather than the farmer, who took up new practices, tried out new seeds, diversified, and attempted to make his plantation as self-sufficient as possible. Having the advantage of a better education, leisure time, and perhaps a taste for reading, the planter subscribed to and read the agricultural journals.[12] These frequently commented on the evils of the one-crop system, the folly of careless tillage, and the consequences of failure to let land lie fallow and to use soil builders. But to be forewarned was not always to be forearmed. Planters' diaries that have survived show considerable attention to land-use problems, but they were kept by the more liter-

[12] Wendell H. Stephenson, in "A Quarter Century of a Mississippi Plantation: Eli F. Capell of 'Pleasant Hill,'" *Mississippi Valley Historical Review*, XXIII (December, 1936), 355–374, tells the story of a self-educated Mississippi planter who built up an estate, partly through inheritance but mostly through accumulation, of 2,500 acres and 80 slaves. Capell is pictured as a "progressive agriculturist" who subscribed at various times to eight different farm journals, which he read carefully and profitably and early began to contribute to them. See also Davis, ed., *Plantation Life*, p. 36; Jordan, *Hugh Davis*, pp. 25 ff.; and Jenkins's Diary. There is much information on the circulation of agricultural periodicals but little on the persons who read them in Albert Lowther Demaree, *The American Agricultural Press* (Harry J. Carman and Rexford G. Tugwell, eds., Columbia University *Studies in the History of American Agriculture*, No. 8; New York: Columbia University Press, 1941).

ate, intellectual, and experimentally inclined and cannot be regarded as evidence of the practices of typical planters. Areas where large plantations predominated and where there was a high state of culture and education, such as southwestern Mississippi, suffered seriously from soil erosion and diminishing production, despite all the preaching of the planters' journals. A writer in *De Bow's Review* scolded cotton planters for their opposition to innovation, to changes in land-use practices, to any thoughtful consideration of their problems. More specifically, he condemned overcropping with insufficient hands, which led to careless and inadequate cultivation, failure to plant only select seed, hasty and reckless gining of the cotton, the use of low-priced gins which injured the cotton, and inadequate packing, pressing, and baling techniques.[13]

A heterogeneous and complex settlement and ownership pattern developed in all parts of the United States as a result of the restless individualism of Americans, the practice of squatting, and the nature of the public-land policies. Nowhere, not even in New England, could one find what a French or Irish peasant or tenant farmer would call small holdings. Throughout every part of the South appeared the squatter looking for land and if he got there early enough he established a squatter's claim. All that was required was residence and some indication of improvement. It was more of an achievement to acquire title, for that took $200 of cash; it was even harder to retain ownership and develop the 160-acre tract when planters appeared, prepared to buy the squatter's title and improvements at a considerable profit to him. Since capital costs of farm making were not light and men of small means could not easily compete with capitalists with slaves, there was a tendency for the better and more desirable land to gravitate into the hands of capitalist-planters. The winnowing process by no means eliminated the small farm maker, but it did bring into large ownerships much of the better land.

Throughout the cotton kingdom the larger number of white people by far were neither large planters having upward of 500 acres and possessing fifty or more slaves, nor medium planters having from 200 to 500 acres and owning from twenty to fifty slaves, but small farmer-planters having less than 200 acres and fewer than twenty slaves. Most small farmers had no slaves.

The researches of Frank L. Owsley and his students at Vanderbilt University in the original census schedules in Tennessee, Mississippi, Alabama, and Louisiana have clearly established, if there was any doubt before, that such yeoman farmers existed in much larger numbers than the planters and poor whites and that they must be distinguished from the poor white farmer, whose economic condition was inferior in that he owned little or no land and such as he did possess provided a substandard

[13] *De Bow's Review*, III (January, 1847), 4 ff.

living. The poor farmers, whether in the piney woods or in the hill regions, may have lost hope of advancing themselves as a result of the poverty of the soil on which they had settled and the hookworm and the nutritional diseases from which they suffered.[14] On the other hand, out of the small yeoman-farmer class came some of the most substantial planters who succeeded because they were shrewd enough to select good tracts, were good farmers, and were fortunate in having good weather conditions, favorable prices, and good health that enabled them to produce good crops.[15]

The studies of the Owsley yeoman-farmer school emphasize the status and number of small farmers, their relative well-being as compared with that of the poor white, and show that their chief ambition was to acquire one or more slaves for social as well as economic reasons and to move into the production of marketable staples. Until they acquired a few Negro hands their farm economy was similar to that of small farmers throughout the country. Their first concern was to raise sufficient corn for the family and the livestock; their next, to be assured of an abundant supply of pork. Live hogs or dressed pork could always be sold. They had a few head of cattle which provided them with beef and allowed for the sale of a number of animals each year. They might also raise vegetables and fruit for the table. Most of them owned their own land, which more than met their own food requirements; if their land was suitable, they might raise small quantities of cotton or tobacco. In the aggregate, their surplus of corn, pork, and beef appears large. It is noticeable that counties outside the cotton belt which could produce some cotton raised larger proportions of corn in relation to cotton than did those in the cotton belt.

Pioneering in the new cotton areas of the West was something very different from the process described by Turner, Paxson, and others of the "frontier" school of historians. There were straggling squatters on the "hither edge" of settlement, but there were also rich planters with their scores of slaves clearing the forests, burning the canebrake, grubbing out the brush, and draining, plowing, and planting. Many great plantations here were not erected by buying out small owners but were acquired as unimproved land in the form of grants, settlement rights, and purchases, direct from the government of the United States, from Spain, from Mexico in Texas. In Alabama the plantations of Andrew and Israel

---

[14] Paul H. Buck, "The Poor Whites of the Ante-Bellum South," *American Historical Review*, XXXI (October, 1925), 41 ff.

[15] Herbert Weaver, *Mississippi Farmers, 1850–1860* (Nashville: Vanderbilt University Press, 1945); Blanche Henry Clark, *The Tennessee Yeomen, 1840–1860* (Nashville: Vanderbilt University Press, 1942); Frank Lawrence Owsley, *Plain Folk of the Old South* (Baton Rouge: Louisiana State University Press, 1949).

FROM PIONEERING TO COMMER-
CIAL FARMING ON THE HOL-
LAND PURCHASE OF NEW YORK
(O. Turner, *Pioneer History of
the Holland Purchase*, 1849,
pp. 562–567.)

1. The Pioneer with his small
   clearing and log cabin.

2. The second year of farm
   making shows a larger clearing, a rail fence enclosing a
   number of acres in corn,
   potatoes, and garden vegetables.

3. The tenth year of farm making shows 40 acres cleared
   and fenced, a block house,
   frame barn, and orchard.

4. The farm in commercial production at 45 years.

WATERTOWN,

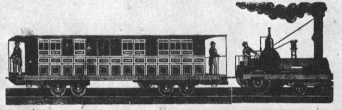

Rome, and Cape-Vincent
RAIL-ROAD.

According to notice in the Jefferson county papers, the inhabitants of this Town will be speedily called on to complete subscriptions towards the above named Road, sufficient to warrant a commencement.

By the charter we have till the 14th of May, 1848, to complete subscriptions, and make an expenditure towards the Road.

The time is short in which to do this business; therefore it is highly important that every citizen, from the St. Lawrence on the North to the Erie canal on the South—from the highlands on the East to the lake on the West, come forward and spread himself to his full extent for the Road.

To stimulate us to action let it be borne in mind that the sun never shone on so glorious a land as lies within the bounds above described. To one who for the first time visits our towns, the scene is enchanting in the extreme. Our climate is bland and salubrious; winters more mild than in any part of New England or southern New York—the atmosphere being softened by the prevalence of southwesterly winds coursing up the Valley of the Mississippi and along the waters of Erie and Ontario, to such degree that for salubrity and comfort we stand almost unrivalled.

Wheat, corn, barley, oats, pease, beans, buckwheat, fruit, butter, cheese, pork, beef, horses, sheep, cattle, minerals, lumber, &c. are produced here with a facility that warrants the hand of labor a bountiful return.

We have water power enough to turn every spindle in Great Britain and America. In fact we have every thing man could desire on this globe, except a cheap and expeditious method of getting rid of our surplus products, and holding communication with the exterior world.

The want of this, places us *thirty years* **behind** almost every other portion of the State. When we might be *first,* we suffer ourselves to be *last.*

Citizens! how long is this state of things to endure? After having lain dormant until we have acquired the dimensions of a young giant, will we, like the brute beast, ignorant of his powers, be still led captive in the train of our country's prosperity—affording, by our supineness, a foil to set off the triumphs of our more enterprising brethren of the East, the South, and the West?

No,—from this moment forward, let us resolve to cut a passage to the marts of the New World, and, by the abundance of our resources, strike their "merchant princes" with admiration and astonishment.

This can easily be done if unanimity, perseverance, and, above all, LIBERALITY, be exhibited. If every farmer owning 100 acres of land, and be not much in debt, will take five shares in the Road, and *others in proportion,* the decree will go forth that the work is done. *Without this,* it is feared the whole must be a *failure.*

Viewed in an enlightened manner, there need be no hesitation on the part of the owners of the soil. They are the ones to be most essentially benefitted. There is no reason why their lands, from having a market and increased price of products, would not be worth fifty to eighty dollars per acre, as is the case in less favored sections, where Rail Roads have been constructed. The very fact that a Road was to be made would add *half* to the value of land—its completion would more than *double* the present prices.

A tax on the land ten miles each side of the Road, to build it, would in three years repay itself, and leave to the present population and their posterity an enduring source of wealth and importance. We lose one hundred thousand dollars annually in the price of butter and cheese alone, when compared with the prices obtained by Lewis and the northerly part of Oneida, simply because they are nearer the Canal and the Rail Road.

But taking stock *is not a tax,* **in any sense of the** phrase. It is only resolving to purchase a certain amount of property in the Road, which, taking similar investments elsewhere as a sample, will pay interest, or can be at all times sold at par, or at an advance, like other property or evidence of value. The owner of shares can at any time sell out, and have the satisfaction of knowing that he has greatly added to his wealth merely by affording countenance to the project while in embryo.

The Directors are powerless unless the people rally to their aid. They have made efforts abroad for capital to build the Road, by adding to the subscriptions on hand at the time they were chosen. Owing to causes not prejudicial to the character of our enterprise, they have not, for the present succeeded. Aid they have been promised, but they are enjoined first to show a larger figure at home. The ability and disposition of our population must be more thoroughly evinced than has yet been the case.

Agents are at work, or speedily will be, on the whole length and breadth of the line from Cape Vincent to Rome. A searching operation is to be had. If the Road is a failure, the Directors are determined that it shall not be laid at their door. Let this be remembered, and every one hereafter hold his peace.

Clarke Rice,
Secretary W. & R. R. R. Co.

WATERTOWN, Aug. 27, 1847.

Circular urging farmers to buy stock in a railroad, the construction of which will, they are told, assure higher prices for grain, dairy products, livestock, and lumber. (Courtesy, Regional History, Cornell University.)

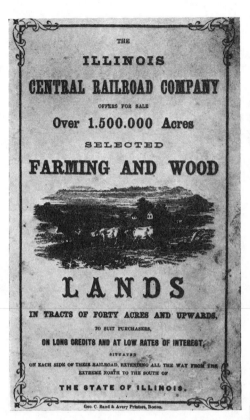

THE

ILLINOIS

CENTRAL RAILROAD COMPANY

OFFERS FOR SALE

Over 1.500.000 Acres

SELECTED

FARMING AND WOOD

LANDS

IN TRACTS OF FORTY ACRES AND UPWARDS,

TO SUIT PURCHASERS,

ON LONG CREDITS AND AT LOW RATES OF INTEREST,

SITUATED

ON EACH SIDE OF THEIR RAILROAD, EXTENDING ALL THE WAY FROM THE
EXTREME NORTH TO THE SOUTH OF

THE STATE OF ILLINOIS.

Geo. C. Rand & Avery Printers, Boston.

Title page of a widely distributed land-advertising pamphlet of the Illinois Central Railroad, 1857. Later land grant railroads patterned their advertising on that of the Illinois Central.

Plat showing selections of land by the Illinois Central Railroad within 6 miles of its line in T 19 & 20 N, R 2 E of 3rd P.M., in DeWitt County. Much of the timbered land and the school sections the railroad did not acquire. (Courtesy, Recorder's Office, Clinton, Illinois.)

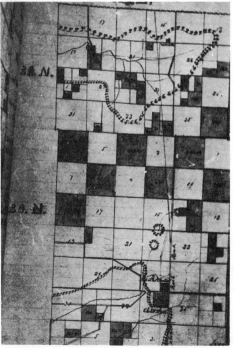

Tobacco growing required much labor throughout the year. (*The Growth of Industrial Art*, p. 192.) **1.** Sowing the seed in a carefully prepared seed bed on which brush had been burned to kill weed seeds and sterilize the soil. **2.** Hilling to keep the roots covered. **3.** Transplanting to the open field. **4.** Laying by and topping to force growth into the leaves. **5.** Worming and suckering, the most unpleasant task. **6.** Cutting and sticking. **7.** Housing in the drying sheds.

Field hands picking cotton. Picking began in August and continued until after Christmas.

Gathering sugar cane. The cane was cut, stripped of leaves, unripe joints removed, gathered into cane wagons, and hauled to the mill. (*Eighty Years' Progress of the United States*, pp. 125, 126.)

Hauling baled cotton to the river landing.

Use of the cradle in harvesting grain was a harsh task
requiring great endurance. From American Banknote Company engravings. (Courtesy, Prints Division, New York
Public Library.)

Compare the easygoing ways depicted in this sketch with the hardworking life of the pioneer
shown in cuts of the Holland Purchase. (*The Hannibal and St. Joseph Railroad Company . . .
offer 600,000 Acres of the Choicest Farming and Wood Lands . . . , 1859, p. 2.*)

Breaking the tough prairie sod was generally done by custom plowmen with their heavy oxen and breaking plows. (Sketched by Theodore R. Davis.) (*Harper's Weekly*, XII [May 9, 1868], 202.)

"The Western Prairie Farmer Running the 'Fire-Guard.' " (Sketched by Theodore R. Davis.) Prairie fires were a constant menace in the late fall and spring. (*Harper's Weekly*, XII [March 28, 1868], 196.)

Grain boats and elevators on the Chicago River. (Courtesy, The Library of Congress.)

Pickens, William R. King, Thomas Bibb, Williamson A. Glover, Eli
Shorter, and Nathan B. Whitfield, builder of "Gaineswood," were erected
on land they acquired directly from the United States. Similarly, the holdings of William Sharkey, Alexander McNutt, Stephen Duncan, James L.
Alcorn, and William Bisland in Mississippi, as well as those of Laurent
Millaudon, John Routh, James and Francis Surget, John Overton, Frederick Stanton (in part), and John Bell in Louisiana were bought directly
from the United States or from the individual states. In Arkansas the holdings of the Ashley, Craig, Craighead, Dabney, and Hill families were
direct purchases. Many other estates either were built on land bought
directly from the federal and state governments or were purchased from
speculators and land companies.

This is not to say that large cotton plantations were not put together
by purchasing smaller farm units. The pattern of landownership has never
been stationary in any part of the United States, and this was particularly
true on the frontier. As in the sugar industry, changes in the capital costs
of land use brought about consolidation of numerous small units into
larger and more efficient plantations. Small owners who managed to pick
up good cotton land could be easily induced to sell out when wealthy
planters made them a generous offer.[16] Speculators' holdings and heavily
mortgaged farms and plantations were highly unstable. Upon the death
of their owners, plantations were commonly divided among the heirs, who
sometimes consolidated the small units or conveyed their shares to neighboring planters.

Throughout the public-land states in the South there was a marked
tendency on the part of successful planters to take advantage of government generosity by engrossing many thousand additional acres. Some of
these purchases were to round out plantations already established; others
were to anticipate future needs resulting from expanding slave population
and declining soil fertility; still others were to establish a second, third,
or fourth plantation by men who had made good on their land and had a

[16] In her sentimental *Memorials of a Southern Planter* (Baltimore: Cushing,
Bailey, 1887), pp. 47, 63, Mrs. Susan Dabney Smedes relates that her father's 4,000-
acre plantation in Hinds County was acquired from six "small farmers" at various
times during and after 1835. This would make the average purchase 666 acres, or
scarcely the holdings of small farmers. Isaac Franklin assembled his 2,000-acre cotton
plantation in Tennessee in eighteen purchases. On the other hand, his 7,767-acre
tract in Louisiana, which was divided into six plantations, was acquired from one
source. Alexander Porter combined six separate tracts to make his 2,400-acre sugar
plantation on Bayou Teche in Louisiana.—Wendell Holmes Stephenson, *Isaac Franklin, Slave Trader and Planter of the Old South* (Baton Rouge: Louisiana State University Press, 1938), pp. 94–102; Stephenson, *Alexander Porter, Whig Planter of Old
Louisiana* (Louisiana State University *Studies,* No. 16; Baton Rouge: Louisiana State
University Press, 1934), p. 116.

surplus of funds for further development; finally, some were made for speculation.[17]

The principal object of all residents of the cotton belt except those living a marginal existence, who had to concentrate upon raising corn and pork for survival, was to produce the greatest possible amount of cotton, the one crop that was always marketable and for which the land seemed best adapted. Cotton provided cash, credit, and the means to buy slaves, to enlarge plantings, and to acquire more land. Nothing was permitted to interfere with producing cotton. As one Georgian phrased it:

Cut down and cripple forest lands and cultivate them, with the sole view of the large annual profits until they will not pay for cultivation, cut down more lands, and remove them field to field, and tract to tract, leaving the exhausted lands to grow up in pine timber, and reclaim themselves . . . such has been the practice among us.[18]

Most methods of cotton cultivation were destructive of the land. The common practice was to plow up and down on slopes and to plant cotton or corn in successive years without using clover or peas to plow under and restore humus to the soil. Clean cultivation of the row crops contributed to the destruction of the humus and reduced the capacity of the land to absorb moisture; the infinitesimal drainage channels became clogged by hard-packed soil, the heavy spring and summer rains, not being absorbed, ran down the slopes and carried off the topsoil in suspension. Sheet erosion was not at first apparent save in declining yields, but when little gullies began to appear and to deepen to the point where they were beyond control, abandonment of the fields was necessary. The Piedmont of South Carolina and Georgia was seriously affected by erosion in the thirties, and during the next two decades was even more grievously damaged. A writer in the *Augusta Constitutionalist* in 1839 observed that thousands of acres of broken land "that were once fertile, and richly repaid labour" were now "worthless to the last degree—nothing but sterile red clay, full of gullies." [19] In 1860 it was stated that the cotton land in middle and southern Georgia, whose owners had believed it inexhaustible, "now present the monotonous and dreary spectacle of bald, barren, red clay hills, marred by deep furrows and yawning red gullies." [20] Even more

[17] James W. Silver, "Land Speculation Profits in the Chickasaw Cession," *Journal of Southern History*, X (February, 1944), 86.

[18] J. S. Whitten in Commissioner of Patents, *Report, 1847* (Washington, D. C.: Wendell and Van Benthuysen, 1848), p. 386.

[19] Quoted in James Silk Buckingham, *The Slave States of America* (2 vols.; London: Fisher, Son & Co., 1842), I, 173. Ralph Betts Flanders, *Plantation Slavery in Georgia* (Chapel Hill: University of North Carolina Press, 1933), pp. 67 ff., summarizes the information on erosion and soil exhaustion in Georgia.

[20] Joseph Jones, *First Report to the Cotton Planters' Convention of Georgia on the Agricultural Resources of Georgia* (Augusta: 1860), p. 13.

alarming was the fact that some of the best cotton land of Mississippi and Alabama had long since passed its prime through overcropping.

Declining fertility and the abandonment of fields did not mean that the Piedmont of Georgia and South Carolina was through as a major cotton-producing area. There was still much land that had not been cleared, and on long-used land it was possible to restore the fertility of the soil if it had not been too seriously impaired. In the fifties the amount of land in cultivation in these two states was increased by 20 per cent over that of the previous decade, while the amount of cotton produced increased by 31 per cent. But even this did not represent, by any means, the capacity of the two states. In 1919 their total output was to be well over three times their greatest crop in the ante-bellum period.

Distressingly low prices for cotton in the forties, as in the twenties, struck hard at a highly capitalized industry, for a large proportion of the cotton was produced by slaveowners. Planters were forced to reconsider carefully their plan of operations and to find places where costs might be cut or production increased.[21] There was much talk about reducing plantings by a third in the hope that a higher price would result. Land already showing declining yields was extensively abandoned and new virgin soils in existing plantations were utilized. Some planters but more small farmers, hard-pressed by low prices, emigrated to the newer states of Alabama and Mississippi, later to Arkansas, Texas, and Louisiana. South Carolina was particularly hard hit by the emigration of both white people and slaves. Between 1810 and 1860 this state lost by emigration 240,737 whites and 173,617 Negroes. For a state that in 1860 had only 703,708 people, this loss was most marked, being equaled only by the losses to the West of a number of New England states.[22] The only alternative to emigration was better farm practices but, with an abundance of cheap and fertile land available farther west, many farmers and planters preferred the risks of emigration to the slow and expensive process of land improvement.

Agricultural reform was the choice of those who cherished the land and their homes. Many of them must have realized that the great profits in agriculture came not from tillage but from buying virgin land cheaply, improving and selling it while its fertility was still rich and its productivity high. But with the right methods good living was still to be made on soils near exhaustion. Nine new farm journals were established in

[21] Weaver, *Mississippi Farmers*, pp. 100–101, shows that in sample Mississippi counties the percentage of cotton produced by slaveowners was 83 in 1849 and 93 in 1859.

[22] *Eighth Census of the United States, 1860, Population* (Washington, D. C.: Government Printing Office, 1864), pp. 616–617; Alfred Glaze Smith, Jr., *Economic Readjustment of an Old Cotton State: South Carolina, 1820–1860* (Columbia: University of South Carolina Press, 1958), pp. 22 ff.

the cotton belt at Raleigh, Charleston, Columbia, Augusta, Montgomery, and Natchez, agricultural societies were organized, and fairs were held to teach the advantages of manuring, horizontal and deep plowing, rotation, cover crops, improved plows and cultivators, selected seeds, pure-bred livestock, draining, tiling, and mulching.[23] Considerable excitement was aroused over the importations of Peruvian guano, which, despite its high cost, was used by progressive planters. A leader in this reform movement was David Dickson, who claimed to have made two half-million-dollar fortunes, one before and one after the Civil War, by the use of guano, potash, and plaster upon his land, and by deep plowing, light cultivation, seed selection, and careful training of his hands to make them efficient. Although somewhat of a controversialist and braggart, Dickson undoubtedly did contribute to the adoption of improved methods, especially the wider use of fertilizer, by his frequently reiterated story that he bought a plantation supplied with slaves, stock, and equipment, and paid for it with one crop of cotton.[24]

PROBLEMS OF THE COTTON PLANTER

Cotton planters faced many of the problems which tobacco planters had to meet: (1) diminishing fertility of the land; (2) rising costs of production; (3) emigration of planters to virgin lands, which provided increasing competition for markets; (4) declining prices resulting from overproduction; and (5) rationalization of planting methods in the older regions and subsequently in the newer planting communities. Cotton's special difficulty was the ease with which it could be grown on different soils in the region extending from North Carolina to Arkansas and from Georgia into the black prairie of Texas. Consequently, too many farmers came to depend on this crop. Settlers moving from North Carolina to Tennessee and Arkansas and those migrating from Georgia and South Carolina to Alabama, Mississippi, Louisiana, and Texas carried with them their experience in cotton planting and immediately set about reproducing

[23] Demaree, *The American Agricultural Press*, pp. 393 ff.
[24] J. Dickson Smith, ed., *A Practical Treatise on Agriculture to Which Is Added the Author's published Letters by David Dickson* (Macon, Ga.: J. W. Burke and Company, 1870), p. 241. It is difficult to determine what part is by Smith and what part by Dickson, for the editor has taken liberties with the original that are not easy to understand. Dickson's eulogy was apparently accepted as trustworthy by the editors of the *Dictionary of American Biography* and by Liberty Hyde Bailey in *Cyclopedia of American Horticulture*, despite its uncritical appraisal. For an account of James Hammond's efforts to improve production in the forties on his extensive plantations in South Carolina, see Robert G. Tucker, "James H. Hammond as an Agriculturist," *Furman Studies, Bulletin* of Furman University, Vol. XXXIV, No. 4 (Winter, 1951), 32 ff.; Flanders, *Plantation Slavery*, pp. 90–92.

the system they had known in their native state. By 1860 the cotton economy had spread thinly over a vast area. The crop of the three gulf states—Mississippi, Alabama, and Louisiana—exceeded that of Georgia, and the crop of each these states as well as that of Texas and of Arkansas was greater than South Carolina's. Between 1815 and 1859 the cotton yield increased from 208,986 bales to 4,541,285 bales of four hundred pounds each. Only sharply reduced prices could enable the market to absorb this tremendous supply. Gone were the days of fifteen-cent cotton. When the price plummeted to below five cents in 1842 and 1844, disaster was imminent for many.

A favorite remedy for planters' distress was to reduce purchases of corn, pork, beef, horses, and mules from the upper Mississippi Valley and of manufactured goods from the Northeast. It was considered "the acme of plantation management to buy no articles which are required by the negroes or in the working of the estate," concluded Robert Russell after visiting a number of large cotton plantations in Mississippi.[25] "Buy neither bread nor meat nor anything that can be made on the place" was the admonition of an Alabama planter. The planter in the black belt wanted to produce at least all the corn, pork, beef, and meal needed by the slaves in their quarters and by the white folks in the big house—at most everything used on the plantations except iron, coffee, and salt.[26]

Noah B. Cloud and Martin W. Philips, two of the Deep South's ablest agricultural reformers, denied that the section was producing too much cotton or that to reduce the amount would improve the price. They took a more moderate position in arguing that more grain, bacon, mules, and wool should be raised. To them diversification and the raising of livestock were essential to maintaining soil fertility. Cloud denied that cotton was king. Corn and hogs were the true kings, and "so long as we continue to enrich the citizens of 'Porkopolis' and kindred hotbeds of abolitionism from our abundance, they will consider a few flattering epithets cheap bids for our favors."[27] Other planters favored legislation to stop the importation of slaves from the older states on the theory that to continue to

[25] Robert Russell, *North America: Its Agriculture and Climate* (Edinburgh: Adam & Charles Black, 1857).
[26] Jordan, *Hugh Davis*, p. 30; Plantation Journal of John Henry Dent, 1850, University of Alabama Archives; Colonel Claiborne in Natchez *Free Trader*, quoted in *South Western Farmer*, I (September 9, 1842), 5. These efforts at self-sufficiency were made with the knowledge, at least on the part of some, that they could not be justified economically.—*Southern Cultivator*, XI (February, 1853), 59. Charles S. Sydnor, *A Gentleman of the Old Natchez Region: Benjamin L. C. Wailes* (Durham, N. C.: Duke University Press, 1938), p. 100, seems to have agreed with the Southern regionalists that they should have produced as much corn and other foodstuffs as conditions permitted.
[27] *American Cotton Planter*, I (January, 1853), 20–21, 23; *American Cotton Planter*, New Series, II (February, 1858), 60.

import would make them free of slavery and hence incline them to join politically with the abolitionists. They also argued that the purchase of slaves was draining the lower South of funds and leaving planters heavily in debt.[28] The abler and more successful planters seem to have thought that they could beat the low prices by enlarging the scope of their operations either by larger individual plantations or by establishing a number of plantations on which they could try out their business methods.

ATTITUDES OF THE LARGE COTTON PLANTER

Low prices, while leading to some attempt at diversification and self-sufficiency, did little to discourage continued rapid expansion of cotton production but contributed to the enlargement of the scale of operations in cotton planting.[29] In each of the five public-land states—Alabama, Arkansas, Florida, Louisiana, and Mississippi—the average size of farms and plantations increased substantially in the fifties, as the table indicates, while in the United States as a whole the average size of farms diminished. In Texas, the trend was toward smaller units of operation, but the average size was still, in 1860, larger than that in any other state.[30]

NUMBER, ACREAGE, AND AVERAGE SIZE OF FARMS, 1850–1860

State	Number		Acreage		Average size	
	1850	1860	1850	1860	1850	1860
Alabama	41,964	55,128	12,137,681	19,104,545	289	346
Arkansas	17,758	39,004	2,598,216	9,574,006	146	245
Florida	4,304	6,568	1,595,289	2,920,228	371	444
Louisiana	13,422	17,328	4,989,043	9,298,576	372	536
Mississippi	33,960	42,840	10,490,449	15,839,684	309	370
Texas	12,198	42,891	11,496,339	25,344,028	942	591
United States					203	194

Source: *Eighth Census of the United States, 1860, Agriculture* (Washington, D. C.: Government Printing Office, 1864), p. 222.

[28] *Planters' Banner and Louisiana Agriculturist*, November 4, 1847; May 11, 1848; June 20 and February 6, 1851; *Natchez Weekly Courier*, January 24, February 13, 27, March 14, May 2, 9, 23, 30, June 6, and December 4, 1849.

[29] *Southern Cultivator*, X (September, 1852), 285.

[30] *Eighth Census of the United States, 1860, Agriculture*, p. 222. The acreage figures are somewhat deceptive because they include both unimproved and improved land. In a state like Texas only 10 per cent of the total land in farms was improved, whereas in Illinois 63 per cent was improved. All the cotton states had a low percentage of improved land in farms in contrast to the northern states, which, with the exception of the new western commonwealths of Iowa, Kansas, and Minnesota, had a low percentage of unimproved land.

Alabama boasted 696 farms and plantations of 1,000 acres or more, and 2,016 of 500 to 1,000 acres. The greater part of these large holdings were in the fertile black belt of south central Alabama, where the average size of farms ranged as high as 770 acres. Here were three plantations having cotton yields of more than a thousand bales each in 1859.

SIZE OF FARMS IN HIGHEST YIELDING COUNTIES IN ALABAMA, 1860

	No. farms	Farms of over 1,000 acres	Farms of 500–999 acres	Average-size farms	Cotton yield in bales of 400 lbs.
Dallas	711	55	138	770	63,410
Marengo	778	62	104	744	62,428
Montgomery	800	60	109	690	58,880
Greene	859	67	99	651	57,858
Average yield of cotton in 52 Alabama counties					19,037

Source: Computed from *Eighth Census of the United States, Agriculture, passim.*

The average production of cotton on the 131 largest plantations in Alabama in 1859 was 525 bales, the gross value of which was $22,000.[31]

Probably the greatest concentration in landownership and cotton production was to be found in the delta country of Mississippi, Louisiana, and Arkansas. A *Picayune* statement that Colonel Joseph Bond of Macon, Georgia, had raised 2,100 bales of cotton in 1858, making him the largest producer in the state,[32] stimulated the *Free Trader* of Natchez to say that there were a half-dozen planters in both Louisiana and Mississippi who had far exceeded this amount. Among these great planters were A. V. Davis of Concordia Parish; Levin R. Marshall, Natchez banker who either owned or had a share in more than 25,000 acres in Louisiana, Mississippi, and Arkansas, and is here listed as a 4,000-bale planter; John Routh, once called the "largest cotton planter in the world," who, after settling much land on his children, still produced in excess of 3,500 bales; Frederick Stanton of Natchez, who raised 2,800 bales; and Dr. Stephen Duncan, 4,000 bales. Mention is also made of Samuel Davis and Francis Surget, who raised from 3,000 to 5,000 bales.[33]

[31] Multiple ownerships in different counties would doubtless increase the concentration of ownership and production of cotton. The three largest productions were 1,250 bales by J. H. Brown in Sumter County, 1,250 bales by Isaac Croom in Marengo County, and 1,150 bales by William Jones & Son in Green County. The largest individual holding of farmland in any one county was 14,000 acres of R. Prewit of Lawrence County.—Computed from original census schedules for 1860 in the State Historical Department, Montgomery, Ala.

[32] Upon the death of Joseph Bond in 1859 his 497 slaves sold for $474,444, or an average of $958.64 each. One slave brought $2,950.—Phillips, *American Negro Slavery,* p. 374.

[33] *New Orleans Picayune,* February 19, 1859.

At the time of his death in 1859 Stanton owned 444 slaves and had five large plantations in Louisiana and a small holding in Mississippi containing 15,109 acres. Three of his plantations in 1859 turned out 3,054 bales of cotton worth $122,000. The probate records of this large estate show that the Liverpool factor to whom two shipments of cotton were consigned debited substantial sums for "false packed cotton" that was unmerchantable, because it contained quantities of leaf and gin balls.[34]

Stephen Duncan may well rate as the greatest planter and slave-owner in the United States in the fifties. Long involved in banking and financial affairs in Natchez, he had built up a large estate including landed property in the North, extensive investments in northern railroads, and six cotton and two sugar plantations. His income in 1850 from the sale of cotton and sugar, after the deduction of the factor's commission and transportation, insurance, lighterage, and other charges, was $169,354. In 1851 he had 1,018 slaves on his eight plantations in addition to 23 at his residence near Natchez.[35] Despite his Whiggish views about self-sufficiency, Duncan found it impossible, or inadvisable, to provide all the foodstuffs used on his plantations. In 1857 he purchased 135 barrels of pork and 7 barrels of flour for "Carlisle." The following year he bought 135 barrels of pork, 13 bags of peas, 34 sacks of corn, numerous potatoes, eggs, 2 barrels of flour, and 1 barrel of whiskey. In 1859 he bought 936 bushels of corn, 12 bushels of oats, 135 barrels of pork, 1 barrel of lard oil, 252 bushels of corn, 12 barrels of flour, and 1 barrel of whiskey.

The Isaac Franklin plantations in West Feliciana Parish, Louisiana, were large and productive. Franklin's wealth had been made in the slave trade from which he gradually withdrew in his later life and established himself as a gentleman planter. The inventory of his estate in 1846 showed six plantations in Louisiana which contained 8,687 acres, and one in Tennessee of 2,000 acres. The 700 slaves on the Franklin plantations produced on the average 1,120 bales of cotton worth approximately $36,000 during each of the three years for which there are records, 1847, 1848, and 1849. Fuel wood and lumber brought an additional income of $12,000 to $25,000 each year. A writer in the Southern Cultivator in 1852, impressed with the magnitude of operations on the Franklin estate, commented on the large steam sawmill and its thirty mechanics, the six overseers, the general agent, the bookkeeper, two physicians, a head carpenter, a tinner,

[34] The records of the estate are in Box 173, Chancery Court, Adams County, Natchez.

[35] Taken from the Journal of Stephen Duncan, 1851–1861, Louisiana State University Archives. "Net proceeds" generally meant the amount the planter was allowed by the factor for the sale of the cotton, with all costs of transportation, freight, insurance, fees, and lighterage deducted. The 1850 figure for net proceeds undoubtedly included the amount received from the sale of both cotton and sugar.

a ditcher, and a preacher who were employed on the Louisiana plantations.[36]

The Surget family of Natchez, through shrewd land purchases, smart management, and intermarriage with the richest families, extended their sway over scores of thousands of acres of cotton land in Arkansas, Mississippi, and Louisiana. In the second generation of the family's stay in Natchez, Jacob, Francis, James, and two sisters, Charlotte Bingamen and Jane White, erected numerous plantations on both sides of the Mississippi, purchased some 50,000 acres in Arkansas, and pushed their total holdings to well over 90,000 acres.[37] In addition to his Arkansas land, James Surget had eight or nine plantations in Louisiana and Mississippi. On six plantations he had 453 slaves, and on five of them his executors produced 1,470 bales of cotton in 1855, which brought $38,174.[38] One writer has stated that James Surget's only son, and heir to half his estate, had 1,000 slaves in 1861, but this is doubtless an exaggeration.[39] Francis Surget seems to have been the most successful member of the family. Called by J. F. H. Claiborne "the most extensive and successful planter ever known in Mississippi," Francis Surget recognized, as too many other planters did not, that current methods of cultivating the land so that the cotton rows ran up and down the hill, permitted the runoff to carry away the topsoil in suspension. To combat this he introduced horizontal plowing.[40] On Surget's 9,969 acres of land in six plantations his executors in 1856, found 813 slaves, that with land and other property brought the value of his estate to a million dollars.[41] Jacob Surget, the third brother, continued to own a large cotton plantation after he moved to New York.

Rich, domineering, and arrogant, the Surgets were not well regarded by their less successful neighbors. When the planters of the back lands tried to get a road built through a Surget plantation to Natchez so that cotton could be shipped by river to New Orleans, they were stopped by a court injunction. At a public meeting the aggrieved planters expressed regret at the action and resolved that it resulted from Jacob Surget's

[36] Stephenson, *Isaac Franklin*, pp. 157 ff.; *Southern Cultivator*, X (August, 1852), 227.

[37] Catherine Surget left an estate of 6,587 acres to her children. To this Francis and James added, by purchase from the United States and from Louisiana, 29,096 acres. Additional purchases from other sources brought their holdings to 85,000 acres. The Jacob Surget, Bingamen, White lands would bring total holdings to 90,000 acres. —Weaver, *Mississippi Farmers*, p. 108.

[38] Material relating to the estate of James Surget is in Box 163, Chancery Court, Adams County, Natchez.

[39] Matilda Gresham, *Life of Walter Quintin Gresham* (2 vols.; Chicago: Rand McNally & Company, 1919), I, 253.

[40] John Francis Hamtramck Claiborne, *Mississippi as a Province, Territory and State* (Jackson: Power & Barksdale, 1880), p. 141.

[41] Probate Real-Estate Record, Chancery Court, Adams County, Natchez.

"disconnection with, and disregard for the permanent improvement of the country." [42] It is very probable that the Natchez *Mississippi Free Trader* had the Surget family in mind as well as some of the other Whig planters when, in arguing for better roads to bring the trade of the small interior planters to Natchez, it said:

They would crowd our streets with fresh and healthy supplies of home productions, and the proceeds would be expended *here* among our merchants, grocers and artisans. The large planters—the one-thousand-bale planters—do not contribute most to the prosperity of Natchez. They, for the most part, sell their cotton in Liverpool; buy their wines in London or Havre; their negro clothing in Boston; their plantation implements and supplies in Cincinnati; and their groceries and fancy articles in New Orleans. The small planter has not the credit nor the business connections to do this; he requires the proceeds of his crop as soon as it can be sold; and he purchases and pays for, cash in hand, almost every necessary wanted during the year, in the same market where he sells his cotton. The small planter hoards no money in these times; he lends none at usurious rates of interest; he buys up the property of no unfortunate debtor for a few dollars; but he lays it all out for the purchase of supplies, and thus directly contributes his mite to the prosperity of our city. [43]

In Arkansas Francis Surget came in for attack for holding unimproved and unused for nineteen years "vast bodies of land" which he would neither sell nor lease. "Rich as Croesus; a nabob of Natchez, Mississippi; making his five or six thousand bales of cotton a year; he appears to care nothing for the wants or desires of the people of Arkansas, and hangs on to his lands (which we understand really cost him nothing or a mere nominal sum) as though his salvation depended upon their being kept back from cultivation." His "dog in the manger" attitude was condemned and the press was urged to speak out and force him to sell or improve his lands, which, being vacant and unimproved, retarded the whole region's growth. [44]

The attitude·of the small planter toward the large is well illustrated in Olmsted's *A Journey in the Back Country.* He quotes a small planter near Natchez as expressing thorough dislike of the owners of great plantations and numerous slaves:

Big plantations, sir, nothing else—aristocrats; swell-heads I call them, sir— nothing but swell-heads. . . .

· · · · ·

[42] Natchez *Southern Galaxy,* January 8, 1829.
[43] *Mississippi Free Trader,* April 14, 1842.
[44] *Memphis Eagle and Enquirer* in *Arkansas State Gazette and Democrat,* February 9, 16, 1855. Francis Surget had entered 11,000 acres in the Batesville district in Arkansas in July, 1836.

Must have ice for their wine, you see, or they'd die; and so they have to live in Natchez or New Orleans; a good many of them live in New Orleans.

．　．　．　．　．

You can know their children as far off as you can see them—young swell-heads! . . . They do want so bad to look as if they weren't made of the same clay as the rest of God's creation.

Olmsted found the "immoral, vulgar, and ignorant newly-rich" more common among the wealthy planters than among men of "refinement and cultivation." [45]

Small-farmer and planter feelings against the very wealthy planters for their snobbishness, their aristocratic ways, their opposition to expenditures for roads and to public aid to railroads,[46] and their withdrawal of lands from development, threatened to come to a head in the Mississippi legislature in 1852.[47] In the discussion of a bill to prohibit the introduction of slaves into the state it was contended that large planters would be able to evade such restrictions, but the small man would be barred by it from further developing his property and acquiring a competence. In the "most important debate of the session" the rich planters, especially those who did not live on their plantations, were called "public nuisances," and a move was under way to have the owners brought before grand juries for indictment as such.[48] On the other hand, the larger planters had no affection for the small farmers. Olmsted quotes a planter as calling the small farmers in his neighborhood "lazy vagabonds, doing but little work, and spending much time in shooting, fishing, and play." He had already bought some of them out and was willing to pay the remainder two or three times the value of their property to rid himself of their presence.[49]

The planter-aristocrats, though small in number, were well entrenched in political parties; in national, state, and local governments; and in the press and the church, and could watch with unconcern and disdain

[45] Frederick Law Olmsted, *A Journey in the Back Country* (New York: Mason Brothers, 1860), p. 27; Horace Smith Fulkerson says the great planters "could illy brook contradiction and opposition from their equals. Indeed they were slow to regard any as their equals except those of their own class."—*Random Recollections of Early Days in Mississippi* (Vicksburg: Vicksburg Printing and Publishing Company, 1885), p. 15. For an unpleasant picture of "cotton snobs," see D. R. Hundley, *Social Relations in Our Southern States* (New York: Henry B. Price, 1860), pp. 163 ff.

[46] Regarding a move to secure aid for the construction of the Greensboro, Newbern, and Woodville Railroad, the Greensboro *Alabama Beacon*, October 29, 1852, said that the small farmers would doubtless favor giving assistance but the large planters would not.

[47] Olmsted, *A Journey in the Back Country*, p. 33, quoted a small planter as saying that the great planters bought "every inch of the land" around Natchez to keep poor men away.

[48] Jackson correspondent in *Natchez Weekly Courier*, May 10, 1852.

[49] Olmsted, *op. cit.*, p. 673.

these scattered evidences of unrest and dissatisfaction among other classes.

In the fifties the number of large farms in Mississippi was greatly increasing, and the number of small farms was sharply declining. In representative counties in the richly productive delta-loess area of Mississippi, Herbert Weaver shows that farms having less than 50 acres of improved land declined from 19 to 7 per cent; farms having 50 to 99 acres of improved land declined from 15 to 8 per cent; and farms having from 100 to 199 acres of improved land declined from 21 to 15 per cent between 1850 and 1860. Increases are noted for all sizes of improved farms above 200 acres, but the big increase was in farms (plantations) having over 500 acres of improved land, the percentage rising from 12 to 26. Economic conditions, the advantages of large-scale production, and the greater capital needs of the highly commercialized agriculture of the principal cotton counties were all working in the direction of squeezing out many of the small farmers or were enabling some of the ablest of them to enlarge their operations, and were creating greater concentration in landownership and production of cotton.[50] Small farmers continued to exist and to flourish, even in the midst of competition from the large planters, but they held a diminishing proportion of the fertile land.

Toward the end of the ante-bellum period, cottonseed, which had earlier been discarded as useless or spread over land as a mulch and fertilizer, was coming to have value for its oil and for the cake left after the extrusion of the oil. A ton of seed which brought $13 at the factory in New Orleans yielded 30–40 gallons of oil worth from 60 to 80 cents a gallon and 700 to 800 pounds of cake worth $40 a ton. England was taking a considerable amount of the cottonseed cake for food for livestock. The oil was used for illumination and for soap. Only planters on navigable streams could take advantage of the market for seed.[51]

COTTON MARKETING

Common to all planters, large and small, was the problem of marketing their staple. Since 64 per cent of the American cotton went to English manufacturers and 29 per cent to manufacturers in New England, New York, and New Jersey, there developed a highly specialized group of brokers, factors, and merchants dealing in cotton at New Orleans, Mobile, Charleston, and Savannah in the cotton area and in New York, Boston, and London.[52] Planters shipped their cotton to factors in one of these

[50] Weaver, *Mississipi Farmers*, p. 72 and elsewhere, comes to different conclusions.

[51] *New Orleans Picayune*, February 24, 1859; *Augusta Evening Dispatch*, July 14, 1860.

[52] Israel D. Andrews reported that 64 per cent of the cotton crop of 1849 went abroad, mostly to England; 29 per cent was used by factories in the United States;

ports, and the factors arranged for storage, insurance, freight, drayage, weighing, and selling. The factor, or commission merchant, took commissions on all these transactions and set up a credit on which the planter could draw. The factor also purchased and shipped goods for the planter, advanced him credit, but insisted that all the planter's cotton be consigned to him.

Inevitably there developed friction between planters and factors over the quality and weight of the cotton, the numerous commissions, prices, the factor's control over the crop, and interest charges. Respectable planters were accused of fraudulent cotton packing, of the "most glaring and unwarrantable trickery and deception." A Memphis paper observed in 1854 that hardly a day passed without some new instance of this disgraceful practice coming to light that had injurious effects upon all planters. Brokers' charges that planters were guilty of false packing, labeling, and weighing were met by planters' accusations that factors and other middlemen were robbing them of a fair return on their cotton. New Orleans cotton dealers were ungrateful tyrants swindling planters of a million dollars a year, said a Mississippian. He urged that every effort be made to sell cotton direct to consumers. Another writer urged that planters use every possible publicity method of conveying to the public the idea that the approaching crop was small by exaggerating adversities and commenting upon the shift from cotton to other crops; at the same time the planters should pick only good cotton and let the poorer quality go unpicked.[53] Planters' grievances, which were extensively aired in the newspapers and agricultural papers, contributed, with abundant crops and low prices, to the calling of a number of planters' conventions between 1845 and 1860. Control of production, price fixing, and the establishment of a monopolistic marketing depot to avoid alleged exactions of the middleman were proposed but little was accomplished. Improved prices were most important in making the planters more conservative in such matters. The factor system received abundant attention at the time, but its ills were considerably exaggerated.[54]

---

6 per cent was consumed in domestic (home) manufacture; and the balance was destroyed by fire or withheld from market.—*Senate Executive Document*, No. 112, 32 Cong., 1 Sess., 1853, p. 816.

[53] *Southern Planter*, I (April, 1842), 7–8; *South Western Farmer*, I (August 26, 1842), 194–195; *New Orleans Bulletin* in *Natchez Courier*, August 20, 1851; *London Chronicle* in *New Orleans Price Current*, May 15, 1852; *Avalanche and Memphis Appeal* in *Southern Cultivator*, XVII (May, 1859), 159; *Memphis Whig* in Helena, Ark., *Southern Shield*, November 11, 1854.

[54] Gray, *History of Agriculture in the Southern United States*, II, 711 ff., 923 ff. The most recent treatment is Ralph W. Haskins, "Planter and Cotton Factor in the Old South: Some Areas of Friction," *Agricultural History*, XXIX (January, 1955), 1–14.

THE ECONOMICS OF SLAVERY

For well over a century the economics of slavery has interested travelers, abolitionists, defenders of slavery, and historians. Much of the writing has been polemical, characterized by sloppy economic analysis and generalizations from sparse data, and reveals an anxiety to present slavery in the best—or worst—possible colors. Yet, both abolitionists and defenders of slavery were convinced that the institution was wasteful, inefficient, and unprofitable. Early twentieth-century historians accepted their arguments while disregarding obvious and well-known facts that invalidate their conclusions. Most of these analyses neglected the capital gains from the rising value of slaves and land in newly opened areas, the profits from rearing slave children, and the high return cotton planters received from selling into the Deep South the surplus slaves of older communities or from rearing their own slaves in the newer areas.

There are other evidences of miscalculation in the efforts of pro-slavery writers of the ante-bellum period, and of historians who have followed their arguments, to prove that slavery was economically unprofitable. On most plantations, particularly on the larger ones, some slaves were used for noneconomic purposes, such as household servants, maids, body servants, coachmen, and gardeners. Stephen Duncan, for example, employed 23 of his 1,041 slaves at his show place, Auburn, in Natchez.[55] These and many other slaves on other plantations had nothing to do with raising cotton, sugar cane, or tobacco but are included in the total number of slaves and in their valuations when analyses of profits and losses are made.

Slavery is blamed for fastening the one-crop system on the South, with its destructive effects on the soil. It is true that planters and farmers, anxious to enlarge their operations and acquire more slaves, became tied to the one-crop system; so also did the small farmer who had no slaves but tried to make a living on poorer land by raising tobacco, cotton, flax, or hemp. It was the cupidity of the planters, not slavery, that was at fault. Furthermore, where some broke away from the one-crop system or experimented with fertilizers, horizontal plowing, seed selection, and "book farming," it was invariably the slaveowner, so far as the records indicate.

The high prices slaves brought in the prosperous fifties tended to drain bondsmen to the sugar and cotton areas of Alabama, Mississippi, and Louisiana; but to maintain that the sale of slaves by planters in the

---

[55] Journal of Stephen Duncan, 1851–1861, Louisiana State University Archives. Mrs. Myrtie Long Candler tells of fifteen house and personal servants in her family in "Reminiscences of Life in Georgia During the 1850's and 1860's," *Georgia Historical Quarterly*, XXXIII (June, 1949), 110 ff.; Smedes, *Memorials of a Southern Planter*, *passim*.

Old Dominion for the current high price was a loss to the region is questionable. The *New Orleans Picayune*, a major spokesman for the cotton interests of the South, was convinced that the inflated prices of the fifties, as long as they coincided with equally favorable cotton prices, not only were good for the region but were also good for all the South. Consequently, it saw no reason to favor the reopening of the slave trade.[56]

To sum up the views of the most recent students of slavery, the following conclusions appear valid: [57] Throughout the entire South, whether in the slave-rearing states of Virginia and Maryland and North and South Carolina or in the newer centers of plantation economy, slavery was profitable. This is not to say that agriculture in Virginia as practiced by the planters was altogether profitable in itself, but it was made so by the profits from the sale of slaves into the new South, where the demand was active, the price high. The rise in the price of slaves, even in the years of great expansion of cotton and sugar cultivation in the fifties, did not outdistance rising productivity, for the ratio of yield per man in the new South was high. Finally, there is no material evidence that slavery or cotton planting had reached its maximum development, as is shown by the enormously greater production within the same slave states in the twentieth century. One cannot accept the notion that slavery was doomed to early extinction.

[56] *New Orleans Picayune*, May 20 and June 7, 17, 21, 1859.

[57] Gray, *History of Agriculture in the Southern United States*, II, 946, and elsewhere; Kenneth M. Stampp, *The Peculiar Institution: Slavery in the Ante-Bellum South* (New York: Alfred A. Knopf, Inc., 1956), pp. 383 ff.; Alfred H. Conrad and John R. Meyer, "The Economics of Slavery in the Ante Bellum South," *Journal of Political Economy*, LXVI (April, 1958), 95 ff.

CHAPTER VIII

Grain Farming

GRAIN production and livestock raising were the basis of agriculture in the North and the Northwest and of many farms in the South. Corn and wheat, cattle, hogs, and sheep provided the principal source of income for the small farmer, whether he was engaged in near-subsistence farming on the frontier or in highly developed commercial farming in the Genesee Valley of New York or in southeastern Pennsylvania.

WHEAT RAISING

Wheat was raised in every state; except for the tobacco and cotton areas of the South, no other crop was so useful to the farmer as a source of cash.[1] In New England it was raised only in very limited quantities as part of a four- or five-year rotation. The section failed to supply its own needs and was obliged to import wheat from surplus-producing states. Efforts of planters in Mississippi and Louisiana to raise their own wheat and make their section independent of supplies from the upper Mississippi Valley also failed. In New York, Pennsylvania, and Ohio, settlers who were buying land on credit from the Pulteney estate, the Holland Land Company, or the Connecticut and Ohio Land Companies, or who were saving to purchase their pre-emption rights from the United States, had no recourse except to raise wheat for their cash crop. Landlords like the Rennselaers and Wadsworths further assured the widespread planting of wheat by insisting on that grain for rental payments.[2] Once begun, and until marketing and transportation conditions changed, it was difficult

[1] C. R. Ball, et al., "Wheat Production and Marketing" (U. S. Department of Agriculture, Yearbook, 1921; Washington, D. C.: Government Printing Office, 1922), pp. 77–160.
[2] Neil Adams McNall, An Agricultural History of the Genesee Valley, 1790–1860 (Philadelphia: University of Pennsylvania Press, 1952), pp. 60 ff.

for farmers, especially those in debt or those anxious to make capital improvements, to free themselves from dependence upon this crop. The first pioneers in New York, Pennsylvania, and Ohio put their land into wheat, which remained the major crop until parasites, plant diseases, soil depletion, rising land values, and competition from grain produced on virgin soils farther west forced its abandonment as a principal crop in the older areas.

Wheat fitted admirably into the farmer's economy. It was everywhere in demand, brought a price that justified hauling it considerable distances to mill or market, and kept well. No great amount of capital was necessary, tools were primitive and some could be made by hand. No elaborate barns were required; floor space for threshing and winnowing and storage bins sufficed.

Heavy, even strenuous labor was necessary in the production of wheat, but only for a short period after the land was cleared. Most difficult and time consuming in wooded areas was the clearing of the land. This extended over almost a generation before a farm was fully developed. In the prairies or oak openings, once the grass sod was broken, careless farmers might run the harrow over the land to stir up the soil, or plow shallow and harrow, then sow the seed and harrow it in or drag the field. Drills were coming into use by the thirties, but sowing broadcast was still much the more common method of seeding. Although the sickle was still in use, the cradle had displaced it on the larger operations and continued to be the principal means of reaping the grain until the fifties, by which time the reaper was being adopted, particularly in the Middle West. Because wheat, when ripe, could not stand for long before it began to shed its grain, it had to be harvested at the right time or the loss would be heavy. At this point all members of a farm family would be pressed into service. Some farmers planted wheat beyond their capacity to harvest and depended on migratory labor to aid them in reaping. When his grain had been cut and shocked, the farmer could breathe a sigh of relief; one of his hardest and most demanding tasks of the year had been accomplished.[3]

For threshing, the flail was still used; even oxen were employed to tread out the grain. On the larger wheat farms in the old Northwest, threshing machines were beginning to be used, and crude winnowing machines were replacing the simpler but awkward and time-consuming devices for separating the wheat from chaff, dirt, and weed seeds. Weed seeds were a particular nuisance. Cockle seed could not easily be separated by winnowing and yet, if found in wheat intended for the mill, it lowered the price of the grain and, if not separated, of the flour. Chess or cheat looked like growing wheat. Its seed was difficult to screen out, and

[3] John Douglas, *The Complete Practical Farmer* (New York: 1835), p. 96.

it was found so commonly with wheat, the production of which it cut sharply, that many thought it was a transmutation of wheat. This notion was discredited as early as 1820, but many farmers clung to it as late as the fifties.[4]

The first concern of the ordinary small farmer was to produce the necessary wheat for the use of his family and his livestock; the second, to raise a surplus to enable him to make payments on his land or mortgage, or to purchase tools and household equipment. Isolated farmers had to grind their own grain, using the same primitive mortar and pestle that had come down from ancient times. Better-located farmers transported their grain on the backs of horses—or mules—over crude trails to the nearest gristmill, where they paid a royalty to the miller for the service. In addition, millers acquired surplus grain, by barter, for shipping elsewhere, or made it into flour for shipment. The miller became a key figure in rural economy, acting as a manufacturer, buyer or middleman, and shipper.[5]

Primitive gristmills with one or more run of stones were often erected on streams and small creeks that could provide only sufficient water to turn the wheels for short periods. When there was no water power cumbersome horse- or ox-powered gristmills were constructed, the tolls of which ranged from one fourth to one sixth of the wheat and one eighth of the corn. A Wisconsin farmer protested against a one-eighth toll on wheat milling which, combined with 12 per cent interest on his debt, he thought too exacting.[6] Larger steam- or water-driven mills which ground the grain and bolted the flour gave from twenty-five to thirty-three pounds of flour for a bushel of wheat.[7] In New York State the toll on wheat milling was commonly 10 per cent, but as much as 22 per cent was taken by some millers. It was suggested that the toll should be limited by law to 10 per cent.[8] The Census of 1840 recorded 4,354 grist or flour mills for the entire country, most of which were small outfits whose total annual grist would not be more than enough to meet the needs of the farmers in their vicinity.

[4] *Plough Boy*, I (March 4, 1820), 316; William H. Brewer, "Report on the Cereal Production of the United States" in *Tenth Census of the United States* (Washington, D. C.: Government Printing Office, 1883), III, 463

[5] Lewis E. Atherton, *The Pioneer Merchant in Mid-America* (University of Missouri *Studies*, Vol. XIV, No. 2; Columbia: University of Missouri, 1939), pp. 90 ff.

[6] David Thomas, *Travels through the Western Country in the Summer of 1816* . . . (Auburn, N. Y.: David Rumsey, 1819), pp. 233–234; *Wisconsin Farmer*, XI (November, 1859), 397. For a contemporary description of the ox-powered gristmill, see William Oliver, *Eight Months in Illinois* (Chicago: W. M. Hill, 1924), p. 125. A reconstruction of the ox-driven gristmill may be seen in New Salem, Ill.

[7] *Prairie Farmer*, XII (April, 1852), 190; Thomas Senior Berry, *Western Prices before 1861* (*Harvard Economic Studies*, Vol. LXXIV; Cambridge, Mass.: Harvard University Press, 1943), p. 160.

[8] *Cultivator*, V (March–October, 1838), 12, 74, 139.

Larger modern mills were located in Baltimore, Rochester, and Buffalo, the principal flour manufacturing cities. Rochester alone boasted twenty-one mills, whose annual output of flour in the late thirties was 500,000 barrels, and 700,000 in 1848.[9]

TRANSPORTATION PROBLEMS

With a bushel of wheat weighing 60 pounds, the load that could be transported by horse or slow-moving oxen over trails or dirt roads was not large. Oats and possibly hay for a number of days had to be carried; otherwise the draft animals had to live off the land on the way and, if through developed areas, at considerable expense. The experience of three men who hauled thirty bushels of wheat to Chicago from Lake County, Indiana, with seven yoke of oxen illustrates the difficulty of providing for forage on the way. Twice the oxen broke into cultivated fields of pumpkins, corn, and cabbages, causing damage that called for compensation. As a result, the nine-day trip involved greater expenses than the return from the sale of the wheat.[10] Over more primitive trails pioneers would carry a "horse load" of three bushels to the mill for grinding.[11] In the twenties and thirties farmers in central Indiana hauled loads of twenty-five bushels a distance of seventy-five miles to the Ohio River, the trip going and coming taking about ten days.[12]

The arduous task of hauling wheat from Lancaster County, Pennsylvania, and from the Genesee country of New York contributed to major improvements in transportation. The Conestoga wagon, with its wide beam, its depth, its bottom slanting toward the middle, and its broad wheels, was designed to carry heavy loads of wheat over the dirt roads from the back country to Philadelphia. A principal argument in behalf of the proposed Erie Canal was that its construction would halve or even quarter the cost of transporting wheat from the interior of New York to market and thereby double the return the farmer received for his crop. When the canal was completed, wheat was one of the principal commodities it carried east. Though upstate New York landowners gave vigor-

[9] Blake McKelvey, *Rochester: The Water-Power City, 1812–1854* (Cambridge, Mass.: Harvard University Press, 1945), p. 209; James F. W. Johnston, *Notes on North America: Agricultural, Economical and Social* (2 vols.; Edinburgh: William Blackwood & Sons, 1851), I, 204

[10] Leon M. Gordon, "Settlements in Northwestern Indiana, 1830–1860," *Indiana Magazine of History*, XLII (March, 1951), 48.

[11] Morris Birkbeck, *Notes on a Journey in America from the Coast of Virginia to the Territory of Illinois* (Philadelphia: Caleb Richardson, 1817), p. 120.

[12] Howard Johnson, *A Home in the Woods: Oliver Johnson's Reminiscences of Early Marion County* (*Publications* of the Indiana Historical Society, Vol. XVI, No. 2; Indianapolis: Indiana Historical Society, 1951), pp. 188–194.

ous support to the movement for its construction, farmers subsequently watched with dismay the unexpected flood of wheat which the canal brought into eastern markets from the West. Produced on virgin land that was subject to little or no taxation, this western wheat demoralized farmers in the older communities, who were already struggling with declining fertility, low yields, parasitic infestations, increasing costs, and declining prices.[13]

The wheat country moved steadily west, as is shown in the table, although Pennsylvania German land and Virginia continued to produce wheat profitably.[14]

WHEAT YIELD IN THOUSANDS OF BUSHELS AND IN PARENTHESES, PERCENTAGE OF TOTAL CROP IN LEADING STATES

State	1839	1849	1859
Ohio	16,571 (20)	14,787 (14)	15,119 (9)
Pennsylvania	13,213 (16)	15,367 (15)	13,042 (8)
New York	12,286 (14)	13,121 (13)	8,681 (5)
Virginia	10,109 (12)	11,216 (11)	13,130 (8)
Illinois	3,335 (4)	9,414 (9)	23,837 (14)
Indiana	4,049 (5)	6,214 (6)	16,848 (10)
Wisconsin	—	4,286 (4)	15,657 (9)
United States	84,823	100,485	173,104

Source: Louis Bernard Schmidt, "The Westward Movement of the Wheat Growing Industry in the United States," Iowa Journal of History and Politics, XVII (July, 1920), 399-410.

Ohio farmers, especially those close to navigable rivers or canals or to Lake Erie, where cheap transportation was available, were producing wheat on low-priced land and were able to drive the New York farmer out of wheat and into a more diversified type of farming. States farther west were even more responsible for upsetting farming plans in older areas. By mid-century, centers of wheat production were developing in northern Illinois and adjacent southern Wisconsin; a decade later these areas became the premier wheat regions of the country. By 1860, seven of the

[13] McNall, An Agricultural History of the Genesee Valley, pp. 106 ff. Squatters in the new West had the use of public lands for one or two years before they had to complete their pre-emption entry and take title. Thereafter the now privately owned land was exempt from taxes for an additional five years.

[14] Louis Bernard Schmidt, "The Westward Movement of the Wheat Growing Industry in the United States," Iowa Journal of History and Politics, XVIII (July, 1920), 399. Statistics of production may be found in the Eighth Census of the United States, 1860, Agriculture (Washington, D. C.: Government Printing Office, 1864), passim.

premium wheat-producing counties, with yields exceeding a million bushels, were located in Wisconsin or Illinois. The seventh was Lancaster County, Pennsylvania. The combined yield of eight Wisconsin counties and thirteen Illinois counties was in excess of the entire output of New York, which had been the third-ranking state in 1839 and 1849 but which fell to seventh place in 1859. By 1860, wheat was being produced in Illinois and Wisconsin, with the best of the farm machines then available and on a commercial scale quite unlike that of the older areas.

Before the coming of the railroad, these areas, too, had their transportation problems. A story of wheat hauling from Rock County, Wisconsin, to Racine on Lake Michigan seems scarcely credible. In the fall of 1844 two farmers broke two hundred acres of prairie with the aid of ten yoke of oxen, sowed the land to wheat, and in the spring harvested 5,000 bushels. In one trip they hauled 205 bushels of this wheat in two wagons to Racine—a distance of at least 50 miles—and received 62½ cents a bushel. The load of more than three tons to the wagon on the roads then available must have been a task even for the ten yoke of oxen.[15] William B. Ogden, a major Chicago entrepreneur, reported in 1841 to an eastern client: [16]

> Wheat is coming in wonderfully fast at least 100 to 150 teams daily bringing from 3,500 to 5,000 bushels which seels [sic] at 87 to 90 cts. You never saw more beautiful wheat, the farmers look cheerly & the town is gay & busy. Many teams come from Sangamon Co. from the Wabash, from west of Rock River (Stephenson Co.) & from as far as two hundred miles in all directions.

In Minnesota in the middle of the century "the mean distance" for hauling wheat to the nearest river was 80 miles. The fortunate farmer who had only three days' haul, or six days for the round trip, brought back no great sum, after paying expenses, for his 30 bushels. It was estimated that farmers in Illinois hauling wheat up to 45 miles brought back from 75 to 85 per cent of the gross sales; for greater distances the net was substantially less. The cost of hauling grain, in 1849, from Janesville to Milwaukee, Wisconsin, a distance of 70 miles, was said to be 18 cents a bushel, which cut deeply into the farmer's return. A much higher estimate of the cost of hauling grain by highway was that of Israel D. Andrews in his classic report on the "Trade and Commerce of the British North American Colonies and upon the Trade of the Great Lakes and Rivers." Andrews held that the cost of transportation per ton-mile was fifteen cents, which is very close to a half cent a bushel for each mile. The significance

[15] *Racine Advertiser*, clipped in *Southern Cultivator*, III (November, 1845), 169.
[16] W. B. Ogden, Chicago, August 28, 1841, to Arthur Bronson, Ogden MSS, Chicago Historical Society.

of the railroads in extending the area open to commercial wheat farming
is made clear by the figure of one and a half cents per ton-mile for wheat
hauling as compared with fifteen cents on the highways.[17]

Farmers unfavorably situated with relation to the railhead or lake or
canal port had to devote many days in the late fall and winter, when the
roads were firm, to transporting their grain. Considering the labor and
capital they had invested in their crop, their returns must not have seemed
favorable.[18] Wheat buyers in interior communities away from water or
rail transportation seem to have paid from 50 per cent to 75 per cent of
the price the grain brought in river and lake ports.[19]

In more remote places, distilleries and breweries sprang up to utilize
grain the farmer could scarcely sell otherwise. New York State, for example, had 295 distilleries and breweries located in 48 of its 60 counties
in 1840; Kentucky had 939 distilleries and breweries located in 90 of its
106 counties; Ohio boasted 449 such business enterprises in 58 of its 79
counties. In many instances the counties for which no distilleries are given
are counties for which the statistical presentation in the census is not complete. Much of the whiskey produced in smaller plants was consumed
locally. It was the distilleries in larger mercantile centers like Cincinnati,
Louisville, St. Louis, and New York that produced quantities beyond the
demands of the local market and shipped elsewhere. In 1850, 14,500,000
gallons of whiskey were shipped south from Cincinnati by way of the
Ohio and Mississippi rivers.[20]

In the forties, wheat dominated the planting operations of farmers
within 250 miles of the infant lake port of Chicago almost as completely
as cotton controlled agricultural life in the lower South. Because Chicago
and, a little later, Milwaukee merchants and brokers could pay higher
prices than could dealers in river ports, who had to ship by a circuitous
route to eastern markets, it was inevitable that most of the wheat should
go through those cities. This flow of wheat, which rapidly reached large

[17] John Griffin Thompson, "The Rise and Decline of the Wheat Growing Industry
in Wisconsin," (University of Wisconsin *Bulletin* No. 292, Economics and Political
Science Series, Vol. V; Madison: 1909), p. 16; *Senate Executive Document* No. 112,
32 Cong., 1 Sess., 1853, pp. 380–381.

[18] Oliver Johnson described his experiences in hauling wheat from the Indianapolis
area to Lawrenceburg on the Ohio.—Howard Johnson, *A Home in the Woods,* pp.
222–224; Henrietta Larson, *The Wheat Market and the Farmer in Minnesota* (Co-
lumbia University *Studies in History, Economics and Public Law,* No. 269; New
York: Columbia University Press, 1926), p. 24; Theodore L. Carlson, *The Illinois
Military Tract: A Study of Land Occupation, Utilization and Tenure* (University of
Illinois *Studies in the Social Sciences,* Vol. XXXII, No. 2; Urbana: University of
Illinois Press, 1951), p. 87.

[19] Larson, *op. cit.,* p. 22.

[20] *Sixth Census; or Enumeration of Inhabitants of United States* (Washington,
D. C.: Blair and Rives, 1841), *passim;* Johnston, *Notes on North America,* I, 276.

proportions—more than 8,000,000 bushels went through Chicago in 1859 —permitted the Chicago Board of Trade and the Milwaukee Corn Exchange to establish standards and grades for wheat marketing. It also enabled grain dealers and speculators on occasion to take advantage of farmers either through a combination to depress prices or by downgrading carefully prepared grain.[21] Northern Illinois farmers on at least one occasion—1849—tried to free themselves of dependence on Chicago elevator men so that they could hold their wheat after hauling it to Chicago until the buyers' prices were satisfactory, but it is doubtful that any considerable success was attained.[22]

THE GEOGRAPHIC SHIFT IN WHEAT FARMING

Continued cultivation of wheat in an area brought upon it infestations of insects and diseases which proved disastrous to growing crops and ultimately forced changes in tillage practices. The grubs from the eggs of the Hessian fly, deposited on the stalk, fed on it and weakened it. Black stem rust shriveled the grain, mildew or blight sapped the strength of the growing plant, which then produced a light and almost unsalable crop. Smut led to degeneracy of the grain, the midge or weevil ate the kernels, and the chinch bug sucked the sap of the growing plants. The Hessian fly drove many farmers to despair in the East until it was found that early frosts killed it; thereafter, late planting was followed. Most damaging was the midge. "Wherever it went," says McNall, "wheat yields dropped heavily." Its "inexorable approach was viewed with something akin to terror." Winter killing and drought were additional hazards, though they were not, like the others, related to overplanting and careless cultivation.[23]

Farmers learned that they could control the ravages of insects and disease to some extent by sowing early in the spring or late in the fall, cleaning their seed carefully, destroying barberry bushes, the host of the rust, draining the land, plowing deeply, and cultivating and preparing the soil with greater attention to weed elimination. Most important, they rotated their crops and did not follow wheat with wheat.[24] Despite these

[21] Bessie Louise Pierce, *History of Chicago* (2 vols.; New York: Alfred A. Knopf, Inc., 1937–1940), I, 128–131, and II, 492–493; *Wisconsin Farmer*, VIII (September, 1856), 410–411.

[22] *Prairie Farmer*, IX (December, 1849), 383.

[23] Douglas, *The Complete Practical Farmer*, pp. 100–107; McNall, *An Agricultural History of the Genesee Valley*, p. 152; Ulysses P. Hedrick, *History of Agriculture in the State of New York* (Albany: New York State Agricultural Society, 1933), p. 334. The spread of the wheat midge in the East and its destructive effects are traced in *Eighth Census of the United States, Agriculture*, pp. 33 ff.

[24] *Plough Boy*, I (April 22, 1820), 371.

and other less useful remedies, the ravages of the Hessian fly and the midge were so disastrous and the reduction in yield so great as to force abandonment of wheat as a major crop in many parts of the East by the thirties.

This decline in production is shown in New York census statistics. In 1845 the yield of its eastern counties ranged from a woefully small five bushels per acre in Dutchess County to thirteen in Otsego County. Monroe in western New York was still enjoying good average yields, though its great day was rapidly passing. Aggravating the problem of soil erosion and declining yield in eastern New York was the high rate of tenancy and the tenants' need to produce wheat to meet their rent.[25] Farmers of western New York, in their anxiety "to make money faster, or build fine houses, make fine lawns, drive fine horses, and ride in fine carriages" were accused of drawing upon their capital by overcropping and exhausting their land.[26] When wheat became no longer a profitable crop, farms were abandoned and the families went west.

On the better soils, farmers gradually ceased to depend on wheat. Cattle raising, dairy farming, and cheese making replaced wheat growing. This meant that the land was put into other grains, clover, and grasses instead of wheat. In central New York, John Johnston, a persistent agricultural experimenter, innovator, and scribe, found a remedy for declining yields and parasitic infestation in tiling the land to provide underdrainage, deep plowing, heavy manuring, and cleaning seed wheat. He fed some of his grain to livestock to assure a second profit, bought oil cake for his sheep which altogether assured that he was putting more back into the land than he took off. Through his prolific writings in agricultural journals and the notable success that came to him from his farming operations in Seneca County, Johnston did much to encourage better farming at a time when the average farmer in the East as well as in the West was merely skimming the land.[27] Other farmers improved their farm practices by leaving their wheatland fallow for a season.[28]

Pennsylvania and Virginia maintained their production of wheat throughout the ante-bellum period as a result of the agricultural revival

[25] David Maldwyn Ellis, *Landlords and Farmers in the Hudson-Mohawk Region, 1790–1850* (Ithaca, N. Y.: Cornell University Press, 1946), p. 187; John H. Klippart, *The Wheat Plant* . . . (Cincinnati: Moore, Willstach, Keys & Co., 1860), pp. 301, 325.

[26] John Johnston in *Country Gentleman*, XIII (February 10, 1859), 90.

[27] Johnston wrote about his operations so extensively in the *Country Gentleman* in the eighteen fifties as to make particular references unnecessary. For a review of his operations, see *Country Gentleman*, XIV (November 10, 1859), 298–299.

[28] Percy W. Bidwell and John I. Falconer, *History of Agriculture in the Northern United States* (Washington, D. C.: Carnegie Institution, 1925), p. 321.

in the Old Dominion and the continuance of good agricultural practices in the Keystone state. Contrast the word picture of Pennsylvania German farm culture of 1853 as drawn by a nineteenth-century German immigrant with the account just given of New York wheat farming:

> Everyone who visits that portion of Pennsylvania where the Germans reside will be agreeably surprised with the appearance of the fields, meadows, and those large barns and manure heaps, the secret of their success. Every strip of land is well cultivated and tended with care; every meadow drained or irrigated. The whole aspect of their estates shows that they love and cherish the soil. They work themselves; their daughters and wives work; all work. They have little hired labor, and yet, with that small amount of labor, they produce large crops, and are very prosperous. To these "Dutchmen" Pennsylvania owes much of her wealth, her prosperity, the high rank which she holds among her sister States, and the fortitude with which she endures the memorable financial crisis. The Germans of Pennsylvania seldom emigrate to the West, to exhaust or ruin another tract of land, and when they are *obliged* to move, in order to make their children also independent tillers of the soil, they always carry with them their industry; and their good farming has become proverbial throughout the Union.[29]

In the newer states the average production of wheat per farm was noticeably greater than was that of the seaboard states. In 1860 it was 44 bushels in New York, 66 in Pennsylvania, 84 in Ohio, 138 in Iowa, 166 in Illinois, and 226 in Wisconsin.[30] Being aided by the construction of canals and the coming of the railroad, midwestern farmers arrived at a state of commercial agriculture with much greater speed than had pioneers on more eastern frontiers in an earlier generation.

As farmers increased their acreage in wheat they became more dependent upon migratory labor or exchange labor, since it was not feasible for them to keep hired hands in sufficient quantity for more than the harvest and threshing season. But, as an Indiana farmer reported in 1852, "Hands are always scarce in harvest, and demand high wages." In consequence, the same farmer noted:

> Machines are being introduced now for harvesting wheat, and some of them are designed to thrash, and partially clean it, also. They are truly labor-saving. The sickle has been laid aside, and the scythe and cradle will most probably soon give place to this machinery, worked by horse or steam power.[31]

[29] Charles L. Fleischmann in *American Polytechnic Journal*, II (1853), 166.

[30] Compiled from *Eighth Census of the United States, 1860, Agriculture*.

[31] Jos. Brady of Brookville, Ind., December 19, 1852, in Commissioner of Patents, *Annual Report, 1852, Agriculture* (Washington, D. C.: Robert Armstrong, 1853), p. 304.

Economic pressure induced farmers to make wheat the core of their operations. It also led them to experiment with hand-operated and horse-drawn drills, with improved plows and harrows, as well as with the reaper and the thresher. Purchase of these farm implements required increasing amounts of capital which only high yields, large operations, and good management could provide. The increasing capital costs of wheat production and the adaptability of the western prairies to large-scale operations, combined with their higher yields, tended to discourage the planting of wheat in the eastern and southern states and to its being abandoned as a major cash crop. Where it was retained, it was usually a part of a three- or four-year rotation. Yields as low as five and ten bushels, which were reported as common in the South, could scarcely justify putting the land in wheat.[32] Although it was commonly said that better tillage practices would improve the yield, the fact remains that in the South, at any rate, the land and climate were not such as to make possible competition with soils better adapted to wheat production.

Wheat on fresh prairie soils, especially in northern Illinois and southern Wisconsin, where the climate seemed just right and disease and parasitic infestation were slight, returned high yields. Here the reaper was extensively introduced in the fifties, and the size of wheat acreages was substantially increased.[33] Without the railroads the wheat could not have been marketed profitably, but without the reaper the large crops of the fifties could not have been harvested. Illinois, Wisconsin, and Iowa accounted for 45 per cent of the increase in the yield of wheat in the United States in 1859 as compared with the yield of 1849.

In the fairly primitive economy which existed before the railroad reached the new wheat-producing centers of Illinois and Wisconsin, wheat was the basis of barter, the standard of value. The *Prairie Farmer* phrased this well in 1850:

> The wheat crop is the great crop of the North-west, for exchange purposes. It pays debts, buys groceries, clothing and lands, and answers more emphatically the purposes of trade among the farmers, than any other crop. The corn is the main crop in home feeding, the pork and beef, butter and cheese, all go to enrich particular districts, but the wheat is the reliance of the democracy of agriculture.[34]

Low prices and heavy winter killing worked hardship for Illinois and Wisconsin wheat farmers in some years, but in 1854 a bumper crop that coincided with the Crimean War and an expanded demand abroad for

---

[32] Abstracted from the *Annual Report* cited above.

[33] William T. Hutchinson, *Cyrus Hall McCormick: Seed-Time, 1809–1857* (New York: Appleton-Century-Crofts, Inc., 1930), pp. 208, 251.

[34] *Prairie Farmer*, X (February, 1850), 52.

American wheat combined to push wheat prices to high levels. Frenzied railroad building brought modern transportation close to wide areas in the upper Mississippi Valley and at the same time brought into the region thousands of land-hungry farmers anxious to share in the boom in wheat production. Buyers of wheat now traveled from farm to farm, offering to purchase the crop at the barn for a dollar a bushel.[35] With the cost of preparing the land for wheat, drilling it in, harvesting, threshing, and marketing an estimated eight to eleven dollars an acre, the farmer who produced 30 bushels to the acre and sold it for one dollar per bushel stood to do very well.[36] Small wonder that pioneers in Wisconsin, Illinois, and in the new communities west of the Mississippi turned so largely to wheat. For the crop year 1859 Wisconsin led the nation in the ratio of wheat to acreage of improved land (4.1 bushels per acre); Minnesota came next with 3.9 bushels for each acre of improved land.

Commercial agriculture developed early in the high-yielding wheat counties. They had a high ratio of horses to farms, a high value of farm implements and machinery, a most favorable ratio of improved to un-improved lands, and high value of land in farms.[37] Absentee ownership, numerous large farm units, tenant farms, and hired laborers were fairly common.

An immense stream of wheat flowed eastward into markets previously satisfied by New York, Pennsylvania, and Virginia farmers, and to England, where it forced farmers to make fundamental changes in their cropping systems. The 72 per cent increase in wheat production in the fifties, which took place entirely in the Mississippi Valley, made possible large sales of wheat abroad during the Crimean War and again during the Civil War. The wheat exports contributed to the prosperity of the United States in the fifties and were a major item on the credit side of her balance of payments and an important factor in her international relations.

Before long, the new West began to experience the same misfortunes that had overtaken areas farther east, where wheat had continually been planted on the same land. The tide of population into the

[35] Thompson, "Rise and Decline of the Wheat Growing Industry," loc. cit., pp. 20 ff.; Joseph Schafer, The Winnebago-Horicon Basin (Wisconsin Domesday Book, General Studies, Vol. IV; Madison: State Historical Society of Wisconsin, 1937), pp. 196 ff.

[36] Estimates of cost of raising wheat are from the Commissioner of Patents, Annual Report, Agriculture, 1853, pp. 137–141. Since they relate to New York State, where land values were much higher than those in Wisconsin, I have discounted them somewhat.

[37] The counties are Dane, Dodge, Rock, Fond du Lac, and Columbia in Wisconsin, and Ogle in Illinois.

AMOUNT AND VALUE OF WHEAT AND WHEAT FLOUR EXPORTED
FROM THE UNITED STATES

Year	Wheat (bushels)	Flour (barrels)	Value
1851	1,026,725	2,202,335	$11,550,063
1852	2,694,540	2,799,339	14,424,352
1853	3,890,141	2,920,918	19,137,797
1854	8,036,665	4,022,386	40,121,616
1855	798,884	1,204,540	12,226,154
1856	8,154,877	3,510,626	44,390,809
1857	14,570,331	3,712,053	48,123,173
1858	8,926,196	3,512,169	28,389,673
1859	3,002,016	2,431,824	17,282,783
1860	4,155,153	2,611,596	19,525,211
1861	31,238,057	4,323,756	62,959,473

Source: Compiled from *Eighth Census of the United States, 1860, Agriculture* (Washington, D. C.: Government Printing Office, 1864), p. cxl.

new wheat country sent land values up, soon the accumulation of diseases and parasites which had ravaged older farm lands began to be felt, yields declined, and costs rose. In 1859, John H. Klippart, a well-known writer on agricultural matters in Ohio, declared that farmers of his state, though expending more money on machinery and more labor in wheat cultivation than formerly, were getting a lower yield per acre, and expressed alarm at the declining fertility of the soil.[38] The following year a writer in the *Indiana Farmer* bewailed the soil deterioration in the Hoosier State resulting from wheat cropping and urged farmers to adopt a rotation system with clover, plowed under to build up humus content. Everywhere in the state, except on farms on deep alluvial deposits, complaints were heard of soil depletion and diminishing production, he said.[39] When Wisconsin was in its infancy, still not a state, the cry was raised that farmers were not learning from the experience of regions farther east, where continued cropping to wheat had been so damaging to soil and land values. Countless statements were made during the bad years, 1849–1851, ascribing the wheat failure to successive seeding to that crop.[40] Nonetheless, high prices in the mid-fifties led Wisconsin farmers to specialize to an excessive and dangerous degree in wheat. It was "radically wrong," said the *Wisconsin Farmer*, for farmers to concentrate upon this grain to the exclusion of other crops and of a proper system of rotation. The writer almost welcomed the wheat setback of

[38] Klippart, *The Wheat Plant*, p. 389.
[39] *Indiana Farmer*, IX (February 4, March 27, 1860), 34, 114.
[40] Thompson, "Rise and Decline of the Wheat Growing Industry," *loc. cit.*, p. 21.

1858 in the hope that it might drive farmers to plant other crops and raise more livestock.[41] When wheat farming failed or yielded unprofitable returns, farmers turned to raising more corn and later more livestock. Wheat farming tended to follow the setting sun, but Illinois, Indiana, Wisconsin, and Ohio continued to be major producing states until the eighties.

CORN GROWING

Corn was the universal grain raised practically wherever there was farming. It was a hardier plant than wheat, being less susceptible to disease and parasitic infestation, yielded more per acre, and was a cheaper grain to feed livestock than was wheat. True, it required a longer growing season, and early frosts sometimes damaged it before the milk stage had been passed. Western pioneers moving into new country could carry their corn seed with them, for only a peck planted an acre, which might produce fifty bushels, whereas it took two bushels of wheat weighing 120 pounds to seed an acre, and the yield might be only fifteen or eighteen bushels. Because corn could be raised easily and cheaply, it was produced in great abundance in areas adapted to its cultivation, and the price was low in relation to the price of wheat. Though corn has almost as many calories per bushel and within 25 per cent of the over-all food value of wheat, it was generally underpriced in relation to wheat. Gray's figures for the price of corn and wheat in Virginia between 1840 and 1860 show that in every year except one, the price of wheat was from 50 per cent to 150 per cent more than the price of corn. The exception was 1851, when wheat brought 42 per cent more than corn.[42]

Wheat was the principal bread cereal, except on the farm, where corn was used more commonly. Corn, the cheaper grain in proportion to its bulk and its food value, was the poor man's food, the pioneer's subsistence, the slaves' usual handout, the feed of hogs, cattle, poultry, and horses. Corn pone, corn bread or johnny cake, corn mush, hominy, and corn fritters were standard items in the farmers' diet, and also became important ingredients in frontier literature. The farmer consumed his own corn at the table or fed it to his livestock, which was the acceptable way of marketing it. Everywhere corn was raised to some extent for fodder for cattle, but in the northernmost sections of the country, where the growing season was too short to permit ripening of the grain, and in

[41] *Wisconsin Farmer*, XI (April, 1859), 115–116.
[42] Lewis Cecil Gray, *History of Agriculture in the Southern United States* (2 vols.; Washington, D. C.: Carnegie Institution, 1933), II, 1039.

the Deep South, where there was insufficient forage for livestock, it was raised mainly for this purpose.

On the farm being newly opened, the first agricultural operation was to get the corn in, whether in a little clearing or in the prairie. Until the farmer had fields in a good state of cultivation, he had to rely on corn for his horses and oxen and other cattle, but later could vary their diet as well as his own when wheat, rye, oats, and vegetables were available.

Corn was planted by hand, or by mid-century, by hand-operated seeders. By using a grub hoe or ax to get through the grass and roots, pioneers on the prairies planted a first crop of corn in the sod without plowing. In areas of shorter growing seasons, only early planting and later frosts would make crops possible. Crows had an uncanny faculty of discovering fields of sprouting corn, which they quickly devastated, and for a time personal attention might be necessary to guard against their menace. Poorly cultivated fields were filled with grass roots and weed seeds that assured an early crop of entangling and choking weeds, if nothing else. For two months frequent hoeing was necessary, especially after each rain, and took much time and energy. Prolonged rains at the wrong time might substantially reduce the crop. When the corn was knee high and the danger from weeds was over, the farmer could "lay by" the corn for the remainder of the growing season.

Unlike wheat, corn could be harvested at the convenience of the farmer. Cutting the stalks and putting them in shocks, where they could dry, was hard labor, frequently undertaken when it was cold and raw in the field. As time was available and when the seeds were dry, the ears were shucked and hauled to the crib for storage until needed. Thereafter, at the farmer's convenience the ears were shelled, by hand at first, later by patented corn shellers. Shelled corn was fed directly to the stock or ground at the nearby mill and fed as meal to assure more efficient use. An easier way that hard-driven farmers had to follow was to throw the unshelled ears to the hogs either when shucked or later, when drawn from the cribs. The most wasteful method of harvesting corn was to turn the hogs into the corn field, but when labor was scarce and expensive and the farmer's burdens were heavy, the waste of grain was less important that the saving of labor.

Weeds, droughts, cool nights, heavy rains that washed the soil and weakened rootholds, windstorms that flattened the stalks, early frost, crows and blackbirds that could destroy much of the early sprouted grain, cutworms that killed the stalk, rats, mice, squirrels, and other wild animals that foraged on the corn in the field, in the shocks, or at the crib were the worst enemies of corn. But with all the devastation they

wrought, the yield in proportion to labor expended was generally good
and it met the needs of the farmer. Never was corn as disastrously affected
by disease and parasites as were wheat and cotton.

Wheat was produced more successfully in the northern counties of
Ohio and Illinois and in southern Wisconsin and Michigan, while corn
was grown more generally in the central and southern portions of Ohio,
Indiana, Illinois, and Kentucky and in Tennessee and Virginia.

In the first year for which there are statistics of corn production—
1839—Tennessee, Kentucky, and Virginia outranked other states, and
were followed closely by Ohio, Indiana, North Carolina, and Illinois.
The Nashville Basin of Tennessee and the Bluegrass region of Kentucky
were concentrated centers of corn planting. Twenty years later, Illinois
had become the top producer, with Ohio, Missouri, and Indiana ranking
next.

CORN PRODUCTION IN LEADING STATES
(*In thousands of bushels*)

State	1839	1849	1859
Illinois	22,634	57,646	115,174
Ohio	33,668	59,078	73,543
Missouri	17,332	36,214	72,892
Indiana	28,155	52,964	71,588
Kentucky	39,847	58,672	64,043
Tennessee	44,986	52,276	52,089
Iowa	1,406	8,656	42,410
United States	317,531	592,071	838,772

Source: Compiled from *Eighth Census of the United States, 1860, Agriculture,*
p. cxl.

Of the twenty-three counties producing over two million bushels of corn
in 1859, eighteen were in Illinois; all four counties producing over three
million bushels were in Illinois.[43] Superior soil, a long growing season,
hot July and August days, combined with sufficient rainfall, created the
modern corn belt in these prairie states.

The demand of southern markets for corn enabled farmers near
navigable rivers and later canals in the Ohio Valley to devote their
land and labor to that grain. Better still, the corn, when fed to hogs
and cattle, might assure two profits instead of one to farmers who had
the capital to engage in such operations. It was thus the adaptability

[43] Compiled from *Eighth Census of the United States, 1860, Agriculture.* For a
different view concerning the relative importance of corn-producing areas, see Donald
L. Kemmerer, "The Pre–Civil War South's Leading Crop, Corn," *Agricultural History,*
XXIII (October, 1949), 236–239.

of the land to corn, the ease with which parts of the crop could be marketed, and the increasing use of the grain for feed for livestock that brought about an ever growing concentration upon that cereal in the farm pattern of the day.

Early settlers, having found a crop to which the land was reasonably well adapted, relied heavily upon corn in their economy, planting it year after year on the same land without rotation or fallowing. A Kentucky farmer with a literary bent that induced him to write frequently to the *American Agriculturist* reported that when he bought his plantation in 1812 a portion "had been in cultivation in one continued succession of corn crops, for some 20 or 25 years." Settlers moving into the prairies regarded the soil as "exhaustless," and therefore not needing applications of manure or other fertilizer. That grain, particularly corn, was being raised regularly year after year on the same land without appreciable reduction in yield seemed to confirm the notion.[44] Rotation was unremittingly urged by farm journals, notably in the corn belt by the *Prairie Farmer*, but without effect except among those who already were addicted to scientific farming.[45]

Prairie soils being perhaps the best in the world for corn, their crops yielded high returns for the labor expended. Fifty to 80 bushels an acre were common yields; on the bottom lands adjoining the Ohio and Mississippi rivers yields ran as high as 100 to 120 bushels to the acre.[46]

In the South, corn produced by high-priced slave labor on the plantations yielded as low as 5 to 15 bushels per acre. Regardless of the low yields, and they were not uncommon in that region, corn continued to be its major crop. When an extensive failure of the corn crop occurred in Georgia and elsewhere in the Deep South, a Georgia paper spoke of it as a greater calamity than a failure of the cotton crop would be.[47] In view of the higher yields and more efficient production on northern farms, growing corn in much of the lower South, particularly on land well adapted to cotton and cane, could be justified only by other than economic arguments.

OTHER GRAINS

Oats, the third major grain, were largely raised for horses, and to combine with corn for cattle and sheep. Every state raised some oats,

[44] *American Agriculturist*, IV (January, 1845), 28, and IX (January, 1850), 16. A Philadelphia capitalist offering 115,000 acres of prairie land in Illinois for sale in 1847 maintained that most of these lands "may be cultivated 100 years or more without manuring, being of the richest alluvial soil."—*Cultivator*, IV (January, 1847), 38.

[45] *Prairie Farmer*, III (November, 1843), 259–263.

[46] Oliver, *Eight Months in Illinois*, pp. 78–80.

[47] *Augusta Evening Dispatch*, July 25, 27, 1860.

but it was essentially a northern grain, well over half of the nation's crop being produced in New York, Pennsylvania, Ohio, and Illinois. Oats followed corn or wheat in rotation on well-run farms, and were in turn followed by clover or timothy grass. The food value of oats was less in relation to its bulk than that of most other grains and it was not profitable to haul it any distances. Like hay, it was needed in cities, and in the South, which did not produce sufficient for its livestock. Where water transportation was available it was shipped there in considerable quantities.

Barley and rye crops were raised for use in breweries and distilleries as well as for human and animal consumption. Buckwheat was a hardy, fast-maturing cereal that was well adapted to high altitudes, short seasons, and poor soils. Needing only eight or ten weeks to mature, it could be planted where corn or wheat had failed and still make possible a crop. During the winter months it provided a major part of the bread diet of farm families in New England and the Middle Atlantic states. The planting of each of these three cereals was centered in New York, Pennsylvania, Ohio, and Illinois; an exception was barley, in which California had the lead in 1860.[48]

Grain farming lent itself to the early appearance of landlordism and tenancy, particularly on land having little value for its timber. On such land there was little or nothing of value to the landlord that might be stolen or destroyed (save soil), and the landlord had only to make sure that a fair division was made of the grain if share rent was the basis of the agreement between him and the tenant. It has already been seen how common tenancy became in the Hudson-Mohawk and Genesee valleys of New York, where wheat was the chief crop, and how it flourished in the early nineteenth century in the wheat and tobacco region of the Piedmont of Virginia until planters engrossed the small allotments in their large estates. An observer in the upper Muskingum Valley of Ohio in 1850 found tenancy not good for the land. In the area around Coshocton he noted "many *large landholders*," some of whom rented their "land on shares, or, for 20 bushels of corn to the acre; (equal to about five dollars). . . ." On such farms corn was raised year after year on the same tracts. "The tenants, occupying only from year to year, naturally want to *get off* all they can; and at the same time bestow as little labor as they can; and as soon as they can accumulate sufficient funds, they are off to the new lands of the west."[49] Here on land originally covered with little but scrub oak a pattern of land use was developing that already

[48] L. H. Bailey, *Cyclopedia of American Agriculture* (4 vols.; New York: The Macmillan Company, 1917), III, 218, 484.

[49] *Cultivator*, VII (November, 1850), 358.

by 1850 was revealing the same unfortunate results of careless cropping that were emerging in the prairies farther west.

THE TRADE THROUGH NEW ORLEANS

Early in the development of the upper Mississippi Valley the bulk of the wheat, flour, pork, and beef went south by flatboat, keelboat, and steamboat to Memphis, Natchez, Vicksburg, and New Orleans, where there was a rapidly growing market and, equally important, where there were facilities to ship to other parts of the South, to the fast-expanding industrial cities of the Northeast, to the West Indies and to Europe. It is scarcely correct to say that the upper Mississipppi Valley was dependent upon the expansion of cotton plantations in the South to absorb its produce. Of the enormous quantities of flour, pork, bacon, corn, whiskey, and many other commodities shipped from this area, large parts were exported from New Orleans.[50]

IMPORTS INTO NEW ORLEANS FROM INTERIOR AND EXPORTS

Year	Flour (bbls.)		Pork (bbls.)		Whiskey (bbls.)		Shelled corn (bbls.)	
	Imports	Exports	Imports	Exports	Imports	Exports	Imports	Exports
1843–4	502,507	300,082	412,928	393,179	86,947	42,127	360,052	204,281
1844–5	533,312	279,137	216,960	181,409	97,651	32,360	390,964	220,295
1845–6	837,985	573,194	369,601	272,319	117,104	58,181	1,166,120	941,689

Source: De Bow's Review, II (December, 1846), opp. 422.

Although corn was widely used for human consumption, the larger part of the crop was fed to hogs and cattle. Hence the areas where corn was produced most abundantly also became the feeding grounds for cattle and hogs. As is seen in the chapter on livestock, the corn belt, stretching from Ohio to Iowa and including Kentucky and Missouri, was the principal meat-producing region of America in the two decades before the Civil War.

The opening of the Erie Canal in New York in 1825 and the building of the Ohio and Indiana canals to connect the Great Lakes with the Ohio River started a reversal of the trade routes that was completed by the construction of east-west railroads. The construction of the Michigan Central and the Michigan Southern railroads to Chicago in 1852, of the Rock Island Railroad to the Mississippi in 1854, and of other railroad connections between Philadelphia and Baltimore and St. Louis completed

[50] Douglas C. North, "International Capital Flows and the Development of the American West," Journal of Economic History, XVI (December, 1956), 496–497.

the transportation revolution. Early in this development the wheat and flour from the more northern portions of the old Northwest began moving east rather than south.[51] Corn and pork, on the other hand, which were raised in the central and southern portions of the old Northwest, tended to flow south even as late as into the fifties. The South used a good deal of the foodstuffs, and for the portion that was to be transshipped elsewhere water transportation was cheaper than combined water and rail shipments.

Flatboats, which offered the cheapest method of transportation, continued to carry a considerable part of the produce of the upriver communities into the Deep South even after the Civil War. At one time the cost of shipping a barrel of flour from Kentucky to New Orleans was one dollar.[52] As many as two and three thousand flatboats annually took produce south from the farms and forests of western Pennsylvania, Ohio, Indiana, Illinois, and Kentucky during the heyday of the steamboat.[53] On these stout but crudely built arks or boats, with their long sweeps, were carried loads that ranged from a few tons to as much as 180 tons of corn, pork, bacon, ham, lard, flour, hay, whiskey, staves, hoops, lumber, hemp, and tobacco. A load of 180 tons, said to be the largest ever brought to New Orleans by flatboat, included 160 barrels of lard and 320,000 pounds of bulk lard.[54]

The composition of the cargo of a number of these flatboats is worth giving in detail for the light it throws on the trade of the upper part of the Mississippi Valley with the Deep South:

FLATBOAT CARGO, INDIANA TO NEW ORLEANS, 1826

18	barrels whiskey
70	barrels oats
8,000	pounds bulk pork
300	barrels corn
7	barrels pork
15	barrels corn meal

[51] De Bow's Review, III (February, 1847), 102; Balthasar Henry Meyer, History of Transportation in the United States (Washington, D. C.: Carnegie Institution, 1917), pp. 487 ff.

[52] Marion Tinling and Godfrey Davies, The Western Country in 1793: Reports on Kentucky and Virginia by Harry Toulmin (San Marino, Calif.: Huntington Library, 1948), p. 83.

[53] De Bow's Review, IV (November, 1847), 395. From September, 1846, to August, 1847, the number of flatboats unloaded at New Orleans was 2,792; a smaller number stopped at Memphis, Vicksburg, Natchez. Of this number, Ohio sent the most, 817; followed by Indiana, 764; Kentucky, 296; Tennessee, 118; Illinois, 109; and Pennsylvania, 108.

[54] New Orleans Picayune, February 28, 1850.

FLATBOAT CARGO, LEAVENWORTH, INDIANA TO NEW ORLEANS, 1830

2,000 pounds bacon in bulk
300 bushels oats
29 hogsheads tobacco
40 kegs lard
35 barrels whiskey
30 barrels flour
30 barrels corn meal

FLATBOAT CARGO, CINCINNATI TO NEW ORLEANS, 1836

850 barrels flour
76 barrels whiskey
110 hogsheads bacon
20 barrels vinegar
21 barrels apples
30 barrels dried apples

FLATBOAT CARGO, INDIANA TO NEW ORLEANS, 1837

90 tons hay

Source: New Orleans Price Current, April 1, 1826; April 24, 1830; December 3, 1836; December 9, 1837.

Two flatboats from Iowa brought to New Orleans in 1844 a highly miscellaneous cargo consisting of the usual pork, bacon, lard, corn, oats, beef, beans, peas, barley, potatoes, and 180 dozen brooms.[55]

In the height of the season there might be several hundred flatboats tied up at Vicksburg or New Orleans with four men to a boat waiting to sell their cargo. The competition of the flatboaters with local tax-paying merchants produced friction and at times violence and punitive action, but the value of the flatboat trade to these communities was too great to jeopardize.[56] Steamboats made inroads into the traffic in agricultural goods of the upper Mississippi Valley, but the flatboat trade in bulkier items continued to flourish throughout the steamboat era.[57]

The volume and variety of goods brought to New Orleans, mostly from the up-river communities and destined for sale throughout the deep South or reshipment may be seen in the following table:

[55] New Orleans Price Current, May 15, 1844.
[56] Franklin, La., Planters' Banner, October 24, 1850; De Bow's Review, VII (November, 1849), 415–416; H. S. Fulkerson, Random Recollections of Early Days in Mississippi (Vicksburg: Vicksburg Printing and Publishing Company, 1885), pp. 97–99.
[57] Louis C. Hunter, Steamboats on the Western Rivers (Cambridge, Mass.: Harvard University Press, 1949), pp. 52–60.

RECEIPTS AT NEW ORLEANS FROM THE INTERIOR, 1848–1849

		Number	Value
Apples	barrels	54,987	$ 174,960
Bacon	casks	32,056	1,282,240
Bacon	barrels & boxes	32,156	803,900
Bacon hams	hogsheads	19,831	892,395
Bacon in bulk	pounds	217,000	10,850
Beef	barrels and tierces	80,590	1,049,016
Butter	kegs	57,972	89,860
Corn meal	barrels	12,097	30,242
Corn in ears	barrels	295,710	133,070
Corn shelled	sacks	1,706,312	1,790,394
Flour	barrels	1,013,177	4,559,296
Hay	bales	54,241	162,723
Lard	barrels & tierces	214,362	3,858,516
Lard	kegs	275,485	1,064,197
Oats	barrels & sacks	266,559	213,247
Pork	barrels & tierces	550,643	5,231,108
Pork	boxes	18,279	365,580
Pork	hogsheads	18,499	739,960
Pork in bulk	pounds	10,273,680	285,263
Potatoes	barrels	140,116	365,290
Wheat	barrels & sacks	238,911	477,822
Whiskey	barrels	125,029	875,203

Source: De Bow's Review, VII (November, 1849), 420–421.

The produce of the upper Mississippi Valley handled by New Orleans merchants actually had greater value than the cotton, sugar, and molasses of the South that went through their commission houses.[58] Chief among these products were pork, lard, and flour. This trade through the southern gateway was vital both to the upper Mississippi Valley and to the lower South. It brought to the Ohio farmer and merchant exchange on which he could draw for the purchase of eastern goods, such as hardware and clothing, and it provided the means with which interest and principal on debts owned on land to eastern creditors could be paid. It provided the South with foodstuffs without which that section could not have existed unless it had ceased to concentrate upon such staples as cotton, sugar, and rice. It also aided materially in building up the commercial business of New Orleans.

In summary, the demand for cotton in England stimulated the great flow of population into the Gulf states, where it concentrated on the production of that staple. Emerging as a deficit food area, the South

[58] De Bow's Review, VII (November, 1849), 420–421.

called for enormous quantities of wheat, flour, pork, and lard, which encouraged and made possible the rapid settlement of the upper Mississippi Valley. As the cotton economy flourished in the South so the corn, wheat, and pork economy flourished in Ohio, Indiana, and Illinois. For a time the one section was dependent for its market on the other. By mid-century, however, the rapid growth of industrial cities in the East was creating a bourgeoning market that called for an ever-expanding amount of the wheat, flour, and pork of the West. First the canals made possible this flow of foodstuffs eastward but they proved inadequate; then came the railroads to accelerate the shipment east of the products of the farm. By 1860 the completion of railroads to Chicago, Rock Island, St. Louis, and St. Joseph, as well as thousands of miles of feeder lines, had brought most of the area from Cleveland to the Kansas border closely in touch with eastern markets; the grain, flour, and pork were largely following these routes to the East.[59]

[59] North, "International Capital Flows . . . ," *loc. cit.*, pp. 493 ff.

CHAPTER IX

Prairie Farming

IT was in the prairies of Indiana, Illinois, Missouri, and Iowa that westward-moving pioneers found it necessary to adapt their techniques to conditions materially differing from those prevailing in the originally forested areas from which they had come. Here the ecological conditions not found elsewhere for a time deterred settlement because they were not understood and because the technology of agriculture had not as yet sufficiently advanced to permit experiment.[1] These differences were recognized by an early compiler of an emigrant guide:

> Upon emigrating to this country [Illinois], it would be well for an eastern farmer to throw off and forget many of his former habits and practices, and be prepared to accommodate himself to the nature of the soil and the circumstances of the country; else he will throw away much labour uselessly, and expend money unprofitably.[2]

Settlers first met with small prairies, a few hundred acres in extent, in Ohio and Michigan, but not until they penetrated into northern Indiana, central Illinois, Missouri, Iowa, and eastern Kansas and Nebraska did they see the great prairies that stretched to the horizon. The prairies were treeless, broken only by narrow timbered areas along the streams, and by groves of oak, hickory, and walnut on the morainal ridges. They were covered with a luxurious growth of bluestem grass up to six feet tall, intermixed with gorgeously colored flowers and, in the sloughs, with a rank growth of reeds and cattails. In the growing season the thick nutritious grass provided excellent forage for game animals or livestock,

[1] O. E. Baker, comp., "Soils of the United States," in *Atlas of American Agriculture* (Washington, D. C.: Government Printing Office, 1936), p. 63.
[2] S. Augustus Mitchell, comp., *Illinois in 1837: A Sketch Descriptive of the Situation, Boundaries, Face of the Country . . . of the State of Illinois* (Philadelphia: S. Augustus Mitchell, 1837), p. 68.

but in late fall, when it dried into brittle straw, a touch of the match or of lightning often set it sweeping in flames over great stretches of country. The ashes and the rotting of the coarse, thickly intermeshed, and deeply penetrating root structure, encouraged by the moist soil, added valuable humus to the generously endowed mineral content of the soil.[3]

The glaciers had been good to the prairies of Illinois and Iowa. These deep, finely powdered, black or brown soils, with their abundant supply of phosphorus, potassium, magnesium and lime, were lavishly enriched by organic matter. They contrasted sharply with the thin forest soils of upland parts of New England and New York, which were acid, stony, and soon exhausted.

DETERRENTS TO PRAIRIE FARMING

Glaciation had leveled off the prairie region, leaving it either gently rolling or quite flat, with little natural drainage. Flat land, such as that north of Lafayette, Indiana, or in what are now Ford and McLean counties, Illinois, could not be brought into cultivation until drainage ditches had been constructed or the land had been tiled. Meantime, their grass cover provided superb forage for the growing feeder-cattle business, which flourished there in the mid-nineteenth century until rising values and taxes forced more intensive utilization of the land. Men of small means were not able to utilize the poorly drained prairies.

There were other deterrents to the development of the prairies that kept them out of the hands of small farmers, who sought, instead, the forest soils to be found along the streams there or in southern Illinois or in Wisconsin. The prairies lacked the timber so essential for buildings, fences, and fuel. Groves of trees near the prairies were almost the equivalent of gold mines, and were grabbed up early by settlers and speculators. Owners who could protect such groves from depredations by neighboring farmers were certain to reap a rich harvest from their timber.[4] Groves near the prairies were generally stripped of their usable trees before they passed into private ownership.[5] Thereafter the demand for lumber could be met only by importing it overland from Chicago, the

[3] The soil survey of a typical prairie county is useful: Cyril G. Hopkins, J. G. Mosier, E. Van Alstine, and F. W. Garrett, *McLean County Soils* (University of Illinois, Agricultural Experiment Station, *Soil Report* No. 10; Urbana: 1915), *passim;* George Ade, "Prairie Kings of Yesterday," *Saturday Evening Post*, July 4, 1931, p. 76.

[4] Isaac Funk sold small lots of his famous Funk's Grove for as high as $90 an acre.—Paul W. Gates, *Frontier Landlords and Pioneer Tenants* (Ithaca, N. Y.: Cornell University Press, 1945), p. 14.

[5] A farmer in La Salle County, Ill., wrote in 1838 that he hired fence rails "made on Uncle Sam's land. . . ."—*Prairie Farmer*, VI (July, 1846), 204.

lumber-marketing center, or from the sawmill towns on the Mississippi. Not until the coming of the railroads to the prairies in the mid-nineteenth century was it possible to meet this demand without excessive cost. Though the railroads lowered its cost to the prairie farmers, lumber was still beyond the reach of many. Nor could Illinois farmers make shift with sodhouses as did prairie settlers farther west in areas of less rainfall.

The deeply penetrating, thick, and coarse root structure of the prairie bluestem grass was impossible to break with the ordinary plows that early settlers brought with them. The wooden moldboard and cast-iron plows that worked fairly well in the lighter and sandier soils of the East were not strong enough for the damp and heavy prairie soils because they did not scour (that is, soil still clung to the plowshare). Improvised awkward and heavy breaking plows were drawn by from two to six yoke of oxen and required the services of two men. Such expensive and heavy equipment was possessed by only a few men, who did custom plowing for others at a rate of $1.50 to $2.00 an acre, or by the larger capitalist farmers.[6]

By the fifties lighter plows made from cast steel imported from England were introduced. Greater smoothness in the moldboard and lightness with strength were thus obtained. Fewer draft animals were needed to haul these new steel plows, which John Deere and competitors produced, and which by the fifties were becoming fairly common.[7] The difficulties of prairie breaking with the awkward and inadequate plows and the high cost of the later steel plows contributed further to make the "tall grass" country of Illinois and Iowa unattractive to immigrants. Prairie farming was to be the work of men of capital rather than that of the ordinary pioneer with little resources save brawn.

Poorly drained prairie soils were held responsible for the ill-health of pioneers. Ague or malarial fever, the most common disease, seemed inescapable. As were bilious ailments or dysentery, the ague was attributed to the miasma or dampness that rose from swampy land. Typhoid may have been caused by the lack of drainage and the resulting contamination of surface water. The ravages of the mosquito were frequently commented upon by travelers, but none suspected then that the insect was a carrier of dread disease germs. A Hoosier landlord in 1846 listed illness as the first factor in accounting for the failure of farmers to

[6] For a description of a breaking plow of 1841, see Herbert Anthony Kellar, ed., *Solon Robinson: Pioneer and Agriculturist* (*Indiana Historical Collections*, Vols. XXI, XXII; Indianapolis: Indiana Historical Bureau, 1936), I, 287–288.

[7] Leo Rogin, *The Introduction of Farm Machinery in Its Relation to the Productivity of Labor in the Agriculture of the United States During the Nineteenth Century* (University of California *Publications in Economics*, Vol. IX; Berkeley: University of California Press, 1931), pp. 21 ff.; Earle D. Ross, *Iowa Agriculture: An Historical Survey* (Iowa City: State Historical Society of Iowa, 1951), pp. 43 ff.

produce any surplus during their first twelve years on the land.[8] Whatever the cause of the excessive illness that affected people on the frontier, the prairie and the poorly drained bottom lands were both blamed and thereby both gained an unenviable reputation.[9]

Efforts to drain the wet prairies met with slight success in the fifties. At the beginning of the decade Congress donated seven million acres of wet lands to the four prairie states to facilitate their drainage. The lands were snapped up by speculators, cattle feeders, or large farmers who did some ditching, but before drainage districts were created individual operators could accomplish little except to divert their surplus water upon neighboring land.[10] Tiling, with its heavy capital costs, was in the future so far as the Middle West was concerned. For the moment only the naturally drained prairie sites were brought into cultivation; the rest were used for livestock.

Prairie trails, for they were little more, were laid out through the seemingly bottomless sloughs rank with coarse grass, weeds, brush taller than a man's head, across the creeks where they could be forded, and over morainal ridges. They took a heavy toll of wagons, which were continually getting mired and being abandoned because of broken axles, wheels, and shafts. One of the principal roads in Indiana—the Michigan Road, built with federal aid in the form of a land grant through the wet area between Logansport and South Bend—was usable only eight months in the year despite the substantial character of its construction. Wagon drivers fared worse on less favored prairie roads. Although heavy commercial loads were hauled "several hundred miles" on the prairies, the cost was high.[11]

With cheap transportation available only by water, those interested in opening up the interior of the prairie states advocated river improvements and canal construction before the railroad era set in. Their demands led to state construction of four canals to connect the Great Lakes with the Ohio and Mississippi rivers across the states of Ohio, Indiana, and Illinois and to the expenditure of much money to improve the navigation of the Des Moines River in Iowa. Areas adjacent to the canals and rivers

[8] Calvin Fletcher, Indianapolis, March 23, 1846, to McFarlin, Fletcher Papers, Indiana State Historical Library, Indianapolis.

[9] Madge E. Pickard and R. Carlyle Buley, *The Midwest Pioneer: His Ills, Cures and Doctors* (Crawfordsville, Ind.: R. E. Banta, 1945), make no mention of dysentery. R. Carlyle Buley, *The Old Northwest* (2 vols.; Indianapolis: Indiana Historical Society, 1950), lists dysentery as a western complaint but concentrates on other ailments. See also Mitchell, *Illinois in 1837*, p. 48.

[10] Margaret Beattie Bogue, "The Swamp Land Act and Wet Land Utilization in Illinois, 1850–1890," *Agricultural History* XXV (October, 1951), 169–180.

[11] Buley, *The Old Northwest*, I, 453, 493; Bessie Louise Pierce, *History of Chicago* (2 vols.; New York: Alfred A. Knopf, Inc., 1937–1940), I, 134.

were aided by all these improvements, but the prairies, being more distant, remained less affected.[12]

Examination of the tract books of the General Land Office for the prairie states shows that before the fifties immigrants had generally settled fairly close to the streams, sought out the wooded areas, or taken positions on the smaller open areas and on the edge of the larger prairies. Some speculative purchasing of prairie land had been made, but the bulk of these lands where surveyed and open to sale was not yet in demand. In contrast, timbered land was well disposed of, except for broken sections, and taken by actual settlers in small tracts.[13] Illustrative of this pattern of settlement is Carroll County, Indiana, a timbered county whose lands passed to settlers through pre-emption in small tracts, mostly in the eighteen twenties and thirties. West of Carroll by two tiers of counties is the prairie county of Benton. Here the bulk of the land was acquired between 1847 and 1852 by speculators or capitalist estate builders who bequeathed to future generations great landed estates operated by tenants, a contrast to the small family-farm ownership pattern early established in Carroll County.[14]

RAILROADS OPEN THE PRAIRIES

It was the railroad that provided the key to the opening of the prairies. It could go wherever there were funds to finance its construction, and the absence of engineering difficulties on the level prairies assured low construction costs. Lines that were not built too far in advance of population could be financed without serious difficulty, as for example, the east-west lines that were primarily designed to connect Chicago, Kansas City, Omaha, and St. Louis with the East but which struck through the heart of the prairies. Feeder lines to tap areas distant from the main routes could be undertaken with local, private, or government aid.

Government land grants on the alternate section pattern, first introduced to aid canal construction, were revived in behalf of the prairie railroads in the fifties. Millions of acres of the best prairie land were given to companies projecting railroads in areas hitherto largely untouched

[12] Balthasar Henry Meyer, *History of Transportation in the United States before 1860* (Washington, D. C.: Carnegie Institution, 1917), pp. 280 ff.

[13] When the Illinois Central Railroad made its selection of land under the Congressional grant of 1850 it found that most of the timbered tracts along its line in central Illinois had been selected long before, but in the predominantly prairie townships there was little or no privately owned land. See *Sectional Maps, Showing Location of Over 2,500,000 Acres Selected Farming and Wood Lands in the State of Illinois* (Chicago: Illinois Central Railroad, 1867), especially Plates 11, 12, 13, and 25.

[14] Paul W. Gates, "Land Policy and Tenancy in the Prairie Counties of Indiana," *Indiana Magazine of History*, XXXV (March, 1939), 11 ff.

184   THE FARMER'S AGE: 1815–1860

by settlement. The Illinois Central, extending from the two northern corners to the southern tip of Illinois, the Hannibal and St. Joseph across northern Missouri, four lines across Iowa, and a number of routes across Wisconsin and Minnesota were thus subsidized to the extent of 19,000,000 acres.[15] Sparked by federal and state aid, a major railroad construction boom developed in the prairie states. Illinois ranked eighteenth among the states in railroad mileage in 1850, being outdistanced even by Connecticut, Georgia, Maine, Vermont, and South Carolina, but it ranked second in 1860 and never again was displaced by any state except Texas. Mileage in Indiana, Illinois, Missouri, and Iowa increased from 339 in 1850 to 6,635 in 1860.[16]

Most important of the prairie railroads was the Illinois Central, with 525 miles of its total of 700 located in the very heart of the Illinois prairie. The road was begun in 1852 and completed in 1856. At the same time nine railroad lines were building across Illinois, establishing connections with lines in Missouri and Iowa which were projected farther west. By 1859 the Hannibal and St. Joseph Railroad was completed through the prairies of northern Missouri to the Missouri River, the westernmost extension of the railroad network. Eastern Iowa was also fairly well provided with railroads. The building of these lines carried far the reversal of the trade routes that had previously been on a north-south axis and opened up the great prairies to settlement.[17]

Since land-grant railroads, somewhat more than other lines, were built through undeveloped areas and were financed in part by mortgages on their grants, which could be retired only through the sale of the lands, the railroads undertook sales promotion and colonization activities on an extensive scale to bring in purchasers for their lands and farmers to

[15] Paul W. Gates, *The Illinois Central Railroad and Its Colonization Work* (Cambridge, Mass.: Harvard University Press, 1934), *passim;* Richard C. Overton, *Burlington West: A Colonization History of the Burlington Railroad* (Cambridge, Mass.: Harvard University Press, 1941); Howard F. Bennett, "The Hannibal & St. Joseph Railroad and the Development of Northern Missouri, 1847–1870: A Study of Land and Colonization Policies." Unpublished doctoral dissertation, Widener Library, Harvard University.

[16] *Poor's Manual of Railroads* (New York: H. V. and H. W. Poor, 1890), p. 6 of Introduction. Maps showing annual construction of railroads in the old Northwest and in Missouri may be seen in Frederic L. Paxson, "The Railroads of the 'Old Northwest' before the Civil War," *Transactions* of the Wisconsin Academy of Sciences, Arts, and Letters, Vol. XVII, Pt. I (1912), pp. 248–266, and Paul W. Gates, "The Railroads of Missouri, 1850–1870," *Missouri Historical Review,* XXVI (January, 1932), 134–141. For railroad mileage and track gauge of prairie states in 1861, see George Rogers Taylor and Irene Neu, *The American Railroad Network, 1861–1890* (Cambridge, Mass.: Harvard University Press, 1956).

[17] Gates, *Illinois Central Railroad, passim,* and Bennett, "Hannibal & St. Joseph . . ." *loc. cit.*

produce traffic for their lines. The Illinois Central and the Hannibal and
St. Joseph railroads distributed pamphlets, posters and handbills by the
hundreds of thousands containing idealized descriptions of the prairies.
Able lithographers, Richard Cobden, a prominent statesman, Sir James
Caird, England's best-known agricultural authority, Dr. J. G. Kohl,
Germany's eminent cartographer and traveler, and numerous journalists
and writers were pressed into service to advertise the prairies. Never
before had real-estate promoters advertised their wares so extensively
or been so successful in bringing them to the attention of so many
prospective immigrants. The flow of westward-moving settlers, many of
them already directed to the upper Mississippi Valley, was now diverted
increasingly to the prairies.[18]

More than 2,200,000 people were added to the population of Illinois,
Indiana, Iowa, and Missouri in the decade of the fifties. This increase was
25 per cent of the total population increase of the forty-one states and
territories. More people were added to the population of Illinois than
were added to any other state, and Missouri's growth was exceeded only
by that of New York and Pennsylvania. Although a considerable portion
of this remarkable growth was concentrated in urban centers like Chicago,
St. Louis, Quincy, and Davenport, and in many smaller county seats
and shipping centers, by far the larger part was rural and agricultural.
Thirty-three per cent of the new farms established during the fifties
were in the four prairie states. The census figure of 199,724 new farms
in these states does not list tenant farms separately from the larger farms
of which they were a part, and doubtless excluded many other tracts on
which operations were just getting under way.[19] It is therefore substantially less than the true figure.

The coming of the railroads, accompanied by a rising index of
commodity prices and credit inflation, triggered a rush for western lands
that swept into private hands all but a fragment of the public lands in
the four states by 1860. A third of Illinois, a fourth of Indiana, two thirds
of Iowa, and a half of Missouri were thus acquired by railroads and
speculators, all prairie boosters anxious to have their holdings improved
so they could sell or lease them.

Immigration, settlement, farm development, and railroad construction were all dependent upon each other. Railroads opened the prairies
to settlement, but it was the immigration and farm development, actual
and prospective, which assured capital for construction and, indeed,
which indirectly provided much capital. The land-grant railroads were
built to a large degree with funds raised by mortgages on the lands and

[18] Gates, *Illinois Central Railroad*, p. 225.
[19] *Eighth Census of the United States, 1860, Agriculture* (Washington, D. C.:
Government Printing Office, 1864), p. 222.

retired from the sale of the lands. Also, a considerable amount of railroad mileage in the prairies was built with local aid provided by municipalities and counties and financed by property taxes.[20] Farmers and speculative landholders in Indiana, Illinois, and Wisconsin contributed to railroad construction by exchanging mortgages on their lands for stock in the transportation companies. The mortgages were sold to eastern financiers and institutions, and when the railroads went into bankruptcy, as most of those financed in this way seem to have done, the farmers found the beautifully engraved stock certificates they had received were valueless but their mortgages inexorably binding.[21]

The building of the railroads made possible bringing into the prairies lumber, farm machinery, breeding stock, and household equipment; and shipping out wheat, hogs, and cattle to Chicago, St. Louis, or the East. Following their construction came a rush of settlers, but settlement problems were not altogether solved prior to 1860.

FENCING

Fencing in wooded or prairie areas was a major improvement and a very costly one in labor and capital. One writer called it "a sore, a blotch, the source of perpetual discontent—the 'fretting leprosy' of the land," all because of the "barbarous practice of suffering stock of all kinds to run at large. . . ." The need for building fences around cultivated land "creates the cause of more rustic quarrels than any other thing, whiskey not excepted." In timbered areas settlers could make the necessary fence rails in the process of clearing. Practiced axmen, and most frontiersmen were that, could cut between 100 and 150 ten-foot rails daily that might be expected to last for a generation or more before needing replacement. In prairie areas, pioneers, if they were not among the fortunate few who had included in their farms a few acres of woods, had to go for miles to find timber and then "hook" it and haul it back across the prairie.[22]

The Virginia or worm fence was commonly used where there was an

[20] Local government aid to railroads in the prairies needs a study comparable to that made by Harry Hubert Pierce for New York State in *Railroads of New York: A Study of Government Aid, 1826–1875* (Cambridge, Mass.: Harvard University Press, 1953).

[21] Frederick Merk has shown that some 6,000 Wisconsin farmers mortgaged their homesteads for between $4,500,000 and $5,000,000 to aid in financing a number of railroads. See his *Economic History of Wisconsin During the Civil War Decade, Publications* of the Wisconsin State Historical Society, *Studies*, Vol. I (Madison: 1916), pp. 238–270. A similar arrangement was used to finance the building of a number of Indiana and Illinois railroads, though in this case the lands that were exchanged for stock of the railroads were mostly held by speculators.

[22] *The Farmer's Guide and Western Agriculturist* (Cincinnati: Buckley, Deforest & Co., 1832); William Oliver, *Eight Months in Illinois with Information to Immigrants* (Chicago: W. M. Hill, 1924), pp. 239–242.

abundance of timber and where land was of little value, but for concentrated commercial farming it scarcely suited. It required more rails than did a post-and-rail fence, was wasteful of land, permitted the growth of noxious weeds, and furnished fuel for destructive fires. Henry L. Ellsworth experimented with a straight post-and-rail fence which he made hog-tight and at the same time provided a drainage ditch by throwing up a furrow on both sides of it.[23]

For the larger prairies the problem of fencing was even more difficult to solve. The few trees early disappeared at the hands of the first to make improvements or were held for a more remunerative use than fencing. That indefatigable agricultural writer, controversialist, and nurseryman, Jonathan Baldwin Turner, having experimented with black and thorn locust, black walnut, poplar, cottonwood, mulberry, privet, gooseberry, sweet briar, crab apple, English thorn, Alabama rose, arbor vitae, American thorns, and Osage orange, settled upon the last as the ideal hedge for fencing purposes. In farm journals and agricultural societies and public addresses he trumpeted the advantages of the Osage orange so effectively that its merits became widely known and it was extensively introduced.[24] The excitement created by Turner and other commercial nurserymen in the farm journals attracted sufficient attention so that it was possible for them to produce and sell the Osage orange seedlings by the hundreds of thousands. They offered to set out the hedge for $100 a mile, or to set out the plants and cultivate and trim them "until a perfect hedge" was produced for $150 to $240 a mile, or to sell seedlings in any quantity.[25]

Major complaints against the Osage orange were that winter killed many plants, leaving gaps through which cattle and hogs could penetrate; the trimming of the plants was an exceedingly difficult and time-consuming job; the hedge absorbed much-needed moisture; teams of horses were so disturbed by the cruel thorns as to be unwilling to approach near the hedge to plow and cultivate; and the land for a distance of ten or twelve feet on each side of the hedge was useless for crops.[26] Notwithstanding such complaints, the Osage orange was the favorite fencing material used in the prairies in the fifties. Within a generation progressive farmers

[23] Commissioner of Patents, *Annual Report, 1845*, p. 387.

[24] *Prairie Farmer*, VII (November, 1847), 346–349. A little earlier Solon Robinson had preached the advantages of the Cherokee rose, about which he seemed to have little information. Though it might make a tight fence in a short time, like the Osage orange, it spread widely, could not be trimmed easily, and could not adapt to the climate of Illinois and Iowa. Other experiments with the Virginia thorn did not yield well.—*Prairie Farmer*, VI (1846), 151, 156, 159, 161, 166, 184.

[25] *The Illinois Central Railroad Company Offers for Sale over 1,500,000 Selected Farming and Wood Lands* (Boston: Rand & Avery, 1857), p. 23.

[26] *Prairie Farmer*, IX (February, 1849), 55. For a detailed description of the cost of and work involved in producing a tight Osage orange fence, see Fred Gerhard, *Illinois as It Is . . .* (Chicago: Keen & Lee, 1857), pp. 355–362.

were beginning to cut it down and grub out the roots, though it continued to dot the prairie landscape until well into the twentieth century.[27] Some still exists.

Since no hedge fence would be hog-tight for a number of years after it was set out, other types of fencing were tried by farm makers anxious to enclose their fields against the encroachments of their neighbors' livestock. Low-grade boards brought in by rail from the pineries partly met the need, but costs were high. Post-and-board fencing cost from $480 to $640 a mile for material alone, while heavy plank fencing cost as much as $750 a mile, as a Missouri railroad found.[28] Sod fencing was also tried but without much success.[29] Plain and woven wire fences, first introduced extensively on the prairies in the fifties, were not altogether successful because the wire, made of wrought iron and not galvanized, rusted and broke in cold weather.[30] Clearly the fencing problem had not been solved, but between Osage orange, board and wire fencing, sufficient progress had been made to permit extensive improvements on the prairies.

CAPITALISTS INVEST IN PRAIRIE LANDS

Farm making in the prairies, conditioned as it was by capital costs, attracted men of substantial means and tended to repel pioneers lacking resources until the pressure on the supply of land induced them to take positions as hired hands, share croppers, or tenants on the property of the large estate builders. Early prairie entrepreneurs were George and Richard Flower, Morris Birkbeck, and Elias Pym Fordham, English farmers of means who migrated in 1817 to southeastern Illinois, where they set themselves up on what was thereafter called the English Prairie in Edwards County. Of the 14,000 acres purchased by this group of English capitalists, 4,000 were to be developed into estates similar to those of rural England, and the remainder was to be held for other moderate capitalists they hoped would join their enterprise.

[27] The Illinois *Pontiac Sentinel*, April 21, 1882, said that the Osage orange was a nuisance because it was homely, took up too much ground, and did not turn hogs.

[28] *The Hannibal and St. Joseph Railroad Company Have Received by Grant from Congress Over 600,000 Acres of the Choicest Farming and Wood Lands* (Hannibal, Mo.: 1859), p. 17; Earl W. Hayter, "The Fencing of Western Railways," *Agricultural History*, XIX (July, 1945), 165.

[29] Much attention is given the fencing problem in the prairies in the *Prairie Farmer* for 1846 and 1847.

[30] Earl W. Hayter, "Barbed Wire Fencing—A Prairie Invention: Its Rise and Influence in the Western States," *Agricultural History*, XIII (October, 1939), 189–207; Clarence H. Danhof, "The Fencing Problem in the Eighteen-Fifties," *Agricultural History*, XVIII (October, 1944), 168–186.

To bring their venture to the attention of English farmers of means, George Flower and Birkbeck wrote a series of pamphlets outlining their experiences and "gilding the lily" in describing the economic opportunities of farming on the prairies of southeastern Illinois. Like so much of the emigrant literature of the period, these pamphlets were widely circulated —one going through eleven printings and another seven—and have since become collectors' items. For a time no other portion of the prairie country was as well known as was the English Prairie. To it there set in a promising flow of emigration from England, and the little settlement became for a time a center of bustle and growth. Unfortunately, internal dissension, overoptimistic disregard of the problems of prairie cultivation, and the costs of farm making in the prairies combined to make the experiment not the success its founders had expected. One may conclude that the Edwards County development had little bearing on the beginnings of agriculture in the larger prairies farther north.[31]

Less is known of the plans of John Grigg and Samuel Augustus Mitchell for developing the 124,000 acres of Illinois prairie land they bought of the government in 1835 and 1836. Grigg was a wealthy Philadelphia publisher; Mitchell, a distinguished geographer, cartographer, and compiler of emigrant guidebooks which were published by the Grigg firm and sold at the rate of 400,000 copies annually.[32] Mitchell, with an interest in the Grigg lands,[33] sought to promote their sale by the publication of a guidebook of Illinois with the title: *Illinois in 1837*. Here it was affirmed that Illinois was "the richest in soil of any [state] in the Union, and of course holds out the greatest prospect of advantage to the agriculturist." In Illinois "the produce of the farmer springs up almost spontaneously, not more than one-third of the labour being necessary on the farms here than is required on those in the east." Naturally, that portion of Illinois in which the Grigg lands were centered was described as "an Arcadian region, in which nature has delighted to bring together her happiest combination of landscape." In short, it was

[31] The literature on the English settlement in Edwards County is extensive. The principal promotional pieces are Morris Birkbeck, *Notes on a Journey in America* (Philadelphia: Caleb Richardson, 1817) and his *Letters from Illinois* (Philadelphia: M. Carey & Sons, 1818); and Richard Flower, *Letters from Lexington and the Illinois* (London: C. Teulon, 1819). The best account of the English settlement is Jane Rodman, "The English Settlement in Southern Illinois as Viewed by English Travellers, 1815–1825," *Indiana Magazine of History*, XLIII (December, 1947), 328–362, and XLIV (March, 1948), 36–38.

[32] *Dictionary of American Biography*, Allen Johnson and Dumas Malone, eds. (New York: Charles Scribner's Sons, 1928–1937), XIII, 61.

[33] Others who had an interest with Mitchell and Grigg in some of the land Grigg entered were Elias B. Bishop of Connecticut, John B. Augur of Illinois, and Cyrus P. Smith of Brooklyn. See mortgage of these five partners to Isaiah Williamson in Christian County Deed Records, I, 84.

"one of the finest agricultural districts in the United States," having a "happy proportion of timber and prairie lands. . . ." Attention was given to the richness of the land, the certainty that it would rise rapidly in value, and the prospects of high returns from investments in Illinois. Mitchell cribbed much of his information from other sources, principally from J. M. Peck, *Gazetteer of Illinois,* published three years earlier, but he omitted Peck's cautionary statements, embroidered his descriptions, and added the most flattering predictions concerning future development.[34]

Mitchell's *Illinois in 1837* was one of the two most widely distributed guides to the Illinois prairies until the appearance of the promotional pamphlets of the Illinois Central Railroad in 1855. Hence it was no accident that the first big push of settlers and speculators into the prairies came in the Sangamon Valley, where the Grigg lands were situated and to which the Mitchell gazetteer gave disproportionate space. Whatever the plans of Grigg and Mitchell for their lands may have been, they sold them over the course of succeeding years at surprisingly moderate prices. Sales were begun almost as soon as the land were patented and continued until into the seventies, though most of them were sold in the forties and fifties. In this long span of years, a portion —55,458 acres in four counties—was sold for an average of $4.93 an acre. These sales were made without raising the usual cries of "monopolist," "speculator," "grasping landlord" that color so much of western political literature.[35]

Another early prairie enterpreneur was Henry L. Ellsworth, a Connecticut Yankee addicted to Democratic politics who became Commissioner of Patents in 1835. Ellsworth, who loved to tinker with farm machinery and to experiment with cropping and feed schemes, used his position to advance the introduction of laborsaving devices on the farm. Having become acquainted with the Indiana prairie, on one of his western trips Ellsworth purchased 18,000 acres in and around Lafayette for himself and other investors, on part of which he planned to develop a modern, tenant-operated agricultural estate. A year's experiment in cultivating prairie land conducted by his son convinced him that the Wabash Valley had "the best soil and most favourable climate," that it was capable of producing "40 bushels of wheat, 70 of corn, 60 of oats, and 450 of potatoes" to the acre and would soon be worth $50 an acre.[36]

[34] Mitchell, *Illinois in 1837,* pp. 5–6, 103; J. M. Peck, *Gazetteer of Illinois, in Three Parts* . . . (Jacksonville: Goudy, 1834), *passim.*

[35] The figures of sales are the result of analysis of the deed books of Christian, Sangamon, Logan, and McLean Counties, Illinois. For a judgment of Grigg, see *Hunt's Merchants' Magazine,* XXV (July, 1851), 28–39.

[36] Mitchell, *Illinois in 1837,* pp. 130–133.

The usual device to promote settlement was the publication of an advertising brochure. In 1838 the Ellsworths, father and son, brought out a booklet of 175 pages in which they tried to outdo the Mitchell book by upholding the virtues and opportunities of the Wabash Valley as against the Sangamon Valley. All that was said about fertility of the soil was correct, and Ellsworth frankly admitted that it took from $3.75 to $9 an acre to bring prairie land into cultivation, but the emphasis upon actual or potential transportation facilities was overdone, sod fencing, which had not worked well in the West, was given favorable attention, its cost was underestimated, and the value of the "inexhaustible" coal deposits at Danville before railroad connections were completed was exaggerated. More serious was the fact that the anticipated profits from prairie cultivation were presented without regard to numerous difficulties settlers were already contending with in the region. The booklet was directed at eastern capitalists, who were urged to invest through the Ellsworth agency in prairie land from which they were assured large profits.[37] No rush of settlers followed the appearance of this extended blurb, but almost $200,000 of eastern capital was invested in Wabash Valley land through the agency of the Ellsworths. Though some of these investors held their land for short periods only, having to sell before the anticipated rise, their activities contributed to the creation of great estates of 20,000 to 40,000 acres and the early appearance of tenant-operated farms.[38]

After retiring from the Patent Office in 1845, Ellsworth took up residence at Lafayette, where he began extensive improvements on his large holdings, now amounting to more than a hundred thousand acres. To confine his herds of cattle and hogs he built 27 miles of heavy plank fence. One hundred and twenty yoke of oxen were used to break the prairie and prepare the land for corn, of which he produced 100,000 bushels in 1851. The corn was fed to his herds of cattle. When fattened they were shipped by canal and lake vessel to the New York market. Ellsworth early resorted to tenancy to assure the necessary labor for his large operations. Tenants were promised the land they improved after they had shared half the crops of corn with him for three years. For other tenants on land which he planned to retain Ellsworth erected dwellings.[39] Because of his prominence in developing the agricultural

[37] Henry William Ellsworth, *Valley of the Upper Wabash, Indiana, with Hints on Its Agricultural Advantages* . . . (New York: Pratt, Robinson & Co., 1838).

[38] Gates, "Land Policy and Tenancy in the Prairie Counties of Indiana," *loc. cit.*, 1–26.

[39] *Wabash Standard*, Lafayette, Ind., July 18, 1845; *American Agriculturist*, VIII (November, 1849), 348; *Davenport Gazette*, October 9, 1851; Elmore Barce, *Annals of Benton County* (Fowler, Ind.: The Benton Review Shop, 1925), pp. 56–58, 66–67; Kellar, *Solon Robinson*, II, 96.

work of the Patent Office, Ellsworth was one of the most widely known men in the field of agriculture and his activities in prairie farming were given much attention in the farm journals.

Birkbeck, Grigg, Mitchell, and Ellsworth, the prophets of prairie agriculture, were somewhat in advance of their time. By the late forties the picture was changing. Now capital in abundance was flowing into prairie ventures. Several scores of large investors and thousands of men with small sums of a few hundred or thousand dollars invaded the prairie country. An Illinois history of 1853 reported, "The prairies are now being brought rapidly under cultivation. . . ." [40]

An illustration of the large investments in prairie land which were being made at the time is that of the Scott family of Lexington, Kentucky. The bulk of the family's 63,000 acres of prairie lands in Iowa and Illinois was acquired in the fifties, and part of it was rapidly developed with gangs of prairie breakers, tenants, laborers, and carpenters. There were twenty tenants on the land in 1860. Scott used a rental-sales agreement that was not uncommon in the West whereby he contracted to convey title to purchasers who agreed to make specified improvements and to pay sixteen bushels of corn for each acre for six to nine years. Much farm land was thus improved for Scott, but only one third of the tenants carried their contract to completion and became owners. [41]

Not far from the Scott holdings in Illinois was the 38,000-acre estate of William Scully, who secured improvements on his land without cost to himself. Scully, whose leasing policies on his substantial Irish estates were being bitterly criticized by both peasants and fellow landlords in the fifties, began the transfer of his capital to prairie land investments in Illinois. Extensive sheep and cattle raising and grain production were accompanied by the renting of tracts to tenants on terms that required them to make all improvements. Within a short time the Scully land was bringing in sufficient surplus to enable the owner to enlarge his holdings and to acquire even greater tracts in Kansas and Nebraska. [42]

Greatest of the bonanza farm makers on the prairies was Michael Sullivant. On his home farm of 5,000 acres adjoining Columbus, Ohio, Sullivant raised purebred cattle. Perhaps the scale of his operations did not satisfy him, for in 1852 he began buying land in eastern Illinois until

[40] W. H. Carpenter and T. S. Arthur, *The History of Illinois from the Earliest Settlement to the Present Time* (Philadelphia: Lippincott, Grambo & Co., 1854), p. 247.

[41] Margaret Beattie Bogue, "Patterns from the Sod: Land Use and Tenure in the Grand Prairie, 1850–1900." Unpublished doctoral dissertation, 1955, Cornell University.

[42] Paul W. Gates, *Frontier Landlords and Pioneer Tenants* (Ithaca, N. Y.: Cornell University Press, 1945), pp. 34 ff.

he held 80,000 acres. With the aid of 100 hired hands, 125 yoke of oxen, and 50 horses he had by 1857 3,000 acres in corn and a smaller number in wheat. Many miles of hedge fencing were set out to protect his grain crops from cattle. For a generation Sullivant's vast farming operations received much attention and considerable criticism, for it was felt locally that the community would have benefited more had the estate been divided into small owner-operated farms. Like other capitalist estate builders, Sullivant provided employment to many immigrants coming into the prairies who lacked the means with which to begin farming and who may have been enabled, through this employment, to become tenant farmers later or, perchance, to begin farming on their own farther West, where cheap lands were available.[43]

Cattle feeding as distinguished from cattle raising early became a specialized feature of prairie agriculture. Since most farmers kept only a few cattle, it was not worth their while to drive them to market; consequently, they were willing to sell to buyers who dropped around once a year to take off their surplus stock. The surplus, whether young steers or old cows, was driven to the feed lots and fattened on a combination of native grasses, bluegrass, and corn. Hogs followed the cattle, salvaging the wasted corn. When the stock was in fit shape it was driven to the market at Chicago, Indianapolis, or Cincinnati. More enterprising drovers would drive stock to New York or Philadelphia, where better prices could naturally be secured. As success came to the feeders and drovers, they enlarged their operations, traveled farther afield, even as far as Texas, in their search for stock.

When the cattle-feeding business first developed, the open prairie, still retained by the federal government, was freely used, and there was no incentive to acquire land other than for a feeding center. As settlers moved into the prairies and speculators began to purchase portions, the drovers found it necessary to protect their interests by engrossing substantial acreages. By the fifties large cattle-feeding estates existed: the 26,000-acre holding of Isaac Funk, the 20,000-acre property of Jacob Strawn, the 16,000-acre ownership of John Dean Gillett, the 33,000-acre ranch of Phineas and Alexander Kent, and the 30,000-acre farming operation of Edward Sumner. These men were constantly buying and selling livestock, and the number they had at any one time is not a true index of the size of their operations. In 1860, one of the most successful, Isaac Funk, reported to the census taker 1,274 cattle, 300 sheep, 150 hogs, and 134 horses and mules, altogether valued at $31,480. He also reported on hand 72,000 bushels of grain.[44]

[43] *Ibid.*, pp. 15–20.
[44] Most of the 35 large Illinois cattlemen receiving attention in Paul W. Gates, "Cattle Kings in the Prairies," *Mississippi Valley Historical Review,* XXXV (Decem-

As landed proprietors the cattlemen raised their own corn instead of buying it, as they had formerly. They employed scores and even hundreds of laborers to operate the breaker plows, the many drags, harrows, cultivators, and other machines then coming into use, and to harvest the grain, feed the stock, and drive it to market. They erected barracks to house their unmarried hands and small cottages for the more permanently employed married help. When migratory labor proved unreliable, careless, and disorderly, and taxes and other costs crept upward, the proprietors divided their large fields and pastures into small farm units, which they rented to tenants on a crop-share basis, or they provided the farm equipment and seed and paid the tenants seven cents a bushel for all the corn they raised. In this way they shared with the tenants responsibility for profits and losses and assured themselves of more dependable labor.

There were other ways in which large prairie estates came into existence. Men who bought and sold lands, dealt in exchange, lent money at 10 per cent or more to hard-pressed farm makers, served as attorneys for railroads, undertook construction contracts for railroads, or carried on a general law and collection business generally acquired a sizable amount of prairie land. There were few communities in which there was not a man who brought to it little cash but much shrewd ability; hung out a shingle; drew deeds, mortgages, and bills of exchange; dabbled in politics; lent money and speculated in land; laid out a town or an addition to an already existing town; dealt in tax titles; and bid in land at foreclosure sales. Such a man became the local squire, the owner of the "big house," the respected but sometimes feared power in the community.

Examples of these self-made holders of large estates in central Illinois and Iowa were Clifton H. Moore, John Warner, and David Davis. Moore was attorney for the Illinois Central Railroad, for which he purchased a part of its right of way through privately owned land; he also acted as agent for its lands. He made loans, foreclosed valuable farm property, made fortunate and wisely selected entries of land at the government sales, and managed investments for others. Warner was a physician who found dealing in lands more remunerative than peddling pills. Intermarriage of the two families brought the estates together. Davis,

ber, 1948), 379–412, were well along in land accumulation by the fifties. Helen M. Cavanagh has brought together more information on the amazingly large cattle business of Isaac Funk in her *Funk of Funk's Grove: Farmer, Legislator and Cattle King of the Old Northwest, 1797–1865* (Bloomington, Ill.: Pantagraph Printing Co., 1952), than we have on any of the other cattle kings of the time. In the discursive *Life of Tom Candy Ponting: An Autobiography*, Herbert O. Brayer, ed. (Evanston, Ill.: The Branding Iron Press, 1952), is useful information concerning cattle droving in Illinois in the fifties.

successively a lawyer, judge, member of the federal Supreme Court, and
of the United States Senate, built up an estate of $2,000,000 in land. Some
45,000 acres of prairie land were acquired by these men, much at less
than the government price of $1.25 an acre. Not all was retained, but the
best tracts were developed by laborers and tenants and before 1860 were
providing considerable rental income. In that year Moore valued his property at $183,900; Warner valued his at $60,000; Davis's property may be
estimated at $100,000 to $150,000. In the same region was another railroad
contractor who invested his profits in land and who valued his holdings
at $275,000.[45]

Capitalist farm makers and livestock breeders were getting large
operations under way in Iowa and Missouri in the fifties. The many-
thousand-acre holdings of the Wearin family, of Horace Everett, of John
Evans, and of Timothy Day in Western Iowa were being fenced and
pastured with great herds of cattle. On the 7,000-acre farm of Richard
Gentry in Missouri were kept 1,000 sheep. Clover, timothy, and bluegrass
were raised on 2,150 acres, corn on 320 acres, and oats on 160 acres.
Twelve grown farm hands and six boys were employed to handle such
large operations. It was these capitalist farm makers and livestock breeders, with their extensive operations, and many others who functioned on
a smaller scale, who brought commercial feeding and breeding activities
to a high place in the prairies.[46] In 1860, Illinois was far ahead of all states
in the number of hogs, was exceeded only by Texas in the number of its
beef cattle, and was outdistanced only by Ohio in the number of horses.

Eastern moneylenders who had put out large sums to buy lands for
squatters on the usual frontier terms not infrequently found their debtors
unable to complete payments on these tracts. The land subsequently
reverted to the creditors, who might make improvements or encourage
the squatters, now their tenants, to continue their development of the
land. Whether they planned it or not, the creditors found themselves
deeply involved in extensive farm-management deals with tenants.[47]

Not all settler-immigrants came to the West without resources. Those
who came from farm backgrounds had sold their old homesteads to get
the funds to take them and their families to the new West. Sometimes
they had enough cash to buy a 160-acre tract, perhaps two or three quarter sections, erect a house, purchase essential farm machinery and some

[45] Taken from the original census schedules in the Illinois State Archives.

[46] *Country Gentleman*, VIII (September 4, 1856), 156–157, X (August 31 and
December 10, 1857), 195 and 381; *Hamilton Freeman*, October 26, 1861; *Genesee
Farmer*, XIX (August, 1858), 247, quoting the *Valley Farmer*.

[47] A private collection, formerly in the hands of Miles White of Baltimore, and
the Easley and Willingham Collection in the manuscript division of the Library of
the University of Virginia offer valuable information concerning loans to squatters
and the numerous forfeitures of their rights through failure to meet payments.

livestock, and hire poorer immigrants to aid in getting farming operations under way. There is abundant evidence that thousands of immigrants moving into the newly developing regions of Illinois, Iowa, Missouri, and even Kansas in the fifties brought sufficient money with them to permit them to purchase land from the government, from speculative companies, or from land-grant railroads with some down payment, and the census figures show that many were also able to invest considerable sums in starting to improve their land. The 47,216 farm laborers who appear in the Census of 1860 for Illinois show that not only the few score of bonanza farmers and extensive cattle ranchers but many other farmers were able to employ hired hands.

FARM LABORERS

Farmers had to compete with railroad construction bosses for their hired hands, and, since the construction season coincided with the busy season on the farms, the competition was keen in periods of expansion, such as the years preceding 1857. Construction bosses scoured the cities for labor, offered $1.25 a day with board in work camps or trains at two dollars a week. Mechanics and artisans were paid from $1.50 to $3.00 a day. But it was farming, not railroad construction or uncertain factory work, that the hordes of immigrants pouring into the prairies wanted to take up for the long pull, provided it offered the road to landownership. Wages of $10 to $20 a month which farmers offered through the year or $2.00 a day with board during the busy planting and harvesting seasons were certainly no short cut to landownership.[48] Nevertheless, the biographical accounts in the county histories show that many farmers started their careers as laborers on farms of others and worked upward through tenancy to ownership. By investing their small savings in livestock, which they were permitted to pasture, or in farm machinery, which they were allowed to use on land allotted them by their employer (perhaps to hold them longer on the job), they gradually built up equipment and stock sufficient to enable them to set up as tenants or as purchasers of land on credit.

The hired hand or farm laborer is the most neglected element of frontier society. Not until 1860 did the Bureau of the Census collect data on farm laborers. The statistics thus assembled have attracted practically no attention though they present a picture of pioneer agriculture quite different from the idyllic scene that historians of the frontier have described. Indiana, for example, contained 40,827 people who were listed as farm laborers in 1860; Illinois, 47,216; and Iowa, 27,196. True, a consider-

---

[48] *Davenport Gazette*, January 26, 1856; Gerhard, *Illinois as It Is*, pp. 316, 447.

able number listed as farm laborers were grown sons who had not as yet left their fathers' farms, but others were immigrants seeking farms who took temporary jobs until they found the land they wanted and had the means to make at least a down payment on it.[49]

Iowa, only fourteen years a state, still but lightly touched by settlement, not able to boast two people to the square mile, had less than a third of its land in farms, but the bulk of its public lands had already gone into private ownership. Despite its slight development, which was largely concentrated in the eastern third of the state, its obvious frontier status, its abundance of raw, unimproved prairie, Iowa reported 40,827 farm laborers in 1860, or 6 per cent of its population. More to the point, of every 100 persons engaged in agriculture, 23 were farm laborers.

Kansas had neither attained the dignity of statehood nor acquired anything but a thin veneer of settlement along its eastern front in the six years it had been a territory; yet census enumerators found here 10,400 farms and, surprisingly, 3,660 farm laborers. Nineteen out of every 100 persons engaged in agriculture were farm laborers. The percentages of farm laborers in the total number of people engaged in agriculture were 23 in Illinois, 19 in Indiana, and 22 in Ohio.

The published census data for 1860 and earlier censuses provide little help in determining the progress settlers were making in their efforts to acquire and develop their farms. That the single-family farm was common throughout the prairies is clear, notwithstanding the number of large farm units that has been shown to exist. Tenancy was growing rapidly and many farmers were buying their land and perhaps going into debt even more heavily to finance improvements: these facts are also clear. In the absence of information in the published census data it is necessary to go back to the original census schedules, which throw much light on the developing labor and tenancy pattern in the prairies. The information is, however, meager because the enumerators were not instructed to deal with tenancy or farm mortgages. Some of the data was gratuitously provided by enumerators who went beyond their instructions.

On the David and Harriet Mark property in Tazewell County, Illinois, for example, there was a well-developed estate amounting to 6,930 acres on which thirty-one tenants paid grain rent in 1863 and 1864. In the census schedules of 1860 these tenants are shown to be accumulating property, such as horses, cattle, hogs, and farm machinery which, with their own labor, they might expect would enable them to buy the farms they were then tilling or perhaps others that might be for sale. Actually,

[49] The statistics of farms and farm laborers in the remainder of this chapter are from the *Eighth Census of the United States, Population,* and from the original schedules of the Eighth Census in the National Archives.

these Mark farms were not to be available for purchase, and ninety years later were still owned by the descendants of David Mark.[50]

More meaningful, though certainly not representative, are the data compiled from four townships in Champaign County, Illinois, which were selected in part because of a large farming operation underway in them. In these four townships there were almost as many farm laborers as farmers, but the fact that farm laborers were working their way up the agricultural ladder is the significant finding.

FARMERS AND FARM LABORERS IN FOUR CHAMPAIGN
TOWNSHIPS, 1860

	Farmers	Farm laborers
With real and personal property	169	20*
With personal only	16*	70*
With real only	1*	1*
Without real or personal	0	89

Source: Compiled from the original census schedules of these townships, in the National Archives. Townships included in this table are Sadorus, Champaign, Scott, and Mahomet.

Of a total of 366 farmers and farm laborers, 108 (marked with an asterisk in the table) appear to be working up the ladder to full ownership of operating farms, and of these 91 were probably tenants. One hundred and sixty-nine were already farmers owning their places and 89 were laborers having no property.

Census takers in Bureau and Kankakee counties provided more information concerning the ownership and renting of farms than is available for most areas in 1860. Tenants were defined as persons who owned all the stock and paid either a cash or a share rent; agents were defined as tenants who owned no stock but were provided with stock and machinery by the landlord and in turn paid a share rent; managers were defined as persons who owned no stock and received no share of the crops, but were paid by the owner to manage the farms. Of 2,826 persons engaged in farming in Bureau County, 2,433 were listed as farmers, 288 as tenants, 81 as agents, and 10 as managers. In addition, 14 were listed as renting land. Approximately 14 per cent of the farms were operated by tenants. In Kankakee County, where there was a flourishing but poor colony of French Canadians, incomplete data show 136 tenants, 1 agent, and 1,467 farmers.

[50] Account of grain sold for the David Mark estate, filed, November 12, 1864, in File Box 38, County Clerk's Office, Pekin, Ill. The value of the Mark land and improvements in 1860 was given as $143,520 in the Census of 1860, but for estate purposes it was listed at $20,000. See abstract of Pekin property compiled for David Mark Cummings, Office of C. R. Cummings, Pekin.

The prairies had not been conquered by 1860. Their lack of natural drainage still remained a major problem which deterred intensive development for nearly a score of years.[51] Only by tiling or ditching and by the establishment of drainage districts with the power to sell bonds and collect taxes was it to be possible to undertake the drainage of the most level land. Land was still withheld from productive use by speculators and farm makers who, in their anxiety to engross as much as their resources permitted, acquired more than they had capital to develop and became land-poor. Whole stretches of land thus undeveloped, though in private ownership, were spoken of as "speculators' deserts." It was this engrossment of land for speculative purposes that drove immigrants looking for land to scatter widely, and explains the demand for the opening of additional territory to settlement. Had more orderly and compact development of land preceded 1854 there might not have been the upsurge of political pressure for the creation of the Kansas-Nebraska territories that produced such mischief.

Notwithstanding these deterrents to progress, no section of the country had been so transformed in the decade before 1860 as the prairies. The modern corn belt was taking shape, with emphasis upon the production of grain for the market and the feeding of livestock. Capital investments in land, improvements, and farm machinery were high, heavy mortgage indebtedness was already showing, tenancy was well under way, but at the same time thousands of farmers from older parts of the country and from northern Europe became freeholders. The prosperity of the mid-fifties was halted by the Panic of 1857 and the consequent precipitous decline in land values and in dollar returns from produce and livestock, but improvements continued to be made, farm development went on, some speculative holdings were liquidated, and the West was soon ready for another era of expansion.

[51] Bogue, "The Swamp Land Act . . ." *loc. cit.*, pp. 169–180.

CHAPTER X

Livestock

THE "suitcase farmer" drilling his wheat in the fall, harvesting it in June, and then leaving the land for an industrial job elsewhere is a twentieth-century type for which there was no counterpart in the nineteenth century. The closest resemblance to such a person was the roving squatter who took up a claim on the outer edge of the frontier, made the rudest improvements, and sold when incoming settlers a few months or a few years later were willing to pay him something for his "right" in land to which he had no title. Such a roving squatter might have had a horse or mule, a scrawny cow or a long-shanked hog, but the value of his stock and his concern for them were slight and did not tie him to his claim. The animals that he had ran wild in the woods.

NEGLECT OF LIVESTOCK

As the original census schedules show, most early nineteenth-century farmers kept stock which tied them to the farm, but they did not give them the attention and care that was customary for English farmers. Timothy Pickering deplored the poor pastures, opened to cattle too early in the spring; the failure to feed grain and root crops; and the lack of care in housing livestock that was generally characteristic of New England farms. Even the best-blooded stock, he warned, would degenerate under such circumstances.[1] Travelers noted that cattle were not housed in the winter, that little or no effort was made to assure good breeding practices, and that the condition of the stock was uniformly low. Thus an English critic observed in 1842 that the cattle on Staten Island were "of the most heterogeneous breeds, bad Lancashires, Scotch, and Welsh, no two bearing the least appearance of consanguinity." The red cattle he saw everywhere in New York State were "degenerated, being of diminutive size,

[1] *New England Farmer,* IV (October 14, 1825), 89.

coarse, and evidently bad feeders, averaging not more than from 25 to 30 stones." Colonel Wadsworth's stock seemed "starved and stunted in their growth, and as miserable in appearance as the worst stock on the bleak sides of our Grampian hills. . . ." His Durham bulls were "so low in condition and so disfigured—appearing as if scalded with hot water—that it is impossible to judge of their properties. He also crosses with half-bred bulls, and the consequence is a heterogeneous mixture which it would puzzle a Wetherell to analyze." [2] Whether sheep, cattle, or hogs, the livestock were required to get most of their forage from unenclosed fields and woods, were given little or no grain or root crops, and rarely had the protection against the wintry blasts.[3] Such feeding practices did nothing to maintain quality.

The condition and care of cattle and other livestock in the South and West was even worse than in the North. A not unfriendly critic said of Louisiana stock in 1818:

The cattle of this part of the country are not often fat. This circumstance is, probably, owing to many causes; some of which are, their being much troubled by flies, not being salted, and the food which they eat being of rapid growth, and of course unsubstantial. The latter does not possess the consistency of the New-England grass.

. . . . . .

The cattle . . . not worth more than one-fourth of the price of New-England cattle. The cows seldom calve more than once in two years, and they give very little milk. The milk of a Yankee cow will make more butter than that of ten of them.[4]

Another traveler, on his way through Georgia in 1845, found the cattle "objects of pity, not to feed upon but to be fed. Left to shift for themselves all winter, their bones look and stare at you. . . ." [5] The Louisiana and Texas cattle were notoriously poor, having "greatly deteriorated" in the generation before 1853, according to Olmsted. Robert Russell thought the cattle throughout the cotton kingdom fared poorly and looked starved.[6]

[2] Captain Barclay, *Agricultural Tour in the United States and Upper Canada* (Edinburgh: William Blackwood & Sons, 1842), pp. 15, 38 ff.

[3] *New England Farmer*, IV (October 14, 1825), 89.

[4] Estwick Evans, *A Pedestrious Tour of Four Thousand Miles through the Western States and Territories During the Winter and Spring of 1818,* reproduced in Reuben Gold Thwaites, ed., *Early Western Travels, 1748–1846* (32 vols.; Cleveland: Arthur H. Clark Co., 1904–1907), VIII, 330–331.

[5] Rev. G. Lewis, *Impressions of America and the American Churches* (Edinburgh: W. P. Kennedy, 1845), p. 140.

[6] Frederick Law Olmsted, *Journey in the Seaboard Slave States . . .* (New York: Dix & Edwards, 1856), p. 628; Robert Russell, *North America: Its Agriculture and Climate* (Edinburgh: Adam & Charles Black, 1857), p. 270.

Had they not known better, European agricultural authorities who journeyed through America in the early nineteenth century and observed the condition of the cattle, particularly in the South, where they were most neglected, might have reiterated the Count de Buffon's earlier hypothesis that the climate of the Western Hemisphere was such as to produce degeneration in man and in domestic and wild animals. Buffon's view had been effectively disproved by Thomas Jefferson in his *Notes on Virginia*, wherein he maintained that the admitted deterioration in domestic animals was the result of neglect and improper feeding and breeding practices.[7]

This all too apparent neglect resulted from the farmer's attempt to accomplish too much. On the frontier he was carving out a farm from the wilderness or subduing the prairie, either of which absorbed his full energies. He needed livestock but he had no time or surplus feed for it and consequently permitted it to shift for itself. Lack of fencing made it impossible for more enterprising farmers to improve the quality of their stock. Consequently, it was easy for farmers to go on year after year devoting their energies to farm making—clearing; fencing out cattle and hogs; erecting barns, frame houses, and corn cribs; even draining wet areas—while doing little for their stock, other than branding them and rounding them up for slaughter or market when they were five or six years old.

Lack of attention, poor feed, and the failure to house the cattle in the winter did not prevent their numbers from increasing rapidly. Between 1840 and 1860 the number of cattle increased from 14,972,000 to 28,963,028. Though the northern and southern states had about the same number of cattle in 1860, the ratio of cattle to human beings and the number per farm was higher in the South. The North developed the feeder and dairy cattle business whereas the South practiced grazing. Professor Frank L. Owsley argues that the piney woods settlers and mountaineers, the poor whites, were essentially cattle graziers who followed the receding frontier and made their living from their livestock while doing a minimum amount of cultivating. Staple-crop planters took the better alluvial and canebrake land; cattle graziers found it possible to do reasonably well in the piney woods and on rough, broken, sandy and hill country.[8] This is not to say that the planters had no livestock; they raised a considerable part of their own beef and pork, but they bought more from the piney woods farmers in addition to barreled beef and pork from the Northwest.

[7] *Notes on the State of Virginia*, Paul Leicester Ford, ed. (Brooklyn: Historical Printing Club, 1894), pp. 69 ff.; *De Bow's Review*, New Series, I (July, 1858), 86.

[8] Frank L. Owsley, "The Pattern of Migration and Settlement on the Southern Frontier," *Journal of Southern History*, XI (May, 1945), 149 ff.

IMPORTS OF PUREBRED CATTLE

Improved breeding practices in cattle raising in the United States date from 1783, when some good-quality cattle of the Patton strain were imported from England and driven to the Bluegrass country of Kentucky. Next came the importation to Kentucky of Herefords by Henry Clay and of Shorthorns or Durhams by Lewis Sanders in 1816. Herefords did not gain favor there at the time, but the two strains of Shorthorns, which were crossed and further improved by new imports, produced cattle famous for their early maturity, great weight in essential places, and economy in feeding.[9] Shorthorns were also imported into New England, New York, Pennsylvania, and Maryland by Stephen Van Rensselaer, "the last Patroon"; by gentleman farmers and cattle fanciers like Lewis G. Morris of Mt. Fordham, New York, and John Hare Powel of suburban Philadelphia; and by professional stockmen and farmers like Felix and George Renick of Chillicothe, Ohio. Group importations were arranged by the Massachusetts Society for the Promotion of Agriculture and the Ohio Company for Importing English Cattle. So numerous were the importations by 1839 that it was remarked that scarcely a ship docked in New York which did not bring purebred stock from England.[10]

It was in Kentucky and New York in 1837 and 1838 that the "Short-horn fever" reached its greatest height. Numerous importations from England were followed by exciting auction sales in which purebred stock sold at from a few hundred dollars to two thousand and more.[11] The *Franklin Farmer*, published in the fast-horse and Shorthorn country, gave more attention in these years to importations, auctions, pedigrees, prices, and cattle fanciers than to all other aspects of agriculture. Similarly, the influential Albany *Cultivator* allotted disproportionate space to the verbal battles that waged in behalf of Shorthorns and Herefords by Lewis F. Allen, E. P. Prentice, Henry S. Randall, and William H. Sotham.[12] The panic, the bank failures, and the Depression of 1837 for a time brought

[9] Lewis Sanders, "History of Kentucky Cattle," *Southern Planter*, X (January, 1850), 19–25; Alvin H. Sanders, *Short-Horn Cattle: A Series of Sketches, Memoirs and Records of the Breed and Its Development in the United States and Canada* (Chicago: Sanders Publishing Co., 1909), pp. 164 ff.; James Westfall Thompson, "A History of Livestock Raising in the United States, 1607–1860" (U. S. Department of Agriculture, *Agricultural History Series*, No. 5, processed; Washington, D. C.: 1942), p. 129.

[10] George F. Lemmer, "The Spread of Improved Cattle through the Eastern United States to 1850," *Agricultural History*, XXI (April, 1947), 84.

[11] Commissioner of Patents, *Annual Report, Agriculture, 1851* (Washington, D. C.: Robert Armstrong, 1852), pp. 98–103; *Cincinnati Daily Gazette*, November 22, 1836, and October 3, 1837.

[12] *Franklin Farmer*, Vol. I (1837), and Vol. II (1838), especially II (January 26, 1839), 183; *Cultivator*, Vol. VII (1840) and Vol. VIII (1841), *passim*.

to a halt the excitement over purebred stock, but it revived in the forties and fifties.

The prosperity of the fifties and the increasing evidence of the value of good stock led to the organization of five stock-importing associations in Ohio, four in Kentucky, two in Illinois, and one in New York, which brought in well over 200 purebred Shorthorns. The diary of an agent of a Kentucky association is illuminating for its account of his travels through England, his examination of numerous herds of cattle and sheep, his failure to persuade some stockmen to part with their best animals, and finally the sale at Paris, Kentucky, at which the imported stock sold at extraordinarily high prices. The Shaker communities also imported purebred Shorthorns for their rich Miami bottom farms of 4,500 acres in Ohio and their 10,000 acres in farms in Kentucky, where they maintained large herds of the best strains of Shorthorns as well as Saxon sheep and Berkshire hogs.[13]

Best advertised and most influential of the stock importers was Lewis G. Morris. On his farm, in what is now Bronx County in New York City, Morris built up a large herd of Shorthorns. His sales were widely advertised and attracted excited bidding. A local historian says that so high a reputation had his stock acquired that English buyers attended his sales and bought and shipped to England some of his choicest animals. The Illinois Breeding Association bought six of Morris's Shorthorns in 1855 for removal to that state.[14]

An agricultural editor from Richmond, Virginia, visiting the Albany-Troy center of purebred cattle, especially the "splendid herds of Messrs. Prentice, Sotham, and Vail" was shown Herefords, Shorthorns, and Ayrshires that surpassed anything he had previously seen. Though he was doubtless familiar with high living among southern planters, he was inordinately impressed with the style of living of these "elegant and accomplished gentlemen" who had "more rural elegancies than we ever dreamed of in our own thoughtless, extravagant harum scarum country." [15]

The "pedigree craze" for purebred Shorthorns was so well established by the middle of the century, and imports were becoming so common,

[13] Wool Grower and Stock Register, VIII (October, 1855), 129; IX (January, 1856), 25; American Agriculturist, X (December, 1851), 365–366; Charles Nordhoff, Communistic Societies in the United States (London: John Murray, 1875), pp. 220 ff.; Register of the Kentucky Historical Society, XXIX (October, 1931), 400–415, and XXX (January, 1932), 37–60.

[14] Ohio Cultivator, VIII (July, 1852), 202; Country Gentleman, V (May 24 and June 21, 1855), 328, 393; VII (May 15, 1856) 38; and VIII (July 3, 1856), 16; J. Thomas Scharff, History of Westchester County, New York (2 vols.; Philadelphia: L. E. Preston & Co., 1886), I, 828.

[15] Southern Planter, IV (June, 1844), 137.

that advertisements of British auctions were carried in American farm journals, and cattle buyers solicited orders for their next trip to England.[16] The foremost American importer sadly reported in 1856 that so great had been the demand for English Shorthorns in the United States, in addition to purchases by cattlemen from the Continent and from Australia, that good stock in England had "diminished most wonderfully" and the number of "good ones left is very small. . . ." [17] Lewis Allen, author of the Shorthorn *Herdbooks* and principal authority on cattle importation, estimated that by 1865 600 Shorthorn cattle had been imported into the United States and 100 into Canada.[18]

Importations of purebred stock into the South, excluding Maryland, Virginia, and Kentucky, were less numerous than those in the North. A Georgia planter knew of the importation of two or three Devons and one or two Ayrshire cows but could detect no considerable movement for the improvement of stock.[19] As late as 1859 one observer thought Mississippi cattle like the lean kine of Pharoah, "their ribs and hip bones about as prominent as their horns, and so run down in flesh that a hydraulic press would not be able to extract either milk or fat from them." A few Shorthorns were brought into Mississippi, but the hot sun, coarse grass, and improper feeding made them unprofitable.[20] One planter deplored as a "sad mistake" the substitution of Shorthorn cattle for the time-tried descendants of Spanish cattle because the Shorthorn and all other oxen from northern breeds were "totally worthless" in heavy hauling in swamps. Furthermore, native cattle, when properly fed, he contended, gave fully as much milk as either the Shorthorn or Ayrshire cows, both of which he had tried. It was held that by judicious selection, good feeding, and kind treatment, southern cattle, without the infusion of northern or English blood strains, could be made to compare favorably with the best in the North.[21]

In Alabama some improvement was made in cattle. At the fair of the Mobile Agricultural and Horticultural Society in 1859 were displayed

[16] *Country Gentleman*, VII (March 13 and May 1, 1856), 183, 288; *Valley Farmer*, V (May, 1853), 1 of advertising section.

[17] Robert Alexander in *Western Farm Journal*, I (September 1, 1856), 98.

[18] Commissioner of Agriculture, *Annual Report, 1866* (Washington, D. C.: Government Printing Office, 1867), p. 305.

[19] *Soil of the South*, III (December, 1853), 746.

[20] *American Agriculturist*, IV (August, 1845), 253; and IX (January, 1850), 30.

[21] *Southern Cultivator*, III (August, 1845), 121; *De Bow's Review*, XVII (December 4, 1854), 627–628. Martin W. Philips of Mississippi had bad luck with his first importation of Shorthorns, a number of which died. He attributed their loss to climate, bad management, inadequate food, and neglect. John C. Jenkins, ordinarily a progressive and experimentally inclined planter, questioned the value of northern cattle for the South.—Franklin L. Riley, "Diary of a Mississippi Planter," *Publications* of the Mississippi Historical Society, X (1909), 326–327.

specimens of Ayrshire, Devon, Shorthorn, Brahman and "many blendings of the different breeds." Some, it was said, were of "monstrous size"; others were of "surpassing beauty. . . ." From the description of the exhibits it appears that most of the stock were mixtures and not pure-breds.[22]

From Texas came conflicting stories about the Shorthorns. A Corpus Christi rancher told of the importation of Shorthorn bulls, Morgan horses, and Merino sheep, and the "judicious crossing" of them with native stock with favorable results. The other side was presented by a Wharton County rancher, who declared that the Shorthorn bulls brought into his area having grown so large and strong from the abundance of feed "as to be dangerous to our herds, were consequently shot." Contentious old Cassius Clay, a Shorthorn enthusiast, held that the Texans would have been wiser to have let the Shorthorns kill off the weaker and less valuable Longhorns. For another decade or two, Texas cattle continued to be chiefly of 'Spanish descent . . . known by the long horns, fierce and savage looks and their apparent dislike of mankind." Despite these unfavorable reports, the *New Orleans Picayune* carried an advertisement on June 4, 1859, announcing arrangements for importing Thoroughbred stallions; Shorthorn, Hereford, Devon, and Jersey bulls, calves, and cows; and Southdown, Merino, Cotswold, Leicester, Hampshire, and Dorset sheep.[23]

Major centers for raising purebred Shorthorn cattle developed in the Bluegrass area of Kentucky; the Scioto and Miami valleys of Ohio; Livingston, Albany, Dutchess, and Westchester counties, New York; and the environs of Philadelphia. Bourbon County, Kentucky, alone had 10 per cent of the registered Shorthorn bulls that were born, imported, or brought in the United States between 1852 and 1856. Five Bluegrass counties had 22 per cent and six Ohio counties had 16 per cent of the Shorthorn bulls. A Kentucky cattle breeder said of the Bluegrass region: "Whoever has limestone land has blue grass; whoever has blue grass has the basis of all agricultural prosperity; and that man, if he have not the finest horses, cattle and sheep, has no one to blame but himself." He went on: "He can hardly avoid doing well if he will try." [24]

By 1860 there were more than 500 breeders of Shorthorn cattle in Canada and the United States, perhaps 100 Devon cattle breeders and a

[22] *Report* of the Sixth Annual Fair of the Mobile Agricultural and Horticultural Society, 1859 (Mobile, Ala.: A. E. Smoot & Co., 1859), pp. 20–21.

[23] *New Orleans Picayune*, January 2, 6, 1859; Commissioner of Patents, *Report, 1854, Agriculture* (Washington, D. C.: Beverley Tucker, 1855), p. 20; *Ohio Farmer*, V (March 1, 1856); *American Agriculturist*, X (May, 1851), 140.

[24] Charles T. Leavitt, "Attempts to Improve Cattle Breeds in the United States, 1790–1860," *Agricultural History*, VII (April, 1933), 61; Charles L. Flint, *Grasses and Forage Plants* (Boston: Crosby and Nichols, 1864), p. 91.

few breeders of Herefords, Ayrshires, and Jerseys. A writer in the *American Agriculturist*, in summarizing the results of this infusion of blood of English cattle stated: "As a consequence . . . the standard, both in weight and quality of our beef, is higher than before it was introduced, while our cows are decidedly better milkers than of old, and of increased size. . . ." Interbreeding with native cattle had greatly changed the livestock picture. So also had better feeding and maintenance practices. Present-day advocates of the progeny test, with its emphasis upon the actual production rate of milk and butterfat by the offspring, may scoff at the emphasis the nineteenth century put on purebred stock and the great excitement the "battle of the breeds" engendered in the agricultural press. There can be no doubt, however, of the salutary influence the purebred stock had upon both beef and dairy cattle. The Ohio writer may be assumed to be correct who maintained that an admixture of one-half or one-fourth purebred stock with the common native catle produced offspring which, if given the best of care and feed, would be worth from 20 to 50 per cent more than common grade stock.[25]

Despite the popularity of the imported Shorthorns and the lavish attention given them in the agricultural press, native or grade cattle of Devon stock continued to be popular in New England and generally elsewhere. Some grade cows gave extraordinary amounts of milk that were duly noted in the local farm journals. The stock was hardy, tough, made excellent oxen, and dressed off satisfactorily. Shorthorns were larger than the Devons, matured earlier, fattened readily, and, in some families, were good milkers. They were, however, expensive to buy, were not so well adapted to the careless management generally given cattle in America, and did not make as serviceable oxen.[26]

Although the Shorthorns constituted the bulk of imported cattle, small numbers of Ayrshires, Jerseys, Holsteins, Herefords, improved Devons, and Brahman cattle were introduced. Holsteins were regarded with disfavor at a time when most surplus farm milk was used for butter making, and high butterfat content was desired. Jerseys won few friends because they gave little though very rich milk, were not hardy, and were not good beef producers. Ayrshires proved hardy, dressed off better than did the Jerseys, and gave large quantities of milk high in butterfat content. The Massachusetts Society for Promoting Agriculture imported two valuable Ayrshire bulls to aid in improving the quality of dairy cattle. Lewis Morris at Mt. Fordham in New York had a small herd of Ayrshires, and elsewhere in New York and New England were found good stock of

[25] Leavitt, "Attempts to Improve Cattle Breeds . . . ," *loc. cit.*, p. 62.

[26] The replies to a questionnaire of the Commissioner of Patents asking preferences in cattle breeds are instructive. See the *Reports, Agriculture,* for 1852–1855, 1861.

this breed.[27] William H. Sotham, the principal advocate of the Herefords, which he imported in considerable numbers to his farm in New York State, waged vigorous warfare against the advocates of Shorthorns, going so far as to maintain that the Herefords were superior milkers.[28] Improved Devons had their suppporters all the way from Massachusetts, which long continued loyal to them, to California. In 1859, an Ohio stock raiser drove eleven "thoroughbred" Devons from Lorain County across the plains to San Francisco, dropping the old bull by the way "being too foot sore . . . to complete the transit of the continent," and adding a young calf. After wintering in the Golden State and adding two more calves, the cattle were sold at auction for $7,467, which was far in excess of what they would have brought in the East.[29]

Despite Sotham's energetic championship of the Herefords and miscellaneous and scattered defense of the Devons, the Shorthorns remained the most popular cattle with specialists breeding for quality beef and were accorded much greater support by editors of agricultural journals.[30] The unattractive Brahman cattle were imported in the fifties because it was thought they would be better suited to the long hot summers of the South. Few could have foreseen the part they were to play in the improvement of beef cattle or, for that matter, that the Shorthorns, the most popular breed in the first two thirds of the nineteenth century, would be pushed aside so completely in the twentieth century by the Herefords.[31]

SUPPLY OF BEEF CATTLE

The specialization in staple-crop economy in the South made this section dependent upon the upper Mississippi Valley for a considerable part of its beef and pork. This southern dependence began almost with

[27] *Cultivator*, IV (February, 1847), 41; Lemmer, "The Spread of Improved Cattle . . . ," *loc. cit.*, pp. 89–90.

[28] *American Agriculturist*, VII (February, 1848), 52–53; Alvin H. Sanders, *The Story of the Herefords* (Chicago: Breeders' Gazette, 1914), pp. 280–282.

[29] These were not the first purebred cattle brought to California; both Shorthorns and Ayrshires had been imported earlier by ship.—*Weekly Alta California*, San Francisco, February 11, March 17, 24 and April 28, 1860; advertising flyer of James E. Wainwright & Co.: "Great Seal of Thoroughbred Cattle!!" Henry E. Huntington Library.

[30] *American Agriculturist*, VII (February, 1848), 53 ff.

[31] *Louisville Journal* in *Wisconsin & Iowa Farmer and Northwestern Cultivator*, III (December, 1851), 235; *Southern Cultivator*, XV (September, 1857), 291; XVII (August, September, 1858), 6, 11; *Wisconsin Farmer*, XIII (October 1, 1861), 341; Commissioner of Patents, *Report, Agriculture, 1853*, pp. 21–22. In 1853, James B. Davis of Columbia, S. C., reported that his half-breed Brahman cattle sold readily for $1,000 a pair.

the commencement of plantations in the newer South and became ever more apparent as time passed. Until 1850, the number of beef cattle had continued to grow in most states, but in the fifties the number actually declined in seven southern states. Texas could have met this deficiency in large part had transportation facilities been available; lacking them, the Texas herds more than quadrupled between 1850 and 1860.[32]

The growth of industry and the resulting rise of cities, whose meat needs could not be supplied locally, necessitated a continuous flow of cattle, sheep, and hogs to city markets. The eastern states, however, were turning to dairy cattle. Their beef cattle, if increasing at all in numbers, were growing slowly while their human population was mounting rapidly. Massachusetts, New York, and Pennsylvania, for example, added 3,138,000 to their population between 1840 and 1860, while their cattle increase was only 183,000. To supply the metropolitan area of New York City, with its million people, 184 pounds of meat per capita were needed in 1860. Here, then, in this northeastern part of the United States was developing a big deficit in beef cattle, and at the same time the South was looking farther afield for cattle and cattle products to fill its own needs.[33] The demands of these two sections, which bid against each other, for supplies, assured a ready market and good prices for the beef and pork of the prairies. It was not so much the railroads that made possible the flow of livestock east as it was the demand of the East which could be met only in the West, whether railroads existed or not.

DRIVING CATTLE TO THE EAST

Long before railroads penetrated into the Ohio Valley the cattle of that area were being driven overland to Baltimore, Philadelphia, and even to Boston. David Thomas, while traveling in Ohio in 1816, met two droves of cattle, one of which contained 300 head, on their way to Philadelphia and Baltimore. The following year, Morris Birkbeck observed in Ohio a drove of "fat oxen" averaging 600 pounds headed for Philadelphia. He was told that the driver expected to sell them at a premium of $20 or $25 a head.[34] In 1817 Felix Renick, a member of a pioneer family

[32] Some Texas cattle were brought to Louisiana by boat, where, because of their poor condition and low quality, they brought less than half the price paid for "western" beef cattle.—*New Orleans Picayune*, June 25, 1859.

[33] Silas L. Loomis has a useful statistical analysis of the deficiency and surplus-producing cattle states in "Distribution and Movement of Neat Cattle in the United States," in Commissioner of Agriculture, *Annual Report, 1863* (Washington, D. C.: Government Printing Office, 1863), pp. 248–264.

[34] David Thomas, *Travels through the Western Country in the Summer of 1816* (Auburn, N. Y.: David Rumsey, 1819), pp. 90, 120; Morris Birkbeck, *Notes on a Journey in America* (London: Severn & Redington, 1818), p. 63.

that did much to introduce Shorthorns into the Scioto Valley, drove to Philadelphia 100 cattle averaging over 1,300 pounds when they started. They brought a premium price of $133 a head. In later years the Renicks sent regular shipments of cattle overland to Philadelphia and New York and, on occasion, to Boston. By the thirties and forties the driving of cattle from Ohio, Indiana, and Illinois had become a well-established business.[35]

Driving cattle to New York from Ohio and Illinois before the railroads were constructed was no easy undertaking. Rivers had to be forded; forage, water, and bedding grounds were needed; weak or lagging animals that could not keep up with the drove were sold or otherwise provided for; and arrangements had to be made to rest and feed the stock for a time before they were sold. Cattle lost from 150 to 250 pounds on the long trip, sometimes more, and they arrived in anything but good merchantable condition.[36] Hogs were sometimes driven after the cattle to utilize the feed the cattle wasted. Droves of 120 cattle accompanied by three attendants were common. The frequency of the drives led farmers on the main routes to establish way stations where cattle could be rested for a noon hour or bedded for the night and provided with the necessary hay, corn, and water. The cost of driving from Ohio or Kentucky was estimated at $15 a head.[37]

Both ends of the cattle business were handled by specialists. In the summer the feeder-cattle man bought three-year-old steers, fattened them on a concentrated diet of corn in confined feed lots during the next four months, and then sold them to the other specialist—the drover—who either drove them or shipped them overland by rail to the stockyards at New York, Brighton, Philadelphia, Baltimore, Buffalo, Indianapolis, or Chicago.[38] To enter the feeder-cattle business a man needed a consider-

[35] William Renick, Memoirs, Correspondence and Reminiscences (Circleville, Ohio: Union-Herald Book and Job Printing House, 1880), pp. 26–31; Prairie Farmer, IX (October, 1849), 305.

[36] Cattle driven a hundred miles from the Connecticut River to the Brighton market in Cambridge in the course of a week were expected to lose a hundred pounds in weight. Henry Colman said they came into market "foot-sore, sunken, in a state of fever, and looking like the victim of cruelty and the picture of misery and exhaustion." —European Agriculture and Rural Economy (2 vols.; Boston: Arthur D. Phelps, 1846–1848), I, 155–156.

[37] Farmers' Library in Western Farmer & Gardener, II (November 15, 1846), 350; Transactions of the American Institute of the City of New York, 1851 (Albany: C. Van Benthuysen, 1852), pp. 115–117, 345–349; New York Semi-Weekly Tribune, August 17, 1855; Renick, Memoirs, pp. 26 ff.; Herbert O. Brayer, ed., Life of Tom Candy Ponting: An Autobiography (Evanston, Ill.: Branding Iron Press, 1952), passim.

[38] Joseph G. McCoy, famous as the historian of the cattle trade, said that before the grass died, cattle were fed small quantities of corn that were gradually increased until the pastures had lost their nourishment, when they were put in feed lots and

able acreage for pasture and for the raising of corn, in addition to substantial credit on which to draw for the purchase of stock. He also had to be an excellent judge of cattle, a shrewd buyer, and to possess an almost uncanny faculty for outguessing the market when it came to selling. Feeder-cattle men scoured their neighborhood in search for stock, gradually widening the area of their buying until they or their agents worked through Missouri and Iowa as well as Ohio, Indiana, and Illinois. One Illinois feeder bought 1,200 Texas cattle for fattening in 1855, the year in which Joseph G. McCoy was reported to have driven 20,000 Texas cattle to Chicago.[39]

The first important and well-recognized feeder regions were the Bluegrass country of Kentucky and the Scioto Valley of Ohio. One Kentucky planter, who fed 300 cattle annually on his farm of 1,800 acres, raised and sold 200 hogs, and produced his own corn, wheat, and rye, figured his profits in 1835 at $9,945 and in 1836 at $10,475. Like many another letter writer, he did not present statistics which would permit one to determine what he meant by profits.[40] There were 64 farmers feeding 100 or more cattle in the Scioto–Miami Valley region of Ohio in 1854.

Because they had prairie grass and cheap corn in greater abundance, Indiana and Illinois feeder-cattle men were crowding the Scioto farmers hard in the last years before the Civil War. There came to the fore a score or more of prairie cattle kings, each with herds of 1,000 or 2,000 cattle grazing in fenced pastures of thousands of acres and cared for by small armies of laborers. Isaac Funk, Jacob Strawn, Benjamin F. Harris, John T. Alexander, and Michael Sullivant, whose family was also heavily involved in the feeder-cattle business in Ohio, were leaders in Illinois. Alexander fattened and shipped to the New York cattle market between 1857 and 1860 from 10,000 to 15,000 cattle.[41] On his acres, Jacob

fed a half bushel of corn a day. In four to six months the usual gain was 200 to 300 pounds, but it was this gain that assured higher quality and better prices than would have been received if the cattle had been sent to market before the grain feeding.— *Historic Sketches of the Cattle Trade of the West and Southwest* (Kansas City, Mo.: Ramsey, Millett & Hudson, 1874), pp. 166 ff. Cf. Renick, *Memoirs*, pp. 26–31.

[39] *Ohio Farmer*, V (February 2, 1856), 17; *Illinois Journal* in *Wool Grower and Stock Register*, VIII (December, 1855), 192. For a somewhat different method of fattening cattle in Kentucky, see Adam Beatty, *Southern Agriculture, Being Essays on the Cultivation of Corn, Hemp, Tobacco, Wheat, Etc., and the Best Method of Renovating the Soil* (New York: C. M. Saxton & Company, 1843), pp. 264–272. *Chicago Press* in *Homestead*, I (September 27, 1855), 31.

[40] Jacob Hughes worked his estate with ten hands.—*Tennessee Farmer* in *Franklin Farmer*, I (September 23, 1837), 26.

[41] *Scioto Gazette* in *Wool Grower and Stock Register*, VI (August, 1854), 59; *Ohio Cultivator*, XII (November 1, 1856), 322.

Strawn, one of the most successful of these feeder-cattle men of the Illinois prairies, fed 1,600 to 2,000 cattle and 700 hogs. He had 2,900 acres in corn divided into 40-acre plots each tended by a laborer, who was paid eight cents a bushel for the corn he raised. All the corn was fed on the place. Steers for feeding were brought in from southern Illinois, Missouri, and Iowa. His gross sales of stock were $100,000 in 1854. Perhaps the size of his operations justified Strawn's being called "The Napoleon of Cattle." [42]

THE ROLE OF THE RAILROADS

The building of the railroad network connecting New York and Philadelphia with the Middle West by way of the Pennsylvania, the Erie, the New York Central, and the Michigan Central eased the path of the drovers and dealers by making it possible for them to ship their cattle most of the way by rail, or by a combination of rail and water, from the point of origin in the prairies to the fast-growing eastern markets. Thus of the 100,000 cattle driven to market from Ohio in 1854, a known 16,364 went partly by water from Cleveland, Toledo, Sandusky, and Cincinnati, a known 24,613 traveled east by the Little Miami and Ohio and Pennsylvania railroads. Doubtless most of the remainder went part of their way by rail.[43] The Erie, completed to Buffalo in 1852, became for a time the principal route to New York City, and the volume of livestock it hauled was large. In the summer of 1855 it carried weekly to New York from 1,100 to 1,900 beef cattle, from 2,500 to 5,700 sheep, and as many as 3,400 hogs. Moved by the public outcry against the suffering imposed on cattle shut up in narrow cars for as much as three days without food or water, the Erie officials established a halfway place near Owego at which the cattle were detrained, rested, watered, and fed. The Erie also ran a special cattle train on Sundays from Dunkirk to New York which shortened the time in transit.[44]

When the New York Central and the Erie railroads raised the price of hauling a carload of cattle from Buffalo to New York by $10 and then announced a second increase of the same amount, the drovers threatened

[42] McCoy, *Historic Sketches of the Cattle Trade*, pp. 166 ff.; Clarence P. McClelland, "Jacob Strawn and John T. Alexander, Central Illinois Stockmen," *Journal* of the Illinois State Historical Society, XXXIV (June, 1941), 201 ff.

[43] *Prairie Farmer*, XIV (November, 1854), 428; *Wool Grower and Stock Register*, VII (January, 1855), 30–31; and VIII (August, 1855), 55; *Ohio Cultivator*, XI (May 1, 1855), 130.

[44] *Ohio Cultivator*, X (January 1, 1855), 12; *New York Semi-Weekly Tribune*, September 21 and October 12, 26, 1855. At Greenbush near Albany the New York Central unloaded, fed, and watered stock it hauled.—Neil Adams McNall, *An Agricultural History of the Genesee Valley, 1790–1860* (Philadelphia: University of Pennsylvania Press, 1952), p. 138.

to direct their stock over the Pennsylvania and the Baltimore and Ohio railroads or even to return to driving them overland. The *New York Tribune* scoffed at the threat:

It is idle to talk about driving beeves, sheep or swine on foot. The loss of time, to say nothing of expense, would ruin any drover. It would take an average of sixty days to drive from Ohio, where it now takes an average of six days by railroad. Besides the loss of time, the loss by shrinkage of the cattle would be much greater on foot than by cars. But this is not all. If all the stock came on foot as it did twenty years ago, it would breed a famine on the road. . . . We doubt very much whether the present average of 4,000 bullocks, 8,000 swine, and 14,000 sheep per week would be fed along the ordinary roads leading to this great meat-consuming city.[45]

By the middle of the century the number of cattle being driven from the prairies to railheads, whence they were hauled to feed lots and slaughterhouses, was in the hundreds of thousands. The previously quoted estimate of 100,000 cattle marketed in the East in 1854 seems conservative, and if to it is added the many thousands from Kentucky, still a major center for high-quality stock, and from Indiana, Illinois, Missouri, and other states, it may be assumed that 200,000 from the West is a low estimate. More than two thirds of the cattle slaughtered for the New York City market came from there. That market alone absorbed 264,000 cattle, 504,000 sheep and lambs, and 400,000 hogs in 1860. Philadelphia, Baltimore, Boston, and many smaller cities also received livestock from the West.[46]

The cattle feeders and drovers of the Scioto Valley organized an Association of Feeders and Drovers of the Scioto Valley to protect their interests by group action. Their principal demands were for the removal of the stockyards to the New Jersey side of the Hudson River and for the adoption of a cash system.[47]

Solon Robinson, the principal agricultural writer of the *New York Tribune,* included in his regular column on cattle receipts caustic remarks about some herds from the West. One lot of eighteen from Ohio were described as the "most contemptible scalawags—the very fag end of hard time. . . ." Two droves from Illinois, he called, "little miserable thin steers" which were "too poor to skin, [so] we skin the owner." Even a New York owner was excoriated for driving to market stock that were "beneath the contempt of every contemptable [sic] thing on earth except their scalawag owner, who ought to be indicted for cruelty to animals. None but a brute would bring such poor little starved brutes here. . . ."

[45] *New York Semi-Weekly Tribune,* November 23, 1855.
[46] Illinois supplied 100,000 cattle for the New York market in 1862.—*Cincinnatus,* III (July, 1858), 310; *Ohio Farmer,* IX (January 14, 1860), 13; *Country Gentleman,* XXI (January 8, 1863), 33; *New York Tribune,* April 12, 1861.
[47] *Ohio Cultivator,* VI (March 1, 1850), 65.

The long six-day train trip from Illinois during which the animals had little or no water and were knocked about by the bumping and shifting of the cars, left them on arrival bruised, feverish, with swollen rumps, hips, ribs, and shoulders and running sores. If taken on arrival to the sales ground they made a poor spectacle and could not bring top prices. Some drovers found it profitable to have their cattle put in fed pens for a period before they were marketed. Robinson commented favorably on the better prices the pen-fed cattle brought. He also noted that cattle from nearby counties brought much better prices in the New York market on the whole than did those coming from a distance.[48]

Even less could be said for the Texas cattle brought into the New York market. Longhorn cattle, bought at four to eight dollars a head in Texas, were driven 1,500 miles overland and hauled 500 miles by railroad to the sprawling New York market. One writer thought their horns constituted the greater part of their weight and said that they gave little evidence of ever having eaten any "fat-producing material." [49]

Meat, although not consumed by the great mass of American people in the astounding quantities that European travelers reported, was nevertheless a major staple in people's diet. Both beef and pork were cheap, butchering was done regularly in larger communities, and meat was generally fresh.

PORK IN THE AMERICAN DIET

The notion that Americans were pork eaters rests in part on the accounts of European travelers, who commented less upon the diet of the genteel class, who feted them generously on everything but pork, than they did upon the food provided them in western and southern steamboats, taverns, and homes of individuals at which they were forced to stop, a menu which consisted largely of pork. One recent writer, obsessed with the notion that "pork was the meat most commonly consumed," documented his conclusion by reference to three travel accounts, two of which lend no support to his statement.[50] In one of his references, on the contrary, is a table showing the average weekly consumption of food at the

[48] New York Semi-Weekly Tribune, August 3, 1855; Ohio Cultivator, X (June, 1854), 181.

[49] Ohio Farmer, IX (October 13, 1860), 324; Wool Grower and Stock Register, VIII (October, 1855), 128; Ralph P. Bieber, introduction to Jospeh G. McCoy, Historic Sketches of the Cattle Trade of the West and Southwest (Vol. VIII of The Southwest Historical Series, Ralph P. Bieber, ed.; Glendale, Calif.: Arthur H. Clark Company, 1940), p. 42.

[50] Edgar W. Martin, The Standard of Living in 1860: American Consumption Levels on the Eve of the Civil War (Chicago: The University of Chicago Press, 1942), pp. 45 ff.

Revere House in Boston, which might have led him to question his own generalization:

WEEKLY CONSUMPTION AT REVERE HOUSE, BOSTON

Food	Pounds	Gallons
Beef	2,000	
Mutton and lamb	1,500	
Veal	400	
Pork	300	
Fish	400	
Poultry	2,000	
Game	500	
Hams	350	
Tongue	100	
Tripe	50	
Oysters		100

Source: Alfred Bunn, *Old England and New England, in a Series of Views Taken on the Spot* (Philadelphia: H. Hart, 1853), p. 40.

The third reference does say "the national taste certainly runs on pork, salt-fish, tough poultry and little birds of all descriptions," but it also devotes much space to a discussion of a sea serpent off Nahant, the "detestable" mint julep, vulgarisms in American food terms, such as "tender line," and misunderstanding American aristocracy.[51] The writer referred to was actually inveighing against the practices of using "lumps of fat pork" in fish soup, of frying fish, or of serving it with chicken or mutton.

Another reason why it has been commonly assumed that pork constituted the major item in the diet of Americans is the emphasis of early writers upon meat packing at Cincinnati, Indianapolis, Chicago, and elsewhere, for it was principally pork that was packed. Hogs were driven shorter distances than cattle. At the slaughterhouses, the bacon, hams, and shoulders were packed in barrels and hogsheads, and the lard was rendered and placed in kegs. Thus the products could be shipped by water to New Orleans and to New York, Boston, and even to England and other remote ports. The role of Cincinnati as "Porkopolis" and the ingenuity displayed in processing and packing huge numbers of hogs were well known throughout America and to many Europeans.

Pork, it is true, was the common item of diet in the West and the

[51] Thomas Colley Grattan, *Civilized America* (2 vols.; London: Bradbury & Evans, 1859), I, 61–64, 106, and elsewhere. James Stuart in his *Three Years in North America* (2 vols.; Edinburgh: Robert Cadell, 1833), I, 307–308, speaking of food provided at a boarding house in Boston and the American preferences in food, said: "They care more for roast-beef, beef-steak, roasted turkey, and apple and pumpkin pie, than for anything else."

South. The western attitude toward pork is seen in Mrs. C. M. Kirkland's story of *Forest Life in Michigan*, published in 1842. Pork, she calls, "the *beau ideal* of good cheer everywhere," more cherished than sweetening or whiskey, something one could never have too much of. Exalted as porkers were, they were allowed unlimited freedom. "Not the sacred cow of Isis was the subject of more reverential attention." [52] The hog was supreme in Arkansas, for example, where there were thirty-three times as many hogs in proportion to the population as there were in Maine, and fifty-two times as many as in Massachusetts. Other states in the South and West also had a relatively high number of hogs.

NUMBER OF HOGS PER CAPITA IN CERTAIN WESTERN, SOUTHERN, AND EASTERN STATES

State	Ratio	State	Ratio
Arkansas	2.6	Iowa	1.3
Indiana	2.2	South Carolina	1.3
Texas	2.2	Pennsylvania	0.3
Tennessee	2.1	New York	0.2
Kentucky	2.0	Connecticut	0.1
Florida	1.9	Vermont	0.1
Georgia	1.9	New Hampshire	0.1
Mississippi	1.9	Maine	0.08
Missouri	1.9	Massachusetts	0.05
Alabama	1.8		

Source: Computed from *Eighth Census of the United States, 1860, Population and Agriculture* (Washington, D. C.: Government Printing Office, 1864), *passim*.

There were no such differences among the states in the ratio of cattle to human beings, though the Northeast was not as well supplied as were the West and the South.

The table on page 217 shows the relative amounts of live pork and beef that were brought into the New York market in the fifties.[53]

Solon Robinson estimated that the average amount of meat yielded by the beeves and cows was 700 pounds; by the calves, 75 pounds; by the sheep, 42 pounds; and by the hogs, 150 pounds. From these figures it may be calculated that, on the average, 128,650,400 pounds of beef, 3,435,700 pounds of veal, 20,532,498 pounds of mutton and lamb, and 53,151,150

[52] Mrs. C. M. Kirkland, *Forest Life* (2 vols.; New York: C. S. Francis & Co., 1842), I, 73–79.

[53] Solon Robinson, *Facts for Farmers, Also for the Family Circle: A Compost of Rich Materials for all Land-Owners about Domestic Animals and Domestic Economy; Farm Buildings; Gardens, Orchards, and Vineyards; and all Farm Crops, Tools, Fertilization, Draining and Irrigation* (2 vols.; New York: A. J. Johnson, 1867), I, 57.

LIVESTOCK RECEIPTS IN THE NEW YORK MARKET

Year	Beeves	Cows	Calves	Sheep	Swine
1854	169,864	13,131	68,584	555,479	252,328
1855	185,564	12,110	47,969	588,741	318,107
1856	187,057	12,857	43,081	462,739	345,911
1857	162,243	12,840	34,218	444,036	288,984
1858	191,874	10,128	37,675	447,445	551,479
1859	205,272	9,492	48,769	404,894	399,665
1860	226,933	7,144	39,436	518,750	323,918
Totals	1,308,807	77,702	319,732	3,422,084	2,480,392
Yearly average	186,972	11,100	45,676	488,869	354,341

Source: See footnote 53.

pounds of pork—all fresh meat—were brought into the New York market anually between 1854 and 1860. Robinson points out "the great bulk of pork from the hogs slaughtered here is packed and sent to other places for consumption; large quantities of it to Europe." Only a small portion of the beef thus brought into the city was sent abroad. He also comments on the "vast quantity" of beef, veal and lamb already dressed that came into the city for use there and in nearby cities and to provision ships and forts along the Atlantic coast.[54] Clearly, it was beef, not pork, which was the principal meat consumed in New York and the New England states.

The early hog made little appeal to the appetite of fastidious people. Travelers commonly noted that in old as well as new cities the hog was a scavenger, running wild and living on the garbage thrown into the streets. Only at branding and slaughtering time did owners round up their hogs.[55] In rural areas hogs ran wild in the woods and swamps; lived on acorns, chestnuts, beechnuts, and roots and grass; bred promiscuously; defended themselves against wild animals; and withal got little attention from their owners. Called razorback, land pike, or alligator, the hog was "long and slim, long-legged and long snouted, slab-sided, large-boned, gaunt bodied, flat eared, with arched back and bristles erect from head to tail." [56] As late as 1858, the author of a popular and practical guide for farmers, commenting on the common hog of the West, said that it "will consume an almost endless amount of corn or other food, and afford little

[54] *Ibid.*

[55] *Cultivator*, VII (January, 1840), 13; Frances Trollope, *Domestic Manners of the Americans*, edited with a History of Mrs. Trollope's Adventures in America by Donald Smalley (New York: Alfred A. Knopf, Inc., 1949), pp. 88–89; Russell, *North America*, p. 84.

[56] Rudolf Alexander Clemen, *The American Livestock and Meat Industry* (New York: The Ronald Press Company, 1923), p. 52.

else than gristle in return. . . ." [57] Another critic called them worthless brutes whose meat was rank and tough. When a farmer had brought sufficient land into corn to satisfy his own needs and those of his horses, oxen, and cattle, he could drive in his hogs from the woods, where they had been feeding on mast, to fatten on the richer diet now available. After five or six weeks of intensive feeding they would be driven to the packing house. "Hogging down" corn was an easy though wasteful and not uncommon way to harvest a portion of the crop. Close penning and intensive feeding from birth, however, were not generally followed save by specialists in swine.

HOG BREEDING

In Ohio, where there was an abundance of cheap corn and where most farmers had surplus hogs which it would scarcely have paid them individually to drive to market, hog buying and fattening became important. Like the cattle feeder, the hog feeder could buy several hundred hogs in his neighborhood, fatten them on a concentrated corn diet, and then either sell to drovers or drive the herd to Cincinnati, Dayton, Columbus, or Cleveland. One Buckeye feeder bought, fattened, and marketed in eastern cities 20,000 hogs yearly.[58]

Corn and hogs thus became the major interest of farmers in the developing corn belt extending from Ohio to Iowa and Missouri. The number of hogs per farm ranged from 24 in Indiana to 31 in Missouri. Even greater numbers of swine were found on the larger farms in the newer southern states, where the number per farm ranged from 37 in Kentucky to 46 in Mississippi.

Good breeding and stock improvement required high feeding and stout fencing. Neither the worm fence of the South nor the stone fence of the Northeast could confine common hogs, which for generations had been forced to roam far and wide for their keep. Hog-tight fencing was expensive to erect and maintain. As a result, improvements in breeding made way slowly and better pork resulted more from high feeding than from good breeding. Improvements in hog breeding could only come with (1) the modern wire or stout board fences, (2) the introduction of better stock, and (3) regular feeding of grain and skim and sour milk.

[57] J. H. Thomas, *Rural Affairs: A Practical and Copiously Illustrated Register of Rural Economy and Rural Taste* (Albany: Luther Tucker & Sons, 1858), I, 94–95 and illustrations.

[58] Russell, *North America*, p. 80; Howard Johnson, *A Home in the Woods: Oliver Johnson's Reminiscences of Early Marion County* (*Publications* of the Indiana Historical Society, Vol. XVI, No. 2; Indianapolis: Indiana Historical Society, 1951), Chap. 12, "Driving Hogs to the River." See also Charles Cist, *Sketches and Statistics of Cincinnati in 1851* (Cincinnati: Wm. H. Moore & Co., 1851), pp. 278 ff.

The story of the introduction of good-blooded swine involves many gentleman farmers as well as stock improvement and importing associations. Among the leaders in importing purebred hogs and improving native stock were Timothy Pickering, prominent Federalist, land speculator, and gentleman farmer; Captain John Mackay of Weston, Massachusetts, after whom a breed of hogs was named; Lewis F. Morris, whose importations of Shorthorn cattle have already been mentioned; Lewis F. and Richard L. Allen, identified with the *American Agriculturist,* whose stock farm near Buffalo was famous for its Shorthorn and Devon cattle and Berkshire hogs; and John Wentworth, organizer of the Illinois Stock Improvement Association. Bedford, Suffolk, Hampshire, and Berkshire hogs were brought in from England, as were Chinese hogs from the Orient, and by crossbreeding a number of American strains were developed. Chief of these American breeds were the Mackay, which had a strong vogue in Massachusetts and Ohio, and the Chester, which came out of Chester County, Pennsylvania. Many importations were made by cattle fanciers, who generally brought in a few breeding hogs along with their Shorthorns, Ayrshires, and Devons.

Some importers of purebred hogs insisted on keeping their blood lines pure and unmixed with other breeds or with native stock. Their object was to sell only breeding stock at the high prices obtainable in the thirties and fifties. Depressed economic conditions in the forties made it necessary for many to disperse their stock through sale. Other importers sought to improve the type of hogs generally and began crossing their purebred Berkshires, Hampshires, or Suffolk hogs with native stock or with grade or part purebreds. Upgrading of swine was continuous, as could be seen in the changing configuration of the hog and the improved quality of the bacon and ham. The expanding demand for lard both at home and abroad contributed to the improvement of hogs by providing a premium for fat stock.[59]

As it was a common practice for farmers and planters to dress off hogs for their own consumption, many hogs were thus used. Hogs were raised commercially mostly in the West, with Ohio leading, and Indiana, Kentucky, and Illinois competing for second place in the fifties. At that time the number of hogs packed in these states annually ranged from 1,818,000 to 2,465,000. Prior to the completion of railroad connections with the East in the early fifties, the bulk of the pork went south by flatboat, keelboat, and steamboat to Memphis, Natchez, and New Orleans or was sold to planters along the way. The coming of the railroad did not so much disturb this flow of meat and lard southward as it drew an expanding volume of live hogs to the East for slaughtering there and drew them somewhat more from the upper portion of Ohio, Indiana, and Illi-

[59] Commissioner of Agriculture, *Report, 1863,* pp. 199 ff.

nois. Thus although the number of hogs packed in the Middle West suffered a drastic decline in 1856–1857, from which it was not to recover
for several years, the number of hogs shipped east increased by an even
greater proportion.[60]

Allusion has previously been made to the alleged dependence of the
upper Mississippi Valley upon the lower South for a market for its wheat,
flour, pork, and beef. As a further corrective it should be pointed out that
long before 1850 the surplus beef cattle of Ohio, Kentucky, Illinois, and
Indiana were driven east to the metropolitan markets. The South took
few live cattle and little dressed beef; indeed, a good portion of its own
surplus beeves from Kentucky and Missouri was destined for eastern
markets. The Northwest depended upon the southern market for the sale
of its pork and lard, but a considerable portion that was sold in the South
was not consumed there and was in fact reshipped to Boston, New York,
Philadelphia, and the West Indies and even to Europe. Because some of
this pork and other foodstuffs were repacked at New Orleans, it is not
possible to determine precisely how much of the imports of the upper
Mississippi Valley was reshipped at New Orleans, but the table of receipts at and exports from New Orleans for 1849 provides an idea of the
magnitude of the reshipments.

RECEIPTS FROM THE INTERIOR AND EXPORTS FROM NEW ORLEANS
FOR YEAR ENDING AUGUST 31, 1849

Goods and packaging	Number of imports	Receipts average value per unit	Total value	Number of exports
Bacon, casks	32,056	$40.00	$1,282,240	N. A.
Bacon, boxes & bbls.	32,156	25.00	803,900	N. A.
Bacon, hams, hhds.	19,831	45.00	892,395	67,202
Bacon in bulk, lbs.	217,000	0.05	10,850	N. A.
Beef, bbls. & tierces	80,590	$11–15	1,049,016	60,058
Beef, dried, lbs.	20,300	0.07	1,421	N. A.
Corn, shelled, sacks	1,706,312	1.05	1,790,394	1,466,861
Flour, bbls.	1,013,177	4.50	4,559,296	778,370
Lard, hhds.	790	60.00	47,400	N. A.
Lard, tierces & bbls.	214,362	18.00	3,858,516	N. A.
Lard, kegs	275,485	3.50	1,064,197	1,249,691
Pork, tierces & bbls.	550,643	9.50	5,231,103	466,050
Pork, hhds.	18,499	40.00	739,960	N. A.
Pork, bulk, lbs.	10,273,680	0.0375	285,263	N. A.
Whiskey, bbls.	125,029	7.00	875,203	53,473

N. A. Comparable figures on exports unavailable.

Source: De Bow's Review, VII (November, 1849), 420–421.

[60] Ohio Cultivator, XIII (March 15, 1857), 89.

In 1859 the export trade of New Orleans was equally important. Three fifths of the flour, one fourth of the pork, two fifths of the bacon, and one third of the whiskey arriving from the interior was reshipped elsewhere.[61]

Pork packing was never centered in one place to the degree that meat packing came to be centered in Chicago after the Civil War. Some slaughtering was done in most towns or villages west of the Appalachians, particularly if they were on or near navigable rivers. By keelboats, flat-boats, or steamboats the heavy barrels and hogsheads of bacon, ham, and pork were easily and cheaply transported to markets in Mississippi, Louisiana, or to southern ports for transhipment to the eastern coast. The state of Ohio early took an interest in meat packing by requiring that pork should be packed in white-oak barrels of 200 to 225 pounds' capacity, strongly bound with at least ten hoops, securely pegged or nailed, and clearly marked with gross and net weights.[62] Public-health and pure-foods legislation to keep diseased meat out of commercial channels had to wait for many years. When acute hog cholera struck down sixty thousand hogs in the great feeding areas of the Middle West in 1856 and 1857, particularly hogs fed on distillery swill, there was no known remedy, nor did the western states take the swift action that Massachusetts took when pleuropneumonia threatened to destroy its dairy herds. Small farmers as well as the great distillery feeders suffered serious losses from hog cholera.[63]

SHEEP RAISING

Raising sheep required less capital and less attention than raising dairy cattle, and although sheep had their parasites and diseases, they were not subject to such dread diseases as hog cholera and pleuropneumonia. During the colonial period it was essential for outlying farmers to have their small flocks of sheep whose wool their wives could scour, card, spin, and weave into cloth. Most of the wool was used on the farm and since little was sold the farmers were not obliged to consider the production of fine-quality fleeces free from dirt. Nor was there concern for the

[61] Computed from *De Bow's Review,* Vol. XXVII (October, 1859). Cf. Henry Clyde Hubbart, *The Older Middle West, 1840–1880* (New York: Appleton-Century-Crofts, Inc., 1936), p. 74.

[62] William T. Utter, *The First Frontier State* (Vol. II of *History of the State of Ohio,* Carl Wittke, ed., 6 vols.; Columbus: Ohio State Archaeological and Historical Society, 1942), p. 155.

[63] *Western Farm Journal,* II (June 29, 1857), 217; *Ohio Farmer,* VI (January 31, 1857), 17; *Cincinnatus,* II (November, 1857), 523; *American Agriculturist,* XVI (December, 1857), 280; *Baltimore Sun* in *Southern Planter,* XVIII (March, 1858), 143–144. The losses of major distilleries ran as high as 4,546 hogs owned by an Aurora firm.—*Veterinary Journal* in *Working Farmer,* IX (July 1, 1857), 102.

mutton, since it was consumed on the farm. One writer described the "native" sheep before the coming of the Merinos as "lank, gaunt, slow-feeding, coarse, short-wooled, hardy, prolific animals—not well adapted to . . . wool or mutton production." [64]

Abroad, particularly in Spain, the Merino sheep had been brought to a high state of perfection by selected breeding and expert attention. Spain, not anxious to share its Merinos with the nationals of other countries, had placed restrictions on their export. During the Napoleonic Wars, however, when Spain was overrun by French troops, these restrictions broke down in practice and the American consul in Spain, William Jarvis, of Wethersfield, Vermont, arranged for the shipment to America of some 6,650 Merinos in 1810 and 1811.[65] When the fine Merino wool brought a premium price there was a scramble to acquire these high-grade sheep, which developed into the famous Merino craze. The War of 1812 shut off further importations of Merinos and heightened the demand for wool, which rose to a peak price of $1.50 a pound in 1815. At this time full-blooded Merinos sold as high as $1,500. Mathew Carey estimated that nearly a million dollars was invested in Merino sheep while the craze lasted. The end of the war, the revived importation of coarse English wool, and the fact that the fine Merino wool proved not well adapted to household manufacture halted the excitement and prices plummeted to depression lows. Dealers lost heavily when the boom collapsed and Merinos went into temporary eclipse, some being sold for mutton by disillusioned farmers. However, despite this absurd destruction, Merinos had been widely distributed over the East and soon improved the flocks.[66]

Improved breeds and breeding practices were not neglected for long. In the northern states most farmers had woodland or hill pastures suitable for sheep and not useful for other agricultural pursuits except the pasturing of cattle and horses. Wool brought a better price in relation to bulk than any other commodity the northern farmer raised and, though he was never content with his marketing opportunities in wool, buyers were rarely lacking. Farmers, therefore, began to raise increasing numbers of sheep and interest in improving stock soon revived.

Despite the earlier revulsion against the fine-wooled but light-fleeced

[64] Henry S. Randall, *The Practical Shepherd* (Rochester, N. Y.: D. D. T. Moore, 1863), p. 43.

[65] *American Agriculturist,* XVII (March, 1858), 71. Cf. Edward Norris Wentworth, *America's Sheep Trails* (Ames: The Iowa State College Press, 1948), p. 84. Another estimate is that 19,651 Merinos were imported in 1810 and 1811.—Liberty Hyde Bailey, *Cyclopedia of American Agriculture* (4 vols.; New York: The Macmillan Company, 1907), III, 619.

[66] Matthew Carey, *Address before the Philadelphia Society for Promoting Agriculture* (Philadelphia: Mifflin & Parry, 1827), p. 35; Chester Whitney Wright, *Wool-Growing and the Tariff* (*Harvard Economic Studies,* Vol. V; Boston: Houghton Mifflin Company, 1910), pp. 36 ff.

Merinos, the revival of interest in quality sheep led paradoxically to concentration upon the importation of the finer-wooled and lighter-fleeced Saxon Merinos. Saxon wool brought a premium price, but the average fleece weighed a pound less than the Merino fleeces. Furthermore, the Saxons were smaller animals, more delicate, needed closer attention than the Merinos and could only thrive in a less hardy climate than prevailed in the North, where labor costs prevented the close supervision of feeding the Saxons enjoyed in Germany. Like the Merino, the Saxon was not a good mutton breed.

To meet the demand for better grades of sheep, stock importers traveled throughout Western Europe in search of improved strains. Spain, France, and Germany were literally ransacked by buyers. Henry S. Randall, the pricipal contemporary authority on sheep raising, himself a practical farmer, accounted for the importation of some 2,800 full- or part-blooded Saxons in this period. So great was the scramble that German papers "teemed with advertisements of sheep for sale, headed 'Good for the American Market.'" [67] The Panic of 1837 halted this importation, and interest in Saxons declined.

Importation of purebred sheep began again in large numbers in the fifties. An importer related his experiences in searching for the best-quality Merino sheep. He toured Spain but found none suitable for buying, because there had been a marked decline in the quality of sheep there since the Napolenoic Wars. In France he purchased a number of the Rambouillet strain of Merinos. He sought out Charles L. Fleischmann, a German-American who had formerly been associated with the agricultural work of the Patent Office and was now serving as American consul at Stuttgart, and secured his aid in locating the best flocks of Merinos in Saxony and Silesia. Here the importer found sheep possessing "more good qualities" than he had seen in any other flocks and he completed his purchases, amounting to 114 animals.[68] About the same time, another Vermonter—Solomon W. Jewett—was in France purchasing 152 Rambouillet sheep. While there he examined different flocks on the government farm and on private model farms, and attended state and district exhibitions of livestock. He returned to Europe in 1852 and again in 1853 to buy more sheep and Suffolk hogs. His importation of 1852 included 160 sheep purchased in Spain for $14,000.[69] When prosperity descended upon farmers in the booming fifties, numerous other Americans went to Europe with

[67] Henry S. Randall, *Sheep Husbandry in the South* (Philadelphia: J. S. Skinner & Son, 1848), p. 140. Randall believed that many nonpurebred sheep were palmed off on American buyers or were bought as grades and sold as purebreds to American stockmen.

[68] *American Agriculturist*, X (August, 1851), 243–244; *American Polytechnic Journal* Vol. I, No. 1 (January, 1853), p. 11.

[69] *American Agriculturist*, X (October, 1851), 301; *Ohio Cultivator*, VIII (June 1, 1852), 165; and X (April 15, 1854), 123.

many thousands of dollars to invest in purebred sheep as well as in cattle and hogs.

For a time the sheep industry proved a major boon to hard-pressed hill areas of New England and New York from which rural folk were emigrating in search of better land and a more satisfactory living. For all but short periods until 1842, the price of raw wool was quite favorable, and farmers expanded their flocks as nature permitted.[70] Once cultivated fields were put into sheepfolds, prosperous farmers bought out their less successful neighbors and in a small enclosure movement consolidated their new acquisitions with old holdings. The peak of the excitement over sheep raising was reached in 1840. All of northern New England was affected by this excitement, Vermont most of all. "Men counted their flocks by the thousands," an old Vermonter later said, "and as they grew more and more rich in money and sheep, they bought farm after farm adjoining their own and turned them into pasturage."[71] In one Vermont county, where the sheep averaged 373 to the square mile, it was said that every bit of land but the kitchen gardens was given up to sheep. Lewis Stilwell makes the point that the lower South "in the heyday of 'King Cotton'" was never "more thoroughly committed to a single crop than was Vermont. . . ."[72] Addison and Rutland counties, Vermont, each had more sheep in 1840 than had any other counties in the country, and in 1850 Windsor, Addison, and Rutland led all counties in number of sheep.[73] Nowhere was there a greater concentration of purebred sheep and horses) and nowhere were there more dealers in Merino sheep than in Addison County, Vermont.[74]

High prices encouraged development of the sheep industry not only in the Northeast but also in Ohio, Indiana, Illinois, and Michigan, where land values and taxes, and therefore costs, were lower, and where sheep could be raised on a larger scale. Cheaply produced wool from Ohio poured into eastern markets, drove the price down, and made it difficult for Vermont or New York sheepmen to compete. The Yankees were not defeated, however, and adapted themselves to the new competition. Marginal sheep farmers with high costs did abandon their hillside farms

[70] Percy Wells Bidwell and John I. Falconer, *History of Agriculture in the Northern United States* (Washington, D. C.: Carnegie Institution, 1925), pp. 495–496.

[71] Harold Fisher Wilson, *The Hill Country of Northern New England* (New York: Columbia University Press, 1936), p. 79.

[72] Lewis D. Stilwell, *Migration from Vermont, Proceedings* of the Vermont Historical Society, V (1937), 172.

[73] Censuses of 1840 and 1850, *passim.*

[74] In 1882, 84 individuals and firms in Addison County advertised purebred Merino sheep in Hamilton Child, *Business Directory of Addison County, Vt., for 1881–82* (Syracuse, N. Y.: Journal Office, 1882).

to blackberry bushes, pine, and hardwoods but farmers with better land and sufficient capital, by a rigid process of selection and the use of pure-bred rams, brought the average weight of their wool fleeces to the highest figure in the country.

Vermont boasted in 1850 an average fleece of 3.3 pounds, which far surpassed the average for any other state. New York's fleeces weighed 2.9 pounds, Michigan's 2.7, Ohio's 2.5, Virginia's 2.1, Illinois's 2.1, Kentucky's 2.0, Tennessee's 1.6—all substantial sheep-raising states. The average fleece of all the New England states was better than the average of any other state. In 1859 the disparity between the New England fleeces and those of other states had further widened. Vermont's fleeces in that year averaged 4.1 pounds. That premier state in quality of sheep and size of fleece, while reducing the number of its sheep by 55 per cent between 1839 and 1859, had kept its yield from falling more than 15 per cent.[75]

Having improved the quality of their sheep and the weight of their fleece to a high point, Vermont farmers found a ready and profitable market for their purebred Merinos. Edwin Hammond, called the leading sheep breeder of his time, whose flocks had a world-wide reputation, A. L. Bingham, Solomon Jewett, and other Addison County sheep breeders were able to sell their rams and ewes for hundreds of dollars each. Shipments of Addison County sheep were made throughout the North and by 1860 they were being sent as far away as California.[76]

Despite the deception in passing off half-blooded stock as purebreds and the general overemphasis upon blood lines, these importations greatly raised the wool-producing quality of American sheep, as is shown in the average amount of wool produced per sheep. In 1839 the average was 1.8 pounds per sheep, in 1849 it was 2.4 pounds, and in 1859 it was 2.7 pounds.[77] It can also be said that the quality of the wool and to a less degree of the mutton was improving.

Spanish Merino, Saxon Merino, and Rambouillet—all varieties of the same stock—while bringing premium prices for their wool, were not appreciated as mutton.[78] They were considered by one authority to be no better than "the gaunt, scrawney, long-legged 'native' sheep" because

[75] Computed from Sixth, Seventh, and Eighth Censuses.

[76] Bailey, *Cyclopedia of American Agriculture*, IV, 581; H. P. Smith, *History of Addison County, Vermont* (Syracuse, N. Y.: D. Mason & Co., 1886), pp. 218–219.

[77] Computed from Sixth, Seventh, and Eighth Censuses.

[78] Differences in Boston prices of various grades of wool as of May 25, 1849, are shown in the *Wool Grower*, I (June, 1849), 35. The prices are in cents per pound.

Saxon	40.0	½ Merino	33.5
Full Merino	37.5	¼ Merino	30.0
¾ Merino	35.0	Common	28.0

their mutton was "coarse, dry, and ill-flavored." [79] It is understandable, then, why the consumption of mutton did not increase during the years when Merino sheep were so popular. It was the importation of improved strains of English short- and coarse-wooled sheep that brought mutton back as an important item of diet. As compared with the Merinos, they were larger in frame, easier to fatten, more vigorous and better able to withstand the penetrating cold and storms, and earlier maturing; consequently they had their place on farms where livestock was raised for the growing urban markets. Most important for their superior mutton were the Leicesters, Cotswolds, South Downs, Hampshire Downs, and Shropshire Downs. Importations of these improved breeds were made by Thorne, Corning and Sotham of New York, Powel of Pennsylvania, and Alexander of Kentucky, all of whom were importers of purebred cattle. William C. Rives, of Charlottesville, Virginia, was also a substantial importer of English sheep. Diminishing profits in raising sheep for their wool in the forties and fifties led to greater emphasis upon the English breeds, particularly in the eastern states. Save for northern New England, they were replacing Merinos in a large measure.[80]

Sheep farmers sought from government not only protection from competition but also compensation from owners of dogs who inflicted damage on their flocks. Over and over again in every sheep state the farmers went to the legislatures asking for effective legislation that would stop the slaughter of their stock. They maintained that the owners of the dogs should provide full compensation for their losses and complained that the legislatures were recreant in not adequately meeting the problem. In the Northeast the dog problem was a factor in leading many marginal farmers to give up their flocks, which returned them little but losses on the wool and dead carcasses to bury. The foot rot also bothered sheep farmers who, having no way of dealing with it individually, turned to the states for assistance. In Ohio they had introduced into the legislature a measure to ban the sale or movement over public roads of sheep afflicted with the disease.[81]

Congressional representatives of the principal sheep states liked to think that their industry could flourish only with the tariff protection they had secured in 1824, 1828, and 1832. Reduction of the rates in 1833 did not affect the prosperity of the New England sheep farmers, but depression struck in the early forties when new high-tariff rates went into effect.

[79] *New York Tribune* in *Weekly Alta California*, July 14, 1860; Henry S. Olcott, *Outlines of the First Course of Yale Agricultural Lectures* (New York: C. M. Saxton & Company, 1860), p. 146; Randall, *Practical Shepherd*, pp. 83–84.

[80] Randall, *Practical Shepherd*, pp. 43 ff.

[81] *Ohio Cultivator*, II (March 1, 1846), 33; *Ohio Farmer*, VI (February 7, 1857), 22.

The notion that the tariff reductions of 1846 and 1857 were responsible for the decline of sheep farming in the Northeast instead of the competition of the low-cost wool raised in the upper Mississippi Valley died slowly.[82]

The raising of sheep, like the raising of beef cattle, swine, wheat, and cotton, was moving west. Ohio lost considerable numbers of sheep in the fifties but was still far in the lead in 1860 as Texas, Illinois, and California were ahead in beef cattle. Wisconsin and the tier of states west of the Mississippi enjoyed increases ranging up to 315 per cent. Most significant for the future was the phenomenal increase in the number of sheep in California, Texas, New Mexico, and Utah. These states were destined to become the sheep-raising area of the future. Dairying replaced sheep raising on some farms in the Northeast, but many farmers could not make the transition; hill farming suffered a heavy blow. The flow of migration westward into the very regions contributing to the plight of the older areas was thus accelerated.[83]

USE OF OXEN

Oxen traditionally provided much of the motive power of the farm. Since most farmers kept some cattle and in the natural process had bull calves bestowed upon them, it was easy to have them castrated, fitted to the oxbow, and trained for ordinary farm work. At the end of their working days they could be fattened and sold to the nearby market or to a drover. While slow and awkward, they were stronger than horses, could pull heavier loads, were not skittish or likely to run away and break expensive equipment, and they needed less grain. They were more used in the extreme northern states, where grain was not as certain a crop as it was farther south. Maine, New Hampshire, Connecticut, Massachusetts, and Wisconsin in the 1850's were the states in which oxen were extensively used. Vermont, which had Morgan horses, used fewer oxen.

Although the number of oxen reached its peak in 1860, well before that date they were being replaced by the faster and more nimble horses and mules. Oxen might be quite satisfactory for drawing great loads of hay to the barn or fuel wood and maple sap to the sugarhouse, but no farmer enjoyed driving his produce to market with them. They were of no

---

[82] Randall, *Sheep Husbandry*, p. 159; Wright, *Wool-Growing and the Tariff*, passim. Harry James Brown has a valuable study of the bickering between the wool manufacturers and the woolgrowers over tariff rates on raw wool, in "The National Association of Wool Manufacturers, 1864–1897." Unpublished doctoral dissertation, 1949, Cornell University Library.

[83] Stilwell, *Migration from Vermont, passim*, and Wilson, *Hill Country of Northern New England, passim*.

use with mowing machines and reapers, which required fast-stepping horses, were too slow and awkward to use with light plows and rakes, and could not easily be used in power devices to run the thresher, the cane grinder, the cotton gin, or the hay baler. The day of the ox was passing, though he was still used in the twentieth century, and the horse in the North and the mule in the South were taking his place.

HORSE BREEDING

Early American horses were descended from Spanish, English, French, and Dutch importations. Well-known English and Arabian strains were brought in for racing and breeding, particularly into Kentucky and Virginia and in other southern states. Racing as a hobby was taken up by planters who maintained a few fast horses purchased in England or from Virginia and Kentucky stables. Michaux spoke of Virginia as having the finest horses for the carriage or saddle in 1805.[84] Early Virginia emigrants to the Bluegrass region of Kentucky who brought these fine horses with them found the area peculiarly well adapted to horse raising. From that time Kentucky was the center for raising fine horses, particularly race horses. Examination of the old files of the *American Turf Register* from its first appearance in 1829 shows how Kentucky led in horse breeding and the southern states led in horse raising. Supplying wealthy planters and urban sports with fast horses brought large returns to Kentucky breeders.

Horse breeding was given a great impetus with the importation of the English Thoroughbred, Messenger, in 1788. From this notable stallion came a line of tough, serviceable, and long-lived horses, including some of the most victorious on the race tracks. Messenger blood mixed with the Morgan strain of American horses produced a combination that seemed unbeatable on the track and in the market.[85]

Justin Morgan, most famous of American horses, and the progenitor of a long line of fast trotters, "spirited chargers," stylish driving, and fairly powerful work horses, was a Vermont product. The Morgan horse, a strong and fast-driving horse despite its somewhat small size, was well adapted to New England, where oxen did the heaviest work and horses were required only for the lighter draft hauling and trips to market. No American stallion had such a far-reaching effect upon horse breeding and has attracted so much historical and genealogical attention as Justin

[84] François André Michaux, *Travels to the Westward of the Alleghany Mountains* . . . (London: J. Mawman, 1805), p. 231.

[85] Massachusetts Board of Agriculture, *Eighth Annual Report*, 1860 (Boston: William White, 1861), pp. 186–187; Bailey, *Cyclopedia of American Agriculture*, III, 501 ff.

Morgan and his descendants. Black Hawk, a third-generation offspring of Justin Morgan, and himself sire of Ethan Allen, claimed to be the fastest trotter in the world, brought to his Bridport, Vermont, owner more than $40,000 in stud fees in addition to substantial earnings at race tracks.[86] In the single year, 1844, thirty-eight Black Hawk colts were sold in Bridport for an average of $590.[87]

Wherever the New Englander migrated he took with him his Morgan horse or a preference for it. Addison County, Vermont, could count on demands from these transplanted Yankees for its Morgans as for its Merino sheep.[88] A Wisconsin critic of the Morgan horses who doubted the purity of their blood said of them:

> Our State is pretty well filled with what is called Morgan Horses, Black Hawks. . . . These Morgan horses have their admirers and Vermont and New Hampshire men bring them, and also many fine-wooled sheep, when they emigrate West.[89]

In the fifties the Morgan horse had reached California, where Morgan and Black Hawk stallions were being advertised for service at fifty dollars. One man drove a herd of horses purchased in Vermont across the plains to California in 1859. One hundred and twenty-two came through the long trek and the losses were few.[90]

Horse-powered treadmills attached to grinders, threshers, corn shellers, hay balers, and gins, and the use of mowers, hay rakes, reapers, and other agricultural machines created a contantly expanding demand for horses. Urban folk, as their income increased, also bought carriage horses. A Georgia planter deplored the increase in the price of horses and attributed it in part to the fact that so many mares were being used to

[86] Daniel C. Linsley, *Morgan Horses* (New York: C. M. Saxton & Company, 1857); Joseph Battell, *The Morgan Horse and Register* (Middlebury, Vt.: Register Printing Co., 1894). A second volume was published in Middlebury by the American Publishing Company in 1905.

[87] Ethan Allen's stud fees for one season were said to be $13,000.—*Ohio Farmer*, V (December 12, 1856), 196; and VI (October 10, 1857), 162; *Boston Cultivator* in *Indiana Farmer*, III (December 15, 1853), 94.

[88] *Wool Grower and Stock Raiser*, IV (October, 1852), 54; *Ohio Farmer*, V (May 31, 1856), 85; *Wisconsin Farmer and North-Western Cultivator*, IX (February, December, 1857), 55, 439; and X (January, 1858), 19; Commissioner of Patents, *Report, Agriculture, 1861*, p. 550. The *Cultivator* ran a series of sketches of outstanding Morgan horses, with engravings which were widely copied for years in other journals. See *Prairie Farmer*, Vol. VIII (1848). The *Valley Farmer* in 1857, Vol. IX, brought some of these sketches up to date by showing that some of the horses were owned in the West.

[89] *Wisconsin Farmer and North-Western Cultivator*, X (February, 1858), 56–57. For a reply see *ibid.*, X (April, 1858), 137. The controversy between the pro- and anti-Morgan horsemen raged over a number of months in this journal.

[90] *Sacramento Union*, March 3, 1857, March 21 and September 10, 1859.

produce "those miserable, ugly, stubborn, sterile, long-eared hybrids," the mules. Where once seventy-five dollars would buy a horse, now it took much more, he said, and anyone who wanted a Morgan would have to pay eight hundred dollars.[91]

In the fifties prejudice against the mule diminished and the number on farms doubled, while the number of horses and oxen increased more slowly. Though mules were concentrated to a large degree in the slave states, it was a New Englander who best summarized their advantages over horses: their life span and working period were longer; they were less subject to disease and accident; they consumed two fifths less food; the expense of shoeing them was less; they could stand up better to hard work in extremely hot weather; they recovered from fatigue more rapidly, pulled more constantly, required no shelter, and were one third less expensive. They exceeded horses in numbers in the lower South. A major reason why the mule was better adapted to the plantation system was that he could be abused, beaten, neglected, improperly fed, worked long hours by slaves who had little incentive to treat him carefully, and show less effects than would horses or oxen under similar circumstances.[92]

Ulrich B. Phillips has pointed out that the deficiency of the cotton belt in hay crops and grazing land made the area dependent upon the region just to the north for its mules.[93] Advocates of self-sufficiency in the deep South were perturbed at this situation, and continued to argue that planters should raise their own mules. They seemed to be almost as much distressed that Georgia and Mississippi planters bought mules from Kentucky and Tennessee as that they bought corn and pork from Ohio. The horse country of Kentucky and the Nashville Basin of Tennessee met the demand of the planters for mules, and the resulting mule trade became one of the chief sources of revenue of farmers in these areas.[94]

Something of the extent of livestock on farms may be seen in the following table, which gives the average number of each kind on farms and

[91] *Southern Cultivator*, XVII (September, 1859), 270–271.

[92] S. W. Pomeroy in John S. Skinner, ed., *The Horse, by William Youatt. Together with a General History of the Horse* (Philadelphia: Lea and Blanchard, 1844), pp. 424–426; *Southern Cultivator*, XIV (August, 1856), 244.

[93] Ulrich B. Phillips, *History of Transportation in the Eastern Cotton Belt to 1860* (New York: Columbia University Press, 1908), p. 68.

[94] *Southern Cultivator*, XV (December, 1857), 363–364; *Working Farmer*, IX (September 1, 1857), 161, quoting the *American Veterinary Journal*; Frederic A. Culmer, ed., "Selling Missouri Mules Down South in 1835," *Missouri Historical Review*, XXIV (July, 1930), 637 ff.; Thomas D. Clark, "Live Stock Trade between Kentucky and the South, 1840–1860," *Kentucky Historical Register*, XXVII (September, 1929), 569 ff.; Russell, *North America*, p. 124; *Ohio Farmer*, VI (March 22, 1856), 48; Robert Leslie Jones, "The Horse and Mule Industry in Ohio to 1865," *Mississippi Valley Historical Review*, XXXIII (June, 1946), 83.

the average value of livestock on farms. This information is presented for
four states as representative of four argricultural regions.

VALUE AND NUMBER OF LIVESTOCK PER FARM IN FOUR STATES
AND IN THE UNITED STATES

	United States	Illinois	Kentucky	South Carolina	Vermont
Horses	3	4	4	2.5	2
Mules	0.5	0.25	1.25	1.5	—
Cows	4.5	3.5	3	5	5.5
Oxen	1	0.5	1.25	0.66	1.25
Beef cattle	7.25	7	5	5	5
Sheep	10.75	5.5	10	7	25
Hogs	16.5	17	26	29	1.5
Value	$536	$505	$269	$724	$521

Source: Computed from *Eighth Census of the United States, 1860, Agriculture.*

CHAPTER XI

Dairy Farming

DAIRY BREEDS

DISTINCT breeds of cattle and the commercial production of milk were slow to be established in the United States. Although utility cows were kept on most farms, their milk and milk products were consumed locally. The original stock of Devons and other breeds brought from England in the seventeenth and eighteenth centuries had deteriorated in size, quality, and milking capacity as the result of poor housing, inadequate feeding in winter, failure to cull out inferior stock, the tendency to sell off the best stock, and the use of scrub bulls. Little grain was provided for cattle, and the hay that was fed in winter on northern farms was poor in quality and insufficient in quantity. Because of the shortage of hay and grain few farmers tried to continue milking through the winter. If, in the spring when the cows freshened, there was an abundance of milk no thought was given to its sale, for there was no established market for it. Calves were permitted to suckle much longer than the modern dairyman would allow, much milk was made into butter and cheese for household use and for commercial sale, and some was fed to hogs. As late as 1848 a report of the Seneca County Agricultural Society of New York could say of farms in the county: "The *dairy* only receives the attention necessary for supplying the inhabitants with milk and butter." [1]

The Shorthorn craze and the New Englanders' liking for the rugged Devon mixtures to which they had long been accustomed delayed the development of dairy cattle. Farmers interested in milking breeds were told that the milking Shorthorns were equal, if not superior, to the Ayrshire, Jersey, and Devon mixtures in milk production and brought premium prices as beef. A leading New York stock importer and breeder

[1] *Cultivator,* New Series, VI (July, 1849), 211.

of quality cattle argued as late as 1844 the superiority of the Herefords as milkers.[2]

Massachusetts, with its flourishing industrial towns and congested population, early acquired an interest in dairy cows. Farmers close to cities were the first to introduce milk breeds. They were likely to be gentleman farmers like the Cushing, Quincy, Adams, Salisbury, Hubbard, and Lincoln families, who turned to Ayrshire cattle on which to build their dairy herds. Importations of Ayrshires and, to a lesser degree of Jersey cattle, brought about substantial improvements in dairy stock in the Bay State as well as elsewhere in New England and New York. By 1860 the Ayrshires gave promise of becoming the leading dairy breed in America. Holsteins were still looked upon with disfavor because of the low fat content of their milk.[3]

Notwithstanding the promotional work undertaken by the breeders of Ayrshires and Jerseys, by the Massachusetts Society for the Promotion of Agriculture, and by the county and state fairs of New York and Massachusetts, these dairy breeds were not widely accepted.[4] The hardy Devon and the fast-growing Shorthorn still attracted a larger following for all-purpose animals and existed in larger numbers.

In 1850 the census showed 6,385,094 "milch" cows, 1,700,741 working oxen, and 10,293,069 other cattle. In 1860 the numbers in these categories were 8,581,735, 2,254,911, and 14,779,373, respectively. Only five states —all in the Northeast—listed more "milch" cattle than "other" or beef cattle.[5] As late as 1860 most of the "milch" cattle listed in the census reports were grade mixtures, largely Devons, with an increasing infusion of Shorthorn.

For a time it appeared that a distinct dairy breed was about to develop in the United States. Colonel Samuel Jaques, on his Ten Hills farm in Somerville, Massachusetts, bred a Shorthorn to a native cow

[2] *Cultivator*, VII (April, October, 1840), 56, 155; and New Series, I (February, 1844), 66.
[3] Thomas R. Pirtle, *History of the Dairy Industry* (Chicago: Monjonnier Bros. Company, 1926), pp. 26, 45 ff.; E. Parmalee Prentice, *American Dairy Cattle: Their Past and Future* (New York: Harper & Brothers, 1942), pp. 231 ff.; Commissioner of Agriculture, *Report, 1863* (Washington, D. C.: Government Printing Office, 1863), pp. 197–198. The first Ayrshire herd book appeared in 1863.
[4] *New England Farmer*, V (October 20, 1826), 102; Charles L. Flint, *The Agriculture of Massachusetts as Shown in the Returns of the Agricultural Societies, 1853* (Boston: William White, 1854), p. 269; Massachusetts Board of Agriculture, *First Annual Report*, Second Series, 1853 (Boston: William White, 1854), p. 85.
[5] *Eighth Census of the United States, 1860 Agriculture,* (Washington, D. C.: Government Printing Office, 1864), pp. 184–186. Unfortunately the usefulness of this comparison is minimized by the action of the Census Bureau in listing an additional 3,347,000 "neat cattle" in 1860, a classification which cannot be broken down into the three categories the Census used elsewhere.

giving phenomenally rich milk, and from the offspring established a herd of cattle whose large milk yields had high butterfat content. At a time when dairy cattle attracted little attention and had less care, the Jaques herd won many premiums and extensive publicity in the farm journals. To keep the herd intact and at the same time assure that it would continue to be bred for the high butterfat content of its milk, a group of Boston merchants took over Ten Hills farm and the Jaques herd, now called "Cream Pot," when the owner became financially embarrassed. Group management failed, however, and the herd had to be dispersed in 1846. Cream Pot cattle might have flourished where dairymen were primarily concerned with making butter, but in the area close to Boston, where the demand for milk was growing, cows with high production records rather than those with high butterfat content in their milk were desired.[6]

MILK PRODUCTION

Estimates of the average production of milk per cow are few but revealing. A writer in the *Cultivator* in 1840 gave the average of the best common dairy cows as ten quarts a day, but this is very different from the average of all dairy cows. Two years later, the Massachusetts Commissioner of Agriculture estimated that the average from good native cows was from five to seven quarts daily. Perhaps most useful is the estimate of Daniel Lee, editor of the *Southern Cultivator* and previously active in New York State agricultural matters, that common cows nowhere gave more than two to four quarts daily.[7]

In the early part of the century, farmers neglected both the all-purpose cows and the beef animals, but as the demand for butter and cheese and, later fluid milk developed, the care and feeding of livestock improved. Experimentally inclined farmers, urged on by their journals and by English commentators, tried feeding carrots, turnips, and potatoes to their dairy cattle without marked success. Corn, which was easier to raise, harvest, and store, did not spoil and, when properly fed, greatly increased the milk flow. In addition to their grass and hay, dairy cows were commonly fed silage made from green corn stalks, corn and cob meal, linseed meal, oats and wheat bran. Cottonseed meal was used to good advantage by the fifties.[8]

⁶*Farmers' Register*, VIII (September 30, 1840), 562; Herbert Anthony Kellar, *Solon Robinson: Pioneer and Agriculturist* (*Indiana Historical Collections*, Vols. XXI and XXII; Indianapolis: Indiana Historical Bureau, 1936), I, 318–319. Cf. *Cultivator*, IX (February, 1842), 36.

⁷*Cultivator*, VII (October, 1840), 150; IX (May, 1842), 77; Lewis Cecil Gray, *History of Agriculture in the Southern United States to 1860* (2 vols.; Washington, D. C.: Carnegie Institution, 1930), II, 846.

⁸*Homestead*, III (November 19, 1857, and January 7, 1858), 152, 254;

For a number of reasons, the sale of fluid milk was not an item of major significance to many dairy farmers until the middle of the century. The market in towns and cities was limited by the high cost of milk, the low income of the workers, poor quality of the milk resulting from adulteration and the methods of feeding city cows, and lack of appreciation of the nutritional value of milk. Distribution costs then, as later, made the retail price high—seven cents a quart in New York in 1860—which placed it beyond the reach of people with low incomes. The large number of deaths from scarlet fever, undulant fever, cholera infantum, scrofula, and consumption attributed to milk further reduced demand.

No. *23.*   **Mr.** *Josiah A. Jennings*

To the City of Boston, Dr.

For a License for one COW to go upon the Common for the year 18 *29* agreeably to an Ordinance of the City Council, $5

Received payment, *May 21. 1829.*

J. M. Cleary   City Clerk.

License to pasture a cow on the Boston Common, 1829 (Courtesy, The Henry E. Huntington Library)

In the absence of rapid transportation facilities and without refrigeration to keep milk fresh, it was impossible to ship it from any considerable distance.[9] Before the coming of the fast milk train, therefore, towns and cities had to depend upon local supplies. Among these supplies were the individual cows maintained by many urban residents in their own stables along with their driving horses and pastured in some outlying field or on the town common during the grass season. As late as 1829 Boston was licensing cows for pasturing on the Common for five dollars a year.[10] When Frances Trollope visited Cincinnati in 1827 she

Percy Wells Bidwell and John I. Falconer, *History of Agriculture in the Northern United States, 1620–1860* (Washington, D. C.: Carnegie Institution, 1925), p. 379.

[9] *Hunt's Merchants' Magazine*, XI (November, 1860), 612; *Scientific American*, VI (December 28, 1850), 114.

[10] Receipt No. 23 to Josiah A. Jennings "For a License for one *Cow* to go upon the Common for the year 1829, agreeably to an Ordinance of the City Council," May 21, 1829, signed by the city clerk.—No. 697, Goodspeed Collection, Huntington Library.

noted that "a large proportion of the families . . . particularly of the poorer class," kept a cow which they milked twice daily and then turned loose to forage at will.[11] Where domestic dairying was impossible and family budgets permitted, milk was purchased from deliverymen who bought milk of cows fed on distillery slops and peddled the thin blue product from a can into the customer's pitcher.

Farmers in the vicinity of crossroads hamlets, county seats, and commercial and industrial centers found a market for milk as well as for other foodstuffs they raised. Thus Colonel Albert J. Pickett, who lived three miles from Montgomery, Alabama, a city with a population of 8,727 in 1850, from twenty cows supplied 80 to 100 quarts of milk a day to customers, and used an equal amount to make butter and to feed his Negroes and swine. A local scribe affirmed that his butter was as yellow, as firm, and as pleasant to taste as the best New York product.[12] A more critical Georgia planter caustically observed that from the ten or twenty cows maintained on the larger plantations, milk was obtained only in the grass season and the owner, if living away from the plantation, would get only from five to ten pounds of "chalky" butter monthly.[13]

MILK STANDARDS

Before the perfection of the Babcock test for determining the fat content of milk in the eighties and the establishment of strict requirements concerning the amount of cream or butterfat that whole milk sold to consumers should contain, the principle of *caveat emptor* prevailed. Adulteration, watering, and skimming off the cream were all practiced by dealers if not by farmers, and city buyers had no way of being sure of the quality of their milk. Robert Smith, president of the Maryland Agricultural Society, and owner of a large dairy two miles from Baltimore, told in 1824 of skimming the cream from his milk and churning it into butter, and of selling the residue or skim milk—a "very pleasant beverage"—to a dealer at two cents a quart. The dealer, in turn, retailed the 250 to 300 quarts thus obtained for three cents and, one may suspect, as whole milk.[14] A New York milkman was quoted as saying that he "always accommodated his customers as to the price" by adding sufficient water to enable him to sell for what they were willing to pay. Another milkman strained water through finely ground corn meal to give it color and then added a little skim milk and sold the concoction

[11] Frances Trollope, *Domestic Manners of the Americans* (2 vols.; London: Whittaker, Treacher & Co., 1832), I, 88.
[12] Montgomery *Alabama Journal* in *Southern Cultivator*, V (March, 1847), 46.
[13] *Soil of the South*, III (December, 1853), 746.
[14] *Southern Agriculturist*, II (February, 1829), 92.

for three cents a quart.[15] Other ingredients added to skim milk were magnesia, arrowroot, flour, starch, sugar, and molasses.

An examination of specimens of milk purchased in 1857 and 1858 in twelve different parts of Boston showed that only one could qualify as being nearly pure milk; three contained 15 per cent water, two contained 22.5 and 25 per cent water, respectively, four contained 30 to 35 per cent water, one was 47.5 per cent water, and the last was skim milk. The editor of the *New England Farmer* was convinced that farmers were not responsible for this adulteration, for the buyers at the dairies watched their purchases carefully. But when the milk was delivered to customers at six cents a quart it was heavily freighted with Cochituate water. At the same time a Cincinnati dealer, when asked whether all dealers diluted their milk with water, replied: "No, the best milk dealers never put water into their milk, but rather put milk into water." [16]

Much of the milk sold in the larger cities came from dairies operated in connection with distilleries, breweries, and piggeries. It was the practice of distilleries and breweries to utilize the by-product of their operations by feeding the hot mash or swill to cows and hogs kept on adjacent premises.[17] Other distilleries sold the hot mash to scores of dairymen operating within the city or on its periphery. The largest New York distillery had adjoining it three huge stables housing 2,000 cows whose only feed was the hot swill that was kept constantly before them. Stalls were rented to dairy managers at four and five dollars a year and the swill was sold for as little as six and a quarter cents a barrel. Cows consumed a barrel a day of the mess and were given no hay or other solid food. The foul atmosphere of the slop dairies resulting from their lack of ventilation and their crowded conditions, plus the fact that the cows had no exercise and had to eat a liquid diet for which their digestive systems was not suited, made many of them ill. Diseased cows were milked, so it was said, until they died.[18]

Contemporary descriptions of city dairies—the story was much the same in most larger cities where distilleries and breweries were located

[15] Henry Colman, *European Agriculture and Rural Economy from Personal Observation* (2 vols.; Boston: Arthur D. Phelps, 1846), I, 196.
[16] *New England Farmer*, X (June, 1858), 292–293; *Cincinnatus*, III (June, 1858), 266.
[17] *Farmers' Cabinet*, XI (January 15, 1847), 175; and XII (September 15, 1847), 41–43; *Daily Placer Times and Transcript*, Sacramento, Calif., August 3, 1855.
[18] *Hartley's Essay on Milk of 1842* in M. Francis Guenon, *Treatise on Milch Cows* . . . (New York: C. M. Saxton & Company, 1856), pp. 29–32; *American Agriculturist*, VII (September, 1848), 266–267; *Pennsylvania Farm Journal*, III (May, 1853), 37–39; *Working Farmer*, XII (June 1, 1856), 79; John Mullaly, *The Milk Trade of New York and Vicinity* (New York: Fowler and Wells, 1853), *passim*; *Scientific American*, VI (December 28, 1850), 114.

—make unpleasant reading. As early as 1838 these conditions were brought to public attention in scorching exposés. One paper spoke with some exaggeration of the wretched milk produced by the 18,000 cows in and near New York City which were fed on the distillery swill from 2,000,000 bushels of grain used in the manufacture of alcoholic drinks.

These grains are corrupt and unhealthy; so much so, that they consume the flesh around the cow's teeth, also rotting the teeth, so that all these cows, becoming sickly in one year, are sent to the market to serve the people as a miserable substitute for beef, and 18,000 new and healthy cows are substituted in their place in one year to share the fate of their predecessors. So poisonous is their milk, that out of 100 children fed with it, 49 die yearly.[19]

The charge that eight or nine thousand children died annually in New York City from drinking contaminated milk is believable. Public outcries, official inquiries, the concern of members of the medical profession, and the newspaper excitement all lent support to such charges.

A rising tide of indignation against the practices of New York's dairy interests led to a series of investigations. After a study of the problem, 105 physicians in the New York Academy of Medicine reported that "the milk of cows fed chiefly on distillery slop [is] extremely detrimental to the health . . ." and urged action to outlaw its sale. A petition to the New York legislature in 1854 spoke of the milk from slop-fed cows as deranging health, inducing lingering and distressing diseases, and destroying life "with impunity," and of the "pernicious dregs of the distillery" as a "horrible evil in all its tendencies and results." With the railroad revolutionizing transportation and making it easy to bring in fresh milk from pasture-fed cows there was no longer any reason to allow the slop-produced milk to be sold, said the petitioners.[20] Investigations resulting from this and other petitions created a demand for legislative protection of the consumers against producers and dealers who were selling adulterated and poisonous milk.[21] It was charged that of the 330,000 quarts of milk consumed daily in New York, 160,000 came from cows fed on distillery mash. To this milk was added 70,000 quarts of water mixed with chalk or plaster of Paris to remove its bluish ap-

[19] *Olive Branch* in *Silk Grower and Farmers' Manual*, I (January, 1839), 154; also copied in *Franklin Farmer*, II (October 13, 1838), 50.

[20] *New York Senate Document* No. 100, 77 Sess., 1854, Vol. II, *passim;* and No. 102, pp. 1, 5–6; *American Agriculturist*, VII (September, 1848), 267.

[21] In 1840 there were 20 distilleries and 16 breweries in New York City and Brooklyn. In 1860 the figures were 33 distilleries and 70 breweries. Most of the larger establishments had dairies in association with them. The figures are from the Censuses of 1840 and 1860

pearance. The balance of the milk was drawn from dairies along the Harlem, Erie, Long Island, and New Haven railroads.

The New York inquiries and the attention given by the press to the problem of adulteration of milk led to similar investigations elsewhere. In Chicago, Cincinnati, Boston, Baltimore, and other cities the newspapers demanded action to outlaw adulteration.[22] Massachusetts was the first state to act by making the adulteration of milk illegal in 1856 and by forbidding the feeding of distillery waste to cows in 1859. To provide a measure of enforcement the state authorized the appointment of an inspector of dairies in 1861.[23] Other states fell into line slowly with similar legislation: New York in 1862, New Hampshire and Wisconsin in 1866, Rhode Island in 1867, Maine in 1869, and Virginia in 1872. New York City and other large centers passed supplementary local ordinances, but the lack of adequate enforcement procedures made these measures largely ineffective. The investigation and publicity did, however, contribute to the demand for milk from pasture- and grain-fed cows in rural areas.[24]

RAILROADS ENLARGE THE MILKSHEDS

The construction of the railroads did more to assure a supply of fresh, relatively pure milk to urban residents than the numerous but unworkable state laws and ordinances of city councils. It also cheapened the price of milk and provided a more wholesome product. Boston was first of the cities to benefit from railroad building in "the reduction of the price and bettering the quality of milk. . . ." By 1842, a large portion of the city's milk was coming by rail from country dairies ten to thirty miles away. Five years later, 14,400 quarts were coming daily to the city over the Fitchburg railroad.[25]

Similarly, the extension of the Erie Railroad to Orange County in 1842 made it possible to bring the milk of the most sanitary dairies of New York State to New York City. Before long, when a second train had been put on, the Erie was hauling more than five million quarts annually. Farmers who received two cents a quart netted more by selling their

[22] *California Express*, Marysville, July 3, 1858.
[23] Pirtle, *History of the Dairy Industry*, p. 129.
[24] Edwin R. A. Seligman, ed., *Encyclopedia of the Social Sciences* (15 Vols.; New York: The Macmillan Company, 1930–1935), X, 475.
[25] *Farmers' Cabinet*, VIII (August 15, 1843), 14, quoting the *Cultivator*; and XII (January 15, 1848), 198, quoting the *Pennsylvania Enquirer*; *Hunt's Merchants' Magazine*, XLI (September, 1859), 382; Edward Harold Mott, *Between the Ocean and the Lakes: The Story of the Erie* (New York: John S. Collins, 1901), pp. 406–409.

fluid milk than by making it into butter and cheese and at far less labor. City people found the new supply of country milk broke the near monopoly enjoyed by distillers' and brewers' dairies and that it provided consumers with a fresher product at lower prices. By 1844, when the Erie was hauling 17,000 quarts daily to the city, the Goshen *Independent Republican* optimistically said: "Orange County milk is driving swill milk from the city." [26]

Meantime, the New York and Harlem Railroad was building its line northward from New York City into another dairy region. Here, as elsewhere, the coming of the iron horse brought swift changes in farm practices. A farmer in Carmel, some 35 miles from the city, related in 1851 how he had shifted from sheep and beef cattle to dairy cows when the Harlem road made possible the shipping of milk to the big market. Milk was kept cool and fresh in cans in large troughs filled with spring water, and, when necessary with ice from the ample ice house, until it was time to take it to the station 1½ miles distant. From his fifty cows he grossed $3,600 in the sale of milk and cream in one year.[27] The Harlem reached Chatham, a distance of 120 miles from New York, in 1852, by which time it had become a major feeder of milk to the city. In 1860, the amount of milk daily moving to New York by rail ranged from 124,871 quarts in January to 188,484 in July, and constituted a major source of income for the companies. Other cities were likewise extending their milksheds and bringing in fresh milk from pasture-fed cows. Notwithstanding all improvements in quality and the reduction in the price of milk made possible by the railroads, the average daily consumption was small: less than half a gill in Washington, half a pint in New York, one gill in Springfield, Massachusetts.[28]

Another promising development that was having some effect in raising the standards of dairy management was Gail Borden's milk-condensing plant at Burrville, Connecticut. Borden eliminated three fourths of the water in milk and in the process sterilized it so that it could keep for a longer time. More important, he set up testing and

[26] Mott, *Between the Ocean and the Lakes*, p. 409, quoting the Goshen *Independent Republican*.

[27] *Cultivator*, IX (October, 1842), 77; and X (June, 1843), 89; see also New Series, VIII (November, 1851), 358.

[28] Silas F. Loomis, "The Consumption of Milk," in Commissioner of Patents, *Report, Agriculture, 1861* (Washington, D. C.: Government Printing Office, 1862), pp. 214–217; *New England Farmer*, XI (January, 1859), 34; David M. Ellis, *Landlords and Farmers in the Hudson-Mohawk Region* (Ithaca, N. Y.: Cornell University Press, 1946), p. 206. Other estimates for the consumption of milk range from one fifth of a pint to fifty-five hundredths of a quart.—Richard Osborn Cummings, *The American and His Food: A History of Food Habits in the United States* (Chicago: The University of Chicago Press, 1940), pp. 54, 77.

sampling procedures to determine butterfat content, purity, and previous care in handling. Milk not measuring up to his standards was rejected. In this way he could assure city consumers good-quality milk and at the same time exert pressure on farmers to take more care of their cows and to keep their equipment clean and their milk cool and free from contaminating odors or dirt. When his plant got under way at Burrville in 1859 *Homestead* predicted that Borden would find the New York city milk dealers solidly opposed to his condensed milk and prepared to use every device to prevent its sale.[29]

BUTTER AND CHEESE

Prior to the building of the railroads and the running of the milk trains, most farm-produced milk was consumed as sweet milk on the farm or made into butter and cheese, the sour, skim, or butter milk being fed to the hogs. Butter and cheese had a high value in proportion to weight and were therefore easy to ship, whether by canal or railroad or even by wagon. Many farmers living within five to fifteen miles of a town or city would load up their buckboard or market wagon once a week with butter and perhaps cheese, apples, and other fruit and vegetables in season and drive to town, there to peddle their wares to individual customers and to take what was unsold to a store for trade. Fresh butter, a standard item in the diet of most families, was always marketable.[30]

Before the separator was invented, the amount of equipment necessary to make butter and cheese was small and inexpensive. Buttermaking was the simpler process. Fresh warm milk was first strained, then put in broad pans, where the cream, when it had risen, could be skimmed off and held until there was sufficient to churn. The churn could be a small device in which the operator moved a dasher up and down to keep the cream in motion until the fat had sufficiently separated from the buttermilk to permit molding the butter. It was then worked over with a wooden paddle to extrude the buttermilk, salted to keep it fresh, and packed into a wooden keg or firkin. In larger dairies the milk was put in a barrellike churn that pivoted on an axle and could be turned by hand or by power provided by a dog or a sheep. Sheep power was considered steadiest, most efficient, and most reliable. Such a device operated by a single sheep, it was said, could churn the butter from twenty cows.

[29] *Homestead*, IV (November 24, 1859), 987–988; Joe B. Frantz, *Gail Borden: Dairymen to a Nation* (Norman: University of Oklahoma Press, 1951), p. 243.

[30] *Farmers' Cabinet*, VII (November 15, 1842), 112; *Transactions* of the New York State Agricultural Society (Albany: Charles Van Benthuysen, 1860), XIX, 105; *Homestead*, II (April 16, 1857), 473.

Butter was made in all counties of the United States and in considerable quantities, though outside the dairy states it was mostly produced for consumption on the farm or plantation. New York, the premier dairy state, accounted for 22 per cent of the butter produced in 1859. St. Lawrence County alone, with more cattle than were found in any other county outside of Texas, produced more butter than did seventeen states, including two in New England, four in the West, and eleven in the South. Butter was in common use on the table of northern farmers, whereas in the South its scarcity confined its use to the upper classes and those small farmers fortunate enough to have milking cows.[31] Maine, not primarily noted as a dairy state, made 18 pounds of butter for each resident, while Alabama made 6 pounds for each resident. Even the richest Alabama planter must have felt that his thirty-five milk cows had not yielded satisfying results in producing milk for only 315 pounds of butter in a year.[32]

There were great differences in the quality of butter, which depended upon cleanliness in the making process, the elimination of the water after washing, the evenness and lightness with which the salt was applied and its purity, and the temperature of the cream at churning and of the room in which the butter was kept. Butter which brought the highest price and was exclusively bought for the United States Navy came from Orange County, New York, or measured up to the high quality of Orange County butter. So high a reputation did it attain that for years the top grade of premium butter was known as Orange County or Goshen butter, no matter where it was made.[33] The cows from which premium butter was made were given careful attention, and their pastures of rich grass mixtures of clover, timothy, and bluegrass were kept in the best of condition by top-dressing. Although the bulk of the Orange County butter was made in the spring, summer, and early fall, some dairy farmers continued to milk their cows and to make butter in the winter by feeding the best of hay and quantities of grain.[34]

During the fall and winter, when cows were fed on hay and grain, the butter lost the deep yellow hue of spring and summer butter.

[31] The per capita consumption of butter in 1860 was 14.62 pounds as compared with 17.28 in the nineteen twenties.—Edgar W. Martin, *The Standard of Living in 1860: American Consumption Levels on the Eve of the Civil War* (Chicago: The University of Chicago Press, 1942), p. 23.

[32] James Benson Sellers, *Slavery in Alabama* (University: University of Alabama Press, 1950), p. 26.

[33] *Cultivator,* New Series, V (July, September, 1848), 206, 271; *Ohio Cultivator,* XI (April 15, 1855), 125.

[34] *Ohio Farmer,* VIII (July 16, 1859), 227. This account of "How Goshen Butter Is Made," by a Mr. Denniston, went the rounds of agricultural papers.

Dairymen commonly colored their fall and winter butter with yellow pepper, marigold water, turmeric, the juice of carrots, or the flowers of saffron. Such practices were relatively harmless, but more questionable additives were also used, such as "bad flour, oat meal, pea flower, large quantities of salt and water, hogs' lard, old or inferior quantities of butter . . . and a soft kind of cheese." As the *American Agriculturist* commented, such practices "conceal the defects, and destroy one of the simplest tests of good butter." [35] The wide disparity in butter prices and quality may be seen from the table of quotations for the week ending February 20, 1861.[36]

QUOTATIONS OF BUTTER IN NEW YORK MARKET, FEBRUARY 21, 1861

	Cents per pound
Orange County	22–25
Extra fall made	19–20
Welsh tub, strictly choice	17–18
Welsh tub, fair to good	15–16
Half firkin, strictly choice	18–19
Half firkin, fair to good	15–17
Firkins, choice	18–19
Firkins, fair to good	15–17
Western Pennsylvania, choice	14–16
Western Pennsylvania, fair	10–12
Western Reserve, good	10–12
Western Reserve, fair to choice	11–13
Western common	9–10
Grease	8½
Roll butter	12–15

Cheese making consisted of mixing rennet—the membrane of a calf's stomach—with the milk as it soured in order to separate the curds from the whey. When separated, the curds were pressed, molded, and cured. Rennet was essential for the separation of the curds, and in remote places, where the demand was greater than the supply, farmers frantically sought a supply elsewhere. The letters of a transplanted New Yorker in Kansas in the eighteen fifties show how anxiously rennets were sought in a region where it was not deemed prudent to kill calves.[37]

[35] *American Agriculturist*, VII (September, 1848), 267. See also the *Ohio Farmer*, IV (January 7, 1860), 2.

[36] *New York Tribune*, February 22, 1861.

[37] *Cultivator*, XI (September, 1843), 147; "Letters of John and Sarah Everett, 1854–1864," *Kansas Historical Quarterly*, VIII (1939), *passim;* R. Bettrang, *A Complete Treatise on Cheese Making* (New York: B. G. Teubner, 1861).

Northern farm women were not commonly expected to work in the field, but butter and cheese making were largely left to them, and there is evidence of their doing much of the milking.[38] Both butter and cheese making required strong arms and backs, and long sustained work if the dairy operations were large. Taking up the cudgels in behalf of her sex, an Oberlin College graduate criticized farmers who required or even permitted their wives and daughters to engage for long periods in such exacting labor, which she held to be little better than "servitude." [39] A male writer similarly argued that "no intelligent man . . . can wish to make a perfect drudge of his wife or daughters" by requiring that they do the work in the dairy.[40] It may be doubted that such sentiments did much to ease the labor of women in the dairy at the time.

The area of cheese making was quite limited. New York produced 46 per cent, Ohio 20 per cent, Vermont 8 per cent, and Massachusetts 5 per cent. The major center of cheese production was in the Mohawk and St. Lawrence valleys of New York, where seven adjacent counties out of sixty in the state produced 29 per cent of the total amount of cheese made in the United States. In Herkimer County, which early produced cheese of a uniformly high quality, the average production per farm in 1859 was 3,541 pounds. Each farm family in that rich dairy county made on the average 8 pounds of butter and 68 pounds of cheese weekly.[41] With butter bringing twelve to twenty-five cents a pound and cheese seven to ten cents, it is apparent that dairy farmers producing at that

[38] John Galt, *Lawrie Todd: Or the Settlers in the Woods* (New York: The Editor, 1847), p. 46; *Homestead*, II (April 23, 1857), 494; Harriet Martineau, *Society in America* (3 vols.; London: Saunders & Otley, 1837), I, 329; Howard Johnson, *A Home in the Woods: Oliver Johnson's Reminiscences of Early Marion County* (*Publications* of the Indiana Historical Society, Vol. XVI, No. 2, Indianapolis: Indiana Historical Society, 1951), p. 164: "It was a universal custom for the women to tend the garden, just as they always milked the cow." Miss Martineau (II, 39) found only German women "seen in the fields and gardens in America, except a very few Dutch, and the slaves in the south."

[39] Mrs. M. B. Bateham deserves more than a footnote for her courageous championship of women's rights. She not only deplored women's milking or working long hours in the dairy but criticized farmers for not mending leaky roofs and broken windows, repairing smoky chimneys, cleaning up muddy yards, and providing cisterns and a "thousand and one household implements and conveniences . . . which a little labor and ingenuity might supply." Mrs. Bateham was also distressed to see, at the communal colony at Zoar, women "perform men's labor in the field, entirely regardless of those habits of delicacy and refinement which we of this country consider so essential to the character of women."—*Ohio Cultivator*, IV (July 15, 1848), 111.

[40] *Wool Grower and Stock Raiser*, IX (May, 1856), 155, quoting the *Cultivator*.

[41] Commissioner of Agriculture, *Report, 1863* (Washington, D. C.: Government Printing Office, 1863), p. 384. All statistics are computed from *Eighth Census of the United States, Agriculture, 1860*.

rate had a substantial source of income. Doubtless an exceptional case, but nevertheless worth citing, is that of Zadoc Pratt of Greene County, New York, who kept detailed records of the dairy operations on his 365-acre hill farm between 1857 and 1861. From 50 cows he made 6,500 pounds of butter in 1857 and 10,860 pounds in 1861, which he sold at 22 to 24 cents a pound. After deducting his expenses, including 7 per cent interest on his investment, he had annual profits ranging from $460 to $1,716. A minister of the gospel in Albany County, New York, summarized his experience in cheese and butter making from the milk of six cows, in the season of 1837, as follows:

1,448 pounds of cheese sold at the door at 7.25 cents	$104.88
452 pounds of cheese at 8 cents	36.16
417 pounds of butter at 18 cents	77.85
	$218.89

The average return per cow, he boasted, was $36.46.[42] New York farmers found in England a rapidly growing market for a portion of their cheese. That country took from New York, in 1840, 723,713 pounds of cheese; in 1849, it purchased 15,380,836 pounds; in 1861, it imported 40,000,000 pounds of American cheese.[43]

CO-OPERATIVE CHEESE MAKING

Cheese making was a trade that required careful attention to details, an art that had to be cultivated with long-continued practice. The labor costs, time involved, and expensive equipment used in large-scale production and the inefficiency of household manufacture on a small scale led some enterprising farmers to take the milk or curds of their neighbors and to make the cheese for them. The entrepreneur's next step was to buy the curds or milk from his neighbors and, after making the cheese, to have full responsibility for selling it. Thus a Connecticut farmer in the fifties bought the curds from the milk of 300 cows of his neighbors, and made cheese of better quality and with less labor than had characterized their individual efforts.[44] Privately operated cheese factories flourished in the Western Reserve of Ohio, a center of cheese

[42] Zadoc Pratt, "The Dairy Farming Region of Greene and Orange Counties, New York, with Some Account of the Farm of the Writer," Commissioner of Patents, Report, Agriculture, 1861 (Washington, D. C.: Government Printing Office, 1862), pp. 411 ff.; Cultivator, V (March, 1838), 15.

[43] Working Farmer, II (August 1, 1850), 137. Kemp & Co. of New York is quoted as saying that the English market could take double the quantity of American cheese it was importing if the quality were improved.—Commissioner of Agriculture, Report, 1863, p. 384.

[44] Homestead, I (August 14, 1856), 738, 745.

production second only to New York. One manufacturer used the curds of 3,000 cows in his four factories.[45]

Co-operative cheese making was begun in Oneida County, New York, about 1850 and rapidly spread throughout the principal dairy counties of that state. By 1864, Oneida County alone had 34 cheese factories operated either by individual owners or by superintendents of co-operating farmers, and making cheese from the milk of 16,000 cows. A single factory in Cortland County, New York, took the curds or milk of 1,400 cows.[46] The next step in co-operative action taken by dairy farmers occurred in Herkimer County, when a group established a marketing society to aid in securing for themselves the best possible price for their cheese and other products. Thus a household industry was moving into the factory stage, and farmers were evolving means by which they could eliminate some of the costly steps in marketing their products.[47]

In addition to butter and cheese, dairy cattle also provided the farmer with quantities of skim, sour, and butter milk for feeding hogs. Young heifers were either used to replace the older animals or sold as veal. It was in the dairy states that the return per acre of land in farms reached the highest figure for the value of animals slaughtered. Thus Connecticut in 1860 could boast $1.25 per acre for the land in farms from dressed livestock, while Georgia could claim only 41 cents per acre. For New York the figure was 75 cents, for Virginia 36 cents. New York, Illinois, Ohio, and Pennsylvania led in the value of dressed livestock followed by Tennessee, Kentucky, and Virginia.[48]

POULTRY RAISING

Prior to 1840, poultry raising almost invariably was a small sideline to provide a greater variety for the farmer's table. Chickens of no named breed were permitted to roam at will through the barns and fields, where they picked up most of their feed. They were given little or no grain except what they could find themselves, laid their eggs in out-of-the-way places, and came forth with new broods of chicks two or three times during the summer. Their eggs were collected irregularly and without regard to their freshness. If a surplus accumulated it was traded off at

[45] Conneaut Reporter in Prairie Farmer, IX (August, 1849), 250; Henry S. Olcott, Outlines of the First Course of Yale Agricultural Lectures (New York: C. M. Saxton & Company, 1860), p. 149.

[46] Homestead, I (August 14, 1856), 738, 745; and II (August 6, 1857), 733, quoting the Ohio Cultivator; Solon Robinson, Facts for Farmers, Also for the Family Circle (2 vols.; New York: A. J. Johnson, 1867), I, 460.

[47] Commissioner of Agriculture, Report, 1863, pp. 403–404; Ellis, Landlords and Farmers in the Hudson-Mohawk Region, pp. 203–204.

[48] Eighth Census of the United States, 1860, Agriculture, p. 187.

the farmers' market for store goods. Farmers' wives commonly managed the poultry and had the benefits therefrom. "The frugal housewife well knows," said the *American Agriculturist*, "the advantage of a basket of eggs for the store, to be returned in a few yards of muslin or calico, a spool or two of thread, a packet of tea, and sundry other 'notions.' She has received many six-pences and shillings of 'pin-money' from the peripatetic chicken merchant." [49]

Growing cities called for an ever larger number of eggs and chickens. To satisfy the demand, some enterprising farmers near such markets entered heavily into the raising of chickens and the production of eggs. In the Quincy market alone in Boston more than 1,100,000 dozen eggs were sold in 1848 at prices ranging from eleven to thirty cents a dozen, and the total value of poultry products sold in the city was estimated at a million dollars. New York was using two million dollars worth of eggs annually by the Civil War. [50]

The introduction of Oriental, African, and European birds during the years of the "hen fever" in the forties and fifties, which is discussed later, directed attention as nothing had previously done to the economic possibilities in poultry. This resulted in a big upsurge. Furthermore, out of the interbreeding of the importations came new varieties, notably the Plymouth Rock. Toward the end of the period the Leghorns were imported from Europe and displayed their unusual combination of desirable qualities: early maturity, large white eggs, heavy laying capacity, and disinclination to become broody. [51]

INCOME OF THE NORTHERN FARMER

The northern farmer, producing his hay and grain for his livestock, and his meat, eggs, dairy products, and vegetables for his table, had less need for major staple products than did his southern counterpart. His income came from many sources. For example, Asa Carter of Jefferson County, New York, produced from his 150-acre farm the following products for which his valuation is given: 1,088 pounds of maple sugar worth $108.80; 35 pounds of wool worth $17.50; 4 veal calves worth $10; 5 lambs worth $10; 5 calves worth $20; 6 pigs sold at $6; 50 tons of hay worth $350; 80 bushels of apples worth $20; 1,535 pounds of cheese worth $122; 280 bushels of potatoes worth $70; 1,482 pounds of pork worth

[49] *American Agriculturist*, XXI (February, 1862), 41.

[50] *Cultivator*, New Series, VII (January, 1850), 55; *American Agriculturist*, XXI (February, 1862), 41; D. J. Browne, *The American Poultry Yard* (New York: C. M. Saxton & Company, 1850), pp. 313–315.

[51] *Homestead*, II (August 6, 1857), 733, 744; *New England Farmer*, XII (February, 1860), 60; *American Agriculturist*, XXI (February, 1862), 41.

$103; 108 pounds of butter worth $19; and growth of 15 one- and two-year-old cattle valued at $105. Other items, including grain, vegetables, and income from the sale of mulberry trees, brought the total to $1,639, not including the butter, cheese, and garden products eaten in the family. Unfortunately, Carter does not tell the amount of his taxes and interest payments, the wages paid hired hands, or the amount of grain and potatoes needed to carry over for seed the following year. His method of farming assured an abundance of manure, which made possible a continued high state of cultivation.[52]

Carter's experience was fairly representative of northern farmers all the way from Maine through New York, Michigan, and Wisconsin. Mixed farming was a year-round occupation which left little free time, and required the energies of all members of the family. At times its rewards seemed meager, but its satisfactions were real: a feeling of pride in achievements, absence of concern about price fluctuations, self-reliance, and security. Among the farmers of this type the differences in social and economic position were small.

[52] *Farmers' Cabinet,* I (April 15, 1837), 299.

CHAPTER XII

Hay, Fruit, and Vegetables

HAY, fruit, and vegetables, while not entering prominently into foreign or even interregional trade, as did cotton, tobacco, wheat, and livestock, were important; and hay certainly was vital to the agrarian economy of the North. Hay was a necessity on practically all farms in the North; fruits and vegetables were sidelines that proved profitable to farmers well located in relation to urban markets.

Hinton Rowan Helper, in his scornful attack upon southern planters who boasted about the importance of "King Cotton," maintained that the hay crop, if valued at the price for which small quantities sold in cities and towns, was king of all crops. True, most of the hay was fed right on the farm but, being consumed there, it produced other income, whereas the cotton shipped abroad contributed nothing further to the American economy than the price the raw cotton brought. Helper was vexed to see northern hay coming into the southern market, although, except to New Orleans, it came in small quantities. Like other advocates of regional self-sufficiency, he maintained that the South should produce its own hay and might be doing so at the time he was writing were it not for the institution of slavery, with its resulting pressure for cash crops.[1] Helper did not recognize that because of its longer growing season, the South derived a greater return from its pastures than did the North, and that its fertile lands were better suited for southern staples than for corn, wheat, or grass.

[1] Hinton Rowan Helper, *The Impending Crisis of the South: How to Meet It* (New York: Burdick Brothers, 1857), pp. 45 ff. The Census of 1850 is reported as valuing the hay crop of 1849 at $96,870,494, and the cotton crop at $93,608,720. Less than 5 per cent of the hay was raised in the southern states.—*Indiana Farmer*, V (November 15, 1856), 343. I have been unable to find this information in the *Census Report* for 1850.

THE HAY CROP

Practical northern farmers doubtless were amused at Helper's state-ment that hay was king of all crops, despite the element of truth in it. Their best and most easily cultivated land was devoted to other crops, and only the poorer tracts were permanently assigned to grass. Heavy clay soils, wet, low-lying meadows, and hillsides subject to washing or too stony to cultivate were used for hay and pasture. Once the pastures dried up in late summer or fall and no longer provided roughage for the livestock, it was necessary to furnish them with hay cut and cured in the height of the season until the pastures were again green in the spring. The farther north the farmer was situated the greater was his need for hay. In laying out and developing his farm he had to allot a considerable portion of his land to grass and pasture, which meant that he had less for grain, potatoes, or fruit, his cash crops. Many farmers must have begrudged the amount of land they had to keep in grass and the time they spent in harvesting the hay crop, which brought in little or no immediate cash.

Like all farm tasks, making good hay called for judgment, skill, and muscle. The grass had to be cut before it was overripe but not before it had reached the proper stage, or the amount and quality of the hay would be lowered. It had to be carefully dried after cutting so as not to bleach it in the hot sun and so as to permit the breezes to do part of the work. At the same time there was pressure to get the hay into the barn before the night dew or July showers should wet it and impair its nutritional value. Cutting with the scythe was the hardest task. It was followed by spreading the swath, then raking and putting the grass in cocks to prevent wetting during the night and to permit additional drying. If not sufficiently dry on the day of cutting, the grass had to be spread in the sun again, raked, and then loaded on the great wagons hauled by muzzled oxen or heavy draft horses to the barn for storing in the mow. Only a man of great energy and muscle could swing the scythe for hours. The workday lasted from sunrise to sunset with a hearty meal at midday. The drive to get the hay down, cured, and safe in the barn was so intensive that the haying season called for all hands from the eldest to the youngest to take part.[2]

Further complicating the problems of northern farmers during the haying season was the fact that the wheat crop ripened in some areas at the same time as the grass became ready for cutting, thereby forcing the

[2] Commissioner of Patents, *Report, 1858, Agriculture* (Washington, D. C.: James B. Stedman, 1858), pp. 308–313; John Douglas, *The Complete Practical Farmer* (New York: 1835), pp. 169–177; U. S. Department of Agriculture, *Yearbook, 1924* (Washington, D. C.: Government Printing Office, 1925), pp. 285 ff.

farmers to do their two hardest tasks within a short period.[3] Migratory workers or hired hands were much in demand at this season for at least a month or six weeks. Rather than thinking of their hay crop as "king," northern farmers may have thought of it as one which brought them in no direct income, cut down on the amount of cash grain they could raise, and actually cost them the wages they had to pay for their hired hands.

The bulky character of hay before baling was introduced necessitated huge barns for storage which were costly to build and maintain. Not all northern farmers housed their livestock and their hay, but in the less temperate areas the more careful farmers did. Pennsylvania German barns were noted for their spaciousness, solid construction, and durability. Frequently the stone barn was built before the permanent house for the family was erected.[4]

When the pastures were dry, hay and oats constituted the diet of the farmers' horses and, together with corn and other grains, were fed extensively to milk cattle, oxen, and sheep. Every farmer had to own a span of carriage horses to get to town, and draft horses or oxen to do the heavy work of plowing and harrowing and hauling hay, grain, and fuel wood. In the haying season they were worked most constantly. In fact, the demand for draft animals was so heavy at that season that horses and oxen were maintained throughout the year without much need for their services except for this month or six weeks of intensive work.

The mower, which came into use in the forties, into common use at least on more progressive farms by the fifties, relieved the farmers of some of their most arduous labor, and, with the horse-drawn rake and tedder, shortened the operation of haying. "Wonderful changes" making the pitchfork and the hand rake lighter and stronger further lessened the toil of the haymaker.[5] All such improvements increased the farmers' capital costs.

Timothy and clover brought over from England in the colonial period were grasses commonly cut for hay. Native and meadow grasses were used and, in the prairies, the bluestem, but they were replaced by timothy, clover, and bluegrass by more progressive farmers. In Kentucky, bluegrass in the pastures furnished abundant feed for most of the year and little hay was put up.[6] Wet areas were commonly left in native grass

[3] Commissioner of Patents, *Report, 1845* (Washington, D. C.: Ritchie & Heiss, 1846), p. 144.

[4] Ralph Wood, ed., *The Pennsylvania Germans* (Princeton, N. J.: Princeton University Press, 1942), pp. 39–40.

[5] Commissioner of Patents, *Report, 1847* (Washington, D. C.: Wendell and Van Benthuysen, 1848), p. 95.

[6] Percy Wells Bidwell and John I. Falconer, *History of Agriculture in the Northern United States, 1620–1860* (Washington, D. C.: Carnegie Institution, 1925), p. 369.

and cut for coarse hay. Elsewhere on cultivable land tame grasses were used to follow in rotation corn, potatoes, and oats or similar combinations. Grass would be cut for two to six years and then corn, potatoes, and oats would follow again. Fields well nurtured with manure would yield longer than those given no such attention.

Towns and cities drew upon the surrounding countryside for hay for their dray horses, livery-stable nags, and carriage horses. Philadelphia, for example, provided a market for 20,561 tons of hay in 1845. Storage and shipping difficulties in the handling of loose hay made inevitable attempts to find ways of compressing the hay for easier handling. As early as 1836 horse-powered hay presses operated by three men and capable of pressing five or six tons of hay a day were offered for $150. Prospective buyers were told, "The Press is not likely to get out of order, and is managed without difficulty by the common laborers of the farm." [7] Over the next few years the original cost of the press declined and its efficiency improved so that hay could be baled and shipped considerable distances, particularly if water transportation was available. [8]

In New York, the biggest market in the East, prices of hay ranged from $8 to $20 a ton in the forties and fifties; in Philadelphia in 1848 hay brought between $12 and $20. In the lower Mississippi Valley, when transportation was cut off from the North, hay for short periods brought high prices. In December, 1833, in Natchez it brought as high as $42 to $45 a ton. A southern sectionalist expressed concern that hay sold in Columbus, Georgia, in 1851, for $35 a ton. On the other hand, hay was quoted in Davenport, Iowa, in June, 1846, at $2.50 to $3.00. [9] Annual shipments to New Orleans ranged from 13,000 to 35,000 tons. Considerable quantities of baled hay were shipped by water from New York to New Orleans, where it brought $5 a ton more than in New York. [10] The bulk of the needs of New Orleans for hay were, however, supplied by the upper Mississippi Valley. Western prairie hay brought lower prices than eastern cultivated hay; clover hay brought the highest price. Farmers not enjoying easy access to city markets or to the lumber camps

[7] *Philadelphia Enquirer* in *Farmers' Cabinet*, X (December 15, 1845), 154; *Cultivator*, III (March, 1836), advertising section.

[8] *Cultivator*, New Series, IV (March, 1847), 99; J. J. Thomas, *Rural Affairs: A Practical and Copiously Illustrated Register of Rural Economy and Rural Taste* (Albany: Luther Tucker, 1858), I, 266, with illustration; *American Agriculturist*, XIX (February, 1860), 190.

[9] The *New York Tribune* regularly provided quotations on hay in the New York market in the forties and fifties.—*Natchez Courier*, December 20, 1838; *Davenport Gazette*, June 25, 1846; Bloomsburg, Penn., *Columbia County Register*, September 7, 1830; *Soil of the South*, II (January, 1852), 197.

[10] *New Orleans Price Current*, 1822, *passim*; *New York Weekly Tribune*, September 20, November 27, 1843.

of Maine, New York, and Pennsylvania, where there was a considerable demand in the winter for hay to feed horses and oxen, reported in normal years that hay brought between $5 and $10 a ton.

It is difficult to arrive at cost figures for nineteenth-century agricultural produce, so meager are the available statistical materials and so inadequate the farmers' methods of bookkeeping. Contemporary estimates of costs are instructive. A Vermont farmer who declared his hay was worth $6 a ton in 1848 maintained that the "cost of labor, etc.," in putting it up was $3 a ton, whereas across the Connecticut in New Hampshire a farmer declared that a gang of four to six men with good tools (not listed) and a team could cut and secure a ton each a day. Since their labor cost from $1.00 to $1.25 a day, this appears to be his estimate of the cost of making hay. Similarly, a New York farmer who valued his hay at $6 a ton determined its cost to him to be only $1.25 a ton. Jacob Kintner on his farm near the Ohio River in Indiana made hay his staple and cash crop. He sold annually 200 tons at the river for $10 a ton and estimated his cost of seeding, sowing, rolling, harvesting, baling, and hauling at $3.75 a ton. As he cut nearly two tons to the acre, he estimated his profit at $10 an acre, or $6.25 a ton. Probably the quotation of $6 a ton as the cost of raising timothy and clover hay in Berks County, Pennsylvania, in 1855, when inflation had produced its effect, is more realistic. It left a good return from the selling price of $24.[11]

John S. Skinner, not one to fall behind in agricultural matters, maintained in 1839 that since hay could be compressed into a small space in much the same way as tobacco, it could be brought to the Baltimore market from as far away as 200 miles instead of the 5 to 20 miles from which it was then being brought. At the price of $15 a ton then prevailing, he urged that hay was a crop too much neglected.[12]

On the other hand, a Maine farmer argued that it was inadvisable for farmers to sell their hay:

The hay crop is the great staple of this State and of New England. The saying is, "the more hay the more manure, and the more manure the more everything." In a climate like this, where the stern necessity exists for feeding cattle from 6 to 7 months in the year . . . any considerable diminution of the hay crop must be followed by serious consequences. . . . The exhausting process pursued very generally by farmers here, of selling off their surplus hay in seasons of plenty, cannot be too seriously condemned. . . .[13]

[11] There is a quantity of information on costs of haymaking in the *Annual Reports* of the Commissioner of Patents. See especially the *Report* for 1848, pp. 370, 446, 808; for 1849, *Agriculture*, p. 291; for 1850, *Agriculture*, p. 223; for 1851, *Agriculture*, p. 211; and for 1856, *Agriculture*, p. 255.

[12] *American Farmer*, New Series, I (May, 1839), 2.

[13] William Upton, Jr., of Dixmont, in Commissioner of Patents, *Report*, *Agriculture*, *1852*, p. 117; *Cultivator*, IV (June, 1837), 69.

In the midst of its campaign to keep Connecticut farmers on the land, the Homestead of Hartford advocated feeding all hay and grain on the farm until the land had been brought to such a high state of fertility that it would yield 75 bushels of corn or two and a half tons of hay per acre. Farmers, the *Homestead* argued, should rely mainly on animal products, such as butter, cheese, wool, pork, beef, and mutton, for income. To the argument that increased production of livestock and the draining and improving of additional land for hay and pasture required much capital and labor, the editor replied that farmers should stop investing their savings in the stocks of railroads, banks, and industrial companies and put them into capital improvements on the farm. Only in this way could Connecticut agriculture be made profitable and capable of competing with the farms of the West.[14] Equally sound advice was urged upon corn-belt farmers at a later period. They were advised to feed their corn to livestock instead of selling it off the farm. In both instances, the purpose was to build up the soil by feeding grain and hay to livestock and utilizing the animal manure to restore fertility. Few farmers were so fortunate as a Mr. Sheaff who, from his 300 acres of well-tilled land near Germantown, Pennsylvania, on which he maintained a few dairy cows and a "first-rate" herd of Shorthorns, was able to sell 100 tons of hay annually and from the proceeds meet all "outlays on the farm. . . ."[15]

New York, the premier agricultural state, first in dairy products and in the value of its livestock, was the first in total hay production with an average yield of 21 tons per farm in 1849 and 18 tons for every farm in 1859. Only three other states—appropriately in New England—exceeded the New York yield per farm though they did not approach its total yield. Vermont, with its long, rigorous winters and short pasture season, reported the highest yields of 27 and 29 tons, respectively, per farm.[16] The short growing and pasture season of the higher elevations of New York and New England, and the need for devoting a large portion of the farms to fodder crops rather than cash crops, made these regions less attractive and their residents more prone to migrate to areas where livestock could browse on growing grass for longer seasons. From the highest Berkshire town in Massachusetts came the plaintive cry in 1852: "It is as much as our farmers can do to keep our mowings any way decent by plowing and manuring. Without ever touching our pastures, most of which produce

---

[14] *Homestead,* II (August 6, 1857), 745–746.

[15] Captain Barclay, *Agricultural Tour in the United States and Upper Canada* (Edinburgh: William Blackwood & Sons, 1842), pp. 121–122.

[16] Computed from *Eighth Census of the United States, 1860, Agriculture* (Washington, D. C.: Government Printing Office, 1864).

from one fourth to one half grass, the rest brakes, hardhacks, etc. If these brakes increase as they have done for four or five years past, we shall have to leave our farms and emigrate to some country that 'eateth not up the inhabitants thereof.' " [17]

The making and feeding of hay required much of the farmer's time, but it enabled him to keep horses which provided him with transportation facilities superior to those enjoyed by most Southerners, who lacked roads and sometimes even horses. More important, hay and pasture grass constituted the principal feed of the cows and sheep, which supplied the butter, cheese, milk, and wool, the principal cash items of many farmers. Moreover, the larger number of animal units per acre in the North made it easy for the farmers to maintain the fertility of their soil whereas southern farmers neglected theirs. Much was said about declining fertility of wheatlands in the North, and the hill areas had certainly suffered from overtillage, but no considerable area of land that was ever really good farm land suffered from erosion in the North as many million acres in the South did. This was not due to greater wisdom on the part of northern farmers. It was owing simply to the fact that northern farmers by necessity had to leave much of their land in grass and pasture and that livestock was an essential part of their economy.

GROWTH OF THE FRUIT AND VEGETABLE INDUSTRY

If hay was the least remunerative of the farmers' crops in direct returns, specialties like fruit, potatoes and other vegetables, and maple sugar were for many northern farmers their most important crops. The fruit helped to vary the farmers' diet, provided the essential for cider and applejack, and aided in fattening hogs. In pioneer days in Vermont is was said that the native apple trees produced so bountifully and the people's appetite for cider was so great that there were more cider mills than schoolhouses, more distilleries than churches. Cider was so plentifully supplied that it sold at times for fifty cents a barrel. The low price of cider—it took eight bushels of apples to produce a barrel of cider—and the onsweep of the temperance and prohibition movement led to neglect of the old orchards.[18]

Whatever the position of Johnny Appleseed may be in American folklore, there is little evidence that his distribution and planting of apple seeds in Ohio and Indiana contributed much to the development of the

[17] *Prairie Farmer*, XII (September, 1852), 415, quoting letter of S. Cone, Peru, Mass., July 14, in *Massachusetts Ploughman*.

[18] *Horticulturist*, VI (January, 1851), 31; Commissioner of Patents, *Report, Agriculture, 1851*, p. 152.

fruit industry there. Good varieties of apples came only with grafted trees, but credit for bringing apples to the Middle West nevertheless belongs to John Chapman, alias Johnny Appleseed.[19]

The growth of the modern fruit and vegetable industry had to wait for the emergence of urban markets, the appearance of a middle class able to afford semiluxuries, transportation facilities which could carry perishables to markets speedily, and the establishment of nurseries capable of providing budded or grafted stock. All these were well under way before 1860. Apples, pears, plums, peaches, and cherries were coming into demand, and nurseries were being established in most sections of the country to provide stock for farmers who were buying in growing volume. In 1855, the *New York Tribune* was quoting retail prices on apples, pears, peaches, plums, blackberries, whortleberries, as well as on green corn, lettuce, beets, turnips, cabbage, tomatoes, peas, string beans, lima beans, cucumbers, squashes, carrots, eggplants, cauliflower, parsnips, melons, and celery.[20]

The most popular apple varieties were as follows: summer, Red Astrachan; fall, Gravenstein; winter, Baldwin, Newton Pippin, Rhode Island Greening, and Russet. Andrew Jackson Downing picturesquely characterized these apples, all of which were still grown in the twentieth century. Of the Red Astrachan he said, "A fruit of extraordinary beauty . . . its singular richness of colour is heightened by an exquisite bloom on the surface of the fruit like that of a plum. It is one of the handsomest dessert fruits." The Gravenstein was a "superb looking German apple . . . and is thought one of the finest apples of the north of Europe." The Baldwin "stands at the head of all New England apples and is unquestionably a first rate fruit in all respects." The Newton Pippin "stands at the head of all apples, and is . . . unrivalled in all the qualities which constitute a high flavoured dessert apple, to which it combines the quality of long keeping . . . retaining its high flavour to the last." The Rhode Island Greening was such a "universal favorite" that it needed no description. Finally, the American Russet "is one of the most delicious and tender aples, its flesh resembling more in texture that of a buttery pear, than that of an ordinary apple."[21]

Fruit and vegetable specialists, called horticulturists, concentrated in the production of one or two kinds of fruit. Robert Pell, of Esopus, New York, said by Downing to have the "greatest orchard in America,"

[19] Harlan Hatcher, *et al., Johnny Appleseed: A Voice in the Wilderness* (Paterson, N. J.: Swendenborg Press, 1945), *passim;* H. Kenneth Dirlam, *John Chapman: Johnny Appleseed* (Mansfield, Ohio: 1953), *passim.*
[20] *New York Tribune,* August 31, 1855.
[21] Andrew Jackson Downing, *The Fruits and Fruit Trees of America* (New York: Wiley & Putnam, 1845), pp. 75 ff.

centered his agricultural operations largely around the production of Newton Pippin apples. From his 2,000 trees he produced 4,000 and more barrels. For the top-quality apples he received $6 a barrel in New York and as high as $30 in England. Apart from his specialty, Pell experimented with many varieties of grapes, peaches, plums, cherries, apricots, and nectarines. Major Philip Reybold of Delaware specialized in peaches on his 1,000-acre farm.[22] He shipped to market during the picking season as much as 5,000 baskets of peaches a day. The New York market alone took 100,000 baskets of the Reybold peaches in 1845, which were brought directly by steamboat.[23] Jonathan Baldwin Turner and Marshall Pinckney Wilder, were well-known pear specialists who dealt in nursery stock. Wilder boasted the possession of 150 varieties of pears; Turner, in his garrulous writings, claimed to have between 800 and 1,000 pear trees in addition to cherry, quince, and apricot trees, gooseberry bushes, and grape vines.[24]

The commercial fruit industry was centered in the North, particularly in New York, Delaware, and New Jersey, where apples, peaches, and plums were the principal fruits; and in Ohio, where grapes were largely grown. The area south of Lake Erie and Lake Ontario in New York and part of New Jersey were becoming noted for their peach orchards. There were to be found growers with 10,000 to 20,000 trees at various stages of development who sent to market in good years as many bushels of fruit. Peaches brought from 50 cents to 4 dollars a bushel in New York. Good-quality freestone peaches sold for 2 dollars a bushel in Rochester, where, it was reported in 1846, the demand was scarcely met and many farmers were setting out additional trees on a large scale. In 1854, when the best peaches were selling in Rochester at a dollar a bushel, the crop of the Genesee country was estimated at 120,000 bushels. Delaware peaches brought premium prices in the Philadelphia and New York markets, but the favorable returns in some years induced fruit specialists to expand their orchards so greatly that the market was soon glutted.[25]

[22] *Cultivator*, II (April, 1848), 466; Commissioner of Patents, *Report, Agriculture, 1853*, p. 271; Andrew Jackson Downing, *Rural Essays* (New York: G. P. Putnam and Company, 1853), p. 460.

[23] *New York Weekly Tribune*, October 4, 1845; U. P. Hedrick, *The Peaches of New York* (New York State Agricultural Experiment Station *Report*, 1916, Vol. II; Albany: J. B. Lyons Company, 1917), p. 99.

[24] Turner wrote frequently to the *Horticulturist*, which welcomed his effusions as it did those of all agricultural authorities.

[25] Downing, *Rural Essays*, p. 454; James F. W. Johnston, *Notes on North America: Agricultural, Economical and Social* (2 vols.; Edinburgh: William Blackwood & Sons, 1851), I, 238; Robert Russell, *North America: Its Agriculture and Climate* (Edinburgh: Adam & Charles Black, 1857), p. 22; *Prairie Farmer*, XII (April, 1852), 195.

The English market early began to draw American apples, particularly varieties that could stand the long voyage across the Atlantic. Baldwins from New England and Newton Pippins from New York were most in demand, though they were to be displaced in part by the Ben Davis. From Boston were exported 120,000 bushels of apples, mostly Baldwins, in the fall and winter of 1858–1859. Small farmers with small orchards produced these apples and others, which found ready markets in local manufacturing cities.[26] Ohio, which was exceeded only by New York in the value of its orchard products in 1860, was selling its Russet and Rome Beauty apples for $1.25 to $2.50 a barrel for shipment to New Orleans, where they brought as much as $7.00. In late fall entire flatboats were loaded with apples for the southern market.

VINEYARDS AND WINERIES

Grape production and wine making had a notable development in the Ohio Valley in the fifties. Cincinnati was the center of the major grape area, where some 1,200 acres were devoted to the crop. Grapes required a heavy investment to start with, and a great deal of labor thereafter. Sufficient grape roots for an acre cost $60; slower-developing cuttings cost $6 an acre. Not until the fourth year could a good crop be expected, by which time the investment would amount to between $200 and $550 an acre. Consequently, most grape orchards were small, ranging from one or two acres to a few score. The production of wine per acre was 200 to 400 gallons, but reports of yields as high as 600 and 800 gallons were published. Nicholas Longworth, the leading vineyardist, worked his estate through twenty-seven tenants. Instead of attempting to naturalize European grapes, he experimented with native American grapes; ultimately concluding that the Catawba was the best wine grape, he concentrated on that.[27] In 1856 he had 300,000 bottles and 200,000 gallons of Catawba wine in casks in his extensive cellars. The best new wine sold in 1854 for $1.00 to $1.10 a gallon, second quality brought 75 to 90 cents, and third quality 40 to 50 cents. Old wine brought higher prices, but the demand was such that little was retained long enough to bring the premium. Ohio outranked all states in wine production in 1859 with a yield of 568,617 gallons; California was moving ahead rapidly, and Kentucky, Indiana, and New York followed.[28] One California vineyardist

[26] Henry S. Olcott, *Outlines of the First Course of Yale Agricultural Lectures* (New York: C. M. Saxton & Company, 1860), p. 45.

[27] Downing, *Rural Essays*, pp. 464 ff.

[28] *Horticulturist*, II (October, 1847), 192; and V (August, 1850), 59; *American Polytechnic Journal*, III (January–June, 1854), 221–224; *Western Farm Journal*, I (August 25, 1856), 90.

—Don Luis Sainservain—already doing things in a big way, had 40,000 vines producing on 40 acres sufficient grapes to make 45,000 gallons of wine and 3,000 gallons of brandy.[29]

GROWTH OF THE NURSERY BUSINESS

The growing commercial demand for fruit, berries, and vegetables in urban centers, and for flowers, shrubs, and ornamental trees in both rural and urban areas made for rapid expansion of the nursery business. The most famous centers in the North were Rochester and Geneva, New York, where individual firms had plantings as high as 500 acres and included hundreds of thousands of specimens. Three Geneva nurseries alone advertised in 1853 470,000 apple, pear, cherry, and peach trees of one to four years.[30] Greatest of all nurserymen was the Rochester firm of Ellwanger and Barry, whose Mount Hope Botanical and Pomological Garden did more business than any other two firms in the country. In their 1845 catalogue Ellwanger and Barry offered 171 varieties of apple trees, 146 of pears, 35 of cherries, 18 of peaches, and numerous strains of apricots, quinces, grapes, nectarines, currants, raspberries, straw-berries, and mulberries in addition to ornamental trees, shrubs, vines, and roses.[31] The firm supplied western nurseries with orders as large as 100,000 trees.[32] In addition to 277 acres in apple, pear, cherry, plum, and peach trees it had 20 acres in evergreens, 7 in roses, 6 in flowering shrubs, and 19 in other miscellaneous trees for the adornment of rural villas and farm homes.[33] The annual volume of sales of a number of Rochester nurseries exceeded $500,000 by 1860.[34] By then there were over a thousand nurseries in the country, which sold between 15,000,000 and 20,000,000 trees for a gross of $5,000,000.[35]

Controversy with a disgruntled customer led William R. Prince of Flushing, New York, to give some details about his nursery business. Fifty gardeners were employed on his 60 acres of nursery ground caring for the 2,000 varieties of fruit seedlings, plants, and flowering shrubs. Great quantities of seedlings and plants were imported regularly from Europe; in a single year the amount of such importations exceeded in

[29] *Vineyard* in *Ohio Farmer*, VIII (January 1, 1859), 3.

[30] *Horticulturist*, Vol. III (September, 1853), advertising section.

[31] U. P. Hedrick, *History of Horticulture in America to 1860* (New York: Oxford University Press, 1950), pp. 243–244; *New York Weekly Tribune*, November 1, 1845.

[32] Russell, *North America*, p. 22.

[33] *Hunt's Merchants' Magazine*, XXXV (September, 1856), 373–375.

[34] See Report of the lectures of Patrick Barry of Ellwanger and Barry on fruit trees in Olcott, *Outlines of the First Course of Yale Agricultural Lectures*, p. 57.

[35] *Ibid.*, pp. 57–58.

weight a hundred tons. Lavishly illustrated catalogues were sent out and became the favorite reading of thousands of families.[36]

Nurseries met a growing demand from farmers and suburban residents for berries and small fruit. William R. Prince found the demand for strawberries so extensive that he advertised 68 varieties for sale.[37] Through scientific plant breeding, Charles Mason Hovey had earlier succeeded in producing a strawberry strain from European varieties which brought him fame and fortune and enabled him to establish the *American Gardener's Magazine and Register* in 1835, later changed to the *Magazine of Horticulture*. For years this was the only horticultural periodical, though many of the farm journals devoted space to fruits, flowers, and vegetables.[38]

Some southern planters, despite their concentration on staple crops, liked to experiment with exotic fruit trees. John C. Jenkins, a highly successful Natchez planter, who, like most planters of the area, sought to make his plantation self-sustaining, experimented intensively with fruit trees, berries, and garden vegetables.[39] Another southern experimenter was Dr. Martin W. Philips, of Edwards, Mississippi, who claimed to have more than 2,000 trees, including 150 varieties of peach trees and many kinds of apple, pear, apricot, fig, and plum trees and grape vines. The cost of these extensive operations was such, he said, as to force him to offer many of his young trees for sale to permit further experimentation. In 1847 he proposed to sell several thousand young fruit trees, but warned that this was the only time his stock would be available to the public.[40]

At the same time peach growing was flourishing in Georgia. Planters had learned how to use fire and smoke to protect their crops from early frosts and were shipping carloads of peaches to the New York market before the war. Southern apples and grapes were able to push their way in competition with northern fruit.[41] Sufficient interest in fruit culture made possible the sale by a Richmond nursery, largest in the South, of 500,000 fruit trees in some years.[42] Notwithstanding these promising developments, fruit growing did not become an important part of southern

[36] *Prairie Farmer*, VI (September, 1846), 281.

[37] *American Agriculturist*, VII (August, 1848), 262.

[38] Hedrick, *History of Horticulture*, pp. 440, 490, 496.

[39] Diary of John C. Jenkins, notations of 1844-1855, Louisiana State University Archives; *Soil of the South*, V (April, 1855), 118-122.

[40] *Southern Cultivator*, V (November, 1847), 176; *Horticulturist*, IV (May, 1850), 494; *Homestead*, IV (May 5, 1859), 522-523. Martin Philips's contributions to the *American Cotton Planter*, 1853-1861, are too numerous to list.

[41] James C. Bonner, "Advancing Trends in Southern Agriculture, 1840-1860," *Agricultural History*, XXII (October, 1948), 250-254.

[42] Hedrick, *History of Horticulture*, p. 283.

agriculture. The day of the Georgia peach and the Shenandoah apple was in the future.[43]

With the rise of the nursery business came the itinerant salesman or "grafter" who carried far and wide apple, pear, plum, cherry seedlings and scions, as well as ornamental shrubs and trees, particularly the Norway spruce. The itinerant salesmen were responsible for gross impositions which, though exposed, continued to defraud innocent people who knew not that the mammoth strawberry, for example, did not measure up to claims for it. Reputable nursery firms like Ellwanger and Barry tried to protect their good names by making every effort to eliminate dishonest salesmen, but not with complete success.[44] Southern and western agricultural writers took advantage of the distress caused by frauds perpetrated by itinerant salesmen to urge that farmers purchasing young fruit trees should patronize only local or regional nurseries, which, incidentally, advertised in the journals in which this advice was given.[45] Judging by the frequency with which persons advertising farms for sale emphasized that they contained many fine and choice fruit trees, one may conclude that many, perhaps most, farmers set out some fruit trees or bushes. Fruit growing was in the process of becoming a major activity with some farmers; with a great many more it was a sideline, but one that entered substantially into the income account.

THE VALUE OF ORCHARD AND GARDEN PRODUCTS

By 1859, the value of orchard products, market garden produce, and wine in the United States was together equal to or greater than that of the total production of any of the southern staples save cotton. Orchard products alone were valued at $17,558,253, and market garden produce at $15,955,390. It seems likely that these figures are considerably below the true value. Marshall P. Wilder, who was more intimately acquainted with the statistics of fruit crops in Massachusetts, declared in 1859 that the value of the fruit of the state in 1835 was $700,000; in 1845, $1,300,000; and that in 1860 it would be not less than $2,000,000. Yet the census figures for 1849 and 1859 were only $463,995 and $925,519.[46] Seventy-three per cent of the value of orchard products was yielded by eleven northern

[43] *American Agriculturist*, III (December, 1844), 363.
[44] *Illinois Farmer*, V (March, 1860), 47–49; Earl W. Hayter, "Horticultural Humbuggery among the Western Farmers, 1850–1890," *Indiana Magazine of History*, XLIII (September, 1947), 205 ff.
[45] *Southern Cultivator*, VII (May, 1849), 78; *Wisconsin & Iowa Farmer and Northwestern Cultivator*, VII (March, 1855), 68–69, 81.
[46] *New England Farmer*, XI (March, 1859), 141; *Eighth Census of the United States, Agriculture, 1860*, pp. 186, 190.

states plus California. The leading northern states were New York, Pennsylvania, Ohio, Indiana, Illinois, and Michigan. As would be expected, the largest production of garden vegetables was found in the counties close to or containing the larger cities, Queens (New York), Middlesex (Boston), Philadelphia, Monroe (Rochester), and Hamilton (Cincinnati). California, at this early date, ranked as a high-yielding state in orchard products, wine, and vegetables.[47]

Producers of fruits, like growers of other products, early found it desirable to organize into associations for the discussion of their problems and furtherance of their interests. In 1829, the Massachusetts Horticultural Society was organized by a group of gentlemen-farmers. With the wealth that flowed into it, this society was well endowed and built up the greatest horticultural library in the country. It also maintained an extensive experimental garden. Under the leadership of its able president, Marshall P. Wilder, the society was one of the most influential agricultural organizations. Mention should also be made of the American Pomological Society, established in 1850, of which Wilder was president for years.[48]

Recognition of the growing importance of fruits and vegetables is seen in the amount of space given them in the agricultural periodicals and in the agricultural volume of the Patent Office. From a sixth to a fourth of the space of this annual volume was devoted to problems of fruits and nuts, a smaller amount being given to vegetables.

THE ROLE OF THE POTATO

There is nothing lowly about the role the potato has played in history, American and European. Despite its name, the Irish potato was a contribution of the New World to the Old. In turn it was introduced into the colonies at an early time, although it did not then become an important item of diet. In the early nineteenth century, potatoes were the cheap food upon which the greatest dependence was placed by millions of peasant farmers in Ireland, England, and Germany and by workingmen in American and English cities. The catastrophic blight which struck the potato in the eighteen forties produced famine and starvation, forced emigration upon millions of Irish and Germans, contributed to major changes in the land-use pattern of Ireland and other countries, and directed to America thousands of emigrants who profoundly changed its social structure.

[47] *Eighth Census of the United States, Agriculture, 1860, passim;* Claude B. Hutchinson, ed., *California Agriculture* (Berkeley: University of California Press, 1946), pp. 36 ff.

[48] Hedrick, *History of Horticulture*, pp. 506–508.

Potatoes thrive best in sandy or well-drained loamy soil and in a fairly cool climate. On newly opened land they produce bountifully and if the land is carefully manured and limed they continue to yield well. Two hundred and four hundred bushels to the acre was not an uncommon yield; five hundred to six hundred bushels were reported. Farmers in the northern tier of states, where soils and climate were peculiarly well adapted to potato culture but not so well adapted to the cultivation of corn and wheat, turned to the potato as a major source of their subsistence and as food for their livestock. The high yields that the most successful of them had would have caused them to agree with Liberty Hyde Bailey that one acre of potatoes may furnish as much food as ten acres of wheat.[49]

To the New England and New York farmers the potato was a godsend. Without too great labor, once they had cleared their land, they could raise a year's supply for their table, the necessary seed for the next year, and perhaps a small quantity for sale or trade in the nearby village. Though potatoes were bulky and heavy in relation to value, farmers could market small quantities in the villages and if they were located near a railroad or close to an industrial center they could sell larger amounts. By the thirties potatoes were well established as a major feature of the farmers' economy in the northern states. In the first year for which there are production figures—1839—Maine, still by no means entirely settled, produced 10,392,280 bushels of potatoes or 20 bushels for every person in the state. Some counties raised as much as 38 bushels for each inhabitant. New Hampshire and Vermont were also large producers in proportion to their size and population. Caledonia County, Vermont, could boast a potato yield of 48 bushels for each inhabitant. All of New England produced 35,180,500 bushels, or one third of the entire production of the country. New York, first in this as in so many products, was the premier potato state, with a yield of 30,123,614 bushels.[50]

Though the farmers' production of potatoes might be large, their gross return from that portion of their crop which they sold was rarely so. Premium prices were obtained only when the old crop was nearly gone and beginning to deteriorate and the first new potatoes were coming into market. But these first potatoes were from more southern climes. For a brief moment they brought as high as $1, $2, and even $3 a bushel at retail in Boston. When the earliest local potatoes reached the market they might sell for 75 cents or $1 or more, but not for long. In the thirties the retail price in Boston was commonly around 50 cents a bushel, and

[49] Liberty Hyde Bailey, ed., *Cyclopedia of American Agriculture* (4 vols., 5th ed.; New York: The Macmillan Company, 1917), II, 520–521.

[50] Computed from *Sixth Census of the United States: Statistics of the United States of America, 1840* (Washington, D. C.: Blair and Rives, 1841).

of this price the farmer would not get more than half. From 1847 to 1851, potatoes averaged 70 cents a bushel in Connecticut at a time when yields were low.[51] Despite these low prices, the farmer, with his odd way of counting costs, could satisfy himself that he was doing well if he sold at such prices, and perhaps he was.

In reply to his circular asking for information concerning crops, prices, costs of production, and methods of cultivating, the Commissioner of Patents in 1851 obtained interesting information on the cost of producing potatoes. A Maine farmer replied that the crop of that year was small but of good quality, the average production being 150 bushels, of which half were marketable. He said that the marketable potatoes brought 80 cents a bushel and cost 25 cents a bushel to produce. At the same time, a Connecticut farmer reported his average yield to be 100 bushels, which he held to be worth 50 cents a bushel. The cost of production was 20 cents. Other replies from farmers in Delaware, Ohio, and Texas reported that the cost of producing potatoes in these states was 18, 13, and 1 cent a bushel.[52]

Few complaints were heard from potato producers other than the usual remarks about parasites until 1843, when calamity struck hard with the first appearance of the "rot," or potato blight. One partial failure was not too serious a problem, since most farmers counted on some grain, hay, hogs, cattle, sheep, and fruit and vegetables to carry them through the winter. True, they might have to buy seed potatoes for the next year, but that could be taken care of by pushing some other crop. Unfortunately, the blight struck even harder in 1844 and again in 1845. Reports from all over the North, particularly from Maine, Massachusetts, New York, and the Middle West, told of partial or complete failure of the potato crop. The vines would be doing well until suddenly they wilted and died, leaving a foul odor. When the potatoes were dug it was found that many of them were similarly affected and those that at the time appeared to be sound were later found to be diseased. Panic was in the air, so serious were the inroads of the blight. No topic so engrossed the attention of the farmers as the nearly complete failure of the potato crop, said a Brattleboro, Vermont, paper. One of the most valuable agricultural products of the northern states was jeopardized.[53]

[51] Quotations from the *New England Farmer* for 1834–1837, and Commissioner of Patents, *Report, Agriculture, 1851*, p. 186; The *New Orleans Price Current* quoted potatoes on December 19, 1835, at $1.625 a barrel.

[52] Commissioner of Patents, *Report, Agriculture, 1851*, pp. 131, 172, 347, 378. The Delaware report is for 1852 and is in the *Report, 1852*, p. 113.

[53] *New England Farmer*, XXIII (October 2, 1844), 107; *Cultivator*, New Series, I (January, October, November, December, 1844), 10, 20, 303, 330, 371; *American Agriculturist*, III (January, November, 1844), 8, 350; IV (December, 1845), 362; *American Farmer*, New Series, VIII (August, October, 1845), 51, 113.

Speculation about the nature of the rot or blight and its cause led to many weird notions, but almost at the outset some keen-eyed observers noted a fungus growth on the diseased plants and attributed the blight to this fungus, correctly, as modern science was later to show. Many suggestions were offered for preventing the rot: careful selection of cuttings, burning the diseased plants and tubers, better drainage, early planting, abandonment of manure for fertilizing the soil, use of lime, sulfur, and other materials for dusting, most of which had some point. Letters from alarmed farmers poured into editors of farm journals, imploring them to publish the latest information concerning protection against the blight, all to no avail. There seemed to be no cure or preventive.[54]

The disease swept rapidly over the northern states and Canada, and sharply reducing yields caused farmers to turn away from this crop. A rhymer in the *Massachusetts Ploughman* said of the potato rot:

> Which everywhere the farmer vexes,
> And all philosophy perplexes.
> Go where you will and search around,
> Where'er they cultivate the ground,
> In every land this curse prevails,
> And all attempt against it fails.[55]

Reports from New England communities expressed doubts that there would be any crop at all.[56] In 1844 imports of potatoes from Ireland reached considerable proportions. *Niles' Register* announced that one vessel had brought in 100 tons, and that a number of other ships carrying potatoes were on the way. In December a ship brought in 7,000 bushels of potatoes which had been bought in Liverpool at 22 cents. A writer in the *American Agriculturist* expressed alarm at this importation, which was "a disgrace of this part of our country," particularly as the imported variety was distinctly superior to the American potatoes.[57] In 1845 the New York State Agricultural Society reported that the average yield of potatoes in New York State had fallen to a paltry 90 bushels to the acre in contrast to average yields of 300 bushels to the acre in former years.[58]

In 1845 the blight was carried across the Atlantic and struck Ireland and part of the European continent. There it wrought havoc incom-

[54] *American Agriculturist,* IV (December, 1845), 362.
[55] Copied in *Prairie Farmer,* XI (March, 1851), 133.
[56] Commissioner of Patents, *Report, 1844,* pp. 204–258, quotes from numerous papers showing the extensive crop failure, and speculating on the nature of the disease.
[57] *Niles' Register,* XVII (October 4, November 30, December 14, 1844), 80, 208, 240; *American Agriculturist,* IV (January, 1845), 15.
[58] *Transactions* of the New York State Agricultural Society, 1846 (Albany: C. Van Benthuysen, 1847), p. 382.

parably greater than the damage done in America. Peasants who were dependent upon the potato for food and for their rent were quickly brought to starvation and death by successive crop failures, for they had little or nothing else to which they could turn when their principal crop failed. American farmers could feel grateful that they had not come to depend upon the potato to the degree that Irish and German peasants had.[59]

The worst effects of the blight were over in the United States by 1845. Indeed, though crops were still short, farmers were getting much more favorable prices. In November, potatoes were selling in Massachusetts at the "unprecedented" rate of 75 cents a bushel.[60] Yields continued to be reported well below those of the years before 1843. From both New York and Connecticut it was reported in 1851 that the average yield was down from 300 bushels to the acre to 100 bushels.[61] Farmers hesitated to resume large-scale planting of a crop that had done so badly over the course of years. The Maine crop of 1849 was down two thirds from its 1839 level, the New York crop was down by one half, and the output of other northern states was down a third to a half. For the nine heavy-producing states of the Northeast the output shrank from 76,911,000 bushels in 1839 to 44,195,447 in 1849. Only in the newer states of the Middle West, where fresh land was continually being brought into cultivation, were more potatoes being planted.[62]

In the fifties, fear of the blight was somewhat dissipated by the development of disease-resistant strains of potatoes, greater care in seed selection, drainage of wet areas, rotation of crops, and better weather conditions than those that had prevailed in the period of its most devastating effects. Meantime, the migration of more than two million Irish and Germans to America had increased the demand for potatoes. Many farmers resumed potato planting, and others were encouraged to take it up by the favorable prices that prevailed. Pennsylvania and New Jersey in 1859 produced more potatoes than they had in 1839, but all other northeastern states still lagged behind. The big expansion came in the old Northwest, where the growth of numerous commercial and industrial communities and the building of the railroads encouraged many farmers to take up potato cultivation in place of wheat. At least one Illinois farmer in the East St. Louis area had made potatoes—"Murpheys"—his principal

[59] Redcliffe N. Salaman, *The History and Social Influence of the Potato* (Cambridge, Eng.: Cambridge University Press, 1949), p. 291; E. C. Large, *The Advance of the Fungi* (New York: Henry Holt and Company, 1940), pp. 13 ff.

[60] *New England Farmer*, XXIV (November 5, 1845), 149, quoting the *Salem Gazette*.

[61] Commissioner of Patents, *Report, Agriculture, 1851*, pp. 172–219.

[62] Computed from the census data of 1840 and 1850.

crop by 1856 and reported that his annual cash returns from them ranged from $600 to nearly $4,000.[63]

Sweet potatoes, largely a southern crop, were mostly raised for home consumption. It has generally been said that they entered very little into the commerce of the time, partly because of the lack of transportation facilities and their poor keeping quality. Yet the *New York Tribune* reporter on household markets in 1845 said that a "hundred vessels came laden with them" to New York, where they were quoted at $2.00 a barrel.[64] High yields were reported, but the boast of 600 bushels per acre was quite exceptional. Sweet potatoes, which were grown uniformly throughout all the lower South in cotton, sugar, and rice counties and in the small farming counties less identified with these major staples, were an important item in the diet.[65]

COMMERCIAL PRODUCTION OF VEGETABLES

Because of their highly perishable character, the commercial production of fresh or garden vegetables was limited to areas close to metropolitan markets, though enterprising farmers were producing many for their own domestic use. How well Bostonians were supplied may be seen in a report of the Faneuil Hall vegetable market in the *New England Farmer* for July 19, 1837. String beans were selling for $1.50 a bushel; cabbages for 6 cents each; lettuce for 2 to 4 cents a head; carrots, onions, and turnips for 6 cents a bunch; peas $1.00 a bushel; radishes for 3 cents a bunch; early summer squash for 50 cents a dozen; new potatoes for $1.50 a bushel; and cucumbers for 25 to 50 cents a dozen. Strawberries, cherries, currants, blueberries, gooseberries, and raspberries were also quoted. A week later more abundant supplies brought prices down substantially and tomatoes were then quoted.[66] Then came in rapid succession shell beans, green corn, celery, cauliflower, melons, thimbleberries, pears, peaches, grapes, apples, and plums. James Stuart, who visited New York in 1830, spoke favorably of the green beans, tomatoes, pumpkins, vegetable marrow, asparagus, and "excellent" peaches, melons, apples, strawberries, and cherries that he had tasted, all being available in great abundance and at little cost.[67]

In 1845, the *New York Tribune*, for long the principal journalistic

[63] Henry C. Brokemeyer, *A Mechanic's Diary* (Washington, D. C.: Henry C. Brokemeyer, 1910), p. 28.
[64] *New York Weekly Tribune,* September 20, 1845.
[65] Lewis Cecil Gray, *History of Agriculture in the Southern United States to 1860* (2 vols.; Washington, D. C.: Carnegie Institution, 1933), II, 827.
[66] *New England Farmer,* XVI (July 19, 1837), 14, 23.
[67] James Stuart, *Three Years in North America* (2 vols.; Edinburgh: Robert Cadell, 1833), II, 540.

innovator, initiated a column of gossipy information about vegetables, fruits, and other items of table economy that are of value to the student of food consumption. The Isabella grapes, for example, were said to have such fragrance that they overcame the fish smell of the Fulton Market. Pumpkins were reported to be so queer in shape as to be almost indistinguishable from squashes. The sugar squash pumpkin, the most desirable for Thanksgiving festivities, was quoted at $3 to $4 a hundred pounds. Lima and snap beans, peppers, cucumbers, onions, melons, and tomatoes (which had long since lost their poisonous reputation), were quoted. The melons were said "to grow melancholy, and will sell themselves at any price from $2 to $8 per 100." Farm women were urged to make more of that "delicious compound called Apple Butter, for which the buxom dames of Pennsylvania are so celebrated." The reporter noted that the "country people" bringing their produce to the Fulton Market "are subjected to great inconveniences" because of the narrowness of the space which "operates to check market gardening in this vicinity." [68] Nevertheless, he was "charmed with the superior neatness and freshness" of the Fulton Market, which was more than many other observers would concede. At Christmas time he said, "Turkeys resign their throats to the inexorable axe as heroically as Grand Sultans of Turkey yield their necks to the bow string." Stewing oysters brought but 50 cents a bushel whereas "strong and leathery clams" sold for 62 cents a bushel. Just before Thanksgiving, pumpkins were found to be "too high, and not enough of them." [69]

In late June, 1846, currants, "blushing with unexpressed wine," were quoted at $1.00 a bushel; asparagus, "getting to be scarce," was quoted at $1.25 for 100 bunches; cucumbers at $2.00 a hundred; watermelons, "warranted to be good for the Cholera," were selling for $1.00; "emphatically small" potatoes brought $2.00 a bushel; string beans, $1.50 a bushel; and the tomato, the "universal favorite," was still scarce and brought $3.00 to $5.00 a basket. A month later, green apples were scored for being "sweetish, sourish, bitterish, greenish things" that might be called "Cholera pills"; raspberries were passing "but like an ambitious beauty of 40 manage still to preserve their admirers and devourers"; whortleberries, "black, fat and saucy" were worth $3.50 a bushel; green corn was in the market and so "tickled" people "that they go on laughing from ear to ear, and pay a shilling a dozen for all that can be got hold of." Tomatoes were still coming from the South, snap beans were down to 25 cents a bushel, and cucumbers sold for a cent apiece, which the reporter thought was exactly one cent more than they were worth. On August 22, the humorous reporter announced that tomatoes, "tart as an offended wife and whole-

[68] New York Tribune, September 21, 27, October 4, 1845.
[69] Ibid., October 25, November 8, 15, 1845.

some as a father's anger," were reduced to 50 cents a bushel; potatoes, "as Collins and as faithful as McShane," sold for $1.25 a barrel; and that "a perfect deluge of watermelons" had broken the price to $5.00 to $20.00 a hundred.[70]

EFFECT OF CITIES ON AGRICULTURE

By 1850, the great growth of commercial and industrial cities was having an ever-widening effect upon agriculture, particularly in the North. Extension of the milksheds for many miles around cities, increasing demand for vegetables and fruits, inability of eastern states to meet their own grain and meat needs, their dependence on the upper Mississippi Valley for wheat, flour, pork, and beef are all evidences of how industry and urban growth were affecting agriculture.

The fifties were years of tremendous immigration, population growth, industrial expansion, and railroad construction, not to speak of the westward movement of population. They were also years in which agriculture in the older parts of the country, the Northeast particularly, was adjusting itself to these changes and the demands they made upon farmers. If the older South, particularly Virginia and Maryland, was going through an agricultural revival in the years just before the Civil War, agriculture in the Northeast was being fundamentally changed by urban needs and western competition. Dairying was replacing grain production; poultry raising was becoming important and profitable; increasing emphasis was being placed upon more intensive use of land and its resources; better grades of cattle, sheep, and hogs were being raised; potatoes, green vegetables, and fruits were being grown. Farmers were tiling their wet areas. Lands not suitable for intensive use was being abandoned, and farmers not able to adopt themselves to the more intensive and capitalistic type of farming were moving into industry or migrating west to farm in their old way there. In the past too much emphasis has been placed upon "rural decline and farm abandonment" in the Northeast, and too little attention has been given to the growing agricultural specialization and readjustment that took place in this area.

The table showing the value of orchard and garden products for 1859 reveals that four states in which industry and urban growth were most concentrated—Massachusetts, New York, New Jersey, and Pennsylvania—plus Ohio, constituted an orchard and truck garden belt. These five states of the thirty-three in the Union produced 47 per cent of the value of fruits and vegetables the country yielded.

[70] *Ibid.*, June 22, July 20, August 22, 1845.

VALUE OF ORCHARD AND GARDEN PRODUCTS, 1859

| | Slave States | | | Free States | |
| | Orchard | Garden | | Orchard | Garden |
State	products	products	State	products	products
Alabama	$223,312	$163,062	California	$754,236	$1,161,855
Arkansas	56,025	37,845	Connecticut	508,848	337,025
Delaware	114,225	37,787	Illinois	1,126,323	387,027
Florida	21,259	20,828	Indiana	1,258,942	546,153
Georgia	176,048	201,916	Iowa	118,377	169,870
Kentucky	604,849	458,245	Maine	501,767	194,006
Louisiana	114,339	413,169	Massachusetts	925,519	1,397,623
Maryland	252,190	530,221	Michigan	1,122,074	145,883
Mississippi	254,718	124,282	Minnesota	649	174,704
Missouri	810,975	345,405	New Hampshire	557,934	76,256
North Carolina	543,688	75,663	New Jersey	429,902	1,541,995
South Carolina	213,989	187,348	New York	3,726,380	3,381,596
Tennessee	305,003	303,226	Ohio	1,929,309	907,513
Texas	48,047	178,374	Oregon	478,489	75,605
Virginia	800,650	589,467	Pennsylvania	1,479,937	1,384,908
			Rhode Island	83,691	140,291
			Vermont	211,693	24,802
			Wisconsin	78,690	208,730
Totals	4,539,717	3,667,837		15,392,512	12,287,553

Source: Compiled from *Eighth Census of the United States, 1860, Agriculture* (Washington, D. C.: Government Printing Office, 1864), p. 186.

CHAPTER XIII

Labor and Farm Machinery

IN the early decades of the nineteenth century, the greatest difference between farming in the Old World and farming in the New was that in America agricultural labor was scarce and its cost relatively high. The American farmer had yet to receive the improved tools and the agricultural machinery that were greatly to increase his productivity and to expand the scope of his operations. He was still limited by what one man's back and arms could accomplish and by the uncertainties and relatively heavy costs to which he became subject if he attempted to rely on hired labor. Henry Colman, Commissioner of Agricultural Survey of Massachusetts, who later was to make an intensive study of European agriculture, best put into words what most Americans familiar with farming appreciated:

> The greatest of all difficulties connected with farming in Massachusetts is labor. It is difficult to be obtained. The prices of labor are enormous. . . . We consider high wages of labor, where there is a sound currency, among the best evidences of the prosperity of the community. . . . But on the other hand, the price of labor should bear a just proportion to the value of agricultural produce, or the farmer cannot pay it.[1]

Similar testimony comes from an Ohio farmer who reported: "One of the greatest deficiencies that affect the interest of farmers in this country is the want of honest, industrious, capable working men, to be hired; and I will here take occasion to say, it is the chief thing in farming, in all its branches, and the most lamentable deficiency."[2]

[1] *New England Farmer,* XIX (July 22, 1840), 22.
[2] *Ohio Cultivator,* I (February 1, 1845), 19.

FARM LABOR

By mid-century, in well-established farming areas, the hired man had become almost as much a part of the agricultural pattern as the 160-acre farm, the milk pail, or the hoe. "All over the country," observed the *Prairie Farmer* in 1846, "on almost every well conditioned farm, are employed more or less persons . . . some for the whole year, some during the summer and others during a short part of the season when work is most pressing." [3] Most farmers needed help in the haying, harvesting, and butchering seasons, and farmers in the maple-sugar country needed extra help in the sugaring season. The *Homestead*, of Hartford, in urging farmers to keep their workers throughout the year instead of merely hiring them in haying time at the high wages they could then demand, said: "It must be truly a poor farm upon which labor during the most of the year, may not be profitably expended in preparing manure and making permanent improvements." *Homestead* complained: "The farmer wants to do all the work himself and grudges every dollar that he pays to the laborer." [4]

Solon Robinson, who also argued for the employment of farm labor the year round instead of for six months, insisted that there was plenty of useful work to do even during the winter months; that the reason farm laborers proved so unsatisfactory, almost the universal complaint, was that they were employed for only six months and then were let go, and that no self-respecting man would want to stay in such a position if better employment were available or if he could move into tenant-farmer or owner-operator status. To maintain good help, farmers should offer employment the year around, he maintained. [5]

Examination of the census data, inadequate as these are, suggests that in the free states there was one farm laborer or tenant for every two farms. This is based on the assumption that many who listed themselves as "farmers" but who were not owners of a farm, though they might have some stock and tools, were really either tenants or laborers. The excess of farmers over farms, which may be seen in the accompanying table, justifies this assumption. True, many farm laborers listed in the original census schedules were older sons tied to the farm until they reached the age of twenty-one, but planned to break away as soon as custom and law permitted.

The first source of labor was the farm family with its many children. From early youth they were trained to do the milking, haying, plowing,

[3] *Prairie Farmer*, VI (February, 1846), 54.

[4] *Homestead*, I (August 14, 1856), 738; and IV (November 18, 1858), 138.

[5] Solon Robinson, *Facts for Farmers, Also for the Family Circle* . . . (2 vols.; New York: A. J. Johnson, 1867), II, 1006–1009.

planting, and hauling; they knew how to handle horses, cows, and oxen; and they were reliable and careful.

NUMBER OF FARMS, FARMERS, AND FARM LABORERS AS SHOWN
IN THE CENSUS OF 1860 IN PRINCIPAL NORTHERN STATES

State	Farms	Farmers	Farm Laborers
California	18,716	20,836	10,421
Connecticut	25,180	30,612	11,489
Illinois	143,310	153,646	47,216
Indiana	131,826	158,714	40,827
Iowa	61,163	88,628	27,196
Maine	55,698	64,843	15,865
Massachusetts	35,601	45,204	17,430
Michigan	64,422	88,657	35,884
New Hampshire	30,501	35,392	10,152
New Jersey	27,646	30,325	18,429
New York	196,990	254,786	115,728
Ohio	179,889	223,485	76,484
Pennsylvania	156,367	180,613	69,104
Vermont	31,556	38,967	14,022
Wisconsin	69,270	99,859	31,472
	1,228,135	1,514,567	541,719

Sources: Eighth Census of the United States, 1860 (Washington, D. C.: Government Printing Office, 1864), *Population*, pp. 662–663 and *Agriculture*, p. 222. Some of the persons listed by the census as farmers were doubtless farm laborers; others may have been squatters improving their tracts but not as yet owning them. For an examination of "farmers without farms," see Merle Curti, *The Making of An American Community* (Stanford, Calif.: Stanford University Press, 1959), pp. 140 ff.

As they grew to maturity and were not needed on their family homestead, they hired out to successful farmers. Some never graduated from this stage of hired hand and remained all their lives workers on the farms of others, faithful in their tasks and grateful for continued employment,[6] although doubtless the object of all was farm ownership. The larger number of farm children moved toward that end by saving their earnings and returns from little ventures their employer might permit them to operate until they felt ready to strike out on their own. Some of them became mortgaged-farm owners, tenants, or squatters, but failed to move up the ladder to ownership; others did not succeed as mortgaged-farm owners or tenants and slipped down the ladder to farm laborer. It should be stressed that the so-called agricultural ladder led both up and down.

Some farm laborers were drifters, moving from one temporary job

[6] *Ohio Cultivator*, X (July 15, 1854), 218–219.

to another, haying, harvesting, picking apples and hops, working on construction jobs and railroads as unskilled labor. Continued complaints of their irresponsibility, their lack of ambition, their careless use of equipment, and disinclination to go rapidly to work in the morning all suggest migratory workers or temporary hands who were waiting for a better opportunity elsewhere and took little interest in their present job. Permanent hands were more dependable but fewer. The Hartford *Homestead* urged farmers to build tenant homes for their hands which would help them to keep a better class of workers and would, at the same time, free their wives of the heavy task of feeding the hired hands.[7]

The second source of supply for farm labor was immigrants from Quebec, Ireland, England, the Scandinavian countries, and Germany. Many of them had been tenant farmers or farm laborers; hence their objective was farm ownership, but that took more money than they had after their arrival. French Canadians and Irish were found on farms in the Northeast in increasing numbers, whereas further to the west people of recent European origin constituted the principal farm labor group.[8]

It might be expected that, as the century progressed, the tremendous influx of immigrant farmers into the United States from these countries would satisfy any demand for agricultural labor and keep its costs down. This was not the case, however, for it was not farm labor jobs that drew immigrants to America, even though the wages offered were higher than farm laborers drew abroad. It was the hope of acquiring a farm as well as the higher wages paid on construction jobs and for factory work that proved attractive to immigrants. Factory and construction jobs might offer year-round, or at least more constant, employment than farmers could provide and at substantially higher wages. By the fifties railroad contractors were offering as high as one dollar a day and board, a wage that farmers could meet only in the harvesting season.[9]

Disregarding the high industrial wages paid in eastern cities, the larger portion of the German and Scandinavian immigrants hastened westward to the public-land states. There they worked on construction jobs or as farm laborers until they could raise sufficient funds with which to start farming on their own, either as tenants or as owners of farms acquired on credit. According to the Census of 1860, the first census to distinguish among farmers, farm laborers, and other laborers, though not

[7] *Ohio Cultivator,* I (February 1, 1845), 19; *Country Gentleman,* VI (September 21, 1855), 186; *Homestead,* IV (September 15, 1859), 827.

[8] *Country Gentleman,* VI (September 20, 1855), 186.

[9] *Illinois Gazette and Jacksonville News,* July 27, 1837; *Indiana Farmer,* II (September 22, 1838), 23. Earlier in 1831 wages on canal construction averaged $10 to $12 a month, though in the winter they fell as low as $5.—George Rogers Taylor, *The Transportation Revolution, 1815-1860,* p. 289. Volume IV in this series.

altogether accurately, there were 795,679 farm laborers as compared with 2,510,456 farmers and planters.[10] Because most of these farm laborers were only waiting for a chance to move up into the tenant or owner class, they did not acquire the class consciousness of the farm-labor population abroad, did little or nothing to make their views known, and had no organization to present their claims upon government. Farm laborers received little or no attention in the agricultural journals, although accounts of farm-labor problems in England were copied from British journals.[11] Such statements on farm labor as did appear were filled with advice as to methods of getting more work out of laborers, and with regrets that they were so careless, so lazy, so disinclined to exert themselves.[12]

FARM WAGES

Some of the best accounts of farm labor were written by British travelers, such as William Cobbett, Patrick Shirreff, and James F. W. Johnston, who are quoted below. William Cobbett, whose travels took him well into the interior of settled America, where he learned much about agriculture in the New World, and who had practical experience as a farmer on Long Island, concluded in 1818 that a good farm laborer could get $120 a year and board, and that a good day laborer could expect $1 a day. In the Middle West the annual wage with board ranged from $100 to $120. Another English traveler reported the lowest price for labor in Illinois to be $13 a month with board. In Maine, which was somewhat off the beaten path, farm laborers in 1818 were getting from $9 to $12 a month with food and clothing and half a pint of rum daily, or $20 a month without provisions. Workers hired by the day drew $1 a day with provisions. Ten years later, in the richer farming areas of southeastern Pennsylvania, farm laborers were drawing $80 to $100 annually; in less well-developed areas they were paid $8 a month in summer and $5 in the winter months.[13] Henry Colman expressed concern in 1840 that

---

[10] *Eighth Census of the United States, 1860, Population* (Washington, D. C.: Government Printing Office, 1864), pp. 662–671.

[11] *Homestead* (1855–1861) is a notable exception to this generalization, for it included many statements about farm labor, more directed, however, to urging farmers to employ more workers and to provide them with better housing, with the thought that such policies would make for intensive utilization of the land and assure steady workers.

[12] *Prairie Farmer*, VI (February, 1846), 54.

[13] William Cobbett, *A Year's Residence in the United States of America* (2d ed.; London: Sherwood, Neeley and Jones, 1819), Pt. III, pp. 320, 508; D. B. Warden, *Statistical, Political and Historical Account of the United States of North America* (3 vols.; Edinburgh: Archibald Constable & Co., 1819), I, 367; Percy Wells Bidwell and John I. Falconer, *History of Agriculture in the Northern United States, 1620–1860* (Washington, D. C.: Carnegie Institution, 1925), pp. 163, 205.

farmers in haying and harvest season had to pay for a day's work the equivalent of a bushel and a half of wheat, three bushels of corn, or eight of potatoes. No farmer, he held, could afford such wages.[14]

Patrick Shirreff, who toured the North in 1833 to study and compare American agriculture with that of Canada and England, found hired men were to be had in all the older parts of the North and also in some- what less abundance in the newer states. He observed of them: "In most cases their reward is ample, and their treatment good, living on the same kind of fare and often associating with their employers. A great deal of farm labor is performed by piece labor." Near Geneva, New York, he found cradlers cutting wheat being paid $1 a day and binders 62½ cents a day, each with board and lodging. On piecework rates they were paid $1.50 an acre for cutting wheat and 87½ cents an acre for binding it, without lodging.[15]

Shirreff made a useful point for prospective English emigrants: the real wages of laborers distant from eastern immigrant centers were much the better, for there they were worth more, at least in food.

The money wages of labour may be stated to be nearly the same from the east to the extreme west, but any difference that exists is towards a rise in the west. In the same direction a decline in the price of produce takes place. Therefore, as the distance from the markets on the coast increases, the farmer pays a greater share of produce to the labourer, and must be remunerated either by the low price of land or its natural fertility. Labourers are of a more unsatisfactory description than in the east, land being so cheap that every prudent man is enabled to purchase a farm for himself in the course of a year or two, and it is only the imprudent who continue labourers. The character of the workmen renders labour dearer than is at first apparent.[16]

It was calculated that the product of an acre of wheat in the West would employ a man twenty-six days without board, whereas the product of an acre of wheat east of the Alleghenies would pay the wages of a hired man thirty-two days. Putting it another way, Shirreff estimated that an Illinois farm laborer would earn in a year the equivalent of 667 bushels of corn, 222 bushels of wheat, or 5,000 pounds of beef. In contrast, an Eng- lish farm laborer earning ten shillings monthly would find his yearly equivalent to be 70 bushels of wheat or 1,560 pounds of beef. Whereas the Illinois farm laborer received yearly the purchase price of 80 acres of government land, the English farm laborer received the value of one tenth of an acre of good land.[17]

[14] New England Farmer, XIX (July 22, 1840), 22.
[15] Patrick Sherreff, A Tour through North America (Edinburgh: Oliver & Boyd, 1835), pp. 78, 341.
[16] Ibid., p. 398.
[17] Ibid., p. 450.

A meticulous Yankee farmer, who kept diary notations of wages he paid the numerous laborers employed in his extensive farming operations, provides useful information. In 1833 he paid cradlers and binders $1.25 a day for their exacting toil. In 1835 he was hiring hands by the month at $10 to $12. In 1838 cradlers and binders were still being paid $1.25 a day, but for general work the pay was $15 a month or 75 cents a day. By 1840 wages had declined to $12.50 a month. This farmer was careful to specify that wages were not paid when work could not be performed.[18]

From the numerous reports farmers made to the Patent Office in 1845 it is possible to reconstruct the wage picture at that time. In New England wages ranged from $12 to $15 a month, or 75 to 83 cents a day with board. In upstate New York they were from $8 to $12 a month with board, which was estimated at $1.25 a week. Farmers in Iowa and northern Illinois had to pay from $12.50 to $20 a month, or 75 cents to $1 a day. In southern Illinois wages of farm labor were from $8 to $10 per month, or 37 to 50 cents a day. In the South, Negro labor was available for from $5 to $10 a month for farm work; slaves who were skilled craftsmen could demand more.[19]

In the better times of the fifties it was increasingly difficult to keep laborers at the old rates. The lure of wages in excess of $1 a day on construction jobs, the excitement about new western communities being opened to settlement, and the rush to the mining camps of California and Colorado drew many from their prosaic and relatively unrewarding positions as hired hands. A Jackson County, Michigan, farmer complained in 1852 that he now had to pay $26 a month to keep hands who, only a few years earlier, had cost him only $11 a month. So strong was California's attraction that 500 farmers in his county were planning to migrate to the gold country.[20] In 1856, a New York farmer sent up a cry for help because many of the older and experienced laborers as well as the younger men had left for the Far West, and the harvesting was being delayed for lack of hands.[21] In the newer public-land states to which immigrants were then flocking, farm labor was so scarce in 1856 that a writer in the *Cleveland Leader* was moved to say "as there is a scarcity of farm hands, it is a pity that a draft cannot be made upon the corps of gentlemen of leisure infesting the city." [22]

James F. W. Johnston alluded to the improved condition of American

[18] John Goodell, ed., *Diary of William Sewall, 1797–1846* (Beardstown, Ill.: John Goodell, 1930), pp. 150 ff.

[19] Commissioner of Patents, *Annual Report, 1845* (Washington, D. C.: Ritchie & Heiss, 1846), pp. 1149–1153.

[20] *Detroit Advertiser* in *Ohio Cultivator*, VIII (March 1, 1852), 75.

[21] *Ohio Farmer*, V (July 26, August 30, 1856), 118, 138.

[22] Works Progress Administration, *Annals of Cleveland* (Cleveland: 1937), Vol. XXXIX, Pt. I, p. 103.

farm labor in 1851. Whereas, at the beginning of the century the laborer's annual wage was valued at the price of one yoke of oxen, now it was equal to the value of two yoke of oxen, or twice as much wheat as earlier.[23] On the 2,000-acre Wadsworth estate in the Genesee Valley of New York, wages ranged from $17.32 a month for the summer season to $12.12 monthly for year-round work, "besides board and lodging, on . . . which they are not likely to find their bones peeping through their skin."

They have meat three times a day—pork five days, and mutton two days in the week—a capital pie at dinner; tea and sugar twice a day; milk *ad libidum;* vegetables twice a day; butter usually three times a day; no spirits nor beer are allowed. The meals are all cooked at the farm, and the overseer eats with the men, and receives from 75 £ to 125 £ a year, besides board and lodging for his family, who keep the farm-house.[24]

The most systematic effort to study farm wages was made by Greeley's *Tribune* in 1859, when industrial and construction work was not abundant and workers' pay was less than it had been in the prosperous years of the earlier fifties. For year-round work, hands were paid as little as $108 in parts of Pennsylvania, $150 in Vermont, $160 in New York, and $175 in Illinois; more common were payments of $120 to $150. In harvest time the monthly pay ranged between $20 to $26; the daily wage was $1.25. For the slack season in winter daily pay was little over 50 cents and monthly pay was $10 to $12.[25]

As the scattered generalizations and data presented here indicate, a long-range improvement in farm wages occurred. Wages of farm labor in the northern states were $8 to $12 a month in the second and third decades, $10 to $15 in the forties, and $12 to $18 in the fifties.

It may not be altogether fair to compare these wages with wages paid English farm labor at comparable times; the English laborer was in most instances a year-round employee, whereas his American counterpart was more likely to be a migratory worker hired for the haying or the harvest season and not at all anxious to remain in his lowly job. Nevertheless, the English statistics are useful. Expressed in American money, they show that the average weekly wage of agricultural labor in England was $2.32

[23] James F. W. Johnston, *Notes on North America: Agricultural, Economical and Social* (2 vols.; Edinburgh: William Blackwood & Sons, 1851), I, 208–209.

[24] Henry A. Murray, *Lands of the Slave and the Free: Or Cuba, The United States and Canada* (2 vols.; London: John W. Parker & Son, 1855), I, 76–77; Robert Russell, *North America: Its Agriculture and Climate* (Edinburgh: Adam & Charles Black, 1857), p. 136.

[25] *New York Tribune* in *Hunt's Merchants' Magazine,* XLI (December, 1859), 758–759. The most valuable collected data on wages of agricultural laborers are found in the Massachusetts Bureau of Statistics of Labor, *Sixteenth Annual Report* (Boston: Wright & Potter Printing Co., 1885), pp. 201 ff., especially 317–318.

in 1824, $2.48 in 1836, and $2.71 in 1860.[26] Living costs in England were lower than in the United States, and the difference in the real wages would doubtless be somewhat less than these figures show.

The high cost of labor and the uncertainty of retaining it made the farmer adopt such laborsaving devices as were available and practicable, provided that in doing so he could reduce his overhead costs and at the same time market a greater volume of goods. Credit and markets, therefore, became major items he had to consider as the flood of inventions of farm machinery gained headway. He was not, however, troubled by opposition to the introduction of laborsaving devices from farm laborers as English farmers were.[27]

IMPROVED FARM IMPLEMENTS

Many of the simpler tools the farmer used were self-designed and self-made. Wooden plows, harrows, cultivators, rakes, forks, shovels, ox yokes, and many items of household equipment that to a foreign traveler looked "clumsy and uncouth" provided farmers with opportunity for whittling and designing that absorbed many winter hours and sharpened their Yankee ingenuity.[28] If they needed a piece of iron for the moldboard or the share, or cutting edge, of the plow, or preferred iron tines to the clumsier wooden fork, or wished for iron spikes to insert in their harrow, or wanted to sharpen an iron shovel, they went to the local blacksmith, who could forge and hammer out almost anything the farmer wished. In this way most of the implement needs of the farmers were taken care of locally. Farmers close to cities, on the other hand, did offer a market for farm tools. Thus the *New England Farmer* in 1826 carried advertisements of Boston houses offering patent hoes, hay cutters, corn mills, cast- and wrought-iron plows, patent hay and manure forks, churns and cheese presses, few or none of which would be purchased by farmers living any considerable distance from Beacon Hill.[29]

[26] Rowland E. Prothero, *The Pioneers and Progress of English Farming* (London: Longmans, Green & Co., 1888), pp. 279–280. Henry Colman, *European Agriculture and Rural Economy, from Personal Observation* (2 vols.; Boston: Arthur D. Phelps, 1846), I, 40 ff. Colman quoted from a Parliamentary report showing that wages of farm laborers ranged from seven to twelve shillings a week. The rent of their cottages was given as one shilling six pence weekly (p. 67).

[27] Colman, *European Agriculture*, I, 462.

[28] Captain Barclay, *Agricultural Tour in the United States and Canada* (Edinburgh: William Blackwood & Sons, 1842), p. 9.

[29] *New England Farmer*, V (August 11, December 1, 1826), 24, 152; Victor S. Clark, *History of Manufactures in the United States* (3 vols.; New York: McGraw-Hill Book Company, 1929), I, 477.

It was the extension of the canals, later the railroads, which was responsible in a large measure for widening the market for farm implements by making it possible to ship plows, harrows, mowers, threshers, and reapers into regions previously cut off from main lines of communication and relatively inaccessible. But, more important, it was the canal and the railroad which provided the necessary facilities to transport to market the growing quantities of wheat, corn, pork, lard, and tobacco that new implements were making possible.

Eighteenth-century plows were either light and flimsy wooden tools that merely scratched the surface without turning over a furrow or were extremely heavy and awkward instruments requiring two to six pairs of horses or oxen to pull them. Neither plow was well designed; both needed constant repairs and two or more workers to handle the plow and the draft animals. The bull plow had a moldboard partly covered with strips of iron and so poorly designed that it made the furrows uneven, the handles difficult to hold, and the labor of man and beast to operate it excessive.[30] Continued and steady progress was made in improving the plow, 372 variations and changes being patented by 1855. The design of the moldboard was improved, cast iron was substituted for wood or wrought iron, parts most susceptible to wear were made readily replaceable, and the lower edge of the share was subjected to cold chilling.

Jethro Wood, an upstate New Yorker, brought together in 1814 and 1819 a number of improvements already in use and perfected a plow that for years was to prove efficient, cheap, and well adapted to use on farms in the eastern states. It consisted of only two wooden parts—beam and handles; and three replaceable cast-iron parts—the share, the moldboard, the brace, and part of the landside, all of which were cast in one piece— the rest of the landside, and the edge of the share. The cast edge, the part that wears the most rapidly, was easily replaced and generally a number were bought with the plow. Here was a plow that was simple in its construction, strong, and durable.[31] These qualities and the fact that it could be sold at a modest price led to its extensive adoption.

Wood's patents did not entirely protect his rights from infringements; moreover, his business associates seem to have taken advantage of him, so that the returns on his ingenuity were not commensurate with the contributions he had made to agriculture. An extension of fourteen years was granted on his patent but, when his heirs sought from Congress a further extension of seven years in 1848 and retained New York's senator, Daniel S. Dickinson, to lobby for it, farmers exploded in indignation. They held that most of the features of the Wood plow were in existence

[30] *Eighty Years' Progress of the United States from the Revolutionary War to the Great Rebellion* . . . (New York: New National Publishing House, 1864), pp. 27–31.
[31] *Plough Boy*, II (September 16, 1820), 123 and illustration.

long before Jethro Wood sought a patent on them, that he had profited sufficiently, and that further extension would increase the cost of the plows fifty cents each and would involve a cost to American farmers of half a million dollars annually. The legislature of New York and the New York State Agricultural Society both condemned the move to extend the patent, as did the *American Agriculturist*, the *Cultivator* of Albany, and the *Ohio Cultivator*.[32] Notwithstanding the vigorous opposition of the farm journals, the Senate passed the measure but it failed of enactment in the House.[33]

The cast-iron plow with replaceable parts early became the most widely used plow in the Northeast. It went through many changes and improvements. By 1850, 200 different patterns and types of plows were being manufactured.[34] As Leo Rogin has said, "The introduction of the casting process transferred the business of plow-making from the village blacksmith to a multitude of small foundries operated by inventors and small producers through the New England and Middle States" and to rapidly growing factories.

As early as 1830, Worcester, Massachusetts, was turning out 1,000 plows a year, and Pittsburgh could boast of a steam factory which had a capacity of 100 plows daily. In 1836 two Pittsburg plow companies were said to have an annual output of 34,000 plows. A Worcester firm was turning out 20,000 plows in a year in 150 different varieties and sizes. Already, American plows were proving the best in the world because of their "simplicity, lightness of draught, neatness and cheapness. . . ."[35]

The great area of agricultural expansion and the largest market for plows and other agricultural machines was in the Middle West. In the sticky soils of Illinois and Iowa the amount of friction was too much for the cast-iron plow because its surface "abounded in small cavities known as blow holes." It would not polish or scour. Nor was it strong enough to break the tough roots of the prairie bluestem. Early experiments were made with steel plows, the most successful being those of John Deere. He made continued improvements, found a ready market for his plows made of cast steel imported from England, and with his partners became the principal plow manufacturer in the upper Mississippi Valley. In 1856

[32] *American Agriculturist*, VII (April, May, 1848), 122, 132, 140; *Cultivator*, V (March, 1848), 97; *Ohio Cultivator*, IV (April 15, 1848), 62.

[33] *Congressional Globe*, 30 Cong., 1 Sess., January 31, 1848, pp. 248–249.

[34] Clark, *History of Manufactures*, I, 477.

[35] Leo Rogin, *The Introduction of Farm Machinery in Its Relation to the Productivity of Labor in the Agriculture of the United States During the Nineteenth Century* (University of California *Publications in Economics*, Vol. IX; Berkeley: University of California Press, 1931), p. 30; Clark, *History of Manufactures*, I, 477; *Eighth Census of the United States, 1860, Agriculture* (Washington, D. C.: Government Printing Office, 1864), p. xviii.

his 65 employees produced 13,400 plows, of which 2,100 were breaker plows for heavy prairie work.[36]

Further major improvements were to come: the riding plow, the gang plow, the steam plow, and a great many minor innovations in existing plows were introduced. In 1860 alone, 109 patents were granted for improvements on plows, of which 25 were taken out by Illinois residents, 9 by South Carolina residents, 8 by Georgia residents, and 7 each by residents of Tennessee and Pennsylvania. Not a Vermont, Massachusetts, or Connecticut Yankee is found among these tinkers on plows.[37] Notwithstanding improvements under way and to come, it could be said that farmers had available to them in mid-century good practical plows that worked reasonably well in almost any soil, except the tough prairie sod, required only one man to operate in lighter thin-sodded soils or previously plowed ground, and were not unduly expensive. As little as seven dollars would buy a plow. A much larger investment had to be made in horses or oxen to pull the plows and other farm machines. So well regarded were the American plows that a substantial demand for them developed abroad. A Boston dealer reported the sale of one hundred plows to a London dealer.[38]

One may puzzle over the fact that Southerners took out patents for improvements in the plow, although the South as a section neglected the new plows then coming into the market. With a plantation system containing great stretches of undeveloped land, a wide and thinly scattered rural population, low land values, and slave labor which had no incentive to use tools and draft animals carefully, the South did not feel the same necessity to make labor more productive through the use of machines. Field work that elsewhere would be done with horse-drawn implements was here done with the hoe; weed chopping was a major occupation of slaves in the growing season. The antiquated shovel plow, which lacked a moldboard, and the scooter plow were commonly used though they did little more than stir the soil.[39] An Ohioan who spent two months in the Abbeville, Edgefield, and Laurens district of South Carolina in 1860 commented on the uncouth character of the farm implements, particularly the clumsy hoe, the awkward ax, the wooden-geared, horse-powered gins, the primitive plows, and the lack of reapers. His comments on the plows and methods of cultivation were scathing:

[36] *Country Gentleman,* X (August 20, 1857), 129; Rogin, *The Introduction of Farm Machinery,* pp. 32–35.

[37] Commissioner of Patents, *Annual Report, 1860, Agriculture* (Washington, D. C.: Government Printing Office, 1861), pp. 487–492.

[38] Johnston, *Notes on North America,* I, 161. Johnston wrote of American agricultural implements: "Ploughs, hay-rakes, forks, scythes, and cooking-stoves, were . . . many of them well and beautifully made." He found the corn shellers and crushers "novel."

[39] *Southern Cultivator,* II (June 26, 1844), 98.

The system of cultivation would seem to me most thriftless and waste-ful imaginable. There is not, as far as I could learn, in those three districts, a *single plow* that a skilled farmer would use in the cultivation of his land.

Plows were so light that they could be carried to the field by young girls on mules. No double-team plows seem to have been employed.[40]
More progressive farmers later came to use the cast-iron plow, but nowhere in the South did it become as common as in the North.[41] At least one Southerner who had visited the New York State Agricultural Fair in 1844 came away greatly impressed with the progress of agriculture in the North and with the "fine roads. . . ." In the North, he remarked, "the best models of the plow, perhaps in the world" were used by experienced and successful farmers. By plowing deeply, and pulverizing the soil thoroughly they secured crops in "greater abundance . . . in comparison with ours." [42]
It may be argued that the southern planters, especially the leading planters, with their abundance of slaves, were not entirely aware of the cost to them of the labor supply they used so prodigally in the production of staples and in less economic enterprises. Staples which could be profit-ably grown with the use of slave labor were those which required the constant application of labor: cotton, tobacco, sugar cane, and rice. None of these crops were to be affected in any important way by improvements in tillage and harvesting machines in the early nineteenth century.
Although the manner in which southern crops were raised was not affected by new machinery, the manner in which they were processed and marketed was. Ginning cotton and compressing it into bales con-tinued to be a time- and labor-consuming task. Horse power was used on the larger machines, and by the thirties steam power was being intro-duced on the great plantations. In 1835 it was said that a gin stand with 60 or 65 saws running constantly from sunrise to eight or nine o'clock in the evening could put through enough cotton to make 3 or 4 bales. The gin stand then cost $500. Ten years later, gins could turn out from 300 to 500 bales of cotton in a season. Improvements in the gin minimized injury to the fiber and cleaned it of dirt and trash. Heavy screw presses operated by horses or mules compressed the cotton into bales of 300 to 325 pounds. With the development of steam presses the bales were increased

[40] *Ohio Farmer,* IX (June 16, 1860), 186. Also see Frederick Law Olmsted, *A Journey in the Seaboard Slave States with Remarks on Their Economy* (New York: Dix & Edwards, 1856), pp. 46–47, who speaks of the heavy clumsy tools that "no man [in the North] in his senses" would use.
[41] Rogin, *The Introduction of Farm Machinery,* pp. 52 ff. Cf. Lewis Cecil Gray, *History of Agriculture in the Southern United States to 1860* (Washington, D. C.: Carnegie Institution, 1933), II, 797 ff.
[42] *Southern Cultivator,* III (January 1, 1845), 12.

to 400 and 500 pounds. The use of iron bands freed the larger planters of their earlier dependence on hemp bags.[43]

On the great sugar plantations of Louisiana the process of extracting the juice from the sugar cane and of manufacturing raw sugar from it involved technical skills of a high order and required increasingly expensive machines to make possible large-scale and efficient operation. Early mills included horse- or ox-powered wooden rollers made of live oak. Clarification, or cleaning of impurities, and evaporation were accomplished in great vats and open kettles of cast iron heated by wood-burning furnaces. In this primitive stage, the cost of setting up a sugar mill was not great. Every plantation ground its own cane and manufactured its own raw sugar. Continued experiments with improved methods and the introduction of devices from abroad eventually quite changed and modernized the industry.

As early as the twenties, steam-powered grinding mills were introduced to replace the cumbersome, slow, and unreliable animal-powered units. Whether the cost of the steam mill was $4,500 or $12,000, it was too much for many planters at the outset, and yet its advantages were apparent: the extraction of a greater proportion of the juice, and savings in fuel. The steam mill, with other capital improvements, slowly eliminated its inefficient competitor and forced the abler of the smaller operators to route their cane through the mills of their more successful neighbors, to enlarge the scale of their operations, or to abandon cane for cotton.

The next major improvement involved the abandonment of the open kettles and the substitution of vacuum pans, which utilized the previously wasted steam for heat in the following process of boiling the syrup. Additional fuel was saved in this process; more important, a higher-quality product was manufactured, assuring a premium of $1\frac{1}{2}$ to 2 cents a pound over the open-kettle sugar.[44] The creole Negro who perfected this new process—Norbert Rillieux—thus made "one of the most important contributions ever made to the technical advancement of the sugar industry." [45] The Rillieux process called for a further heavy capital investment of as much as $50,000 on the larger plantations.

The steam engine also came to the assistance of the rice and cotton planters. Steam-powered rice threshers capable of threshing a thousand bushels of rice a day were in operation by the middle of the century.

[43] J. H. Ingraham, The South-West (2 vols.; New York: Harper & Brothers, 1835), II, 288–290; Gray, op. cit., II, 680, 704, 736; John H. Moore, Agriculture in Ante-Bellum Mississippi (New York: Bookman Associates, 1956), p. 48.

[44] Reynold M. Wilk, Steam Power on the American Farm (Philadelphia: University of Pennsylvania Press, 1953), pp. 6–9.

[45] J. Carlyle Sitterson, Sugar Country: The Cane Sugar Industry in the South, 1753–1950 (Lexington: University of Kentucky Press, 1953), pp. 133 ff., especially p. 150.

Their cost of $3,000 to $7,000 was prohibitive, however, except for all but the larger planters. Others could have their threshing done at the new units on a custom basis. The cotton gin, when operated by steam power, speeded up the ginning process greatly, but the complex gears frequently broke and held up operations. Since most plantations had blacksmith shops it was not difficult to repair them, but the repaired gear was not strong.[46]

Wheat was the crop that called forth the most continuous, concerted efforts by tinkers and inventors to improve the methods of production and reduce labor costs. In the generation before the Civil War various inventions were made to replace broadcast sowing; the use of the sickle, cradle, and flail; and the crude methods of winnowing the wheat from the chaff.

Broadcasting, or sowing grain by hand, rarely proved an economical and certain way of starting a field in wheat. Part of the seed was lost to birds, and the coverage of the field was likely to be incomplete. Harrowing, rolling, or even thin plowing after sowing worked the wheat into the soil to some degree. Experiments were made with broadcasting devices carried by the sower, who turned a crank attached to the seed box and forced the seed out in all directions, with considerable uniformity. Though it distributed the seed more evenly than could be done by hand, the "hand rotation sower" did not aid in covering the seed to assure germination. A few English drills may have been imported prior to 1840, and some drilling devices were patented, but none proved very workable. After 1840 experiments were made with heavy and awkward drilling devices which proved usable on level and well-cleared ground. Continued tinkering brought forth a number of fairly efficient grain drills by 1860, at which time much of the wheat in the commercial region of the Middle West was drilled, not sown.[47]

THE REAPER

Cutting grain with a sickle, or cradle, and grass with a scythe was a backbreaking and expensive job in terms of man-hours. At most, an expert with a cradle could cut only four acres a day; the average cut was two and a half acres.[48] Inventively minded farmers had long tried to perfect

[46] Wik, op. cit., p. 8 and passim.

[47] Rogin, The Introduction of Farm Machinery, pp. 192 ff.; Russell H. Anderson, "Grain Drills through Thirty-Nine Centuries," Agricultural History, X (October, 1936), 157 ff.

[48] Joseph Schafer, A History of Agriculture in Wisconsin (Wisconsin Domesday Book, General Studies, Vol. I; Madison: State Historical Society of Wisconsin, 1922), p. 87.

a horse-drawn machine to lighten this arduous task and to speed up the harvest. All the basic features of such a machine had been invented, but had not been combined to make a workable device until 1830, when Cyrus McCormick contrived to bring these features together in a feasible but still not a practicable reaper. For another decade the McCormick family turned its attention to the manufacture of plows and reapers, to the invention and sale of a hemp break, and to the iron industry. The reaper did not absorb the attention of the McCormicks exclusively nor did they show any awareness of its future possibilities.

Meantime, the Hussey machine had been brought into production with a cutter bar superior to that of the McCormick reaper and was being actively marketed. The McCormicks now improved their machine and under the leadership of Cyrus, one of the ablest businessmen of the day, pushed it to the front. To relieve the worker who raked the cut grain from the platform while standing, a seat was installed on the machine. The cutter bar and the guards were improved and the machine was strengthened to make it stand up in midwestern prairie fields, where grain was coarser and harder to cut. Cyrus McCormick negotiated contracts with manufacturers to produce his machine for which a royalty of $35 was to be paid him. In 1848, having found no large market in the East and South for his reaper, McCormick established his main plant at Chicago. No shrewder move could have been made. Chicago was still a small community in comparison with Cincinnati or St. Louis, but McCormick may have realized that the future wheat-producing center of America would be west and northwest of Chicago and would become in a large measure tributary to that city.

McCormick had to share the market with a number of competitors when his efforts to destroy them by costly suits for patent infringements met with signal failure. Furthermore, his competitors' machines had certain improvements: the self-raking device of the Atkins reaper, which freed the labor of one man; and the stronger and more effective cutter bars of the Manny reaper, which for a time worked better in Illinois wheat and were also better for mowing grass. The keen competition was helpful in stimulating rapid improvements on all the machines, had some effect in holding their prices at around $100 to $150, and did much to advertise the merits of the new machines.

When in 1860 the McCormicks began another move to secure from Congress an extension of patents on their reaper and mower, the *New York Tribune* issued a warning to farmers and others that a hearing on their motion was coming up before the Patent Office and that anyone wishing to file objections should do so promptly. In this, as in earlier efforts to secure extension of patent rights on the reaper, McCormick was unsuccessful. The examining committee as well as Congress seems to have been convinced that he had profited sufficiently by his previous enjoyment of a monopoly of some of the basic features of the successful reaper.[49]

Extensive advertising and popular trials of competing reapers at state fairs brought the reaper to the attention of farmers in a period of expansion, easy credit, rapid broadening of the market for wheat, and favorable prices. With wheat well above the dollar mark from 1853 to 1858, Illinois, Wisconsin, Iowa, and Minnesota farmers enjoyed real prosperity and were in a position to buy and pay for reapers. Sales of the new and improved machines doubled and tripled. By 1860 close to 80,000 reapers had been sold.[50]

The new reapers, which "harvested grain more thoroughly, and seven times more rapidly than the cradle; with one half the labor force" had a tremendous effect upon the scale of farm operations. Leo Rogin estimated that a man with a sickle could cut one half to three quarters of an acre of wheat in a day, with a cradle he could cut two to three acres a day, and with a self-rake reaper he could cut ten to twelve acres a day. Harvesting with a self-raker, which left the wheat easier to bind than when it had been cut by a cradle, saved the labor of four men in a day's work of ten or twelve acres.[51] Since harvest hands cost at least a dollar a day, the reaper thus reduced the labor outlay for harvesting by fifty cents an acre. Further saving resulted from the fact that with a reaper the farmer could cut his crop closer to the ideal time and would sustain less loss. Since the amount of wheat a man could sow was limited by the short period in which it had to be harvested and by the man-days of labor required to cut it, it can readily be seen how much the reaper expanded the possibilities of wheat growing.

The effect of the adoption of the reapers upon the agriculture of the newly developing states and territories was tremendous. Farmers turned from corn to wheat, wheat acreage more than doubled, the capitalization of wheat profits sent land values up sharply, and the deficit in farm labor became less pronounced for a time. In the Northwest the development of the new railroad network made the farmers' wheat a cash crop readily marketable. A major wheat-producing center came into existence in northern Illinois and southern Wisconsin. Farms in this area had the highest acreage in wheat and the highest yield of wheat per farm

[49] Ohio Farmer, IX (December 15, 1860), 397; William T. Hutchinson, Cyrus Hall McCormick: Seed-Time, 1809–1856 (New York: Appleton-Century-Crofts, Inc., 1930), pp. 276 ff.

[50] Hutchinson, op. cit., pp. 467–471.

[51] Rogin, op. cit., pp. 125–126.

in the country. Eleven of these high-producing counties in northern Illinois purchased approximately one fourth of the total number of McCormick reapers sold in the years 1849 to 1857.[52]

Threshing the wheat, rye, barley, and oats and separating the grain from the chaff also came in for mechanization. The flail and oxen continued to be used, and grain was still trodden out by oxen, particularly in the South, but as wheat fields were increased in size, the need for mechanical threshers became more acute. Crude, hand-powered threshers with mallets as beaters were invented, numerous patents were taken out on such devices, and some machines were sold, but they offered little advantage over the flail. Then came the cylinder-and-concave arrangement which used power more effectively and, when connected to the horse tread, accomplished much laborsaving. Meantime, fanning machines had been perfected to separate wheat from chaff. In the late thirties John and Hiram Pitts, Maine farmers and mechanics, combined threshing and winnowing devices to produce a complete workable machine called the thresher-cleaner. With a horse-power attachment it sold for approximately $230.[53] In 1840 John Pitts moved to Albany and found in the Genesee country a ready market for his machine. Within three years several hundred were in use. Most of these early machines were simple threshers, but by the fifties threshing and winnowing were ordinarily combined. The market was now shared by the Pitts factories in Buffalo, Massillon, Ohio, and Alton, Illinois, and the J. I. Case factory in Racine, Wisconsin. Experiments were made with portable steam engines to replace horse treads for threshers, but they were not generally successful before the Civil War.[54] The heavy cost of threshers forced most farmers to hire custom threshers to do their work. Thus early wheat threshing became a migratory occupation manned by workers who were employed by the operators of the machines.[55]

An Illinois agricultural editor who visited the Wisconsin State Fair in October, 1851, before the big rise in the price of wheat had occurred, mentioned favorably the display of corn and cob crushers, a new type of wagon spring, a flax puller, a churn, a water ram, five threshing machines operated either by sweep or tread power, reapers, and drills. He did not

look upon these threshing implements with as much interest as formerly. Think, for instance, of buying a drill, price $125, reaper, price $125 and then a threshing machine, price $175—total $425, as a necessary preparation for wheat sowing; and then ten bushels per acre at 40 cents per bushel! Then

[52] Hutchinson, op. cit., map and tables opposite p. 469.
[53] American Farmer, New Series, I (August 14, 1839), 92.
[54] Wik, Steam Power on the American Farm, pp. 19 ff.
[55] Rogin, op. cit., pp. 154 ff.

think of corn, 60 bushels per acre at 30 cents per bushel, and no additional implement required but a sheller costing $25, or so![56]

Early efforts to adapt the reaper to mowing grass were not wholly satisfactory. Reel, platform, and self-rake were removed, thereby lightening the weight and making the machine more maneuverable, but most of the early machines, when they worked at all in grass, were rough in performance, especially in thick grass. In the late forties a one-wheel mower was brought on the market that was reported to work in all but thick grass. By 1852 the Ketchum mower was said to function well on smooth ground. It could cut ten acres a day. At a cost of $100, however, it was out of the reach of many farmers, and, in view of its uncertain performance on rough ground and in thick grass, could scarcely be justified. Only in the middle fifties, when a second traction wheel was added to the separately designed mower, an adjustable cutter bar introduced, and the draft lightened did the mower become an effective agricultural machine. Thus the farmer was relieved of another backbreaking task. It was estimated in 1858 that the mower reduced the cost of cutting grass by one half.[57]

DEVELOPMENT OF OTHER FARM MACHINES

Other machines were introduced to reduce the labor of haying and were gradually brought to efficient operation. Of these, the most important was the horse-drawn hay rake, which made it possible to mass the hay in rolls, after which it could more easily be picked up and drawn to the barn. The tedder, or kicker, was employed in the field to turn the hay over to permit drying of all parts. The baler or press was used to compress the bulky hay into small bales that could be shipped to nearby cities or by water to southern ports and even to England. The horse fork was a large steel fork attached to a rope which was drawn over a pulley by a horse. When the fork, loaded with hay, was drawn to the top of the barn it ran along a rail or groove to the point where the farmer wanted to store the hay; at this point a release mechanism was tripped, dropping the hay into the mow. All these devices or machines went through the usual process of crude improvising, frequently on the farm or in the neighboring blacksmith shop, the making of numerous improvements, patenting, and finally manufacturing by factory methods.

Corn, the most widely raised of all crops, fell behind wheat in the mechanization of its cultivation, partly because of technological difficul-

[56] *Prairie Farmer*, XI (November, 1851), 482.
[57] *Cultivator*, New Series, V (November, 1848), 330; and X (March, 1852), 109; Rogin, *op. cit.*, p. 91; Bidwell and Falconer, *History of Agriculture*, p. 296.

ties and partly because it required less labor and could be harvested when other tasks did not demand attention. In 1838 and 1839 experiments were made with hand-operated and horse-drawn planting devices. Four different types of horse-drawn planters were constructed, and at least one was offered for sale in Massachusetts. They were somewhat awkward and heavy, the release mechanism was not perfect, and their cost doubtless seemed high. Continued improvements were made on planters, and by the fifties the commercial farmers in the corn belt employed them quite generally with considerable saving in labor.[58] Farmers had a long time to wait for harvesting machines for corn.

Improvements in the manufacture of drain tile were made possible by the immigration to this country of skilled English workers and drainage engineers, capable of laying out accurate drainage plans for farms. They contributed to a small drainage boom, mostly confined to the Northeast.[59] John Johnston on his farm near Geneva, in the Finger Lakes area of New York, began experimenting with tile draining early in the fifties. His yields of wheat, other grain, and grass were pushed up to high levels, and he maintained that the midge damaged his wheat appreciably less than it did the wheat grown on worn and ill-drained soils. He attributed his success to tiling and went ahead with an intensive program of drainage on his 300-acre farm until, by 1856, he had laid 210,000 tiles stretching fifty miles.[60] Johnston's long-maintained campaign in behalf of draining and high farming, and the excellent crops that resulted from his efforts, drew much attention to his personal success and led to a considerable development of drainage activities in areas of high land values.

Amazing varieties of other farm implements were ingeniously contrived and brought into use in the forties and fifties. Progressive farmers, seeking to expand their operations and faced with rapidly rising labor costs, eagerly turned to contrivances that would free them of dependence upon hired labor. With horse or ox power available to operate these contrivances, the cost was not beyond their means. Among the devices were cotton-seed planters, corn shellers, improved cultivators, potato diggers, cheese presses, churns, iron rollers, flax pullers, corn and cob crushers, water rams, and incubators.[61]

A breakdown of the patents granted for agricultural appliances in 1849 shows 20 were for seed planters, 15 each for harvesting machines and plows, 10 for churns and butter workers, 9 each for threshing ma-

[58] *Boston Cultivator*, February 23, September 28, 1839; Bidwell and Falconer, *op. cit.*, pp. 300–302.

[59] *Farmer's Monthly Visitor*, VII (October 31, 1845), 156; *Country Gentleman*, I (June 23, 1853), 399; II (August 4, 1853), 71; and XII (September, 1858), 144.

[60] Johnston was a prolific writer for the *Country Gentleman* in the fifties. See especially Vols. VII–XIV.

[61] *De Bow's Review*, VI (August, 1848), 131 ff.

chines and separators, 8 for grain hullers, 7 for corn shellers, 6 for cultivators, 5 each for straw cutters and beehives, 4 for rakes, and 2 for curry
combs and ox yokes.[62] A decade later, the Patent Office reported 659
patents for agricultural implements of which 116 were for seed drills and
planters, 113 for harvesters for cutting small grain, corn, sugar cane, and
the like, and 43 were for plows, of which 5 were steam-propelled. Other
patents were granted for cheese vats, cotton-seed cleaners and hullers,
corn huskers, and potato diggers.[63]

It is instructive to look at the statistics of the value of farm machinery
as tabulated by the census takers in 1860. New York, as might be expected,
came first with $29,166,695, Pennsylvania followed with $22,442,842, then
came Louisiana, with its heavy investment in sugar grinding and manufacturing equipment, with $18,648,225. Ohio and Illinois followed with
$17,538,532 and $17,235,472, respectively. The average value of machinery per farm was highest in Louisiana: $1,064. Other states with high
averages were Mississippi, $210; New York, $148; and Pennsylvania, $143.
Among the low-ranking states were Ohio, $97; New Hampshire, $87;
Connecticut, $84; and North Carolina, $78. The averages of southern
states were high not only because sugar-refining and cotton-ginning machines were expensive but, more important, because the large plantations
were almost congeries of farms. The value of farm machinery per acre of
improved land is a better index. For representative southern states, the
figures are Virginia, $0.82; North Carolina, $0.90; Alabama, $1.16; Missis-
sippi, $1.74; and Louisiana, $6.80. For representative northern states, the
figures are Massachusetts, $1.80; Ohio, $1.38; New York, $2.03; and
Pennsylvania, $2.14.[64]

Progressive critics of farm practices complained of farmers' unwillingness to buy new tools and machines when they had been proved
useful and good investments, and charged that farmers preferred to invest
their profits in land for speculation or in railroad and bank stocks. "Caution, a dread of new ways and the prejudiced conclusion that whatever
is new in farming is necessarily untrue, are the great obstacles to improved culture," said the forthright *Homestead* in 1859. Men hesitated
year after year about buying a horse rake or corn planter which were
so obviously laborsaving and money-making. No other class of Yankees,
the editors emphasized, was "so obstinately perverse" in taking advantage of new machines, tools, and cropping methods.[65] England's foremost
critic of American agriculture, though a gentle one, made similar obser-

[62] Commissioner of Patents, *Annual Report, 1849*, Pt. I, *Arts and Manufactures*
(Washington, D. C.: Printers to the Senate, 1850), p. 455.

[63] *American Agriculturist*, XIX (July, 1860), 199.

[64] Computed from *Eighth Census of the United States, 1860, Agriculture*, pp. 184
and 222.

[65] *Homestead*, IV (February 3, 1859), 320.

vations. James F. W. Johnston maintained that too little capital was used in farming, and was distressed to find that farmers possessed of a few hundred dollars "prefer to lend it on mortgage at high interest, or to embark in some other pursuit" than to invest it in further development of their farms.[66] This same reluctance was not shown in the rice- and sugar-producing areas of the South or the rapidly growing wheat regions of the upper Mississippi Valley.

The manufacture of agricultural implements, machines, and other goods peculiarly identified with farming was a major industry by 1860. If one half the value of goods produced by blacksmiths and by manufacturers of wagons and carts, saddles and harnesses are included, the total value of goods produced that year was $34,000,000. This figure made the farm-servicing trades rank among the top ten industries in the country.[67]

Invention of farm machinery was not left entirely without government patronage. The United States had a benevolent patent system, designed to encourage inventions, which permitted investors to have a monopoly of the sale of their machines for seventeen years. True, the patent system did not always assure the man who had perfected the machine the sole right to produce and rent or market it, as Eli Whitney, the inventor of the cotton gin discovered, but in many instances the system did work well from the standpoint of the inventor or the manufacturer who bought the inventor's rights.

State and county fairs also sought to stimulate inventions by offering prizes for the best implements and machines of various sorts. Thus the Massachusetts Agricultural Society gave a prize of $20 to a Mr. Prouty for a sward plow which "appears to have been the result of a continued attention and minute observations, with practical skill as a farmer in the use of the plough, as well as mathematical calculation in the principles of its construction. . . ." For the next fair the same organization offered $30 for the best subsoil plow and $20 for "any newly invented agricultural implement or machine superior to any designed for the same use." [68] In 1842 a prize of $50 was offered "for the best improvement on the Subsoil Plows now in use, adapted to reduce the draught." [69] At the New York State Fair in Auburn, in 1846, silver medals, diplomas, and volumes of the *Transactions* of the New York State Agricultural Society were awarded for cultivators, fanning mills, horse-power rigs, corn-stalk cutter, threshing machine and separator, corn planter, straw cutter, corn and cob

[66] Johnston, *Notes on North America*, I, 207. For a similar point of view see *Cultivator*, New Series, VIII (November, 1851), 359.

[67] *Eighth Census of the United States, 1860, Manufactures, passim.*

[68] *New England Farmer*, XVII (April 17, 1839), 322–323; and XVIII (July 24, 1839), 24.

[69] *New England Farmer*, XX (March 2, 1842), 274.

crusher, horse rake, hay and manure forks, corn sheller, axes, hoes, and "the greatest collection of agricultural implements." [70]

By the middle of the century competition among farm-implement manufacturers—in an industry now grown to large proportions—led to keen contests at the fairs, and more generous awards. Prizes as high as $200 and the prestige of winning in the very exciting exhibition contests helped in bringing out the latest improvements and in perfecting the machines.[71]

By 1860 some phases of American agriculture had been completely revolutionized. The most remarkable of the changes which had occurred during the preceding half century had come in plowing, drilling, reaping and threshing wheat, ginning cotton, hulling rice, and making cane and maple sugar. Although all the machines used in producing wheat were subsequently to be improved and made more efficient, they had already been brought to successful operation. With their aid wheat farmers could devote much larger acreages to the grain than formerly. Similarly, farmers in the corn belt could work up larger fields with the improved plows and cultivators and manage a larger acreage in corn than their fathers could have taken care of a generation earlier. Cutting and shucking the corn were still time-consuming and unpleasant tasks, but shellers provided a good deal of relief. In dairying, the establishment of cheese factories and the rise of the market for whole milk in cities greatly lightened the burdens of farm women. Horse-tread power and horse sweeps ran the threshers, corn shellers, corn and cob grinders, cotton gins, cheese presses, balers, and many other instruments.[72] Steam power used with sugar apparatus and steam and tidal power in the processing of rice had become basic features of plantation economy. Smaller instruments, such as shovels, hoes, axes, and rakes, had been lightened and made more effective.

SOCIAL EFFECTS OF IMPROVEMENTS

Through all these improvements the labor of man had been made more productive, though not without social costs. The capital needs of farm making had increased, making it more difficult for farm laborers and tenants to climb the agricultural ladder; the increased efficiency of labor permitted production to outrun the market at times, and prices fell to distressingly low levels; farmers had become more dependent upon banks and other lending agencies for credit to carry them from planting to harvest, and upon middlemen for marketing their output. The farmer

[70] *American Agriculturist*, V (November, 1846), 356–357.

[71] Hutchinson, *Cyrus Hall McCormick*, p. 340.

[72] Rogin, *The Introduction of Farm Machinery*, pp. 173–174.

was no longer the independent individual the Hoosier pioneer had been when he plunged into the wilderness ahead of civilization, free of all restraints and under obligations to no man. His increased well-being had brought with it problems and difficulties over which he had no control, and which were to become increasingly serious in a later period.

In the South, dependence upon the labor of slaves, who lacked the incentive to use equipment and livestock carefully and who were forced to do their work under the threat of the lash, made it inadvisable to use expensive field equipment. The hoe continued to be the principal tool used in planting and cultivating cotton and rice. The agricultural revolution that machines made possible came to the South in the processing and manufacturing of rice and sugar, but not in the field. Hand labor using primitive tools continued to prevail on the plantations.

CHAPTER XIV

Search for New Species

THE quarter century before the Civil War was a period of continuous agricultural experimentation. Knowledge of chemical analysis and of the methods of applying it to crops and soils to determine plant needs was brought to America through the writings of German and British scientists and by the thin stream of Americans who had gone abroad to study under the masters of the new science at Giessen, Jena, Durham, and other university centers. Agricultural periodicals took up the findings of the chemists and geologists and sought to utilize them to rebuild exhausted soils and to improve production on other land. Few readers of the agricultural periodicals could fail to be aware of the new scientific techniques.

Forward strides were also being made in what was later called animal husbandry. At one time it was thought that the importation of high-quality stock like Spanish Merino sheep or English Shorthorn cattle was all that was necessary to assure rapid improvement in the native American stock. Without proper feeding practices, carefully kept records, and selection of the best stock for breeding, little progress was made. By mid-century, after a long process of trial and error, American livestock specialists were producing such superior cattle that English buyers were regretting the sales they had made to Americans and were beginning to purchase some of the best American Shorthorns at public auctions. British cattle, sheep, and hogs were still on the average far superior to those of the United States, but the cattle of Scioto County, the sheep of Vermont, and the hogs of the cornbelt were second to none.

Plant breeding was still a young science and yet much progress had been made by 1860. Hybridizing was practiced by plant specialists, new varieties of grain, tobacco, cotton, apples, pears, and plums had been perfected and time-tried vegetables had been improved. Little can be said, however, for entomology other than that progress was being made in the taxonomy of insects.

295

INTRODUCTION OF NEW CROPS

In the midst of this period of agricultural experimentation, interest developed in the introduction of new crops or varieties of crops and unusual varieties of poultry. Agricultural writers and leaders of agricultural societies seized upon new introductions without always examining their claims cautiously before pressing them upon the public as important innovations. The fact that many agricultural writers and editors were proprietors of, or employees in, seed, nursery, and livestock businesses and had a direct interest in the new ventures they were urging upon farmers did not lead them to write with restraint. There was much humbug in the claims set forth by sponsors of new varieties of seeds, fruits, and poultry and the excesses to which these sponsor-editors went created suspicion and distrust of much that appeared in the farm journals and seemed to provide justification for the enemies of book farming. Yet, despite the harm that false and ill-justified claims—did, there came out of this period of experimentation important gains for American agriculture.

Early efforts to introduce new crops were the result of scientific and exploring expeditions, in part government-sponsored and -financed, and in part privately outfitted. The Lewis and Clark expedition was one of the most productive of these, though it was not accompanied by any scientists.[1] From this expedition came the Osage orange which, in the middle of the century, became the principal fencing tree, many thousand miles of it being set out. The Oregon grape, the golden currant, the western snowberry bush, varieties of beans, corn, and flowers, not all of practical value, were also found by Lewis and Clark. The nursery business benefited largely from these and other seeds and plants brought back from the western country, as did agriculture generally.[2] Later, John Bradbury and Thomas Nuttall, the first trained botanists who toured part of the trans-Mississippi West—getting as far as the Mandan villages of North Dakota in 1809–1811—and William Baldwin, physician-botanist with the Stephen Long expedition to the Colorado Rockies in 1818–1820, brought back specimens, cuttings, and seeds that were classified, described, and experimented with in botanic gardens.[3]

The first botanical exploration undertaken by an American official

---

[1] U. P. Hedrick, *History of Horticulture in America to 1860* (New York: Oxford University Press, 1950), p. 183, says that Lewis was sent to Philadelphia for nine months to study botany as preparation for his exploration.

[2] *Ibid.*, pp. 183, 204, 401, 402.

[3] Susan Delano McKelvey, *Botanical Exploration of the Trans-Mississippi West, 1790–1850* (Jamaica Plain: Arnold Arboretum of Harvard University, 1955), pp. 63 ff.

in South America was made by the same William Baldwin in 1817 and 1818. Although there was no mention of botanical explorations in his official instructions—he was assigned as ship's surgeon—Baldwin devoted much of his time to collecting specimens of plants in Brazil, Uruguay, and Argentina. He examined methods of cultivation and discussed his findings and compared notes with other botanists. Cuttings of muscatel and other fine grapes, roots of flowering plants for which new methods of drying for preservation were developed, and club wheat from Chile were brought to the United States for taxonomic study and for planting in botanical gardens. Although club wheat did not become a permanent wheat in the eastern United States, it had earlier been introduced into California, where it flourished. Wayne D. Rasmussen concludes that the plant specimens of the South American expedition which were placed in the Academy of Natural Sciences in Philadelphia, and Baldwin's notes and newspaper accounts of his investigations awakened "interest in importing improved varieties of plants, an interest that was eventually to mean much to American agriculture." [4]

In the same year that Baldwin was dispatched to South America, Congress undertook to encourage the cultivation of grape vines and olive trees by granting a group of French refugees pre-emption rights, with credit for four years, to four townships of land (92,160 acres) on which they were to carry out their horticultural work. Though grape vines and olive trees were set out on the tract on the Tombigbee River in Alabama, the grapes did not prove suitable for wine making and the olive trees were killed by frost. Other difficulties that brought failure to the experiment were trouble with squatters, confusion over the location of the lands, and the fact that the French officers were not ideal frontier farm makers.[5] The experiment of granting pre-emption rights for agricultural diversification was not again tried. Congress did, however, grant a township of land in Florida to Dr. Henry Perrine to encourage the introduction of tropical plants. Perrine imported 200 varities of tropical plants, including sisal hemp, tree cotton, and the Indian rubber tree.[6]

[4] Wayne D. Rasmussen, "Diplomats and Plant Collectors: The South American Commission, 1817–1818," Agricultural History, XXIX (January, 1955), 22–31.

[5] Albert James Pickett, History of Alabama and Incidentally of Georgia and Mississippi (2 vols.; Charleston, S. C.: Walker and James, 1851), II, 386. An earlier attempt to promote the culture of the vine in Ohio by authorizing John J. Dufour and associates to purchase four sections of land at the two-dollar price was made in 1802, but met with failure.

[6] Commissioner of Patents, Report, Agriculture, 1857 (Washington, D. C.: James B. Stedman, 1858), p. 19; Nelson Klose, America's Crop Heritage: The History of Foreign Plant Introduction by the Federal Government (Ames: Iowa State College Press, 1950), pp. 20–23, 25.

Efforts to collect useful seeds, plants, and trees in foreign countries for experiments in the United States were undertaken in 1819 and again in 1827, when the Secretary of the Treasury requested American consuls abroad to solicit seeds, plants, and cuttings and to arrange for their shipment home. In the former year they were instructed to collect "forest trees useful for timber; grain of any description; fruit trees, vegetables for the table, esculent roots; and in short, plants of whatever nature useful as food for man or the domestic animals, or for purposes connected with manufactures or any of the useful arts." In 1830 the House of Representatives requested the Navy Department to secure new varieties of sugar cane in the West Indies, and cuttings were brought back and distributed in Florida.[7] Unfortunately there was no adequately supported government agency equipped to receive such importations and to transmit them to farmers, nurserymen, and others who might have been interested in experimenting with the specimens and seeds. Nevertheless, the large Lima bean was successfully introduced from Peru in 1824, and importations of alfalfa were made in the twenties.[8]

Botanical gardens were well under way in a number of places by 1815. Most famous and long-lived was that established on the Schuylkill by John Bartram in 1728. As a nursery dealer and botanist Bartram imported from Europe during the next fifty years varieties of pears, plums, nectarines, apricots, alfalfa, lilacs, laurels, horse chestnuts, lilies, and seeds of many vegetables and flowers. His son William, a professor of botany at the University of Pennsylvania, continued the garden until his death in 1833.[9] The Elgin Botanic Garden, where Rockefeller Center now towers, contained 2,200 species of plants collected under the direction of Columbia University in 1814. Another famous botanical garden flourished in Charleston. The United States Botanic Garden in the District of Columbia was established in 1820, but it was inadequately supported and survived for only a short time. In 1850 a new botanical garden was established on the Mall in Washington.[10]

Greatest of the scientific undertakings of the federal government was the famous Wilkes Expedition of 1839–1842, in which some of the best-known scientists of the day participated. From South America, the

---

[7] Harold T. Pinkett, "Records of the First Century of Interest of the United States Government in Plant Industries," *Agricultural History*, XXIX (January, 1955), 39, quoting from circular letter of the Secretary of the Treasury to United States Consuls, March 26, 1819.

[8] Klose, *America's Crop Heritage*, p. 28.

[9] Hedrick, *History of Horticulture*, pp. 84–92.

[10] *Ibid.*, pp. 423–430.

Pacific Coast of present California and Washington, the Hawaiian and other Pacific islands, and Singapore were collected some 40,000 specimens of 10,000 species of plants, 100 living plants, and a large variety of seeds. The collections were all sent to Washington and turned over to the newly created National Institute for the Promotion of Science. Charles Pickering, a botanist who had immediate responsibility for the collection though no certain place to store the numerous items, must have been troubled when the invoice of the shipment reached him: 98 boxes, 27 packages, six barrels, six half barrels, and ten kegs of material for which he had to find space. The only place available was the Gallery of the Patent Office, and here they were put.[11]

News of the arrival of the specimens, plants, and seeds led nursery firms, seed salesmen, gentlemen-farmers, and wealthy urban people interested in embellishing their property with exotic shrubs and flowering trees to urge their claims for plants and seeds upon influential Washingtonians.[12] Some plants were distributed to people of influence, but from the point of view of agriculture little benefit was derived from the very large expenditure of money that had been made. Congressional wrangling and bureaucratic bickering minimized to some degree the scientific contributions of the expedition. The greatest harm done was in delaying indefinitely the publication of many of its important findings.[13]

Since his appointment as Commissioner of Patents, Henry L. Ellsworth had made his office efficient in its major responsibility and at the same time had developed within it an increasingly valuable and widely appreciated agricultural service. There is no evidence that he was hostile to pure science, but his duties and his inclination led him to favor the application of science to practical matters. He thought the Smithson fund could best be used to establish an agricultural and technological school. Similarly, he favored using the seeds, cuttings, shrubs, and trees from the Wilkes Expedition for experimental work in practical agriculture and would have liked them to be distributed to nurseries and farmers capable of making the best use of them. Since 1837 he had been distributing seeds and cuttings and, though the results

[11] The invoice is in the Robert Alonzo Brock Collection, The Huntington Library.

[12] Letters of Jeremiah Brown, February 10, 1845; James Buchanan, February 21, 1843; N. G. Pendleton, September 17, 1842; J. B. Russell, February 25, 1843; and Gideon B. Smith, January 13, 1842 [1843], Robert Alonzo Brock Collection, The Huntington Library. Other requests for seeds and cuttings that went directly to the National Institute are also in the Brock Collection.

[13] G. Browne Goode, "The Genesis of the National Museum," Board of Regents of the Smithsonian Institution, *Annual Report, 1891* (Washington, D. C.: Government Printing Office, 1892), pp. 273 ff.; Harley Harris Bartlett, "The Reports of the Wilkes Expedition and the Work of the Specialists in Science," *Proceedings* of the American Philosophical Society, LXXXII (June 29, 1940), 601 ff.

were not altogether favorable, he had developed the machinery for such distribution. For another agency now to manage the distribution of items brought back by the Wilkes Expedition seemed unwise to Ellsworth. Furthermore, in the Patent Office he had created an agricultural and technological museum where were displayed models of patented devices and to it came many curious visitors. The hall used for such exhibitions had the only space available for storing and displaying the material collected by the expedition. Ellsworth favored putting on these exhibits for popular, practical use rather than allowing a scholarly institution such as the National Institute for the Promotion of Science to preserve them. He was thus forced to oppose an agency whose ideas ran in other directions than his.[14] Difficulties with the National Institute weakened his standing and may have contributed to his removal in 1845.

Plant and seed importations were continued in the fifties by the government. A representative of the Patent Office accompanied Commodore Perry on his expedition to Japan in 1854 to exchange implements and seeds with that country. Varieties of rice, beans, wheat, tea, cotton, cabbages, turnips, broom corn, soybeans, tobacco, and fruits and flowers were introduced into the United States through this means. Most important of all introductions in the fifties, says Nelson Klose, was the rough purple Chile potato from South America. Through crossing with this strain to give potatoes immunity from disease, most of the varieties of potatoes in the twentieth century have been derived.[15]

Daniel J. Browne, head of the agricultural work of the Patent Office in the fifties, made two trips to Europe to collect seeds and cuttings for further distribution. In his report of 1855 he included an elaborate defense of his importation and distribution, of which he claimed, with somewhat less than justification, that the benefits of this work had called forth the "expressed gratification and general approval of the agricultural portion . . . in all sections of the Union." That the seeds and cuttings with all their deficiencies were anxiously sought by farmers and gardeners none could deny. Browne described importations of Turkish flint wheat from Greece, sorghum from France and Africa, the Chinese yam, the earth almond, the Persian walnut, the cork oak, meadow fescue, trefoil, alsike, Guinea grass, the opium poppy, the vanilla plant, the ginger plant, the castor-oil plant, the asafetida plant, dyer's madder, and the deodar

[14] Bartlett, "The Reports of the Wilkes Expedition . . . ," loc. cit., p. 621n.

[15] Klose, America's Crop Heritage, pp. 33–36. Published documents of the Perry Expedition include accounts of agriculture in the Lew Chew Islands, Cape of Good Hope, Japan, and China which provide information on crops, diseases and parasites, and farm machines.—Narrative of the Expedition of an American Squadron to the China Seas and Japan, 1852–1854, under the Command of Commodore M. C. Perry, House Executive Document No. 97, 33 Cong., 2 Sess., 1856, 3 vols., II, 3 ff.

Butter making, except among New Englanders, was commonly done by farmers' wives. (Sketched by Alexander Anderson.) (Courtesy, Prints Division, New York Public Library.)

Southern Pine Woods Hog

Progress in hog raising resulting from use of purebred stock and improvements in feeding, housing, and care. (*Eighty Years' Progress of the United States,* p. 61.)

Western Beech Nut Hog

Improved Suffolk

1839.

CATALOGUE OF

GARDEN SEEDS,

RAISED AND SOLD
BY THE

UNITED SOCIETY.

Pittsfield, Berkshire Co. Mass.

Papers.		Cents.	Papers.			Cents.
6 EARLY PETERSBURGH PEAS,...		6	2 Tomato, ...			6
5 Large White Marrowfat do.		6	Pink, ...			6
1 Green Dwarf Marrowfat do.		6	Burnet, ...			6
Strawberry do.		6	Rue, ...			6
Berkshire Dwarf Beans, ...		6	4 Large early curl head Lettuce,...			6
Early Bush do.		6	Frankford head do. ...			6
Red Cranberry do.		6	Cabbage head do. ...			6
Mangel Wurzel Beet, ...		6	4 Hardy Green do. ...			6
6 Blood do.		6	4 Early do. ...			6
2 Orange do.		6	Large Head do. ...			6
3 Turnip do.		6	2 Ice do. ...			6
3 Red do.		6	10 Drum-head Winter Cabbage,....			6
3 White do.		6	6 Early Dutch do.			6
3 Sugar do.		6	2 Red Dutch do.			6
6 Scarcity do.		6	2 Early Yorkshire do.			6
12 Yellow Onion, ...		6	3 Savoy do.			6
3 White do.		6	1 Sugar Loaf do.			6
15 Red do.		6	Cauliflower do.			6
5 Long White Parsnip, ...		6	1 Sage, ...			6
3 Guernsey do.		6	2 Summer Savory, ...			6
Salsify do.		6	1 Celery, ...			6
4 Orange Carrot, ...		6	2 Curled Parsley, ...			6
3 Yellow Swedish Turnip,........		6	Garden Cress, ...			6
White Swedish do. or Ruta			2 Pepper Grass,................			6
Baga,.....................		6	Prickley Spinnage,.............			6
4 English Turnip,.................		6	2 Saffron,.......................			6
French do.		6	8 Watermelon, ...			6
3 Scarlet Turnip Radish,........		6	3 Rusty-coat Muskmelon, ...			6
14 Scarlet do.		6	3 Nutmeg do			6
2 Salmon do.		6	2 Yellow Crookneck W. Squash,..			6
1 Yellow do.		6	3 Crookneck Summer do. ..			6
1 Black Spanish do.		6	5 Dutch Bush do. ..			6
2 Squash Pepper, ...		6	15 Early Cluster Cucumber, ...			6
2 Cayenne do.		6	15 Early do.			6
Asparagus, ...		6	10 Long do.			6

30 Papers, at 12½ cts....	3	75	114 Papers, at 6 cts.....	6	84
82 do. at 6 cts....	4	92	Bro't forward,.....	8	67
	8	67	Total amount,.. $	15	51

All orders to be directed to Pittsfield Post-Office.

Jos. Patten Agent.

An early invoice of seed orders showing numerous varieties, 1839. (Courtesy, New York State Historical Association.)

Do you see that fine Cider Mill and Press?

This Mill and Press will be your own,
When I to you this plan make known.

KNOWDEDGE IS WEALTH—IMPROVEMENT THE LIFE OF BUSINESS.

A NEW PLAN

OF

REFINING CIDER.

BY JOHN COPELIN, Jr. TROY, N. Y.

First, apples are indispensable; which should be gathered clean and free from decay. Grind and let the pumice stand twenty-four hours, if circumstances will permit; lay up the cheese and press it gently with flannel cloth, suspended where the cider runs off, through which it may filtrate. The cider thus made will have a fine flavour and richness of colour, not surpassed by the choicest wines of France or Spain. Fill your casks, which must be pure and sweet. (The most effectual method of restoring casks impregnated with must or taint, is by stone lime.) The casks being full, let the cider work till it forms a crust on top; draw it off immediately into other pure casks,—then to fine and preserve it, put in each barrel the *white of four eggs Beat together* put into each barrel, at the same time, two thirds of half a pint *gray mustard seed unpulverised* and in a hogshead, a little more in proportion. Stir the liquor a little when the ingredients are in, by means of which they will settle through the cider and it thus becomes impregnated with the oil they contain. Which oil refines and prevents its fermentation. Bung tight. Lay the casks in a cool cellar; the cider will retain its sweetness, and become transparent. The cider should be racked again about the first of March; and to prevent a future fermentation, through the heat of summer, or in southern states, pour into each barrel one pint of pure English or American, *Linseed oil* and in a hogshead in *proportion*. Bung tight—your cider will be good.

☞$ To be paid John Copelin Junr. in spring 183   and experiment to be made first year, or responsible for amount.
N. B. Not to be made known under penalty of $50.

Directions for making and preserving cider. (Courtesy, New York State Historical Association.)

Pitching fresh made hay on the hayrack preparatory to hauling it to the barn.

Mowing machine cutting grass, a primitive horse-drawn rake, and a hayrack. From American Banknote Company engravings (Courtesy, Prints Division, New York Public Library.)

McCormick reaper of 1851 that required a second man to rake the wheat off the platform. (Courtesy, McCormick Historical Library, Wisconsin State Historical Society.)

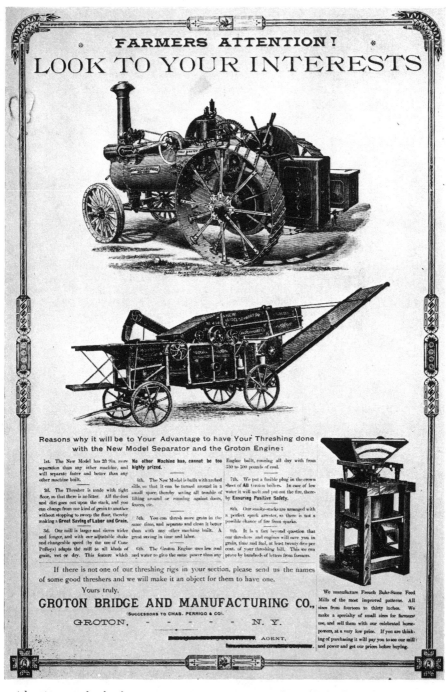

Advertisement of a thresher, a steam engine to operate it, and a small grinding mill. (Courtesy, Regional History, Cornell University.)

Horace Greeley, whose *New York Tribune* was read by farmers for its extensive news coverage, its detailed columns of information on the marketing of farm products, its sound advice on farm procedures, and its vigorous championship of land reform. (Courtesy, Prints Division, New York Public Library.)

Marshall Pinckney Wilder, a leading horticulturist, fruit specialist, and leader in the Massachusetts Horticultural Society and the United States Agricultural Society. (*Harper's Weekly*, I [September 26, 1857], 612.)

Machinery Hall, Fifth Annual Exhibition of the United States Agricultural Society, Louisville, 1857. (*Harper's Weekly*, I [September 26, 1857], 612.)

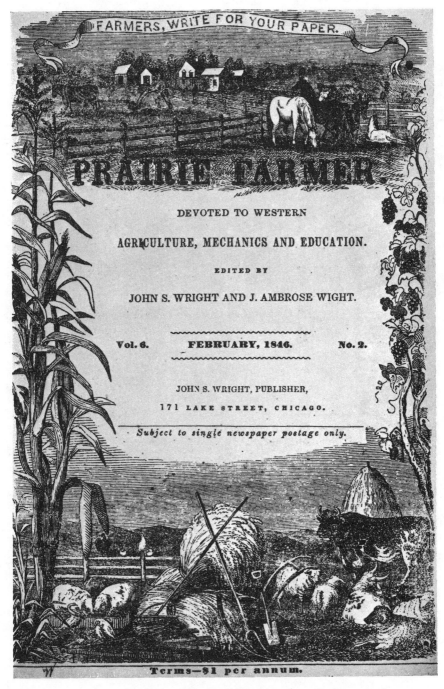

FARMERS, WRITE FOR YOUR PAPER.

PRAIRIE FARMER.

DEVOTED TO WESTERN

AGRICULTURE, MECHANICS AND EDUCATION.

EDITED BY

JOHN S. WRIGHT AND J. AMBROSE WIGHT.

Vol. 6.   **FEBRUARY, 1846.**   **No. 2.**

JOHN S. WRIGHT, PUBLISHER,
171 LAKE STREET, CHICAGO.

Subject to single newspaper postage only.

Terms—$1 per annum.

Cover page of the *Prairie Farmer,* à long-lived, Midwestern farm journal.

A leading agricultural college, now Iowa State University, aided by the land grant of the Morrill Act of 1862. (From an early announcement reproduced in Earle D. Ross, *The Land Grant Idea at Iowa State College*.)

tree.[16] At the time the nursery and seed business may well have derived more benefits from this government activity than did the farmers, but in the long run the empirical methods that were persistently followed to diversify and improve agriculture succeeded.

New varieties of cotton seed, corn, wheat, and other grains and vegetables, whether imported or developed in the United States, were given much attention by the farm journals and, if successful, were quickly adopted. The importation of Mexican seed about 1805 had a most important influence on the short-staple or upland cotton industry. Earlier varieties of upland cotton had deteriorated, the length of the fiber had become shorter, the plants were subject to rot, and their pods did not open sufficiently to make picking easy. Tales of Mexican opposition to the exportation of the seed of its superior cotton may be apocryphal, but the value of the importation of this plant to American planters is quite beyond estimate. It was not subject to rot, its bolls opened widely, the fiber was longer and easily picked. With Mexican cotton, field hands could pick in a day several times the amount they could pick of the older varieties of upland cotton. Next to the cotton gin, the introduction of Mexican cotton, which was improved further by careful seed selection and was later called Petit Gulf, was the most important development in spreading cotton cultivation throughout the Deep South.[17]

Sorely beset in the forties by low prices and declining yields, planters looked for other miracles comparable to the introduction of Petit Gulf cotton. New varieties, or strains that were said to be new, were given much attention in the press, advertised effectively by stories of their high yields, and sold at absurd prices. Mastodon seed sold for "one bit a piece," later $5 a bushel, and Hogun seed was said to have brought $250 a peck. Other alleged varieties of cotton that were ardently pushed by seed salesmen passed under such fancy names as Banana, Multiboll, Pomegranate, Sugar Loaf, Silk, and even Accidental Poor-Land Cotton. Some of them were outright frauds.[18] In a brilliant article on

[16] Commissioner of Patents, *Report, Agriculture, 1855* (Washington, D. C.: Cornelius Wendell, 1856), pp. x–lxiii, "Report on Seeds and Cuttings Recently Obtained by the Patent Office, with Suggestions as to the Expediency of Introducing Others."

[17] James L. Watkins, *King Cotton: A Historical and Statistical Review, 1790–1908* (New York: James L. Watkins & Sons, 1908), pp. 13, 75, 164–165. Lewis Cecil Gray, *History of Agriculture in the Southern United States* (2 vols., Washington, D. C.: Carnegie Institution, 1933), II, 689, 302.

[18] *New Orleans Picayune*, November 11, 1844; *Alabama Beacon*, Greensboro, April 16, 1850; *Feliciana Whig*, April 2, 1851. Martin W. Philips's discussions of cotton seed in the *Southern Cultivator* were brought together in J. A. Turner, *The Cotton Planter's*

"Cotton Breeding in the Old South," Professor John Hebron Moore has shown that most of these hybrid varieties were improvements over the earlier Mexican Petit Gulf seed. Such prices could not be justified except for experimental or nursery purposes.[19] The numerous agricultural crazes caught the fancy of editors of farm journals, who pushed them with force and were responsible to a large degree for the excesses to which each obsession of the time went.

On occasion, farmers were warned by some of the more critical and disinterested of the agricultural editors to be on their guard against fraudulent and deceptive advertising by nurserymen and seed dealers. Edmund Ruffin's *Farmers' Register* printed an instructive article in 1838 "On Agricultural Hobbies and Humbugs," in which readers were warned against spectacular claims for new varieties of seeds.[20] The Yankee editor of *Homestead* warned his readers about the outlandish claims made for the *Dioscorea batata,* which nursery advertisers in the *New York Tribune* presented as "the most priceless boon God ever bestowed upon the human race, at ten dollars a dozen bulbs":

> Some twenty years since, France—that land of beautiful things and Mississippi bubbles—brought out the Rohan Potato, and, from a coarse, rank, yellow-fleshed vegetable, made a dish that gods might have envied. After a long gestation, and with exemplary patience, prophetic of the coming prodigy, this mother of rare things is again parturient, and the world looks on with admiration and astonishment while the offspring is baptized *Dioscorea batata;* a bubble more injuriously framed and carefully nurtured than the Rohan, but just as truly filled with wind.[21]

Though the editor of *Homestead* continued to scoff at the *Dioscorea batata* it carried in its own columns advertisements of patent medicines and fertilizers that had been discredited, and it did nothing to disillusion its readers about other current frauds. Similarly, the *Prairie Farmer* and the *Ohio Farmer* both expressed disenchantment with Wyandott corn, but stimulated interest in its pretensions and those of other humbugs by frequent items about them.[22]

Manual (New York: C. M. Saxton & Company, 1857), pp. 98-125; Watkins, *King Cotton,* p. 151.

[19] *Agricultural History,* XXX (July, 1956), 95-104.

[20] *Farmers' Register,* VI (April 1, 1838), 47-48.

[21] *Homestead,* I (February 28, 1856), 355, 368, 499, and II (June 4, 1857), 602. A missionary was quoted as saying that the Chinese potato was "only eaten by the poorer classes as an accompanyment to rats and young puppies . . . ."

[22] *Ohio Farmer,* V (February 16 and March 8, 1856), 26, 37, including quotation from the *Prairie Farmer.*

THE SILKWORM CRAZE

The most pervasive and costly, in terms of lost time, energy, and money, was the craze for raising silkworms and growing a species of the mulberry tree, the *Morus multicaulis*. The possibility of producing another cash crop by utilizing the "spare time" of women and children, as so many advocates put it, in unwinding the silk cocoons aroused interest in this exotic industry. It was further stimulated by the farm journals, which published and republished short accounts of silkgrowing that were calculated to arouse the cupidity and interest of readers. Writers and journals in all parts of the country rushed into print with stories about easy success in silk culture, and scores of nurserymen turned to raising *Morus multicaulis* trees by the tens of thousands to meet the expected demand.

Caught up by the excitement at a time when farming in the state was not doing well, the legislature of Massachusetts appointed a committee to consider a proposal to aid the culture of silk. The committee reported "that we have the power to produce and manufacture Silk in this Commonwealth to an immense extent, and that no difficulty is to be encountered either from soil or climate." Members of the legislature were sufficiently impressed with the report to appropriate $600 for the preparation and distribution of a manual on the mulberry tree and silk culture. Various states undertook to subsidize silk production by offering bounties. Massachusetts took the lead in 1835 and was most generous; [23] Vermont, Pennsylvania, Maryland, Georgia, and New Jersey followed. Indiana passed the issue on to county commissioners, who were authorized to offer bounties for silk cocoons and reeled silk.[24]

Advocates of raising mulberry trees and producing domestic supplies of silk solicited aid from the federal government, as did most promoters of economic and agricultural matters. They induced it to publish three brochures on silk culture, which were widely distributed.[25] In 1830 and

[23] J. H. Cobb, *A Manual Containing Information Respecting the Growth of the Mulberry Tree, with Suitable Directions for the Culture of Silk* (Boston: Carter and Hendee, 1832), pp. iii ff.

[24] Commissioner of Patents, *Report, 1845* (Washington, D. C.: Ritchie & Heiss, 1846), pp. 822–824. For the story of silk culture in Ohio and the part Oberlin College played in it, see Robert Samuel Fletcher, *History of Oberlin College* (2 vols.; Oberlin: Oberlin College, 1943), II, 648 ff.

[25] "Growth and Manufacture of Silk," *House Report* No. 158, 20 Cong., 1 Sess., February 7, 1828, Vol. IV, 220 pp.; "Letter from James Mease transmitting a treatise on the Rearing of Silk-Worms by Mr. De Hazzi of Munich," *House Report* No. 26, 20 Cong., 1 Sess., February 2, 1828, Vol. IV, 108 pp.; "D'Homergue upon American Silk. Report of the Committee on Agriculture on the Growth and Manufacture of Silk . . . with Essays on American Silk with Directions to Farmers for Raising Silk Worms by John D'Homergue, Silk Manufacturer and Peter Stephen Duponceau,"

1832, in response to petitions from citizens asking for such aid, House committees recommended appropriations to encourage silk culture. A fantastic proposal which had strong support provided for an appropriation of $40,000 to establish a "normal school of filiature" for instruction of young people in "reeling, manufacturing, and dyeing silk. . . ." The usual parliamentary delay prevented a vote for two sessions, during which the excitement in Washington subsided a little, and in 1832 the proposal was defeated by a vote of 97 to 74.[26] The movement for government aid to silk culture did not die, however, and for years thereafter it was kept before Congress and its committees. The most far-reaching proposal called for putting the federal government into the business of silk production.[27]

Seven journals devoted to the silk business were established, with imposing titles: *American Silk Grower and Agriculturist,* published in 1836–1839, in Keene, New Hampshire; *Silk Culturist and Farmer's Manual,* published in 1835–1839, in Hartford; *Fessenden's Silk Manual and Practical Farmer, Devoted to the Culture of Silk, Agriculture, and Rural Economy,* published in Boston, 1835–1837; *Journal of the American Silk Society,* published in 1839–1841, in Baltimore; *Silk-Grower and Farmer's Manual,* published in Philadelphia, in 1838–1839; and *Southern Silk Manual and Farmer's Magazine,* published in Baltimore, in 1838–1839. At least two editors or compilers of these magazines, and perhaps all, were large growers and sellers of the *Morus multicaulis* and used every device to promote sales of their trees.[28] One of the journals claimed a circulation in excess of 10,000.[29]

At the height of the excitement over silk production and the *Morus multicaulis,* speculation in this plant reached fantastic proportions. Not only editors of the silk journals but editors and proprietors of old and well-established journals like the *New England Farmer* and the *American Farmer* were deeply involved in raising and selling the *Morus.*[30] When large numbers of these trees succumbed to the withering blasts of the northern winters, one of these salesmen-editors explained the casualties away by saying that "injudicious methods" of preserving them were at fault.[31] Only wise old Jesse Buel, of the Albany *Cultivator,* expressed

May 24, 1830, *House Report* No. 126, 21 Cong., 1 Sess., Vol. IV; *Southern Agriculturist* I (August, 1828), 337.
[26] *Register of Debates,* 22 Cong., 1 Sess., March 24, 1832, p. 3096.
[27] *Silk-Grower and Farmer's Manual,* I (July, 1838), 21–24.
[28] *Ibid.,* I (December, 1838), 132.
[29] *Ibid.,* I (June, 1839), 276.
[30] The editors of both the *New England Farmer* and the *American Farmer* offered *Morus multicaulis* for sale in 1831 at one dollar each.—*New England Farmer,* X (September 7, 1831), 61; *American Farmer,* XIII (August 26, 1831), 191–192.
[31] *Silk-Grower and Farmer's Manual,* I (May–September, 1839), 252.

doubt about the adaptability of the *Morus* to northern climate, for which he was scolded for his misinformation by an editor with 100,000 trees for sale.[32] Other editors disregarded the hazards of weather, the great volume of labor involved in unwinding the cocoons, and the high cost of labor.

The silk craze coincided with the rugged nationalism of the Jacksonian period and the movement for self-sufficiency. Patriotism and the profit motive went hand in hand in the nursery business and the agricultural press, and few dared to raise their voices against the excitement. Farmers were anxious to find new marketable crops to enable them to get away from their concentration on grain, tobacco, and cotton, to diversify their operation, and to make them less dependent upon world markets. They were easily influenced by the current nationalism and its corollary, economic self-sufficiency. Excited public auctions of the *Morus* were held by nurserymen at which throngs bid wildly for the plant. At such an auction near Germantown, 3,000 people were said to have bought 260,000 trees for $81,218.[33]

Some doubts about the success of the silk industry having crept in, "a large number of gentlemen interested in the culture and manufacture of Silk" met at the American Institute in New York to pass upon the question in 1843. Here were presented enthusiastic reports from numerous individuals as to their success in feeding leaves of the *Morus* plant to silkworms and the amount of cocoons and silk these had produced. It appeared that Massachusetts had paid out over $9,000 through its subsidy program, and even the tight-fisted Yankees of Vermont had expended nearly $6,000 in its silk subsidy program. The American Institute, which included among its members some of the most solid gentlemen-farmers of the time, awarded seventeen gold and silver medals and diplomas to persons exhibiting the silk products of their industry. At the same time its officers denied that they had any "pecuniary interest whatever in the silk business. . . ." Though the results of the National Convention of Silk Growers and Silk Manufacturers held at the American Institute were published in a pamphlet entitled *The Silk Question Settled: The Testimony of One Hundred and Fifty Witnesses,* the silk bubble was about to burst.[34] A good index of the interest in the

[32] *Cultivator,* II (March and June, 1835), 4, 50; and III (March, 1836), 2–4; *Silk-Grower and Farmer's Manual,* I (July, 1838), 12–13. Interestingly, the editors of the *Homestead,* ordinarily well informed, attributed the excitement about the *Morus multicaulis* many years before to the fact that farmers had no periodicals to warn them of humbugs such as the silk craze.—*Homestead,* II (June 11, 1857), 602.

[33] *Niles' Register,* Fifth Series, I (September 28, 1839), 69.

[34] *The Silk Question Settled: The Testimony of One Hundred and Fifty Witnesses. Report of the Proceedings of the National Convention of Silk Growers and Silk Manufacturers Held in New York, Oct. 13th and 14th, 1843* (New York: Saxton and Miles, 1844), *passim.*

silk craze and the *Morus multicaulis* is the number of notices, sketches, and accounts of the silk business in the Albany *Cultivator*. Between 1835 and 1842 the number of such insertions ranged from six in 1837 to twenty-six in 1842. In 1843 the number fell to fourteen, in 1844 to eight, and in 1845 to one.

Despite this sharp reduction in interest in the silk business among the contributors to the *Cultivator* it was a long time before all hope for silk culture in the United States ended. For half a century after its establishment in 1862, the United States Department of Agriculture was to continue efforts to revive the earlier interest in silk production.[35]

The agricultural journals had no reason to be proud of the major role they had played in fanning excitement about silk culture. The fact that their editors had been misled or had taken part in it because of their own participation in the sale of *Morus* resulted in considerable disillusionment with the press.[36] Yet, although editors of farm journals frequently made scornful allusions about those who had contributed to earlier hoaxes, none of them apologized for the harm they had done in wasting the time, labor, and money of farmers in the *Morus multicaulis* mania.[37]

OTHER AGRICULTURAL CRAZES

Other agricultural crazes followed in rapid succession, and were promoted in a similar fashion by the advertisements of nurseries and by the farm journals. Most of them were exploded fairly soon. Wyandott corn, the "greatest agricultural wonder of the age," which sold for a penny a grain or $800 a bushel; Iverson's fescue grass seed, which brought five dollars a peck; the sugar beet; the mangel-wurzel; Chinese tree corn; Chinese sugar cane; and Shanghai chickens—all were pushed vigorously by editors. When the Chinese sugar cane was being promoted, one of the rare skeptical editors wrote:

"Can any good thing come out of Nazareth?" The spirit of this proverb may well be applied to China which after sending us Chinese tree corn, Shanghai's, and lastly the Dioscorea Batata has not a very enviable reputation for productions valuable to the American Farmer.[38]

His skepticism seemed justified in view of the many times that excitement over new species or crops had swept away balance and judgment, with

[35] U. S. Department of Agriculture, *Yearbook, 1904* (Washington, D. C.: Government Printing Office, 1905), p. 85.
[36] Henry S. Olcott, *Sorgho and Imphee: The Chinese and African Sugar Canes* (New York: A. C. Moore, 1858), p. 57.
[37] For a humorous account of the *Morus multicaulis* excitement, see the *New England Farmer*, XVIII (September 4, 1839), 76. For a statement on "Humbugs and the Troubles of Agricultural Editors," see *Ohio Farmer*, VI (January 17, 1857), 10.
[38] *Homestead*, II (January 8, 1857), 252.

the result that farmers paid high prices for seed which produced crops of little worth.

Seeds of the Chinese sugar cane, or sorghum, were brought by Daniel J. Browne to the United States from France in 1854, where he had been sent by the Patent Office to collect seeds and cuttings. The plant had earlier been brought to France from China for experimental purposes. Just why a substitute for sugar cane was introduced when Louisiana sugar interests were so powerful in national politics is difficult to determine. Sugar-cane crops had reached their peak in 1853–1854—449,000 hogsheads —fell to 73,000 hogsheads in 1856–1857, and never again came within 87,000,000 pounds or 87,000 hogsheads of the 1853–1854 yield in the ante-bellum period. Poor crops, apprehension that the sugar cane was deteriorating in Louisiana, and the high price of sugar, 6⅛ to 10¼ cents, as compared with 4¼ cents in 1854, may have been responsible for the prevailing interest in the Chinese sugar cane.[39]

Sufficient seed of the Chinese sugar cane was imported to plant 100 acres, and it was distributed to farmers in all sections except New England. A critic admitted that there was one good thing about the interest in it: the fact that its seed had been so widely disseminated by the Patent Office as to make it impossible for seed speculators to exploit the public as they had with other humbugs. At the same time, seedsmen were reported to have imported some tons of seed for sale. Early results of planting led Browne optimistically to announce that 25,000,000 acres were suitable for planting to the crop, and that from this acreage might be expected 50,000,000 tons of fodder worth $500,000,000, a sum greater than the value of all the crops at the time.[40] Equally optimistic were statements spread over the pages of the farm journals about the saccharine content of the cane and the prospects of making sugar and molasses from it. Here was a crop that was adapted to planting anywhere from St. Paul in the North to Louisiana in the South, and that had both a high value as fodder for livestock (much needed in the South) and the capacity to replace some of the lost sugar production of Louisiana.

About the same time the Chinese sugar cane was brought in, the Patent Office introduced the seeds of imphee, an African sorghum.[41] Henry Olcott brought together in a book called *Sorgho and Imphee: The Chinese and African Sugar Canes*, published in 1858, all that was favorable about the new crop. Surely few could read it without feeling that

[39] Olcott, *Sorgho and Imphee*, pp. ii–iv.

[40] Commissioner of Patents, *Report, Agriculture, 1855*, p. xiii; Olcott, *Sorgho and Imphee*, p. iv. Olcott says that the Patent Office distributed 100,000 packets of seed, but the Patent Office *Reports* give no evidence of such lavish distribution.

[41] See Liberty Hyde Bailey, *Cyclopedia of American Agriculture* (4 vols.; New York: The Macmillan Company, 1907), on this as on most other topics relating to agriculture.

one or more of the sorghum varieties promised to become a major silage crop for livestock as well as a crop capable of meeting the sugar and molasses needs of a considerable part of the country.

Frank Ruffin, editor of the *Southern Planter*, of Richmond, took a more cautious view of the sorghums than did many of his contemporaries. He conceded that the Chinese sugar cane provided good forage for stock and held that for Virginia planters this was its best use. He deplored, however, the notion that Virginians should attempt to produce sugar or molasses or other agricultural products for which their soil was not as well suited as that of other regions, adding: "The day has gone by when a man thought it his duty to 'make everything himself'; and though a few require the daily task, of three cents' worth of carding and spinning in order to employ negro women, yet that class of managers is nearly extinct." [42] Had the South paid more attention to these words it might have avoided some of the excesses to which it went in attempting to meet its food needs. *De Bow's Review* likewise was not overimpressed with the possibilities that Chinese sugar cane would replace Louisiana sugar cane as the major source of sweetening for the American table.[43]

Sorghums were planted quite generally throughout the country, except in New England and Louisiana, 6,749,123 gallons of sorghum molasses being produced in 1859. Largest producing states were Iowa, Indiana, Illinois, and Missouri in that order.[44] Sugar that could compete with Louisiana sugar was not successfully refined from sorghum molasses, notwithstanding all the optimistic predictions. The full usefulness of sorghums was not to be realized until settlement moved farther west in the Great Plains.[45]

The deterioration of sugar cane caused much concern, and the government made numerous efforts to import species from the Far East and South America to improve yields. In 1851, the Secretary of the Navy instructed the commander of an American squadron in the Far East to secure specimens of fruits and cane from countries he visited, but unfortunately, when the sloop of war *Malta* returned, it was found that all the cane had rotted. Additional importations were ordered from Penang, and again when the naval ship unloaded its canes they proved too decayed to use.[46] The small sugar output of 1855 and 1856 increased the government anxiety about the sugar industry, and in 1856 the annual appropriation for the agricultural work of the Patent Office was raised

[42] *Southern Planter*, XVII (January, 1857), 10–12.
[43] *De Bow's Review*, XXVI (March, 1859), 309–310.
[44] *Eighth Census of the United States, Agriculture, 1860* (Washington, D. C.: Government Printing Office, 1864), p. 187.
[45] Bailey, *Cyclopedia of American Agriculture*, II, 574 ff.; Fred A. Shannon, *The Farmer's Last Frontier*, p. 219. Volume V in this series.
[46] *De Bow's Review*, XIX (September, 1855), 98–99, 369.

from $30,000 to $75,000 to permit the fitting out of a ship to collect and to bring back from South America slips of sugar cane.[47] This expedition may have been more successful in introducing new cane, but it was also held responsible for importing the cane borer that threatened heavy damage until early frosts eliminated it.[48] Tragically little thought was given at this time to the danger of importing insects and diseases along with plants and seeds.

The hen fever was another agricultural craze that raged in the late forties and early fifties, stimulated by foreign importations. During this period giant Cochin China, Canton, Shanghai, Brahma Pootra, and Chittagong hens and cocks, as well as bantams and game birds, were imported from the Orient, specimens of Dorking poultry were brought from England, and Leghorns and other birds were brought from Spain and Italy. Absurd laying capacity was claimed for these birds, and editors of the farm journals threw themselves into the effort to make every reader a poultry fancier. The *New England Farmer,* published in the center of the area where interest in fancy breeding was strongest, permitted the poultry suppliers almost to monopolize its space for a time with full-page accounts, including engravings, of the more exotic of these birds, such as the Bankiva, spangled Hamburg, black Spanish, red Shanghai, and Sumatra game fowl.[49] Poultry fairs and societies were established; a spate of books appeared with such titles as *American-Fowl Breeder, New England Poultry-Breeder, American Poultry Yard, American Poulterer's Companion,* and *The Poultry Book,* all borrowing heavily from English works; specialists fought among themselves concerning distinctions between breeds; and the business of supplying eager buyers mounted rapidly.[50] Prices of purebred fowls went as high as $50, $80, and even $100 a pair, and setting eggs brought up to $12 a dozen.[51]

George P. Burnham, one of the largest and more fortunate dealers in this mushrooming industry, whose *New England Poultry-Breeder* went through thirteen printings in as many weeks, forwarded stock to all parts of the country, particularly to the South. Two of his largest buyers were from Louisiana; one took $2,330 worth in a single order,

[47] 11 *U. S. Stat.* 89; Klose, *America's Crop Heritage,* pp. 34–37.

[48] J. Carlyle Sitterson, *Sugar Country: The Cane Sugar Industry in the South, 1753–1950* (Lexington: University of Kentucky Press, 1953), p. 130.

[49] Ten such engravings and accompanying accounts appeared in Vol. II, 1850. See also the *Albany Cultivator,* New Series, II (January, August, 1850), 22–23, 113.

[50] *Cultivator,* New Series, II (June–August, 1850), 209–211, 227–230, 264–268; *Southern Cultivator,* Vol. VII (1849), Vol. VIII (1850), Vol. XI (1853), and Vol. XII (1854).

[51] *Cultivator,* New Series, II (July, 1850), 251; *Southern Planter,* XV (June, 1855), 182–183; *Soil of the South,* V (June, 1855), 177–179.

and the second paid over $10,000 for stock imported in one year. This same dealer, chuckling over his reminiscences, when he thought the business was declining, said that these southern buyers "had long purses," for they cheerfully paid $40 to $50 a pair for birds without "cavil or complaint. . . ." Between 1849 and 1855 Burnham made gross sales of $70,000 and in addition had income from his books, one of which was a satirical account of the activities of himself, his competitors, and his customers.[52] When the hen fever began to decline in 1855, and when a number of imported varieties, not yet crossed with other poultry, had fallen short of success, it was easy for disillusioned buyers to blame the farm journals for the excitement and the fantastic prices, and to denounce them all as propagators of humbuggery unduly influenced by advertisers or the special financial interests of their proprietors and editors.[53]

The unethical conduct of editors of some farm journals should not cause the reader to overlook the very constructive achievements that resulted from the importation of foreign birds. Interbreeding of the heavy Brahma and Cochins with the lighter English and Mediterranean poultry produced a general-purpose fowl that was both a good layer and a good table bird. Already becoming a standard American breed and standing high in the farmers' esteem was the Plymouth Rock, which was said to be half Cochin, one fourth Dorking, one eighth Malay, and one eighth "wild India." [54] Their Asiatic ancestors gave the Plymouth Rocks and Wyandottes their breadth, weight, and smaller combs, as they gave the Rhode Island Reds their buff color. Leghorns, with their white eggs and small frames, were not as popular; heavier birds for roasting and stewing were more in demand. The Leghorns, however, were important for crossing with other breeds to raise their laying capacity. Furthermore, as the demand for eggs in the cities expanded, the Leghorns early proved

[52] George P. Burnham dedicated his reminiscences "To the Amateurs, Fanciers, and Breeders of Poultry, the Successful and Unfortunate Dealers, throughout the United States; and the Victims of Misplaced Confidence in the Hen Trade, Generally." —*History of the Hen Fever: A Humorous Record* (Boston: James French and Company, 1855), pp. 89, 163. Having sold to Southerners many hundreds of birds that he frankly thought little of, Burnham had his disillusioning book advertised in their midst. —*Soil of the South*, V (June, 1855), 191. Burnham's *History of the Hen Fever* claimed to have advanced orders for 12,000 copies and went through two printings. See *New England Farmer*, VII (March, 1855), advertising pages.

[53] In 1857 prices of fancy birds in New York were as follows: Cochin China, $4–$5; Shanghai, $3–$4; speckled Dorking, $12; white Dorking, $8; Poland, $4; white Bantam, $8; Japanese, $8.—*New York Tribune* in *Homestead*, III (September 24, 1857), 13. Cf. *Southern Planter*, XII (November, 1852), 360; and XVIII (February, 1858), 81–82; "Humbugs and the Troubles of Agricultural Editors," *loc. cit.*, p. 10.

[54] D. J. Browne, *The American Poultry Yard* (New York: C. M. Saxton & Company, 1850), p. 76.

valuable for their high laying capacity. Their white eggs were preferred in the New York market.[55]

Despite the slowness with which the poultry business grew, census valuation of poultry on farms in 1840 was over $12,000,000.[56] In the absence of census figures for 1850 and 1860, it may be estimated that this figure doubled in each decade.

All these crazes and fads had their day, were tried, and some proved of great value. In their efforts to diversify their agricultural economy, Americans experimented freely and sometimes threw discretion and common sense to the winds, as they did during the first Merino craze. Nevertheless, generally more was gained than mere experience.

[55] Bailey, *Cyclopedia of American Agriculture*, III, 529.
[56] Browne, *The American Poultry Yard*, p. 315.

CHAPTER XV

Government Concern for the Farmer

FARMERS, specifically the elite among farmers—the gentry living near Boston, Philadelphia, and Charleston—learned as early as the seventeen eighties that by organizing they could achieve progress unattainable otherwise. They formed societies for the promotion of agriculture, offered prizes for the importation of purebred livestock, for the discovery of remedies for animal and plant diseases, and for improvements in tillage practices. The Massachusetts Society's officers and members included Lowells, Cabots, Winthrops, Warrens, Russells and other notables who rarely followed the plow or pitched manure, but, nevertheless, were deeply interested in agricultural problems and devoted much time to improving farm practices on their estates and to the activities of their organization. In 1801 they offered substantial prizes for remedies for the canker worm and the slug worm, the importation of high-quality sheep, the best method of making compost, the discovery or introduction of new and useful grass for forage, and for a method of determining and replenishing the constituents of the soil.[1] These early societies were limited by the nature of their appeal to gentlemen-farmers, and the results of their activities, as set forth in their publications, could not have influenced the general practice of agriculture much at the time.

ROLE OF THE COUNTY FAIR

It was the county fair, rather than the publications and meetings of societies, which reached the lower strata of farmers. The fairs became the principal means by which farmers displayed the progress they were making, encouraged their neighbors to follow the best and most modern practices, and invited purchase of the good stock they had for sale.

[1] *Papers on Agriculture Consisting of Communications Made to the Massachusetts Agricultural Society* (Boston: Young and Minns, 1801), pp. 6–8.

Elkanah Watson, a wealthy Albany merchant and gentleman-farmer, had much to do with initiating the movement for agricultural fairs. Having taken up the raising and sale of purebred Merino sheep, he was anxious to have local fairs at which his sheep and the products of other progressive farmers could be displayed. The Berkshire County Agricultural Fair, which met in October, 1810, was the promising beginning that Watson hoped to see established in every county. Partly through his efforts, Massachusetts in 1817 and New York in 1819 appropriated funds to aid county societies in offering premiums at their fairs. New York appropriated $10,000 a year for such fairs, to be distributed among the counties on the basis of population, with the proviso that the local societies should expend equal amounts.[2]

The gentry supported the county fairs as they had the agricultural societies, and for years managed to dominate displays and to take an undue proportion of the prizes. Timothy Pickering, John Lowell, Josiah Quincy, and Thomas H. Perkins were among the most active leaders. Quincy—whose biographer declared, "His agricultural experience, like that of most gentlemen-farmers, were rather profitable to others than to him"—experimented with improved farm implements, modern soil practices, and hawthorne hedges, about which he wrote essays for the enlightenment of less fortunate farmers.[3] Gentlemen-farmers with fat steers, superior produce, and walnut-paneled barns that were show places also took up much space in the farm journals, particularly the *New England Farmer,* with descriptions of their model farming practices in which a good deal of hired labor was employed. The gulf was great between John P. Cushing, who, on his lavishly planned 60-acre estate nead Watertown, Massachusetts, employed ten or fifteen hands throughout the year and maintained imported cattle and hogs, a large "conservatory," and acres of flowers; and the small farmer who had grade stock, used little hired labor, and was dependent upon the produce of his farm and the small surplus he might exchange in a nearby town.[4]

Working farmers resented the domination of the agricultural societies and journals by these gentlemen-farmers, felt that their expensive and uneconomic show places did agriculture little good, and refused to join with them in support of the fairs. The "Honorable John Lowell"[5] was chairman of a committee of the Massachusetts Agricultural Society,

[2] Wayne Caldwell Neely, *The Agricultural Fair* (Columbia University *Studies in the History of American Agriculture,* Vol. II; New York: Columbia University Press, 1935), II, 59 ff.; Hugh M. Flick, "Elkanah Watson's Activities on Behalf of Agriculture, *Agricultural History,* XXI (October, 1947), 193 ff.

[3] Edmund Quincy, *Life of Josiah Quincy of Massachusetts* (Boston: Ticknor & Fields, 1858), p. 365.

[4] *Farmers' Cabinet and American Herd-Book,* VI (June, 1842), 338–339.

[5] *New England Farmer,* V (August 25, 1826), 38, thus alluded to Lowell.

which maintained in 1826 that the "substantial yeomanry" were forgetting their earlier jealousy of the city or gentlemen-farmers and were coming to support the fairs.[6] This was wishful thinking, however, for the fairs were on the way out under a barrage of criticism from the Albany *Plough-Boy,* the *Albany Argus,* and other papers for their undemocratic and impractical character.[7]

AGRICULTURAL SOCIETIES

Interest in agricultural societies revived in the forties. County and state societies, as well as many town and city groups, were organized with programs of a more popular and useful nature than those characteristic of the earlier movement. By 1856 there were 912 local and state organizations, of which all but 165 were in the North and West. These were followed by the establishment of state boards of agriculture in many states. The societies revived the country fairs and made them and the state fairs highly successful. The state legislatures, which were urged to appropriate funds for these boards and societies, did so with increasing generosity. New York State appropriated $40,000 to aid the county societies over a period of five years, gave $700 a year to the state society, and published its annual volume. Massachusetts appropriated annually $6,000 to its state board of agriculture and $600 to every county society. Nine other states, including Missouri, Kentucky, and Tennessee, voted financial aid.[8]

From these societies and boards of agriculture flowed an ever-growing stream of volumes containing statistics of crops and livestock, in addition to short sketches of innovations in agricultural practices. The annual volumes of the New York State Agricultural Society were notable, for they included accounts of the important research and agricultural activities of such authorities as James F. W. Johnston of Scotland and John P. Norton of Yale. The annual transactions of the agricultural

[6] *New England Farmer,* V (October 27, 1826), 105.
[7] *Plough Boy* and *Argus* quoted in *New England Farmer,* I (April 5, 19, 1823), 285, 298. See also the defense of the gentlemen-farmers who controlled the Massachusetts Agricultural Society and the Massachusetts Horticultural Society in *New England Farmer,* I (March 23, 1823), 255. Lowell defended gentlemen-farmers, who, he maintained, were responsible for the introduction of the best fruit grown in the state and implied that they had brought to the notice of practical farmers the principal root crops.—*New England Farmer,* IV (October 28, 1825), 107. As late as 1854 Charles L. Flint, Secretary of the Massachusetts Board of Agriculture, argued in defense of gentlemen-farmers.—Massachusetts Board of Agriculture, *First Annual Report* (Boston William White, 1854), pp. 12–14. For the decline of the early fairs see Neely, *The Agricultural Fair,* pp. 69–71.
[8] *Rural Register* in *De Bow's Review,* XXVIII (April, 1860), 470.

societies of Ohio, Michigan, and Wisconsin also rated well.[9] Altogether, the importance of these local and state societies and boards of agriculture, in focusing attention upon the knowledge of scientific agriculture then becoming available, cannot be overestimated.[10]

The new agricultural societies and fairs were conducted somewhat more for the larger group of practical farmers than the earlier ones had been, but there was still ground for criticism on this point. Gentlemen-farmers, wealthy livestock breeders, and business and professional men whose major responsibilities were in the cities, bought, and developed to a high state of perfection farm land outside the city limits. Here they experimented with every new idea that came along in farm practice, applied heavy quantities of guano and other soil-enriching compounds, brought in purebred Shorthorns and Merinos, took an active part in the agricultural societies, and offered their newly imported stock for premiums at the county and state fairs, and, of course, carried away many prizes. A Connecticut farmer in 1857 questioned whether the landed gentry should compete with working farmers for awards at the fairs.[11] Another criticism not easily answered was that the state fairs emphasized horse racing, and that prizes or purses for winners were much larger than those offered for livestock or other exhibits.[12] Races brought the crowds, which in turn supported the fairs, and it was not unusual for farmers to take an interest in the races and even to bet. Next to the races in popularity and attraction were the heavy-pulling contests of beautifully paired teams of oxen driven by skillful handlers who knew how to get the most co-operation and power out of their lumbering beasts.

State fairs and agricultural societies or boards proving successful, the next step was to establish a national society that might conduct a national fair. In 1852, the United States Agricultural Society was organized by leaders in agricultural work, chief of whom was Marshall P. Wilder of Massachusetts, who served as president for six years. It conducted investigations of farm machinery, published regular transactions, held annual conventions in Washington, at which issues affecting government policy toward agriculture were threshed out, and held national fairs at various cities in successive years.[13] The practice of buying and selling the livestock exhibited at county and state fairs was made a basic feature of the national fairs also, at which auctions were authorized. The fairs of the United States Agricultural Society on occasion drew

[9] Daniel Lee, "American Agricultural Literature," in Commissioner of Patents, *Report, Agriculture, 1852* (Washington, D. C.: Robert Armstrong, 1853), pp. 21–22.
[10] Neely, *The Agricultural Fair,* p. 85.
[11] *Homestead,* II (January 29, 1857), 298–299.
[12] *Wisconsin Farmer and North-Western Cultivator,* IX (February, 1856), 45–47.
[13] Neely, *The Agricultural Fair,* p. 97.

public support from nearby county and state fairs, and the resulting complaints were influential in bringing about their discontinuance.[14]

SOIL SURVEYS

Increasing familiarity with the newly developing agricultural and soil science led representatives of agricultural societies and fairs to urge the states to make surveys of the status of agriculture within their boundaries and to employ geologists and chemists to analyze the formation and content of their soils. Assisted by others who were eager to promote mining, they secured the establishment of geological bureaus that carried out intensive research in the geology and chemistry of soils. Beginning with Massachusetts in 1830, eighteen states, including every southern state but Florida and Louisiana, established geological bureaus or appointed geologists to make such detailed surveys of their rocks, soils, and minerals.[15] The surveys included information useful for agriculture at the time, and for agricultural experimental work later. The most intensive and detailed of these surveys was that undertaken by New York in 1836, *The Natural History of the State of New York*. In the course of the next twenty years at least twenty quarto volumes with superb illustrations were published at an expense of more than half a million dollars. The five volumes on agriculture included analyses of soils and the chemical composition of vegetables, grain, and milk, and treatises on meteorology and on injurious insects. Professor James F. W. Johnston, the distinguished British authority on agriculture, thought the volumes "very creditable" to the state but superficial in their analyses, wasteful in their treatment of questions already handled better elsewhere, and "insular" in that they revealed unawareness of, and perhaps unwillingness to profit from, scientific investigations abroad.[16]

The less technical and more useful portions of the geological surveys of the states were copied extensively in the agricultural journals, and were thereby brought to the attention of many farmers. The *New England Farmer*, for example, included thirty-one columns from the reports of Massachusetts, Maine, and New York.[17] Contributors in this journal early

[14] *Sixth National Exhibition by the United States Agricultural Society and the Virginia Central Agricultural Society to Be Held in the City of Richmond, Virginia . . . 1858* (Washington, D. C.: W. H. Moore, 1858), p. 5; Lyman Carrier, "The United States Agricultural Society, 1852–1860," *Agricultural History*, XI (October, 1937), 278 ff.

[15] Dirk J. Struik, *Yankee Science in the Making* (Boston: Little, Brown & Company, 1948), p. 188; Charles S. Sydnor, "State Geological Surveys in the Old South," in David Kelly Jackson, ed., *American Studies in Honor of William Kenneth Boyd* (Durham, N. C.: Duke University Press, 1940), pp. 86–109.

[16] James F. W. Johnston, *Notes on North America: Agricultural, Economical and Social* (2 vols.; Edinburgh: William Blackwood & Sons, 1851), II, 283–286.

[17] *New England Farmer*, Vols. XVII and XVIII (1838 and 1839).

accepted the work of the famous German scientist, Justus von Liebig, who taught that plants were dependent upon minerals in the soil, and that as these minerals, notably potash, lime, phosphorus, and sulfur, were depleted, they should be restored by the use of artificial manures or fertilizers to keep land in a good state of production.[18]

Edmund Ruffin, having long since undertaken his crusade in behalf of the application of "Calcareous Manures" to the soils of Virginia to restore their fertility, threw the influence of his powerful *Farmers' Register* in support of the movement for a geological survey of Virginia. In the first volume of this journal some thirty-two columns were devoted to long extracts from the writings of leading geologists, such as Amos Eaton and George W. Featherstonhaugh, and to the movement, ultimately successful, to induce the legislature to provide for the appointment of a state geologist. In 1837, the *Register* printed extensive extracts from the reports on the geology of Virginia, Maryland, and New York. True, much of this matter was devoted to precious minerals and to coal, iron, and building stone, but it also included such a useful item as Professor Eaton's "Application of Geology: As the Basis of the Science of Agriculture."[19] Science in the form of chemical analysis of soils was furthered by the appointment of agricultural chemists by several states. Maryland led off in 1847. The appointee was required to make studies of soils and soil needs, to prepare a report describing his findings, and to make public lectures throughout the state that would be useful to farmers. Virginia shortly followed this example.[20]

STATE AID TO AGRICULTURE

In an era when state governments developed their economies by state assistance to private enterprise, agriculture came in for its share of state aid. Bounties were offered to diversify and sustain agriculture, marketing regulations were enacted to prevent the sale of inferior produce, state warehouses were established, and state funds were spent to find remedies for potato rot and dangerous animal diseases. Wheat was not a new crop to Maine and Massachusetts in 1837 and 1838; on the contrary, its production was declining and farming in hill areas was being abandoned. It was thought that a bounty might serve to halt the decline.[21] Maine promised two dollars for the first twenty bushels of wheat produced by any farmer, and six cents for each additional bushel. Massachusetts gave ten cents a bushel. Neither state was successful in

[18] *New England Farmer*, XXIV (December 31, 1845), 212–213.
[19] *Farmers' Register*, Vol. IV (1837), *passim*, and I (September, 1833), 246–249.
[20] *Pennsylvania Farm Journal*, I (May, 1851), 42.
[21] Margaret Richards Pabst, "Agricultural Trends in the Connecticut Valley Region of Massachusetts, 1800–1900," (Smith College *Studies in History*, Vol. XXVI; Northhampton, Mass.: 1940), p. 14.

stimulating production or in checking decline. In the midst of the mania for silk production, numerous states offered bounties to encourage experimentation, despite failure that had met such efforts in the colonial period. Massachusetts, also caught up in the excitement about the sugar beet, offered a bounty for its production, but with little success.[22]

In the two great calamities which struck the farmers of Massachusetts most seriously, the state came to their aid. In the forties, when the potato blight was working its havoc, the commonwealth offered a bounty of $10,000 for a remedy.[23] Unfortunately, botanical science had not developed sufficiently at this time to cope with this dread plague, which ran its course unhampered by man. Pleuropneumonia was brought to Massachusetts in 1859 by cows imported from Holland. The disease spread swiftly, carrying with it a high death rate that threatened panic-stricken dairy farmers with ruin. The only method of treatment seemed to be to destroy infected cattle and to isolate those that had been exposed to the disease. A farmers' petition to the legislature for aid in combating the disease was met, after thirty-five days of deliberation, by an act authorizing the appointment of a commission and an appropriation of $10,000 to fight it. Unfortunately, during this long wait the disease had spread into large herds in Worcester County, and rumors of its appearance elsewhere were bruited about. The funds were quickly exhausted and an additional $15,000, privately pledged, proved insufficient to stamp out the disease. Two hundred and ninety thousand head of cattle worth $15,000,000, which were basic to the farmers' welfare, were at stake.

Governor Nathaniel P. Banks answered the cry for help by summoning the legislature into special session and urging it to take more drastic action. The legislature responded by requiring all infected animals to be killed and all suspected cattle to be quarantined, and providing compensation for losses. Heavy penalties were established for transporting or selling diseased animals. Never before had government moved so swiftly and so effectively to meet a calamity.[24] Other states watched

[22] L. P. Brockett, *The Silk Industry in America: A History* (New York: Silk Association of America, 1876), pp. 35 ff.; Commissioner of Patents, *Report, 1845* (Washington, D. C.: Ritchie & Heiss, 1846), pp. 805-875. *Boston Cultivator*, March 14, 1840; Oscar and Mary Flug Handlin, *Commonwealth: A Study of the Role of Government in the American Economy: Massachusetts, 1774-1861* (New York: New York University Press, 1947), p. 226.

[23] *Cultivator*, New Series, IX (October, 1852), 350-351.

[24] Massachusetts Board of Agriculture, *Eighth Annual Report, 1860* (Boston: William White, 1861), pp. 10 ff.; *New England Farmer* (June and July, 1860), 289-290, 293, 307, 321, 329-330; Commissioner of Patents, *Report, Agriculture, 1861* (Washington, D. C.: Government Printing Office, 1862), pp. 239-267, contains two articles on pleuropneumonia.

with concern the "terrible scourge," and seven—Maine, Vermont, Rhode Island, New York, Pennsylvania, Kentucky, and Ohio—appointed commissions to visit the infected district and gather information respecting methods of fighting the disease.[25] Connecticut appointed cattle commissioners who barred the admission of cattle from Massachusetts until cold weather ended fear of the epidemic.[26]

Growing awareness of the ravages of insects and plant diseases led farmers to ask for state aid in the field later called entomology. Tobacco worms; cotton bollworms; the wheat midge, rust, and the Hessian fly; squash bugs; potato bugs; and the curculio, or apple moth, all received frequent attention in the agricultural press, where many homely cures were proposed. Most of the suggestions for the destruction of insects were useless, and the only effective method of fighting the potato bug and the tobacco worm was to shake or pick the insects from the plants by hand and then destroy them. Arsenic compounds and other effective insecticides were to come later. In 1853, New York State, the first state to do so, appropriated $1,000 for the appointment of a state entomologist to study insects injurious to vegetation. Asa Fitch, the first appointee to this office, produced valuable descriptions of insects but little practical advice on how to combat the pests.[27]

New Hampshire farmers, troubled by the damages done by crows to cornfields, prevailed upon their legislature to offer a bounty for the destruction of the birds, only to find it necessary to repeal the measure shortly because people were hatching crow eggs and offering the young brood for the bounty.[28]

Another way in which the states showed their concern for farmers and planters was by enacting inspection laws and establishing standards for staple products. Cotton merchants complained about the trash, metal, and other extraneous objects they found in the bales, which necessitated repacking the cotton. They succeeded in getting some southern states, notably Mississippi and Georgia, to enact inspection laws to compel more careful packing.[29] From colonial times the legislature of Virginia had attempted to define standards for tobacco to be sold outside the state. Further tightening of these measures came in the nineteenth century. Practically all tobacco was subject to inspection in

[25] Ohio Farmer, IX (June 2, 30, 1860), 180, 202.
[26] Wisconsin Farmer, XII (October 1, 1860), 309.
[27] L. O. Howard, History of Applied Entomology (Smithsonian Miscellaneous Collections, Vol. LXXXIV; Washington, D. C.: Smithsonian Institution, 1930), pp. 43, 63–64.
[28] Homestead, IV (February 17, 1859), 347.
[29] Lewis Cecil Gray, History of Agriculture in the Southern United States to 1860 (2 vols.; Washington, D. C.: Carnegie Institution, 1933), II, 706.

private warehouses or in three public warehouses owned by the state and by the city of Richmond. Inspectors were nominated by the county courts and appointed by the governor, but after 1852 the power of selecting them was solely in the hands of the governor. In Virginia, as in North Carolina, inspection, although enforced with some vigor, was always involved in politics and a matter of frequent dispute and angry recrimination.[30] Maryland, South Carolina, Kentucky, Georgia, Missouri, and Louisiana also provided for inspection and warehousing facilities at various points.[31] The Louisiana law, modeled after Virginia and Maryland legislation, required the removal of the tobacco from the casks to determine the tare, the sampling of the tobacco in four places, and the sealing of the tobacco after inspection. Such measures came only after extensive deception and fraud had been practiced.[32] The success of the warehousing and inspection system was due to the fact that the warehouses were coming to be the centers in which most of the tobacco was sold at auction.[33]

New York State, anxious to raise the standard of its flour to a level equal to that of Baltimore flour, set up an inspection system for all flour exported to other countries. The inspection was not entirely satisfactory, however, for underweight contents and overweight tare on barrels continued to be reported. Other states adopted measures providing for the inspection of flour in barrels, more to protect consumers than to aid in marketing surpluses elsewhere.[34] Ohio laws specified that pork was to be packed in white-oak barrels, clearly marked with gross, tare, and net weight. Only clean meat, assorted according to grade, was to be packed. Louisiana established standards of meat packing in 1820 by requiring the use of two pecks of coarse salt with 6 per cent saltpeter and a saturated salt solution for each barrel of pork, and even more salt for beef. The act also provided for the appointment of a meat inspector and three repackers, and for assessing the owners the cost of repacking meat carelessly put up. Kentucky also lent its weight to the movement for high standards in meat packing.[35]

[30] Joseph Clarke Robert, *The Tobacco Kingdom: Plantation, Market and Factory in Virginia and North Carolina, 1800–1900* (Durham, N. C.: Duke University Press, 1938), pp. 76 ff.

[31] Ulrich Bonnell Phillips, *History of Transportation in the Eastern Cotton Belt to 1860* (New York: Columbia University Press, 1908), p. 55; James Neal Primm, *Economic Policy in the Development of a Western State: Missouri, 1820–1860* (Cambridge, Mass.: Harvard University Press, 1954), pp. 116–118.

[32] *De Bow's Review*, II (July, 1846), 42–46.

[33] Robert, *The Tobacco Kingdom*, p. 93.

[34] *United States Commercial & Statistical Register*, III (October 7, 1840), 228, quoting the *Journal of Commerce; Placer Times and Transcript*, Sacramento, August 12, 1853.

[35] *Southern Cultivator*, II (September 18, 1844), 151; Thomas Senior Berry, *Western Prices before 1861: A Study of the Cincinnati Market* (*Harvard Economic*

The importation of Peruvian guano having reached large proportions through increasing demand from the tobacco, wheat, and cotton plantations of the South, and its price being high, dealers mixed the bird manure with ground stone, clay, mortar, and sawdust, and sold this mixture, sometimes adulterated as much as 97 per cent, as pure guano. Beginning in 1846, Maryland and Virginia tried by law to regulate the quality of commercial fertilizers but not, however, with any substantial effect.[36]

Not all this state intervention in the business affairs of its citizens was wholly appreciated. Frank Ruffin, editor of the *Southern Planter*, driven to intense indignation by the increasing government interference in private business through the multiplication of inspection devices by states, hurled a terrific blast against them all. Inspection of guano, tobacco, wheat, gypsum, and packaging methods violated all principles of good government, he declared. They did not ensure stable quality nor prevent adulteration or fraudulent packing and marking, and their costs were excessive and unfairly levied; furthermore, they protected European buyers of American goods at the cost of Americans, but did not protect American buyers of European goods.[37]

Although many farmers and their representatives in Congress regarded the central government as one of limited and, indeed, closely circumscribed authority, they rarely permitted limitations to concern them when they sought favors. The development of the agricultural press, societies and fairs, state boards of agriculture, and farmers' clubs enabled the spokesmen of agriculture to bring their issues out into the open, to marshal support for common ends, and to exert influence upon the federal government in behalf of measures designed to aid specific interests. Increasingly the view was expressed that the government should aid agriculture through grants for farmers' education, experimental work, the collection of agricultural statistics, and distribution of new seeds and plants. Bounties, tariff protection, and an aggressive effort to secure a larger share of the world market for those agricultural goods of which the United States had a surplus—all had their advocates. Manufacturers were being aided through tariff protection, inventors through patent laws, merchants and traders through grants for internal improvements, and bankers through federal charters. Why should not the farmers also have the government's fostering care?

Studies, Vol. LXXIV; Cambridge, Mass.: Harvard University Press, 1943), p. 147; R. Carlyle Buley, *The Old Northwest: Pioneer Period, 1815–1840* (2 vols.; Indianapolis: Indiana Historical Society, 1950), I, 532; William T. Utter, *The First Frontier State*, in Carl Wittke, ed., *History of the State of Ohio* (6 vols.; Columbus: Ohio State Archaeological and Historical Society, 1942), II, 155.

[36] *American Cotton Planter*, II (February, 1854), 43; Gray, *History of Agriculture in the Southern United States*, II, 806.

[37] *Southern Planter*, XVI (March, 1856), 80–90.

In 1843 the Allen brothers brought together most of these proposals in an effective editorial in *The American Agriculturist*, although they conceded it was too early to press for them:

> What benefits might not result to the community of this broad Union, from the diligent selection of foreign seeds; their careful cultivation by scientific farmers; and the gratuitous and general distribution of such as on experiment were found to be adapted to increase our comfort and prosperity? The collection of the latest and best information and means of agricultural improvement, and its distribution among the citizens of the United States; the establishment of a great national school for the exclusive education of farmers; the employment of men of science to investigate and develop new principles on the subject, all these are objects which would seem to commend themselves to an assembly that once voted themselves "the most free and enlightened body in the world." [38]

FEDERAL AID TO AGRICULTURE: TARIFFS

Agriculture acquired a sounding board in 1820 and 1825, when the United States House of Representatives in 1820, and the Senate in 1825, established standing committees on agriculture. This was not accomplished without a struggle, however, for although commerce and manufactures already were well served by committees, there was doubt in the minds of some members of Congress of the need for committees on agriculture. A senator from Maine even questioned whether any issues would rise that would call for study by a committee on agriculture. The existence of the committees assured a more favorable attitude by Congress toward the wishes of special interests among the farmers and their societies.[39]

When the silk craze hit the country in the late twenties, the House of Representatives authorized the compilation of a manual on silk culture and its possibilities in the United States, and the federal government published two other brochures to stimulate the fast-growing business of *Morus multicaulis* and the silk industry.[40]

Both tobacco and rice planters felt aggrieved at the tariff discrimination that their commodities suffered in foreign markets. Since their inclination was strongly toward free trade for the United States, it was not inconsistent of them to urge that their government take steps to secure lower rates abroad for American tobacco and rice.

[38] *American Agriculturist*, I (February, 1843), 332.
[39] *Annals of Congress*, 16 Cong., 2 Sess., November 15, 1820, p. 439, and 19 Cong., 1 Sess., December 9, 1825, pp. 3–7.
[40] For references see note 25 in Chapter XIV. Also, J. H. Cobb, *A Manual Containing Information Respecting the Growth of the Mulberry Tree, with Suitable Directions for the Culture of Silk* (Boston: Carter and Hendee, 1832).

Tobacco planters' indignation at foreign discrimination reached a high point in 1837. At a convention in Washington they urged the United States to make every effort to secure concessions, particularly from the German states. In response Congress created a select committee to examine the tobacco trade with foreign nations and authorized the appointment of special consular agents to negotiate for more favorable treatment for American tobacco. For the next three years numerous meetings and conventions were held to urge action, even punitive action, against foreign countries if they were not amenable to negotiation. Three successive Congressional resolutions urging additional pressure were adopted, and the American position was strongly presented at London. The American minister took the matter up with English tobacco importers and manufacturers, the Chancellor of the Exchequer, the President of the Board of Trade, and members of Parliament, all without effect.[41] Again in 1859 and 1860, agitation against the high duties levied on American tobacco abroad led to the introduction of a resolution in Congress protesting against discriminatory duties and limitations on importation and urging the government to take steps to secure their abatement. Instructions were forwarded to American ministers requesting that they bring the matter to the attention of the governments to which they were accredited.[42] For the protection of the tobacco planters as well as of the rice planters, Southerners could favor the use of governmental powers when those interests were in jeopardy and raised no constitutional scruples as they did when other sections also sought to use federal powers, implied or explicit, to further their interests.

Although there were many fewer rice planters than tobacco producers, their influence on national economic policy was more persistently felt and produced favorable action. As early as 1829 the Agricultural Society of South Carolina expressed dismay that rice constituted no part of the diet of the personnel of the United States Army, though many thousands of barrels of wheat flour were used to feed the soldiers. It urged upon the War and Navy departments "the great advantages and benefits which would attend the introduction of Rice as a part of the food of the Army and Navy . . ." as well as the benefits which such patronage would bring to South Carolina planters.[43] The pressure of the rice planters

[41] *Farmer and Gardener* quoted in *Farmers' Register,* IV (April, 1837), 747–748. The *American Farmer,* which became the official paper of the tobacco producers represented in the Washington convention in 1840, contains many references and accounts of the proceedings of these planters' meetings. See especially New Series, I, 332, 353, 364, 369, 377, 387. Bingham Duncan treats of this episode in "The Tobacco Trade in Anglo-American Diplomacy, 1830–1850," *Emory University Quarterly,* V (March, 1949), 48–55.

[42] *Rural Register,* I (January 15, 1860), 213.

[43] *Southern Agriculturist,* II (December, 1829), 574.

and traders induced the national administration to urge through its diplomatic and consular agents that England and the German states should make more favorable rates on the importation of American rice. A claim for a rebate of £80,000 for overpayment resulting from a change in the impost was also asked of England. Skillful negotiations persistently followed through four administrations produced favorable action; the claims were allowed, impost rates were reduced, and American rice flowed more freely abroad.[44]

Cotton planters, apprehensive lest they lose some of their foreign markets, were also fearful that the production of cotton might expand more rapidly than the market could absorb it. They watched with foreboding the emergence of cotton planting in India, speculated about its future, condemned Great Britain for attempting to make itself independent of American cotton, and besought their government to collect data about cotton produced elsewhere.[45] They feared discrimination against southern cotton in favor of cotton from Egypt or India, and were successful in having a provision written into a commercial treaty with the Kingdom of the Two Sicilies that made sure there would be no penalties invoked against American cotton in that country.[46] In 1856, in compliance with a Congressional resolution, the Department of State submitted a detailed analysis concerning the "tariff duties and custom-house regulations applicable to American cotton." [47] The following year Congress appropriated $3,500 to enable the Commissioner of Patents to collect information on the consumption of cotton in the industrial nations.[48] Like all good bureaucrats, John Claiborne, who was appointed to make the survey, protested that the appropriation was wholly inadequate, but he found it sufficient to cover the cost of a pleasant jaunt to Europe, where he collected a *potpourri* of miscellaneous information requiring one hundred pages in the agricultural volume of the Patent Office.[49] Notwithstanding their anxiety, producers of short-staple cotton had little to fear from foreign competition.

[44] Bingham Duncan, "Diplomatic Support of the American Rice Trade, 1835–1845," *Agricultural History*, XXIII (April, 1949), 92–96.

[45] In 1840 and 1841 the *Farmers' Register* copied from other journals a number of accounts of cotton planting in India.—VIII, 406, 582, 653; and IX, 274, 536. Other examples are in *Southern Cultivator*, II (February 21, December 25, 1844), 24, 206; *De Bow's Review*, I (April, 1846), 318–319; *New Orleans Price Current*, October 4, 1851, quoting *London Globe*; Ft. Pickering, Tenn., *American Eagle*, March 7, 1842, quoting *New Orleans Advertiser*.

[46] Treaty of October 1, 1855; 11 *U. S. Stat.* 654.

[47] J. A. Turner, *The Cotton Planters' Manual* (New York: C. M. Saxton & Company, 1857), pp. 249–276.

[48] Act of March 3, 1857; 11 *U. S. Stat.* 226.

[49] Commissioner of Patents, *Report, Agriculture, 1857* (Washington, D. C.: James B. Stedman, 1858), pp. 319 ff. For criticism of overemphasis on cotton in the com-

While southern rice, tobacco, and cotton producers expressed anxiety about their status in foreign markets, sugar, hemp, and flax producers sought to preserve the American market for themselves by government action and were ardent supporters of protection.

Congress early showed its sensitivity to the welfare of the sugar planters. The establishment of a high revenue rate of 2½ cents a pound on sugar imports in 1800 was kept at that level or higher until 1833, by which time the duty had become highly protective. Thereafter Louisiana Democrats could favor high sugar rates for revenue purposes, and Whigs could support them for protective purposes. Despite this unanimity of opinion, import rates on sugar were reduced in 1833, 1846, and 1857, but not disastrously. Furthermore, sugar production was no longer an infant industry, but was a lusty adult that employed all the best techniques and machines and operated on a large commercial scale. The tariff no longer affected the prosperity of the industry as it had earlier; sugar planters firmly supported the Whig party, not solely because of its views on the tariff but also because it was more receptive to planter interests on other questions and less influenced by the attitudes of the small farmer.[50]

Congress's concern for the sugar industry led it to instruct the Secretary of the Treasury to prepare a manual on the most modern methods of producing sugar. In response to these instructions, Benjamin Silliman, the great Yale chemist, compiled in 1833 a *Manual on the Cultivation of the Sugar Cane and the Fabrication and Refinement of Sugar,* which analyzed the industry and made recommendations for improvements in methods of growing the cane and refining the sugar. Some of Silliman's recommendations were far in advance of the time, but were to be introduced by some of the most modern producers by the fifties.[51]

The Democrats were not oblivious to the needs of the sugar planters, certainly not John Slidell. When the House of Representatives in 1856 had under consideration a deficiency item to increase the appropriation to the Agricultural Branch of the Patent Office for procuring and dis-

missioner's reports, see *Wisconsin Farmer and North-Western Cultivator,* IX (February, 1857), 75.

[50] J. Carlyle Sitterson, *Sugar Country: The Cane Sugar Industry in the South, 1753–1950* (Lexington: University of Kentucky Press, 1953), pp. 177 ff.; Arthur Charles Cole, *The Whig Party in the South* (Washington, D. C.: American Historical Association, 1913), *passim,* including maps in rear; Roger W. Shugg, *Origins of Class Struggle in Louisiana* (Baton Rouge: Louisiana State University Press, 1939), p. 151. *The Plough, the Loom and the Anvil,* I (November, 1848), 288–289, contains a "Planters' Manifesto," signed by prominent Natchez planters, in which they declared their approval of the high rates of 1842. Among the signers were the most influential sugar and cotton planters of the area, including William Bisland, Levin R. Marshall, Stephen Duncan, Benjamin L. C. Wailes, and William J. Minor.

[51] Benjamin Silliman, *Manual on the Cultivation of Sugar Cane . . .* (Washington, D. C.: F. P. Blair, 1833).

tributing cuttings and seeds and for collecting agricultural statistics, strict constructionists from Missouri, Virginia, Arkansas, Kentucky, and Georgia opposed the item, while northern representatives from Pennsylvania, Indiana, Maine, and New York favored it. Later, in the same session, an appropriation of $75,000 was voted for the identical purpose but without discussion. To the discomfiture of Northerners, particularly the watchful and suspicious Horace Greeley, the Pierce Administration seemed to favor the use of the enlarged appropriation for the encouragement of the cultivation of tea and, more important, the improvement of the sugar industry, neither offering anything to the North.[52]

Sheep farmers and hemp and flax producers were the most assiduous of all agricultural groups in their efforts to secure tariff protection. Sheep were raised more largely in New England, New York, and Ohio; flax and hemp were principally identified with Kentucky, Missouri, and Ohio. Representatives of these states had won adequate protection for these goods in the tariffs of 1816 and 1824, but in 1828 the rates were pushed to higher levels. Flax and hemp duties were made $60 a ton; wool was to pay 4 cents a pound plus an ad valorem tax of 40 per cent. In 1832, flax producers lost their protection, and the duty on hemp was cut to $40 a ton. Sheep farmers were able to marshal sufficient support to prevent any substantial change in the duties on wool. The rapid emergence of sheep raising in the Northeast in the thirties and its almost equally rapid decline thereafter are not to be attributed to changes in tariff rates.[53]

Supporters of hemp production continued to work for additional government aid. In 1841 they induced Congress to direct the purchase of American hemp for the Navy wherever possible. Two years later, Congress appropriated $4,000 to establish hemp-buying agencies and, in 1845, $50,000 to buy American hemp. Halfhearted efforts were made to carry out directives of Congress, but the Navy clearly preferred Russian hemp, and its bungling efforts to find the right quality and quantity of American hemp were of little benefit to the western hemp interests. Nor was the restoration of the $40-a-ton impost of foreign hemp in 1842

[52] *Congressional Globe*, 34 Cong., 1 Sess., 1855–1856, pp. 958–960; *New York Tribune* in *Indiana Farmer* and comments thereon, V (December 1, 1856), 360–361; Commissioner of Patents, *Report, Agriculture, 1856* p. viii; Nelson Klose, *America's Crop Heritage: The History of Foreign Plant Introduction by the Federal Government* (Ames: Iowa State College Press, 1950), pp. 34–37.

[53] Henry Stephens Randall, *Sheep Industry in the South: Comprising a Treatise on the Acclimation of Sheep in the Southern States and an Account of the Different Breeds* (Philadelphia: J. S. Skinner & Son, 1848), pp. 158 ff.; Frank W. Taussig, *Tariff History of the United States* (New York: G. P. Putnam's Sons, 1910), pp. 90 ff.; Chester Whitney Wright, *Wool-Growing and the Tariff* (Boston: Houghton Mifflin Company, 1910), Chap. 5; Harold Fisher Wilson, *The Hill Country of Northern New England* (New York: Columbia University Press, 1936), p. 82.

markedly successful. Later tariff reductions in 1846 and 1857 did no good to the hemp people. In seeking high tariff protection the hemp bloc in Congress came into conflict with the more powerful cotton bloc, which felt pinched by the high cost of cotton bagging made from hemp.[54]

GUANO IMPORTS

Tobacco, cotton, and wheat planters of the South, the principal users of guano, brought the ills of the fertilizer trade to the attention of the government and urged aid in solving them. This valuable bird manure had been imported from the Chincha Islands off the coast of Peru in growing volume since the early forties. The limited supply and active demand for it in England, in Europe, and in the southern states, combined with the system of state control instituted by the Peruvian government, which had pledged to its British creditors, revenues derived from the monopoly, permitted the maintenance of a high price for the rich manure, ranging from $45 to $60 a ton.[55] Experimental work in its use was carried on by gentlemen-farmers in the North and planters in the South, who did not have to figure outgo too closely. Their early favorable reports and the vigorous promotion given to guano by dealer-editors, such as Solon Robinson and Anthony B. Allen of the *American Agriculturist,* and the editors and publishers of the *American Farmer* and the *Rural Register,* created a widespread interest in guano just at the time when agricultural science was beginning to flourish. The demand for guano led to importation in some years in the fifties of as much as 175,000 tons— at $50 a ton, $8,750,000.[56]

Congress was repeatedly urged in conventions, memorials, petitions, and resolutions to take action to lower the price, to break the monopoly, and to question Peru's ownership of the guano islands. It was even proposed that the railroads be compelled to transport guano and lime at the lowest possible rates.[57] Presidents Fillmore, Pierce, and Buchanan

---

[54] James F. Hopkins, *History of the Hemp Industry in Kentucky* (Lexington: University of Kentucky Press, 1951), pp. 87 ff., 177.

[55] *Southern Planter* in *American Cotton Planter,* II (January, 1854), 14.

[56] The *New York Tribune,* July 4, 1855, gives the following figures of guano imports (in tons):

1848–1849	21,243	1851–1852	50,054
1849–1850	11,740	1852–1853	36,034
1850–1851	97,881	1853–1854	175,849

See also *Southern Cultivator,* IX (June, 1851), 82; Rosser H. Taylor, "Fertilizers and Farming in the Southeast, 1840–1850," Pt. I, "Introduction of Guano," *North Carolina Historical Review,* XXX (July, 1953), 305 ff.

[57] *Southern Planter,* XV (January, 1855), 20; and XVI (June and August, 1856), 178, 244; *Southern Cultivator,* XVII (October, 1859), 302.

and Secretaries Webster, Everett, and Marcy struggled with the issue. In his first annual message to Congress in 1850, Fillmore, egged on by Congressional interest in the guano trade, declared:

> Peruvian guano has become so desirable an article to the agricultural interest of the United States that it is the duty of the Government to employ all the means properly in its power for the purpose of causing that article to be imported into the country at a reasonable price. Nothing will be omitted on my part toward accomplishing this desirable end.[58]

That this was no idle threat was shown by the action of Daniel Webster, Secretary of State, in denying the validity of the claim of Peru to the nearby Lobos Islands—like the Chincha group, valuable for their guano deposits—and setting up the basis for an American claim. At the same time, an American naval vessel was ordered to proceed to the islands to protect American ships loading guano. Belief in Manifest Destiny was widespread, being strengthened in this instance by agricultural and commercial interests. Fortunately, on second thought, top officials of the State Department became convinced that the United States had not the shadow of a claim to the islands and, somewhat mortified, withdrew the naval vessel and the claim.[59]

Interference in Peruvian government matters did not stop here, however, for the Peruvian monopoly was creating great indignation. Clashes between Americans attempting to load guano on their vessels and Peruvian authorities regulating the trade led to demands for redress.[60] Long delays in the resulting diplomatic negotiations having produced no relief from the high price of Peruvian guano, angry Southerners, with the aid of the powerful *De Bow's Review,* proposed to levy a punitive tariff, not for revenue or to protect a rival American industry, but to compel the Peruvian monopolists to sell their guano in the American market at $40 a ton instead of at the prevailing price, which ranged from $45 to $60. Guano imported when the domestic price was $40 was to be allowed free entry; when it sold for $40 to $47, the duty was to be $4 a ton; when it sold for $47 to $50, the duty was to be $10; when it sold for more than $50, the duty would be 60 per cent. *De Bow's* editor conceded that the "principles of the bill are somewhat at variance with our revenue

[58] James D. Richardson, comp., *Messages and Papers of the Presidents, 1789–1897* (10 vols.; Washington, D. C.: Government Printing Office, 1896–1899), V, 83.

[59] For conflicting views on the handling of these negotiations, see the treatments by Clyde Augustus Duniway and Foster Stearns in Samuel Flagg Bemis, *The American Secretaries of State and Their Diplomacy* (10 vols.; New York: Alfred A. Knopf, Inc., 1927–1929), VI, 110 ff.; and Roy F. Nichols, *Advance Agents of American Destiny* (Philadelphia: University of Pennsylvania Press, 1956), pp. 156 ff.

[60] Richardson, *Messages and Papers,* V, 212.

policy. . . ." [61] The measure did not become a law, but the issue was kept before Congress till the eve of the Civil War. [62]

In 1856, Congress was persuaded by the senators of Virginia, Maryland, and Delaware, acting in conjunction with William E. Seward of New York, who was not often caught supporting Virginia interests, to adopt a peculiar and potentially dangerous bill that sought to assure guano at a fair price to southern planters and high profits to discoverers of guano-bearing islands. The measure provided that where there was no adverse claims by another country, the discoverer of such islands should have exclusive right to exploit the deposit under the protection of the American government and could sell the guano *in situ* for $4 a ton or loaded on vessels for $8 a ton but only to Americans and for consumption solely in the United States. [63] Thus did a combination of northern politicians concerned for the welfare of commercial interests and southern planter representatives enact a measure that smacked of the dollar diplomacy of a later generation. Within a short time this Congressional indiscretion brought the United States into near conflict with Haiti and Hawaii over islands claimed by them. It was a sorry story that brought no relief in lower prices to the planters. [64]

THE PATENT OFFICE AND AGRICULTURE

Farm spokesmen were not content with the government's concern for special crops but urged that an agency or board of the government was necessary to do for farmers what the Treasury Department was doing for commercial interests. Thus the *Quarterly Journal of Agriculture, Mechanics and Manufactures* came out in 1835 with a memorial to Congress urging that an agricultural survey of the United States should be undertaken to provide statistics of crops planted, yields, the amount of labor

[61] *De Bow's Review*, XVIII (January, 1855), 33–34; Gray, *History of Agriculture in the Southern United States*, II, 805–806; *Congressional Globe*, 24 Cong., 1 Sess., July 22, 1856, pp. 696–700, and 36 Cong., 1 Sess., March 26, 1860, p. 1362, for discussions of guano imports and costs.

[62] For the documents, see *Senate Executive Document* No. 59, 31 Cong., 1 Sess., June 29, 1850, Vol. XII; *Senate Executive Document* No. 80, 31 Cong., 1 Sess., September 27, 1850, Vol. XIV; *Senate Executive Document* No. 109, 32 Cong., 1 Sess., August 21, 1852, Vol. X; *House Executive Document* No. 70, 33 Cong., 1 Sess., March 1, 1854, Vol. X; *House Report* No. 347, 33 Cong., 1 Sess., July 31, 1854, Vol. III; *Senate Executive Document* No. 63, 35 Cong., 1 Sess., June 8, 1858, Vol. XIII; *Senate Executive Document* No. 25, 35 Cong., 2 Sess., February 5, 1859, Vol. VII.

[63] Act of August 18, 1856; 11 *U. S. Stat.* 119; *Congressional Globe*, 34 Cong., 1 Sess., July 24, 1856, p. 1741.

[64] For the difficulties into which the American government fell as a result of the Act of 1856, see Nichols, *Advance Agents of American Destiny*, pp. 185 ff.

employed, and the character of farm implements, after the model of the great English surveys. To carry out this survey the *Journal* recommended that a board of agriculture be constituted that should make reports to Congress, and publish the findings for distribution among farmers.[65] "Agriculture should be patronized by the Government," said Jesse Buel in the *Cultivator*, in September, 1837.[66]

Conditions seemed ripe in the thirties for the federal government to use the survey method of facilitating agricultural improvement. Therefore, when Henry L. Ellsworth was appointed Commissioner of Patents in 1836, action soon followed. The combination of his practical experimental work in Indiana, which he brought frequently to the attention of farmers in their journals, and his promotional activities in Washington made Ellsworth one of the best-known figures in agriculture.[67]

Ellsworth collected data concerning crops and methods of plowing, planting, cultivating, and feeding. He wrote widely to agricultural authorities and had forwarded to American consuls abroad circulars requesting information about crops and the collection of seeds and cuttings of plants that he planned to set out in the "propagating garden" run by the Patent Office. Sketches of farmers' experience in experimenting with new crops, fertilizers, methods of planting, and breeding practices were brought together and provided the basis, along with the statistics, for the printed material included in the *Annual Report* of the commissioner.[68] In 1837, before he had any public funds for that purpose, Ellsworth began the free distribution of seeds. Two years later, Congress was persuaded to make the first appropriation—$1,000—to the Patent Office for the collection of agricultural statistics.[69] In his reports to Congress, Ellsworth urged it to establish an agricultural bureau to collect and disseminate useful information for farmers, and when constitutional scruples threatened to intrude, he suggested the use of a portion of the Smithson Fund for this purpose.[70]

Ellsworth also collected information about agricultural machinery.

[65] *Quarterly Journal of Agriculture, Mechanics and Manufactures* in *New England Farmer*, XIII (April 1, 1835), 300–301.

[66] *Cultivator*, IV (September, 1837), 113.

[67] Paul W. Gates, "Land Policies and Tenancy in the Prairie Counties of Indiana," *Indiana Magazine of History*, XXXV (March, 1939), 6 ff.

[68] From his first *Annual Report* as Commissioner of Patents for 1837, Ellsworth showed his keen concern for agriculture and desire to foster it. See also *Union Agriculturist*, January, 1842, with communication from Ellsworth in Herbert Anthony Kellar, *Solon Robinson: Pioneer and Agriculturist* (*Indiana Histsorical Collections*, Vols. XXI and XXII; Indianapolis: Indiana Historical Bureau, 1936), I, 296–299.

[69] *Cultivator*, IV (March, 1837), 8; 5 *U. S. Stat.* 354.

[70] Arthur Charles True, *History of Agricultural Experimentation and Research in the United States* (U. S. Department of Agriculture, *Miscellaneous Publication* No. 251; Washington, D. C.: 1937), pp. 25–26.

This work tied in well with his duties as Commissioner of Patents. Samples of implements used in the United States were exhibited in the National Gallery, where it was hoped farmers would examine them. Under the imaginative and literate pen of Ellsworth, the *Annual Report* of the Patent Office, with its numerous articles and sketches devoted to farm machinery and farm practices, in addition to the usual detail of patents, became a much-sought document. True, the statistics of crops produced an angry response from some states, which felt that their yields were underestimated.[71] All agreed, however, that the descriptive articles were valuable. Ellsworth declared early in 1844 that, despite the large printings of the *Report*, it had not been possible to supply the demand for the previous year.[72] Old John Quincy Adams, embittered because he heard that Ellsworth was to be displaced for political reasons, sat long on March 31, 1845, reading the previous *Report*, which he found

. . . so interesting . . . the House ordered twenty-five thousand extra copies of it to be printed for circulation by the members. He [Ellsworth] has for a succession of years been improving it from year to year, till it now forms a volume of five hundred pages, and a calendar of mechanical and agricultural inventions and discoveries more sought after than any other annual document published by Congress. Ellsworth has turned the Patent Office from a mere gimcrack-shop into a great and highly useful public establishment.

After more than two hours devoted to reading, Adams "was finally obliged to break off so as not to lose the whole day." [73]

Later-day readers will not find quite so absorbing the 520 pages of the *Report*, of which 428 are devoted to agriculture, with articles on the alpaca, mills for grinding bones, the manuring and steeping of seeds, and the saline matter of grain.

Ellsworth's successor, Edmund Burke, was responsible for the *Report* for 1845, a huge volume of 1,376 pages, of which 1,085 were devoted to agricultural problems. Much of it was copied from farm journals. Objections were made to its eclectic character and to its excessive cost, estimated at $11,000, and questions were raised concerning the constitutional authority for a government agency to deal with matters that were essentially private. It was even stated by some that the collection of agricultural statistics by the government "would endanger the liberties of the people." Solon Robinson, no unfriendly critic of the agricultural work of the Patent Office, called the 1845 volume a "bundle of trash." The outcry influenced

[71] *Southern Planter*, III (May, 1843), 112.

[72] Commissioner of Patents, *Report, 1843* (Washington, D. C.: Blair & Rives, 1844), p. 3.

[73] Charles Francis Adams, *Memoirs of John Quincy Adams* (Philadelphia: J. B. Lippincott Company, 1877), XII, 188–189.

Congress, which refused to appropriate money for the agricultural work of the Patent Office, and it lapsed for a time.[74] Popular demand and the anxiety of congressmen to have something more attractive than the *Congressional Globe* to distribute among their constituents led to a quick reversal and, beginning with 1847, Congress regularly appropriated funds for the collection and dissemination of agricultural statistics and seeds and for special investigations. Forty-five thousand copies of the *Report* for 1848 were ordered printed.[75]

Meantime, the political character of the agricultural work of the Patent Office, especially after the displacement of Ellsworth, its subordinate position, and the inadequate support it received irked many agricultural leaders, who flayed the agency for its "lamentable lack of judgment," its award of positions to political spoilsmen, its favoritism in the distribution of seeds and publications, "its agricultural Farce. . . ." [76] Mapes's *Working Farmer* wrote of its "apology for a seed room, located in the cellar," and called its agricultural work a "miserable subterfuge for calming the anxiety of the agricultural public, by the distribution of a few seeds. . . ." [77] The *American Agriculturist* called the free seeds "worthless trash"; their distribution was "a jobbing affair, for the benefit of a few favorites, instead of a public project. . . ." The Massachusetts Horticultural Society appointed a committee to memorialize Congress to stop the abuses in the agricultural section of the Patent Office. To the question, Where is the agricultural department? this answer was offered:

Pent up in the cellar of the patent office, and cannot be found at midday without a candle; and when found, a single clerk struggling to get up the report.

De Bow's Review, while conceding that the "Agricultural Branch of the Patent Office undoubtedly does some good" expressed alarm at the "enormous sums" it spent, the class of duties it performed, and the dangerous precedent it set in giving away seeds.[78] *Homestead* insisted that private enterprise could print the *Report* more expeditiously and less expensively.[79] The *American Agriculturist* conducted a vendetta of a personal character against the Patent Office but it did bring out the major weak-

[74] *American Agriculturist,* V (August and December, 1846), 261, 377; Commissioner of Patents, *Report, 1848* (Washington, D. C.: Wendell and Van Benthuysen, 1859), pp. 11-12.

[75] Commissioner of Patents, *Report, 1848,* title page.

[76] *Southern Planter,* XI (February, 1851), 62-63; *Rural New Yorker* in *Ohio Cultivator,* IX (February 1, August 15, 1853), 44, 250.

[77] *Working Farmer,* V (May 1, 1853), 49.

[78] *American Agriculturist,* XVI (April, 1852), 430; and XVII (February and April, 1853), 40, 104; *Indiana Farmer,* III (May 15, 1854), 248; *De Bow's Review,* XXIII (July, 1857), 77.

[79] *Homestead,* III (January 7, 1858), 249.

ness of continuing the pseudoscientific and statistical work relating to agriculture under an agency with which it had no functional relationship:

> This tacking agriculture as a sub-department on to still another sub-department, is not only placing it below its proper position in point of importance, but this very fact so depreciates its dignity, that little attention is given to placing at its head a man of acknowledged superior abilities.[80]

Daniel J. Browne, as editor and compiler of the agricultural volumes of the Patent Office from 1854 to 1859, and as head of the agricultural work of the agency for most of that period, came in for sustained and bitter attack from the *Cultivator*, the *Ohio Farmer*, and the *American Agriculturist*, with which he had formerly been associated. These journals maintained that most of Browne's compilations were "old stuff" drawn from the agricultural press of years before; that the seeds he distributed had long since been tried and found worthless, or were filled with weed seeds; and that the *Reports* contained many other "errors and absurdities. . . ." Browne was "either intentionally guilty of deception, or ignorantly guilty, by lack of knowledge," and his opinions were the "merest twaddle" compiled by a man who secured his position by political influence.[81] Some of the most vehement critics of Browne's work in the Patent Office were in the seed business and disliked the free distribution of seeds by the government.[82]

Horace Greeley maintained that the Agricultural Branch of the Patent Office, by spending taxpayers' money in compiling material for the annual volume, and printing, binding, and conveying hundreds of thousands of copies of it to people in all parts of the country, was undermining and threatening to destroy by unfair competition the agricultural press. He held that "the gigantic Book and Pamphlet manufacture, now carried on at the public cost, in Washington, is in every way wrong and pernicious—that it robs some of their hard earned means to confer a doubtful and undeserved advantage on others. . . ."[83]

Within his own division Browne's actions produced friction and sharp conflict, reminding one much of the not uncommon bureaucratic bickering and jealousy of more recent days. A subordinate, who subsequently

---

[80] *American Agriculturist*, XVIII (April, 1859), 104. See also the attack of the Philadelphia *North American* in *American Agriculturist*, XVII (August, 1858), 230.

[81] *Ohio Farmer*, V (March 1, 1856), 33. The same editor belabored the *Tenth Annual Report* of the Ohio State Board of Agriculture equally vigorously for its flimsy paper, small type, feeble presswork, typographical blunders, pictures of mangy cattle, and long delay in printing.—*Ohio Farmer*, V (December 20, 1856), 202.

[82] *Dictionary of American Biography*, Allen Johnson and Dumas Malone, eds. (21 vols.; New York: Charles Scribner's Sons, 1928–1937), II, 165. For a defense of Browne, see *American Cotton Planter and Soil of the South*, New Series, II (September, 1858), 276–282.

[83] *Ohio Farmer*, IX (July 7, 1860), 212.

became a distinguished entomologist, resigned in 1859 after clashing with Browne over the latter's insistence on appearing as the author of everything written by employees of the Agricultural Section of the Patent Office. Townsend Glover, on resigning, called Browne "a notorious plagiarist & wants to take all the credit he can from other men's brains—nay the last report was actually cabbaged by him from other authors, & then strung together . . . without any knowledge of the subject he was writing about. . . ." Browne was said to be jealous of Glover's growing reputation.[84]

Serious political charges were brought against the Patent Office in 1856 and 1857, to the effect that the $75,000 appropriated for the distribution of seeds was being used solely for the "purchase, transportation and distribution of sugar-cane slips for the sugar-growing states, leaving all other requirements unprovided for," and that the person in charge of the search for disease-free cane "perhaps had never seen the plant in cultivation. . . ."[85] Southerners were offended because sorghum was advanced by the Patent Office as a substitute for cane sugar. Others were disgruntled because the agency had provided quantities of its free seeds to agricultural periodicals, which were used by them as bait to secure subscriptions.[86]

This barrage of criticism against the Agricultural Section of the Patent Office, in sharp contrast to the highly favorable press it had received when Ellsworth was commissioner, reached a high point when the Buchanan Administration was under attack from many angles. Some defense of the Patent Office seemed advisable. Officials tried to meet the criticisms by the publication of a document justifying its actions, which the *American Agriculturist* called nothing but a whitewash.[87] Though he was upheld by his superiors for a time, Browne was dropped from the Patent Office in 1859 because he was too much of a liability to the administration.

Notwithstanding the attacks upon the agricultural work of the Patent Office, Congress showed increasing liberality in voting it appropriations ranging from $3,000 in 1847 to $75,000 in 1857.[88] Consequently, the agricultural operations of the agency were ambitiously expanded. A chemist

[84] L. O. Howard, *History of Applied Entomology* (*Smithsonian Miscellaneous Collections*, Vol. LXXXIV; Washington, D. C.: Smithsonian Institution, 1930), p. 37.
[85] *Working Farmer*, VIII (December 1, 1856), 217; *De Bow's Review*, XXVII (November, 1859), 611.
[86] *Wisconsin Farmer*, X (March, 1858), 113.
[87] *American Agriculturist*, XVII (July, 1858), 198. Cf. *Congressional Globe*, 35 Cong., 1 Sess., January 6 and June 1, 1857, pp. 206, 2587.
[88] 9 *U. S. Stat.* 160; 11 *U. S. Stat.* 89. The figures of the Commissioner of Patents in his *Report, Agriculture, 1857*, differ considerably from the total for 1856, being shown there as $105,000.

was employed to make quantitative analyses of soils, experiments were made with grape culture and wine making, insects and diseases affecting the cotton plant were studied by the agency's entomologist, and attention was paid to imported varieties of grains and vegetables.

The most valuable and, on the whole, the most interesting parts of the *Reports* were the detailed statements of individual farming experiences that were submitted to the commissioner in response to a questionnaire concerning the success of farmers with various crops, livestock, fruit, the use of manures, and the methods of attacking diseases and parasites. Naturally, there is wide variation in the replies, which are published *in extenso,* but the quality of the information is high and constitutes a major source for a study of agriculture of the time. This scattered, diffuse, and unintegrated information, together with the articles and statistics, made the Patent Office *Annual Report* "a work of real worth and utility, a treasure, indeed, to the farmer who is fortunate enough to get a copy. If the supply were equal to the demand, it would give greater satisfaction." Thus spoke Chester Hunt of Somerset, Michigan, whose own contribution to the *Report* for 1852 was one of the best.[89]

With such an array of practical and impractical information, accompanied by interesting, and in some years colored, illustrations of fruits and animals, it is understandable why congressmen were so much concerned to have copies of the *Annual Report* for distribution among their constituents. In 1849, when the Patent Office was placed under the jurisdiction of the newly created Department of the Interior, it separated the agricultural matter from the business of patents and printed it thereafter as Volume 2, with the title "Agriculture." Editions of 145,420 were printed in 1851, 167,920 in 1854, and 267,920 in 1855.[90]

The *Report* in 1851 contained a number of articles long remembered for their significance then and for the future. Professor John P. Norton contributed a scientific article on "The Mineral Manure Theory," which brought together the best information concerning methods of fortifying soil. Representative John L. Taylor of Ohio prepared a "History of the Ohio Company for Importing English Cattle," which is a basic document on early importations of cattle. Jonathan B. Turner submitted his "Plan for an Industrial University" that was widely copied and was the most influential document in the movement for industrial and agricultural education.

As is true of the farm journals which continually adjured farmers to follow the best of modern practices, it is difficult to assess the significance of the work of the Patent Office. Editors could easily find fault with

[89] Commissioner of Patents, *Report, Agriculture, 1852* (Washington, D. C.: Robert Armstrong, 1853), pp. 273–280.

[90] Commissioner of Patents, *Report, Agriculture, 1857,* p. 25.

its volumes for their poor organization, repetition, heavy borrowing, and poor printing, but they had to concede that there was much of value in them. The volumes compared well with the general run of agricultural periodicals.[91]

CREATION OF THE DEPARTMENT OF AGRICULTURE

Fearful that the agricultural work of the Patent Office might be cut off or harmed by its subordination to the major obligations of that office, farm groups became convinced that it should be established as a separate office. Beginning in 1849, efforts were made to have Congress establish a separate bureau of agriculture in the Department of the Interior or, better still, a new department to which the agricultural work of the Patent Office should be transferred. Memorials and resolutions of numerous state legislatures and agricultural societies were transmitted to Washington in behalf of this objective, and bills were introduced to carry it out. Meetings of the United States Agricultural Society were annually wracked by bickering over resolutions favoring the creation of such a department.[92] Like other reforms then under consideration, the move ran into opposition from southern conservatives and legalistically minded congressmen who doubted both the wisdom of and the constitutional authority for such legislation. Time was with the advocates of the movement, but throughout the fifties a minority succeeded in holding it back.[93]

The transfer of the Patent Office to the newly established Department of the Interior in 1849 was accompanied by the segregation of the agricultural work of that agency in what amounted to a separate division but one that was still subordinate to the Commissioner of Patents. The beginnings of work in entomology, the propagation of plants in a small botanical garden, chemical analysis of vegetable foods, improvement in the collection of agricultural statistics, and expansion of efforts to collect abroad new species of plants and encourage their cultivation all date from this period. By 1860 the Agricultural Division of the Patent Office was important enough to have a superintendent, an entomologist, a gardener, four clerks, and a number of assistants. No one could doubt that the Agricultural Division, to function properly, needed to be separated from the Patent Office. In 1862, when the blighting influence of the opponents of

[91] New England Farmer, III (November 22, 1851), 378.
[92] Rural New Yorker in Southern Planter, XII (August, 1852), 241.
[93] Congressional Globe, 31 Cong., 1 Sess., January 8, April 18, and May 13, 1850, pp. 119, 769, 983; Horticulturist, IV (June, 1850), 544, 572; New England Farmer, II (January 19, 1850), 30; Southern Planter, XII (August, 1852), 241; and XVIII (January, 1858), 29–30; De Bow's Review, XVI (April, 1854), 427 ff.; Working Farmer, IV (August 1, 1852), 122–123; American Farmer, Fifth Series, I (February and May, 1860), 240, 347; Cincinnatus, Vols. IV and V, passim.

change was gone from Congress, the Agricultural Division was elevated to a separate Department of Agriculture with authority to employ chemists, botanists, entomologists, and other scientists trained in modern agricultural fields.[94] This measure, with the land-grant act for agricultural colleges of the same year, marked the end of a quarter century of struggle by friends of the farmer to induce the federal government to adopt a definite agricultural policy which included the fostering of agricultural education and scientific work to improve farm practices.

By 1860 it could no longer be said, as it had been earlier, that farmers were neglected by the government, that society was not interested in their problems, or that agriculture was backward, slow to change. Farmers were recognized politically as a potent group and, when not divided by extraneous issues, could make their influence felt. Some of agriculture's special interests, such as the cotton, sugar, and tobacco planters and the sheep raisers in the early period, ranked among the country's most influential pressure groups. Farmers supported a flowering of agricultural journalism and numerous societies and fairs, which, together with the publications of the state boards of agriculture and the agricultural volumes of the Patent Office to which they contributed their experiences, were making possible a widespread familiarity with the best of modern farm practices. An increasing number of farmers could subscribe to periodicals, could experiment with new techniques, including the use of guano, lime, and other soil-improving minerals, and could buy the new farm machines. Agriculture had come a long way in the period between 1815 and 1860.

[94] True, *History of Agricultural Experimentation*, pp. 28 ff.

CHAPTER XVI

Agricultural Periodicals
and Journalists

NO other economic group in the early nineteenth century was the recipient of so much free advice, practical as well as impractical, as were the farmers; nor, by the thirties and forties, was any other group so well represented by state and national societies, by fairs, by weekly and monthly journals, and by numerous "experts" who wrote on its problems regularly for newspapers and periodicals.

THE ALMANAC

Prominent in early rural literature was the almanac. George Lyman Kittredge went far afield to make amusing, as well as instructive, his *Old Farmer and His Almanack*, a study of the farmers' chief reading matter other than the Bible.[1] *The Farmer's Almanack*, published annually in Boston from 1793, was followed by farmers' almanacs in New York (1802), Vermont and Maine (1807), New Jersey (1809), Connecticut (1816), and Pennsylvania and South Carolina (1817), most of them published for state agricultural societies. In addition to the calendar and the usual play with astrology, these almanacs contained bits of information about mammoth cabbages, rye grass, the grubworm, and mildew in wheat; advice on choosing a horse; and numerous homilies on manuring land, careful attention to breeding animals, the maintenance of fences, early planting, weeding of crops, draining low lands, and seed selection.[2] Like the gar-

[1] George Lyman Kittredge, *The Old Farmer and His Almanack* (Boston: William Ware & Co., 1904).
[2] Clarence S. Brigham, *An Account of American Almanacs and Their Value for Historical Study* (Worcester, Mass.: Antiquarian Society, 1925). *passim.*

deners' page in modern newspapers, a Connecticut farmers' almanac in 1820 succinctly summarized for each month the various tasks farmers should pursue to have orderly and successful operations.[3] Considerable space was devoted to reprinting articles from British and American serials of agricultural import. The farmers' creed was thus summarized in one of these almanacs:

> Let this be held the Farmer's Creed—
> For stock, seek out the choicest breed;
> In peace and plenty let them feed;
> Your land sow with the best of seed;
> Let it not dung or dressing need;
> Inclose, plough, reap, with care and speed;
> And you will soon be rich indeed! [4]

One farmer, claiming to have taken the *Old Farmer's Almanac* from the first in 1793, noticed that its predictions about the weather " 'Expect a storm about these days,' etc., answered just as well for the weather in the house as for the weather out doors." [5] Whatever the value of predictions concerning the weather, the advice and suggestions concerning farm practices were on the whole sound and useful. One may question whether the almanacs fell into the hands of people most needing that advice. However, judging by the large number which have survived and have been acquired by libraries it would appear that they were widely distributed and read.[6]

WEEKLY NEWSPAPERS

The weekly newspaper appearing in most county seats and other growing communities gradually replaced the almanac as the principal medium for disseminating information. Supported as they were by the official advertising patronage of town, county, state, and national governments, these papers were invariably committed to some political faction or party and perforce devoted much of their space to defending "true principles." [7] Papers with titles like the *Farmers' Chronicle* of Richmond, Kentucky, the *Farmers' Museum* of Keene, New Hampshire, the *Republican Farmers' Free Press* of Herkimer, New York, and the *Republican*

[3] *An Agricultural and Economical Almanac, for the Year of Our Lord 1820* . . . (New Haven, Conn.: Sidney's Press, 1820), *passim*.

[4] *An Agricultural and Economic Almanack, for* . . . *1817* . . . (New Haven, Conn.: Hezekiah Howe, 1817), p. 4.

[5] *Homestead*, IV (February 17, 1859), 347.

[6] Bibliographies of almanacs published in all the New England states, New Jersey, and New York have appeared.

[7] Milton W. Hamilton, in his *The Country Printer* (New York: Columbia University Press, 1936), Pt. IV, briefly treats some of the forms of government patronage.

Farmer of Bridgeport, Connecticut, were not truly farm journals, but were filled with political bickering and the usual borrowing from metropolitan papers.[8] On the other hand, the *Gloucester Farmer* of Woodbury, the *Bergen Farmer* of Hackensack, and the *Hunterdon Gazette and Farmers' Weekly Advertiser*, all of New Jersey, did have useful information for farmers.[9] Many papers of the time made a point of printing an occasional column with captions: "Agricultural," "To Farmers," or "Farmers' Work."[10] Admonitions on soil treatment, early planting, seed selection, weed elimination, and directions for the making of cider were thus offered. As was true of the almanacs, much of the material in these columns was borrowed, but that did not affect its usefulness.

The mid-nineteenth-century city newspaper sought patronage among the rural as well as the urban reading public. Best known and most influential was the *New York Tribune,* which came nearest to being a truly national paper. Horace Greeley, its crusading editor, was deeply interested in both rural and urban problems, and thought that if the unemployed classes in the cities were encouraged to emigrate to the public lands of the West the position of the workingman would be improved. Under Greeley's editorship, the paper was outstanding for the breadth of its news coverage and the vigor with which it championed reforms. The *Tribune's* period of greatness was the fifties, when it fought the slave states on such questions as the admission of free states, the free distribution of the public lands, and government aids to agriculture. Its arguments carried conviction deep into rural America. Northern farmers had good reason to approve the *Tribune's* position on Kansas, slavery in the territories, free homesteads, and government aid to agriculture, but the paper's coverage of agricultural matters doubtless seemed more important to them. For three dollars a year farmers could subscribe to the semiweekly edition, with its minutely detailed accounts of crops and their prices in all parts of the country, and its sundry long and practical articles on such subjects as sprouted wheat, turnips as feed for cattle, the culture of cranberries, farm work for winter, and methods of improving corn culture.[11] Veterinary and horticultural matters received attention; indeed, scarcely

[8] In the Huntington Library there are at least fourteen newspapers for 1830, each from different communities, with "Farmer" or "Farmers" in the title.

[9] Carl Raymond Woodward, *Development of Agriculture in New Jersey, 1640–1880* (New Brunswick: New Jersey Agricultural Experiment Station, 1927), pp. 89 ff.

[10] Examples: *Lewisburg Journal,* Lewisburg, Penn., July 17, 1830; *Anti-Masonic Sun,* Watertown, N. Y., September 7, 1830; *Constitutionalist,* Augusta, Ga., July 30, 1830; *Vermont Chronicle,* Windsor, August 13, 1830. Both Woodward, *Development of Agriculture in New Jersey,* and Richard Bardolph in his *Agricultural Literature and the Early Illinois Farmer* (University of Illinois *Studies in the Social Sciences,* Vol. XXIX; Urbana: University of Illinois Press, 1948), pp. 58 ff., examine the volume and nature of agricultural information in the newspapers of their respective states.

[11] *Semi-Weekly New York Tribune,* July 3, October 12, November 27, 1855.

a phase of agriculture was neglected. Greeley's own fertile mind and facile pen were supplemented by those of a half-dozen other able agricultural journalists.[12]

Other papers, such as the *New York Times,* the *Chicago Tribune,* and the *Cleveland Plain Dealer,* found it useful to include agricultural columns. Illinois newspaper readers were probably as familiar with the practical and thoughtful writings of M. L. Dunlap and Dr. John Kennicott as readers of the *New York Tribune* were with Solon Robinson's sage counsel.[13] *Harper's Weekly* included numerous bits of practical advice to farmers. Under the caption "Winter Work for Farmers" they were urged to prepare their wood supply for the following winter, repair fences, make rails, protect the manure piles, and house their stock from the wintry blasts.[14]

FARM JOURNALS

It was in the agricultural periodicals that farmers found the most practical articles and information. They were written specifically for rural folks, had little or nothing in them that was not of interest to farmers and their wives, and their contents were presented in a homey fashion. The *Agricultural Museum,* the first of the farmers' journals to appear in the nineteenth century, lasted for only two years (1812–1814).[15] The publication of agricultural periodicals really dates from 1819, with the appearance of the *American Farmer* (1819–1834) in Baltimore, edited by John S. Skinner, and of the *Plough Boy* (1819–1823) in Albany, edited by Solomon Southwick.[16] They were followed by the establishment of the *New England Farmer* (1822–1845), edited by Thomas G. Fessenden, of Boston; the *Genesee Farmer* (1831–1839), edited by Luther Tucker, of Rochester; the *Farmers' Register* (1833–1842), of Shellbanks and Petersburg, Virginia, edited by Edmund Ruffin; and the *Cultivator* (1834–1865), of Albany, edited by Jesse Buel. Thereafter a host of other farm journals appeared, many of which had but short careers.

Edmund Ruffin's *Farmers' Register* established a high standard of agricultural journalism by its unremitting efforts to improve farm practices, the intellectual and literary quality of its material and the idealism

[12] Earle D. Ross, "Horace Greeley and the Beginnings of the New Agriculture," and Roy Marvin Robbins, "Horace Greeley, Land Reform and Unemployment," *Agricultural History,* VII (January, 1933), 3–41.

[13] Bardolph, *Agricultural Literature and the Early Illinois Farmer,* pp. 60 ff.

[14] *Harper's Weekly,* I (January 24 and February 7, 1857), 62, 91.

[15] Claribel Barnett, "The Agricultural Museum: An Early American Agricultural Periodical," *Agricultural History,* II (April, 1928), 99–102.

[16] Harold S. Pinkett, "The American Farmer: A Pioneer Agricultural Journal, 1819–1834," *Agricultural History,* XXIV (July, 1950), 146–151.

—sometimes perverted—of the editor. Like all southern farm journals, it was intended for planters and had little appeal for the small farmer. Unfortunately, the zeal with which Ruffin warred against banking and currency vagaries and the amount of space he gave to these questions repelled readers and ultimately forced suspension of the paper.[17]

Next to the *American Farmer* and the *Farmers' Register* in influence and circulation among southern journals stood the *Southern Agriculturist* (1826–1846) of Charleston, South Carolina; the *Southern Planter* (1841—) of Richmond, edited for a time by the able Frank Ruffin; the *Southern Cultivator* (1843–1935) of Augusta, Georgia; and the *American Cotton Planter* (1853–1861) of Montgomery, Alabama, which claimed 10,000 subscribers.[18] Elsewhere in the South was a scattering of meagerly supported journals with small formats and a large proportion of articles cribbed from northern periodicals. A writer in *De Bow's Review*, answering his own rhetorical question, "How many agricultural newspapers are there in the [cotton] country?" said, "Two or three seven-by-nines, starving for patronage." [19]

Most influential of the farm journals were the four great New York state periodicals: the Albany *Cultivator*, successively edited by Jesse Buel and Luther Tucker; the *American Agriculturist* (1842—), founded in New York City by A. B. and R. L. Allen and pushed to the top by Orange Judd, a former student of agriculture at Yale; *Moore's Rural New Yorker* (1849—) founded at Rochester, by D. D. T. Moore; and the *Country Gentleman* (1853–1955), established at Albany by the indefatigable Luther Tucker. These journals succeeded in stirring up farmers to write of their experiences and had as many as 400 to 600 correspondents penning homely little articles or notes about yields, prices, weather, Yankee inventions, fairs, and fertilizers.[20]

In the trans-Allegheny country, the *Ohio Farmer* (1852—), edited and published at Cleveland by Thomas Brown, and the *Ohio Cultivator* (1845–1864), edited at Columbus by M. B. Bateham, set high standards by the comprehensiveness of their agricultural matter, the persistence with which they pushed purebred livestock, particularly Shorthorn cattle, and the trenchant articles of Mrs. Bateham on women's labor on the farm. Like those of the *New England Farmer* and the *Farmers' Register*, their columns were allotted to subjects of more concern to the large capitalistic

[17] Avery Craven, *Edmund Ruffin, Southerner: A Study in Secession* (New York: Appleton-Century-Crofts, Inc., 1932), pp. 61 ff.

[18] Weymouth T. Jordan, "Agricultural Societies in Ante-Bellum Alabama," *Alabama Review*, IV (October, 1951), 249.

[19] *De Bow's Review*, III (January, 1847), 4.

[20] Albert Lowther Demaree, *The American Agricultural Press, 1819–1860* (Columbia University *Studies in the History of American Agriculture*, No. 8; New York: Columbia University Press, 1941), *passim;* William Edward Ogilvie, *Pioneer Agricultural Journalists* (Chicago: Arthur G. Leonard, 1927), pp. 29 ff.

farmer than to the small operator. The *Prairie Farmer* (1840—), edited by that eccentric and speculatively inclined booster of Chicago, John S. Wright, has had a long and notably influential career. In the Far West the *California Farmer* (1854–1889), was well known for the forcefulness of its editorial views, particularly on the need for early adjudication of California land claims.

The historian of the *American Agricultural Press* estimates that more than 400 farm journals were published in the ante-bellum period, and of these he gives bibliographical information for 100. Most of these slowly withered away through inadequate support, but some flourished. In 1840, 30 or more farm journals were being published with a combined circulation in excess of 100,000. A contemporary writer boasted of the "pregnant fact" that more agricultural journals were "published in the United States than in all the world beside." [21] On the eve of the war there were between 50 and 60 such journals, with an estimated circulation of 250,000 to 350,000. Another estimate allowed for 25 or more journals in the northern states, with a circulation of 250,000, and 6 or 8 journals published in the southern states, with a circulation of 35,000.[22] Allowing for duplications, it appears that one farmer of ten subscribed to an agricultural journal. Many more were among the 250,000 to 300,000 buyers of the semiweekly edition of the *New York Tribune.*[23]

All agricultural periodicals had much in common; at the same time they reflected the individual interests of their editors as well as state and sectional differences. Editors and other contributors, some of whom were practicing farmers, assumed that most farmers employed crude and simple extractive methods to get as much from their land as possible with the least effort, destroyed the forest cover without regard to future needs of fuel in their desire to get land cleared, cultivated thinly, planted crops on the same tracts year after year without rotation, plowed up and down slopes, did nothing to maintain or protect soil, permitted their manure to waste away, kept nothing but the poorest grade of stock, and did not properly house or feed them. The editors continually admonished their

[21] Commissioner of Patents, *Annual Report, 1852, Agriculture* (Washington, D. C.: Robert Armstrong, 1853), p. 16. For a list of seventy-eight agricultural and horticultural periodicals published in 1868, see Commissioner of Agriculture, *Annual Report, 1868* (Washington, D. C.: Government Printing Office, 1868), pp. 608–611.

[22] Demaree, *The American Agricultural Press*, pp. 17–18; *Eighty Years' Progress in the United States from the Revolutionary War to the Great Rebellion* (New York: New National Publishing House, 1864), p. 98. The *Mark Lane Express*, quoted in *Homestead*, IV (September 15, 1859), 829, gives slightly different statistics: twenty-one journals in the free states enjoying a circulation of 233,600, and six journals in the slave states with a circulation of 32,250.

[23] *Eighth Census of the United States, 1860, Population* (Washington, D. C.: Government Printing Office, 1864), p. 663; Jeter Allen Isely, *Horace Greeley and the Republican Party, 1853–1861* (Princeton, N. J.: Princeton University Press, 1947), p. 338.

readers to discard wasteful practices, make full use of manure, apply lime, marl, or gypsum to the land, rotate their crops, plow deeply, use selected seed, and improve their livestock.[24] This was all very practical, but most readers, who presumably were the better educated among farmers and generally the better farmers, were already sufficiently familiar with such elementary ideas and were following them.

More valuable were the discussions of tillage practices; analyses of the results of the application of lime, marl, or guano to land; reports on plant and animal diseases and parasites and the methods of combating them; descriptions of the various breeds of horses, cattle, hogs, and sheep; and discussions of specialized treatment of fruits and vegetables and of veterinary problems.[25] On all these questions there were differences of opinion, and the wise editor sought to stimulate discussion and controversy. Contemporary readers surely found these controversial treatments the spiciest and most rewarding, though at times they were long drawn out.

COMMON CRITICISMS OF THE PRESS

A common theme in the agricultural press was criticism of farmers' efforts to acquire and to operate too much land. Advocates of the new scientific agriculture urged that small farms intensively cultivated by deep plowing, frequent weedings, the application of manure, rotation, horizontal rows, and due regard for seed selection promised more than large farms extensively cultivated. Western periodicals took up the theme, urging that few immigrants had the means to bring as much as 160 acres into cultivation, and maintaining that they should be content with 40 or 80 acres. Larger purchases would so scatter settlements as to delay the coming of roads, schools, churches, and other social facilities.

In *The Plow*, which lasted for only one year, Solon Robinson excoriated as "barbarous cruelty" the law that "gives one man power . . . to wrest from another and his hopeless family, their only shelter, however humble, while it bears the name of home" and called for homestead exemption from forced sale for debt.[26] He moved toward the views of Horace Greeley and Henry George of a later time in suggesting that farm

[24] Typical of the somewhat carping criticisms directed at farmers is the editorial in the *Southern Planter* entitled "Common Errors of Farmers" in which "land skinners," the policy of cultivating too much land, waste of manure, and defective soil culture, are condemned.—XVIII (September, 1858), 562–565.

[25] George F. Lemmer analyzes the contents of Colman's *Rural World* in "The Agricultural Program of a Leading Farm Periodical, *Colman's Rural World*," in *Agricultural History*, XXVIII (October, 1949), 245 ff.

[26] *The Plow*, I (May, 1852), 164. Robinson's views on homestead exemption earlier propounded in the *Indiana State Sentinel*, December 14, 1847, are reproduced in Herbert Anthony Kellar, *Solon Robinson: Pioneer and Agriculturist* (Indiana His-

homes be made inalienable. Robinson's humanity and his awareness of the pressing character of farmers' debts are thus shown. On the other hand, Robinson swallowed all the sophistries and pseudoscientific nonsense preached by the most blatant slavery defenders, whom he ardently cultivated on his travels through the South. His defense of slavery written for the arch exponent of the slave system—*De Bow's Review*—must have pained his northern friends, who could not fail to realize what a distorted picture his southern planter-hosts had given him of their unique institution.[27]

John S. Skinner expressed a political and social philosophy similar to Robinson's in his revived *American Farmer* (1839-1897) of Baltimore. He stated in 1840 his opposition to usury laws and to distributing to the states the proceeds from the sale of public lands, and fulminated against the extravagance of state legislatures and their misdirected energies. Instead of distribution, he favored grants of land to aid in construction of internal improvements.[28]

Agriculture profited greatly from the work of the brilliant German scientist, Justus von Liebig. When his *Organic Chemistry in Its Application to Agriculture and Physiology* appeared in the United States it was widely quoted. Crotchety old Edmund Ruffin, who apparently felt that some of his own well-known ideas should have been considered by Liebig, differed from him in a number of ways but conceded that his book had received "more respectful attention and applause than any on agriculture" and proceeded to borrow whole pages from it.[29] Skinner's *American Farmer*, whose editor had no professional position at stake, went the whole way in accepting Liebig's work. In the months after its publication, the *American Farmer* made numerous allusions to Liebig, borrowed long extracts, and urged that his book be placed in every library.[30] Readers

---

torical Collections, Vols. XXI and XXII; Indianapolis: Indiana Historical Bureau, 1936), II, 161.

[27] The headings of the long article shows the nature of the argument: "Early History of Negro Slavery; Slavery in the States; The Bible Question of Slavery; Physical Characteristics of the Negro; Safety of the Slave Institution; Fidelity of Negro Slaves; Slavery compared with English Poor Labor; Misery of British Operatives, etc." It appeared in *De Bow's Review*, VII (September and November, 1849), 206-225 and 379-389, and is reprinted in Kellar, *Solon Robinson: Pioneer and Agriculturist*, II, 253.

[28] *American Farmer*, New Series, I (January 22, February 26, and April 15, 1840), 273, 314, 370.

[29] *Farmers' Register*, IX (August 31, 1841), 459-469.

[30] *American Farmer*, New Series, III (1841-1842), 17 ff. Adam Beatty cribbed whole sections from Liebig in his *Southern Agriculture, Being Essays on the Cultivation of Corn, Hemp, Tobacco, Wheat, Etc. And the Best Method of Renovating the Soil* (New York: C. M. Saxton & Company, 1843), pp. 131 ff. For a later but strong attack upon Liebig's "ammoniacal theory," see the *Prairie Farmer*, XI (October, 1851), 447.

of Liebig were provided with much information about soil constituents and the chemical actions that plants produce in soil. They were made aware that lime, marl, and gypsum, when applied to soils, revived crops, though just why was not entirely clear. Liebig's notion that plants drew upon the mineral deposits in the soil, which had to be replenished, led to searches for ways of restoring depleted stores of potash, phosphorus, and sulfur.

Farmers, becoming increasingly aware that their past practices had wrought great damage to many areas, were receptive to the ideas of the new chemical age which agriculture was now entering and avidly read about the new discoveries. Their leaders experimented with a wide variety of ways of restoring fertility, including the spreading on the land of both coal and wood ashes, old wool, human excrement, cottonseed, seaweed, ground fish, salt, muck and mud, as well as manures, guano, lime, marl, and gypsum.

Enterprising promoters were prompt in attempting to aid farmers in reversing the soil losses about which the social scientists were now lecturing. Mixtures of guano with ground phosphoric rock, lime, and other minerals appeared on the market under a rash of fancy names such as Improved Superphosphate of Lime, Phosphatic Lime, Reese's Manipulated or Phospho-Peruvian Guano, and Ammoniated Super Phosphate of Lime.[31] One dealer, taking the name of the German chemist, styled himself the Liebig Manufacturing Company and advertised that its poudrette —dried contents of privies—would mature vegetables ten days earlier and more perfectly than would any other manure.[32] Many frauds were perpetrated on farmers, and a good deal of nonsense was written by advertisers and serious writers who were beyond their depth in the knowledge of chemistry. Fantastic claims were made for the new fertilizers and many impractical suggestions were put forth. As one kindly critic said at the time, concerning much of the popular writing about chemistry and soil analysis,

. . . with what is true and practical, not a little, too, that is visionary and impractical often finds a place in our agricultural journals, under the name of agricultural chemistry. . . .[33]

[31] For these and other trade names, see the advertising section of the *Southern Planter*, Vol. XVIII (1858).

[32] *Homestead*, I (February 21, 1856), 350.

[33] Charles L. Fleischmann in the *American Polytechnic Journal*, I (January–June, 1853), 59. The same critic gently chided editors of farm journals and, inferentially, managers of country fairs for their emphasis upon large animals, large vegetables, and large crops without providing "the details of management, proportions, etc., which may render them practically useful." This practice of publishing details of the largest ox, the heaviest pumpkin, and the biggest egg lasted far beyond our period.

Farmers were urged to build up the humus as well as the mineral content of their land. This, it was pointed out, could be accomplished through the use of clover in rotation with other crops. Liberal use of straw and shavings for bedding livestock would absorb the urine and, when spread on the land, would contribute humus as well as ammonia to it. Even the compost piles on which table refuse was discarded would be beneficial to the soil.[34]

Northern farms had a larger number of animal units to the cultivated acres and a greater quantity of manure than the depleted farms and plantations of the South, and were therefore not as much in need of guano. Furthermore, there was more rotation of crops in the North, including grass and clover, which tended to maintain soil quality. Northern farm journals, instead of devoting space to discussions of the miraculous effects resulting from the use of guano, urged farmers to preserve and protect their manure and to spread it on the land at the right season.

Southern journals other than the *American Farmer* were more provincial in their outlook and coverage than were those elsewhere because of the unique character of southern staples and also because they found it necessary to defend slavery. Space was devoted to arguing the inferiority of the Negro race and the economic indispensability of slavery, and to essays on the duties of overseers and the free Negro "nuisance." [35] The fact is that the contents of southern journals were designed for planters; rarely was there anything in them written particularly for the yeoman-farmer.[36] Not having the popular support enjoyed by such northern journals as the *Country Gentleman* and the *American Agriculturist*, they were generally one-man affairs and in consequence had to borrow heavily from other periodicals. Since there were few southern journals, and all of them were in the same boat, each copied lavishly from northern periodicals.[37] True to the section's views on strict interpretation of the federal constitution, some southern journals expressed grave doubts as to

[34] *Ohio Farmer*, VIII (January 22, February 12, 1859), 25, 56.

[35] "Moral Benefits in Slavery," *American Cotton Planter*, I (June, 1853), 172–174, and in *Southern Planter*, XIII (August, 1853), 244–245. Also *Southern Planter*, XVI (May, 1856), 149–153; XVII (July and November, 1857), 414–415, 671; XIX (October, November, December, 1859), 643–651, 664, 672, 723–740; *American Cotton Planter*, I (September and December, 1853), 283–285, 353–356; Craven, *Edmund Ruffin, Southerner*, pp. 130 ff.

[36] A communication from an overseer on one of Colonel Joseph Bond's many plantations in Georgia in which success in producing a high ratio of cotton, corn, and pork to the number of slaves is attributed, at least in part, to the owner's shrewdness in providing the former with a subscription to the *Soil of the South*, is effusively welcomed by the editor. The suggestion is made that other planters should similarly provide their overseers with the journal.—*Soil of the South*, IV (March, 1854), 70–71.

[37] *Farmers' Register*, IX (March, April, May and June, 1841), 156, 163, 244, 277, 324, 362, 372, 375.

the wisdom of creating a federal Department of Agriculture and of sub-
sidizing through grants of land to each state the establishment of agricultural colleges. They also found fault with the effort of the Patent Office
to disseminate information concerning farm practices through the publication of an annual volume on agriculture and to diversify crops through
free seed distribution. It should be added that southern journals were not
alone in such criticisms.[38]

In the North, *The Plough, the Loom and the Anvil,* of Philadelphia,
and Jesse Buel's *Cultivator* took up cudgels for protection which, they
maintained, by aiding the laborer and the manufacturer would benefit the
farmer.[39] Condemnation of slavery was expressed by the *Boston Cultivator* and opposition to the extension of slavery in the territories was
announced by the Utica *Rural American.*[40] Western farm journals were
solidly for government aid to agriculture but had doubts about providing
that aid through grants of land that might become the prey of speculators.[41] With these exceptions, political discussion was rigorously pro-
scribed in the farm journals.

Agricultural editors centered their attention upon farm practices.
They were not drawn into religious or political controversies nor did they
suffer the sickly sentimental fiction of the time to mar their columns. They
did do a great deal of moralizing and devoted space to the temperance
movement. They neglected, however, two of the farmers' greatest problems—credit and marketing—but on the whole they provided the sub-
scribing farmers with trade journals that compare well with other special-
interest periodicals of the time.

There is surprisingly little of interest, and less of use, to farm women
in the agricultural press. A few journals contained columns for women,
but ordinarily they did not appear for long, which perhaps indicates lack
of interest. The *Ohio Cultivator* contained trenchant editorials by the
wife of the editor, in which she criticized the kind of farm work many
women had to perform.[42] Its rival, the *Ohio Farmer,* not to be outdone,
carried an account of the tasks the farmer's wife had to perform in the
course of her day, which made her a mere drudge:

[38] *Southern Planter,* XVII (January and March, 1857), 3–10, 135; *New England
Farmer,* XI (April, 1859), 172–173. The *Southern Planter,* XVII (April, 1857), 211,
copied from the *Ohio Farmer* an attack upon the Morrill bill, then under consideration to grant land to the state for agricultural colleges. See also Bardolph, *Agricultural
Literature and the Early Illinois Farmer,* pp. 88–89.

[39] *The Plough, the Loom and the Anvil,* II (July, 1849), 1–11; *Cultivator,* IV
(June, 1837), 61–62.

[40] Demaree, *The American Agricultural Press,* pp. 82–83.

[41] Paul W. Gates, *The Wisconsin Pine Lands of Cornell University* (Ithaca; N. Y.:
Cornell University Press, 1944), pp. 8 ff.

[42] *Ohio Cultivator,* IV (May, 1856), 111.

her life is one of the most unremitting toil. It is nothing but mend and patch, cook and bake, wash and iron, churn and make cheese, pick up chips and draw water, bear children and nurse them. The family enlarges, the husband grows wealthy, becomes important in the community, rides to town each day, takes his ease when he chooses; but the cares of his faded and broken down wife, know no relaxation.[43]

Two Yankee farm sisters, anxious to dispel the notion that New England farm girls did not perform manual work, boasted that in addition to washing, ironing, dusting, scrubbing, cooking, spinning, and dress-making, they milked and churned, and molded butter.[44] When the hydraulic ram was proved an effective device to conduct water to a higher elevation than its source, it was offered as a means to ease the path of the farmer in watering his stock, not as a way of getting water into the house for the many tasks of the housewife.[45] An illustration of thinking then current concerning the position of women in farm economy as taken from the *Southern Cultivator* is instructive:

To Select a Good Wife

Choose a woman who has been inured to industry, and is not ashamed of it. Be sure she has a good constitution, good temper, and has not been accustomed to "*dashing*" without knowing the value of the means, is not fond of novels, and has no giddy and fashionable relations, and you need inquire no further—*she is a fortune.*[46]

In this same connection James F. W. Johnston related a story he picked up about Canadian women as farm wives as compared with New York women. A New York farmer is quoted as saying:

I'll go over to Canada for a wife when I marry. When I come home at night she'll have a nice blazing fire on, and a clean kitchen, and a comfortable supper for me; but if I marry a New Yorker, it'll be, when I come home, "John, go down to the well for some water, to make the tea;" or, "John, go and bring some logs to put on the fire, to boil the kettle." No, no; a Canadian woman's the wife for me.[47]

[43] *Springfield Republican* in *Ohio Farmer,* VI (March 7, 1857), 40.

[44] *Homestead,* II (April 23, 1857), 494. A "Massachusetts Lass" replied to this communication, saying that in her region the spinning wheel had given way to the sewing machine, the butter churn was operated by water power, and wood was sawed by wind power.—*Ibid.,* II (May 21, 1857), 558.

[45] *American Agriculturist,* VII (February, 1848), 50–51; *Homestead,* III (November 19, 1857), 144.

[46] *Southern Cultivator,* II (March 20, 1844), 48.

[47] James F. W. Johnston, *Notes on North America* . . . (2 vols.; Edinburgh: William Blackwood & Sons, 1851), I, p. 263.

PROBLEMS OF THE PRESS

Having to manage advertising, circulation, editorial, and printing departments, few editors had time to dig out information and to write original material sufficient to keep their journals supplied with copy. Consequently, they borrowed heavily from each other and from the publications of the state agricultural societies, the United States Patent Office report on *Agriculture,* farm columns in the metropolitan newspapers, and English books and serials on agricultural problems. On occasion this borrowed material, written as it was by specialists, was quite valuable. Farmers were urged to write of their experience with crops, livestock, and fruit, and as the period progressed, more and more of their accounts were published. Inevitably these included a vast deal of repetition, for they went over the same ground time after time without bringing out anything new or a fresh point of view, but the writing was of such a homely character that the reader finds interesting bits of local information so lacking in much of the copy.

As subscription lists grew and income increased, the editors were able to afford assistance in getting out their journals and to journey though regions of heavy patronage, soliciting additional subscribers and preparing the inevitable "Notes by the Way" on their experiences and observations. In these notes, which appear in practically every journal by the fifties if not before, are to be found some of the best descriptions of contemporary farm practices, though one suspects that they were not altogether typical. Furthermore, criticism, in the rare instances in which it was offered, was very light so as not to give offense to patrons.

Advertising was not always the major source of income that it has become in more recent times. The *Farmers' Cabinet* of Philadelphia not only subsisted without such patronage but actually refused to accept it when offered. In one instance in 1838, when it was proposed to insert an advertisement of a farm for sale, the editor, in rejecting it, said he did so because otherwise his journal would soon "be entirely filled with them." He then went on to give the substance of the proposed advertisement gratuitously. Conditions soon changed, however, and by 1844 the same editor was soliciting advertising.[48]

Advertising, however, became a more and more important source of revenue to farm journals, and at times editors permitted the insertion of advertising that exceeded the bounds of propriety, good taste, and honesty. Distributors of patent medicines did not clutter up the pages of the farm journals quite as much as they did after 1860, but advertise-

[48] *Farmers' Cabinet,* III (October 15, 1838), 103; and VIII (August 15, 1843), 40.

ments of nurseries, seed and guano salesmen, and agents for agricultural machines were far from restrained. A number of editors and proprietors were personally interested in the sale of agricultural machines or fertilizer, and gave numerous and elaborate puffs to them. Among the most flagrant examples were James J. Mapes, editor of the *Working Farmer* and producer of Mapes's Superphosphate of Lime; John S. Wright of the *Prairie Farmer* and manufacturer of the Atkins Automaton Reaper; A. B. and R. L. Allen of the *American Agriculturist*, who were prominent in the importation of livestock and proprietors of a farm-machinery business; and Joseph Breck, publisher of the *New England Farmer*, proprietor of the Agricultural Warehouse and Seed Store of Boston and manufacturer of Howard's plow.[49] The *New England Farmer* justified its refusal to print advertisements of competing manufacturers and salesmen of plows.[50] It was this same Breck who used the pages of the *New England Farmer* to puff the sale of Rohan potatoes, Chinese tree corn, *Morus multicaulis,* eggs of the China silkworm—all of them humbugs.[51]

Professor James J. Mapes, LL. D., Consulting Agriculturist or Agricultural Chemist, as he variously appeared before the public, was the most blatant of these editor-salesmen. He used the columns of his *Working Farmer* to urge farmers to consult his advisory service, for which he charged liberally, and to buy the various combinations he sold as fertilizer. In no other farm journal was so much space devoted to the speeches, farming practices, commercial success, and pet theories of its editor as appeared in Mapes's journal. When his "nitrogenized superphosphate of lime" and other mixtures were subjected to chemical analysis by Samuel W. Johnson of Yale, and found deficient in potash and phosphorus, and in no sense measuring up to advertising claims or justifying their price, the facts were brought out in other farm journals. Mapes's "trashy mixtures," his "persistent braggery and humbuggery," his false claims to being a professor, were all exposed in detail.[52] Mapes replied in the usual journalistic billingsgate of the time.[53] Though his sins may have been many, Mapes produced a journal of a fairly high order, filled with information about soils and their chemical content, the need for fertilizer, drainage, and careful cultivation. He

[49] Woodward, *The Development of Agriculture in New Jersey,* pp. 127–149; Demaree, *The American Agricultural Press,* pp. 97, 143 ff.; Bardolph, *Agricultural Literature and the Early Illinois Farmer,* p. 138.

[50] *New England Farmer,* XVII (January 18, 1839), 222.

[51] See the *New England Farmer* for 1837 and the following years.

[52] *Homestead,* IV (October 6 and December 15, 1859), 1035–1036. For other references to such attacks, see Demaree, *op. cit.,* pp. 68 and 97.

[53] See especially the *Working Farmer* for 1853 and 1854.

copied more widely from British farm journals, notably, the *Mark Lane Express,* than did his American contemporaries and thus brought more fresh material to his readers.[54]

Some editors, Thomas Brown of the *Ohio Farmer,* was one, rode their hobbies in which they had an important economic interest, but they were at the same time sincerely convinced of the correctness of their judgment. Brown, a Shorthorn breeder, used his columns as a vehicle for praising his favorite cattle. The largest Hereford breeder in the country, and himself not free from prejudice, accused Brown of writing the "most extravagant and extraordinary accounts" of Shorthorns "to puff and keep up extreme excitement" at auction sales. Brown did keep interest in Shorthorns at a high pitch and did neglect other breeds. On the other hand, he was not alone responsible for the preference shown for Shorthorns; cattlemen generally, as well as the editors of most agricultural journals, favored them.[55]

Inevitably, considering the credulity of the age, there was a good deal of humbug in the farm press, and one may conclude that the editors were almost as easily gulled as their readers. For example, a great deal of space in the periodicals was allotted to the controversy that raged for half a century as to whether wheat could be transmuted into chess. Although David Thomas had discredited the notion in the *Plough Boy* as early as 1820, and some editors were aware that there was no basis for it, not all would take a position on it; without exception, they permitted, indeed encouraged, its discussion to run on to questionable length in their columns. Equally absurd were the "scientific" evidence for phrenology that was offered to prove the inferiority of the Negro race, and

[54] Mapes impressed some men of high standing with his technical knowledge and the quality and usefulness of material he included in the *Working Farmer.* An example is Charles G. Page, one-time chief examiner of the Patent Office and in 1853 editor of *The American Polytechnic Journal: A New Monthly Periodical Devoted to Science, Mechanic Arts, and Agriculture,* who wrote of him: "Upon the subjects of agricultural chemistry, proper manuring, rotation, etc., Prof. Mapes is quite 'at home,' bringing into the field as he does his valuable stock of chemical knowledge; and this added to extensive practical knowledge of mechanics and the arts generally, admirably fit him for his position."—*American Polytechnic Journal,* II (1853), 160. See also the long account of a visit to Mapes's farm and the favorable impression received from it by M. L. Holbrook in *Ohio Farmer,* IX (April 21, 1860), 122, 130; Horace Greeley and other members of the American Institute of New York were favorably impressed with Mapes. Of recent writers, Carl Raymond Woodward, *The Development of Agriculture in New Jersey,* pp. 127 ff., is the most favorable.

[55] Brown published William H. Sotham's attack, which originally appeared in the *Mark Lane Express,* answered it, and then refused to give him additional space. In view of the great quantity of controversial material he allowed in his columns on the merits of different families of Shorthorns, his refusal was not in good taste.—*Ohio Farmer,* V (November 18, 1856), 180.

therefore to justify slavery, and the arguments about the influence of the moon on crops and farm events.[56]

In addition to the great agricultural editors, such as John S. Skinner, Luther Tucker, Jesse Buel, and Edmund Ruffin, there came into prominence a group of writers who specialized in farm subjects and whose work appeared in many journals, was widely copied, and added substantially to the variety and quality of current agricultural literature. The most professional writer on agricultural topics, and one who succeeded in making a living from it, was Solon Robinson, traveling correspondent of the *Cultivator,* the *American Agriculturist,* and the *New York Tribune,* subscription agent, and salesman for nursery stock and seeds. Robinson's accounts of his travels in various parts of the country and his reviews of agricultural books and periodicals are his most valuable work. His travel accounts are not as perceptive as those of Frederick Law Olmsted but are more practical.[57] Martin W. Philips, a small Mississippi cotton planter, wrote extensively in behalf of diversification and the use of laborsaving devices, and warned against fraudulent claims of seed salesmen.[58] Noah B. Cloud of Alabama and Thomas Affleck of Mississippi shared their farm experiences with other cotton planters in their numerous letters and sketches that appeared in southern journals. They advocated soil building, fallowing, rotation, use of guano, horizontal plowing, and limited government aid to agriculture.[59]

NOTABLE FARMER-WRITERS

One of the most original and forward-looking of the practical farmer-writers was John Johnston, whose farm, on which he conducted constant experiments, was located near Geneva, New York. Over and over Johnston wrote to the *Country Gentleman* and other agricultural publications urging farmers to drain their land. His advice did not go unheeded. The demand for tile led to the establishment of the Albany Tile Works, which was capable of turning out 20,000 to 25,000 tiles a week. In the *Country Gentleman* a professional land-draining engineer advertised his services.[60]

[56] *Southern Cultivator,* I (April 19, 1843), 55. Illustrations are too numerous to list.

[57] Kellar, *Solon Robinson, passim.*

[58] Lewis Cecil Gray, *History of Agriculture in the Southern United States to 1860* (2 vols.; Washington, D. C.: Carnegie Institution, 1933), II, 702, 706–707, 781; John Hebron Moore, "Cotton Breeding in the Old South," *Agricultural History,* XXX (July, 1956), 101–103.

[59] Weymouth T. Jordan, "Noah B. Cloud's Activities on Behalf of Southern Agriculture," *Agricultural History,* XXV (April, 1951), 55 ff.

[60] *Country Gentleman,* I (June 23, 1853), 399; II (August 4, 1853), 71; and XII (September 2, 1858), 144. Isaac Hill's *Farmer's Monthly Visitor* of Concord, N. H., had earlier taken up the cause of tile draining. See especially these issues: VII

The great day of tiling, however, was not to come until the late nineteenth century.

Marshall Pinckney Wilder of Massachusetts ranks among the leading agricultural writers and organizers of the time. His experiments in hybridizing fruit trees, both native and imported, the leadership he provided in the establishment of the Massachusetts Horticultural Society, the Massachusetts State Board of Agriculture, the United States Agricultural Society, and his frequent articles in the publications of these societies and in the *New England Farmer* and other farm journals made him one of the best-known writers on agricultural topics.[61]

Henry Colman became a prolific writer on agricultural matters after retiring from the ministry. His numerous contributions to the *New England Farmer*, the *Cultivator*, the *Genesee Farmer*, and other periodicals brought him into such prominence that in 1837 he was appointed Commissioner of Agricultural Survey of Massachusetts, with funds to enable him to assemble detailed information on the progress of agriculture in Massachusetts such as was not available for other American states. Accounts of his personal investigations of farming operations and the statistics elicited by his questionnaires, when published, pushed him into the lead in agricultural matters. His reports warranted the conclusion that "Massachusetts is capable of yielding more than triple the amount of agricultural products, which have hitherto been obtained." [62] Coming as they did at the time when the state's agriculture was suffering severely from the competition of better lands elsewhere, they must have brought great comfort to many people.

While carrying out his official duties for Massachusetts, Colman acted as editor of the *New England Farmer* whose proprietor, Joseph Breck, was also managing his agricultural warehouse as well as his publications. Colman wrote copiously on banking, credit, horticulture, and many other subjects, but came to resent the limitations on his freedom of expression which Breck imposed. He was not permitted to condemn "frauds practiced upon the poor Indians, in the robbery of their lands," Negro slavery, and gross mismanagement of state banks, or to advocate temperance, and had always to strive not to annoy political partisans, manufactures, and the clergy, lest sensitive souls order the paper stopped and threaten suit for libel. After "several hard raps over the knuckles," and a promise "to say nothing which could offend any one" he found the position too stultifying and resigned.[63]

(October 31, 1845), 156; VIII (January 31, 1846), 15; and IX (September 30, 1846), 149.

[61] *Horticulturist*, New Series, V (March, 1855), 111–120; *Dictionary of American Biography* (New York: Charles Scribner's Sons, 1928–1937), XX, 210.

[62] *North American Review*, CIV (July, 1839), 241.

[63] *New England Farmer*, XIX (December 30, 1840), 206.

Colman's writings on Massachusetts agriculture were sufficiently impressive to leaders in farm economy so that he was urged to visit Europe, particularly England, Ireland, France, and Italy, for the purpose of making a similar survey. To finance the trip advance subscriptions were taken for the expected reports. Leading agricultural societies, such as those of New York and Massachusetts, ordered 100 copies each, and gentlemen-farmers like Thomas H. Perkins, John P. Cushing, Samuel Appleton, Nathan Appleton, Abbott Lawrence, and John A. Lowell ordered from 25 to 100 copies. Altogether, some 2,325 sets of Colman's account of his observations were ordered in advance at thirty to thirty-two shillings each, thus helping to pay the expenses of the trip. Colman went abroad in 1843 and remained five years, traveling widely and writing his observations in two notable collections of essays, one of which went through six printings. His *European Agriculture and Rural Economy* combines some naïve observations on nonagricultural matters with acute and detailed examinations of farm practices and agricultural problems, all written with urbanity and good taste, something often lacking in English travelers' accounts of America.[64] A writer in the *Edinburgh Review* found Colman's work "full of kindly and benevolent feeling."[65] The agricultural historian can only regret that there was no foreign traveler sufficiently interested in American agricultural problems to do for the United States what Colman did for England.

Colman, impressed with England's fairs, agricultural education, and the diffusion of information about improved farm practices, thought well of the emphasis upon methods of selecting good seed, but did not detect any superiority in its wheat, grasses, root crops, or hogs. Its farm implements did not appear to be better than those in use in the United States, except for the clod crusher. His principal recommendation to his American readers was that which most English travelers had made: turnips, beets, and carrots should be grown as feed for livestock. Other admonitions offered by Colman were the usual advice appearing constantly in farm journals: deep plowing, liming, preservation and use of manure, draining, and crop rotation.[66] Because of Colman's prominence and the extraordinarily wide circulation of his views in the press, his description of the best of English and European farm practices doubtless had considerable influence in America.

[64] Henry Colman, *European Agriculture and Rural Economy* (2 vols.; Boston: Arthur D. Phelps, 1846). Colman also wrote *European Life and Manners: In Familiar Letters to Friends* (2 vols.; Boston: C. C. Little and J. Brown, 1849). Also in *New England Farmer*, XXI (January 4, April 5, 1843), 213, 214, 317; and XXII (July 5, 1843), 1.

[65] *Edinburgh Review*, XC (October, 1849), 386–387.

[66] Clarence H. Danhof, "American Evaluations of European Agriculture," *Journal of Economic History*, IX (Supplement, 1949), 66–67.

BOOKS ON FARMING

Despite the oft-repeated charge that American farmers were suspicious of "book learning" and "book farming," many books on agricultural problems were published and had wide circulation. Most popular was the all-embracing compendium, covering every activity of the farmer and providing him with an abundance of practical advice in dealing with everyday problems. Of the dozen or more of these in circulation in the ante-bellum period, Thomas Green Fessenden's *Complete Farmer and Rural Economist Containing a Compendious Epitome of the Most Important Branches of Agricultural and Rural Economy*, first published in Boston in 1834, seems to have sold the most widely. As editor of the *New England Farmer*, Fessenden had written copiously on agricultural subjects and from this writing he borrowed for his book. The compendium reached its fourth edition in 1839 and its tenth, "revised, improved and enlarged," in 1854. His other major agricultural work, *The New American Gardener*, was advertised as being in its twentieth edition in 1850 and two years later appeared as the thirty-sixth edition with the title *The American Kitchen Gardener*. Both works are compilations; there was nothing fresh in them, but they did bring together some of the best of Fessenden's earlier work. That they sold widely is clear, but Fessenden seems not to have profited to any extent from royalties.[67]

Another prolific writer on agricultural subjects whose books sold well was Daniel Jay Browne, who became the most controversial figure in the agricultural work of the Patent Office. Browne's *American Muck Book*, his *American Poultry Yard*, and his *American Bird Fancier* went through a total of eight printings.

The works of significant English agricultural authorities likewise circulated extensively in the United States. William Youatt, *History of the Horse*, sold 25,000 copies; *Youatt on the Structure and Diseases of the Horse* sold 20,000 copies; Youatt and W. C. L. Martin, *Cattle*, sold 10,000 copies, and Youatt, *The Hog*, had at least two printings in the United States.[68] Many other works by English authorities were reprinted in New York, Philadelphia, or Boston and given extensive circulation. James F. W. Johnston's fame had preceded his visit to America in 1849, where his *Catechism of Agricultural Chemistry and*

[67] Porter Gale Perrin, *The Life and Works of Thomas Green Fessenden, 1771–1837* (University of Maine *Studies*, Second Series, No. 4; Orono: The University Press, 1925), pp. 162–165 and *passim*.

[68] *Homestead*, IV (September 15, 1859), 829, quoting the *Mark Lane Express*. See also *Eighty Years' Progress in the United States*, p. 98. Other large-selling agricultural books were George H. Dadd, *American Cattle Doctor*, 20,000 copies; Daniel Chipman Linsley, *Morgan Horses*, 5,000 copies; Henry Steel Olcott, *Sorgho and Imphee*, 4,000 copies.

Geology and his *Elements of Agricultural Chemistry and Geology* went through two American printings and others of his books were extensively sold.[69]

Mention should be made of two off-quoted works: Henry Stephens Randall, *Sheep Husbandry in the South,* and Lewis Falley Allen, *American Shorthorn Herdbook,* of which three numbers appeared.[70]

Andrew Jackson Downing belongs among this galaxy of writers on agricultural topics for, according to the dean of agricultural writers, Liberty Hyde Bailey, he was the creator of American landscape gardening who "affected country life in its every aspect." A rural architect, authority on flowers, and America's greatest horticulturist, Downing's influence was expressed through his books, which went through many printings, and through the *Horticulturist,* which he edited from its founding in 1846 to his death in 1852. In his efforts to improve rural architecture and to embellish home landscaping, Downing stood for the "simple, natural, and permanent as opposed to the intricate, artificial and ephemeral." [71] Downing's *Architecture of Country Houses* reached its sixteenth printing in 1861, his *Cottage Residences* was in its fourth printing in 1852, his *Fruits and Fruit Trees of America* was in its fourteenth printing in 1853, and his *Treatise on Theory and Practice of Landscape Gardening* went through at least six printings before 1860.

With agricultural literature in the best-seller class, publishing houses sought out books to meet the growing demand, and one or two houses concentrated their activities entirely in this field. C. M. Saxton of New York offered more than a hundred books on agricultural and rural activities in 1854, including works of Cobbett, Youatt, Skinner, Browne, Johnston, Liebig, Buel, Colman, Allen, Samuel L. Dana, Randall, and Fessenden.[72] Some of these books sold for as little as twenty-five and thirty-eight cents.

Through these low-priced books and the agricultural periodicals, whose subscription rates ranged from fifty cents to two dollars a year, and the farm columns in newspapers, information about the latest discoveries and the best methods of pursuing scientific agriculture was brought within the reach of a wide circle of farmers. Agricultural writers and editors played a major role in the great advances being made in farming in the half century preceding 1860.

[69] Titles and editions are from the Library of Congress catalogue.

[70] Bardolph, *Agricultural Literature and the Early Illinois Farmer,* has a chapter on "Books and Farmer Education."

[71] L. H. Bailey, *Cyclopedia of American Horticulture* (4 vols.; New York: The Macmillan Company, 1900), I, 501.

[72] *Ohio Farmer,* V (March 22, 1856), 48; *Farm Journal,* VI (January and May, 1856), 30, 154; advertising section in Thomas G. Fessenden, *New American Gardener* (30th ed.; New York: C. M. Saxton & Company, 1854).

CHAPTER XVII

Education for Future Farmers

AGRICULTURAL periodicals, county and state fairs, and the annual publications of agricultural societies and of the Agricultural Division of the Patent Office together constituted an educational force of growing significance. The periodicals reported the latest discoveries in agricultural science, reviewed the works of leading authorities, and on occasion gave extensive accounts of their lectures. Some, such as the *Farmers' Register* and Mapes's *Working Farmer*, copied liberally from the best British periodicals. Similarly, the publications of the state agricultural societies and of the Patent Office contained much original matter in addition to the borrowed material bearing on agricultural improvements. Yet the editors and principal contributors were not satisfied. They deplored the farmer's opposition to "book farming," his disinclination to change his ways and adopt new methods. They particularly resented his unwillingness to subscribe to agricultural periodicals which were trying to improve his status. They came to feel that if it was too late to teach the old-style, practical farmer the new agricultural science, the coming generation at least should have every opportunity of learning what their fathers had refused to profit from.

Formal instruction in the techniques of scientific agriculture was what was necessary, the leaders came to believe: instruction that could be available in the common schools, academies, and publicly supported colleges. Such instruction should be provided by men trained in the newly developing sciences and skilled in their practical application. Agricultural chemistry or modern soil science, geology, meteorology, anatomy, physiology, botany, and entomology were all suggested fields of learning that should be opened to the younger generation in the schools.[1] At all times it was stressed that practical farm experience should accompany the more formal training.

[1] R. L. Allen, "Agricultural Colleges," *American Agriculturist*, III (February, 1844), 52–54.

THE MOVEMENT FOR VOCATIONAL EDUCATION

As early as 1823 Jesse Buel introduced a measure into the New York legislature "looking to the establishment of a state agricultural school," and throughout the remainder of his career worked stanchly to that end. A little later, Edmund Ruffin, in the *Farmers' Register*, recognized that the message he was seeking to carry to Virginia planters—the use of marl, horizontal plowing, rotation of crops, and addition of humus to the soil —could be more effectively transmitted if it were supplemented by the teaching of agricultural science at the state university.[2] The *Register* gave attention to agricultural schools abroad, applauded the proposal of Governor James Barbour to establish a "professorship of agriculture" at Charlottesville, and added to it a plan for an experimental farm.[3] The *Southern Agriculturist*, the *Southern Planter*, the *Southern Cultivator*, the *Ohio Cultivator*, the Albany *Cultivator*, the *Horticulturist*, and the *New England Farmer* all gave editorial support to the move to have individual states either create agricultural schools or establish professorships of agricultural chemistry in the state universities.[4]

The *American Agriculturist* was bold enough to suggest that some rich men might be induced to endow agricultural schools. With "legislatures constituted as at the present day, we can not . . . look to a single one of our 26 state governments for the object desired; and as for Congress, nothing can be hoped from that quarter," it opined. From a third to a half-million dollars would be needed as an endowment for a private institution. With such support it would be possible to bring to the United States the Liebigs and other great scientists of Europe, the *American Agriculturist* held.[5] A speaker before the American Institute of New York urged that there be established an agricultural college and experimental farm in every state in the Union.[6]

How strong the movement for vocational education became among farmers it is not possible to determine. Suspicion of "book larning" was

[2] *Ohio Cultivator*, VII (June 15, 1851), 184; Harry J. Carman, *Jesse Buel: Agricultural Reformer* (New York: Columbia University Press, 1947), p. 72.

[3] *Farmers' Register*, I (December, 1833), 90; III (September, 1835), 274; IV (February, 1837), 639; V (May, 1837), 14–17; VI (December, 1839), 707–709.

[4] *Southern Agriculturist* in the *Cultivator*, III (October, 1836), 133; *New England Farmer* in the *Cultivator*, II (February, 1836), 190–192; and III (March, 1838), 14–15; *Farmers' Register*, IX (June, 1841), 339; *Southern Cultivator*, III (April, 1845) 56; and IV (October, 1846), 153; *Southern Planter*, III (January, 1843), 14; XIII (July, 1853), 217; XVI (February, 1856), 43; XVII (March, 1857), 177; *Horticulturist*, IV (December, 1849), 19.

[5] *American Agriculturist*, II (May, 1843), 47; III (February, 1844), 52–54; V (April and December, 1846), 105, 377; VI (January, 1847), 9.

[6] Peter B. Mead in *Transactions* of the American Institute of the City of New York, 1850 (Albany: Van Benthuysen, 1851), p. 111.

extensive, and practical farmers' antipathy for progressive or gentlemen-farmers has been seen. Certainly mass inertia and obscuratism made the role of the agricultural leaders not an easy one to pursue.[7]

Despite the lukewarm attitude of farmers, who feared anything that might mean higher taxes, the movement of agricultural education began to achieve results. Semiprivate and public schools were set up to teach practical agricultural science. Some of these were associated with manual training and corrective institutions, but the technical education replaced the emphasis upon religion in such schools only slowly.[8] The *Ohio Cultivator* of July 1, 1846, contains descriptions of three agricultural institutes that were then getting under way: the Western New York Agricultural School at Wheatland, New York, the Dutchess Agricultural Institute of Poughkeepsie, New York; and the Mt. Airy Agricultural Institute near Germantown, Pennsylvania. Tuition and fees of the first two were $100 and $200 a year.[9] Of these ventures the Mt. Airy Agricultural College and its promoter, James Gowen, received the most attention, but none of them survived for long. Insufficient patronage, meager resources, and lack of an able supporting organization brought them to an early end.[10]

Other indications of promotional interest in agricultural education rather than sustained support were the appointment of a lecturer on agricultural chemistry and mineralogy at Amherst College in 1843 and a series of lectures on the application of science to agriculture at Oberlin in 1854. In the Oberlin announcement were scheduled lectures on soils, manures, animal and vegetable life, geology and botany, and veterinary medicine.[11]

Some wealthy philanthropists supported the movement for scientific education at an early date, but their gifts did not accomplish much for agriculture. Stephen Van Rensselaer, "the last patroon" and landlord of some 3,000 tenant farmers, established a school at Troy, New York, in 1824 to teach "the application of science to the common purposes of life." The school grew into Rennselaer Polytechnic Institute, where agricultural chemistry, botany, and geology were taught with special attention to the

[7] A writer in the *American Farmer*, VIII (February 2, 1827), 367, in advocating the establishment of agricultural schools, said that farmers made "the warmest opposition to them."

[8] John R. Commons, *et al.*, *History of Labour in the United States* (4 vols.; New York: The Macmillan Company, 1926), I, 328.

[9] *Ohio Cultivator*, II (July 1, 1846), 97; Alfred Charles True, *History of Agricultural Education in the United States, 1785–1925* (U. S. Department of Agriculture, *Miscellaneous Publication* No. 36; (Washington, D. C.: 1929), pp. 35 ff.

[10] *Ohio Cultivator*, III (August 1, 1847), 109.

[11] Robert Samuel Fletcher, *History of Oberlin College* (2 vols.; Oberlin, Ohio: Oberlin College, 1943), I, 355–358.

growth of plants, organic functions of their parts, and chemical examination of soils.[12] The principal interest of the school, however, came to be in engineering, not agriculture. A decade later, Benjamin Bussey of Roxbury, Massachusetts, left to Harvard University an endowment of $150,000 to provide "a course of instruction in practical agriculture," gardening, botany, and other natural sciences, but the widow's life interest in the estate prevented action until 1870. Again, in 1847, Harvard was given $50,000 and a similar sum in 1859 by Abbott Lawrence, the leading wool manufacturer, for the establishment of a school of engineering, mining, machinery, and science. Lawrence's purpose in part was to "make better farmers, through the application of chemical and agricultural science." It was the Lawrence endowment which made possible the bringing to America of the distinguished Swiss zoologist, Louis Agassiz. Agricultural science was not, however, to be the major interest of the Lawrence Scientific School. Nor were Theodore Lyman's bequests of $10,000 to the flourishing Massachusetts Horticultural Society, $10,000 to the Boston Farm School, and $50,000 to the State Reform School in 1849 to accomplish anything for agriculture.[13]

LECTURES ON SCIENCE IN AGRICULTURE

Meantime, the movement for scientific education for farmers and mechanics was given considerable impetus when James F. W. Johnston came to America to lecture. Johnston was Great Britain's leading agricultural scientist and popularizer of Liebig's theory of the relation between the nutrition of plants and the composition of the soil. It had been hoped that Liebig himself might come to America, where, as one journal said, he would be preferred "to many a swaggering tourist, whose only claims to notoriety consist in flying over the country with post haste, ridiculing our institutions, because they require more than shallow investigations of blockheads, and rewarding our hospitality by sneers at republican vulgarity, and contemptible fawning to the aristocratic tendencies of society in the old world." [14] Liebig could not make the trip, but Professor Johnston, of the University of Durham and of Edinburgh University, proved an able substitute.[15] Johnston was invited by the government of

[12] *Cultivator*, New Series, IV (June, 1847), 174.

[13] *Cultivator*, New Series, V (April, 1848), 127; *Farmer's Monthly Visitor*, IX (January 31, 1847), 87; *Southern Cultivator*, IV (October and November, 1846), 153, 168; *Horticulturist*, IV (September, 1849), 143; Samuel Eliot Morison, *The Development of Harvard University* (Cambridge, Mass.: Harvard University Press, 1930), 414, 509.

[14] *Wool Grower*, II (December, 1851), 134.

[15] Rowland E. Prothero, *English Farming, Past and Present* (London: Longmans, Green & Co., 1912), p. 366.

New Brunswick to survey that Canadian province and to make a report on its agriculture and recommendations for its improvement. Some months of investigation of farming in New Brunswick in 1849 and 1850 were followed by travel, study, and lectures in eastern United States and in Upper and Lower Canada. Johnston delivered a major address in 1849 at the New York State Agricultural Fair [16] and followed that by "a short course of lectures" extending over four weeks on "The General Relation of Science to Agriculture," which, one hearer said, had "an eminently practical bearing on the farmer's art." Though sandwiched between lectures by artists, humorists, and temperance advocates, Johnston's course was well attended and was influential "in giving a further impulse to the progress of scientific agriculture in this part of the Union." [17] Under the same title Johnston delivered twelve lectures at the Lowell Institute in Boston and a number at the newly established Smithsonian Institution in Washington.[18] Through these lectures, which were reported at length in the farm journals, and through Johnston's numerous manuals and textbooks on the chemical basis of agriculture, one of which went through seventeen printings, the best of European scientific learning in so far as it related to agriculture was transmitted to the new world.

The intense interest shown in the Johnston lectures at Albany was partly responsible for the arrangement of a second series on agricultural problems in the same city in 1851. A fee of $10 to $25 was charged for attendance. Professor John P. Norton of the Department of Scientific Agriculture of Yale lectured on the nature of soil, plants, and animal economy; Professor James Hall, New York State Geologist, lectured on the bearings of geology and mineralogy on agriculture; Dr. Henry Goadby, formerly of the Royal College of Surgeons of London, discussed the action of insects on vegetation; and other lectures on chemistry and agriculture were given.[19]

Norton's contributions to scientific agriculture in the United States was noteworthy. His training included study with Benjamin Silliman, Sr., at Yale, two years with Johnston at Edinburgh, and nine months at Utrecht. While engaged in his studies and travels abroad he wrote twenty-eight letters about his experiences and observations, which were published in the Cultivator and the American Agriculturist in 1844-1847.

[16] Cultivator, New Series, VII (February, 1850), 71-77.

[17] James F. W. Johnston, Notes on North America: Agricultural, Economical and Social (2 vols.; Edinburgh: William Blackwood & Sons, 1851), II, 234.

[18] Ibid., p. 394; New England Farmer, II (November 9, 1850), 369; Boston Cultivator, XII (February 16 through March 30, 1850), 52-106, gave meaty and practical summaries of the Lowell lectures of Professor Johnston, but see the criticism of the same, ibid., XII (April 13, 1856), 115.

[19] Prairie Farmer, XI (December, 1851), 565.

The appearance of these letters in journals of such wide circulation and Norton's easy style and the practical information he imparted made him, while in his twenties, one of the best-known authorities on agriculture. In 1846 at the age of twenty-four he was appointed Professor of Agricultural Chemistry at Yale to which the title of Professor of Vegetable and Animal Physiology was later added. He lectured and wrote in a semipopular vein, without using the scientific jargon affected by some of the pseudo scientists of the day, on topics relating to soil and its chemical components; methods of maintaining soil quality by rotation of crops, draining, subsoiling, trenching, the application of lime, mineral and animal manures; the composition of crops; and better feeding practices.[20]

Norton's lectures and extensive writings embodied the results of his own fruitful research and that of other forerunners of soil and plant science, whose investigations he corrected and extended. His *Elements of Scientific Agriculture* was well received, won a $100 prize offered by the New York State Agricultural Society in 1850 for the best work on scientific agriculture, and went through at least four printings.[21] Like most of the younger scientists, Norton was a follower of Liebig, whose mineral manure theory that plants drew their nourishment from minerals in the soil and ammonia from the air was enjoying a great vogue. He struck hard at the notion of Edmund Ruffin that the application of lime, marl, muck, or gypsum alone would restore fertility to the land and revive worn soils. Such treatment of acid soils might revive their productivity but in no sense was it adequate. Only by careful analysis of the chemical composition of soils and plants would it be possible, Norton thought, to achieve the real potential of the land.[22] Norton, aware of the adulteration in and fraudulent claims for commercial brands of fertilizer then being advertised, warned that farmers should never purchase them in any large quantity without first obtaining chemical analyses to determine the amount of ammonia and phosphates they contained.[23] In this he was anticipating the work of his student and successor, Samuel W. Johnson.

The impetus Norton had given to scientific agriculture at Yale was not lost at his death in 1852, but was carried further by Johnson, who had a long and notable career as chemical analyst, teacher, extensive writer, and lecturer.[24] After study with Norton, and with Liebig at Munich,

[20] *Cultivator*, V (June 1 and 15, 1848), 81–83, 89.

[21] John P. Norton, *Elements of Scientific Agriculture* (Albany: Erastus H. Pease & Co., 1851).

[22] *American Cotton Planter*, I (August, 1853), 232 ff.

[23] *Soil of the South*, II (April, 1852), 245.

[24] Johnston, *Notes on North America*, I, 135.

Johnson turned to the analysis of the commercial fertilizers and guano combinations whose manufacturers and dealers listed their chemical constituents without regard to their actual contents. Finding differences between the advertised analyses and his results, and being certain of fraud and adulteration, he brought the matter into the open in a series of articles in the *Country Gentleman* and the *Homestead,* in which he named names and brands, some of which were being advertised in the *Homestead.*[25] Despite the furor his researches produced, and the fact that some very eminent men of integrity gave testimonials in behalf of the dealers and manufacturers, Johnson continued his investigations, applying to them the same rigorous type of analysis that was to characterize the work of the Bureau of Standards at a later time. His attack upon false advertising and the use of adulterants in fertilizers had the effect of improving quality, minimizing fraud, and driving charlatans out of the fertilizer business.[26] Johnson was one of the earliest of modern scientists to utilize laboratory methods to test the quality of goods and the truth of advertising.[27]

John Addison Porter, Professor of Chemistry at Yale, who, like Johnson, had been deeply influenced by Liebig while studying with him at Giessen, persuaded his institution to offer a five-week lecture course in agricultural chemistry in 1856.[28] Its success and Porter's continued interest in agricultural experimentation led him to propose the establishment, in association with the Yale Scientific School, of an agricultural school that should have a practical farm, an experimental farm, a museum of agricultural products, a collection of farm implements, and a veterinary hospital.[29] As a step in this direction an agricultural department was established in which were to be taught agricultural and analytical chemistry; practical agriculture, with experiments and observations on a farm; geology and mineralogy; agricultural engineering, surveying, draining,

[25] The persistence of the attacks upon James J. Mapes in the *Country Gentleman* and his use of the *Working Farmer* to advance his fertilizer business are partly accounted for by the fact that its editor, Orange Judd, had earlier been a colleague of Johnson and a student of Norton at Yale when some of the investigations on fertilizers were being undertaken.

[26] I have relied on the letters of Professor Johnson, which are published in the book edited by his daughter, Elizabeth A. Osborne, *From the Letter-Files of S. W. Johnson, Professor of Agricultural Chemistry in Yale University, 1855–1896* (New Haven, Conn.: Yale University Press, 1913), pp. 81, 109–120, and the *Homestead* for the years 1855–1860.

[27] The most important of Johnson's analyses are described in *Homestead,* as follows: I (1856), 562–564, 613–615, 677–680, 709–711; II (1857), 225, 461, 604; IV (1859), 603, 876.

[28] *Homestead,* I (December 27, 1855), 239.

[29] *Ibid.,* I (April 3 and May 1, 1856), 440, 509.

trenching, and leveling; entomology; botany; veterinary medicine and surgery; and meteorology.[30]

Funds were not forthcoming to support such a grand edifice. In 1857, however, lectures were offered in chemistry and general principles of agriculture, practical agriculture and rural economy, and botany and vegetable physiology.[31]

The success of the lecture series in agricultural problems at Yale led in 1860 to a most ambitious program under which a brilliant group of authorities from many areas and institutions lectured in a four-week session. Marshall P. Wilder discussed pomology; John Johnson, tile draining; Benjamin Silliman, Jr., meteorology; Lewis F. Allen, fruit trees; Samuel W. Johnson, chemistry; Cassius M. Clay, beef cattle; and John Addison Porter, agricultural education. Other subjects covered were destructive insects, nursery management, dairy farming, and agriculture abroad. Seventeen of the twenty-five lecturers thus brought together were later accorded space in the *Dictionary of American Biography*. Probably not again in the nineteenth century was there such a galaxy of authorities in the field of scientific agriculture associated in teaching as were together in this promising but short-lived Yale experiment. An Ohioan who faithfully attended all the lectures reported that the audiences ranged in number from 100 to 350, including Yale students, city and rural folk from near and far, and some women. His detailed reviews of the lectures suggest that they were sufficiently weighty and profitable to satisfy an agricultural journalist, and yet had a lightness of touch that kept the audience returning for more.[32] Wide circulation of the lectures was given through full reporting in the *New York Tribune* and through their publication in *Outlines of the First Course of Yale Agricultural Lectures,* edited by Henry Steel Olcott.[33] The success of the experiment led to the announcement at the final lecture that a similar series would be presented at Yale the following year.

Meantime, Professors Porter and Johnson worked closely with the Connecticut State Agricultural Society to improve farm practices. As chemist of this society, Johnson made numerous analyses of advertised

[30] *Ibid.,* I (April 24, 1856), 481–482.

[31] *Ibid.,* II (January 1, 1857), 247.

[32] M. L. Holbrook in *Ohio Farmer,* Vol. XI (February 11 to March 24, 1860); *American Agriculturist,* New Series, XIX (February, 1860), 59; *California Culturist,* II (May, 1860), 487–493; *Wisconsin Farmer,* XII (April 1, 1860), 102; *Rural Register,* I (1859–1860), 275, 278, 303, 310, 326; George Wilson Pierson, *Yale College: An Educational History, 1871–1921* (New Haven, Conn.: Yale University Press, 1952), p. 50; True, *History of Agricultural Education,* pp. 39 ff.

[33] Henry Steel Olcott, *Outlines of the First Course of Yale Agricultural Lectures* (New York: C. M. Saxton, Barker & Co., 1860).

brands of fertilizer to determine their actual worth. The results were published in the proceedings of the society, summarized in addresses given by Johnson at the anual meeting, and given in detail in *Homestead*, which acted as the society's unofficial organ. In 1859 Porter and Johnson toured the state together, visiting and counseling farmers' clubs and individual farmers in the interest of "progressive agriculture."

No other institution in America had developed scientific research, particularly in its relation to agriculture, as had Yale by 1860 under the leadership of the younger Silliman, Norton, Johnson, and Porter. Pure science and practical science had gone hand in hand and had achieved remarkable progress for the time.[34] This combination and the intellectual leadership of the men who made it explains why Yale was made the beneficiary of the Morrill land-grant act of 1862 by the state of Connecticut. Other considerations subsequently led to the transfer of the grant to Connecticut Agricultural College.[35]

THE SMITHSON BEQUEST

Well before these events, the largest and most imaginative public bequest that was to be made until well into the twentieth century set in motion an unrivaled scramble for its use. At his death in 1829, James T. Smithson, an illegitimate son of an English nobleman, left his estate valued at approximately half a million dollars to a nephew, with a proviso that if the latter died without issue it was to go to the United States "to found at Washington . . . an Establishment for the increase & diffusion of knowledge among men." Nine years later, the nephew having died without heirs, the benefaction came to the United States, and interested people in and out of Congress began maneuvering to have this large endowment devoted to their pet projects. Among the suggestions were the establishment of an astronomical laboratory; a school for the blind; an art gallery; courses of lectures; a meteorological office; encouragement of better methods of raising sheep, horses, and silkworms; the development of a national university; and a science museum or science library to supplement the Library of Congress.[36]

The spokesmen for agriculture rushed into the fray with the argument that farmers, the country's largest economic interest, had no satisfactory way of learning the scientific developments that affected their occupation and that therefore the Smithson bequest should be devoted to the creation of a national university for applied agricultural science. The

[34] *Homestead*, IV (November 3, 1859), 944.
[35] Pierson, *Yale College*, p. 454.
[36] Webster Prentiss True, *The Smithsonian Institution* (Smithsonian Scientific Series; Washington, D. C.: 1929), I, 238 ff.

Patent Office, with its popular and widely distributed *Reports*,[37] the United States Agricultural Society with Solon Robinson and Henry L. Ellsworth its chief promoters, and some of the farm journals worked together to induce Congress to establish a national university of agriculture. Charles L. Fleischmann, a graduate of the Bavarian Royal Agricultural Institute, who became an employee of the Patent Office and later produced three guides for German immigrants and a treatise on American economy, in two memorials to Congress in 1838 urged that a botanical garden and agricultural school be set up with the aid of the Smithson fund. Among the courses of instruction he advocated were vegetable crops, veterinary science, animal husbandry, and agronomy.[38] Thereafter increasing pressure was exerted on Congress to create a national university with the aid of the Smithson fund.

Congress was confused by all this advice and uncertain what to do about the bequest. Some of its members even doubted the wisdom and constitutionality of accepting the gift and urged that it be turned back to England. This confusion and uncertainty delayed action until 1846, by which time some of the odd plans for use of the fund had been dropped. Actually, at the outset, more time was given by congressmen to discussing the unfortunate investment of the principal in the securities of states which repudiated their obligations, than to plans for the utilization of the bequest. In 1845, Senator Benjamin Tappan's bill for the establishment of a university in the District of Columbia with professorships of natural history, chemistry, geology, astronomy, and agricultural and rural sciences came up for consideration. Doubts about the constitutionality of a national university, though Washington, Jefferson, and Madison had repeatedly recommended the establishment of such an institution in the national capital, led Southerners, despite the paucity of opportunities for higher education in their section, to oppose it. Fears that a national university might encroach upon the many colleges already in existence aroused the opposition of such stout New Englanders as Rufus Choate and John Quincy Adams. The opposition of Adams was the more noteworthy because as President he had followed the example of his predecessors in urging the creation of a national university.[39] When New England intransigence defeated the bill in the

[37] Commissioner of Patents, *Report, 1837*, p. 5, and *1842*, p. 2.

[38] Memorials of April 14 and December 8, 1830, *House Document* No. 334, 25 Cong., 2 Sess., Vol. X, and *House Document* No. 70, 25 Cong., 3 Sess., Vol. III; *Franklin Farmer*, II (January 19, 1839), 169; *New England Farmer*, XVII (January 2, 1839), 202; *Cultivator*, VI (March, 1839), 24; *Silk-Grower and Farmer's Manual*, I (April, 1839), 232.

[39] *Congressional Globe*, 28 Cong., 2 Sess., January 8, 1845, and later, pp. 105 ff.; *ibid.*, 29 Cong., 1 Sess., April 20, 1846, p. 748; James D. Richardson, comp., *Messages*

Senate, David Dale Owen, like his father long friendly to the working class, took the leadership in the House to put through what was essentially the Tappan plan.

The Owen bill provided for a national normal school to train teachers in science, an experimental farm and botanical garden, conservatories, a chemical laboratory, natural history exhibits and a library, scientific lectureships at which attendance was to be free, and the publication and sale at low prices of bulletins for the dissemination of scientific knowledge. Demagogic attacks by southern strict constructionists again stripped the bill of all its agricultural features before it passed.

The Smithsonian Institution was not to be the means of attaining improvements in agriculture that Ellsworth, Robinson, Fleischmann, and others had hoped for, but was to be an institution for the advancement of pure science through research, publication, and a museum.[40] For years some agricultural leaders looked with disfavor upon the work of the Smithsonian as shown by the comment of one of them, who was associated with the *Ohio Cultivator*. In a page entitled "A Chapter on Humbugs" the Smithsonian was called "little better than a political hospital for the hungry pensioners of government." [41] Because of these attacks, Joseph Henry, Director of the Smithsonian, made much of its meteorological work, which he held to be highly beneficial to farmers. Efforts to move the federal government to do something for agricultural education did not cease with the failure to secure anything of importance from the Smithson fund, but agricultural leaders now turned to the states for action.

The clamor for vocational education became strident in the fifties as farmers became increasingly aware of its importance, workingmen's groups began to give the movement their support, and industrialists recognized that technical education of workingmen at public expense would be beneficial to them. Harrison Howard of New York and Jonathan Baldwin Turner were the leaders in the movement to organize workingmen into industrial conventions and leagues for the purpose of focusing their strength in behalf of the movement for the creation of industrial universities. Howard was influential in the calling of the Industrial

and Papers of the Presidents, 1789-1902 (10 vols.; New York: Bureau of National Literature and Research, 1904), I, 66, 410, 485, 568; II, 312.

[40] Richard William Leopold, *Robert Dale Owen* (Cambridge, Mass.: Harvard University Press, 1940), pp. 219 ff.; A. Hunter Dupree, *Science in the Federal Government: A History of Policies and Activities to 1940* (Cambridge, Mass.: The Belknap Press, 1957), pp. 66 ff.; Samuel Flagg Bemis, *John Quincy Adams and the Union* (New York: Alfred A. Knopf, Inc., 1956), pp. 504 ff. Smithson's will and other basic documents are in *Eighth Annual Report of the Board of Regents of the Smithsonian Institution, 1854* (Washington, D. C.: A. O. P. Nicholson, 1854).

[41] *Ohio Cultivator,* IX (August 15, 1853), 250.

Legislature at Lockport, New York, in 1851, at which vigorous support was offered for a state measure to establish a technical and agricultural school.[42] The powerful support of Greeley's *Tribune* and of the American Institute of the City of New York was gained.[43] The institute was a combination of industrial and agricultural interests in the downstate area, which included some of the most influential journalists and gentlemen-farmers in the state.

Turner was the flamboyant, self-assured, and contentious leader in the West who started the ball rolling by initiating "industrial" and "agricultural" conventions in 1851 and 1852. At these gatherings Turner declared that industrial education could be furthered only through an entirely new institution, a state university. His scheme embodied, and elaborated upon, previous suggestions for agricultural colleges and experimental farms and blossomed out into a 6,700-word tract, "Plan for an Industrial University for the State of Illinois." The tract was published in full in one of the West's most widely read agricultural periodicals, *The Prairie Farmer;* the more important part was included in the *Annual Report* of the Commissioner of Patents for 1851, of which 145,420 copies were printed; and all or part was copied in the *Transactions* of the Illinois State Agricultural Society, the *Valley Farmer,* the *Horticulturist,* and the *Buffalo Patriot.* Favorable comments were made on it in the *Southern Cultivator,* the *Philadelphia North American,* the *New York Tribune,* the *Illinois State Register,* and elsewhere. A series of industrial conventions inspired by Turner's clarion call kept the industrial university before the people.[44] *The Prairie Farmer* devoted 57 columns to the proposed university in 1852 and 26 pages in 1853. John A. Kennicott, its horticultural editor, Bronson Murray, a bonanza sheep farmer, and Governors Joel A. Matteson and Augustus C. French of Illinois joined Turner in urging the Illinois legislature to take action. Only partial success was achieved in Illinois with the chartering of Illinois Normal University near Bloomington, but before the excitement had lapsed, the state legislature was induced to memorialize Congress urging that public lands to the value of $500,000 be donated to each state for the endowment of industrial universities.[45]

[42] Earle D. Ross, *History of the Iowa State College of Agriculture and Mechanic Arts* (Ames: Iowa State College Press, 1942), pp. 21 ff., and his *Democracy's College: The Land-Grant Movement in the Formative Stage* (Ames: Iowa State College Press, 1942), pp. 14 ff.

[43] *New York Tribune,* September 5 and 9, 1851.

[44] *Prairie Farmer,* XII (February, 1852), 68–74; Commissioner of Patents, *Report, Agriculture, 1851,* pp. 37–44; Burt E. Powell, *The Movement for Industrial Education and the Establishment of the University, 1840–1870* (Semi-Centennial History of the University of Illinois,* 2 vols.; Urbana: 1918), I, 14 ff.

[45] *Prairie Farmer,* XII (March, 1853), 114; Powell, *op. cit.,* Vol. I, Chap. 3.

During the great ferment in behalf of agricultural education Charles L. Fleischmann, who had previously sought to have the Smithson funds used for this purpose and was now, with others, editing *The American Polytechnic Journal*, came forth with a plan for agricultural colleges which showed his familiarity with the best of the technical schools abroad. In addition to the usual studies advocated by others, Fleischmann urged attention to farm management and agricultural economics. Time and efficiency studies, soil and cost analyses, planning of farms and their operations, the use and application of labor, bookkeeping, civil engineering, and mechanics were all included in his program. Had the men in charge of the new institutions that were created in the sixties and seventies carefully examined Fleischmann's treatise, they might have avoided some of the blunders into which they fell.[46]

DEVELOPMENT OF AGRICULTURAL COLLEGES

A swift flowering of institutions and agricultural professorships followed this agitation for vocational education at the college level. Though the movement floundered in Virginia, it led to the establishment of agricultural professorships at the Universities of North Carolina and Georgia in 1853 and 1854, and to efforts to organize agricultural colleges in Tennessee and Maryland.[47] The University of Georgia was given $20,000 as endowment for an agricultural professorship, with the recommendation that the position be given to Daniel Lee, then editor of the *Southern Cultivator*.[48] Formerly editor of the *Genesee Farmer* and active in the movement to establish an agricultural school in New York, Lee had become nominal editor of the *Cultivator* while maintaining his residence in Rochester. He wrote copiously on southern agricultural problems and was promptly accepted by southern leaders, the more so after he attacked the *New York Times* and northern abolitionists for their views on slavery and presented a stout defense of the peculiar institution.[49]

Michigan, Pennsylvania, Iowa, and Maryland pioneered in the fifties in actually getting under way agricultural schools that have grown into great modern universities. With state appropriations of $50,000 in 1855

[46] "Agricultural Education," *American Polytechnic Journal*, II (July–December, 1853), pp. 166–177.

[47] *Soil of the South*, IV (October, 1854), 297; True, *History of Agricultural Education*, p. 65; Lewis Cecil Gray, *History of Agriculture in the Southern United States to 1860* (Washington, D. C.: Carnegie Institution, 1933), II, 791–792.

[48] A similar sum was given the Virginia Military Institute in 1859 to endow a professorship of agriculture.—*Wisconsin Farmer*, XI (October, 1859), 377.

[49] *Southern Cultivator*, XII (April, June, and August, 1854), 105, 169, and 233.

and $40,000 in 1857, Michigan acquired a tract of 700 acres at Lansing, erected buildings, and began instruction in Michigan Agricultural College in 1858. Students were taught "English and scientific education as will render" them intelligent citizens and practical farmers. Pennsylvania established the Farmers' High School (later to become Pennsylvania State College) and appropriated for it $50,000, which was to be matched by residents of Center County where the school was situated. An experimental farm and orchard were laid out, barns and instruction buildings were erected, professors of horticulture, literature, and natural science were appointed, and classes began in 1859. Iowa, a younger state, created in 1858 the Iowa State Agricultural College and Farm, to which was voted $10,000 for development. Maryland chartered a semiprivate institution in 1856, to which it appropriated $6,000. Maryland Agricultural College opened in 1859 with chairs of agricultural science, exact sciences, and languages, and with more than a hundred students in attendance. On the eve of the Civil War a promising beginning in veterinary medicine was made in the chartering by Pennsylvania of the Veterinary College of Philadelphia, with a distinguished board of trustees and an able faculty.[50]

At Cincinnati, Farmers' College could boast in 1858 a record of ten years of operation in which it had developed its experimental farm and botanical garden, a body of 250 students, "one of the finest Chemical Laboratories" in the country, and an agricultural department that was both theoretical and practical. What was more important, perhaps, it had an effective farm journal, which it used to advance agriculture and Farmers' College.[51] At the other end of the state, in Cleveland, another venture in agricultural education was begun with the Ohio Agricultural College offering instruction in chemistry, vegetable life, comparative anatomy, geology, agricultural mechanics, political economy, and other fields.[52] It survived briefly.

New York State was not far behind in the movement for vocational education.[53] In 1853, the state chartered two colleges to provide higher education in agricultural and mechanical arts. People's College at Havana

[50] Commissioner of Patents, *Report, Agriculture, 1857* (Washington, D. C.: James B. Stedman, 1858), p. 26; *Rural Register*, I (August 1, 1859), 39; True, *History of Agricultural Education*, pp. 57 ff.; Ross, *Democracy's College*, p. 14; Wayland Fuller Dunaway, *History of the Pennsylvania State College* (State College: Pennsylvania State College, 1946), p. 17; *Southern Planter*, XIX (September, 1859), 587.

[51] *Cincinnatus*, III (February, 1858), 83.

[52] *Ohio Cultivator*, XII (December 1, 1856), 368; Fletcher, *History of Oberlin College*, I, 355.

[53] *Horticulturist*, IV (December, 1849, and February, 1850), 249, 353, 381; *Prairie Farmer*, IX (July, 1849), 227.

with a distinguished board of trustees, including Horace Greeley, received no state aid in the fifties, though it had a liberal charter, but attracted sufficient local benevolence to enable it to begin construction and appoint a president.[54]

The New York State College of Agriculture was situated at Ovid. A state loan of $40,000, matched by an equal amount of private subscriptions, enabled the college to acquire 750 acres for a campus and experimental farm, and to build a "pretentious edifice." The college opened with twenty-seven students in 1860, but with the coming of the war it languished, never to recover. For a generation the Empire State was to leave vocational education to a private institution—Cornell University—which was made the state's beneficiary under the Agricultural College Act of 1862.[55]

Farmers were not ready to follow their leaders in the movement for agricultural education. This was pointed out by James F. W. Johnston, whose associations with the members of the New York State Agricultural Society and conversations with many farmers of New York make his opinions worthy of serious consideration. He found "the farmers averse to change, and more averse still to the opinion that they are not already wise enough for all they have to do." Although lawyers and other special-interest groups in the New York legislature were willing to appropriate public money for their own peculiar concerns, the farmers could not bring themselves to favor aid to agricultural colleges "on the ground that the knowledge to be given in the school is not required, and that its application to the soil would be of doubtful benefit." Johnston observed:

There is something in the habit of mind which is common to the cultivators of both sides of the Atlantic, which makes them difficult to convince that any thing they have been accustomed to do, has been done in a wrong way, or that, by any other way you can describe, the same thing could be done cheaper, sooner, better, or with more profitable results.

Johnston also sagely remarked that any rural member might be induced to support a bill for state aid to a college if it were to be located in his district, but fear that he might not land the plum inclined him to

---

[54] The papers of Harrison Howard, an active leader in the movement for agricultural education in New York, are in the Cornell University Library. Albert Hazen Wright brought together much scattered material about the New York State Agricultural College (of Ovid) in *Pre-Cornell and Early Cornell: I, Cornell's Three Precursors; II, New York State Agricultural College* (Ithaca, N.Y.: State College of Agriculture, 1958).

[55] Paul W. Gates, *The Wisconsin Pine Lands of Cornell University: A Study in Land Policy and Absentee Ownership* (Ithaca, N.Y.: Cornell University, 1944), pp. 49 ff.

favor, if anything were to be done, the establishment of a dozen small institutions instead of one well-supported college.[56] Parochialism, distrust of farmers, and sectarian-dominated colleges, fearful of a secular rival, were all responsible for New York's failure.[57]

From the slight success the friends of vocational education had won by the eve of the Civil War, one may conclude that despite the clamor, the resolutions, and the publicity, representatives of the people were not, on the whole, ready to appropriate money for this purpose. Only four states had made any outright grants, and they were for buildings and grounds. Failure to induce the states to act led those interested in agricultural education to make another onslaught on the federal government in the hope that it might be induced to provide aid, if not by establishing a national university, then by making grants of land or money to the states to enable them to succor the feeble colleges they had spawned or to create new ones.

GOVERNMENT AID TO EDUCATION

Government aid to education from common schools to colleges was firmly grounded in the American tradition. When the Land Ordinance and the Northwest Ordinance were adopted in 1785 and 1787 for the administration of the lands and the establishment of government in the territory north of the Ohio, the sixteenth section in each township was reserved for aid to common schools, and two townships (46,080 acres) were to be given each state for the endowment of a university. These endowments were not to be turned over to sectarian institutions but to be used to establish state, and therefore secular, institutions.[58] By mid-century a dozen or more colleges had come into existence as a result of these grants, but most of them received little support, followed the curriculum of the older eastern institutions, showed little tendency to experiment in technical education, and drew few students. Apart from the University of Michigan, none of them had made any impact upon educational theory or development. True, at the University of Wisconsin, agriculture, chemistry, and natural history were taught by a member

[56] Johnston, *Notes on North America*, II, 281, 572.

[57] Carl Becker, *Cornell University: Founders and Founding* (Ithaca, N. Y.: Cornell University Press, 1943), *passim*.

[58] George W. Knight, *History and Management of Land Grants for Education in the Northwest Territory* (*Papers* of the American Historical Association, Vol. I, No. 3; New York: G. P. Putnam's Sons, 1885), p. 13; Matthias Nordberg Orfield, *Federal Land Grants to the States, with Special Reference to Minnesota* (University of Minnesota *Studies in the Social Sciences*, No. 2; Minneapolis: 1915), Chaps. 2 and 3.

of the staff, but there is no evidence that he satisfied the agricultural leaders.[59]

Federal aid in the form of land grants to the states offered the best prospect of making the struggling state agricultural institutions successful, or at least those that were situated in public-land states. By mid-century, constitutional scruples against the employment of the public lands for schools, universities, canals, roads, railroads, and public buildings had been fairly well dissipated, save among the most hardened Southerners. But how could aid be given to the original states, in which the federal government had no public land? If eastern states were given land in western states and territories, would not a conflict over jurisdiction of the lands develop such as had threatened in New York, Ohio, and Maine at an earlier time? It was suggested that the way to get around this difficulty was to grant money instead of land, but money grants for education were still far in the future. Few members of Congress were so bold as to intimate there might be constitutional authority for such a radical innovation.

The prevailing public-land theory of the older states, North as well as South, was that the land cessions of the older states and the purchase of Louisiana, Florida, and the Southwest by the federal government gave to all states a right to share in the proceeds from the sale of these lands. Older states therefore looked unfavorably on donations of land to settlers or grants to western states for internal improvements, education, or other purposes. For political reasons it had been found necessary to satisfy the demand of the West for donations and grants, but the older states gave way only reluctantly. As the revenue features of public-land policy declined with the enactment of laws for land donations, land subsidies, pre-emption, graduation, and military land bounties, the older states saw that they were drawing less and less benefit from the public lands and that, if a free-homestead policy were adopted, the public lands might entirely cease to be of value to the federal government and therefore to them.

The northeastern states now came forth with a proposal to share directly in the disposal of public land as well as in the rapid rise in real estate values which was occurring. The proposal first appeared in a bill sponsored by a feminine reformer and lobbyist, Dorothea Dix. Improvement in the care of the insane was her overwhelming interest, and to achieve that object she sought aid from the federal government in the form of grants of land to every state; from the proceeds of these grants new buildings were to be constructed very different from the

[59] Merle Curti and Vernon Carstensen, *The University of Wisconsin, 1848-1925: A History* (2 vols.; Madison: University of Wisconsin Press, 1949). See also True, *History of Agricultural Education*, pp. 57 ff.

dungeon-prison type of buildings in which insane people were then confined. By lobbying at state capitals, where she induced the legislatures to memorialize Congress in behalf of her bill, and in Washington, Miss Dix, over the course of six years, succeeded in building up sufficient support in Congress to secure passage of the measure.[60] The Dix bill provided for a donation of ten million acres of land, to be apportioned among the states "in the compound ratio of geographic area and representation . . . in the House of Representatives."[61] Before its adoption, the bill was amended to meet the objection of western states that it would permit older states to gain ownership of great tracts of land in the West and would thus lead to jurisdictional disputes. The amendment provided that states containing no federal lands were to receive scrip for land, which they were required to sell at not less than $1.00 an acre. Purchasers could use it to acquire western land subject to entry at $1.25 an acre.[62] Franklin Pierce vetoed the Dix bill and thus brought to a halt the effort to use the public lands as a means of achieving social reforms.[63]

The Turner-inspired Illinois memorial, calling for donations of land worth $500,000 to each state for the aid of "industrial colleges," was presented a year before the final action on the Dix bill. Previously, the Michigan legislature had asked for a grant of 350,000 acres for a state agricultural college, and the New York legislature had urged a land grant for educational and other useful purposes. The Illinois memorial, however, was the first to ask for aid for colleges in every state.[64] It differed from the Dix bill in that it proposed equal grants to all states, whereas the Dix bill provided for grants based on the size and population of the states on the assumption that the large and populous states needed greater aid. Advocates of the Illinois plan argued that the populous states, such as New York and Pennsylvania, were well able to finance their own agricultural colleges and only needed a modest donation to get them started; the newer states, on the other hand, lacking a broad tax base, should have at least an equal grant, since it would be years before

[60] *Congressional Globe*, 35 Cong., 1 Sess., April 22, 1858, p. 1742.

[61] *Senate Journal*, 33 Cong., 1 Sess., May 3, 1854, pp. 372–374; Francis Tiffany, *Life of Dorothea Lynde Dix* (Boston: Houghton Mifflin Company, 1890), pp. 166 ff.; Helen E. Marshall, *Dorothea Dix: Forgotten Samaritan* (Chapel Hill: University of North Carolina Press, 1937), p. 129.

[62] *Congressional Globe*, 33 Cong., 1 Sess., February 2, 1854, p. 455.

[63] Here, and in the treatment of the movement for the adoption of the bill to grant lands to agricultural and mechanical arts colleges, I have followed an earlier and more detailed analysis in my *Wisconsin Pine Lands of Cornell University*, pp. 11 ff.

[64] Edmund J. James, *The Origin of the Land Grant Act of 1862 and Some Account of Its Author, Jonathan B. Turner* (University of Illinois *Bulletin*, Vol. VIII; Urbana: 1910), p. 14.

they could devote any considerable revenue to higher education and experimental farming.

That the West was favorable to the establishment of industrial or agricultural colleges none could deny, but it was by no means united in support of a plan that would permit eastern states to gain ownership of western land or scrip. The influence of western land reformers was growing rapidly in the fifties, and they looked upon the scrip plan as only slightly less obnoxious than donations of land in their midst to eastern states. They knew on the basis of past experience that the scrip would be used by speculators to acquire large tracts of land. Also, agricultural-college lands to be granted directly to public-land states were required to be sold at $1.25 an acre and would thus be another block in the way of the free homesteads. For these reasons political leadership in the movement for the creation of agricultural colleges passed into the hands of members of Congress from older states in which there was no public domain: Justin Smith Morrill and Jacob Collamer of Vermont, Israel Washburn of Maine, John Parker Hale of New Hampshire, and John Bell of Tennessee. Charles E. Stuart of Michigan and James Harlan of Iowa were also active in support, but without the solid vote of New England little progress would have been made.

Morrill, representative and later senator from Vermont, led the movement in the House to secure land donations for agricultural colleges. His measure, introduced in December, 1857, provided for a grant to each state of 20,000 acres for each of its two senators and representatives to which it was entitled, to aid in establishing colleges of agricultural and mechanical arts. New states with but slight population would receive 60,000 acres, in contrast to the 660,000 acres New York State would receive. In this way it was less palatable to the West than was the Dix bill. Before its adoption, the Morrill bill was amended to provide that neither eastern states nor institutions chartered as beneficiaries under the bill could themselves enter land directly or hold land entered with the scrip; they were to benefit from selling the scrip to others. Morrill rightly anticipated that despite the increasing liberality with which the Constitution was being interpreted in the fifties, particularly with respect to the disposal of the public lands, strict constructionists would find reason to doubt the power of Congress to enact such a measure. In one of the keenest speeches of his career, he said:

I know very well that when there is a lack of arguments to be brought against the merits of a measure, the Constitution is fled to as an inexhaustible arsenal of supply.[65]

[65] *Congressional Globe*, 35 Cong., 1 Sess., April 20, 1858, p. 1692.

A minority of Southerners allowed their desire to have their states share in the proceeds from the sale of the public lands to override their constitutional scruples. Some representatives of New England and Middle Atlantic states likewise were influenced by this motive. Members of Congress squirmed in attempting to reconcile their politico-constitutional views with their desire to support a measure so ardently wanted by agricultural interests.

Joseph R. Williams, President of Michigan Agricultural College, whipped up sentiment in behalf of the bill in a communication to editors of agricultural papers, wherein he urged them to "arouse public attention . . . in an earnest article, and send a number to each of the gentlemen composing the committee on public lands and agriculture, in both House and Senate at Washington. Will you ask your State and County Societies to make themselves heard *at once* at Washington on the subject? Will you bring all the personal influence you can bear on individual members of your delegation in Congress?" [66]

Williams's appeal elicited an unexpected response from Noah B. Cloud, editor of the *American Cotton Planter and Soil of the South*, and a well-known leader of agricultural reform, and the editors of the *Southern Cultivator*.[67] Cloud favored the establishment of an agricultural college in Alabama and found no fault with the proposal to grant lands to each state to aid in establishing such institutions, but he held that Williams's plan for colleges organized on the manual labor system, in which all students should participate in farm tasks, was not suited for the South. Southern students should not be employed in field or barn; all such tasks should be performed by slaves. "Our plan is to educate the proprietor," Cloud maintained. There was no provision in his scheme for educating the young men of yeoman-farmer status. Similarly, the *Southern Cultivator* favored the establishment of an experimental farm in Georgia "worked by negroes" and an agricultural college to supply "educated overseers and mechanics and common school teachers." [68] Cloud gave active support to the Morrill bill and did not hesitate to criticize southern congressmen for their opposition to it. He averred that the *Farmer and the Planter* of Columbia, South Carolina, was the only

[66] *Ohio Cultivator*, XIV (January 1 and 15, 1858), 9, 25. Cf. *De Bow's Review*, XXVI (March, 1859), 250 ff.; *Homestead*, III (February 4, 1858), 316.

[67] *Germantown Telegraph* in *American Cotton Planter and Soil of the South*, New Series, II (April–September, 1858), 133, 137, 169, 200, 233, 265.

[68] *American Cotton Planter*, II (June, 1853), 183; *American Cotton Planter and Soil of the South*, New Series, III (June, 1858), 169; *Southern Cultivator*, XVII (September, 1859), 259. Cf. Blanche Henry Clark, *The Tennessee Yeomen, 1840–1860* (Nashville: Vanderbilt University Press, 1942), pp. 103 ff.

agricultural journal on his exchange list of twenty or thirty opposing the bill.[69]

It was not an easy matter to push the Morrill bill through Congress over the nearly unanimous opposition of the Old South, the solid opposition of the southern public-land states, and with only weak support from the West. Even some eastern agricultural journals expressed doubts about the bill.[70] The *American Agriculturist* feared the proceeds from the sale of the lands might go to "build asylums for broken down politicians, or to the beneficiaries of political parties, and that the . . . agricultural colleges to be erected, will be nurseries of scientific nonsense. . . ." [71] True to its conservative tradition, the *New York Times*, no agricultural paper, opposed the bill on grounds that (1) it was class legislation, (2) the government had already done sufficient for agriculture, (3) few working farmers would send their children to agricultural colleges, and (4) existing institutions were beginning to offer instruction in agricultural chemistry and further offerings were unnecessary.[72] On the other hand, the *Valley Farmer* of St. Louis, though it disliked some features of the college bill, disagreed with the Missouri delegates in Congress and supported it. The *Cincinnatus*, which might expect to benefit from a federal grant, expressed strong favor.[73]

What may well have tipped the scale in support of the Morrill bill was a smart maneuver that brought numerous leaders in the movement for agricultural education to Washington at government expense. The Commissioner of Patents, whose agricultural work was under attack, summoned to the capital leaders to draft plans for future agricultural work that might be less subject to criticism. After completing its work the group dissolved and the next day the members convened with others as the United States Agricultural Society, which proceeded to urge adoption of the land-grant measure, its members lobbying vigorously in the halls of Congress for that end.[74]

[69] *American Cotton Planter and Soil of the South*, III (May, 1859), 167, 169. Cloud seemed to reverse himself in declaring that agricultural colleges in this country were intended for "proprietors who labor with their own hands, and who combine . . . all the characteristics of landlord, tenant and laborer, in the same man."

[70] The *New England Farmer* thought Massachusetts might not take advantage of the bill for forty years and feared that the task of managing the land grants would be too great and that little profit would result from them.—XI (April, 1859), 173.

[71] *American Agriculturist*, XVII (June, 1858), 166.

[72] *Homestead*, IV (February 24, 1859), 361.

[73] *Valley Farmer*, X (February, 1858), 43; *Cincinnatus*, III (February, 1858), 49.

[74] *Cincinnatus*, IV (February and March, 1859), 78, 128; *Wisconsin Farmer*, XI (March, 1859), 83; *Ohio Farmer*, VIII (February 26, 1859), 66; *De Bow's Review*, XVI (February, 1859), 237; Ross, *Democracy's College*, p. 55. At the 1859

One of the South's most stiff-necked opponents of federal aid to agricultural education—George W. Jones of Tennessee—who watched with suspicion the use of funds not specifically allocated by Congress, secured the adoption of a House resolution calling upon the authorities to explain both the justification of bringing to Washington, and the basis of selection of, members of the Patent Office Advisory Board of Agriculture. He doubtless was offended that only three delegates came from slave states as against nineteen from the free states, but was more troubled at the direction the board's deliberations took. Principal attention was given to expansion of the agricultural work of the Patent Office and the desirability of creating a government department of agriculture as well as of declaring in behalf of the Morrill bill. Commissioner Holt, in reply to the resolution, listed the names of all participants brought to Washington at government expense, gave the payments to each, and explained that authorization for the expenditure was in an act of the previous year appropriating $60,000 "for the collection of agricultural statistics, investigations for promoting agriculture and rural economy, and the procurement of cuttings and seeds." [75]

It was the able lobbying of Joseph R. Williams,[76] Freeman G. Cary, Amos Brown, Marshall P. Wilder, James Gowen, and the supporters of five other agricultural colleges, backed by forty-five petitions and memorials, thirteen of them from state legislatures, that won over hesitating members of Congress to the support of the Morrill bill. On the other hand, some western opposition was based on the belief that the non-public-land states should not profit directly or indirectly from the sale of lands. Rising land values in the West were, they maintained, the result of improvements Westerners were making, and they alone should draw the benefits. After more than a decade of active discussion of the need for agricultural colleges, Congress passed the bill and sent it along to James Buchanan for his signature.[77]

President Buchanan, long responsive to the views of the South, which had cast only seventeen votes in both houses for the bill in contrast to eighty-three cast against it, could scarcely be expected to sign the Morrill bill. In his veto message, as Morrill had predicted, he resorted to the

---

meeting of the United States Agricultural Society, Joseph Henry tried hard to show how the Smithsonian Institution was aiding farmers through its studies of weather.

[75] *Congressional Globe*, 35 Cong., 2 Sess., January 7, 1859, p. 268; *Cincinnatus*, IV (March, 1859), 126.

[76] For a powerful speech in behalf of agricultural education and the Morrill bill, which President Williams delivered before the New York State Fair in October, 1858, see *Cincinnatus*, III (December, 1858), 530–556.

[77] I have discussed the sectional alignment on the bill and the motives therefor in *Wisconsin Pine Lands of Cornell University*, Chap. 1.

Constitution "as an inexhaustible arsenal of supply" for arguments in opposition, but he also embodied in his veto message the antispeculation plea that Westerners had made.[78] Even on this latter point one may doubt Buchanan's sincerity: his action in forcing squatter-occupied public lands into the market in 1858 to 1860 shows how little concern he had for frontier squatters. Freeman G. Cary struck hard at the fallacy in Buchanan's reasoning. If the measure was unconstitutional, the veto needed no other supporting argument. If it was constitutional to give land "to land-pirates for the construction of railroads," to spend "millions in a grand crusade to Utah," or "to waste thirty millions . . . to purchase Cuba," surely it was proper to aid agriculture through land endowments to agricultural colleges. The President showed "the most profound ignorance of the wants of agriculture. . . ."[79]

The drive for federal aid in establishing agricultural colleges was thus held up by a minority element or section, but not for long. After the withdrawal of the South from the Union, Senator Morrill reintroduced his measure, enlarged the acreage to be given to 30,000 for each senator and representative the states had in the Congress, and pushed it through in June, 1862. Again, the eastern states were overwhelmingly favorable while the West was lukewarm. Not only would the measure contribute to speculative accumulation of land and thus reduce the value of the homestead measure, which was in process of adoption at the same time; it would provide for large grants to wealthy and populous eastern states while giving inadequate aid to the new states whose taxable resources were small. Little could be accomplished during the war years toward creating agricultural colleges, but afterward the states carried out the purpose of the act, either by creating wholly new agricultural colleges, such as those at Manhattan, Kansas; Davis, California; and Lafayette, Indiana; or by grafting agricultural colleges on existing states universities as at Madison, Wisconsin.[80]

By the middle of the century, farm organizations and farm leaders had learned much about their obligations to government and the benefits that government might bestow on them. Because it was difficult for them

[78] Congressional Globe, 35 Cong., 1 Sess., February 26, 1859, pp. 1412-1413.
[79] Cincinnatus, IV (April, 1859), 145-151.
[80] Much ink has been wasted in a fruitless effort to determine the person most responsible for the adoption of the Agricultural College bill of 1859 and the Act of 1862. Partisans of Morrill and Turner have been vigorous in their efforts to prove their heroes' shares. In fact, Morrill's friends were claiming credit as early as 1860 for initiating the move. See the Illinois Farmer, V (July, 1860), 113; William Belmont Parker, The Life and Public Services of Justin Smith Morrill (Boston: Houghton Mifflin Company, 1924), pp. 262 ff. Most useful are True, History of Agricultural Education, pp. 23 ff.; Ross, Democracy's College, Chaps. 2 and 3; and Powell, The Movement for Industrial Education, Vol. I, passim.

to agree on political objectives, they had not taken full advantage of their potential political power. For example, they constituted far the largest element in the New York Assembly in 1850, and yet little of significance for them was adopted.

EMPLOYMENT MAKE-UP OF THE NEW YORK HOUSE OF
REPRESENTATIVES, 1850

Farmers	54	Gentlemen	6
Lawyers	26	Manufacturers	5
Merchants	16	Merchants	3
Physicians	9	Others	9
		Total	128

Source: James F. W. Johnston, *Notes on North America: Agricultural, Economical and Social* (Edinburgh: William Blackwood & Sons, 1851), II, 238. See also II, 415 for a breakdown of membership in the two Houses of the Massachusetts Legislature, which likewise shows a strong predominance of farmers over any other trades.

They had learned to bear without complaint state and federal taxes that were inescapable since they were based either on ownership of property or on the importation of goods. Outside the South they were generally favorable to the tariff, which, while protecting sheep farmers from competition from abroad, brought them little good and some harm in the way of higher prices on goods they purchased. They went along with the commercial and mercantile elements in favoring federal grants of land to aid the construction of internal improvements, knowing as they did that though they would materially benefit from these improvements they would have to pay for them in high prices for the land thus given. They knew that credit, which was available to them, whether by federal or state banks, was costly, uncertain, and subject to call at inconvenient times.

On the credit side, farmers had materially influenced the shaping of federal land policies, which were becoming increasingly liberal and by 1862 included free homesteads. They had learned some of the advantages of association through agricultural societies and fairs, and in their support of agricultural periodicals. Slowly, but long after industrialists, bankers, shippers, exporters, and great planters had secured major concessions from the federal government, they had begun to experiment with using their associations to secure such concessions as help in the sale of crops abroad, the collection and publication of agricultural statistics and articles about new techniques in agriculture, the free distribution of seeds, appropriations to aid state and county fairs, the establishment of agricultural schools and colleges, and the creation of a federal Department of Agriculture that would assume the work being done by the Patent Office,

American farmers had learned the way to political action, but they had no agrarian program to promote. They were working wholly within a conservative framework in expressing their wants. They sought no radical measures, no method of distributing the tax burden more equitably, no means of assuring themselves a larger share of the national income, no devices to protect themselves against the unfair monopolistic practices of manufacturers of farm implements or of processors, warehousemen, and factors. At a time when England was beginning its long-sustained efforts to improve the lot of Irish and English tenants, no such measures were in progress in this country, nor was there any effort to secure them, though tenancy was rapidly growing in the newer West. American farmers advanced no leveling measures such as their descendants were to fight for at a later time, organized no party, and, save for the class-conscious planters, rather blindly followed the leadership of other economic groups. In the midst of adversity the farmer sought no stay legislation, though many were threatened with foreclosure. They permitted their emotions to carry them away on matters not immediately affecting their welfare, such as slavery, abolitionism, "fifty-four forty," but seem never to have examined the effect of federal, state, and local taxes upon their economy.

Farm leaders placed their hope for improvement of the position of rural people in vocational education to make the farmer a more intelligent businessman in the use of his land, livestock, equipment, and labor. Long since they had been influential in securing public support for common schools, and now, with the Morrill bill, they thought they had a measure that would produce great improvement in agriculture. Perhaps it was fortunate that they could not foresee how ineffective for a generation the new crop of agricultural colleges that came after 1862 was to be.[81]

[81] Ross, *Democracy's College*, pp. 86 ff.

CHAPTER XVIII

New Land and Farm Problems in the Far West

IN the distribution of the public domain, extraordinary developments in farm practices and in public policy toward natural resources occurred in the area beyond the Rockies in the years just preceding 1860. Here, where rainfall was meager and soil alkaline, where rivers were mostly dry beds in the summer, markets remote, and communication with the outside world was slow, incoming settlers were adapting themselves to this new environment and, in the process, were introducing major innovations in agriculture and in the public management of land and water.

PROBLEMS OF THE MORMONS

Because the Mormons were engaged in a bitter conflict with the federal government, Utah, unlike other territories, was denied the benefits of the federal land system. No land offices were established, no surveys were made, and no squatters' or locally recognized rights to land had any standing in federal law. No grants for schools, roads, railroads, and public buildings were made. In consequence, the Mormons improvised their own land system. They made their own surveys and assigned land to individuals on the basis of need and capacity to develop it. Continued ownership of land was conditioned on approved use, not on prior concessions. In areas that could be irrigated and intensively developed, the 160-acre unit was discarded in favor of five-, ten-, twenty-, and forty-acre tracts. Larger units were assigned where grazing only could be conducted. Such large holdings of cultivable land as existed were held by the church fathers and were claimed to be held for the church and were

383

well utilized.[1] Firm theocratic control of the territory and an obedient homogeneous population enabled Mormon Utah to avoid many of the difficulties and much of the malfunctioning associated with the federal land system elsewhere. The Mormons' system was based on the principle that improvements brought title to land. Thus they avoided claim conflicts, difficulties with squatters (except where "Gentiles" intruded into the picture), and litigation over mortgages, foreclosures, tax titles, and other liens and disputes that wracked the early history of California, Kansas, Iowa, and Illinois. They also escaped the blighting effects of land booms and busts, inflated values, speculator-retarded communities, extortionate interest charges, and numerous foreclosures.

From the outset of their settlement in the Great Basin, the Mormon leaders were aware that only through irrigation could the valley lands be made to produce.[2] Consequently, they early set about the making of small diversion dams and ditches to conduct water by gravity from the streams draining the west side of the Wasatch Mountains to the parched but fertile basin of the Great Salt Lake. Small projects to utilize the water of the Jordan River, which drains Utah Lake into the Great Salt Lake, and the water of the American Fork River and the Spanish Fork River, which flow into Utah Lake, were undertaken at the very beginning of Mormon colonization. The age-old doctrine of riparian right—the right to use water of a stream flowing through or by land, provided such use did not materially damage other riparian owners—was found inapplicable and there was substituted for it the doctrine of beneficial use or appropriation. Water was not to be associated with individual property but was to be utilized for the benefit of the greatest number in the most efficient way. In practice this meant that riparian owners on the upper benches were not entitled to take water that could be more productively used on the richer lands in the valley.[3]

The Mormons early established the principle that public ownership and control of basic natural resources other than soil was essential. Forests, water, and minerals were thus grouped together, and rights in them

[1] Leonard J. Arrington, "The Settlement of the Brigham Young Estate, 1877–1879," Pacific Historical Review, XXI (February, 1952), 1 ff.

[2] George Thomas, Early Irrigation in the Western States (Salt Lake City: University of Utah, 1948), passim.

[3] George Thomas, The Development of Institutions under Irrigation (New York: The Macmillan Company, 1920), pp. 42 ff.; R. P. Teele, a leading authority on irrigation, has considerable historical material on the beginnings of irrigation in Utah in Elwood Mead, et al., Report of Irrigation Investigations in Utah (U. S. Department of Agriculture, Office of Experiment Stations, Bulletin No. 124; Washington, D. C.: 1903), pp. 40 ff. For the trials of one irrigation development, see Leonard J. Arrington, "Taming the Turbulent Sevier: A Story of Mormon Desert Conquest," Western Humanities Review, V (Autumn, 1951), 393 ff.

were held for the benefit of the Mormon community as a whole rather than for the individual. Here, as in irrigation development, the Mormons were far in advance of Americans generally, who were not to realize for another generation the importance, the vital necessity, of establishing some form of social control over perishable and rapidly disappearing resources.

Mormon tithing houses came to be the equivalent of communitarian or co-operative marketing and exchange centers for farmers and other business groups. The tithe, which was paid on everything the farmer raised, including grain, vegetables, butter, eggs, pigs, cattle, and chickens, was collected at the tithing house. Farmers brought not only their tithes but their surpluses, to exchange for food, clothing, household goods, or other items that came in from other farmers or household industries as tithes or as surpluses for exchange. The tithing house distributed these goods where needed in the immediate community and sent surpluses to the central tithing house in the capital, whence such commodities as wheat and livestock might be sent to California or elsewhere. In this way the federated tithing houses solved the problem that small farmers in frontier communities everywhere faced of not having the means of bartering surpluses, whatever they might be, for essentials they could not produce.[4]

Only as a result of the communitarian character of their economy and their stress on self-sufficiency was it possible for the Mormons to survive and prosper in a poorly endowed area, and in the face of government hostility and the droughts and calamitous crop failures of 1855 and 1856. By 1860, there were 40,273 people, 3,635 farms, and 77,219 acres of improved land in cultivation in the Utah Territory. The wheat yield was nine bushels for each person in the territory. Most significant was the fact that the Mormon principle of individual responsibility for land use kept the amount of unimproved land in farms at a low figure as compared with every other state and territory. Only Illinois and Ohio had more improved than unimproved lands in farms in 1860. The ratio of improved to unimproved land in Dakota was one to twelve, in New Mexico one to eight, in Nebraska one to four, in Washington one to three, in Oregon one to one, but in Utah it was one to sixteen.[5] This was no small achievement. In the face of great adversity the Saints not only had survived but had created a successful community capable of feeding itself and of supplying

[4] Leonard J. Arrington, "The Mormon Tithing House: A Frontier Institution," *Business History Review*, XXVIII (March, 1954), 24 ff., and his *Great Basin Kingdom: An Economic History of the Latter-Day Saints, 1830–1900* (Cambridge, Mass.: Harvard University Press, 1958), pp. 134 ff.
[5] Computed from *Eighth Census of the United States, Agriculture, 1860* (Washington, D. C.: Government Printing Office, 1864), *passim*.

surpluses to emigrants passing through and to mining communities. More, it had shown that with group action and intelligent leadership the arid lands could be farmed successfully.

OREGON TERRITORY

Oregon Territory, unlike Utah Territory, was treated exceedingly generously by the federal government. It was promptly created as a territory in 1848, only two years after British surrender of joint occupation, and was admitted as a state in 1859, before it had the 60,000 population considered proper for admission. Early provision was made for surveys, which were pressed forward rapidly. Liberal donations of land were made to public institutions, and the most generous homestead policy ever to be authorized by the United States was instituted to attract immigrants to the territory. Settlers who resided there on December 1, 1850, were given, if married, a full section of land on condition of occupying and improving it for four years; if unmarried, 320 acres on the same conditions. People who emigrated to Oregon between December 1, 1850, and December 1, 1855, and who occupied and improved land were given 320 acres if married, 160 acres if single. The motivation of Congress in so generously treating a border territory, and it applied to the Washington Territory, is clear: here, in Oregon, was the actual beginning of the homestead policy that was to flower in the Act of 1862.[6] Such generosity was not to be duplicated until 1904, 1909, and 1916, when Congress experimented with 640- and 320-acre homestead offers. The enlarged homesteads obtainable in the twentieth century, however, were thinly grassed tracts in the semi-arid region which had little value except for grazing, whereas the Oregon grants were of choice land. That it was necessary to offer such inducements for settlement in the Willamette Valley, described by Hall Jackson Kelley as "the most favoured spot of His beneficence," having a climate the "most healthful in the world" may be doubted.[7] The government's bounty did not substantially accelerate the flow of population to Oregon, because of the greater attractions of California's gold and the excitement over Bleeding Kansas, which brought these areas an overwhelming amount of publicity. The growth of the Oregon Territory was not spectacular, but it was steady and sound.

[6] Acts of September 27, 1850, and February 14, 1853; 9 *U. S. Stat.* 496 and 10 *U. S. Stat.* 158; *Congressional Globe*, 31 Cong., 1 Sess., September 17, 1850, pp. 1839–1848; James M. Bergquist, "The Oregon Donation Act and the National Land Policy," *Oregon Historical Quarterly*, LVIII (March, 1957), 17 ff.
[7] Hall J. Kelly, *A Georgraphical Sketch of the Part of North America Called Oregon* (Boston: J. Howe, 1930), pp. 18, 25.

STATUS OF FARMING IN WASHINGTON AND
OREGON, 1860

	Popu-lation	Grants	Farms	Farmers	Acreage of Grants	Acreage in farms Improved	Un-improved
Oregon	52,465	7,317	5,657	7,861	2,563,757	896,414	1,164,125
Washington	11,594	985	1,259	1,260	290,215	81,869	284,287

Source: Compiled from *Eighth Census of the United States, Agriculture*, pp. 184, 222, and *Population*, p. 663; Thomas Donaldson, *The Public Domain* (Washington: Government Printing Office, 1884), pp. 295–297. The number of farm laborers for Oregon is given as 1,653 and for Washington as 257.

The table suggests either that the census officials erred badly in collecting data on the number of farms (which may well be the case), or that the privilege of free donations was seriously abused in Oregon. The census figures also suggest that in the fifties the settlers in Oregon turned their attention to farming more seriously than did those in the other new states of Kansas, Minnesota, and California. They had an average of seventeen acres of improved land in farms for each inhabitant, as compared with seven for California, four for Kansas, and three for Minnesota. The Census also shows, perhaps for the last time, that Oregon was producing four times as much wheat as Kansas. Jayhawkers absorbed in the Kansas conflict and the Californians in the gold rush expanded the agriculture of their respective states but slowly. Oregon happily escaped the excessive speculation in land to which both Kansas and Minnesota were subjected during the prosperous fifties.

Congress was somewhat less interested in New Mexico than in Oregon, but it did grant to citizens living there prior to 1853 a free homestead of 160 acres. Few took advantage of the offer, however, for only 135 certificates for 20,104 acres were issued.[8]

CALIFORNIA

Congressional generosity in granting free homesteads to settlers in Oregon and New Mexico was not extended to California. In fact, California in its infancy was treated like an unwanted child. In other areas with an alien population, the residents who had no land had been given a free grant when the territory was transferred to American control. This had been true of Michigan, Indiana, Illinois, Missouri, Louisiana, Florida, Alabama, and Mississippi. But the landless residents of California were not given free homesteads. Also, surveys were so delayed that years

[8] Thomas Donaldson, *The Public Domain: Its History* (Washington, D. C.: Government Printing Office, 1884), p. 297.

elapsed before settlers could gain any rights on government land. Not until 1853 were settlements authorized on unsurveyed land, and then the privilege was inapplicable to much of the better land since it had not yet been determined what was private and what was public land. Congress was slow in providing for the establishment of a Board of Land Commissioners to adjudicate the land claims dating from the Spanish and Mexican period. The board, in turn, was slow to get under way and slower to act; not until 1856 did it complete an investigation of the 813 claims presented to it. Only after the claims had been confirmed and surveyed, or rejected and returned to public-land status, was it possible to determine what was public and what was private land.

Included in the 813 claims was most of the better agricultural land in the coastal valleys and along the Sacramento River. These claims had been granted by the Mexican-appointed governors of California as ranchos for the raising of cattle, and ranged from one to eleven square leagues of 4,438 acres each.[9] A few grants of mission lands included as much as 60,000 to 133,000 acres. Practically none of the claimants had perfect titles, and few had bothered to conform to the conditions and requirements for securing them. Many claims were unsurveyed and had the vaguest of boundaries; some had not even been located; others were conflicting and overlapping. Until this tangle of inchoate, incomplete, conditional, unsurveyed and unlocated grants had been cleared, ownerships established, surveys made of the confirmed claims, and the location of public lands determined, there was little prospect of peaceful development of California's agricultural possibilities. The rush of population to California before Congress had initiated surveys and provided for the extension of the land system to it, and the backwash of disappointed miners looking for land to make into farms all created a pressure upon the supply of land that resulted in conflicts over public lands, squatter intrusions on the private claims, and small-scale warfare between squatters and claimants.

The Land Act of 1851 for the adjudication of the land claims was based on past practice and embodied the results of long experience in dealing with French, Spanish, and British claims ranging from Michigan, Indiana, Illinois, Missouri, Arkansas, and Louisiana to Florida. In adjudicating some 20,000 claims in these states, the federal government had met practically every problem that the California claims presented, and had evolved machinery for considering them which safeguarded the rights of legitimate owners, though the issuance of the patent might be delayed for years. The Act of 1851 provided for the usual board to examine and confirm or reject the claims as the documentary evidence justified. Both

---

[9] The end papers in Robert G. Cowan, *Ranchos of California* (Fresno: Academy Library Guild, 1956), show the confirmed grants.

the claimant and the government had the right of appeal to the district court and to the Supreme Court of the United States for reconsideration. Final determination of ownership was made by the Supreme Court on appeal. After confirmation, the grants had to be surveyed and the surveys approved by the General Land Office and, if appealed, by the courts. Dubious claims and those which claimants sought to stretch to include mining and farming improvements made by others might not be decided for years. On the other hand, most claims supported with adequate documents and evidence of continued occupation and improvement, and whose survey presented no difficulties, easily won confirmation by the commission and the district court.

California historians have harshly judged the Land Act of 1851. They maintain that many native Californians were so impoverished by the costs of litigating their claims that they lost the land on which they had lived for years. Many early Californians did lose their land but not solely—not even largely—because of the cost of litigation. In fact, between a quarter and a third of the claims had been acquired by Americans and other recent immigrants before the transfer of the territory to the United States in 1848. Well over half of the grants had been made in the forties—eighty-seven of them in 1846—and had not been developed at all. These had been given to friends, business and political associates, and relatives of the last governor in anticipation of the transfer of the territory to American control, and were not intended as colonization grants or as rewards for the development of the land. The fact is that the Mexican or native Californians, like the Creoles of Louisiana in the early part of the nineteenth century, had less regard for landownership than had Anglo-Americans, less foresight, and little realization of the increase in land values that might occur with American occupation. They lived extravagantly, were hard hit by taxes and drought, borrowed on their claims, and had to pay 1 to 8 per cent interest monthly; they showed little of the concern for their obligations that other mortgage-ridden Americans felt; and thus they were brought to bankruptcy or to foreclosure of their estates. A considerable number of the claims had been antedated, their title tainted with fraud.

Early transfer of claims did not necessarily mean division of the large holdings. Shrewd buyers, such as Abel Stearns, John Forster, and Edward F. Beale of southern California, added to their already extensive holdings until they ran into the hundreds of thousands of acres. Farther north, however, where there was greater pressure on the supply of good land, the large holdings were being subdivided.

Squatters, disappointed because they found no land open to preemption and contemplating the great areas of uncultivated land within the private claims, settled upon them, made their improvements, and started farming operations. In a short time they had spread over most of the northern claims and were reported to be killing the cattle, cutting down the trees, and threatening the life of the claimants if they were disturbed. Ejectment proceedings were attempted but not always with success, for settlers had learned long since that, if united, they could resist the law effectively, at least for a time.[10]

The Board of Commissioners proved so liberal in confirming questionable titles that its lenience aroused criticism and brought forth suggestions for tightening the Act of 1851. At the same time the increasingly favorable sentiment toward squatters, caused partly by the confirmation of obviously fraudulent claims and by a growing realization of the extent of land monopoly in California, led the legislature and Congress to adopt measures to protect squatters in peaceful possession of their land against claimants having defective titles. When the judges struck down these measures the squatters had recourse only to the election of friendly local officials and to mass action to prevent ejectments.[11] The slow grinding of the judicial mills gradually settled the title to claims, though the surveys of the confirmed claims remained for many years longer an unsettling and disturbing problem. By the end of 1860 only 88 patents had been issued for land claims; by 1870, 320; by 1875, 456; by 1880, 517.[12] Some grantees who won confirmation not only tried to exact the full value of land they might sell the occupants but also demanded back rents for the years in which the latter had been on the land.[13] Until well into the seventies, ejectment suits and other title cases filled the calendars of the state courts and added largely to the cost of securing title to farm land in California.

The legacy of the California land claims was a concentrated pattern of ownership of land, a small number of farms in relation to the population, large bonanza farms, and a high proportion of farm laborers and tenants.[14] It was also responsible, so California writers affirmed, for

[10] For the work of the Land Commission I have borrowed heavily from my "Adjudication of Spanish-Mexican Land Claims in California," *Huntington Library Quarterly*, XXI (May, 1958), 213–236.

[11] Act of March 26, 1856; *Statutes of California*, Seventh Session of the Legislature, 1856 (Sacramento: James Allen, 1856), pp. 54–56; *Los Angeles Star*, April 21, 1855, and April 5 and 12, 1856; Act of April 26, 1856; *Statutes of California*, Ninth Session of the Legislature, 1858 (Sacramento: John O'Meara, 1858); p. 345; *Weekly Alta California*, May 15 and June 19, 1858; Act of May 18, 1858, 11 *U. S. Stat.* 290.

[12] *Corrected Report of Spanish and Mexican Grants in California Complete to February 25, 1886*, prepared by the California Surveyor General and published as a supplement to his *Office Report* for 1883–1884 (Sacramento: 1886), *passim*.

[13] *San Francisco Telegram* in *Sacramento Union*, December 10, 1859.

[14] The first tenancy figures of the Census of 1880 show the California counties having the highest rates of tenancy to be those in which the greater proportion of their land was in Spanish and Mexican claims.

thousands of settlers who found no land which they could take up and improve, going elsewhere to begin farming.

Mishandling of federal grants of land was quite the rule on the part of the states, and California's experience in prematurely and improperly selling warrants for its 500,000-acre grant for internal improvements was not unusual. By an Act of 1852 the state provided for the sale of scrip in amounts of 320 acres to be used to acquire public land before any such land had been segregated from the land claims, before surveys, and, in fact, before any federal land was open to acquisition. Speculators bought up much of the scrip, sought out what appeared to be the best lands outside the Mexican claims, whether settlers were on it or not, made application for titles, and proceeded to sell their rights to others. In so doing they violated federal law by filing on unsurveyed land, and also the California law of 1852, which did not permit the scrip to be used on land occupied by squatters. Settlers coming into areas claimed by scrip holders squatted upon the tracts, holding that location by the scrip holder before survey was illegal. So it was, but so also was the settlement of the squatter before 1853. Another series of conflicts thus emerged between new groups of land claimants and squatters. In the Humboldt Bay region, squatters organized an asociation for mutual protection, appointed a vigilante committee to prevent scrip holders from locating on land held by their members, and drew up a memorial to Congress condemning the speculators who were taking advantage of a badly framed law.[15]

In 1853, the slowness with which surveys were made in California and the bitterness of the squatters at the quantity of land claimed by Mexican holders, induced Congress for the first time to extend the preemption privilege to settlers on unsurveyed lands.[16] In the following year the privilege was extended to settlers in a number of other territories. The pressure for opening the public lands before the survey was great, but, in letting down the bars, Congress was neither making easier the efforts of legitimate owners of private land claims to develop their property nor easing the burdens of the local land officers, who thereafter were to be deluged with conflicts between two or more settlers claiming preemption rights on the same quarter section whose boundaries were not established when they made their improvements. Extension of preemption to unsurveyed lands was an invitation to squatters, which they readily accepted, to take up lands near the private claims. Thus a rapidly deteriorating situation was aggravated.

[15] Act of May 3, 1852; *Statutes of California,* Third Session of the Legislature (San Francisco: G. K. Fitch & Co., 1852), p. 41; *San Francisco Herald,* January 20, 1853; *Placer Times and Transcript,* Sacramento, October 25, 1853; *Alta California,* November 10 and December 29, 1853.

[16] Acts of March 3, 1853, and March 1, 1854; 10 *U. S. Stat.* 246, 268.

Extension of pre-emption to unsurveyed lands could quiet the discontent of the landless, but it could not expedite the passage of land to patent. In November, 1857, four and a half years after the enactment of the pre-emption law, only 28 pre-emption entries had been completed— for 4,352 acres. An additional 862 declaratory statements (intentions to pre-empt) had been filed, and 2,160 notices of intentions to pre-empt were filed when the surveys had been run. Over the course of the next three years the government sold 148,989 acres and accepted entries of a somewhat larger amount of land for military bounty warrants. Never had the government been so tardy in bringing land into market for purchase and settlement in a region being flooded by a great wave of immigration.[17]

In the fifties California and territorial Kansas were simultaneously in much the same situation. In neither was land available for purchase for years after settlers had moved in. Titles on claims could not be secured, borrowing to make improvements could be done only at excessive interest because of the risks involved in lending on uncertain titles, squatters' associations flourished, and numerous conflicts occurred when squatters found their improvements had been made on land claimed by others. Government failure to deal promptly with the land problems of California and Kansas produced bitter agrarian feelings. It left a heritage in California that Henry George was to make much of in his attacks upon large ownerships of land.[18] In Kansas its fruits were seen in the heavy mortgage indebtedness that made Jayhawk farmers especially vulnerable to price fluctuations and responsive to the outburst of agrarianism in the nineties. Utah, notwithstanding its even greater neglect by the federal government, made few complaints, and shaped its own land system with controls that avoided the excesses and harmful results seen elsewhere.

Despite all the confusion, bickering, and turmoil over land titles and survey lines in California, the demand for food by a rapidly growing population induced many, including those disillusioned at the mines, to turn to agriculture. In the past, native Californians had not been interested in farming, that is, in cultivating the land and raising crops. They were rancheros or vaqueros, and cattle raising was their major economic interest. They had not, however, shown concern about improving the quality of their cattle. This is understandable for, before American occupation, cattle had little value aside from their hides and tallow and their meat for domestic consumption. Through long neglect the cattle had

[17] Argus in California Farmer, VIII (November 20, 1857), 152; Commissioner of the General Land Office, Annual Reports, 1857, 1858, 1859, 1860, passim.

[18] Henry George, Our Land and Land Policy (New York: Doubleday and McClure Company, 1901), Chap. 1, "The Lands of the United States," and Chap. 2, "The Lands of California."

become small, tough, rangy, and slow-growing, and had little but coarse-grained meat. The sheep, hardy and coarse-wooled, provided unappetizing mutton.

California's transfer to American control and the inrush of population created a demand for meat animals, a demand which brought prosperity to southern rancheros and led to the importation of quantities of grade and purebred cattle and sheep from the East and the Middle West. Where formerly the value of cattle lay in their hides and tallow, now the demand in the mining camps and growing cities for beef was such as to make it profitable to drive cattle the five hundred miles and more from the southern "cow counties" to rapidly growing northern markets. Cattle brought such favorable prices that rancheros found themselves wealthy almost over night. Shrewd dealers like Abel Stearns, whose herds amounted to 20,000 cattle in 1853, were able to lend money to less efficient rancheros and ultimately to acquire their holdings. The era of lush prosperity lasted for a number of years, but the high prices that livestock brought led to such extensive importations as to flood the market and lower prices.[19] For the long pull, however, the importations of eastern cattle and sheep brought overland and by sea worked their magic in improving the quality of native stock.[20]

The usual conflict between stockmen and farmers showed itself early. Farmers were distressed that cattle and sheep were destroying their wheat, which they could not afford to fence, and they urged legislation to compel the "stock lords and cattlemongers" to be responsible for the damage their stock did to growing crops. Stockmen were accused of pre-empting forty- or eighty-acre tracts in the midst of farming communities, where their cattle could subsist chiefly on the crops of neighboring farmers.[21]

The great ranchos of the Mexican period, though granted for grazing

[19] Abel Stearns, October 14, 1853, to A. Randall, copy, Stearns MSS, The Huntington Library; Robert Glass Cleland, The Cattle on a Thousand Hills (San Marino, Calif.: The Huntington Library), pp. 72 ff.

[20] A cattleman held that a two-year-old steer by an American bull was equal to a three-year-old "California Novillo," and that the meat was far better. The difference between the quality and size of native and imported cattle was shown in the San Francisco market, where the former were quoted at $20 to $30 and the latter at $55 to $67 a head.—Letters of Lewis Belcher, Stockton, September 10, 1852; S. A. Pollard, Rancho Nipomo, May 4, 1855; and Charles R. Johnson, Martinez, August 19, 1856, to Abel Stearns, Stearns MSS, The Huntington Library; California Farmer, V (March 7, 1856), 72, and VII (June 19, 1857), 180; John S. Hittell, Resources of California (San Francisco: A. Roman & Co., 1863), p. 284; Alta California, September 18, 1853. In 1868 Los Angeles County assessed Merino and other fine sheep at $5.00 each, "improved" sheep at $1.50 each and "California" sheep at $1.00 each.—The People of the State of California v. Flint, Irvine & Co., p. 50.

[21] Alta California, April 28, 1860.

livestock, proved adaptable to grain. In the drier areas, the possession of water rights and the construction of irrigation and drainage canals, all requiring heavy capital investments and feasible only for large tracts, gave to the entrepreneur with resources a big advantage over men of limited means. Consequently, from the outset of its agricultural development, California had many large farms ranging up to several thousand acres.

Wheat and barley were the principal cash crops on the large farms. Gang plows permitted the preparation of broad areas for sowing. Fields of 100 to 250 acres of grain were common, but some ranged as high as 1,000 to 1,500 acres. Good prices, and the ease with which these cereals could be produced, harvested, threshed, and hauled to market, induced farmers and rancheros to place heavy reliance on the two crops. In adapting midwestern planting methods to California, farmers learned to prepare the land for grain in the fall after the first rain had loosened the hard-baked crust. Shallow plowing aided in retaining the moisture in the soil by preventing evaporation. Mechanical reapers were essential for cutting the grain, for in the searing heat of summer it ripened quickly and losses were likely to be heavy unless it was harvested promptly. Heavy reliance on the production of grain led to predictions that over-croping would soon impoverish the land,[22] if indeed it had not already done so.

By 1859, California was raising a surplus of grain not easy to market, and its farmers were harvesting the highest average yield of wheat per farm in the country—316 bushels as compared with 166 for Illinois, the leading wheat state.[23] Abundant crops and lower prices brought trouble to farmers, who were urged to diversify more and to feed their poorer wheat, mixed with barley, to horses and mules. By 1860, nearly a third of the wheat of California was being exported, either as grain or flour. The glut in the market had one advantage in that it defeated speculators who sought to corner the supply and create and artificial scarcity.[24]

In the heyday of their missions, the Franciscan padres had successfully irrigated fertile tracts of land and produced abundant crops of fruit and grain. Although long neglected and run down, the missions remained as mute evidence of what the land could be made to do. In the fifties artesian wells were used to provide water for irrigating farm land. In some of the narrower valleys and in locations close to the foothills, wells

[22] *Transactions* of the California State Agricultural Society, 1858 (Sacramento: 1859), pp. 166 ff.; *Sacramento Bee* in *Alta California*, January 21, 1860.

[23] *Eighth Census of the United States, Agriculture, 1860*, pp. 185, 222.

[24] *Alta California*, December 8, 1860; Horace Davis, "Wheat in California," *Overland Monthly*, I (November, 1868), 446 ff.; Charles E. Johnson, San Francisco, July 21, 1856, to Abel Stearns, Stearns MSS, The Huntington Library.

could be drilled without great difficulty. By 1855, there were two hundred artesian wells in the San Jose Valley alone. These wells were used to irrigate a few acres of orchard, vineyard, or truck gardens. Unfortunately, it was found that a flowing well lowered the level of other wells from which people were pumping. Proposals were made to restrict the use of flowing wells, but the people were not yet ready for effective control of valuable water resources.[25] In the mining country, farmers secured some water for irrigation from the flumes built to aid the miners in extracting the gold from the alluvium. Californians were learning the possibilities of irrigation farming. The *Alta California* anticipated the move that culminated in the Desert Land Act of 1877 when, in 1855, it called upon the federal government to donate to entrepreneurs such lands as they irrigated by stream diversion and ditch construction.[26]

Before they came to California farm makers had had more experience in reclaiming wet lands than in irrigating dry lands and, as might be expected, in the first decade of American occupation they made more progress in reclamation than in irrigation. The tule lands along the San Joaquin and Sacramento rivers were rich and fertile, but they were overflowed much of the time and were not suitable for cultivation unless drained. Under the Swamp Land Act of 1850, California received these tule and other wet lands to the amount of 2,159,303 acres, with the understanding that it would drain them. Instead, the state authorized their sale at one dollar an acre on five years' credit and pledged the proceeds to the retirement of bonds issued for the erection of a state prison. Sales were made before the swamp land had been surveyed, selected, or approved by the federal government. Squatters on the wet lands came into dispute with the buyers of the lands, and another source of irritation, litigation, and conflict over titles, was thus created.[27] State administration accomplished nothing toward the draining of the lands, but private initiative was more successful. By 1860, extensive tracts of rich tule land divided into hundreds of "snug farms" were being brought into cultivation as a result of the construction of levees and ditches to shut out and drain the low areas along the San Joaquin and Sacramento rivers and in the San Francisco Bay area. Heavy, deep-cutting plows, one operated by steam, dug ditches as deep as three feet, throwing up the earth on one side for levees.[28]

[25] *Alta California*, January 28, 1860; *Los Angeles Star*, September 28, 1855.

[26] *Alta California*, December 27, 1853.

[27] *Alta California*, February 18, 1852; *San Francisco Herald* in *Daily California Express*, Marysville, August 28, 1858. Act of May 1, 1852; *Statutes of California*, Third Session of the Legislature (San Francisco: G. K. Fitch & Co., 1852), p. 133; and Act of April 28, 1855; *Statutes of California*, Sixth Session of the Legislature (Sacramento: B. B. Redding, 1855), p. 189.

[28] *Weekly Alta California*, June 16 and 30, July 6, 1860.

In 1860, 35 per cent of California's farms contained less than one hundred acres, and their ability to compete with grain farms of one thousand acres and more was being questioned. An advocate of the small farm maintained that on a tract of fifty or sixty acres, a farmer, with the aid of his family, could harvest sufficient grain to assure him a profit, whereas the big farmer who had to pay wages to laborers of $20 or $25 a month could not prosper. He was promptly answered by others who held that grain farming could flourish in California only if conducted in a big way through the use of the gang plow, the reaper, and the drill. The small farmer could not afford such expensive machines, which would be idle much of the year, but on the large farms operations could be so arranged that the machines could be kept in use for longer periods.[29]

Small farmers had their opportunity, however, when they learned how admirably adapted the soil and climate of California were to raising grapes, apples, and other fruits and vegetables. These crops could be produced on small tracts as well as on large ones and had a ready market in the fast-growing cities and in the mining camps. The native or Spanish-Mexican grapes were inferior for wine making and had early to be abandoned. Grape farmers and wine makers showed initiative in importing different varieties of grapes. Most responsible for the early lead California took in grape raising and wine making was a Hungarian immigrant, Ágoston Haraszthy. By successfully introducing foreign cuttings on his rancho near Sonoma and by experimenting to determine the best grapes and best procedures for wine making, Haraszthy showed other farmers what could be done with small acreages in grapes. Large wineries in Sonoma, the Napa Valley, and near Los Angeles bought the grapes of farmers who did not have their own equipment for processing them and making wine. Haraszthy had 80,000 vines growing on his farm in 1858, while in the entire state there were 8,000,000 vines under way or already producing. Troubles in wine making and marketing, such as adulteration, the use of improper casks, lack of adequate storage facilities, unfamiliarity of the producers with the best techniques of wine making, and the poor quality of their product, gave California wines a poor reputation, but the influence of Haraszthy brought about continued improvement.[30]

The truck gardening business came to be as flourishing as the fruit industry. The average value of garden produce per farm for California in 1859 was the highest of all the states—$62—and its average value of

[29] Alta California, April 14 and May 12, 1860.

[30] Alta California, July 28 and September 1, 1860; Transactions of the California State Agricultural Society, 1858, pp. 242–246, 283–287; Ágoston Haraszthy, Grape Culture, Wines, and Wine-Making (New York: Harper & Brothers, 1862), pp. xv ff.; Vincent P. Carosso, The California Wine Industry, 1830–1895 (Berkeley: University of California Press, 1951), pp. 38 ff.

orchard products per farm—$40—was exceeded only by that of Oregon, $82. California farmers raised two dollars' worth of fruit for every person in the state, while New York, the chief fruit state, produced less than a dollar's worth for each person. Similarly, in garden produce California farmers raised three dollars' worth, whereas New Jersey raised a little over two dollars' worth.[31] California's eminence in fruit and vegetable production is partly explained by the higher prices that prevailed there, but more important was the fact that farmers had learned how, on small truck gardening and fruit farms, they could, by intensive farming and irrigation, make the land yield a variety of products for which there was a rapidly expanding demand.

By 1860, a new section had come into existence in the American Union to complicate the old division of the Northeast, the South, and the upper Mississippi Valley. In their farming operations its occupants pursued practices as different from those of northeastern farmers as the latter differed from practices in Louisiana. Experiments in dry and irrigation farming and issues over water rights were forcing changes in farm practices and pointing to the need for modification of land policies. Careful and precise planning of the time of sowing and harvesting grain, larger operations and the greater use of machines, mulching the soil, and dependence on crops tolerant of droughts were among the changes in farm practices. Years of bitter conflicts over water rights and land policies lay ahead, during which government policies were but slowly adapted to practical needs.

[31] *Eighth Census of the United States, Agriculture, 1860,* p. 186.

CHAPTER XIX

Economic Problems

FARMING, wherever carried on, was a complicated business involving many different operations and requiring many skills. In addition to raising field crops and livestock and tending orchards and gardens, the farmers were retailers in a small way, disposing of some of their surplus products locally. The more intelligent of them subscribed to a newspaper or farm journal and watched market quotations closely. On a small scale the farmer was often an employer as well as a craftsman and a mechanic. Above all, the farmer was a creator of capital and an investor, holding down his standard of consumption so as to be able to make improvements, investing his own life and labor, and the labor of his hired men and slaves, in the land. To put it as would the frontiersman who had the notion that labor was the source of all wealth, it was the farmer, the cultivator of the soil, who made the land valuable.

Improving land and creating farms was not the work of a decade or two; it went on for a generation or more. Gradually the farmer brought more of his acreage under cultivation, cleared brush and trees, ditched or tiled wet areas, fenced all his land, erected larger barns and sheds, and built a frame house to replace what was often a log hut. He also wanted to improve his livestock, to purchase the new machinery that was coming on the market, and to bring running water into the barn and perhaps into the house, by gravity flow or by the much-talked-of hydraulic ram. He thought not only of his own family's needs but also of the community; hence he wished for better school facilities, better roads, a nearby church, the building of canals and railroads. All these he helped to create by paying his taxes, performing his road services, by voting local aid to transportation companies, which increased his taxes, and by donations of money and labor for the building of churches. These improvements added to the capital value of his farm. Unlike the urban laborer working in mine or mill his twelve or fourteen hours daily, creating profits and capital for others, the farmer on his own land was creating capital for himself as well as for the community.

The community was also creating capital value for him. As population pressed into an area, the demand for land and its market value increased. Part of the value of an improved farm was therefore the consequence of the capital and labor the owner-operator invested in it, and part was the contribution of society, the unearned increment. The pioneer farmer was well aware that in the end his profits would come largely from rising land values. Usually he bought or tried to buy more land than he could utilize and sometimes more than he could finance with safety. As a squatter he might sell his crude improvements and his claim and obtain some advantage from the advance in land values. As a permanent settler he might sell off a surplus forty or eighty, garnering some unearned increment. Or he might gradually bring all his land under improvement and leave his children a valuable property, part of whose capital value would be of his own creating and part would be unearned increment. But the successful pioneer did not use the term "unearned increment." If he was a simple man he explained his success by saying, "I came west and grew up with the country." If he was pompous he attributed his success to "hard work, plain living and high thinking."

In the numerous county histories are to be found accounts of many thousands of farmers who started life with limited resources and ended up with a substantial amount of property, the major part of which was land, stock, and machinery. This is a record of solid success despite adversity. Unfortunately, from the historian's point of view, only those who succeeded appear in these volumes, for only they could afford to buy space in them and purchase the books. The squatter who bought his claim at the government auction with a loan that cost him 30 or 40 per cent a year and who never could pay off his obligation and so ultimately lost his farm, the farmer who incurred debts through ill-health, crop failures, or diseases among his animals, or who optimistically bought an additional eighty when times looked right and found he could not swing it, all these and others who failed and lost their property are not in these histories. Some slipped down the ladder to tenant or hired-man status, others wiped the dust of the region from their feet and set out for the land of the setting sun where they might try again.

Except in the Pennsylvania-German area, and with individual exceptions elsewhere, American farmers regarded their land as the means of quickly making a fortune through the rising land values which the progress of the community and their own individual improvements would give it. Meanwhile they mined the land by cropping it continuously to its most promising staple. They did not look upon it as a lifetime investment, a precious possession whose resources were to be carefully husbanded, whose soil they could enrich and would ultimately pass on to their children more valuable and more productive than when they acquired it. To them land was not an enduring investment but a speculation which they were prepared to part with when the opportunity came to sell at a favorable price. James F. W. Johnston noted this tendency:

. . . there is as yet in New England and New York scarcely any such thing as local attachment—the love of a place, because it is a man's own—because he has hewed it out of the wilderness, and made it what it is; or because his father did so, and he and his family have been born and brought up, and spent their happy youthful days upon it. Speaking generally, every farm from Eastport in Maine, to Buffalo on Lake Erie, is for sale. The owner has already fixed a price in his mind for which he would be willing, and even hopes to sell, believing that, with the same money, he could do better for himself and his family by going still further west.[1]

Similarly, Arthur Carpenter, writing from Iowa, in 1853, said that nearly every man in his neighborhood was ready to sell his farm.[2]

In considering the question "Is Farming Profitable?" a contributor to the *Ohio Farmer,* in 1856, held that it was in a rich country like Ohio where settlers could take up government land and a generation later have a productive farm worth $5,000 or $10,000 on which they could live "as comfortably as mechanics. . . ." The writer conceded, however, that the profits, aside from the increased value, came from continued grain cropping which had rapidly exhausted the soil.[3]

When a farm reached the point beyond which additional labor and capital could not economically be expended upon its further development, it might still increase in value if its situation were in demand and the fertility of the soil were maintained by good practices. If, on the other hand, its agricultural pattern had become archaic, if through poor tillage practices the soil was being washed away, or if it was meeting competition from richer and more productive areas elsewhere, the owner's chances of enjoying rising land values were limited if not ended. Beyond that point the owner-operator was no longer creating capital. These diverse possibilities may be observed in Massachusetts, Vermont, Kentucky, and Pennsylvania.

Land values in Worcester County, Massachusetts, were in a state of near equilibrium in the fifties and also in the sixties. During these inflationary decades, when land values were increasing generally, the value of Worcester County farm land (with acreage diminished through abandon-

---

[1] James F. W. Johnston, *Notes on North America: Agricultural, Economical and Social* (2 vols.; Edinburgh: William Blackwood & Sons, 1851), I, 162.

[2] Arthur Carpenter, Montezuma, July 22, 1853, to his brother, Redfield MSS, The Huntington Library.

[3] *Ohio Farmer,* V (April 19, 1856), 62.

ment) increased less than 1 per cent in the fifties and slightly more than 1 per cent in the sixties. Production of butter, cheese, and wool, as well as the number of sheep and swine in the county, declined sharply. On the other hand, the number of cattle remained stationary while their value increased. Farmers in this county were adapting themselves to western competition by giving up or reducing their flocks of sheep, eliminating poorer land from cultivation, using better farm equipment, resorting to truck gardening and fruit production, improving their livestock, especially dairy cows, and selling fluid milk. The opportunity for profit making from rising land values in Worcester County was over. Small wonder then that from this area farmers were emigrating.

A perceptive student of "Migration from Vermont" found much the same situation in the Green Mountain State, despite the fact that as late as the fifties agriculture was still expanding somewhat. The older cultivated lands, especially the hilly areas which had lost much of their topsoil by erosion and had been exhausted by continued wheat cropping, gave out. "Vermonters' profits in the past," Lewis Stilwell contends, had been "derived as much from increasing land values as they were from agriculture. When the unearned increment ceased with the cessation of new settlements, the land itself was not enough to make a living." Contrasting their situation with that of farm makers in the West where "land values were rising, markets were improving and everything was 'on the make,'" the Vermont farmers were brought to despair and to the decision to emigrate. Vermont and the hill country of other northeastern states "were exporting men, because they could find little else to export." The unearned increment having long since been skimmed off, the farmers sought other regions where they could participate in the prosperity of a dynamically expanding economy.[4]

Contrast the situation in Worcester County and the New England hill region with that in Fayette and Bourbon counties, Kentucky, where the acreage in farms was in a state of near equilibrium. Both Fayette and Bourbon listed practically no unimproved land in farms in either 1850 or 1860. Their improved acreage expanded only slightly, but the total value of the land in farms increased by 67 per cent and 40 per cent, respectively. The explanation of the rising land values of these two counties is not that new land was brought under cultivation, but that large amounts of capital were invested in purebred livestock to utilize the extraordinarily rich bluegrass pastures. This is shown by the increase in the value of livestock for the decade: Bourbon, 123 per cent; Fayette, 60 per cent. At the same time, the richest farming county in the United States, Lancaster, in the heart of Pennsylvania German country, while

[4] Lewis D. Stilwell, *Migration from Vermont, 1776–1860, Proceedings* of the Vermont Historical Society, V (1937), 232.

increasing its land in farms by a mere 4 per cent, added to the value of its farms by 48 per cent. This old, well-established county was able to obtain such a large increase in value through its excellent farming practices, the improving quality of its livestock, and its high yields of grain.

Until the Panic of 1857, the fifties were a period of marked prosperity for farmers. Prices of staples were high, land values were pushing upward, farmers were putting into cultivation a larger proportion of their lands, more new farms were being created, and more additional areas in older farms were brought under cultivation than in any previous decade. Between 1850 and 1860, 587,976 new farms were created in the United States. During this same period farm-land values, including those of the newly created farms, increased by more than three billion dollars or 100 per cent. This increase in the value of farm land was unevenly distributed among the states and even in counties within states. It was highest, excluding California and Oregon, which were in their beginning stages, in Mississippi, where the value of all farm land increased by a thumping 176 per cent while the acreage of farms increased by 50 per cent. Other states with large increases in the value of their farm land were Illinois (121 per cent), Missouri (114 per cent), Tennessee and Louisiana (both 110 per cent), and Alabama (107 per cent). Twelve states, including Georgia, New Jersey, and Pennsylvania, failed to keep up with the national average. New England fell farthest behind, with only Vermont (40 per cent) coming close to the national average. Here again is evidence of the fact that the profits in rising land values in the Northeast had already been skimmed off by an earlier generation.[5]

Farmers went on making improvements in depression and in prosperity. Such improvements might not show in land values on a declining market but when the economic trend was reversed the added values became apparent. Those who held title to and retained ownership of the tracts they were improving were beneficiaries of the long-sustained rise in land values that went on progressively, although with violent fluctuations from 1815 to 1860. True, rising land values did not necessarily mean rising net returns. Yet, with greater net worth, the farmers' credit was better. They could borrow at lower interest rates, they could withhold their crops or stock from markets and thereby take advantage of better prices, they could feed their grain to their own livestock instead of having to sell it as soon as it was harvested, they could buy the new and improved reapers, plows, threshers, and drills, they could erect tighter fences, and they could drain their lowlands.

Tenants, whose numbers were increasing, particularly in the corn belt, where land values were climbing rapidly, had no share in the rising values. Commonly they worked out their rent by making improvements

[5] Computed from Censuses of 1850 and 1860.

on the land, which added to its value, made it possible for the landlord to exact larger rents in a few years' time, and this diminished their prospects of buying the farms they operated.

In well-established areas where farming was prosperous land values were expected to rise in a regular rate of progression. A writer in the Albany *Cultivator* expressed this in 1836 as follows:

Who ever heard of a man buying and selling a farm at the same or a lessened price? It is so well understood that the seller is to have more than he gave, that it has become almost a settled principle in the purchase of real estate. This percentage is sometimes very high, but in almost all cases, it adds materially to the profits of the investment. Besides, it is correct in principle; a tract of land under judicious culture, must be enhanced in value at least five per cent per annum . . . nine-tenths of all our property has been derived from this source alone, the increased and the increasing value of real estate.[6]

When commodity prices, new settlements, and farm making were all booming, many people emigrated to fast-growing areas *"to live by their wits,* rather than by cultivating the soil," as one writer put it. "It is undoubtedly true that many young men who have sought the West, are seeking for sudden wealth by the rise of land, or exorbitant interest, rather than by honest toil." With more insight than possessed by many he added, "It is certain that all cannot become rich in this way. All cannot be *shavers* —some must be *fleeced*."[7]

CREDIT AS A PROBLEM

The chief problems that the pioneer farmer had to meet in the process of developing his raw land into a productive farm were credit and markets. Few farmers had anything more to invest in their lands than their labor. Little actual money was brought into new communities by immigrants, who had generally exhausted their resources on moving themselves and their families to the new El Dorado. Capital goods, however, were brought: household effects, a plow, an ax, a shovel, a hoe, perhaps a few chickens, a hog, a cow, and horses or oxen. Most farmers were not able at the beginning to pay for their land, much less to stock or equip it, and they made their start either as squatters or by buying land on credit. In the goods economy the pioneer's capital was chiefly his labor. If, however, he could obtain credit for supplies, he could utilize his own labor to better advantage, create a productive farm more rapidly, and hasten the process of capital formation.

[6] *Cultivator,* II (January, 1836), 172.
[7] E. D. S., New York, May 23, 1857, in *Ohio Farmer,* VI (June 6, 1857), 90.

The pioneer farmer carried little capital in cash westward, but money went there through many other channels. For Indian occupancy rights, the payment of Indian annuities, the purchase of beef and pork for Indian and army rations, the surveying of land, the payment of territorial officers, and receivers and registers of land offices, the government had either to transmit funds to the West or to draw upon money received at the land offices. Fur traders, army officers, European travelers, land speculators, loan sharks, and representatives of eastern land and transportation companies altogether brought to new communities a great deal of money. Much of this money rapidly returned to the East. One portion went to the federal treasury as land-office receipts, another portion went to repay eastern speculators for land or loans. Eastern holders of western internal-improvement bonds also drew interest from the West. More money went east for the purchase of essential goods the West was not yet able to produce.[8] It has been seen how desperately new communities tried to produce commodities they could exchange for the goods they needed, but the balance was against them. In consequence, practically every transaction on the frontier involved credit.

The country storekeeper provided the pioneer with both credit and a market. In timbered areas he took from him the ashes obtained from clearing the land, perhaps staves and cordwood, even furs. He provided him with farm tools, ironware, salt, harness, logging chains, clothing, perhaps food. In prairie areas the farmer would more quickly have a crop to sell, but meanwhile he would need farm implements, ironware, tools, clothing, food, rough boards, and planed lumber.

Farmers in debt to a country merchant were virtually compelled to take their produce to him and he, in turn, discounted it heavily in both quality and quantity to aid in making up for losses suffered at the hands of absconding debtors. As long as the farmer had attachable property in the form of livestock, implements, land, or growing crops, he could expect credit within reason. The merchant was quite prepared to wait for payment because he himself had received credit from eastern capitalists and wholesalers, but meanwhile he kept "an eagle eye upon the last cow and prosecutes in season," if necessary.[9] Merchants took in the farmers' butter, cheese, grain, eggs, hogs, and cattle, which they would sell to a large dealer or drover, always on credit. These barter and credit deals permitted the transaction of a great volume of business without the use of money. When sufficient farm goods had accumulated to warrant shipment, the country storekeeper was able to replenish his stock in trade and his own credit. Successful merchants who thus accumulated capital were soon in a position to lend to farmers wishing to enlarge their operations,

[8] George L. Anderson, "Some Phases of Currency and Banking in Territorial Kansas," (University of Kansas Social Science Studies; Lawrence: 1954), p. 109.
[9] Plough Boy, I (April 8, 1820), 356.

to buy feeder cattle, or to complete payments on their land contracts in order to secure a clear and mortgageable title. At this point the small merchant, who had begun on a shoestring, emerged as an influential moneylender or banker, and the book credit previously extended to the farmer was changed into a loan secured by a mortgage on the farmer's property.[10]

Farmers borrowed to buy land either to begin farming operations or to enlarge them, and their need of credit expanded with their prosperity. They borrowed to carry them through till harvest, or until their stock was ready for slaughtering, or to purchase feeder cattle. They borrowed to build themselves a better house or barn, to buy some new and expensive equipment, such as a reaper, a thresher, a heavy plow, or a cheese press—whatever might improve their farm operations or save labor. They borrowed to drain their wet lands by ditching or tiling, to meet taxes, to relieve themselves of compulsory road work. These and many other developments on the farm required capital which the farmer could not provide without borrowing. In borrowing he was, perhaps, taking a risk, but he was doing much more; he was expanding the capital invested in his farm, thereby increasing its productivity and its value. Debt and mortgages might be a sign of progress, not a sign of distress.

The *New England Farmer* wrote perceptibly of the credit needs of farmers in older areas:

Their hired hands must be paid in autumn, if not sooner, and if they expect to get store goods and mechanics' work at a reasonable rate, they must pay as they go along. A farmer sells his pork, butter, cheese, grain, etc. from January to April. The cost of producing all these, was paid, (or ought to have been,) the summer and autumn before. His sheep are sheared in May, and should be able to convert their fleeces immediately into money, (which he cannot always do,) still the whole expense of producing this wool, excepting about two months spring pasturing, was paid the year before, a considerable portion of it the August before.

It cannot be denied that a farmer can get along after a fashion with little or no capital, because it is done by thousands every year. . . . A farmer without capital in the first place, will not perhaps hire more than half as much labor as his farm requires; of course all his work is slighted, and all done out of season, and half crops is the consequence. When the time arrives for paying his laborers, perhaps he will get some things out of the store for them on trust, or borrow a little money to pay them in part, and put off paying the remainder until winter or spring, to the no small injury of his credit, otherwise he must force sale of some of his scanty produce

[10] J. M. D. Burrows, *Fifty Years in Iowa* (Davenport: Glass & Company, 1888), *passim;* Lewis Eldon Atherton, *The Pioneer Merchant in Mid-America* (University of Missouri *Studies,* Vol. XIV, No. 2; Columbia: 1937); and Thomas D. Clark, *Pills, Petticoats and Plows: The Southern Country Store* (Indianapolis: The Bobbs-Merrill Company, 1944).

at a reduced price, to make out the pay. In the next place he buys of the storekeeper wholly on a long credit, and pays a price accordingly, say twenty to thirty per cent more than the cash price. His dealings with the blacksmith, shoemaker, and mechanics in general are after the same fashion. And thus he passes his life continually pinched for the want of a little money, incessantly harassed by duns, and once in a while appalled by a tap on the shoulder, though gentle it may be, of the practised hand of the constable.[11]

It was when farmers borrowed for speculation that they took serious risks. If they borrowed to buy a half or whole section of land without any expectation of improving more than a quarter of it, the income from their improved portion was often insufficient to meet the heavy interest they had to pay on their total speculative investment. Taxes might also hurt them, as they did absentee speculators.

It was not always a lack of credit that troubled farmers; sometimes credit came too easily, notably in the flush periods of the middle thirties and fifties, when banks and lending agencies were pressing their funds on prospective borrowers, though at high rates, particularly in newly developing areas. Land agents, representatives of land-grant canals and railroads, and farm-machinery companies urged their land or machines on farmers whose notes and mortgages they willingly took for payments extending over several years. Farmers, borne along on the tide of prosperity, enjoying favorable commodity prices, and witnessing the appreciation in land values, wanted to secure a larger share of it. Though their agricultural papers cautioned farmers against buying too much land and urged that their funds be put into improvements, their advice had little effect. When the era of inflation came to a halt and there was a sudden tightening of credit, calling in of loans, suspension of specie payments, and closing of banks, many a farmer found his overoptimism had brought him to the point where he was threatened with the loss of his home or perhaps the surrender of part of his land. He might also stand to lose his livestock, the agricultural machines he had bought on credit, and possibly his growing crops on which he had previously given liens.

The needs of southern planters for credit are too well known to need repetition. The planters, and, indeed, the small southern farmers, anticipated their returns from crops by drawing on their factors in advance against future deliveries of cotton, tobacco, or sugar. Once they had acquired a line of credit, it seemed difficult for them to liquidate their debts.[12] There is some evidence, however, that southern planters, at least

[11] Quoted in Percy Wells Bidwell and John I. Falconer, *History of Agriculture in the Northern United States, 1620–1860* (Washington, D. C.: Carnegie Institution, 1925), pp. 247–248.

[12] Ralph W. Haskins, "Planter and Cotton Factor in the Old South: Some Areas of Friction," *Agricultural History*, XXIX (January, 1955), 8 ff.

some of them, were not as much distressed by the exactions or charges of their factors and as dependent upon them as has been maintained. Roger Shugg found the indebtedness of Louisiana planters to New Orleans factors in 1861 to be $8,000,000, secured by plantation mortgages, crop liens, and notes.[13] He does not indicate whether this was the total debt of the planters, and doubtless it was not, but it probably was the larger part of their debt to banks or to previous owners. This debt was less than 4 per cent of the total value of the farms and plantations of Louisiana and was less than 20 per cent of the combined value of the cotton and sugar crops for 1859. Some planters and farmers were no doubt troubled by their obligations, but these figures provided little warrant for the view that the planters of Louisiana were overburdened with debt. True, they had to pay interest of 8 to 12 per cent, and sometimes an additional fee, and ship all their cotton or sugar to their factor, but such charges were not exorbitant for the time.

That some Southerners had either surplus capital or easy access to abundant credit through banks they controlled is apparent from the extensive investments they made in northern lands and railroads. Such outstanding planters as Loose of Maryland, Scott of Kentucky, Brent and Cabell of Virginia, Blanding and Grayson of South Carolina, Cobb and Shorter of Alabama, Duncan of Mississippi, and Slidell of Louisiana invested many hundreds of thousands of dollars in public lands in Indiana, Illinois, Iowa, Kansas, Wisconsin, and Minnesota. Dr. Stephen Duncan, owner of cotton and sugar plantations in Mississippi and Louisiana and Natchez banker, held more than a million dollars worth of securities of northern railroads. E. E. Malhiot, a substantial sugar planter of Assumption Parish, Louisiana, was not so burdened by this responsibility as to be prevented from purchasing 22,000 acres of Illinois prairie on which he settled one hundred Cajun and French-Canadian colonists. Close to a million acres of farm land, town and city property, and railroad securities of the North, at a conservative estimate, drew between four and eight million dollars for investment from the South.[14]

Land companies, speculators, nurseries, farm-implement manufacturers, and lumbermen were all aware that business in the West could be transacted only on a credit basis. Cyrus Woodman, one of a group of

[13] Roger W. Shugg, *Origins of Class Struggle in Louisiana* (Baton Rouge: Louisiana State University Press, 1939), p. 110.

[14] Paul W. Gates, "Southern Investments in Northern Lands before the Civil War," *Journal of Southern History*, V (May, 1939), 155 ff. For large investments in northern municipal securities and city property by two of Georgia's greatest planters, one of whom ultimately moved to New York City, see Ralph Betts Flanders, *Plantation Slavery in Georgia* (Chapel Hill: University of North Carolina Press, 1933), p. 104 and Savannah Writers' Project, Mary Granger, ed., *Savannah River Plantations* (Savannah: Georgia Historical Society, 1947), p. 308.

eastern capitalists who had a large investment in land in Illinois, found they did little business because they gave only one year's credit, whereas three or four years was usual.[15] On the other hand, in the late fifties Cyrus McCormick went on selling reapers to hard-pressed prairie farmers on credit. Because of poor crops resulting from unfortunate weather conditions and commodity prices affected by the depression, the farmer-debtors could not meet their obligations, which accumulated until they amounted to more than a million dollars. Other farm-machinery competitors faced the same degree of delinquency but, lacking McCormick's abundant resources, were forced to the wall, the only "consoling aspect of the hard times," to McCormick.[16]

In the prosperous years a great volume of capital flowed west and southwest, attracted by the high interest available there. Prior to 1820, however, credit facilities in the rural areas, including those provided by merchants, implement manufacturers, land companies, absentee speculators, and the federal government failed to satisfy the demand, and the cry went up for banks which would lend on real estate. To meet this demand the states experimented with a variety of banking institutions. One variety that flourished for a time in the South was the real-estate or property bank. The capital of these curious and unstable institutions was provided by stockholders who presented mortgages on their plantations for their stock subscriptions. These mortgages, in turn, were the security for bonds of the bank, which were sold to eastern banks or exchanged for state bonds that were similarly sold. Stockholders would borrow up to one half the amount of their stock subscription. State banks, whose capital was raised to a considerable degree abroad, were also set up with extraordinarily liberal procedures for lending money to farmers and planters on mortgage security. Between 1830 and 1837, some three hundred new banks established with a capital of $145,000,000, state-bank-note circulation increased from $50,000,000 to $149,000,000, and loans from $137,000,000 to $525,000,000.[17]

All the evils predicted by opponents of these banks came to pass. Farmers and planters, or the more speculatively inclined of them, hastened to take advantage of the credit now so easy to secure. They used it to acquire more land when they had not yet improved much of the land they already had, thus adding to the amount of land privately owned that was not yielding anything. More practical men used their borrowed

[15] Larry Gara, *Westernized Yankee: The Story of Cyrus Woodman* (Madison: State Historical Society of Wisconsin, 1956), p. 28.

[16] William T. Hutchinson, *Cyrus Hall McCormick: Harvest, 1856–1884* (New York: Appleton-Century-Crofts, Inc., 1935), p. 71.

[17] Earl Sylvester Sparks, *History and Theory of Agricultural Credit in the United States* (New York: Thomas Y. Crowell Company, 1932), pp. 83, 111, 236.

funds to expand their operations, but within the one-crop system. When the crash came in 1837 the former had difficulty in carrying their lands, and the latter found it quite impossible to dispose of their enlarged crops at prices that would return even a small profit.

It was the quickening tempo of western development and the rapid rise in land values in the thirties and again in the fifties that induced settlers to try to get title to their land as quickly as possible in order to borrow on it for the purchase of farm equipment and more land. In earlier periods pioneers had not been so hurried in their efforts to acquire ownership and had not entered into debt so readily. Horace Greeley was convinced that a large proportion of settlers in the new public-land states was in debt and paying from 12 to 50 per cent interest.[18]

The range of interest rates was fully as wide as that mentioned by Greeley. In 1829 the *Southern Galaxy* complained that the 12 to 50 per cent interest being charged planters meant irretrievable ruin.[19] In hard times the higher rates were likely to bring disaster, but in flush times, when land values were rising and cotton and wheat prices were high, money was easily carried at 40 or 50 per cent interest. Thus Benjamin F. Parke, writing from the rich black belt of Alabama in 1835, when cotton was selling at fifteen cents and corn and flour and land were equally high, had no complaint to make about the 40 or 50 per cent interest he reported money was bringing.[20] Such rates were charged only in periods of unusual financial stress or for loans of a speculative character. John Carmichael Jenkins, for example, a wealthy Natchez planter, could borrow in 1844 for 12 per cent, though less successful planters in the neighborhood had to pay as high as 15 and 18 per cent.[21]

In the upper Mississippi Valley, interest rates were not dissimilar. In 1837, rates on large sums ranged between 10 and 20 per cent; on small sums they ran to 36 per cent.[22] At land-office sales, where squatters had to enter and pay for their land or risk losing it, interest on small sums

[18] *New York Weekly Tribune*, February 11 and 18, 1846. Fourteen years later, in denying similar comments by Greeley, on the number of debt-ridden farmers, the *Wisconsin Farmer*, XII (April 1, 1860), 125, maintained that not one fourth of "our whole people are in debt at all" and declared that those who did have debts could easily discharge them with one or two good crops.

[19] *Southern Galaxy*, July 30, 1829.

[20] Benjamin F. Parke, Sumter County, Ala., July 6, 1835, to Lewis Hill, Box 92, Robert A. Brock MSS, The Huntington Library.

[21] The Jenkins Diary, Vol. II, April 4, 1844, Louisiana State University Archives.

[22] Thomas Senior Berry, *Western Prices before 1861: A Study of the Cincinnati Market* (Cambridge, Mass.: Harvard University Press, 1943), pp. 411, reports interest of 10 to 18 per cent as common on good real-estate loans in fairly normal times and 24 per cent in periods of stress. Such interest rates are indications of the tightness of the money market rather than of poor credit.

ranged from 60 per cent per annum to 10 per cent a month.[23] On a rising market in a period of optimism and expansion, farmers were not afraid of assuming such obligations, being willing to gamble that a good crop would enable them to pay their debts.

Evidence of the amount of farm debt and of the numbers of farmers involved is difficult to come by except by detailed examination of county instruments in representative or sample areas. Scattered statements can be taken only as indicative of the situation. The president of the Genesee County Agricultural Society, of New York, declared in 1820 that in the five counties west of the Genesee, $5,000,000 was owed on land purchases, and that only $150,000 of the $350,000 annual interest on this debt was being paid, leaving $200,000 to be added to the debt.[24] The *Christian Examiner,* of Boston, in 1831, spoke of the distressing burden of pecuniary obligations, "the incredible proportion of the community" that labored under a load of debt, and added that in "some of the most beautiful townships in New England" half the farms were mortgaged. Probably New England farmers were not as deeply in debt as the writer assumed. The *Windsor Chronicle* of Vermont hastened to say in 1831 that those who were in debt were paying off their obligations.[25] In 1827, a writer in the *New York Evening Post,* committed to the fight against bank charters on the ground that they encouraged farmers to borrow for speculation or for useless or nonproductive expenditures, remarked that he had seen half a county foreclosed.[26] In 1851, James F. W. Johnston was told that many farmers in central New York had bought their land on mortgage, paying 7 per cent, but were gradually retiring their debt. He expressed some skepticism about their success in meeting their debts, however, for he had heard much to the contrary, particularly in western New York.[27]

Following the financial crashes of 1819, 1837, and 1857, there were wholesale foreclosures. Many of the banks that failed in this period came to destruction because they had lent sums too generously on absurd appraisals of land which, when commodity prices fell, could not be sold after foreclosure for a fraction of the sum they had lent on it. During these periods of depression, court dockets in the newer parts of the country were clogged with foreclosure cases. Four thousand purchasers

[23] *Springfield Journal* in *Memphis Enquirer,* October 5, 1838; letters of William B. Ogden, February 21, 1836, to Alexander McGregor, and October 15, 1839, to John D. Ledyard, letter book, 1836–1839, Ogden MSS, Chicago Historical Society.

[24] *Plough Boy,* I (April 8, 1820), 355.

[25] *Christian Examiner* in *New England Farmer,* X (July 20, 1831), 1, and Windsor, Vt., *Chronicle,* cited in the same issue, p. 60.

[26] Copied in *American Farmer,* VIII (February 16, 1827), 383.

[27] Johnston, *Notes on North America,* I, 173 ff.

of lands of the Illinois Central Railroad forfeited their contracts because of failure to meet payments.[28]

There is no evidence that great land companies, like the Holland Land Company, which had long and tedious conflicts with its purchasers, or the Illinois Central Railroad, or other large land-selling companies wished to regain title to land they had sold on credit and which was now in default. Nor is there any substantial evidence that the large speculators and eastern capitalists who lent money to impoverished squatters to enter their claims were pleased with resulting defaults or anxious to foreclose mortgages. There were too many political risks in large-scale absentee ownership. Investors, whether institutional or individual, preferred to keep their funds in more liquid investments than farm property that had come back on their hands because of failure of the purchaser to meet the terms of the contract. Furthermore, real-estate values in new communities fluctuated violently as the business cycle changed. What seemed like safe loans on conservative valuations in flush times became, when the cycle plunged downward, most unsound. Creditors, particularly absentee creditors, early found it better to play along with their delinquent debtors, if in doing so they could preserve their equity, rather than to evict them.

The stereotyped notion of the grasping Shylock who loaned money on mortgage in the hope of acquiring ownership, however, need not be completely discarded. Local squires, living in the big house in the county seat, lending their personal funds or those of the bank they controlled, undoubtedly did make loans on choice property which they anticipated might fall into their hands when crops failed, prices fell, or some other calamity struck. Asahel Gridley of Bloomington, Illinois, is an illustration of a shrewd moneylender who conformed in this period to the description penned by a rabid anti-bank man:

Did you ever see a cat watch a mouse, reader? Just so will the little country bank director, who has lent cash to a farmer on the mortgage of his place, watch him. Sixty day renewals, with fresh meals of interest, are an eating moth. The speculation fails—the note is now as big as half the value of the farm—the Daniel S. Dickenson of the law tightens the screws—the farm is the banker's and its owner on his way to Iowa.[29]

Gridleys existed in every flourishing agricultural community but were not always insistent on their full pound of flesh.

[28] Paul W. Gates, The Illinois Central Railroad and Its Colonization Work (Harvard Economic Studies, Vol. XLII; Cambridge, Mass.: Harvard University Press, 1934), pp. 260 ff.

[29] William MacKenzie, The Life and Times of Martin Van Buren: The Correspondence of His Friends, Family and Pupils, Together with Brief Notices, Sketches and Anecdotes (Boston: Cook & Co., 1846), p. 87.

It was the fear that they could not make enough out of additional improvements introduced with capital borrowed at high interest that deterred many farmers from borrowing to enlarge or intensify their operations, experiment with farm machines, drain, clear, or fence additional land, and add to the number and quality of their livestock.[30] Progressive agriculturists pointed out that only by the application of capital along with his labor could the farmer expect to improve his lot. They argued that borrowing to improve land use and hence farm income, if done with caution, might not involve more risk than holding back, refusing to introduce the most modern and productive methods, and allowing an archaic farm pattern to come into existence. The *New England Farmer* for 1854 and 1855 contains a running argument between a Massachusetts man, whose own experience with mortgages led him to shudder at the word, and a Connecticut farmer, who advocated borrowing on mortgage when there was no other way of financing improvements. The Connecticut farmer was even more certain that the weakest point in New England farming was the reluctance of farmers to employ capital in their business. "Better be in debt than not have money to improve the farm with," it held.[31]

The editors of *Homestead* and a writer in the *New England Farmer* charged that the profits of New England farming were being invested in loans or stock of banks, railroads, and manufacturing companies, instead of being plowed back into the farm.[32] Northeastern farmers held too much land and failed to develop it even though they had the capital to do so. Instead, attracted by the high interest rates they could secure, they invested their cash elsewhere. Farmers in the vicinity of Hartford were said to have invested in the stock of city banks as much as $3,500,000, some of which was lost as a result of the Panic of 1857.

Northeastern farmers were also niggardly in the employment of labor, not recognizing that the investment of additional labor in the farm would mean improvements, would increase their ability to care for a larger quantity of livestock, and would add materially to the productivity and capital value of their farm. These charges were related to that most commonly leveled against farmers in all parts of the country: they were skimming the land of its fertility and topsoil by attempting to extract as much from it as possible.

Western farmers needed no encouragement to borrow for improve-

[30] J. C. Mandeville, Freedom, N. Y., August 2, 1852, to James W. Mandeville, Mandeville MSS, The Huntington Library.

[31] Quoted in *Indiana Farmer*, IV (September 1, 1855), 327.

[32] *New England Farmer*, VII (March and July, 1855), 118, 299; *Homestead*, III (October, 1857), 80; *Cultivator*, New Series, IV (May, 1847), 155.

ments. With the optimism characteristic of frontiersmen who witnessed their region changing almost overnight, they were ready to rush into debt to buy land, machinery, or stock, or to make improvements. They were cautioned to free themselves from debt and not to borrow any further until this desirable end had been reached. A secretary of a county agricultural society in Wisconsin maintained:

It is seldom or never safe to build, or enlarge your estates; to engage in new enterprises, or grant yourself and families new indulgences, except as the accretion of your industry and economy afford the means of paying as you go.[33]

True, the advice was offered after Wisconsin farmers had been badly burned in the crash of 1857 and again in the contraction of 1860.

NEED FOR MARKETS

If the farmer's need for credit was acute, his need for markets was equally serious. Self-sufficiency, if attainable, was not the goal of intelligent farmers; instead, they planned to produce something they could trade—better still, something they could sell. Though necessity forced them to produce much that they consumed, even though that required an inefficient expenditure of labor, they continually struggled to wrest from their land a marketable surplus. Commercial farming developed rapidly in the Middle West. Merchants complained that some religious groups were poor spenders because they attempted to satisfy all their needs from the farm, but these minorities were exceptional.

The channels of marketing varied widely from region to region. In back-country and frontier areas the farmer was dependent on the country storekeeper, who took his surplus in trade and allowed him book credit. Farmers within driving distance of towns or cities of any size enjoyed a cash market. They hauled their dressed pork or beef, vegetables, fruit, butter, and cheese to market or they might peddle their products on a regular route. Sometimes professional buyers of country produce sought them out. Staples, such as wheat, rice, tobacco, cotton, and sugar, were handled at Buffalo, Chicago, Cincinnati, New Orleans, Mobile, Charleston, or Richmond by brokers, factors, or commission agents who were specialists in their line. The factor who handled the planter's cotton also performed numerous other functions for his client.

He held the planter's funds subject to order, extended credit through a system of advances, procured bills of exchange, discounted notes, and re-

[33] *Wisconsin Farmer*, XII (December 1, 1860), 364.

mitted specie . . . he was not only a banker but a personnel agent as well —investment counsel, stock-broker, collector, real estate operator, and jack-of-all-trades . . . a veritable "planter's factotum." [34]

With the growth of markets and the expansion of agriculture, the machinery of buying and selling the farmers' produce became increasingly complex. Simple barter deals and sales by farmers to customers in nearby communities were displaced by sales to buyers, wholesalers, jobbers, drovers, and other specialists. Buyers operating on any considerable scale had access to the latest available market reports, watched prices closely, could sometimes anticipate changes, and, with their abundant credit, could pay cash at a time when the farmers needed it and could thereby take advantage of them. Farmers were no match for the wily buyers, who know quality and grades as they did not. Rarely were farmers offered a competitive price by these itinerant buyers, and too often were they reminded that the only alternative to the price offered was a long trip to market with its time-consuming delays, expenses, and uncertainties. Farmers felt at the mercy of the buyers, whom they distrusted, and groped for some way of marketing that would free them of dependence upon these "speculators."

A writer in *Homestead* averred that "there is a growing dissatisfaction with our present way of making sales of produce of all kinds."

Nothing is more evident than that the hundreds of speculators that scour the country, picking up apples, potatoes, tobacco, poultry, mutton, veal, wool, cider, etc., have an object in so doing at least commensurate with their troubles. We have not a doubt that our producers lose on an average at least a quarter in the long run, by selling to speculators; and if they, under our present system of city marketing, attempt to peddle their produce in town, their actual loss, though they may get the higest retail prices, is even greater.

Homestead proposed using town fairs to bring farmers, butchers, and retailers together for mutual trade, thereby avoiding the middlemen.[35] Market fairs were tried in New Britain, Connecticut, and Albany, New York, and were under consideration in Massachusetts to provide a means for direct sale by farmers to consumers.[36] Dairy farmers were the most advanced in arranging for co-operative cheese-making plants and sales agencies.

Woolgrowers likewise came to see the necessity of group or co-

[34] Alfred Holt Stone, "The Cotton Factorage System of the Southern States, *American Historical Review*, XX (April, 1915), 557 ff.; Ralph H. Haskins, "Planter and Cotton Factor in the Old South: Some Areas of Friction," *Agricultural History*, XXIX (January, 1955), 2.

[35] *Homestead*, IV (November 18, 1858), 140; *Boston Cultivator*, XII (December 21, 1850), 403; and XIII (May 3, 1851), 140.

[36] *Homestead*, IV (March 10, 1859), 393.

operative action in marketing their produce. Sheep farmers in the two principal states of New York and Ohio were influential in establishing wool depots at Buffalo and Cleveland, to which they assigned their wool. There it was graded and offered at public auctions which buyers from the mills attended. The depots also provided the farmers at low cost with sacks and twine for binding. Proprietors of the wool depots worked closely with the sheep farmers, furnishing them information on marketing, grades, breeds, and care of sheep. For their compensation and costs, they took a small percentage of the price for which the wool sold. In Ohio, a woolgrowers association was organized to protect the members' interests. Ohio sheep farmers tried to organize a woolgrowers' bank to furnish credit to farmers unable to secure loans from existing institutions.[37]

Connecticut Valley tobacco raisers were likewise brought to the point of organization for mutual aid. They united in a series of conventions, first supported and then assumed charge of a warehouse, to which they consigned their leaf, and which, through its superintendent, provided information to members concerning production, parasites, processing, marketing, prices, and prospects. Members claimed that their tobacco, when sold by the warehouse, brought them from two to three times what individual sales had earlier yielded them.[38]

Transportation costs in time and money were so heavy for farmers remote from navigable streams, turnpikes, or the later railroads that it was early found necessary to concentrate goods intended for market. Wheat, corn, and barley were turned into whiskey; corn was fed to hogs and cattle; milk was made into butter and cheese; wheat was hauled to the nearest mill, where it was ground into flour. Tobacco and cotton were made less bulky by presses; rice was hulled, cleaned, and polished; only better qualities of tobacco and rice were shipped to market. Cattle and hogs could be driven many hundreds of miles, though not always with the best results.

Along the major waterways there gradually developed centers to which farmers brought their commodities for sale or shipment. Pittsburgh, Wheeling, Marietta, Cincinnati, Chillicothe, Louisville, Lexington, Evansville, Terre Haute, and St. Louis flourished as trading and processing centers for farmers' goods. The merchants, tradesmen, commission agents,

[37] *Ohio Farmer,* V (February 16 and May 31, 1856), 26, 80; VI (January 3, 1857), 3; VIII (August 13, 1859), 260. John S. Wright, the flamboyant editor of the *Prairie Farmer,* used fifteen pages of his paper to bring to the attention of sheepmen the wool depot he established in Chicago.—*Prairie Farmer,* XII (March, 1852), 150–164.

[38] *Homestead,* I (January 17, 1856), 274; II (October 30, 1856), 96; and III (November 5, 1857), 109.

and wholesalers in these communities joined with farmers and land speculators in the interior in advocating public aid to internal improvements. Thus was formed a formidable political bloc of town and country supporters working for financial aid from local, state, and federal governments for the building of roads, canals, and railroads. Constitutional scruples, political nostrums, old party ties—all fell before this unbeatable combination.

Through feverish construction of canals in the thirties and railroads in the fifties there was accomplished a transportation revolution,[39] that greatly changed agriculture. Livestock could be moved a thousand miles in a few days and with less loss of weight than they had sustained in half that distance when driven. Grain could reach markets faster to take advantage of current quotations. Fruit and other perishable goods, as well as milk, were shipped considerable distances by rail. Farmers equipped with the new mowers, reapers, patented plows, rakes, threshers, and harrows now available at nearby centers could concentrate upon the most profitable crop and not worry about whether there would be buyers.

Not all farmers benefited from the coming of the railroads. During the fifties the major lines and affiliates completed to Chicago and St. Louis engaged in a series of rate wars that so cheapened transportation as to make it possible for western goods to flood the eastern markets and seriously depress prices. The result was a collapse of commodity prices and farm-land values. New York farmers, for example, had to pay more per bushel on way freight than through-shippers from Chicago paid for the same quantity. Their plight drove them to join in a movement to require that rates be levied on a prorata basis.[40] Failure to secure such relief made them more responsive to the appeal of the Granger movement at a later time.

The building of the railroads further damaged New England agriculture, which was already suffering from declining fertility, high costs, and archaic methods. Corn, which could be raised in Illinois for twelve to sixteen cents, cost from forty to fifty cents to produce in New England. Nor did the cost of transporting the grain from the West make up for this difference. Pork and beef, as well as corn, were falling to unprofitable levels, further aggravating the distress of the New England farmer. Worst of all was the inpouring of Ohio, Michigan, and Indiana wool that depressed prices and threatened to drive the Vermont sheep raisers

[39] This is the title of Volume IV in this series by George Rogers Taylor. See also George Rogers Taylor and Irene D. Neu, *The American Railroad Network, 1861–1890* (Cambridge, Mass.: Harvard University Press, 1956), *passim*.

[40] Frederick Merk, "Eastern Antecedents of the Grangers," *Agricultural History*, XXIII (January, 1949), 7.

out of business.[41] Another harmful effect the railroads had upon the hill areas of New England was that, by providing cheap, easy, and fast transportation to the new West, by advertising extensively these easy routes and cheap rates, and by picturing the West as possessing all the advantages for farming that the hill areas of the Northeast lacked, the railroads contributed greatly to drawing to the West many thousands of farmers.[42] As population left these hill communities, the burdens on those who remained became doubly heavy.

These seemingly unfortunate results of railroad building upon northeastern agriculture were offset by other new developments. When the Erie Canal was constructed, northeastern farmers had been adversely affected by western competition and had learned to make adjustments. Many of them left for other occupations or journeyed west. Those on better land rationalized their agricultural patterns by utilizing more fully the special advantages their locations gave them. The railroads brought about further changes. Urban milksheds were now extended, fluid milk replaced cheese and butter as the easiest and most remunerative dairy product to market, and many eastern farmers turned to dairying as a major feature of their economy.

A somewhat different situation developed in the South. The new competition of fresh lands in the Gulf states induced residents of the older communities, who felt their region's economy was slipping, to advocate the construction of internal improvements to make possible the opening up of portions of the Piedmont. Ulrich B. Phillips maintains that the building of railroads in the cotton belt "intensified the popular engrossment in the one great staple" and produced "something of a cutthroat competition" among planters.[43]

Publicly supported internal improvements proved a mixed blessing to farmers. Whether it was state, county, municipal, or federal aid that was given to canals and railroads, in the end the farmer had to bear a large part of its cost. Rural counties and states which had optimistically

[41] Harold Fisher Wilson, *The Hill Country of Northern New England: Its Social and Economic History, 1790–1930* (Columbia University *Studies in the History of American Agriculture*, No. 3; New York: Columbia University Press, 1936), pp. 65, 82.

[42] Stilwell, *Migration from Vermont*, p. 220; Gates, *Illinois Central Railroad, passim.* Railroads were also accused of killing many cattle, horses, and sheep along their unfenced right-of-way; of setting fire to woods, ripe grain, and buildings of farmers by sparks from their locomotives; of causing floods and drainage problems by their high embankments; and of spreading pernicious weeds over cultivated fields by allowing thistles and other weeds to flourish on their line.—*Homestead*, II, (July 16, 1857), 690; Charles Hirschfeld, *The Great Railroad Conspiracy: The Social History of a Railroad War* (Lansing: The Michigan State College Press, 1953).

[43] Ulrich B. Phillips, *History of Transportation in the Eastern Cotton Belt to 1860* (New York: Columbia University Press, 1908), pp. 70, 388.

voted public aid expected that profits from their railroad securities would enable them to pay off the bonds they had sold to raise capital for the roads. This rarely proved to be the case. Instead, the major part of these bonds was retired over the course of many years by farmers through taxes levied on their property. Land grants to canals and railroads were sold by them at more than double the original price of government land, and again it was the farmer who had to pay. Farmers could set off against these factors the greater ease with which they could market their produce and bring in goods from industrial centers.[44]

Americans had dispersed themselves widely over the eastern half of the country by 1860, picking and choosing their land and leaving great acreages in the aggregate that were not within farms. In addition, as the Census of 1860 shows, 241,943,671 acres of unimproved land were included within farms and plantations. Some of this unimproved land was not worth developing, but a large part of it was and subsequent censuses show that it has been steadily reduced. Except for New England and New Jersey, not a state has failed to enlarge its acreage of improved land since 1860. This is particularly true of the South, despite the oft-repeated view that the cotton kingdom was approaching, if it had not already attained, full use of land suitable for cotton and had therefore to look elsewhere for land to which cotton and slavery could be transferred.

Agriculture had made great strides in the decades before 1860. Farmers were hearing and reading more about the new agricultural science, with its emphasis upon soil and fertilizer analysis, and were putting to effective use this new knowledge. Favorable economic conditions in the fifties enabled them to buy mowers, reapers, improved plows, hay rakes, corn shellers, and numerous other machines that permitted larger operations with less drudgery. Steam-operated gins and cotton presses relieved numerous hands on the cotton plantations of their heaviest labor. Better livestock and more knowledge of animal husbandry gave farmers more favorable returns from their capital and labor.

Even the comforts of life were being introduced not only by the landed gentry, North and South, but to some degree by the ordinary farmer. Drafty log houses, with their crude interiors, were being abandoned for frame structures with decorative fireplaces, sturdy stoves

---

[44] Harry Pierce, *Railroads of New York: A Study of Government Aid, 1826–1875* (Cambridge, Mass.: Harvard University Press, 1953), pp. 25, 46, has shown that the $47 million contributed by the state and municipal governments of New York to aid railroad building was most important in making possible the beginning of numerous railroads, particularly branch lines. He shows that farmers at the time the grants were under consideration were convinced they would profit from the construction of the railroads through rising land values.

with provisions for heating water, sufficient bedrooms to provide for the growing family, and a well-shuttered parlor for the entertainment of visiting clergymen, politicians, and relatives. Emphasis upon self-sufficiency was declining, spinning and weaving were moving into the new factories, cheese making was just beginning to be centered in modern establishments, and increasing dependence was being placed on store goods. New and tighter barns, with great mows overhanging the stalls and with rope and pulley devices for unloading hay, were lightening the work load and providing greater comfort for man and beast in winter.

Increasing specialization on the farm did not necessarily mean the continuation of a one-crop system that wrecked havoc with land. Vegetable crops, fruit, and dairy products were produced near metropolitan markets on land whose value was such that owners early learned to conserve the soil and prudently manage it. Diversification was being brought about, though very slowly, through the growing recognition that in it lay the solution for some of the major ills of the farmers' economy.

Government showed increasing responsiveness to the needs of the agricultural population. The land system was being rapidly liberalized, and free homesteads were near. Agriculture had been assisted by the work of the Agricultural Division of the Patent Office, which had assembled valuable agricultural statistics and had published information about new farm techniques, machines, and varieties of seeds and plants; the advantages of fertilizers and lime; and the use of soil-enriching plants, such as clover and alfalfa. Most important, the Patent Office had successfully focused attention upon farm problems. By 1860, state governments were showing a growing tendency to use their powers to encourage the holding of agricultural fairs, to publish annual volumes dealing with agricultural problems, and to vote appropriations for combating plant and animal diseases and rural decay. Government aid to railroads was bringing modern transportation close to thousands of previously isolated farmers. America's wide-open immigration policy, encouraged by state and railroad promotion of immigration, permitted the inflow of millions of northern Europeans, who assured a rapidly expanding domestic market for food and fiber crops.

A benevolent attitude toward the rush of population into new territories, which were promised self-government, public aids to education and internal improvements, and the benefits of a liberalized land policy all contributed to rapid farm and state making. Slavocracy's blighting hand on the Democratic party threatened to slow the rapid growth of the West, but the election of 1860 brought to power a new party pledged to give free homesteads, support transcontinental railroads, and aid agricultural education.

CLOSE OF AN ERA

Yet the great age of the American farmer was drawing to a close. In 1860 everything appeared to be going his way, while in reality new economic forces were developing within the nation which were to exercise a stronger influence than he upon its political life. New economic problems, such as excessive and discriminatory freight rates, uncurbed inflation followed by swift deflation, and monetary and banking questions, were just over the horizon in the solution of which the farmers' cries were to go unheard. The old problem of an inadequate credit structure that was inflexible when flexibility was most needed, and which took a high toll of farmers, had not been solved. Increasing commercialization of agriculture made farmers doubly dependent on credit, but the instruments of credit were not expanded as agricultural needs grew. A startling fact revealed by the Census of 1860 was that agriculture was the occupation of only 40 per cent of those whose employment was listed that year.[45] At a time when farmers and planters needed to unite more firmly for mutual interest, against threatening influences in national affairs that were inimical to them and were waxing powerful, division and discord broke these groups apart. It was to be many years before they were to come together in support of common objectives.

[45] *Eighth Census of the United States, 1860, Population* (Washington, D. C.: Government Printing Office, 1864), *passim.* To get this 40 per cent I have included apiarists, dairymen, drovers, graziers, herdsmen, horticulturists, overseers, planters, rancheros, shepherds, threshers, and vineyardists.

Bibliography

EVERETT E. EDWARDS, A *Bibliography of the History of Agriculture in the United States* (U. S. Department of Agriculture, *Miscellaneous Publication* No. 84; Washington, D. C.: Government Printing Office, 1930), long since out of print and listing little that appeared before 1900 or after 1929, is still useful for any work on agricultural history. Edwards, "A Guide for Courses in the History of American Agriculture" (U. S. Department of Agriculture, *Bibliographical Contribution* No. 35; Washington, D. C.: 1939, processed), is also useful. Supplementing Edwards's bibliographies are two valuable bibliographies also prepared in the U. S. Bureau of Agricultural Economics on land settlement and land use: Louise O. Bercaw, A. M. Hannay, and Esther M. Colvin, *Bibliography on Land Settlement with Particular Reference to Small Holdings and Subsistence Homesteads* (U. S. Department of Agriculture, *Miscellaneous Publication* No. 172; Washington, D. C.: Government Printing Office, 1934); Bercaw and Hannay, *Bibliography on Land Utilization, 1918–1936* (U. S. Department of Agriculture, *Miscellaneous Publication* No. 294; Washington, D. C.: Government Printing Office, 1938). Oscar Handlin, *et al., Harvard Guide to American History* (Cambridge, Mass.: Harvard University Press, 1954), is indispensable.

A valuable list of contemporary works on agricultural and rural affairs, including some travel accounts but with notable omissions, is found in the U. S. Commissioner of Agriculture, *Report, 1868* (Washington, D. C.: Government Printing Office, 1869).

The greatest collections of printed source materials on agricultural history are found in the serial documents published on authorization of Congress and original manuscript records of the Bureau of the Census, the Patent Office, the General Land Office, the Treasury Department, the Department of Agriculture, the House, and the Senate. Neither of the guides to federal documents is wholly reliable, and searchers must work through indexes to the Senate and House Executive Documents, Miscellaneous Documents, and Reports of Committees of each session of Congress to make certain they have found everything on their subject. The two guides are Benjamin Perley Poore, *Descriptive Catalogue of the Government Publications of the United States, 1774–1881* (*Senate Miscellaneous Document* No. 67, 48 Cong., 2 Sess.); and *Tables of and Annotated Index to the Congressional Series of United States Public Documents* (Washington, D. C.: Government Printing Office, 1902).

Guide to the *Records in the National Archives* (Washington, D. C.: Government Printing Office, 1948) is the first place to turn to in the use of manuscript materials in the National Archives. An amazing number of guides, inventories, and surveys of manuscript records in state, county, municipal, and federal buildings in the states, prepared under the aegis of the Historical Records Survey of the Works Projects Administration, are recorded in Sargent B. Child and D. P. Holmes, *Bibliography of Research Projects Reports: Check List of Historical Records Survey Publications* (Works Projects Administration, Technical Series, *Research and Records Bibliography* No. 7; Washington, D. C.: 1943).

For the South, Duke University and the state universities of North Carolina and Louisiana have superb collections of diaries, plantation journals, letters, and other original materials relating to agriculture. Each of these institutions has guides to its collections. The Historical Society of Wisconsin, with its unrivaled McCormick Collection and other groups of material, is strong for the old South, notably Virginia, and for the upper Mississippi Valley.

The published documents of a number of states relating to economic matters are listed in Adelaide R. Hasse, *Index of Economic Material in Documents of the States of the United States* (13 vols.; Washington, D. C.: Carnegie Institution, 1907–1922).

Grace Gardner Griffin's *Writings on American History, 1906—* (variously published), is a useful guide through the maze of primary and secondary materials in print on American history.

The *Encyclopedia of the Social Sciences*, Edwin R. A. Seligman and Alvin Johnson, eds. (15 vols.; New York: The Macmillan Company, 1930–1935), stands up well a generation after it appeared because of the high standards of selection of subjects and authors and the careful bibliographical apparatus. Indispensable is the *Dictionary of American Biography*, Allen Johnson and Dumas Malone, eds. (20 vols. and index vol.; New York: Charles Scribner's Sons, 1928–1937), in which agricultural journalists, editors, and innovators are given generous space.

No one working on any topic in American agriculture, past or present, should neglect Liberty Hyde Bailey, ed., *Cyclopedia of American Agriculture* (4 vols.; New York: The Macmillan Company, 1907), which is a mine of practical information that becomes increasingly valuable as the agriculture of the period preceding the utilization of the gasoline engine recedes into the past.

Max Meisel, *A Bibliography of American Natural History: The Pioneer Century, 1789–1865* (3 vols.; New York: The Premier Publishing Co., 1924–1929), is useful for source material and articles concerning the great exploring expeditions sent out by the United States government.

GENERAL AND REGIONAL WORKS

The student of agricultural history is fortunate to have two fine mono-
graphic studies of American agriculture for the period beforce 1860: Percy
Wells Bidwell and John I. Falconer, *History of Agriculture in the Northern
United States, 1620–1860* (Washington, D. C.: Carnegie Institution, 1925),
and Lewis Cecil Gray, *History of Agriculture in the Southern United States to
1860* (2 vols.; Washington, D. C.: Carnegie Institution, 1933). Their tables,
charts, illustrations, and bibliographies, as well as their text, are useful for
every phase of agricultural history. More modest but thoughtful is Joseph
Schafer, *Social History of American Agriculture* (New York: The Macmillan
Company, 1936). In Louis Bernard Schmidt and Earle Dudley Ross, *Readings
in the Economic History of American Agriculture* (New York: The Macmillan
Company, 1925), is brought together some of the best but otherwise scattered
writing on American agricultural history. Norman Scott Brien Gras, *History of
Agriculture in Europe and America* (New York: Appleton-Century-Crofts,
Inc., 1925), is generalized but informative. U. P. Hedrik, *History of Horticulture in America to 1860* (New York: Oxford University Press, 1950) is
excellent.

A number of state and regional agricultural histories are available, of
which the best are Neil Adams McNall, *An Agricultural History of the Genesee
Valley, 1790–1860* (Philadelphia: University of Pennsylvania Press, 1952);
David Maldwyn Ellis, *Landlords and Farmers in the Hudson-Mohawk Region,
1790–1850* (Ithaca, N. Y.: Cornell University Press, 1946); Merrill E. Jarchow,
The Earth Brought Forth: A History of Minnesota Agriculture to 1885
(St. Paul: Minnesota Historical Society, 1949); Joseph Schafer, *History of
Agriculture in Wisconsin* (*Wisconsin Domesday Book, General Studies*, I;
Madison: State Historical Society of Wisconsin, 1922); Carl Raymond Wood-
ward, *The Development of Agriculture in New Jersey, 1640–1880* (New
Brunswick: New Jersey Agricultural Experiment Station, 1927); Harold Fisher
Wilson, *The Hill Country of Northern New England: Its Social and Economic
History, 1790–1930* (Columbia University *Studies in the History of American
Agriculture*, No. 3; New York: Columbia University Press, 1936); Margaret
Richards Pabst, *Agricultural Trends in the Connecticut Valley Region of Massa-
chusetts, 1800–1900*, William D. Gray, *et al.*, eds. (Smith College *Studies in
History*, Vol. XXVI, Nos. 1–4; Northampton, Mass.: 1940); Cornelius Oliver
Cathey, *Agricultural Developments in North Carolina, 1783–1860*, Fletcher
M. Green, *et al.*, eds. (*The James Sprunt Studies in History and Political
Science*, Vol. XXXVIII; Chapel Hill: The University of North Carolina Press,
1956); Herbert Weaver, *Mississippi Farmers, 1850–1860* (Nashville: Vander-
bilt University Press, 1945); John Hebron Moore, *Agriculture in Ante-Bellum
Mississippi* (New York: Bookman Associates, 1958); Theodore L. Carlson,
*The Illinois Military Tract: A Study of Land Occupation, Utilization and
Tenure* (University of Illinois *Studies in the Social Sciences*, Vol. XXXII, No.
2; Urbana: University of Illinois Press, 1951); Robert Leslie Jones, *History of
Agriculture in Ontario* (Toronto: The University of Toronto Press, 1946);
Edward Van Dyke Robinson, *Early Economic Conditions and the Develop-*

ment of Agriculture in Minnesota (University of Minnesota *Studies in the Social Sciences*, No. 3; Minneapolis: 1915). Others that are useful are U. P. Hedrick, *A History of Agriculture in the State of New York* (Albany: New York State Agricultural Society, 1933); Stevenson Whitcomb Fletcher, *Pennsylvania Agriculture and Country Life, 1640–1840* (Harrisburg: Pennsylvania Historical and Museum Commission, 1950); Claude B. Hutchinson, ed., *California Agriculture* (Berkeley: University of California Press, 1946); Willard Range, *A Century of Georgia Agriculture, 1850–1950* (Athens: University of Georgia Press, 1954); Clarence Albert Day, *A History of Maine Agriculture, 1604–1860* (University of Maine *Studies*, Second Series, No. 68; Orono: The University Press, 1954); W. C. Latta, *Outline of Indiana Agriculture* (Lafayette: Purdue University Agricultural Experiment Station, 1938); Lewis D. Stilwell, *Migration from Vermont, 1776–1860* (*Proceedings* of the Vermont Historical Society, New Series, Vol. V, No. 2; Montpelier: 1937).

A brilliant study that shows mastery of soil science is Avery Craven, *Soil Exhaustion as a Factor in the Agricultural History of Virginia and Maryland, 1606–1860* (University of Illinois *Studies in the Social Sciences*, Vol. XIII, No. 1; Urbana: University of Illinois, 1926). Russell H. Anderson, "Agriculture among the Shakers, Chiefly at Mount Lebanon," *Agricultural History*, XXIV (July, 1950), 113–120, is an interesting study of a communitarian group that excelled in agriculture.

For a generation the works of Ulrich Bonnell Phillips comprised the standard treatment of slavery and the plantation system. They are now quite dated because of their too generous treatment of the planter class, the patronizing account of the "peculiar institution," and their questionable treatment of the economics of slavery; yet they are still valuable for detail. Phillips's two volumes of documents in *Plantation and Frontier*, in John R. Commons, *et al.*, eds., *A Documentary History of American Industrial Society* (Cleveland: Arthur H. Clark Co., 1910), Vols. I and II, show this same preoccupation with the plantation, which may be unavoidable because of the paucity of documents relating to small farmers. His *American Negro Slavery: A Survey of the Supply, Employment, and Control of Negro Labor as Determined by the Plantation Regime* (New York: Appleton-Century-Crofts, Inc., 1928) needs to be compared with Frederic Bancroft, *Slave-Trading in the Old South* (Baltimore: J. H. Furst Company, 1931), John Hope Franklin, *From Slavery to Freedom: A History of American Negroes* (New York: Alfred A. Knopf, Inc., 1947), and Kenneth M. Stampp, *The Peculiar Institution: Slavery in the Ante-Bellum South* (New York: Alfred A. Knopf, Inc., 1956). Phillips's most mature work is embodied in *Life and Labor in the Old South* (Boston: Little, Brown & Company, 1929), and in his unfinished *The Course of the South to Secession* (New York: Appleton-Century-Crofts, Inc., 1939).

The economy of the plantation system with its slave labor has been the subject of long controversy from the appearance of Hinton Rowan Helper,, *The Impending Crisis of the South: How to Meet It* (New York: Burdick Brothers, 1857). Phillips's views on the low profits that slaves brought their masters have been sharply reversed by Thomas P. Govan, "Was Plantation Slavery Profitable?" *Journal of Southern History*, VIII (November, 1942), 513 ff.;

Gray, *History of Agriculture in the Southern United States,* previously cited; Stampp, *The Peculiar Institution;* and Alfred H. Conrad and John R. Meyer, "The Economics of Slavery in the Ante Bellum South," *Journal of Political Economy,* LXVI (April, 1958), 95 ff.

MUSEUMS

The further we are from the pre-tractor age in agriculture the more valuable become the great agricultural and industrial museums which have sprung up in recent years. Among these are the Henry Ford Museum and Greenfield Village of Dearborn, Michigan, the Museum of Science and Industry in Chicago, the Museum of the State Historical Society of Wisconsin at Madison, the Farmers' Museum and rural village of Cooperstown, New York, Old Sturbridge of Sturbridge, Massachusetts, and reconstructed New Salem Village in Illinois. Here may be seen ancient shovels, rakes, wooden plows, Conestoga wagons, primitive drills, reconstructions of the early reapers, and hundreds of other tools and machines. At Cooperstown may be seen a blacksmith shop in operation and some of the farm work actually being done with the tools of the early nineteenth century.

GOVERNMENT PUBLICATIONS

From 1837, when Henry L. Ellsworth began the compilation of facts and statistics on agriculture, to 1862, when the first Commissioner of Agriculture was appointed, the *Annual Reports* of the Patent Office include material relating to agriculture. Between 1837 and 1849 the agricultural material was included in the same volume with the detail on patents; from 1849 to 1861 separate volumes on agriculture appeared as *Annual Reports, Agriculture.*

On public lands the early documentary material was assembled and republished in *American State Papers, Public Lands,* 8 volumes. The Gales and Seaton edition (Washington, D. C.: 1832–1861) is the best. From 1817 to 1848 the reports of the Commissioner of the General Land Office are in the *Annual Reports* of the Secretary of the Treasury. Beginning with 1849, when the General Land Office was transferred to the newly established Department of the Interior, the commissioners' reports are in the *Annual Report* of the Secretary of the Interior.

STATE PUBLICATIONS

In many states agricultural societies or state boards of agriculture were early established whose transactions or annual reports were published by the states as one of the first aids to agriculture. In 1841 New York was the first to publish these materials, then Massachusetts in 1845, Michigan and Ohio in 1849, New Hampshire and Pennsylvania in 1850, Indiana and Wisconsin in 1851, Illinois in 1853, Iowa in 1854, Maine and Tennessee in 1856, North Carolina in 1857, and California in 1858. Local information concerning fairs, awards, proceedings of county and state societies, prize essays, orations by distinguished leaders praising agriculture and the homely virtues of the farmer, and notable essays and lectures on the new agricultural science are found here. A number of states appointed geologists and entomologists, whose reports have value for the student of agricultural history.

Agricultural History, published quarterly since 1927 by the Agricultural History Society, is largely devoted to the United States. It is an indispensable tool for any work touching on agriculture. The *Mississippi Valley Historical Review, A Journal of American History,* and the regional and state historical journals need attention.

A useful treatment of a number of early agricultural journalists, including John Stuart Skinner, Jesse Buel, Luther Tucker, and Orange Judd, is William Edward Ogilvie, *Pioneer Agricultural Journalists* (Chicago: Arthur G. Leonard, 1927).

Jesse Buel, founder of the Albany *Cultivator,* receives proper attention in Harry J. Carman, ed., *Jesse Buel, Agricultural Reformer* (Columbia University *Studies in the History of American Agriculture,* No. 12; New York: Columbia University Press, 1947). Solon Robinson, one of the most prolific writers, is sensitively treated by Herbert Anthony Kellar in *Solon Robinson: Pioneer and Agriculturist (Indiana Historical Collections,* Vols. XXI and XXII; Indianapolis: Indiana Historical Bureau, 1936). Unfortunately, Robinson's astringent comments on the cattle trade, which appeared in the *New York Tribune,* receive no attention. Edmund Ruffin, that tartar of Southern controversialists and editors, is critically evaluated by Avery Craven in *Edmund Ruffin, Southerner: A Study in Secession* (New York: Appleton-Century-Crofts, Inc., 1932). Porter Gale Perrin, *Life and Works of Thomas Green Fessenden, 1771–1837* (University of Maine *Studies,* Second Series, No. 4; Orono: The University Press, 1925), is more concerned with Fessenden's literary than with his agricultural activities, but it is a valuable study. See Weymouth T. Jordan, "Noah B. Cloud's Activities on Behalf of Southern Agriculture," *Agricultural History,* XXV (April, 1951), 53–58, and his "Noah B. Cloud, and the American Cotton Planter," *Agricultural History,* XXI (October, 1957), 44–49; Harold T. Pinkett, "The American Farmer: A Pioneer Agricultural Journal," *Agricultural History,* XXIV (July, 1950), 146–151; Richard Bardolph, "A North Carolina Farm Journal of the Middle 'Fifties," *North Carolina Historical Review,* XXV (January, 1948), 57–89. George F. Lemmer, *Norman J. Colman and "Colman's Rural World": A Study in Agricultural Leadership* (University of Missouri *Studies,* Vol. XXV, No. 3; Columbia: 1953) is useful although it is primarily concerned with the postwar period. The same author's "Early Agricultural Editors and Their Farm Philosophies," *Agricultural History,* XXXI (October, 1957), 3–22, treats most of the prominent editors of the antebellum period. Hugh M. Flick, "Elkanah Watson's Activities on Behalf of Agriculture," *Agricultural History,* XXI (October, 1947), 193 ff., is a summary of a doctoral dissertation on Watson in the Columbia University Library. Dr. Martin W. Philips, prominent in agricultural reform in Mississippi and prolific writer for agricultural journals, left a valuable plantataion diary for the years 1840–1863. Franklin L. Riley edited the diary and prepared a sketch of Philips in *Publications* of the Mississippi Historical Society, X (Oxford: 1909), 305 ff.

For a listing with bibliographical information of agricultural periodicals, see Stephen Conrad Stuntz, *List of the Agricultural Periodicals of the United States and Canada Published During the Century July 1810 to July 1910* (U. S. Department of Agriculture, *Miscellaneous Publication* No. 398; Washington, D. C., Government Printing Office, 1941). Albert Lowther Demaree provides useful sketches of the more important journals and their editors in *The American Agricultural Press, 1819–1860* (Columbia University *Studies in the History of American Agriculture*, No. 8; New York: Columbia University Press, 1941). Gilbert M. Tucker, *American Agricultural Periodicals: An Historical Sketch* (Albany: Privately printed, 1909), is a meticulously careful study in the dating of the beginning and suspension of periodicals which was excluded from the Bailey, *Cyclopedia of American Agriculture* because of a controversy with the publisher of one of the journals.

Following is a selected list of the more useful of these periodicals: *American Agriculturist*, New York, 1842—; *American Cotton Planter*, Montgomery, Alabama, 1853–1861; *American Farmer*, Baltimore, 1819–1834, 1839–1897; *Boston Cultivator*, Boston, 1839–1876; *Cincinnatus*, Cincinnati, 1856–1861; *Country Gentleman*, Albany, 1853–1955; *Cultivator*, Albany, 1834–1865; *Farmers' Register*, Shellbanks and Petersburg, Virginia, 1833–1842; *Genesee Farmer*, Rochester, New York, 1831–1839; *Homestead*, Hartford, 1855–1861; *Horticulturist*, Albany, 1846–1875; *Moore's Rural New Yorker*, Rochester, 1849—; *New England Farmer*, Boston, 1822–1846, 1848–1913; *Ohio Cultivator*, Columbus, 1845–1864; *Ohio Farmer*, Cleveland, 1852—; *Pennsylvania Farm Journal*, Lancaster and West Chester, 1851–1857; *Prairie Farmer*, Chicago, 1840—; *Soil of the South*, Columbus, Georgia, 1851–1857; *Southern Cultivator*, Augusta, Georgia, 1843–1935; *Southern Planter*, Richmond, 1841—; *Valley Farmer*, St. Louis, 1849–1864; *Wool Grower and Magazine of Agriculture and Horticulture*, Buffalo and Rochester, New York, 1849–1856; *Working Farmer*, New York, 1849–1875.

Three other contemporary periodicals contain valuable information on agricultural problems: *Niles' Register*, Washington, D. C., 1811–1849; *Hunt's Merchants' Magazine and Commercial Review*, New York, 1839–1870; and *De Bow's Review*, New Orleans, 1846–1880. Able exponents of southern positions are treated in Norval Neil Luxon, *Niles' Weekly Register News Magazine of the Nineteenth Century* (Baton Rouge: Louisiana State University Press, 1947), and Robert F. Durden, "J. D. B. De Bow: Convolutions of a Slavery Expansionist," *Journal of Southern History*, XVII (November, 1951), 441–461.

<h3 style="text-align:center">FARMERS' GUIDES</h3>

Of the host of farmers' guides and manuals of agriculture providing information on every aspect of farm work and farm life, the following have been useful: Anon., *The Farmer's Guide and Western Agriculturist* (Cincinnati:

Buckley, Deforest & Co., 1832); Henry Heermance, *The Farmer's Mine, or Source of Wealth* (New York: Henry Heermance, 1843), which shows how heavily Americans depended upon the agricultural science of England; Josiah T. Marshall, *The Farmer's and Emigrant's Hand-Book* (New York: D. Appleton & Company, 1845); Adam Beatty, *Southern Agriculture, Being Essays on the Cultivation of Corn, Hemp, Tobacco, Wheat, etc., and the Best Methods of Renovating the Soil* (New York: C. M. Saxton, 1843); Solon Robinson, *Facts for Farmers; Also for the Family Circle: A Variety of Rich Materials for All Land-Owners about Domestic Animals and Domestic Economy* (2 vols.; New York: A. J. Johnson, 1868). This was the fourth printing of a book which first appeared in 1864.

TRAVEL ACCOUNTS

A stream of Englishmen, some possessing and others lacking literary pretensions, came to the United States in the first half of the nineteenth century to tour a part of the country, visit its major scenic spots in the East, take a glance at slavery, meet distinguished Americans, and set forth their reactions in volumes they hoped would attract buyers. The flood of books, guides, and brochures was appalling for its volume, repetition, plagarism, superficiality, distortion, and contemptuous misrepresentation of American traits and morals. It was also useful to Americans and to later historians, for it was a mirror in which could be seen the vanity and pomposity of American aristocracy, the vulgarity and crudeness of the common people, the shallowness and sordidness of their political leaders. It also provided Americans with a better understanding of their political institutions, the idealism of their reform leaders, the unique character of their scenic wonders, the extent of their natural resources, the reasons for their unparalleled success in erecting republican institutions, in spreading their settlements over half a continent, and in developing industry, commerce, and agriculture on a relatively democratic basis. Andrew D. White wrote of these travelers who spent "a week in one great state, a day in another, an hour in a third—pirouetting from great city to great city—not deigning to look at the vast intervening spaces where the strongest elements in the new civilization were developing—gathering husks and rinds to be paraded in England as fruit—too dignified to suffer acquaintance with the sturdy men who were grappling with the great problems presented; only condescending in noting the idioms of wagon-drivers and bar-keepers. . . ."—*A Word from the North-West to Dr. Russell, Sometime American Correspondent of "The Times"* (Syracuse, N. Y.: 1863), pp. 4–5.

A general appraisal and guide to this literature is needed and was under way at one time under Solon J. Buck for the American Historical Association, but it seems to have fallen by the way, though the materials collected are available in the Library of Congress. More limited in its scope is the ambitious project: *Travels in the Old South: A Bibliography*, edited by Thomas D. Clark (Norman: University of Oklahoma Press, 1956–1959), in three excellent volumes. The South is broadly interpreted to include the Ohio Valley. Brief but illuminating sketches of the authors and evaluation of the various accounts make this bibliography particularly valuable. The compilers are unduly concerned with the "fairness" or "unfairness" of the accounts, especially toward slavery.

Solon J. Buck, *Travel and Description, 1765–1865* (*Collections* of the Illinois State Historical Library, Vol. IX, Bibliographical Series, No. 2; Springfield: 1914), is most useful despite the fact that it only includes travel accounts that have some bearing on Illinois. The perceptive essays and individual sketches of travelers and the bibliography in Allan Nevins, *America through British Eyes* (New York: Oxford University Press, 1948), constitute a useful introduction. Also see Frank Monaghan, *French Travellers in the United States, 1765–1932* (New York: New York Public Library, 1933).

Among the more useful of the travel accounts by Europeans for their comments on agriculture are Captain Barclay, *Agricultural Tour in the United States and Upper Canada* (Edinburgh: William Blackwood & Sons, 1842); Morris Birkbeck, *Notes on a Journey in America* (London: Severn & Redington, 1818); William Cobbett, *A Year's Residence in the United States of America* (2d ed.; London: Sherwood, Neeley & Jones, 1819); James F. W. Johnston, *Notes on North America: Agricultural, Economical and Social* (2 vols.; Edinburgh: William Blackwood & Sons, 1851), one of the most useful of the British travel accounts for science and agriculture by a prominent agricultural chemist; Robert Russell, *North America: Its Agriculture and Climate* (Edinburgh: Adam & Charles Black, 1857); Patrick Shirreff, *A Tour through North America; Together with a Comprehensive View of the Canadas and the United States as Adapted for Agricultural Emigration* (Edinburgh: Oliver & Boyd, 1835). Unwary writers have frequently been taken in by what appear to be objective though critical comments on American agriculture and land. For example, a bevy of writers hired by, or investors in, the Illinois Central Railroad wrote accounts which have to be used with extreme care. Among them are James Caird, *Prairie Farming in America; With Notes by the Way on Canada and the United States* (London: Longmans, Brown, Green, Longmans, & Roberts, 1858); J. G. Kohl, *Reisen im Nordwesten der Vereinigten Staaten* (New York: D. Appleton & Co., 1857); and William Ferguson, *America by River and Rail; or, Notes by the Way on the New World and Its People* (London: J. Nisbet & Co., 1856). Two other widely used books on the West were written to foster land-speculating schemes: Samuel A. Mitchell, *Illinois in 1837* . . . (Philadelphia: Mitchell, 1837) and Henry W. Ellsworth, *Valley of the Upper Wabash, Indiana, with Hints on Its Agricultural Advantages* . . . (New York: Pratt, Robinson & Co., 1838). Birkbeck was also writing for the purpose of drawing English immigrants to the English prairie of southeastern Illinois.

A number of travel accounts by Americans have detailed treatments of agriculture. At the top of the list must stand Frederick Law Olmsted, *A Journey in the Seaboard Slave States, with Remarks on Their Economy* (New York: Dix & Edwards, 1856); *A Journey in the Back Country* (New York: Mason Brothers, 1860; and *The Cotton Kingdom: A Traveler's Observation on Cotton and Slavery in the American Slave States* (New York: Mason Brothers, 1861). The third is in part a compression of the two earlier accounts. Timothy Dwight made some interesting observations on rural life in his *Travels: In New England and*

New York (4 vols.; New Haven, Conn.: T. Dwight, 1821). David Thomas, who became an outstanding horticulturist at a later time, described his western tour of 1816 in *Travels through the Western Country in the Summer of 1816, Including Notices of the Natural History, Antiquities, Topography, Agriculture, Commerce, and Manufactures; With a Map of the Wabash Country Now Settling* (Auburn, N. Y.: David Rumsey, 1819).

Agricultural journalists made numerous journeys through regions they were cultivating for additional circulation and wrote their observations, which are virtually travel accounts, for publication in their periodicals. The best of these travel letters or "Traveling Memoranda" were accounts of their observations while on tours of the South by Solon Robinson and Richard L. Allen, both prominent agricultural authorities associated with the *American Agriculturist*. Herbert Anthony Kellar edited Robinson's letters in *Solon Robinson: Pioneer and Agriculturist*, cited above. Allen's meaty and incisive accounts are in the *American Agriculturist*, Vol. II (1847).

SETTLEMENT AND ECONOMIC DEVELOPMENT

Three co-operatively planned and written regional and state histories and one ambitious but never completed individual project brought local history out of the doghouse and established it on a high professional basis. They are listed here because of their attention to agriculture. The ten-volume *History of the South,* Wendell Holmes Stephenson and Ellis Merton Coulter, eds. (Baton Rouge: Louisiana State University Press, 1947—), contains two volumes important for this period: Charles Sackett Sydnor, *The Development of Southern Sectionalism, 1818–1848* (1948), and Avery Craven, *The Growth of Southern Nationalism* (1953). *The Centennial History of Illinois,* Clarence Walworth Alvord, ed., has the following volumes for the period from 1815 to 1860: Clarence Walworth Alvord, *The Illinois Country, 1673–1818* (Vol. I; Chicago: A. C. McClurg & Co., 1922); Solon Justus Buck, *Illinois in 1818* (Introductory Volume; Springfield: Illinois Centennial Commission, 1917); Theodore Calvin Pease, *The Frontier State, 1818–1848* (Vol. II; Chicago: A. C. McClurg & Co., 1922); Arthur Charles Cole, *The Era of the Civil War, 1848–1870* (Vol. III; Chicago: A. C. McClurg & Co., 1922).

Four volumes of the *History of the State of Ohio,* Carl Wittke, ed. (Columbus: Ohio State Archaeological and Historical Society, 1941–1944), need citation: Beverley W. Bond, *The Foundations of Ohio* (Vol. I); William T. Utter, *The Frontier State, 1803–1825* (Vol. II); Francis P. Weisenburger, *The Passing of the Frontier, 1825–1850* (Vol. III); and Eugene H. Roseboom, *The Civil War Era, 1850–1873* (Vol. IV). Period studies of individual states are Jarvis Means Morse, *A Neglected Period of Connecticut's History, 1818–1850* (New Haven: Yale University Press, 1933); Richard J. Purcell, *Connecticut in Transition, 1775–1818* (Washington, D. C.: American Historical Association, 1918); Lewis D. Stilwell, *Migration from Vermont, 1776–1860* (*Proceedings* of the Vermont Historical Society, Vol. V; Montpelier: 1937); Ruth L. Higgins, *Expansion in New York with Special Reference to the Nineteenth Century* (The Ohio State University *Studies,* No. 14; Columbus: 1931).

Joseph Schafer's studies of the early settlement and economic development of portions of Wisconsin were landmarks in historical writing when they appeared: *Four Wisconsin Counties* (*Wisconsin Domesday Book*, Vol. II; Madison: State Historical Society of Wisconsin, 1927); *The Wisconsin Lead Region* (*Wisconsin Domesday Book, General Studies*, Vol. III; Madison: 1932); *The Winnebago Horicon Basin* (*Wisconsin Domesday Book, General Studies*, Vol. IV; Madison: 1937). Attention is also directed to Thomas Perkins Abernethy, *From Frontier to Plantation in Tennessee: A Study in Frontier Democracy* (Chapel Hill: University of North Carolina Press, 1932); the same author's *The Formative Period in Alabama* (*Publications* of the Alabama State Department of Archives and History; Historical and Patriotic Series, No. 6; Montgomery: 1922); Roscoe Carlyle Buley, *The Old Northwest Pioneer Period, 1815–1840* (2 vols.; Indianapolis: Indiana Historical Society, 1950); and Solon J. and Elizabeth Hawthorn Buck, *The Planting of Civilization in Western Pennsylvania* (Pittsburgh: University of Pittsburgh Press, 1939).

For the role of the railroads in promoting settlement, see Paul Wallace Gates, *The Illinois Central Railroad and Its Colonization Work* (*Harvard Economic Studies*, Vol. XLII; Cambridge, Mass.: Harvard University Press, 1934); Richard C. Overton, *Burlington West: A Colonization History of the Burlington Railroad* (Cambridge, Mass.: Harvard University Press, 1941); and Howard F. Bennett, "The Hannibal & St. Joseph Railroad and the Development of Northern Missouri, 1847–1870: A Study of Land and Colonization policies." Unpublished Ph.D. dissertation, 1941, Harvard College Library.

LAND POLICIES AND LAND COMPANIES

Thomas Donaldson, *The Public Domain: Its History* (Washington, D. C.: Government Printing Office, 1884), is the great compendium of statistics on the disposal of the public lands largely compiled from the *Annual Reports* of the General Land Office. Benjamin Horace Hibbard approached his *History of the Public Land Policies* (New York: The Macmillan Company, 1924) from the point of view of an agricultural economist who had been profoundly influenced by Frederick Jackson Turner. His treatment may be supplemented by Roy Marvin Robbins, *Our Landed Heritage: The Public Domain, 1776–1936* (Princeton, N. J.: Princeton University Press, 1942), which is somewhat stronger on western concern for land reform but, like Hibbard, is weak on disposal of the public lands and the actual functioning of the land system. Payson Jackson Treat, *The National Land System, 1785–1820* (New York: E. B. Treat & Co., 1910), is still good for the limited period. Two useful studies of land problems in the politics of the time are Raynor G. Wellington, *The Political and Sectional Influence of the Public Lands, 1828–1842* (Cambridge, Mass.: The Riverside Press, 1914), and George M. Stephenson, *The Political History of the Public Lands from 1840 to 1862* (Boston: Richard G. Badger, 1917). For workingmen's influence on land policy, see Helene Sara Zahler, *Eastern Workingmen and the National Land Policy, 1829–1862* (Columbia University *Studies in the History of American Agriculture*, No. 7; New York: Columbia University Press, 1941).

For the disposal of the public domain see the following works by Paul Wallace Gates: *The Wisconsin Pine Lands of Cornell University* (Ithaca, N. Y.: Cornell University Press, 1944); *Fifty Million Acres: Conflicts over Kansas Land Policy* (Ithaca, N. Y.: Cornell University Press, 1954); "Southern Investments in Northern Lands," *Journal of Southern History*, V (May, 1939), 155–188; "Land Policy and Tenancy in the Prairie States," *Journal of Economic History*, I (May, 1941), 60–82, "The Role of the Land Speculator in Western Development," *Pennsylvania Magazine of History and Biography*, LXVI (June, 1942), 314–333; "Frontier Landlords and Pioneer Tenants," *Journal* of the Illinois State Historical Society, XXXVIII (June, 1945), 143–206; "Private Land Claims in the South," *Journal of Southern History*, XXII (May, 1956), 166–183.

Indian allotments, which were later to be so important in Oklahoma, come in for study in Alabama and Mississippi by Mary E. Young in "The Creek Frauds: A Study in Conscience and Corruption," *Mississippi Valley Historical Review*, XLII (December, 1955), 411 ff., and in "Indian Removal and Land Allotment: The Civilized Tribes and Jacksonian Justice," *American Historical Review*, LXIV (October, 1958), 31 ff. Speculation in a part of these same lands is discussed by James W. Silver in "Land Speculation Profits in the Chickasaw Cession," *Journal of Southern History*, X (February, 1944), 84 ff. One of the many land grants which went awry is discussed by Leonard F. Ralston in "Iowa Railroads and the Des Moines River Improvement Land Grant of 1846," *Iowa Journal of History*, LVI (April, 1958), 97 ff. Before a definitive study of the disposal of the public domain can be made, a great deal of intensive research in the entry volumes of the various land offices needs to be done preparatory to the history of disposal in states like Michigan, Minnesota, Alabama, South Dakota, Washington, and New Mexico. Also, more work is needed on pre-emption, the use of scrip, military bounty land warrants, the swamp land grants and internal improvement, and railroad land grants.

Efforts to deal comprehensively with public-land policies in individual states are Addison Erwin Sheldon, *Land Systems and Land Policies in Nebraska* (*Publications* of the Nebraska State Historical Society; Lincoln: Nebraska State Historical Society, 1936), Vol. XXII, the most useful; Roscoe L. Lokken, *Iowa Public Land Disposal* (Iowa City: Iowa State Historical Society, 1942); William Elgin, *The Animating Pursuits of Speculation: Land Traffic in the Annexation of Texas* (Columbia University *Studies in History, Economics and Public Law*, No. 547; New York: Columbia University Press, 1949); Milton Sydney Heath, *Constructive Liberalism: The Role of the State in Economic Development in Georgia to 1860* (Cambridge, Mass.: Harvard University Press, 1954); Enoch Marvin Banks, *The Economics of Land Tenure in Georgia* (Columbia University *Studies in History, Economics and Public Law*, Vol. XXIII, No. 1; New York: Columbia University Press, 1906).

One of the best investigations into a segment of American and state land policies—military bounties—has never been published: William Thomas Hutchinson, "The Bounty Lands of the American Revolution in Ohio," Ph.D. dissertation, University of Chicago, 1927.

Valuable on Louisiana land claims are Harry C. Coles, Jr., "Confirmation of Foreign Land Titles in Louisiana," *Louisiana Historical Quarterly*, XXXVIII

(October, 1955), 1–22, and "Applicabilty of the Public Land System to Louisiana," *Mississippi Valley Historical Review*, XLIII (June, 1956), 39–58. On the Indian cessions in the South and the speculation in the Creek lands, see Mary E. Young, "The Creek Frauds: A Study in Conscience and Corruption," cited above.

Few of the major land companies have been treated, because of the destruction of their records. Since some of the better-known companies were failures, or at least not successes, it has been assumed that most of them produced little profit to their investors. One of the best of the studies is Paul Demund Evans, *The Holland Land Company* (*Publications* of the Buffalo Historical Society, No. 28; Buffalo: 1924). Less useful for economic analysis but withal a charming study is Helen I. Cowan, *Charles Williamson: Genesee Promoter—Friend of Anglo-American Rapprochement* (*Publications* of the Rochester Historical Society, Vol. XIX; Rochester, N. Y.: 1941). Edith M. Fox, in her small treatise, *Land Speculation in the Mohawk Country* (*Cornell Studies in American History, Literature and Folklore*, No. 3; Ithaca, N. Y.: Cornell University Press, 1949), provides a model study which needs to be duplicated for other regions. Florence May Woodard, *The Town Proprietors in Vermont: The New England Town Proprietorship in Decline* (New York: Columbia University Press, 1936), continues the earlier work of Roy H. Akagi, *The Town Proprietors of the New England Colonies* (Philadelphia: University of Pennsylvania Press, 1924). There is some information on public land distribution and policies in Maine in Richard G. Wood, *History of Lumbering in Maine, 1820–1861* (University of Maine *Studies*, Second Series, No. 33; Orono: The University Press, 1935). Elizabeth K. Henderson, "The Northwestern Lands of Pennsylvania, 1790–1812," *Pennsylvania Magazine of History and Biography*, LX (April, 1936), 131–160, shows what good work can be done in state land policy.

COTTON

An early book of value on cotton planting is J. A. Turner, *The Cotton Planter's Manual: Being a Compilation of Facts from the Best Authorities on the Culture of Cotton* (New York: C. M. Saxton and Company, 1857). Guion Griffis Johnson, *A Social History of the Sea Islands* (Chapel Hill: University of North Carolina Press, 1930), deals with sea-island cotton. For general economic studies of cotton, see M. B. Hammond, *The Cotton Industry: An Essay in American Economic History* (*Publications* of the American Economic Association, New Series, No. 1; New York: The Macmillan Company, 1897), and James L. Watkins, *King Cotton: A Historical and Statistical Review, 1790–1908* (New York: James L. Watkins & Sons, 1908). Useful for Alabama is Charles Shepard Davis, *The Cotton Kingdom in Alabama* (Montgomery: State Department of Archives and History, 1939). Studies of slavery in the Deep South that have much bearing on cotton economy are Ralph Betts Flanders, *Plantation Slavery in Georgia* (Chapel Hill: University of North Carolina Press, 1933); James Benson Sellers, *Slavery in Alabama* (University: University of Alabama Press, 1950); and Charles Sackett Sydnor, *Slavery in Mississippi* (New York: Appleton-Century-Crofts, Inc., 1933). Frank Lawrence Owsley, *King Cotton*

434   THE FARMER'S AGE: 1815–1860

Diplomacy: Foreign Relations of the Confederate States of America (Chicago: The University of Chicago Press, 1931) is a brilliant study. Valuable biographies of cotton planters are Wendell Holmes Stephenson, *Alexander Porter, Whig Planter of Old Louisiana* (Baton Rouge: Louisiana State University Press, 1934), his *Isaac Franklin: Slave Trader and Planter of the Old South* (Baton Rouge: Louisiana State University Press, 1938), and Charles Sackett Sydnor, *A Gentleman of the Old Natchez Region: Benjamin L. C. Wailes* (Durham, N. C.: Duke University Press, 1938).

GRAIN

Old but dependable is John Giffin Thompson, *The Rise and Decline of the Wheat Growing Industry in Wisconsin* (University of Wisconsin, *Bulletin* No. 292; *Economics and Political Science Series*, Vol. V, No. 3; Madison: 1909). See also Henrietta M. Larson, *The Wheat Market and the Farmer in Minnesota* (Columbia University *Studies in History, Economics and Public Law*, Vol. CXXII, No. 2, Whole No. 269; New York: Columbia University Press, 1926), and Charles Byron Kuhlmann, *The Development of the Flour-Milling Industry in the United States with Special Reference to the Industry in Minnesota* (Boston: Houghton Mifflin Company, 1929). Donald L. Kemmerer, "The Pre-Civil War South's Leading Crop, Corn," *Agricultural History*, XXIII (October, 1949), 236–238, is suggestive.

HEMP

James F. Hopkins, *History of the Hemp Industry in Kentucky* (Lexington: University of Kentucky Press, 1951), is indispensable for this minor crop.

RICE

Albert V. House, Jr., has appraised the literature of rice planting and presented useful documentary material in the following articles: "The Management of a Rice Plantation in Georgia, 1834–1861, as Revealed in the Journal of Hugh Fraser Grant," *Agricultural History*, XIII (October, 1939), 208–217; "Charles Manigault's Essay on the Open Planting of Rice," *Agricultural History*, XVI (October, 1942), 184–193; "Deterioration of a Georgia Rice Plantation during Four Years of Civil War," *Journal of Southern History*, IX (February, 1943), 107–113; and *Planter Management and Capitalism in Ante-Bellum Georgia: The Journals of Hugh Fraser Grant, Rice Grower* (Columbia University *Studies in the History of American Agriculture*, No. 13; New York: Columbia University Press, 1954). Also see James Harold Easterby, ed., *The South Carolina Rice Plantation as Revealed in the Papers of Robert F. W. Allston* (Chicago: The University of Chicago Press, 1945); Duncan Clinch Heyward, *Seed from Madagascar* (Chapel Hill: University of North Carolina Press, 1937); and Savannah Writers' Project, Mary Granger, ed., *Savannah River Plantations* (Savannah: Georgia Historical Society, 1947).

SUGAR

A basic source for the sugar industry is P. A. Champomier, *Statement of the Sugar Crop Made in Louisiana,* which was published annually in New Orleans from 1845 to 1860. J. Carlyle Sitterson has a model history of the sugar industry, *Sugar Country: The Cane Sugar Industry in the South, 1753–1950* (Lexington: University of Kentucky Press, 1953). Also see V. Alton Moody, "Slavery on Louisiana Sugar Plantations," *Louisiana Historical Quarterly,* VII (April, 1924), 191–301.

SILK

Three brief studies of the silk craze in different parts of the country are Sidney Glazer, "The Early Silk Industry in Michigan," *Agricultural History,* XVIII (April, 1944), 92–96; Robert Price, *"Morus multicaulis,* or, Silk Worms Must Eat," *Ohio State Archaeological and Historical Quarterly,* XLV (1936), 265–272; and Elizabeth Hawes Ryland, "America's 'Multicaulis Mania,'" *William and Mary College Quarterly Magazine,* Series 2, XIX (January, 1939), 25–33.

TOBACCO

The literature on tobacco is voluminous, but reference need be made here only to three modern studies whose bibliographies are extensive: Joseph Clarke Robert, *The Tobacco Kingdom: Plantation, Market and Factory in Virginia and North Carolina, 1800–1860* (Durham, N. C.: Duke University Press, 1938, and his *The Story of Tobacco in America* (New York: Alfred A. Knopf, Inc., 1949); and Nannie May Tilley, *The Bright-Tobacco Industry, 1860–1929* (Chapel Hill: University of North Carolina Press, 1948).

LIVESTOCK

Still useful is James Westfall Thompson, "History of Livestock Raising in the United States, *1607–1860* (U. S. Department of Agriculture, *Agricultural History Series,* No. 5, processed; Washington, D. C.: 1942). Rudolf Alexander Clemen, *American Livestock and Meat Industry* (New York: The Ronald Press Company, 1923), deals more with meat packing but is useful for the early trade in cattle and hogs. An incredible amount of ink was expended in England and America in the middle of the nineteenth century in controversies on the origin of the Shorthorn cattle in both countries. The controversy waxed so acrimonious in the *Ohio Farmer* in 1858, abetted by Cassius M. Clay and others, as to threaten to take up most of the space for many issues and finally to lead to the editor's refusing to publish additional communications. Lewis Falley Allen was the most prolific contemporary writer on the Shorthorns. In addition to his *Herdbooks,* which contain much of value, see his *History of the Short-Horn Cattle: Their Origin, Progress, and Present Condition* (Buffalo: The Author, 1883); *American Cattle: Their History, Breeding and Management* (New York: Taintor Brothers & Co., 1868); and "Improvements in Native Cattle" (U. S. Commissioner of Agriculture, *Annual Report, 1866*; Washington, D. C.: Government Printing Office, 1867), pp. 294–320. Alvin Howard Sanders has also written extensively on cattle; his most valuable work for the period before 1860 is *Short-Horn Cattle: A Series of Historical Sketches, Memoirs and Records of the Breed and Its Development in the United States and Canada* (Chicago: Sanders Publishing Co., 1901).

Improvements in cattle breeds are analyzed in Charles T. Leavitt, "Attempts to Improve Cattle Breeds in the United States, 1790–1860," *Agricultural History*, VII (April, 1933), 51–67, and in George F. Lemmer, "The Spread of Improved Cattle through the Eastern United States to 1850," *Agricultural History*, XXI (April, 1947), 79–93. Early cattle driving is outlined in Paul C. Henlein, "Cattle Driving from the Ohio Country, 1800–1850," *Agricultural History*, XXVIII (January, 1954), 83–95. Useful for the introduction of Shorthorns into Kentucky is Otis K. Rice, "Importations of Cattle into Kentucky, 1785–1860," *Register* of the Kentucky State Historical Society, XLIX (January, 1951), 35–47.

For the rise of the cattle barons on the prairies south of Lake Michigan, see Paul Wallace Gates, "Hoosier Cattle Kings," *Indiana Magazine of History*, XLIV (March, 1948), 1–24, and his "Cattle Kings in the Prairies," *Mississippi Valley Historical Review*, XXXV (December, 1948), 379–412.

The milk trade, dairying, and the public health movement all call for study. Despite its organization, there is useful information in Thomas Ross Pirtle, *History of the Dairy Industry* (Chicago: Majonnier Bros. Company, 1926). E. Parmalee Prentice, *American Dairy Cattle: Their Past and Future* (New York: Harper & Brothers, 1942), is contentious but has much material on the dairy breeds in Europe and America.

A valuable study of the conflicts between the woolgrowers and the wool manufacturers over tariff rates is Harry James Brown, "The National Association of Wool Manufacturers, 1864–1897." Unpublished Ph.D. dissertation, Cornell University, 1949.

Daniel Chipman Linsley, *Morgan Horses* (New York: C. M. Saxton, 1857), pays much attention to blood lines and New England breeders, as do the two volumes by Joseph Battell, *The Morgan Horse and Register* (Vol. I; Middlebury, Vt.: Register Printing Company, 1894; and Vol. II; Middlebury. American Publishing Company, 1905).

On the horse and mule trade, see Thomas D. Clark, "Livestock Trade between Kentucky and the South, 1840–1860," *Kentucky State Historical Register*, XXVII (September, 1929), 569 ff.; Frederic A. Culmer, ed., "Selling Missouri Mules Down South in 1835," *Missouri Historical Review*, XXIV (July, 1930), 637 ff.; and Robert Leslie Jones, "The Horse and Mule Industry in Ohio to 1865," *Mississippi Valley Historical Review*, XXXIII (June, 1946), 61 ff.

Henry Stephens Randall, the principal contemporary authority on sheep, produced three significant treatises: *Sheep Industry in the South: Comprising a Treatise on the Acclimation of Sheep in the Southern States and an Account of the Different Breeds* . . . (Philadelphia: H. S. Skinner & Son, 1848); *The Practical Shepherd* (Rochester, N. Y.: D. D. T. Moore, 1863); and *Fine*

Wool Sheep Husbandry (New York: Orange Judd & Company, 1863). See also L. G. Connor, "Brief History of the Sheep Industry in the United States," *Annual Report* of the American Historical Association, 1918 (2 vols.; Washington, D. C.: Government Printing Office, 1921), I, 89–197. Edward Norris Wentworth casts his net more widely in *America's Sheep Trails: History, Personalities* (Ames: Iowa State College Press, 1948), which is a compendium on sheep in the United States.

AGRICULTURAL MACHINERY

All works on agricultural history deal with this topic in some degree. Most useful is Leo Rogin, *The Introduction of Farm Machinery in Its Relation to the Productivity of Labor in the Agriculture of the United States During the Nineteenth Century* (University of California *Publications in Economics,* Vol. IX; Berkeley: University of California Press, 1931). Hadley Winfield Quaintance has an interesting essay: *The Influence of Agricultural Machinery on Production and Labor, Publications* of the American Economic Association, Third Series, Vol. V, No. 4 (November, 1904). G. E. Fussell, *The Farmer's Tools, 1500–1900* (London: Andrew Melrose, 1952), though concerned with English agricultural implements, is of interest to American students. Of specialized value are Victor S. Clark, *History of Manufactures in the United States* (3 vols.; New York: McGraw-Hill Book Company, 1929), and William T. Hutchinson, *Cyrus Hall McCormick: Seed-Time* (New York: Appleton-Century-Crofts, Inc., 1930), on the development of the reaper and controversies revolving around it; Reynold M. Wik, *Steam Power on the American Farm* (Philadelphia: University of Pennsylvania Press, 1953), for the substitution of steam power for the treadmill. A contemporary account by a recognized authority is that of M. L. Dunlap, "Agricultural Machinery," in U. S. Commissioner of Agriculture, *Annual Report, 1863* (Washington, D. C.: Government Printing Office, 1863), pp. 416–435. Russell H. Anderson, "Grain Drills through Thirty-Nine Centuries," *Agricultural History,* X (October, 1936), 157–205, is the work of much time and insight. On farm machinery in the South, Cornelius O. Cathey, "Agricultural Implements in North Carolina, 1783–1860," *Agricultural History,* XXV (July, 1951), 128–135, is helpful.

MARKETING PROBLEMS

Valuable for his recollections of many business operations in which he engaged as a small-town merchant is J. M. D. Burrows, *Fifty Years in Iowa* (Davenport, Iowa: Glass & Company, 1888). Lewis Atherton has made the country merchant and the small town of the Midwest his major interest in *The Pioneer Merchant in Mid-America* (University of Missouri *Studies,* Vol. XIV, No. 2; Columbia: 1937); in *The Southern Country Store, 1800–1860* (Baton Rouge: Louisiana State University Press, 1949); and in *Main Street on the Middle Border* (Bloomington: Indiana University Press, 1954). Thomas D. Clark shows the important credit position of the southern country store in *Pills, Petticoats and Plows: The Southern Country Store* (Indianapolis: The Bobbs-Merrill Company, 1944).

For a comprehensive account of the internal and external trade of the United States, see Emory Richard Johnson, *et. al., History of Domestic and Foreign Commerce of the United States* (Washington, D. C.: Carnegie Institution, 1915). Norman Sydney Buck, *The Development of the Organization of Anglo-American Trade, 1800–1850* (New Haven, Conn.: Yale University Press, 1925), deals with cotton, grain, and flour. Arthur H. Stone, "The Cotton Factorage System of the Southern States," *American Historical Review*, XX (April, 1915), 557–565, has long been the principal study of cotton factors.

Louis Bernard Schmidt, "The Internal Grain Trade of the United States," *Iowa Journal of History and Politics*, XVIII (January, 1920), 94–124, and his, "The Westward Movement of the Wheat-Growing Industry in the United States," *Iowa Journal of History and Politics*, XVIII (July, 1920), 296–412, are helpful. Douglass C. North has a provocative analysis of intersectional economic relations in "International Capital Flows and the Development of the American West," *Journal of Economic History*, XVI (December, 1956), 493–505.

FOOD CONSUMPTION

Two fruitful studies on American food habits show what can be done and, more, what needs to be done in this field: Richard Osborn Cummings, *The American and His Food: A History of Food Habits in the United States* (Chicago: The University of Chicago Press, 1940), and Edgar W. Martin, *The Standard of Living in 1860: American Consumption Levels on the Eve of the Civil War* (Chicago: The University of Chicago Press, 1942).

THE ROLE OF GOVERNMENT

Alfred Charles True has written most extensively on the role of Federal government in agriculture. See especially his *History of Agricultural Education in the United States, 1785–1925*, and his *History of Agricultural Experimentation and Research in the United States, 1607–1925* . . . (listed under Agricultural Education). Oscar Handlin and Mary Flug Handlin, *Commonwealth: A Study of the Role of Government in the American Economy: Massachusetts, 1774–1861* (New York: New York University Press, 1947), and Louis Hartz, *Economic Policy and Democratic Thought: Pennsylvania, 1776–1860* (Cambridge, Mass.: Harvard University Press, 1948), are both brilliant studies. James Neal Primm, *Economic Policy in the Development of a Western State: Missouri, 1820–1860* (Cambridge, Mass.: Harvard University Press, 1954), follows well-beaten paths. Milton Sydney Heath, *Constructive Liberalism: The Role of the State in Economic Development in Georgia to 1860* (Cambridge, Mass.: Harvard University Press, 1954), the fourth study of the state as an entrepreneur, is sponsored by the Committee on Economic History.

FARM LABOR

See Paul S. Taylor, "Plantation Laborer before the Civil War," *Agricultural History*, XXVIII (January, 1954), 1–21; and Albert V. House, *"Labor Manage-*

ment Problems on Georgia Rice Plantations, 1840–1860," Agricultural History, XXVIII (January, 1954), 149–155.

AGRICULTURAL EDUCATION

Alfred Charles True, *History of Agricultural Education in the United States, 1785–1925* (U. S. Department of Agriculture, *Miscellaneous Publication* No. 36; Washington, D. C.: 1929), and his *History of Agricultural Experimentation and Research in the United States, 1607–1925: Including a History of the United States Department of Agriculture,* (U. S. Department of Agriculture, *Miscellaneous Publication* No. 251; Washington, D. C.: 1937), are mines of information on the role of the federal government in agriculture.

On the movement for the adoption of the Morrill Act, with its aid for agricultural colleges, see Earle D. Ross, *Democracy's College: The Land-Grant Movement in the Formative Stage* (Ames: Iowa State College Press, 1942). For a somewhat different analysis of the Act of 1862, see Edmund J. James, *The Origin of the Land Grant Act of 1862 and Some Account of Its Author, Jonathan B. Turner* (University of Illinois *Bulletin,* Vol. VIII; Urbana: 1910); and Paul W. Gates, "Western Opposition to the Agricultural College Act," *Indiana Magazine of History,* XXXVII (March, 1941), 103–136.

Of the plethora of histories of land-grant institutions, see Merle Curti and Vernon Carstensen, *The University of Wisconsin, 1848–1925: A History* (2 vols.; Madison: University of Wisconsin Press, 1949); W. H. Glover, *Farm and College: The College of Agriculture of the University of Wisconsin: A History* (Madison: University of Wisconsin Press, 1952); Earle D. Ross, *History of the Iowa State College of Agriculture and Applied Science* (Ames: Iowa State College Press, 1942); and Wayland Fuller Dunaway, *History of the Pennsylvania State College* (State College: Pennsylvania State College, 1946).

Index

West, attitude on public land policies, 66
  on absentee speculators, 87–88
  views on squatters, 88
Westward movement, 5
Wheat, buyers, 162
  Chicago marketing center, 162–163
  commercial production of, 167
  decline in New York, 164
  diseases, 163
  distribution of planting, 156
  drills, 157
  exports, 20, 167–168
  harvest hands, 165
  hauling of, 159–162
  improved cultivation of, 164, 288
  Maine bounty for, 317
  major crop in New York, 35
  milling tolls, 158
  Pennsylvania Germans' crop, 44–45
  pests, 163
  prairie cultivation, 166
  prices in Crimean War, 166
  production improved in Old South, 109
  rental payments of, 173
  shift from, 163, 169
  produced soil deterioration, 168
  in Virginia, 4
  westward movement of, 160–161
  in Wisconsin, 160–161, 166–169
Wheeling, market center, 415
Whigs, sugar planters supported, 129
Whiskey, in New Orleans trade, 174
  production in New York, 35, 36
  principal states in, 13
  shipments of, 162
White, Miles and Elias, extensive money
    lenders, 74
  foreclosures, 75
Whitfield, Nathan, cotton planter, 141
Wilder, Marshall P., fruit hybridizer, 257
  fruit statistics, 261
  leading pomologist, 354
  lectured at Yale, 365
  supported Morrill bill, 379
  President, U.S. Pomological Society,
    315
Wilkes Expedition, scientific results of,
    298–299
  scramble for specimens of, 299
Willamette Valley, 386
Williams, Joseph R., lobbyist for agricul-
    tural education, 377

Williamson, Charles, land agent, 36
Willingham, William W., extensive money
    lender, 74
  foreclosures of, 75
Windsor County, Vt., sheep center, 224
Wine, making in Ohio, 258
Wisconsin, railroad farm mortgages in
    politics, 93, 186n
  state fair, farm machine display, 288
  stay law, 92
  wheat, 160–161, 166–169
Women, in farm press, 348–349
  work in dairy, 244
Wood, fuel, market for, 26
Wood, Jethro, opposition to extension of
    patent of, 280–281
  perfected improved plow, 280
Woodman, Cyrus, creditor, 408
Wool, fleeces, 225
  grades and prices, 225
  marketed through cooperatives, 415
  tariff rates, 326
  western depressed New England prices,
    416
Wool growers' association, 415
Wool growers' bank, attempt to establish,
    415
Worcester County, Mass., land values in,
    400
  pleuropneumonia in, 318
Worcester, Mass., plow manufacture in,
    281
Working Farmer, ties with fertilizer busi-
    ness, 351
Worm fence, 186–187
Worthington, Thomas, 49
Wright, John S., editor, *Prairie Farmer*,
    343
Wyandott corn, 302, 306

Yale, agricultural science at, 362–365
Yankees, farming in Virginia, 113
  restlessness of, 27
Yellow fever, slave deaths from, 128
Yeomen farmers, dislike of snobbish plant-
    ers, 151–152
  in Kentucky, 12
  largest group in South, 139
  Owsley school on, 140
Yerby, George, 83n
Youatt, William, writer, 356